NOT THE SLIGHTEST CHANCE

THE DEFENCE OF HONG KONG, 1941

Tony Banham

HONG KONG UNIVERSITY PRESS

Hong Kong University Press
14/F Hing Wai Centre
7 Tin Wan Praya Road
Aberdeen
Hong Kong

© Hong Kong University Press 2003, 2005

First published in hardback edition 2003
This paperback edition 2005

ISBN 962 209 780 4

All rights reserved. No portion of this publication may be reproduced or transmitted in any form or by any means, electronic or mechanical, including photocopy, recording, or any information storage or retrieval system, without prior permission in writing from the publisher.

British Library Cataloguing-in-Publication Data
A catalogue record for this book is available from the British Library.

Secure On-line Ordering
http://www.hkupress.org

Printed and bound by ColorPrint Production Ltd., Hong Kong, China.

Contents

Preface ix

Acknowledgements xiii

Abbreviations xvii

Introduction 1

1. **The Background** 3
   Hong Kong, 1841 to 1941 3
   The Causes of the War 7

2. **THE BATTLE** 11
   The Week Immediately Preceding the Fighting 11
   The Battle 17

3. **Phase I: The Loss of the Mainland** 21
   8 December Monday 23
   9 December Tuesday 32
   10 December Wednesday 40

	11 December Thursday	47
	12 December Friday	56
4.	**Phase II: The Siege of the Island**	**65**
	13 December Saturday	66
	14 December Sunday	73
	15 December Monday	78
	16 December Tuesday	83
	17 December Wednesday	89
5.	**Phase III: The Invasion of the Island**	**93**
	18 December Thursday	95
6.	**Phase IV: The Forcing of Wong Nai Chung Gap**	**115**
	19 December Friday	117
7.	**Phase V: Pushing the Line West and Encircling Stanley**	**165**
	20 December Saturday	168
	21 December Sunday	185
	22 December Monday	199
	23 December Tuesday	214
	24 December Wednesday	230
	25 December Thursday	248
	26 December Friday	276
8.	**The Week Immediately Following the Fighting**	**283**
9.	**Conclusion**	**289**
10.	**Epilogue**	**293**

Appendices		**295**
1.	Additional Casualties	295
2.	The Defenders on the Eve of Invasion	298
3.	Massacres	305
4.	Civilian airmen operating from Kai Tak	313
5.	Casualty Summary Tables	313
6.	British Military Losses	317

7.	Civilian Losses	318
8.	Japanese Losses	318
9.	Hospitals	319
10.	Military Cemeteries	320
11.	Japanese Artillery Records	321
12.	Fates of HKVDC Air Unit Personnel	322
13.	The HKDDC	322
14.	The British Army Aid Group (BAAG)	322
15.	HKRNVR Personnel Transferred Outside Hong Kong	323
16.	Arrival and Appointment Dates of Significant Personnel	323
17.	Tables of Ships	324
18.	Occupants of Repulse Bay Hotel	327
19.	Personnel at West Brigade HQ	329
20.	Japanese Order of Battle	330
21.	British Artillery Specifications	332
22.	Population	332
23.	Canadian Popular Histories and British Popular Histories	333

Notes 335

Annotated Bibliography 385

Index 411

List of Maps

1	Gin Drinkers Line, 8 December	24
2	Shing Mun Redoubt, 9 December	37
3	Fixed Royal Artillery Positions, 8 December	67
4	Topography: Hong Kong Island 1941	94
5	Initial Positions, Hong Kong Island, 18 December	96
6	The North Face, 18–19 December	100
7	Hong Kong Island, 19 December at 00.01	118
8	Wong Nai Chung Gap, 19 December	127
9	Wan Chai Operations, 20–25 December	167
10	Hong Kong Island, 20 December at 00.01	169
11	Hong Kong Island, 21 December at 00.01	186
12	Hong Kong Island, 22 December at 00.01	200
13	Hong Kong Island, 23 December at 00.01	215
14	Hong Kong Island, 24 December at 00.01	231
15	Stanley, 23–25 December	238
16	Hong Kong Island, 25 December at 00.01	249
17	Hong Kong Island, 26 December at 00.01	277

Preface

> One is not conscious of living history; the burst of bombs, the sense of personal danger, anxiety for one's friends, hunger and, thank goodness, an occasional episode that strikes one as amusing, do not make for the necessary detachment. It is for the historian afterwards, in the calm of his study, to piece hundreds of such personal stories together into one connected whole.
> — Phyllis Harrop, *Hong Kong Incident*, 1943

Not the Slightest Chance was the story that could never be written. More than 10 per cent of the Colony's defenders had been killed in battle; a further 20 per cent died in captivity. Those who survived the fighting and three years, eight months in brutal POW camps seldom spoke about their experiences. Many died young. Anything written down during the fighting was burnt during the painful years of occupation, and the little 'primary' material that we have was written in-camp from memory, or years after the events. No wonder these records are contradictory, fragmented, and confused.

I knew nothing of this when I moved permanently to Hong Kong in 1989, but within months of arriving I had been given a book, *The Lasting Honour*, by Oliver Lindsay. I didn't know it then, but I couldn't have found a better book to spark my interest. I read it overnight, and the next day being a Sunday, visited one of the battlefields mentioned —

Wong Nai Chung Gap. Less than five minutes after arriving I found a 6.5-mm cartridge from a wartime Japanese Arisaka rifle hanging out of an earth bank near the old police station.

What made the battle of Hong Kong unique was the scale. This was no battle of Berlin with millions of men involved; instead, just 14,000 defended the Colony. But, in an isolated location like this, those 14,000 formed a microcosm of Imperial forces of the time. Navy, air force, army, and every supporting unit was represented. Inside this force was a microcosm within a microcosm, the Hong Kong Volunteer Defence Corps. They too had everything from an air unit to a navy (through the Hong Kong Royal Naval Volunteer Reserve), to an army with all its units.

It occurred to me that it might just be possible to write a new *type* of history — a history based on the individual — *all* the individuals, rather than the big battalions so beloved of Napoleon and traditional historians.

I set to work. First, I put together a basic chronology of the fighting here. On top of that, I overlaid the records of the Commonwealth War Graves Commission (CWGC) for Hong Kong (including civilian records where they existed, and the hard-to-separate naval records). This immediately highlighted fatalities without incidents, and incidents without fatalities. The detective work had begun.

The next step was to identity all published (and whenever possible, unpublished) accounts, diaries, and records of the fighting, and correlate them with the data already assembled. This involved processing some 180 works, and almost immediately highlighted a problem: diarists, in particular, habitually make reference to individuals by surname or nickname without any other particulars. Who was 'Gow', for example? Why was he at that place at that time? What else did that tell us?

There was no option but to compile a database of the entire garrison's personnel. The Hong Kong Public Records Office had reasonably complete hospital records from the fighting (almost the only records to have survived from the time), and a partial list of POWs completed in January 1942. All went into the computer, and suddenly I knew who I was dealing with. In fact, by looking for groupings of wounded in particular units on certain dates, I was even able to do primary research from within my own book.

I now had a map of an entire Colonial garrison of the mid-twentieth century. It soon became apparent that historians up till now had completely ignored some less fashionable units, and others had received more than their fair share of attention. I determined that I should take the opportunity to write the first comprehensive and balanced account of the fighting, giving fair coverage to each unit involved.

And then it started to get interesting. The scene shifted from a backroom historian sifting through dusty papers in the archives, to the world of modern communications and face-to-face dialogue with veterans.

My first contact with veterans came as early as 1991 when, through the kindness of the then adjutant of the Volunteers, Captain Albert Lam, I was invited to the fiftieth anniversary memorial service at Sai Wan military cemetery. There I met two survivors of the Middlesex regiment, both wounded at Stanley ('there was no option, there was so much stuff flying around') and survivors of the *Lisbon Maru*, and also the late Terry Leonard (one of the 3 Coy. HKVDC heroes) and many others. But it was too early in my research to make full use of these contacts.

For the next few years, whenever time enabled, I continued doing my homework. Finally I felt I had a good understanding of events, and needed some way to calibrate what I had done so far. Now it was time to enlist the help of the veterans. I started to build a worldwide network of contacts with similar interests — including the veterans themselves.

By now I had learned how to interview these survivors. It is no use asking, 'What did you do in the war, Daddy?' when that war happened sixty years ago. At best, you will receive a muddled response. But if you have done your homework, worked out where the interviewee was and when, and what incidents he or she might have been involved in, then you can ask very exact questions. Suddenly the years are stripped away, and shockingly precise recollections replace the muddle.

After these interviews (face-to-face, or via letter, email, fax, and phone) many details were falling into place. Days spent walking the ground, picking up shrapnel and bullets and working out how units moved from one place to another filled in many more. By 2002, I realized that enough was enough; I had reached the point of diminishing returns.

Writing this Preface today, I find that the piecing together of the story in *Not the Slightest Chance* has indeed been the satisfying intellectual puzzle I was hoping for — and yet at some point in the last few years the human aspect took over. It was no longer 'Private Agerbak', but 'Carol's dad'; Drummond Hunter was no longer just a name on a scrap of paper, he's a gentleman with a fine Scottish accent calling me from Edinburgh; and when I walk through the Stanley cemetery today I feel I know everyone there.

It's a little like looking at an old school photograph.

Acknowledgements

Firstly, to six people without whom this work could not have been completed in its current form:

David Roads, ex-journalist and intelligence man, who once told me he was one of the few US Marines to have fought the Japanese in all five major campaigns. He would be worth a book in his own right. Part Native American, he also married a Miss Philippines, and took a dollar off Al Capone as a youngster. David (I knew him for three years before he told me his surname) could find me anything. I once asked him if there was any way that I could get hold of original copies of the *South China Morning Post* for the period 8–25 December 1941. The next day he invited me for lunch at the Hong Kong Foreign Correspondents' Club (of which he was twice president) and handed me a package of newspapers tied in twine. They were the papers I had asked for, wrapped in no less than three copies of the first *South China Morning Post* to have been published after the liberation in 1945. Unfortunately, I had to photocopy them and hand them back, as David needed to return them whence they came — he wouldn't tell me where, of course — by noon the following day.

Richard Hide, son of the stoker of MTB 07, whom I met through his excellent web site covering the topic of the Motor Torpedo Boats' escape.

Dick has been a mine of information and has put me in touch with several survivors of the fighting or their descendants. His web site was responsible directly or indirectly for many of the contacts described below.

Anne Ozorio, a staunch member of Hong Kong's Portuguese community, who lost several relatives during the war. Anne has been instrumental in tracking down many important records in the UK on my behalf, including vital documents from the Kew Public Records Office and the Commonwealth War Graves Commission. This book would have been less comprehensive, by an order of magnitude, without her invaluable assistance.

Professor James 'Jimmy' Cummins, executor of Major Charles Boxer's will and long-time friend of Charles and 'Mickey', who put me in touch with many survivors in London and elsewhere and was a delight to correspond with throughout.

Ian Quinn, a Cathay Pacific pilot and an expert in the American bombing raids on Hong Kong from 1943 to 1945, who hopes to be publishing a book on that subject. Ian often took time out from his own researches to aid mine, and provided much useful information from local sources.

H. W. 'Bunny' Browne, CBE. Of all the veterans I have corresponded with, Bunny has been the most prolific. His memory of events and people sixty years ago has been of enormous assistance.

The second group are survivors (although several, sadly, have not lived to see the book in print) of the December 1941 fighting, who answered questions, provided documents, and generally aided the author:

Borge Agerbak (Winnipeg Grenadiers), Barbara Anslow (ARP), Dr Solomon M. Bard (HKVDC Field Ambulance), Gloria Barretto (NAAFI), Professor Brian Baxter (HKDDC), Bill Bethell (schoolboy), George Bristow (Royal Navy), H. E. 'Bunny' Browne CBE (HQ China Command), Landon Burch (2 Coy HKVDC, and the son of 'Pop' Burch of the HKVDC Hughes Group), Phil Doddridge (Royal Rifles), E. H. Field (Royal Artillery), Pat Fallon (HKVDC Field Ambulance), James Ford MC (Royal Scots), Arthur Gomes MBE (5 Coy. HKVDC), Albert Haines (HKDDC), Major F. S. C. Hancock (Hong Kong Mule Corps), John Harris (Royal Engineers), 'Buster' Hollands (HKVDC), Dick Hooper (Royal Artillery), Drummond Hunter (Royal Scots), L. D. Kilbee (HKRNVR), Tom Middleton (Royal

Navy), Raymond 'Ron' Parry (Royal Navy), David Parsons (Z Force), Sir Albert Rodrigues (HKVDC Field Ambulance), Roger Rothwell (Middlesex and HQ China Command), Edward Shayler (Winnipeg Grenadiers), Raymond A. Smith (Royal Rifles), Steve Smith-Dutton (Royal Artillery), Ralph Stephenson (RNVR), Osler Thomas (HKVDC Field Ambulance, BAAG, and Force 136), Jim Wakefield (Royal Engineers), Geoffrey Wilson (Hong Kong Police), and Michael Wright (3 Bty. HKVDC).

The third group are descendants of members of the 1941 garrison:

Rowena and Lauren Avery (daughter and granddaughter of Archibald Drover, Royal Rifles), Les Bowie (stepson of Sgt. Parkin, RAMC), Pam Broadhead (daughter of Cpl. John Marriott, RE), Isabella Cooper (daughter of James McHarg Miller, Royal Scots), Dr A. E. Dormer (son-in-law of W. R. N. Andrews, Field Company Engineers), Tony Dudman (son of Sgt. Dudman, HKVDC Air Unit), Cheryl Foundling (second cousin of Geoffrey Coxhead, HKVDC), Liana Frenette (granddaughter of John Edward James, Winnipeg Grenadiers), Ian Gow (son of Pte. Gow, Royal Scots), Carol Hadley (daughter of Borge Agerbak, Winnipeg Grenadiers, and my main contact for the Hong Kong Veterans Commemorative Association in Canada), Lori Halliday (granddaughter-in-law of Norman Halliday, HKDDC), Dig Hastilow (grandson of Major General C. M. Maltby), Pam Heinrichs (daughter of Ferdinand Poitras, Winnipeg Grenadiers), Ian Hemsley (son of Frederick Martin Hemsley, RAF), Verna Karpetz (niece of Frank Woytowich, Winnipeg Grenadiers), Patricia Osborn (daughter of Sgt. Osborn, VC), Cathy McAllister (great-niece of William Kohut, Winnipeg Grenadiers), John Matthews (son of Pte. Clifford L. Matthews and nephew of Alf Matthews, both Winnipeg Grenadiers), Tom Middleton (son of Tom Middleton senior, Royal Navy), Barry Mitchell (son of Lt. William Vaughan Mitchell and nephew of Lt. Eric Lawson Mitchell, both Winnipeg Grenadiers), Pat Mulligan (son of Gunner James Patrick Mulligan, Royal Artillery), Veronica Needa (daughter of Victor Needa), Nick Nigel (son of Lt. F. G. Nigel, HKVDC), Ron Parker (son of Maj. Parker commanding D Coy. Royal Rifles, and himself an authority on Canadian operations in Hong Kong), Judy Prieston (daughter of Riley Prieston, Winnipeg Grenadiers), Elizabeth Ride (daughter of Lt. Col. Lindsay Ride, ever helpful and herself an authority on irregular warfare in South China), Warwick Ross (son of Ted Ross, Ministry of Information), Joe Schell (grandson of Thomas

Chester Budd, Winnipeg Grenadiers), Dr Mary Seed (daughter of Sir Selwyn Selwyn-Clarke), Gillian Shave (great-niece of executed civilian Frederick Bradley), Paul Sinclair (son of William Henry Sinclair, Royal Artillery), Peter Thompson (son of Capt. Thompson of the RAPC), Donald Wagstaff (son of Donald Wagstaff senior, HKRNVR), Bill Wiseman Jnr. (son of Bill Wiseman, RASC), and Marina Earley (daughter of Isaac G. Williamson, Royal Scots).

The fourth group provided their own expertise on the topics covered:

Michael Benbow (General Cohen), Phillip Bruce (Hong Kong history), Carol Cooper (FEPOWs), Martin Heyes (Hong Kong military history), Tim Ko (who provided the photographs used in this book), Captain Albert Lam (Adjutant, The Volunteers), Vicky Lee (Stanley camp), Bob Massey (the HKVDC Air Unit), David Mather (ordnance), Dr Charles Roland (medical conditions in Hong Kong's POW camps), Rosemary Seton and Alison Field (SOAS Library, London), *South China Morning Post*, Rob Weir (who gave invaluable help with Hong Kong's fixed defences), and Tim Wolter (sports in POW camps).

Thanks also to Dr Solomon Bard, Peter Moss, CBE, and Cyril Pereira for reviewing a very early version of the manuscript.

Lastly, thanks to the PRO in Kew, the Hong Kong PRO, the Commonwealth War Graves Commission, Pen & Sword Books, and *Battlefields Review* for permissions to quote, and to Colin Day and Hong Kong University Press for backing this rather formidably academic project.

In the final analysis, I have tried to do what Phyllis Harrop suggested some sixty years ago. I hope that the descendants of those who fought in the battle will regard this work as a fitting tribute to their ancestors, and as a useful record of a colonial garrison as it was in the mid-twentieth century.

The errors that persist in this work, despite the advice of these kind contributors, are of course entirely my own.

Note: Many of the battlegrounds referred to in this book still contain unspent ordnance. Hong Kong's Explosive Ordnance Disposal unit is called out hundreds of times each year, dealing with everything from homemade fireworks to 500-pound bombs. It is inadvisable to touch such items.

Abbreviations

Burial Records

K	Known grave at Stanley or Sai Wan military cemeteries unless otherwise stated.
CCC	Cape Collinson Roman Catholic Cemetery
HKC	Hong Kong Cemetery
HKJ	Hong Kong Jewish Cemetery
HKM	Hong Kong Muslim Cemetery
HKR	Hong Kong Roman Catholic Cemetery
U	Unknown grave. Commemorated in Hong Kong unless otherwise stated.
UC	Unknown grave. Commemorated in Chatham
UCWD	Unknown grave. Commemorated in the list of Civilian War Dead
UP	Unknown grave. Commemorated in Plymouth
UPO	Unknown grave. Commemorated in Portsmouth
UT	Unknown grave. Commemorated at Tower Hill
UX	Unknown grave. Not in CWGC records.

Dates in [square brackets] are original CWGC dates that this work has corrected.

Hospital Abbreviations

BRH	Bowen Road Hospital (also known as BMH, British Military Hospital).
CSUC	Chinese School University Compound
HKH	Hong Kong Hotel Relief Hospital
IGH	Indian General Hospital
RNH	Royal Naval Hospital
SAH	St. Albert's Convent Relief Hospital
SSH	St. Stephen's College Relief Hospital
STH	St. Teresa's Hospital
UH	University Hospital
WMH	War Memorial Hospital

Other Abbreviations

2IC	Second in Command
AA	Anti Aircraft
A/C	Armoured Car
ADC	Aide De Camp
ANS	Auxiliary Nursing Service
APV	Auxiliary Patrol Vessel
ARP	Air Raid Precautions
ASC	Army Service Corps
ASP	Assistant Superintendent
ATS	Auxiliary Transport Service
BAAG	British Army Aid Group
BOP	Battery Observation Post
BOR	British Other Rank
BSM	Battery Sergeant Major
CWGC	Commonwealth War Graves Commission
CNAC	China National Aviation Corporation
CO	Commanding Officer
CSM	Company Sergeant Major
DOA	Dead on Arrival
DOW	Died Of Wounds
FAA	Fleet Air Arm
GC	George Cross

GSO	General Staff Officer
HAA	Heavy Anti Aircraft
HKDDC	Hong Kong Dockyard Defence Corps
HKH	Hong Kong Hotel
HKMC	Hong Kong Mule Corps
HKPF	Hong Kong Police Force
HKRNVR	Hong Kong Royal Naval Volunteer Reserve
HKSRA	Hong Kong and Singapore Royal Artillery
HKVDC	Hong Kong Volunteer Defence Corps
IGH	Indian General Hospital
IHC	Indian Hospital Corps
IOR	Indian Other Rank
IWM	Imperial War Museum
JLO	Jardines Lookout
KCRC	Kowloon Canton Railway Corporation
KIA	Killed In Action
KL	Kowloon
LAA	Light Anti Aircraft
LMG	Light Machine Gun
MAP	Medical Aid Post
MB	Mountain Battery/Medium Battery
MC	Military Cross
MiD	Mentioned in Despatches
ML	Motor Launch
MO	Medical Officer
MTB	Motor Torpedo Boat
OP	Observation Post
OR	Other Rank
PB	Pillbox
POW	Prisoner Of War
PWD	Public Works Department
QAIMNS	Queen Alexandria's Imperial Military Nursing Service
QF	Quick Firing
QM	Quarter Master
QMS	Quarter Master Sergeant
RA	Royal Artillery
RADC	Royal Army Dental Corps
RAF	Royal Air Force
RAFVR	Royal Air Force Volunteer Reserve

RAMC	Royal Army Medical Corps
RAOC	Royal Army Ordnance Corps
RAPC	Royal Army Pay Corps
RASC	Royal Army Service Corps
RAVC	Royal Army Veterinary Corps
RBH	Repulse Bay Hotel
RCAMC	Royal Canadian Army Medical Corps
RCAOC	Royal Canadian Army Ordnance Corps
RCASC	Royal Canadian Army Service Corps
RCCS	Royal Canadian Corps of Signals
RE	Royal Engineers
RIASC	Royal Indian Army Service Corps
RN	Royal Navy
RNR	Royal Naval Reserve
RNVR	Royla Naval Volunteer Reserve
RSM	Regimental Sergeant Major
VAD	Volunteer Aid Detachment
VC	Victoria Cross
VCO	Viceroy Commissioned Officer
WDV	War Department Vessel
WNCG	Wong Nai Chung Gap

Introduction

Not the Slightest Chance is focused on a single month of Hong Kong's short but exotic history — December 1941. The hundredth anniversary of the Crown Colony, this was also the moment when its ownership changed hands for the second of three times in its history.

This work has three aims. The first is to bring together into one volume the salient points of all known accounts of the eighteen-day battle between the Japanese invaders and Hong Kong's garrison, so that the various different versions of the story can be compared and — hopefully — reconciled into a single comprehensive narrative.

The second aim is to establish (so far as it is possible after some sixty years) the exact fates of each of the approximately 1,600 men and women killed in action on the allied side during the battle.[1]

Lastly, through the medium of the World Wide Web, a companion site contains the first serious attempt yet made to put together a man-by-man, woman-by-woman listing of the 14,000 or so personnel of this isolated garrison as it stood on the day of invasion, 8 December 1941.

For the story, I have examined almost all known published sources, and all the unpublished sources that I could gain access to. There are many agreements in these documents about events, but many disagreements about times and dates. Even in those cases where all secondary sources agree on a date and time, it is often simply because they all rely on a single source document which may itself have been written post-war, and whose precision is therefore also questionable. The reconciliation has been attempted by researching all versions of the story, and checking them against movements of forces and personnel. Walking the area where the fighting took place has in turn supported this. As a final check, the accounts have been correlated against the records of deaths at the Commonwealth War Graves Commission, and admission records of the various Hong Kong hospitals.

As an attempt to cover all units equally, this book has been limited by the available documentation. The 2,000 Canadians who joined the garrison just weeks before the invasion are covered in great (though often questionable) detail in many recent works. Coverage of the British units varies from good for the two infantry battalions, through poor for the many supporting units. Documentation on the Indian units — by nationality, the biggest component of the garrison — is almost entirely missing. This cannot help but cause inequalities in the amount of text dedicated to each component of the garrison.

While this book is focused purely on those who actually fought and died during December 1941, this is not the full story. The survivors still had nearly four years of war in front of them. Without a doubt the most unpleasant document I consulted during this research was that entitled 'List of Patients Unlikely to Recover Before 12 Months' (145). It had been laboriously typed in early 1942 on the paper of a long-forgotten Dutch Company, and listed in detail the wounds of men who had been ripped apart by flying fragments of steel slicing into their bodies, and tearing through them quite indiscriminately. No other document exposed modern warfare for what it is quite so viscerally. Many of these men, of course, died of their wounds in the Prisoner of War camps later, and many more died of mistreatment, disease, starvation, or drowning on their way to camps in other countries. For example, of the 144 officers and men of the 8th Coast Regiment Royal Artillery who died before the final Japanese surrender, only fourteen had actually been killed in action in Hong Kong. *Not the Slightest Chance* is just the beginning.

Readers interested in the fatalities listed for each day should note that the details of the deaths are taken, unless stated otherwise, from the records of the Commonwealth War Graves Commission (CWGC). Those entries followed by a date in square brackets indicate that the date under which the death is listed here is derived from researches for this book, and contradicts the records of the CWGC; the date ascribed by the CWGC is that in square brackets. Occasionally, if a date of death is uncertain, the CWGC may ascribe a range of possibilities, such as 19/25 December.

1 The Background

HONG KONG, 1841–1941

As an island and tiny peninsula on the south coast of China, Hong Kong's one and only asset in the middle of the nineteenth century was the remarkable deep-water harbour for which the 'Fragrant Harbour' was named. It was just what the British needed, as Guangzhou — at that time the only Chinese port at which trade with foreigners was permitted — was a little further up the Pearl Estuary, and they were looking for a good harbour on its doorstep as a staging post for their latest 'merchandise'. This ever-exotic colony was founded on the opium trade

By Britain's military might in the region, China was compelled to sign the extremely one-sided Convention of Chuanbi, which — among other concessions — granted the island of Hong Kong to the British. Despite the British Government disagreeing with the document, the local British commander sent a certain Captain Edward Belcher to lay claim to the island with his ship, HMS *Sulphur*.

As he raised the Union Flag on 25 January 1841, he surveyed a largely 'barren rock' on which an estimated 7,450 Chinese villagers and fishermen lived. He could never have imagined that the establishment of the harbour as a naval base was to be the cause of the Colony's undoing one hundred years later.

While the British Government was slow to recognise the value of their new colony, traders were swift. Within a month, Matheson — soon to be a well-known local name — put up a matshed godown on the middle of the shoreline below present-day Flagstaff House. It was soon converted to stone, which was fortunate as the Colony's first typhoon struck on 21 July and flattened most of the nascent town. Typhoons, plagues, and fires would regularly punctuate the island's history.

Hong Kong grew up as a haphazard settlement, perched on an uncomfortable narrow strip of relatively flat land between the hills and the sea, and administered by sometimes incompetent officials who were often out of their depth. Disease was rife, with the first Colonial Surgeon himself dying within a year, and his successor surviving just eight months. Despite this, by November 1844, there was a population of some 20,000 Chinese and a few hundred British. Growth continued, with the population more than doubling between 1853 and 1859, and reclamation of land from the sea — another recurring theme for Hong Kong — began. As part of this expansion, on 26 March 1860, the area south of a line (today's Boundary Street) drawn between Kowloon Fort and a point opposite Stonecutters Island was granted to Britain in perpetuity.

By 1865 — just twenty-four years after the Colony's founding — the population, a mixture of Chinese, Indians, and Europeans, had grown to 125,504. Four years later, Hong Kong was considered important enough for a royal visit, and the Duke of Edinburgh arrived on HMS *Galatea*.[1] Growth of commerce in Hong Kong thereafter was rapid. In 1876 there were 142 brokers, 215 hongs, and 67 marine compradors. By 1881 the figures were 455, 293, and 113 respectively, and the population topped 160,000 for the first time. The terrible typhoon of 1874, the great fire of Christmas night 1878, and the constant outbreaks of cholera and malaria did nothing to stop the population growth.

On 2 May 1888, the Peak Tramway opened and paved the way for the population of the Peak by affluent Europeans who had previously lived in Mid-Levels. Two years later, electric lamps superseded the civic gas lighting that had been progressively installed since 1865, and in 1891 Hong Kong celebrated fifty years as a British Colony. By this time it was an island of great prosperity, admirably positioned to exploit the combined strengths of the British and Chinese in commerce. No one would have guessed what another fifty years would bring.

However, the Colony was severely shaken by an outbreak of bubonic plague in 1894. The causes were not understood at the time, and attempts to bring the disease under control through destroying buildings in the affected areas were of uncertain effectiveness. Finally, cold weather brought it to an end — but not before 2,500 had died and another 80,000 fled.

On 9 June 1898, China and Britain — not realising that this was to morph into the Colony's eventual death warrant — signed documents ceding the New Territories to the Colony for 99 years, primarily to better enable defence in the event of an attack from the Mainland. The approximately 100,000 Chinese inhabitants of the area (who had of course not been consulted) formed small bands and attacked British positions, leading to an armed confrontation with the militia — the Volunteers — near Kam Tin on 17 April 1899.

By the beginning of the twentieth century, commerce was already dominated by Chinese merchants. By 1900, some 41 per cent of the trade with China passed through Hong Kong. However, the international political situation was beginning to affect the Colony. In January 1902, Britain and Japan signed the Anglo-Japanese Alliance, and two years later Japan attacked Russia, sank its fleet, and emerged as the dominant power in the Far East.

Typhoon, turbulence, and terror struck, with the great storm of 18 September 1906 leaving 10,000 dead, the Chinese revolution of 1911 producing yet another stream of refugees, and an assassination attempt on Governor Sir Henry May at Blake's Pier in 1912.

The Colony was not greatly affected by the First World War, though they had their own tragedy in February 1918 when a fire at the Happy Valley racecourse killed about 600 spectators. By this time the population was an estimated 561,000.

In 1919, following an increase in the price of rice, an organised workforce of local Chinese asked for a 40 per cent pay rise. European intransigence provoked an all-out strike, not settled until the employers grudgingly offered 32.5 per cent. The old balance of power was changing, and a general strike in 1922 led to a longer dispute and boycott of British goods in 1925–6. The Colony was slow to recover financially, and by the time the recession of 1931 struck, the Hong Kong dollar — which had been valued at over five shillings in 1919 — was worth less than one.

Fortunately, these problems coincided with the 1925 appointment of arguably Hong Kong's most intelligent Governor, Sir Cecil Clementi. Fluent in spoken and written Chinese, he was a practised diplomat and instigated a wide range of improvements, from slum clearances and the foundation of the Queen Mary Hospital to the building of the Shing Mun reservoir and the formation of the Hong Kong Flying Club (in 1929). While the latter point may seem minor, by 1938 Kai Tak was handling almost 10,000 passengers.[2]

However, by now the rise of Japanese power was a cause for concern in the Colony. Singapore, Hong Kong, and Hawaii were preparing for war. The Sino-Japanese war had begun on 7 July 1937, and within a year Beijing,[3] Nanjing, and Shanghai had fallen. In October 1938, 30,000 Japanese troops landed at Bias Bay, just 24 kilometres north-east of Hong Kong. Within two weeks of landing, they had captured Guangzhou. Thousands of refugees fled to Hong Kong — a quarter of a million in the twelve months ending July 1938 alone — and the camps opened to house them were soon to house British and Commonwealth POWs. By December 1938, the total population was estimated at 997,982.

The border became a flashpoint, and Japanese cross-border incursions intensified, culminating in the bombing of Lo Wu in February 1939. In June 1940, the Hong Kong Government suddenly announced the compulsory evacuation of European women and children, and by August, 3,474 had left for Australia.[4] In July, conscription had been introduced.[5]

Many aircraft were fired upon; Japanese fighters shot down one DC2 of China National Aviation Corporation just after leaving Kai Tak, and on 27 September 1940 — some three weeks after all schools for British children had been closed — an RAF Vildebeeste was attacked. Hong Kong's defences were steadily improved meanwhile, with the rebuilding of the Gin Drinkers Line defences in the New Territories, the construction of massive air raid shelters, and fortification of the north shore of the Island. However, the Washington Treaty of 1922, in an attempt to balance the Pacific powers of the USA, Great Britain, and Japan, forbade strengthening the fortifications of any base east of the 110th meridian. Hong Kong's major defences were therefore 'fossilised' in their largely seaward-facing state.[6]

Refugees continued to arrive, with a March 1941 census giving a total of 1,444,337 people in the urban areas, and an estimated further 200,000 in the New Territories.

By mid-year it was clear that war was coming. In October, the Americans placed an embargo on their citizens trading with Japan, and in November the Hong Kong Government issued a circular to the population giving advice in case of attack. That same month, two new

Canadian battalions arrived to bolster the garrison. The strategic locations in the east had been reinforced as far as the fighting in Europe would allow, and everyone settled down to wait.

By late 1941, Hong Kong, still the peaceful and successful trading port that it had been since inception, was celebrating its hundredth birthday.[7] It was an uneasy celebration. With the Japanese forces just over the border, and the number of cross-border incidents flaring, everyone knew that peace could not last much longer.

THE CAUSES OF THE WAR

By 1941, war with Japan had become inevitable. In the nineteenth century, with the re-establishment of intercourse between Japan and the West, the Japanese had realised the extent of their technical and organisational inferiority. Immediately — and successfully — they set about a programme to reduce this gap, using the dominant European colonial powers as their models.

The brilliance of their achievement was crowned by Japan being both recognised as an ally of the British, and defeating Russia in war, in the first five years of the twentieth century. However, Japan was not recognised as an equal. The Treaties of Washington in 1922 made concessions to Japan by restricting British and American fortifications in the Pacific, but balanced these by setting a ratio of 5:5:3 in capital ships for America, Britain, and Japan respectively.

This was interpreted as a denial of Japan's status as a 'Great Power'. In the 1930s, reactionary and militant forces gained the upper hand in Tokyo. Soon these elements were actively pressing for greater Japanese expansionism, beyond Korea and Taiwan to China and South-East Asia.

In 1931, Japan attacked Manchuria, and established the puppet state of Manchuguo under Pu Yi, 'The Last Emperor'. Japanese troops were landed at Shanghai in 1932, and the Japanese Government's reaction to censure by the League of Nations was to withdraw from that organisation the following year — the year in which they also withdrew from the naval limitation treaties. Japan's argument that there could be no stability in east Asia except under their leadership was threatened by Chiang Kai Shek's success in uniting China.

Japan then (in 1937) staged the infamous Marco Polo Bridge incident, south of Beijing. On the pretext that they had been attacked, they demanded the withdrawal of Chinese forces. The Chinese refused, and the invasion of China began. The Chinese Government fled to Chungking in the western part of the country, and one by one, starting in the east, the other cities fell. Nanjing was the scene of horrific atrocities, the films of which gave Western cinemagoers in Hong Kong and Singapore much food for thought. In 1938, Guangzhou fell and there was nothing to stop the Japanese from coming south to Hong Kong.

The year 1939 saw the Yangtze and Pearl Rivers being closed in the face of American and British protests. In Japan the decision was already all but taken — they would pre-emptively strike at the existing powers, and present them with a fait accompli that they believed would have to be accepted.

The basic philosophy of the Japanese at the time seemed to be that if there were to be colonialists in Asia, they should be Asian colonialists. However, to fuel — literally — their planned domination of the area, they would need to take the natural resources of South-East Asia. Knowing that the European powers, together with America, would not stand idly by (and certainly would no longer provide them with oil), the Japanese carefully planned a numbing blow that would destroy Western naval power and bases in one move. The oil they needed so desperately was available in Indonesia, but the sea-lanes from there to Japan were long and vulnerable. The only way to protect them was to destroy the enemy naval assets first.

In June of 1941, Hitler attacked Japan's old enemy, Russia. With Russia at war on her western borders, Japan felt safe from attack, and by July had made the decision to advance south. By this time, Japanese–American negotiations had reached crisis point. America was demanding that Japan leave China, but Japan regarded this as an impossibility. The Japanese continued their preparations for a simultaneous pre-emptive strike on the Anglo-American naval bases of Manila, Singapore, Wake, Hong Kong, and Pearl Harbour.

In this context we can now understand that whether Hong Kong had been garrisoned by four, six, or even twelve battalions, the Japanese strategy would have been unaffected. Had the Colony been strengthened further, the Japanese would simply have been forced to employ a larger force in their attack. Hong Kong — a major enemy naval harbour — had to be eliminated. With Hong Kong and Manila (the two guardians of the South China Sea) in their hands, Japan's supply of oil would be protected.

On 6 November 1941, the Japanese Imperial Headquarters ordered the China Expeditionary Army to prepare to attack Hong Kong on the understanding that participation in the attack must not imperil the security of the zones already occupied. They were ordered to assemble at Shen Chuan, and to start operations immediately after those in Malaya.

> Objective: Neutralise air power and destroy vessels and installations. Method: after crossing the border, occupy Tai Mo Shan and press forward to the line running east to west beyond the hill. After forcing that line and occupying Kowloon, the main attack would be on the north shore of Hong Kong Island, but preparations should be made to land a detachment on the southern beaches to lead the defenders to believe an attack would be made there. (123)

2 The Battle

THE WEEK IMMEDIATELY PRECEDING THE FIGHTING

Responsibility for the defence of Hong Kong and its grotesquely swollen wartime population lies squarely on the shoulders of Major General C. M. Maltby. Maltby, a highly respected career soldier of the old school, has a garrison of some 14,000 men behind him.[1]

There are six infantry battalions[2] in the Colony. Two, the 5/7th Rajputs[3] and the 2/14th Punjabis, are from the old Indian army that Maltby himself — he is fluent in Hindustani — has served with for some thirty years. Two are famous British names, the 1st Middlesex (the 'Die Hards') and the 2nd Royal Scots (the 'First of Foot'). The final two are Canadian, the Royal Rifles of Canada, and the Winnipeg Grenadiers.[4]

There are also the Hong Kong Volunteer Defence Corps (HKVDC) — virtually an army within an army — who, being locals, know the ground better than most of the professionals.

These are supported by a large Royal Artillery contingent — including the Hong Kong and Singapore Royal Artillery (HKSRA) — who man guns ranging from massive 9.2-inch fixed coastal defences to 40-mm Bofors anti-aircraft guns.

Aside from these are all the support arms: the Royal Army Service

Corps (RASC), the Royal Army Ordnance Corps (RAOC), the Signallers, the Royal Engineers (RE), the medics, and so forth.

Hong Kong is also home to a bustling naval community, comprised of both professionals and local volunteers, and a small RAF unit at Kai Tak which — on the first day of the week (Monday, 1 December 1941) — receives a new commander in the form of Wing Commander H. G. 'Ginger' Sullivan.

From this day onward there is a considerable increase in Japanese naval and aerial activity around Hong Kong. Preparation work continues on the fixed defences on the mainland, and 100 rounds of ammunition are delivered to each artillery piece with the same held in reserve at West Fort and a further 200 rounds per gun stored at the Mau Tau Kok ordnance depot (93: 127).[5]

In 1937, a loosely fortified defensive line known as the Gin Drinkers Line had been constructed across the New Territories from Gin Drinkers Bay to Tide Cove, then east to Port Shelter. Initially on his posting to Hong Kong, Maltby had not intended — through sheer lack of manpower — to defend this line at all. However, with the addition of the two Canadian battalions[6] to the garrison he changes his mind. The defenders are therefore split into two brigades, with the Mainland Brigade charged with the defence of the Gin Drinkers Line, and the Island Brigade charged with 'Home Defence'.

The Mainland Brigade, under Brigadier Wallis,[7] consists of the Royal Scots (commanded by Lt. Col. White), the Punjabis (commanded by Lt. Col. Kidd), the Rajputs (commanded by Lt. Col. Cadogan-Rawlinson), and elements of the HKSRA, Royal Engineers, Hong Kong Mule Company, and HKVDC.

The Island Brigade, under Brigadier Lawson,[8] consists of the Middlesex (commanded by Lt. Col. Stewart), the Royal Rifles (commanded by Lt. Col. Home), the Winnipeg Grenadiers (commanded by Lt. Col. Sutcliffe), and all remaining supporting units and elements of the Royal Artillery and HKVDC.

The Gin Drinkers Line, defended by (from west to east) the Royal Scots, the Punjabis, and the Rajputs, has been manned since mid-November. A Company of the Royal Scots occupies its positions on the 11th, B Company on the 12th, C Company on the 18th, and D Company on the 22nd. The Punjabis man their posts on the 27th, with the Rajputs coming into the line a little earlier. The HKSRA begins preparing gun positions on the mainland on the 20th (139).

By Monday, 1 December, the defences are prepared.

On Tuesday, war or no war, Hong Kong's glitterati (including the Governor, Sir Mark Young) lavishly celebrate the philanthropist Sir Robert and Lady Ho Tung's diamond wedding anniversary at the Hong Kong Hotel in Central.[9]

On Wednesday, General Maltby — aware of Chinese intelligence reports (95: 24) stating that on the following day ten to twenty thousand Japanese troops will arrive at Sham Chun, just over the Chinese border from Hong Kong — tours the frontier and observes Japanese troops through binoculars. Meanwhile, the Grand Christmas Bazaar held by the British War Fund Committee at Maltby's residence, Flagstaff House, attracts a large crowd and is declared a success (94: 13).

Thursday sees the Hong Kong Volunteer Defence Corps, on exercises at Fan Ling near the Chinese border, ordered to strike camp early and return to the Island — a clear indication of intelligence of Japanese plans. That evening, Maltby dines with the officers of the 1st Middlesex (96: 31).[10]

By Friday, the situation is considered serious enough for the number one degree of readiness order to be issued at Kai Tak. All personnel are confined to the station, the defences are manned and the RAF aircraft are bombed-up and dispersed (61: 58).

Wallis has delegated a key task — interference with any Japanese advance through the New Territories — to Major George E. Gray, commander of C Company of the 2/14 Punjabis. Gray is an old soldier who had enlisted in the Sussex Yeomanry at the age of sixteen, and had celebrated his nineteenth birthday at Gallipoli. His job is to slow down the Japanese advance, largely through road and bridge demolition, until they reach the first defensive positions on the Gin Drinkers Line.

On this day, Gray takes his company to Fan Ling, together with the Field Company Engineers and other elements of the HKVDC[11] (including a demolition party of HKVDC engineers under Lieutenant I. B. Tamworth, Signallers, four Bren carriers under Second Lieutenant Edwards, and two armoured cars under Second Lieutenant M. G. Carruthers)[12] and establishes his Company HQ.

On the other side of the border, the main force of the Japanese 38th Division — tasked with the invasion of the Colony — together with other units (some 60,000 men in total),[13] leaves the San Shui/Nan Hai area to prepare for the invasion at To Kat, some eight miles from the frontier.

More pragmatic, Hong Kong's Japanese newspaper ceases publication (the number of Japanese in Hong Kong had dropped to about 80), but the English-language version continues (44: 25).

On Saturday, 6 December, the main elements of the Japanese 38th Division are assembled. Captain Batty-Smith (the Governor's ADC) calls Thomas Harmon (the Public Works Department's inspector of furniture) and Von Kobza Nagy (a Hungarian picture restorer) to Government House to discuss the hiding of the more valuable works of art there (including the famous Chater collection) in the grounds (probably in a bricked-up annex to the air-raid shelter which ran under the house). The PWD itself, less interested in art than defence, sets up barbed-wire entanglements along the waterfront, running from pillbox to pillbox.

Despite these military activities, peacetime attitudes die hard. In this uneasy blend of peace and war, the Middlesex Regiment plays South China Athletic at football (94: 14), the Hong Kong Cricket Club plays Hong Kong University (150), and the band of the Royal Scots plays at the Happy Valley racecourse as the day's races run. According to one witness there, Mabel Redwood, an auxiliary nurse who would find herself on the front line just twelve days later, 'by tiffin time there seemed to be tenseness. Military police were advising soldiers to return to barracks immediately' (95: 33).[14]

That night, in a *fin de siècle* atmosphere, parties are the mode. In the Peninsula Hotel, the Tin Hat Ball, attended by the Governor amongst others, is in full swing, hoping to raise £160,000 towards the purchase of bombers for the RAF. A noted beauty of the time, Hilda Yen, sings, but then at nearly midnight T. B. Wilson, the president of the American Steamship line, appears on the balcony above the dance floor, announcing: 'any men connected with any ships in the harbour — report aboard for duty. At once' (95: 33).

At a Canadian officer's party at the same time, a witness recalls: 'suddenly interrupted by a telephone call. Major Lyndon, the Brigade Major, left immediately, Captain Bush half an hour later, and Colonel Hennessey never reached the party at all' (95: 33). Both Lyndon and Hennessey would be dead within a fortnight.

Another party at the Hong Kong Hotel, after the Middlesex Regiment plays rugby at the Cricket Club (now Chater Garden), goes on until 4.30 a.m. (95: 33). While these parties are in progress, the Anti-Aircraft Defence Commander receives orders to place all guns at Immediate Readiness (93: 127).

On Sunday, 7 December, the new Colonial Secretary, Mr F. C. Gimson, arrives in Hong Kong. He is to spend the entire war in internment. Had he but known it, the Japanese across the border had just received their orders. They read:

> Objective: The main objective of the Hong Kong Operation is to capture Hong Kong by destroying the enemy forces.
>
> Policy: In co-operation with the Navy, an element of the 23rd Army will attack Kowloon Peninsula and Hong Kong Island from the mainland.
>
> Strength (Refer to Analysis): In strict secrecy, the 23rd Army will assemble powerful units of its attack force in the vicinity of Shen Chuan Hsu while its main force will assemble in the vicinity of Hu Men, Shih Lung, and Canton.
>
> The operation will commence immediately after the operation in Malaya is definitely known to have started. As soon as battle has begun, army and navy air units will strike Hong Kong and its environs. Enemy air power will be neutralized and all important military installations, as well as all vessels in the harbour, will be destroyed. The invasion force, timing the action with the progress of the air attack, will break across the boundary near Shen Chuan Hsu, occupy Mount Tai Mo Shan, and press forward to a line running east to west of the hill.
>
> At this line, the invasion force will prepare for a major attack. It will advance and destroy enemy positions aligned east to west near Jubilee Reservoir (Shing Mun) and drive down to the southern tip of Kowloon Peninsula. To support the advance of the main invasion force, a small sea advance unit will operate near Tsing I. Then, depending upon the battle situation, troops may be landed to the west of Mount Ma On Shan in order to attack the enemy's right flank.
>
> Immediately after the capture of Kowloon Peninsula, troops will prepare to attack Hong Kong. Enemy military installations on such small islands as Tsing I, Stonecutters, and others must be destroyed before the major operation is launched. In attacking Hong Kong, troops will first land on its northern beach and from there enlarge their gains. To facilitate this operation, as large a demonstration movement as possible will be staged on the southern beach of Hong Kong to lead the enemy to believe forces will land there.
>
> The invasion will be carried out in close co-operation with the navy.

> If battle exigencies demand, part of the army and navy air units already in action in other areas, may be called upon to support the Hong Kong operation.
>
> Movement after the capture of Hong Kong: The 23rd Army will resume the mission of maintaining the security of the already occupied zones as well as the vicinity of Hong Kong.
>
> The army will assemble the 38th Division and other troops in the vicinity of Hong Kong and prepare them for new missions in other zones.[15]

Waiting for them, apart from Major Gray's border force, is the Mainland Brigade manning the Gin Drinkers Line.[16]

The Royal Scots are on the west side, holding a line from Gin Drinkers Bay to the Shing Mun Redoubt and the southern slopes of the Tai Mo Shan mountain. The Punjabis continue the line to Sha Tin and thence to Tide Cove and the sea, and the Rajputs are on the eastern side south of Tide Cove to prevent the Japanese crossing there.[17] The Mainland Brigade is supported by three mobile elements of the HKSRA, the 2nd Mountain Battery, the 3.7-inch howitzers of the 1st Mountain Battery (under Maj. Hunt), and the 25th Medium Battery.[18] No. 1 Company HKVDC is stationed at Kai Tak under Captain A. H. Penn.

The RAF — what little there is of them — is also ready:

> I take a Vildebeeste with full bomb load on a test climb during which I try to imagine where would be the best place to drop them and what would be my chances if attacked by fighters. But everything is peaceful and Hong Kong looks quite beautiful far beneath. We park the Walrus on the water and disperse the Beests but what wonderful targets they make. (Squadron Leader Donald Hill (89))

Maltby is called out of the Church Parade at St John's Cathedral by an officer who tells him that the Japanese are almost certainly mustering at the border (95: 34). At the same time, some elements in Hong Kong seem to underestimate the likelihood of attack: 'the reports are certainly exaggerated and have the appearance of being deliberately fostered by the Japanese who, judging by their defensive preparations around Canton, appear distinctly nervous of being attacked' (95: 25).

However, at eleven in the morning Maltby orders the entire garrison to stand-to in their battle positions (95: 34). A call for all personnel to report to their units is put out on the radio and at the cinema and a State of Emergency is announced.

By six in the evening of 7 December, all military personnel are at readiness in their positions[19] and the gunboat HMS *Cicala* is at two hours' readiness to steam (95: 35).

As the carnival rides and sideshows of the last day of 'Tait's Carnival' amuse the Colony's children (113: 206), the waiting is almost over.

THE BATTLE

Before approaching the details of the battle, it is advisable to understand a summary that can be used as a skeleton upon which the flesh of detail will be built. The eighteen days of fighting can neatly be summarized as six phases:
- The Loss of the Mainland
- The Siege of the Island
- The Invasion of the Island
- The Forcing of Wong Nai Chung Gap[20]
- Pushing the Line West
- Encircling Stanley

In fact the last two phases are concurrent, but as the Stanley battle is the final engagement, it will be left to last.

The Loss of the Mainland, 8–13 December

Beginning in the early hours of 8 December, the Japanese slowly but irresistibly move south towards Kowloon. A small force of Punjabis and Field Engineers, supported by infantry of the HKVDC, delay their progress by sabotage until the Gin Drinkers Line is reached.

Here, at the Shing Mun Redoubt, is the first — and telling — skirmish in which the Royal Scots are pushed out of their position and fall back to Golden Hill. Golden Hill is very exposed, and in a far bigger battle the next day it is given up. From then until the evacuation of the Mainland there is only one other significant engagement, at the Ma Lau Tong line, as the Indian rearguard defends their retreat.

The Siege of the Island, 13–18 December

With all defending forces now tied up on the Island, the Japanese start a concerted effort to bomb and shell all militarily significant areas. The Peak and the fixed defences (gun batteries and pillboxes) are the major targets, though civilian areas in Central, Mid-Levels, Causeway Bay, and Wan Chai are also hit with many casualties.

The Invasion of the Island, 18 December

On the evening of 18 December, the invasion begins. Japanese landings commence between North Point and Shau Kei Wan in conditions made all the more confusing for the defenders by poor weather and thick smoke from bombed industrial sites. The Rajputs, with elements of the Middlesex, HKVDC, Royal Artillery, and Royal Rifles becoming involved as the beachhead moves inland, put up the initial resistance. By midnight, almost the whole north-eastern corner of Hong Kong is in Japanese hands, with the line as far south as the northernmost point of Jardine's Lookout, and as far west as the North Point power station.

The Forcing of Wong Nai Chung Gap, 19 December

The Japanese strategy is simple: to take Wong Nai Chung Gap and continue south along Repulse Bay Road to split the Island in two. This necessitates keeping East Brigade busy so they cannot organize any useful counter-attack, while other Japanese forces concentrate on knocking out defences on Jardine's Lookout and Mount Nicholson (overlooking the Gap from the east and west respectively), and in the bottom of the Gap itself. Once this is done, and the strategically important police station at the south of the Gap is captured, the fighting moves south along Repulse Bay Road. In 1941 it is relatively sparsely populated, thus the skirmishes on this and later days are generally named after the houses at or around which they occur: from north to south, Postbridge, Altamira and The Ridge, Twin Brooks, Overbays, Repulse Bay Hotel, and Eucliffe.

    This is by far the hardest day's fighting, with the defenders incurring in twenty-four hours approximately one-third of their total fatalities. Losses to the attackers are probably in a similar ratio.

By midnight, although there are still pockets of resistance, the Gap and the majority of the road are in all practical terms in Japanese hands.

How far south Japanese forward patrols advance along the road that day is uncertain, but there is a distinct possibility that a few small groups or individuals reach the south coast itself.

Pushing the Line West, 19–25 December

As early as the night of the 18th, the defenders have the genesis of a line running south from the power station through the developed north coast to the hills, preventing the Japanese from advancing to Central. Over the next few days this 'northern sector' is pushed steadily west with the northernmost anchor moving from Caroline Hill quickly back to Leighton Hill (which is defended energetically) and finally Morrison Hill and Mount Parish, while street fighting is rife in Wan Chai. The southern anchor moves from Wong Nai Chung Gap to Mount Nicholson, then Mount Cameron, and finally Wan Chai Gap and a little west.

Further south is the 'central sector'. Here Mount Nicholson is taken with ease, but Mount Cameron is a hard struggle, with Wan Chai Gap being held almost to the end. Finally, there is the 'southern sector' which falls back in stages from Shouson Hill, to Brick Hill, to the stoutly defended Bennet's Hill.

It is this relentless western progress that prompts the surrender on the 25th, by which time it is felt that Wan Chai cannot be held any longer. Central is already within the range of small arms fire from the central sector.

As this phase and the next, although independent, occur simultaneously, they will be covered in parallel in the text.

Encircling Stanley, 19–26 December

When East Brigade HQ at Tai Tam withdraws towards Stanley on the 19th, fighting on two fronts becomes impossible to avoid. Delaying actions at Red Hill and Bridge Hill cannot prevent the Japanese advance from the north-east, and the Repulse Bay Hotel area cannot be held against their advance from the north-west. The circle tightens around Stanley Mound and Stone Hill, where Canadians and Volunteers fight it out with the invaders in particularly tough country, and finally squeezes them into the Stanley peninsula itself. By the time of the official surrender on Christmas Day, the first two of three defensive lines have fallen. However, defence of the final line is maintained until the early hours of 26 December, when written orders to surrender are finally delivered to Brigadier Wallis.

Now read the war diary as the events unfold hour by hour.

3 Phase I: The Loss of the Mainland

The task of the Mainland Brigade is expressed in very simple terms: hold the Gin Drinkers Line as long as possible (134).

Once the Japanese cross the front line, the Royal Engineers, covered by the Punjabis and elements of the HKVDC, begin their delaying action. Interestingly, even at this time the delay seems to be for delay's sake. All preparations have been made already, and with the simultaneous attacks on Malaya and other areas, no reinforcements can be expected to rush to Hong Kong's aid from Singapore.

The strongest point of the line is the Shing Mun Redoubt. However, 'Redoubt' is a strong word for a sparsely defended (with just five pillboxes) twelve-acre patch of hilly ground with a perimeter some three-quarters of a mile long, manned — as it transpires — by about forty-five personnel all told. Its defence — when it comes some thirty-six hours after the initial Japanese advance — is less than epic. Only some twenty-two British Other Ranks (BOR) and one Indian Other Rank (IOR) are not trapped underground. Of these, four BORs and one IOR retreat to the Observation Post (OP) for safety, five are wounded and left behind (one dies), and Sergeant Robb with the survivors withdraws east to join the Rajputs (134). There is no great battle. The Redoubt falls with very little fighting.

Once the Redoubt has fallen, the Royal Scots fall back to a new position on Golden Hill. Maltby and Wallis plan a counter-attack at dawn on the 10th. At both 07.30 and 09.30, Wallis encourages Lieutenant Colonel White commanding the Royal Scots to launch this action against the Japanese now holding the Redoubt, but White has no faith in the plan (or, possibly, his own troops), and nothing materializes.

Wallis in turn has little faith in the Royal Scots. In his own words, written in a POW camp some two months later:

> I was none too happy re the state of discipline of the Battalion as exemplified by:
> a) The numbers of courts martial, some of them on officers
> b) The high rate of venereal disease
> c) The high percentage of malaria (indicative perhaps of lack of discipline)
>
> During this fighting, men of the Royal Scots are found drinking in Wan Chai on the Island. Later, on taking over the east infantry brigade on the Island, I sent to my H.A. a captain Harold Sheldon (a judge), to frame [courts martial] charges against these deserters. Subsequent fighting precluded their trial and justice was not possible. (134)

Maltby, on being asked, post-war, what reliance could be put on Wallis's negative reports about the Royal Scots: 'Wallis was not quite up to the job he was asked to take on. He was a tremendous talker and during the operations constantly referred to me for advice. He was a good fighter and I think you can accept his evidence as correct. His report on the Royal Scots is in my opinion 90% correct' (134).[1]

When questioned about White, he said: 'White was a bad CO. I suggested to Wallis that he should relieve him of the command of the Battalion but the latter pointed out that there was no senior officer in the Battalion who was any better or in any way worthy to take his place.' 'His adjutant[2] was useless, as was also his second in command.'[3] 'The QM (Bowes?)[4] was a menace, and there was an old and doddery dug out, I think by the name of Walker, I think he was a Major[5] and I can't remember what he commanded' (134). However, Maltby blamed the rot on White's predecessor, McDougall: 'I only saw Lt. Colonel McDougall for a few weeks. He was sodden with gin and completely ruined his Battalion' (134).

He commented on Jones, nominally in command of the Shing Mun

Redoubt: 'Captain Jones was of course an utterly useless Company Commander.' On the fall of the Redoubt itself, he continued:

> I am however convinced that:
> a) Jones had no standing or moving patrol out on his front.
> b) He and his men were all caught below ground in the pillboxes and complicated communication trenches of the Shing Mun Redoubt.
> c) A number of the garrison immediately escaped and joined up with Newton [Rajputs] and the remainder were pinned below ground until Jones decided to surrender. (134)

The Japanese thought along similar lines: 'the collapse resulted from shortcomings in establishing the system of fortifications and by their failure to exercise proper security measures against our forces' (122).

Once the Redoubt has fallen, no defence in depth has been prepared. The Golden Hill positions to which the Royal Scots fall back are useless militarily, and when these are lost it is clear that the further defence of Kowloon will not be possible. The challenge then becomes to evacuate as many men and as much material as possible to the Island.

The Royal Scots and D Company Winnipeg Grenadiers (who, with a few supporting Canadian elements, had been brought to the Mainland at the last minute) are evacuated from Tsim Sha Tsui. The Indian units fall back along the line of peaks to Devil's Peak itself in a very well-managed rearguard action. Later, minus some mules, they too will be brought back to the Island.

8 DECEMBER MONDAY

> I can't remember being frightened. My parents seemed, my mother seemed terrified ... but I can't remember fear. To me it was an adventure if you want to put it that way ... but you're watching something that you've never experienced before. (Bill Bethell)[6]

For the Japanese, the war begins in the pre-dawn hours. At the same time as Japanese troops move forwards to attack Hong Kong from across the Chinese border, other Japanese forces attack Pearl Harbour, the Philippines, and Malaya.

For Maltby, war begins just forty-five minutes later with an intercepted

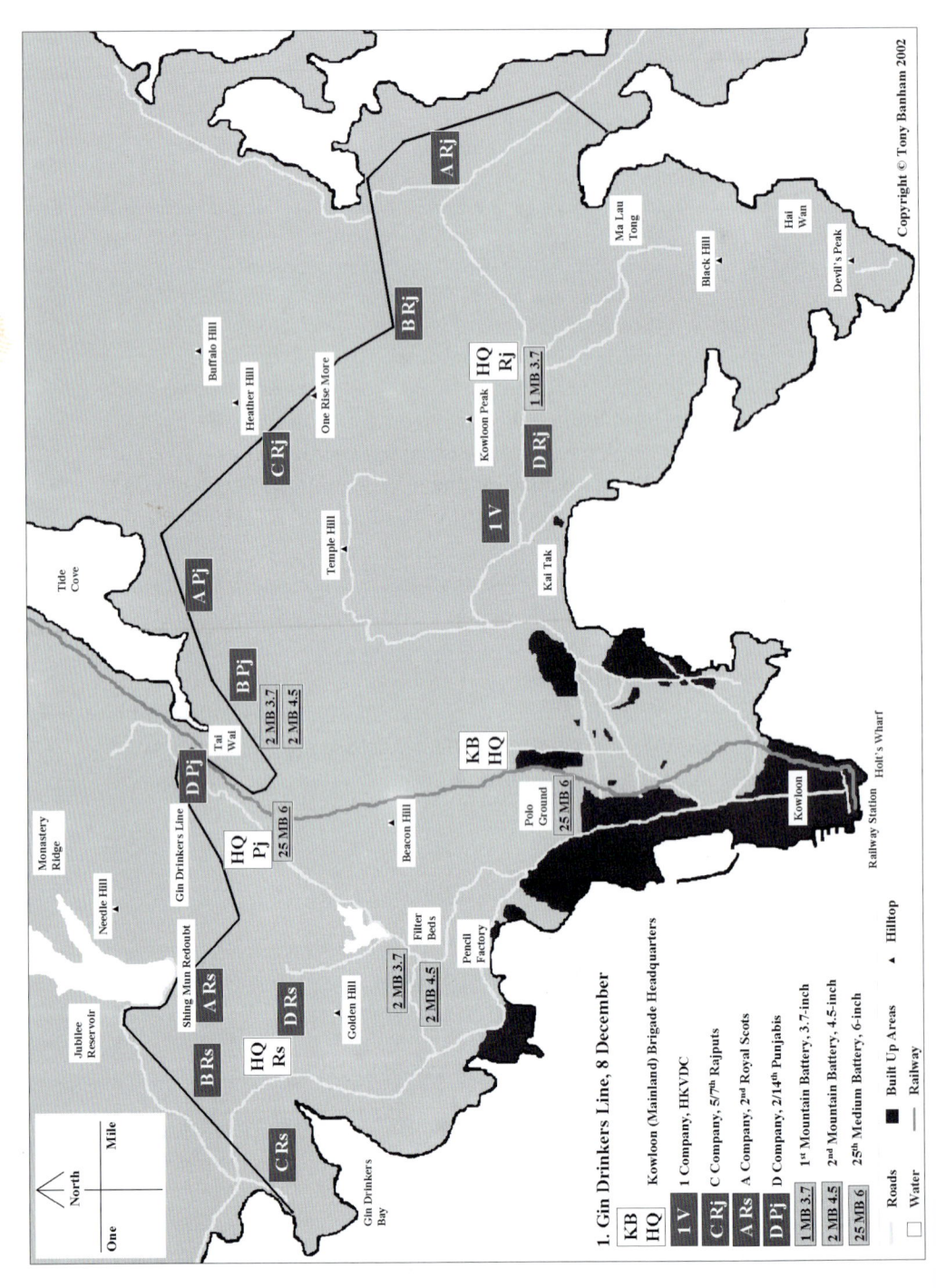

radio signal. Immediately, the Battle Box[7] is manned and the order goes out to start demolition work on the roads and bridges leading from the Chinese border to Kowloon. These demolitions continue all day, accompanied by a series of small delaying actions by the Engineers, Punjabis, and Volunteers, causing a large number of Japanese casualties.[8] Royal Scots forward patrols also encounter the Japanese.

The garrison receives official notification of hostilities two hours later, but civilians are not informed. However, at eight in the morning, the Japanese bomb Kai Tak and Sham Shui Po, thus alerting the population at large to the fact that they are at war. The day is punctuated by further air attacks, and by midnight, the Japanese are as far south as Tai Po.

Maltby's order of the day reads:

> It is obvious to us all that the test for which we have been placed here will come in the near future. I expect each and every member of my force to stick it out unflinchingly and that my force will become a great example of high-hearted courage to all the rest of the empire who are fighting to preserve truth, justice and liberty for the world. (91: 54)

As he speaks, Chinese refugees at the Kam Tin (now Sek Kong) camp decapitate the British commandant[9] and steal all the food stores (32: 65) in a taste of things to come in Kowloon. In a last breath of peace, at St John's Cathedral, Mr C. Bramall Burgess[10] marries Miss Sessan Lilian Fjord Christensen (147). Some 355 Chinese soldiers are released from Argyle Street internment camp for first aid duties (131).[11]

Gray's delaying force does its job well, but the Japanese learn to bypass the well-defended roads by travelling across open country to the east of Cloudy Hill. At the end of the day, Gray withdraws his men south of the Tai Po Causeway. Of the Japanese forces, the 228th are ordered to take position between the southern foot of Grassy Hill and east of Needle Hill. The 230th are sent to the foot of Tai Mo Shan, and the 229th to cross Tide Cove to Buffalo Hill in preparation for attack.

The Japanese are tired, but morale is high: 'Although the morale of the 228th Regiment was very high and they were full of fighting spirit, they were also greatly fatigued from a long and constant march and the heat of South China. The march for the day covered a distance of 48 kilometres and the troops had taken no sleep at all since the previous day' (122).

Those are the positions by nightfall on this first day of fighting. At sea, all Motor Torpedo Boats are at war stations. MTBs 10 and 08 are off Po Toi Island (near Stanley), 07 and 09 off Lamma Island, and 27 and 26 at the Tathong Boom[12] (as there was no accommodation on the Thorneycroft boats, the crews of 27 and 26 stayed on HMS *Robin* near the Boom) (143e). Meanwhile, HMS *Tamar* (the old wooden-hulled ship from which the naval base gets its name) is taken out of the naval dockyards to her buoy in the harbour (99: 37). All *Tamar* personnel are re-housed in the China Fleet Club[13] (130: 19), and the Water Police are kept busy evacuating the outlying islands (98: 169).

At dawn, the HKSRA — with the garrison's only mobile guns — are occupying seven section positions and seven observation posts on the mainland (90). Other units are sent to new battle stations: 'We were to be dispatched to Stonecutters Island[14] instead of to Magazine Gap where we had done most of our training. On Stonecutters we were considered beach defence, as well as protection for British and Indian artillery units that had been firing effectively on advancing Japanese troops in the New Territories. We had some casualties from dive bombers responding to our machine-gun activities': Matthews of 3 Company HKVDC (23: 231).[15]

In the hours of darkness, the Royal Artillery concentrates on putting down harassing fire from Stonecutters Island's 6-inch and 60-pounder guns on Japanese positions at Lok Lo Ha and north of Pai Tau valley.[16] The 5 AA Regiment Wong Nai Chung Section is despatched to Queen's Road recreation ground, and the Albany Road section is sent forward to King's Park, Kowloon.[17]

Diary for 8 December

00.01   A small bomb explodes in a side lane near Waterloo Street (131).

00.10   A mystery explosion is reported in Russell Street, Wan Chai (147).

00.45   A second mystery explosion is reported near Luen Fat Street, Southorn Garden, Wan Chai (147).

02.00   An unexploded bomb is found at the entrance to the cinema at the foot of Hung Hom station (131).

PHASE I: THE LOSS OF THE MAINLAND   27

04.00   The Japanese command order their troops to attack Hong Kong.

04.45   Tokyo makes a radio broadcast warning Japanese citizens that war with the US and its allies is imminent: 'The Army and Navy divisions of Imperial Headquarters jointly announced at six o'clock this morning (Tokyo time), 8 December, that the Imperial Army and Navy forces have begun hostilities against the American and British forces in the Pacific at dawn today' (21: 45). The broadcast is intercepted by Major Charles R. Boxer (a fluent Japanese speaker) in Fortress HQ.[18] A second broadcast from British forces in Singapore confirms that Malaya is being invaded. The Engineers and Punjabis are immediately ordered to blow all forward demolitions (95: 36).

05.00   Major General Maltby and staff descend, via an entrance immediately north of Kennedy Road near today's British Consulate, into the Battle Box fifty feet under the Murray Barracks.

05.00   Work starts on demolition of the Kowloon Canton Railway Corporation (KCRC) bridges over the Sham Chun river north of Fan Ling (79: 221).

05.30   The forward bridges are blown.

06.25   Dr Newton, based in the Kowloon Hospital, receives a call from the MO (Medical Officer) in charge telling him that a 'Precautionary Stage' had been declared (95: 43).[19]

06.30   Staff Officer Operations relays a message to destroyer HMS *Scout*'s First Lieutenant Briggs to pass to the Captain, 'tell your Captain that we are at war with Japan and to get the ship ready for sea' (31: 1).

06.45   The garrison is warned that Japan and the Empire are at war (20: 6).

07.00   Kai Tak airfield receives warning of a Japanese air attack.[20]

07.30   More bridges across the frontier are blown and roads through Fan Ling made impassable. Gray states that 'There was complete silence and nothing happened until about 7.30 am when it was reported to me from an observation post that several thousand Japs were pouring over the frontier on my right flank' (91: 68). Gray falls back to Tai Po, where he is met by Major Bottomley's HKVDC Field Company Engineers.

08.00 A dozen Japanese Ki 36 bombers of the 45th Sentai escorted by nine Ki 27 fighters of the 10th Independent Chutai, operating from Guang Zhou, approach Kai Tak from the west in a V formation. They machine-gun and dive-bomb the barrack blocks and the RAF's three dispersed Vickers Vildebeeste torpedo bombers. They then attack the two surviving Supermarine Walrus amphibians and sink them both.[21] 'Both Walrus are gone, one Beeste is ablaze, another badly damaged, leaving one plane intact. We attempt to put out the fire praying that the bombs won't explode. The blaze is too fierce and she is completely burned with two red hot heavy bombs amongst the ruins' (89).[22]

Turning their attention to the civil aircraft in the airport or moored offshore, they destroy, the PanAm Clipper (Sikorsky S-42B NC16735),[23] the impressed HKVDC training aircraft of the Air Unit,[24] five Curtis T-32 Condors of the CNAC, and three Junkers 52/3m of Eurasia Air Corporation (XIX, XXII, XXIV). A fourth, Junkers 52/3m (XV), is undamaged, as is the Junkers W.34 (II) and a sixth T-32 (which was later captured intact by the Japanese and re-used) (11: 98).

Joyce Basset (secretary to Governor Sir Mark Young): 'I heard "crumping" sounds from Kai Tak and looked out of the window. You could see the planes diving in with their bombs' (15: 6). '[S]houts of delight came from onlookers when one or more planes were seen to be falling but their delight died when the planes pulled out of their dives after releasing their bombs' (147). 'Orange flames and grey-black smoke indicated direct hits on grounded planes' (30: 16).

A civilian market nearby is hit: 'The wounded and dead are still lying under the wreckage. The walls of the building and pavement are spattered with human blood and flesh and people are moving out of the houses that have been hit' (117: 22). Bombs fall in Ta Ku Ling Road and Yen Chau Street. The latter causes forty-one casualties (131).

The Sham Shui Po Barracks and police station are also strafed, and two Canadians in the Jubilee Buildings (142) are wounded (95: 37).[25] Captain E. L. Hurd, Winnipeg Grenadiers:

> I was discussing the alarm with Capt. Thompson, and at the same time noticed three bombs dropping from one plane... We dashed into Capt. Barnett's room, just as the bombs hit. Some hit in the Jubilee Building near where our officers were quartered. Another hit still closer, probably forty feet from where we were taking cover. Two others hit in front of the Ration Stores near the main gate. There were several casualties in this area but with the exception of two O.R. of Brigade Staff, they were all Chinese servants. (100: 45)

Meanwhile the first reports are coming in from forward positions that Japanese are pouring in to Laffan's Plain (3: 6). They are crossing the Sham Chun river at Lo Wu (heading for the Castle Peak Road) and Sha Tau Kok (heading for the Tai Po road) (44: 71).

08.15   Dr Newton arrives at the Kowloon Hospital.

08.30   Tamworth's engineers destroy two bridges at Lo Wu as planned. He then withdraws to Gill's Cutting,[26] blocks the road and railway there, and pulls back further to Tai Po market (3: 7).

08.30   HMS *Cicala* receives a signal ordering her to proceed to Castle Peak Bay (91: 80).

09.00   Before 9 o'clock, Sister Sybil Spencer of the Colonial Nursing Service attached to Kowloon Hospital is in her ward, receiving the first casualties from the bombing (91: 53). By day's end there will be 103 (95: 44).

09.00   Japanese forces from the 38th Division are now confirmed to be attacking across the border, with the 228th and 230th in the west, and the 229th via Laffan's Plain towards Tide Cove.

09.05   First air raid ends (147).

10.00   Bokhara Battery (on Cape D'Aguilar) engages an enemy patrol vessel at extreme range (93: 128).

10.00   The Special Branch lock up Japanese consular officials and staff under police guard at number 7 Conduit Road (131).

10.15	Six Royal Scots 'commando sections', each consisting of an NCO and two men, move forward to watch the tracks leading eastwards from the Castle Peak Road (134).
11.00	Two Japanese aircraft attack HMS *Cicala*. Captain Boldero states: 'It was a frightening, but at the same time, an intensely exhilarating experience. *Cicala* was fitted with triple rudders and could be turned almost on a sixpence' (91: 81).
12.00	Captain K. S. Robertson destroys three more bridges on the Tai Po road and the KCRC at Pineapple Pass[27] (3: 7).
12.00	A further bridge is destroyed as the first Japanese run across it (27: 16).
13.30	A second air raid starts: a dive-bombing raid on Kowloon (147). The Kowloon Docks are hit (131).
13.30	APV *Shun Wo* — under HKRNVR Lieutenant D. P. Ralph — returns from Aberdeen patrol,[28] having been informed by Eastman[29] in a motorboat at 05.20 that war had been declared (130: 14).
14.00	APV *Minnie* returns from Tathong patrol and *Indira* takes her place (130: 13). On this voyage, APV *Indira* — under HKRNVR Lieutenant Desmond Hindmarsh — is attacked by aircraft, and three of those on board (Cadet Mike Laloe and two gunners from the training sloop *Cornflower*) are wounded, one fatally.
14.00	The forward Bren carriers of the Royal Scots make contact with the Japanese near Yuen Long (134).
14.30	A second attack on *Cicala* commences.
15.00	The Japanese advanced party attacks Gray's line and are driven off (20: 6). They are repulsed. Sources claim that there are up to one hundred Japanese casualties (91: 70).[30]
15.40	The second air raid ends (147).
16.00	The Japanese 230th occupy the top of Tai Mo Shan (44: 72).
16.00	The last MTB leaves the Kowloon base to move to Aberdeen,[31]

following the first that had left at 12.00. MTB 12 remains in Hong Kong Dockyard undergoing repairs (143e).

17.00 APV *Han Wo* returns from Beaufort patrol having been unsuccessfully attacked by three bombers (130: 14). APV *Perla* replaces her.

17.30 Another air raid commences on Kowloon, lasting till dusk (15: 8).

18.00 APV *Stanley* starts Aberdeen patrol (130: 14).

18.30 The railway tunnel south of Tai Po is destroyed. Japanese forces walk into an ambush prepared by the Punjabis on the left of Gray's line. The Punjabis, astride the Tai Po road, decimate the advancing Japanese units as they come down the hillside on a track towards Tai Po. Japanese casualties are again estimated at around one hundred (95: 41).

19.00 The first of the three surviving CNAC aircraft takes off for Namyang (61: 59), evacuating CNAC personnel and their families. The total number rescued by the 10th is 275.[32] Escorting the Soong sisters (Sun Yat-Sen's widow and her sister) to their waiting plane, Cohen reports: 'It was a pretty grim farewell. We all knew that it was likely to be our last. For once I found myself absolutely tongue-tied. I couldn't think what the hell to say. We shook hands and I just blurted out, "We'll fight to the bitter end anyway"' (113: 207).[33]

19.30 The HKVDC armoured cars take part in a second ambush on the Tai Po road, destroying another Japanese platoon as it attempts to advance down the highway (20: 6).
19.30 The forward British units fall back to Cheung Shiu Tan (3: 7).[34]
19.30 The destroyers HMS *Scout* and HMS *Thanet* leave for Singapore, leaving only HMS *Thracian* to defend the colony (106: 109). However, *Thanet* only survives another seven weeks.[35] Briggs, whose wife would be interned at Stanley for the next three years and eight months, reports: 'The two ships left the dockyard at about 6.30 pm and went to an anchorage in Kowloon Bay, then

through the boom gate at 9.15 pm. which was open and ready for us to pass through.' Colin MacDonald of *The Times* is also on board as an evacuee (31: 9).[36]

20.30   Captain Robertson blows up the railway tunnel north of Cheung Shiu Tan (3: 8).

22.00   The next road bridge on the Tai Po–Sha Tin road is destroyed (3: 8).

22.25   Enemy guns are reported on Kam Tin airfield (93: 128).

22.30   A further road bridge is destroyed while Japanese are crossing (3: 8).

23.06   A false air raid alarm sounds (147).

24.00   Forward troops are now withdrawn to Tai Po Mai (20: 6), coming under attack from the left flank.

Roll of Honour for 8 December

ENGINEERS — 1 Killed

| Price, Herbert James[37] | Sapper, 22 Fortress Coy. RE | U |

Died Combined Military Hospital Kowloon. Possibly buried (126).[38]

ROYAL NAVY — 1 Killed

| Wong Yuk Wah | Ordinary Seaman, HKRNVR | UP |

Killed by bombing (133).   [1 Dec.][39]

9 DECEMBER TUESDAY

We were subject to high-level bombing daily from 9 till 5, but we suffered only minor damage & near misses. (Ralph Stephenson)[40]

The early hours reveal the shocking truth that far from being the daytime-only soldiers that the British forces had been led to expect, the Japanese can operate very effectively at night. The day is characterized by a slow withdrawal of British forces from the northern New Territories back to the Gin Drinkers Line, to the accompaniment of almost constant Japanese bombing attacks and artillery duels.

In the morning, HMS *Cicala*'s 6-inch gun engages enemy vehicles at Brother's Point (91: 82). During the day, the Japanese close up to the Gin Drinkers Line, and at nightfall, they attack at its key point — the Shing Mun Redoubt manned by the Royal Scots. This strong point is woefully undermanned. It consists of the headquarters of A Company (Capt. 'Potato' Jones and nine other ranks), No. 8 Platoon (2nd Lt. J. Thomson, Sgt. Robb, and twenty-six other ranks), and an Artillery Observation Post from 2 Mountain Battery HKSRA (Lt. L. Willcocks, with two British and two Indian Other Ranks). The A Company HQ troops and the 2 Mountain Battery men are in the Observation Post, bar one IOR posted as a sentry, and one signaller manning the exchange (134).

During the day, the only good news for the defenders is the report of a Japanese seaplane shot down at Aberdeen (at which the Navy has a shipyard and barracks for its Chinese seamen and reservists). However, with a cash prize having been offered in the papers for any planes shot down, some ten anti-aircraft sites claim the victory.

Meanwhile, Hong Kong moves onto a war footing as the Government requisitions motor lorries, vans, and motorcycles, calls out all the civilian Auxiliary Corps for service, and orders food shops to stay open from 08.00 till sunset (147).

Diary for 9 December

00.30   No. 25 Medium Battery HKSRA lays down harassing fire on Lok Lo Ha on the Tai Po road (134).

01.00   Gray's troops withdraw further down the Tai Po road into the Fo Tan valley (20: 6), and by dawn are at Tau Fung Shan Monastery ridge (44: 72).

02.00   The Field Company Engineers withdraw to Kowloon railway station (79: 222).

02.15   Fortress HQ's War Diary reads: 'the lesson of today is that the enemy can operate strongly on a moonlight night' (92: 96).

03.30 All demolitions are now successfully completed (20: 6).

05.00 APV *Poseidon* rendezvouses with minelayer *Man Yeung*, escorting her safely to Aberdeen at 11.00 (130: 15).

05.00 The Royal Scots commando sections make contact with the Japanese on the Tai Mo Shan–Telegraph Hill line, engaging them at 05.40 (134).

06.10 D Company of the Rajputs, under Captain H. R. Newton, is ordered up from Kai Tak to fill the gap between the Royal Scots on Smuggler's Ridge and the Punjabis at Sha Tin. They take position off the Tai Po road, their HQ being at Kowloon upper reservoir at the head of the Sha Tin valley (44: 72).

06.30 The MTBs return to Aberdeen (143e).

07.00 The first air raid alarm of the day sounds. It lasts only five minutes, but sets the scene for the rest of the morning (147).

07.00 The forward troops withdraw within the perimeter (134).

08.50 The second air raid alarm is sounded. Aircraft are seen off Aberdeen, which is bombed severely. The MTBs scatter (143e). The all clear is sounded at 09.15 (147).

09.00 Captain Jones makes contact with Newton to his east, and learns that the Japanese are moving towards Shing Mun (134).

09.35 The third alarm sounds. HMS *Cornflower* is straddled by bombs in Aberdeen harbour (143e). The all clear is sounded at 10:17 (147).

10.30 Official Communiqué:

> It has been a quiet night and there is nothing of special interest to report. In accordance with the defence plan contact has been maintained with the enemy in the neighbourhood of Tai Po and along the Castle Peak Road, and there has been patrol activity on both sides. There were no air raids, but the alert was sounded at 9 a.m. this morning. The Chinese Company of sappers have so far taken a leading part in operations and they continue to perform

Phase I: The Loss of the Mainland 35

their duties admirably. Some time to-day certain demolitions may be carried out in the harbour area. The public should not be alarmed as these demolitions are part of the defence plan. By means of a Bren Carrier patrol we engineered a highly successful ambush of a Japanese Platoon which was practically annihilated on the Castle Peak Road. (147)

10.40 Fourth, short, alarm (147).

10.50 Fifth alarm. The all clear is sounded at 11.38 (147).

11.20 The HKSRA reports that the enemy OP on Grassy Hill (Tso Shan) has been destroyed (93: 128).

11.45 Sixth alarm. The all clear is sounded at 12.08 (147).

12.58 The HKSRA reports an enemy working party and light gun at Lo Wai.[41] They are engaged by the 2nd Mountain Battery (93: 128).

13.00 Seventh alarm. The all clear is sounded at 14.09 (147).
13.00 *Indira* returns from patrol, damaged, and *Minnie* takes her place (130: 13).
13.00 Jones reaches Battalion HQ, where he discusses patrolling with his commanding officer, White (134).[42]

14.37 Japanese infantry at Wo Liu Hang[43] are engaged by Polo Battery with infantry observation (93: 128).

15.00 Colonel Doi observes the British from summit of Needle Hill: 'my impression was that the enemy was still inactive perhaps because of their estimate that it would take at least several more days for the Japanese troops to approach their position. Heavy fog suddenly reduced the visibility to about twenty metres.'
  He decides to attack that night (despite the fact that the Redoubt lies in another regiment's sector), and orders the 2nd Battalion to carry out a reconnaissance and secure a start line, and the 3rd to assault at 23.00 (95: 48).

17.00 Official Communiqué:

All defences on the mainland are being successfully maintained. Some artillery fire has been put down on enemy parties and their progress brought to an abrupt end. Desultory air raids have been taking place, but at least as much must be expected in the future. No serious casualties. Our anti-aircraft guns have received some excellent training on targets of which they have long dreamed. One enemy plane at least has been badly crippled. (147)

17.40   Tai Wai Battery (the 3.7-inch troop of 2 Mountain Bty. HKSRA) engages the Japanese in a nullah. The fire is reported effective by infantry (93: 128).

18.00   Gray withdraws his units to the Gin Drinkers Line (95: 42).
18.00   Meanwhile, although the war is still just a distant sound to most civilians, it is coming closer. Their movements are restricted by order. 'No person shall enter a defence area, whether from another defence area or elsewhere, unless he is [a member of the armed or auxiliary forces, or Government]' (147).

19.40   The Mount Davis Battery attempts a predicted shoot[44] on Brothers Point (Tai Lam Kok) to finish a demolition attempt.

20.00   After visiting 7 and 9 Platoons, Jones returns to the Shing Mun Redoubt (134).

21.00   In the darkness,[45] the Japanese 3rd Battalion of Colonel Doi's 228th Regiment leaves its position. Approximately 150 men of the 9th and 10th Companies are assigned to make the attack on the Shing Mun Redoubt (15: 15). Their forward obstacle-clearing teams break the defenders' wire undetected for the next hour. Inside waits 8 Platoon of A Company Royal Scots under Lieutenant Thomson (27: 18), plus A Company HQ under Captain 'Potato' Jones, and an artillery observation post under Lieutenant Willcocks of the HKSRA (95: 46). The remainder of A Company extends 400 yards towards what is now Sheung Kwai Cheung, with 7 Platoon holding Pineapple Hill and 9 Platoon on its left in touch with B Company which is on the south-western side. C Company holds the ground from there to the

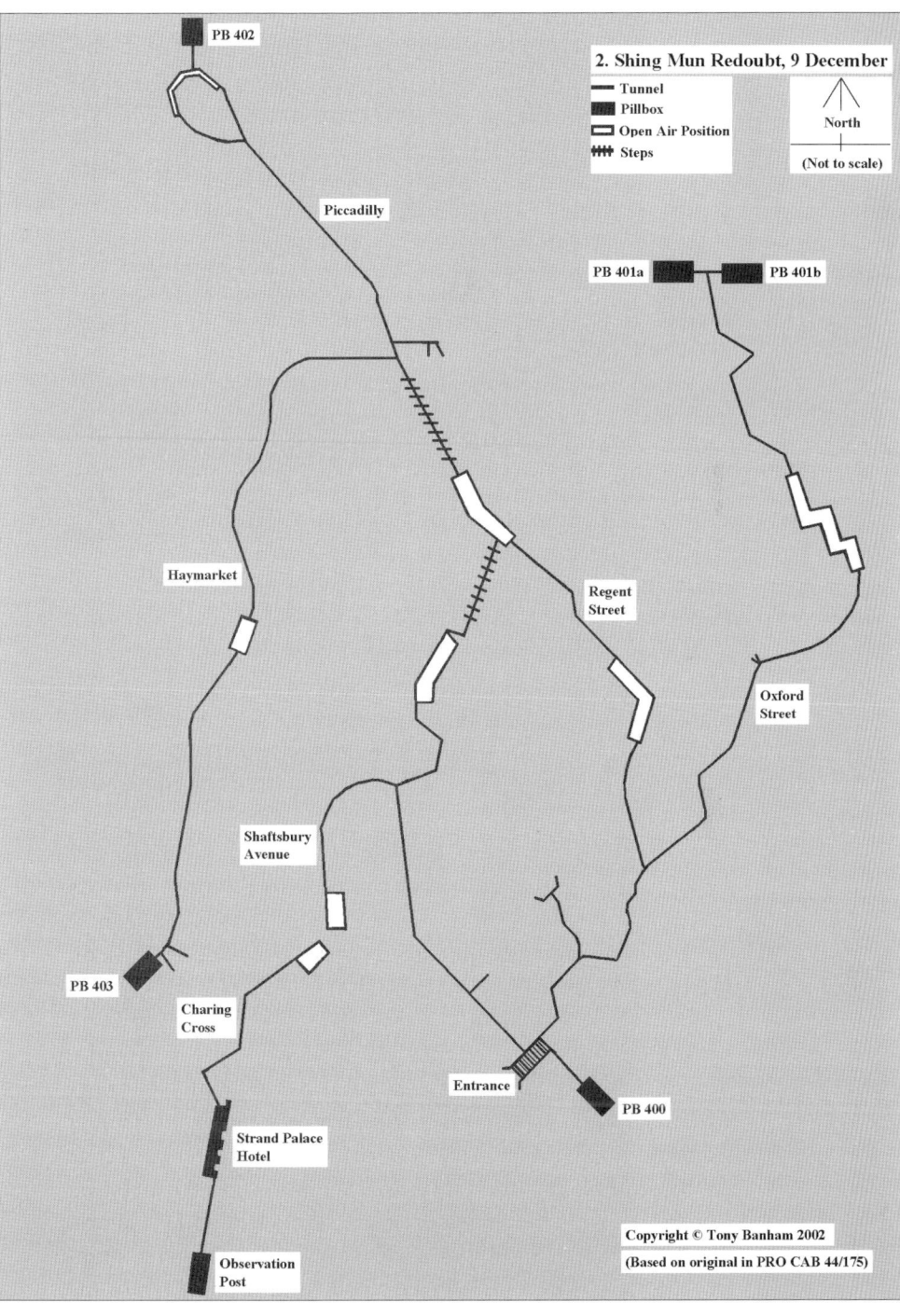

sea at the Texaco Peninsula, D Company is technically in reserve on Golden Hill, and battalion HQ is at Skeet Ground on Castle Peak Road. The forward troops under Major Burn (with five Royal Scots Bren carriers, two HKVDC armoured cars, and the engineers) are in the Ping Shan–Au Tau area (134).

22.00   Avoiding the Royal Scots 22.00 patrol of one officer and nine men, the 3rd Battalion 228th crosses the river south of (and below) the dam at the end of the Shing Mun reservoir. They climb the steep hill to a position above the Shing Mun Redoubt, move north along Smuggler's Path, and turn to the east to attack the easternmost part of the stronghold. Doi: 'Men silently making their way in darkness in gripping tension, stumbling and falling without even raising a cry, were a grim picture indeed' (122).

        The Royal Scots patrol returns without detecting them,[46] and reports to Sergeant Robb, the platoon sergeant (95: 48).

        The platoon commander reports to the company commander in the artillery observation post. They hear that the leader of Z Force[47] wishes to come up from B Company and brief them. 'That first night Kendall, the Chinese and Colin McEwan returned to our HQ at Shing Mun to obtain further maps and to report on the progress of the Japanese forces, as our lines of communication had been destroyed' (132b: Parsons).[48] A runner is sent to guide Kendall to the redoubt.[49] They wait.

22.00   The last aircraft leaves Kai Tak, carrying Lieutenant Colonel H. Owen Hughes of the HKVDC to Chung King (3: 8).

22.50   Dr Isaac Newton treats last case of the day at Kowloon Hospital (15: 18).

23.00   Lance Corporal Laird, on sentry duty to the east of the Redoubt, nearest the Shing Mun river, challenges figures approaching the wire (95: 49). They disperse and he engages them with his sub-machine gun. They reply with rifle fire and grenades. The Japanese attack the Redoubt (initially around PBs 401b and 402) from above, throwing grenades down the airshafts. While they attack the eastern parts, they are fired on from the western (and by Cpl. Campbell with a Vickers gun in a position fifty yards north of PB 402) with the 3rd Battalion HQ elements being caught in the open and suffering casualties. Sergeant Robb leads a counter-attack. Men are ordered to suppress the fire, and the battle degenerates into short blind chases through claustrophobic concrete tunnels. Sergeant Robb's party of thirteen men receive five casualties (L/Cpl. Bankier, Prts. Basnett,[50] Coyle,[51] Casey, and Jardine). They are left behind as Robb withdraws. Casey is killed when the Japanese enter. The others — apart from Jardine[52] — are captured.[53] Lieutenant W. Willcocks (the artillery observation officer of HKSRA) calls fire down on the Redoubt itself to try and dislodge Japanese forces in the open (92: 98).

23.30 Captain H. R. Newton, commanding the Reserve Company of Rajputs at the point on the Gin Drinkers Line where the Punjabi's line joins the Royal Scots, reports seeing Japanese forces coming down the Shing Mun river below the dam.

23.30 The Kowloon Police Emergency Unit is called out to a fire at Sham Shui Po Barracks caused by an arsonist. One saboteur is shot (131).

23.45 A Rajput patrol runs into a party of 200 Japanese in the Shing Mun valley about 800 yards south-east of the dam (134).

24.00 It is clear that an officer needs to leave the observation post and take command of the fighting for the Redoubt. There is a telephone conversation between the Redoubt and White, and Thomson is told to take command. He tries to leave but finds the main door locked, and the top grille already under attack. Before this, a total of four Royal Scots other ranks, and the Indian sentry, have been admitted into the observation post via the top grille (134).[54]

24.00 Newton suspects that the Redoubt[55] has already fallen. This loss leaves the Gin Drinkers Line untenable.[56]

Roll of Honour for 9 December

PUNJABIS — 1 Killed

Puran Singh   Havildar   U
  Most probably shelling on the Gin Drinkers Line, or Gray's unit.[57]

ROYAL SCOTS — 3 Killed

Casey, John   Private   U
  Left behind, wounded, at the Shing Mun redoubt on Dec 9th (92: 100). [19 Dec.]

Moore, William   Private   U
  Missing 9 Dec. (145: 179). Missing Castle Peak Road west of dairy farm, [10 Dec.]
  9 Dec (126).

Peacock, Percy Charles   Bandsman   U
  Missing 9 Dec. (145: 179). Missing Castle Peak Road west of dairy farm, [10 Dec.]
  9 Dec (126).

10 DECEMBER WEDNESDAY

> The Dockyard staff were then given the option of joining the Volunteer defence forces of the Colony, or of remaining a civilian. I don't remember anyone choosing the latter option. We duly took the oath of allegiance and received uniform. (Albert Haines)[58]

The day starts with the loss of the Shing Mun Redoubt — the defensive position that was intended to be the key to the Gin Drinkers Line holding out for a week. The Japanese are slow to take advantage of the situation — Colonel Doi's superiors even try to persuade him to withdraw from the Redoubt as he has intruded into territory allotted to the 230th — and little further fighting takes place as the Royal Scots fall back to some very inadequate positions on Golden Hill where they are machine-gunned and mortared in the morning (92: 103).

The day is again punctuated by Japanese bombing attacks and artillery duels. The pillboxes along the hill slopes above Tide Cove are systematically shelled and put out of action, and a newspaper article states that Mr Lim K. Chu (associate General Secretary of the Chinese YMCA), his wife, and some of his children are killed in Kowloon (147).[59] This news item reveals the tip of the iceberg. As the fighting moves closer to urban areas, civilian casualties start to mount, but no official record is kept.

Concerned by the rapid defeat on the Gin Drinkers Line, Maltby orders D Company of the Winnipeg Grenadiers to be hurried across from the island to take up positions at the junction of the Tai Po and Castle Peak roads. He also orders the evacuation of Kai Tak airfield. RAF personnel are evacuated from Kai Tak to Aberdeen by lighter (61: 60) after sabotaging the facilities in an effort to deny it to the Japanese. Squadron Leader Hill: 'I left late in the afternoon on the last lighter with twenty men and all the arms and ammunition. Aerodrome strewn with all kinds of obstacles to prevent use by the enemy. Chinese loot our mess as the lighter leaves' (89). RAF Corporal Tug Wilson sets fire to the radio shack as the Japanese approach. He crosses by boat to the Island with bullet wounds in his back (61: 60).

Apart from the Shing Mun Redoubt and some probes south (including a reconnaissance across Tide Cove by two boats of the 229th), there is little ground fighting and the Japanese rely on shelling and air attack as they position to consolidate their gains.

In the afternoon, Stonecutters Island is shelled and No. 1 gun is hit. Later shelling is heavier, with one havildar killed in Parade Battery and one Indian Other Rank killed in West Fort (93: 129).

During the night, as a foretaste of the future, Hong Kong Island is shelled for the first time. Hits are recorded in the vicinities of the Albany Road AA site, Kennedy Road, Bowen Road, and the 188-bed Military Hospital there (134).

Diary for 10 December

00.18   No. 2 Mountain Battery's 4.5-inch howitzers at Filter Beds — directed by Willcocks — open fire at the Japanese in areas opposite the western front of the Royal Scots (near Lo Wai and south-east of Chuen Lung). This is the last order recorded from the observation post, as communications with it are cut between 01.00 and 02.00 (134).

00.30   Captain Bowman's D Company Winnipeg Grenadiers is ordered to the mainland by Maltby (134).

01.00   The Japanese consider themselves in control of the redoubt. A Japanese inscription found in the Redoubt post-war, and still visible today, reads: 'Captured by Wakabayashi Unit'.[60]

01.19   White orders D Company Royal Scots to move their left Platoon from west of Castle Peak Road up towards Golden Hill, and C Company on the Texaco peninsula to leave one platoon guarding the road junction in Tsun Wan Wai village and the road block, and to move to the vicinity of Battalion HQ on Skeet Ground (134).

02.40   Royal Scots situation report:
      A Coy.:   Sergeant Robb and the survivors of 8 Platoon are heading towards the Rajputs, 7 and 9 Platoons are in their original positions
      B Coy.:   In its original position
      C Coy.:   In PBs 406, 407, 408
      D Coy.:   In L. 115, 116, 117, 118[61]
      HQ Coy.: Still in the OP (134)

02.45   The Japanese blow in the main steel shutter of the observation post, instantly killing two Indian signallers. Thomson is badly wounded by a grenade (92: 98). Stunned, the artillery OP (garrisoned by three officers, fifteen British ORs, and IORs) surrenders with a total of eleven casualties (134).[62]

03.15   British artillery fire is put down on the western portion of the Redoubt (20: 7).[63]

03.30   Captain Harold Newton of D Company Rajputs reports that eighteen[64] Royal Scots have reached his position from the Redoubt. In confused fighting, the Rajputs push the Japanese back up the valley and into the Redoubt (95: 50).

04.00   The Redoubt is now considered fallen to the Japanese, though one pillbox is still occupied.[65]

04.00   The police are asked to evacuate villagers from Sha Tin Pass, as the Japanese have previously used civilians as shields and to clear landmines. The evacuation is largely successful, though some villagers panic and run into minefields when Japanese start firing (131).

04.00   The Reserve Company of the Winnipeg Grenadiers arrives at Mainland Brigade HQ (20: 7). They are in dispersed positions around the polo ground by 04.30 (134).

PHASE I: THE LOSS OF THE MAINLAND 43

05.30 Wallis considers the Canadians 'too untrained' to use in a counter-attack on such difficult ground (134).

07.30 PB 402, the last still holding out at the Redoubt, is severely damaged by a British shell. Four soldiers (Cpl. Robertson's section) are dug out alive[66] by the Japanese at 14.00 (92: 102).

07.45 About one-and-a-half Japanese companies attack along the Shing Mun ridge. The attack is easily held by D Company Rajput (134).

08.00 No. 23 godown in Western District is shelled, with two civilians killed and three wounded (131).

08.30 Air raid alarm. All clear at 09.00 (147)

09.00 APV *Perla* returns from Beaufort patrol and is relieved by APV *Poseidon* (130: 14).

09.30 Japanese move south from the Redoubt and attack the Royal Scots and the Rajputs (whose battalion HQ is at Customs Pass) (3: 9). The Punjabis in the centre of the Gin Drinkers Line are also heavily shelled.

10.00 A 3.7-inch section temporarily sited at Causeway Bay (the Wong Nai Chung section) reports hitting a plane. It is later confirmed as having force-land in Tide Cove (93: 129).

10.00 Official Communiqué:

> The Japanese launched a heavy attack on our positions at 1 a.m. this morning from Shing Mun Valley and the direction of Needle Hill. Some penetration of our forward defences occurred but the attack has for the moment been halted. Fighting is continuing. In spite of extremely poor visibility our artillery of all natures has put in some very effective shooting. Shortly before 6 p.m. last night our light artillery caught a Company of Japanese who had advanced incautiously; this Company suffered severe casualties. Our casualties have so far been light. (147)

10.00 Wallis reports the Royal Scots' (Lt.- Col. White's) refusal to counter-attack the Shing Mun Redoubt to Maltby.[67] The only course available is to allow them to withdraw (134).

10.34 MTB 07 proceeds to Joss House Bay to clear it of junks (143e).

11.20 White issues a warning that the Royal Scots should prepare to move back to the Smuggler's Ridge–Lai Chi Kok Peninsula line (134).

12.00 No. 1 gun from the West Battery (Stonecutters Island) is ordered to fire on Shing Mun Redoubt (76: 63). Shortly after this, Stonecutters Island is dive-bombed and shelled (with some guns being put out of action) from a Japanese 5.9-inch howitzer battery on the Kam Tin airfield. Parade Battery's two 60-pounder, and Mount Davis No. 3 gun also fire on the Redoubt (93: 129).

12.00 Colonel Doi, having captured the Redoubt without official permission, is finally given permission for his troops to remain in the captured position (106: 122).

13.00 The Senior Superintendent of Kowloon Police meets Brigadier Wallis of the Mainland Brigade and explains that the police may be evacuated any time after 18.00. Wallis expresses surprise and claims that he can hold Kowloon indefinitely (131).

14.00 Police sent to Sai Wan Ho market find around 1,000 looters and take 'drastic action' (131).[68]

14.30 Official Communiqué:

> Two attacks from the direction of Shing Mun have been beaten off and the situation has stabilised at approximately this morning's position. There has been no substantial change. A Japanese plane crashed this morning in Tide Cove at 9.30 a.m. Two boat-loads of the enemy attempted to cross Tide Cove and land on the East shore. Both boats were sunk by machine-gun fire and the remnant of the landing party was wiped out on the beach. Reports reaching headquarters testify to the effectiveness of our artillery fire last night. (147)

14.41 The air raid alarm is sounded. All clear at 15.44 (147).

15.00 Japanese aircraft begin an attack on HMS *Cicala*, which is shelling their attempts to remove obstacles on Castle Peak Road (3: 10).

PHASE I: THE LOSS OF THE MAINLAND   45

15.00   Nos. 19 and 23 godowns in Connaught Road West are shelled, causing civilian casualties (131).
15.00   Police open fire on a Japanese aircraft which is strafing civilians on Lai Chi Kok Road and Tai Nam Street (131).

15.30   All remaining Royal Scots previously holding the Redoubt and the area around it are ordered to fall back to Golden Hill (20: 7).
15.30   Mathers, commanding D Company Punjabis: 'Capt [sic] Boxer and F/Lt. M. Oxford came to visit me, little information to give them' (140).

16.00   MTB 10 tows MTB 12 from Hong Kong Dockyard to Aberdeen for completion of refit (143e).
16.00   A Company Punjabis claim that their machine-gun fire from PB 210 destroys two sampans filled with Japanese soldiers (140).

16.15   HMS *Cicala* (near Chung Hue Island) is attacked by nine aircraft, claiming two damaged. It is hit on the stern by a bomb (143f) — wounding Able Seaman Wilkinson (who returns to Aberdeen)[69] — and is replaced by HMS *Tern* in the shelling of Japanese positions.

16.37   Another air raid alarm is sounded. All clear at 17.04 (147).

17.00   Official Communiqué:

>   Positions on the mainland were maintained during the afternoon. The enemy brought up artillery support on the Castle Peak Road and engaged Stonecutters Island. Our naval units in the vicinity replied, and those were later supported by Stonecutters and Island coast defence guns. Our field artillery on the mainland hotly engaged enemy troop concentrations during the afternoon. Good results were observed. Our casualties during these engagements were very light. (147)

17.32   Air raid. All clear at 17.53 (147).

17.42   The last of Eastern Telegraph Company's cables between Hong Kong and the outside world are cut by enemy action (20: 8).

18.00   An artillery duel between Japanese guns shelling Stonecutters Island and British guns firing at their batteries on Castle Peak Road ends.

18.00   Second Lieutenant J. A. Ford is ordered to establish his platoon on the highest part of Golden Hill. Hunter reports: 'the next thing I recall was the order to move Don Company out of the lower ground onto Golden Hill. We did this overnight, with Sgt. Sandy Sutherland and myself leading the Company along the appropriate paths or tracks, with intermittent low whistles to those behind us' (132b: Hunter). 'Once on Golden Hill I experienced a strange and quite unaccountable feeling of relief. Perhaps I felt that our initial positions could have become a trap for us. Essentially ours was a delaying operation, and it was good to feel that we had recovered some freedom of manoeuvre by getting on the right side of Golden Hill': Hunter (78: 72). After an impossibly difficult climb, they occupy crumbling defensive positions constructed (like the Shing Mun Redoubt) in 1937.[70] D Company (under Capt. D. Pinkerton)[71] covers Smuggler's Ridge. The remainder of the Royal Scots (B and C Coys., two platoons of A Coy., and Battalion HQ) occupy positions on lower ground to the west, with C Company covering the main road. Battalion HQ itself is established at Filter Beds House (134).

18.00   The Rajput defenders of PBs 205 and 206 are forced, by shellfire, to withdraw to Dome Hill. On the Punjabi front, PBs 208 to 214 are all engaged and 211 is destroyed (134). Later, PB 208 and PB 214 are also destroyed (140).

18.00   Houses and godowns near Belcher's Fort are damaged by shellfire (131).

18.30   APV *Perla* starts Aberdeen patrol (130: 14).

19.30   There is another air raid on Victoria (147).

23.00   PB 308 is fired upon, wounding one B Company Punjabi sepoy (140).

Roll of Honour for 10 December

ARTILLERY — 4 Killed

Basant Singh	Gunner, 2 Mountain Bty. HKSRA	U
Shing Mun Redoubt OP.		
Kishan Singh	Lance Naik, 2 Mountain Bty. HKSRA	U
Shing Mun Redoubt OP.		
Sawan Singh	Havildar, 35(M) CB Bty. HKSRA[72]	U
Killed Parade Battery, Stonecutters.		[9 Dec.]
Tek Singh	Cook, 20 HAA Bty. HKSRA[73]	U
Killed West Fort, Stonecutters Island. Body not recovered (126).		[9 Dec.]

ROYAL SCOTS — 1 Killed

Jordan, Herbert	W.O.I. Bandmaster	U
(145: 180) agrees killed 10 Dec. Shot by British sentry during night after failing to respond to challenge.[74]		

RAJPUTS — 2 Killed

Hakim Singh	Havildar	U
Buried Heather Pass between Buffalo Hill and Tate's Cairn (126).		
Rala Ram	Lance Naik	U
Buried Heather Pass between Buffalo Hill and Tate's Cairn (126).		

11 DECEMBER THURSDAY

> On December 11th we opened fire on a flotilla of junks thought to be carrying Japanese troops from Lamma; they wasted little time in returning. (Michael Wright)[75]

Predictably, the weak Royal Scots positions on Golden Hill are attacked by the Japanese, and — initially in some disarray — they fall back with heavy losses.[76] By late morning it is obvious that the position is very serious, and at midday Maltby orders the Mainland evacuated. In the afternoon — under the usual shelling and bombing — the evacuation starts.

With nothing now to prevent the Japanese from occupying the New Territories and Kowloon, the Governor calls on all Hong Kong Police Force, Police Reserve, naval establishments police, and special constables to perform combatant duties as militia force until further notice (147).

The Auxiliary Quartering Corps issues a communiqué to Peak and Mid-Levels residents who had received notice that their houses would be taken over by the Government in an emergency, telling them to pack up and be ready to leave by 17.00 (147). Unattended road vehicles are ordered to be immobilized.

Stonecutters Island is shelled all day (93: 130), as is the British Military Hospital, with one Chinese employee being killed and several wounded (27: 42). A friendly round falls on the officers' quarters (no. 13, The Peak) killing a Chinese batman and damaging the Command Pay Office severely (27: 46). The shelling of military targets is also taking a psychological toll: '[Major] Anderson [commander of 24th Coastal Artillery at Mount Davis] and [Captain] Hammett still in hiding and haven't seen daylight for three days', RSM Ford (15: 30).

As the Japanese advance, British positions near Tate's Cairn are destroyed and Tsing Yi Island is captured. HKSRA (26th Bty.) and HKVDC (two platoons of 3 Coy. under Maj. E. G. Stewart) units are evacuated from Stonecutters Island, and British units start destroying anything on the Kowloon Peninsula which might be useful to the Japanese.

In Kowloon, terrible rioting and looting in the Nathan Road district follows as word gets round that the British are pulling out (15: 29). No. 1 Company HKVDC has the job (among others) of riot control (3: 12), but it is an impossible task.

At sea, the situation is no better, with the Hong Kong Royal Naval Volunteer Reserve (HKRNVR) Auxiliary Patrol Vessel (APV) *Indira* being attacked, causing the death of two crew members (143e). Japanese forces land on Lamma Island and attempt to cross to Aberdeen. They are driven off by a platoon of Winnipeg Grenadiers and 3 Battery Volunteers (95: 54). The Aberdeen Industrial School becomes the HQ of both the Navy and the RAF. Commander Millet (OC AIS) asks Squadron Leader Donald Hill to form anti-aircraft and defence posts for Aberdeen, as the RAF is the only force there with machine guns. Hill positions four posts on the roof with tommy-gun posts on the verandas (89).

The Royal Artillery starts pulling its guns back from the mainland and exposed positions. The 5 AA Regiment Wong Nai Chung section moves back from Queen's Road recreation ground to Wong Nai Chung Gap,[77] where it will be destroyed on the 19th. The Albany Road section moves back from King's Park, Kowloon, to Albany Road. The 965 Defence Battery's Stanley Bay 18-pounders are sent forward to Braemar, where they will be destroyed on the 18th. RA Mainland HQ moves from

Waterloo Road, Kowloon, to join the HQ 1st HK Regiment Wong Nai Chung Gap, where they will be wiped out on the 19th. The HKSRA 1st Mountain Battery 3.7-inch howitzers stay on the Mainland for the moment, and move from Customs Pass leaving one at Tate's Cairn, two in forward positions, and four on Devil's Peak. The 2nd Mountain Battery 3.7-inch guns move from the Mainland, one being lost, one going to Victoria, and two to Stanley Gap. Two of their 4.5-inch guns move to Coombe Road, and two to Tai Tam Hill. The 25th Medium Battery also leaves the Mainland, moving two guns to Caroline Hill and two to Tiger Balm.

In the evening, the surviving Royal Scots and the Canadians embark for the Island at Sham Shui Po Barracks and the Jordan Road ferry terminal. It is, not to mince words, a rout.

Diary for 11 December

02.00   Kowloon is shelled most of the morning.

05.30   The evacuation of police families from Kowloon gets under way (98: 171).

07.00   The Royal Scots positions on Golden Hill are attacked by the 230th with mortars. Second Lieutenant Ford says: 'from then on throughout the day we were heavily mortared. That was the worst of it. There could be no fighting back. And the mortaring was carried out with deadly accuracy. Every time we disclosed that some of us were still alive' (95: 52).[78]

British counter-battery fire starts immediately, but because of lack of communication, British shells start landing in the Royal Scots' positions. Captain Douglas Ford[79] manages to reach a field telephone and has the range of the artillery extended beyond their front line. The artillery duel is followed by hand-to-hand fighting in which the Japanese try to drive a wedge between D Company, and B and C Companies on the lower ground.

Wave after wave of Japanese attack B and C Companies. Richardson — commanding B Company — is killed while going forward on reconnaissance. There are heavy casualties on both sides with some twenty-nine Royal Scots killed.[80] Platoons commanded by Second Lieutenants F. R. Haywood (13 Platoon) and G. C. Houstoun-Boswell (14 Platoon) succeed in pushing the Japanese back, but Houstoun-Boswell is killed by a Japanese sword (100: 106) in the close-quarter fighting. Captain Rose — commanding C Company — goes to Haywood's 13 Platoon to give instructions about withdrawal, but is killed in the attempt (15: 32). Haywood takes over command of C Company.

08.00   The left of the line of the Royal Scots gives way. B and C companies fall back in disarray and reestablish a line with A Company.

Captain Pinkerton of D Company leads a bayonet charge to clear the top of the Golden Hill ridge and the slope down to his left, towards the main road and C Company — an action for which he is decorated with the MC (91: 76). D Company then takes over Golden Hill in exposed northern positions, eroded weapons pits dug some three years earlier, and itself now receives the full weight of the Japanese attack, and are ordered to pull back to less exposed ground. Second Lieutenant Ford, with a section of seven men, stays near Golden Hill to cover D Company's withdrawal. After one hour, Ford and one survivor also pull back. 'We tried to take one of the seriously wounded on the knoll with us, but it was rough going down to the road and he died on the way.' Of the officers of D Company, Second Lieutenant J. M. M. Dunlop is hit in the thigh and bleeds to death, Second Lieutenant J. Nicoll is hit in the stomach by machine-gun fire and dies later, Lieutenant Drummond Hunter is carried back unconscious having been hit.[81] Second Lieutenant Ford's 17 Platoon, of twenty-six men, that day lost six killed and seven wounded (95: 53).

08.00   A Japanese reconnaissance plane is spotted over Hong Kong.

08.00   Wallis holds a briefing for second in commands to prepare plans for the ultimate withdrawal from the Mainland (134).

08.00   The Japanese start shelling Hill 70, held by 10 Platoon, B Company Punjabis. At the same time, PB 300 is hit and destroyed. B Company is shelled until 11.15 (140).

09.15   White reports by phone to Wallis that B and C Companies are retiring and he 'cannot explain why'. Wallis therefore despatches

Major Burn up Castle Peak Road to Lai Chi Kok to rally the troops (134).

09.20 APV *Shun Wo* starts Aberdeen patrol (130: 14).

10.00 Colonel L. Newnham[82] (General Staff Officer 1st Grade at Fortress HQ) visits Kowloon Infantry Brigade HQ in Waterloo Road: 'Here a very bleak picture was painted ... Japs broken through on Castle Peak Road ... arrive in Kowloon at any minute' (79: 224).

10.00 Brigadier Wallis tells the Royal Scots commanding officer that 'the good name of the Battalion was at stake. It was emphatically stressed that further withdrawals must stop' (95: 53).

10.00 Official Communiqué:

> It has been a quiet night and there is nothing to report. Some shelling of the Island took place but it had only a nuisance value. Damage and casualties are insignificant. (147)

10.00 The Japanese are reported to be landing on Lamma. Aberdeen and Jubilee batteries are brought to bear (20: 8).

10.00 A shell falls in Nathan Road killing around sixty people (131).

10.15 Burn reports that the 'enemy have broken through along the Castle Peak Road. Two Platoons [B Coy.] holding road at World Pencil Factory' (134).

10.30 Police Inspector Saunders at Sham Shui Po patrols the Castle Peak Road and comes across Japanese forward units. Soon after, Lance Sergeant Watson reports that the Japanese are in Cheung Sha Wan (98: 171).

11.00 The Royal Scots are permitted to withdraw towards Lai Chi Kok, supported by the Reserve Company of the Winnipeg Grenadiers (who have been ordered up Castle Peak Road to prevent Japanese breakthrough into Kowloon), the Volunteers' armoured cars and Bren carriers, and a platoon of 1 Company Volunteers (95: 53).

11.25 Orders are given by RA Mainland for Tai Wai and Filters Batteries to withdraw to the vicinity of Polo battery. At this time, the 4.5-inch battery is engaging targets at ranges as close as 600 yards (93: 130). The Punjabis and D Company Rajputs are ordered back to the line of the passes (Sha Tin Pass, Garter Pass, Kowloon Pass, Railway Pass, Beacon Hill, Tai Po road) (134).

11.30   The Police Training School in Kowloon is surrounded by Japanese street fighting in plain clothes (131).

11.55   Police Sub-Inspector A. Wallingford reports that the Japanese are cutting through Cheung Sha Wan to attack the Sham Shui Po Barracks.

12.00   Lieutenant. R. J. F. Stanton, Royal Scots, and his 10 Platoon leave Castle Peak Road.

12.00   Fifth columnists attack an ammunition convoy of Royal Scots in Prince Edward Road (20: 8).

12.00   Maltby makes the decision to evacuate the Mainland and issues orders to this end (20: 8). During the withdrawal, a shell bursts among a section of 3.7-inch howitzers of 2nd Mountain Battery in the vicinity of Railway Pass, causing casualties (93: 130).

12.00   'C' Watch of the Hong Kong Dockyard Defence Corps (HKDDC)[83] — about one-third of its personnel — are ordered under Major D. Campbell to proceed to the RN Yard at Aberdeen (133: 3). In the evening, the remainder follow, minus some thirty staff accommodated in the Rotary Converter House and acting as a skeleton staff for the Hong Kong Yard.

13.00   A Japanese party in Chinese sampans are reported landing on Aberdeen Island. They are driven off by machine guns (20: 8).

13.30   All available armed ships are ordered to sink all junks in East Lamma Channel (130: 15).

13.30   A Company Punjabis reaches Sha Tin Pass. B Company reaches the second line, then continues to the line of the passes. D Company moves to Beacon Hill. C Company remains in the reservoir area. D Company Rajputs takes a position between Beacon Hill and the Tai Po road. A Company Rajputs is ordered to reach Hammer Hill by 17.00, B Company to occupy right sector east of Mau La Tong, C Company to withdraw to the Hai Wan Line (134).

13.45 All available motor torpedo boats are ordered to east of Kowloon Peninsula to evacuate troops retreating to Kai Tak piers. MTBs 07, 08, 09, 10, 11, 26 and 27 proceed. Kai Tak west pier is unavailable due to a sunken aircraft lying off it,[84] but the east pier is usable. MTB 26 embarks twenty soldiers, and MTB 10 thirty, and they take them to Hong Kong Dockyard (143e).

14.00 HMS *Robin* and Gate Vessels *Aldgate* and *Stargate* are ordered from Sai Wan moorings to Aberdeen (143f).

14.00 Police from the Kowloon stations start to arrive at the Canton Road godowns for evacuation to the island (98: 172).

14.30 Official Communiqué:

> Our forces continue to engage the enemy, who has been pressing his attack, and who has made some little progress. Our artillery has been causing many casualties among the enemy and preventing the enemy guns from any accurate fire on the Island. Some long-range enemy shell fire was directed at various points on the Island, but little damage was done. Air activity has been slight, except for some dive-bombing attacks on Stonecutters Island. Our Indian infantry and gunners are, as usual, living up to their already great reputation as first class fighters. (147)

14.30 All available ships are ordered to assist in the evacuation of Kowloon. *Thracian*, *Tern*, and APV *Indira* proceed via Tathong. APVs *Poseidon*, *Shun Wo*, *Minnie*, *Britannia*, *Stanley*, *Frosty*, and *Han Wo* proceed via the East Lamma Channel (130: 16).

14.30 Police Coxswain 100 is severely wounded by shrapnel on a police launch on duty in the harbour (131).

15.00 By this time, West Battery at Stonecutters alone has received over forty direct hits (76: 63). Stonecutters and the forward observation posts at Port Shelter and High Junk are ordered to withdraw during the night. On the way out, 3 Company HKVDC break into a store and help themselves to Thompson sub-machine guns, later to be used at Wong Nai Chung Gap.

15.15   All ferries are in position for the evacuation (106: 124).

16.00   Four heavy bombs hit Mount Davis Fort.[85] Later, a stick of three bombs is dropped near the Lye Mun officers' mess, causing casualties amongst the Chinese staff (30: 21).

16.00   White holds a conference at Filter Beds House to discuss the night's withdrawal. Bowman of D Company Winnipeg Grenadiers is present (134).

18.00   APV *Indira* starts Beaufort patrol (130: 14).

19.30   B Company Punjabis reach the Sam Ka Tsun pier (at the southern end of Devil's Peak) (134).

20.00   APVs *Perla* and *Poseidon* go alongside the 8,000-ton coastal freighter SS *Yatshing* to investigate lights (130: 16).

20.00   The Mainland Brigade HQ is evacuated by the Kowloon city ferry (98: 172).

22.30   The surviving Royal Scots, having embarked at Sham Shui Po Barracks and the Jordan Road ferry terminal, reach Hong Kong. Ford: 'We drove down to Kowloon Point. A strange journey. After all the Battalion had been through, we left the battlefield in buses, as if we were going back to barracks after an exercise in the hills. The ferry boats were waiting for us at the pier' (95: 59).

23.30   A Company Punjabis reaches the Sam Ka Tsun pier (134).

24.00   A vehicular ferry brings over the surviving armoured cars and Bren carriers.

24.00   The Hong Kong Telephone Company cuts all communication between Kowloon and Hong Kong (20: 9).

Roll of Honour for 11 December

ROYAL SCOTS — 29 Killed[86]

Akers, Munro Sumerville   Private   K
    Died 11 Dec. (145: 180), Golden Hill (126).   [15 Dec.]

Armstrong, James	Private		K
Died 11 Dec. (145: 180), Golden Hill (126).			[15 Dec.]
Cairns, James William	Corporal		U
Died 11 Dec. (145: 181)[87]			[15 Dec.]
Coutts, James	Private		K
Died 11 Dec. (145: 180), Golden Hill (126).			[15 Dec.]
Douglas, James	Private		K
Died 11 Dec. (145: 180), Golden Hill (126).			[17 Dec.]
Dunlop, James Maxwell	Second Lieutenant		K
Hit in thigh, bled to death, 11 Dec., Golden Hill.			[4/18 Dec.][88]
Falconer, Albert Scott	Private		K
Died 11 Dec. (145: 180), Golden Hill (126).			[15 Dec.]
Gibb, Duncan	Private		K
Killed Golden Hill area (126).			
Giblen, David	Lance Corp.		K
Missing Golden Hill area (126).			
Glasgow, Henry Moir	Corporal		K
Golden Hill (126).			
Habberley, Thomas	Private		K
Missing 11 Dec. (145: 179), Golden Hill (126).			[12 Dec.]
Hadden, John	Private		K
Died 11 Dec. (145: 180), Golden Hill (126).			[15 Dec.]
Henderson, George	Private		K
Died 11 Dec. (145: 180), Golden Hill (126).			[15 Dec.]
Horne, James Adamson	Lance Corporal		K
Killed Golden Hill area (126).			
Houstoun-Boswell, George	Second Lieutenant		K
Killed by sword-stroke,[89] 11 Dec., Golden Hill.			[8/14 Dec.]
Lee, John	Private		K
Died of wounds (Shing Mun Redoubt?), RN Hospital.			
Lough, George	Private		K
Died 11 Dec. (145: 180), Golden Hill (126).			[15 Dec.]
Macleod, John	Private		K
Died 11 Dec. (145: 180), Golden Hill (126).			[15 Dec.]
Mitchell, Thomas Martin	Private		K
Died 11 Dec. (145: 180), Golden Hill (126).			[15 Dec.]
Nicoll, James	Second Lieutenant		K
Hit in stomach and died, 11 Dec., Golden Hill.			[8/14 Dec.]
Paterson, Archibald King	Private		K
Golden Hill (126).			

Pow, Peter Johnston	Private	K
Died 11 Dec. (145: 180), Golden Hill (126).		[15 Dec.]
Richardson, Frederick Stanley	Captain	K
Killed going forward on reconnaissance, Golden Hill B Coy.		
Rose, Walter Ross	Captain	K
Killed visiting Haywood's platoon below south-western spur of Golden Hill.		
Semple, Robert Malcom	Private	K
Died 11 Dec. (145: 180), Golden Hill (126).		[15 Dec.]
Smith, Joseph Thomas	Private	K
Died 11 Dec. (145: 180), Golden Hill (126).		[15 Dec.]
Spinks, Henry Victor	Lance Corporal	K
Died 11 Dec. (145: 180), Golden Hill (126).		[15 Dec.]
Wilson, James	Corporal	K
Died 11 Dec. (145: 180), Golden Hill (126).		[15 Dec.]
Wood, Thomas	Lance Corporal	K
Died 11 Dec. (145: 181), Golden Hill (126).		[15 Dec.]

PUNJABIS — 5 Killed

Gurdayal Singh	Sepoy	U
Cremated vicinity of PB 208, slope of Sugar Loaf Hill (126).		
Jaswant Singh	Havildar	U
Cremated vicinity of PB 208, slope of Sugar Loaf Hill (126).		
Kapur Singh	Naik	U
Cremated vicinity of PB 208, slope of Sugar Loaf Hill (126).		
Karnail Singh	Naik	U
Cremated vicinity of PB 208, slope of Sugar Loaf Hill (126).		
Nanta Singh	Sepoy	U
Cremated vicinity of PB 208, slope of Sugar Loaf Hill (126).		

POLICE — 1 Killed

Tam Tin	Coxswain, HKPF	U
Almost certainly Coxswain 100, who was severely wounded at 12.30.		

12 DECEMBER FRIDAY

[I was told that] 'the Lighter' which had been earmarked to take the 'mules' across to the Island had been destroyed by enemy action. So we had 'sadly' to turn our mules 'loose'. The men were taken over to the Island by Launch to our HQ. (F. S. C. Hancock)[90]

With the retreat of the Royal Scots, the Volunteers, and the Canadians complete, the remaining Punjabis, Rajputs, and HKSRA detachments fall back overnight to the Devil's Peak line. By dawn, together with Wallis's Mainland HQ, they are in position except for two Punjabi companies delayed by rearguard action. Six Lewis guns of the 5 AA Regiment are sent from Wong Nai Chung to Devil's Peak to cover them for the night. However, in the evening all British units will be ordered to withdraw.

There is panic in Kowloon as the populace is caught between the Japanese in the north and the harbour — and presumed safety of Hong Kong Island — in the south. As the Japanese advance southwards, they start a pattern of rape that would characterize the civilian experience of the Hong Kong campaign (3: 94). In the early hours of the morning, the last police party on the mainland, under Assistant Superintendent Searle, is taken off from the Star Ferry pier by Marine Police Launch No. 1. The harbour itself is full of refugees fleeing to the island on ferries, and a European nurse is shot by Japanese snipers on the last ferry from Kowloon and dies the next day (95: 57). Mrs Briggs[91]: 'When we got to the ferry, the crowd was terrific. We were bombed all the way as we crossed — they were trying to hit the wireless station at Stonecutters Island quite close to our route. When I got across I found that I had been on the last ferry' (35: 96). By dawn, an advance party of Japanese occupy Kowloon railway station (3: 13), and by 10.00 the last British troops leave the Kowloon Peninsula.

> Each day the fighting crept nearer the waterfront. The sound of gunfire was almost constant during the day. At night shells whistled into the nearby godowns. A terrific stench filled the air. The bodies of the dead were rotting in the bright sun. Sewage seeped into the streets from broken mains. The refrigeration system had broken down in the godowns, and the goods stored there began to rot. Putrid fish and salted cabbage added their odours to that of death. Exhausted soldiers slept in the lobby of the 'Y' and buried their faces in their arms in order to keep out the stench of death, excreta and putrefaction. (42: 12)

Starting today, Japanese artillery in Tsim Sha Tsui (firing from warehouses, in positions allegedly built while they were rented to Japanese companies)[92] pound allied positions on the north-eastern shore of Hong Kong Island. Japanese bombers dive-bomb Allied positions. Leiper (attached to 4 Coy. HKVDC):

> When we reached Bowen Road several cars and houses were blazing; water mains had burst; and the Peak Tram station and the track had been demolished by a bomb. An anti-aircraft battery near the station had been knocked out and two guns were heaps of twisted metal. An Indian gunner was propped up on the pavement with the top of his head sliced off as one would cut off the top of a boiled egg and his brains were visible in what remained of his skull. Some of his comrades were standing round his body and they looked dazed and demoralised. (5: 41)

Siu-Feng Huang:

> Air-raids and shelling all day long. We were not afraid as our office was in that stone massive building of H&SBC. When I left office in PM for HKH to catch the bus, a shell came from KL side and hit the roof of that building opposite BoEA,[93] leaving plenty of debris on the streets. Everybody was running so did I until arrival at the Gloucester Arcade. (156)

A Sikh temple in Victoria is hit, and many are killed (95: 58). The evening also witnesses Hong Kong's biggest ever explosion, when the lighter *Jeanette* — laden with dynamite — is mistakenly fired on in the harbour.[94]

Return fire is put down on Customs Pass and Anderson Road. Throughout the day, the 3.7-inch howitzers of 1st Mountain Battery HKSRA (firing some 400 rounds) and 6-inch howitzers of East Group fire at the Japanese approaches to Devil's Peak Peninsula.

Japanese naval forces stay off the southern shore of Hong Kong as the British move the naval base from the China Fleet Club on the Mainland-facing coast of the Island to the Industrial School at Aberdeen (143f). HMS *Moth* — refitting in Hong Kong Dockyard dry dock — is scuttled, as is HMS *Tamar* at her buoy. Mrs Briggs: 'Later, I was talking to one of the dockyard policemen who had done the job and he told me that it was fantastic to see the number of rats leaving the sinking ship' (35: 97).[95]

Brigadier Lawson's diary reads: 'I am in command of all troops on island. Quite impossible with staff and facilities available. I go to Fortress HQ for discussion. Arrangements made for East and West commands.'

Diary for 12 December

01.30   After covering the retreating British troops, the Punjabis fall back (with the main body travelling via a steep incline — covered by the Japanese position at Tate's Cairn — to the Clearwater Bay Road and Anderson Road) to Devil's Peak, but the headquarters group under Lt. Nigel Forsyth get lost and come down from the hills at Kai Tak. They make their way towards the Star Ferry pier, guided by Private B.A. Gellman of No. 1 Company HKVDC. Here they guard the ferries and assist refugees (3: 13).

01.20   The RA stores evacuated from Stonecutters arrive at RN Dockyards (93: 130).

02.00   F. W. Shaftain, Director of Criminal Intelligence with the Hong Kong Police Force, meets with the Triad leaders to negotiate a way out of their plan to massacre all 'white' people at 03.00 on 13 December (7: 91).

02.00   A and B Company Punjabis leave the Sam Ka Tsun pier (134).

02.00   A and B Company Rajputs are established on the Ma Lau Tong line (134).

04.45   A and B Company Punjabis disembark on the Island (134).

06.00   Military cables to Kowloon are cut at the RN Yard cable hut (20: 9).

06.30   The Rajputs fall back to Ma Lau Tong line. Behind them are Brigadier Wallis with his Mainland Brigade HQ, and the remaining Punjabis (95: 59).

07.30   HQ, C and D Companies Punjabis arrive at Devil's Peak after a twenty-mile march and no food for thirty-six hours. D Company Rajputs arrives at the same time (134).

08.25   An RA party from Jubilee arrives to offload stores, but finds that the ferry is already sinking, having been scuttled by the Royal Navy (93: 130).

08.25   Short air raid alert (147).

08.47 Short air raid alert (147).

10.00 The main body of the Japanese appear at the southern tip of Kowloon. Holding them at bay at point-blank range, Forsyth's Punjabis — about 300 men — embark with ferry-loads of fleeing refugees and in RAF launches, firing from the stern (3: 13) as they cross the harbour.[96]

10.00 The Japanese unsuccessfully dive-bomb Devil's Peak positions (95: 59).

10.00 Official Communiqué:

> The Island was subjected to a certain amount of sporadic bombardment by aircraft and artillery during the day, and for a short period during the night, but casualties were very low, and damage negligible. It is probable that during the next week or so, the Island will be subjected to some bombing and shellfire, but if the public profits by its experience of taking cover and of dispersal, casualties can be kept very low. The G.O.C. would like to congratulate the civil population on their calm confidence and steadiness, and assures them that if they will continue on this gallant manner they have nothing to fear. (147)

10.46 Air raid alert. The all clear is at 11.06 (147).

12.45 Police are sent to clear No. 9 Air Raid Tunnel at Smithfield of people, to make room for dynamite[97] to be delivered that night (131).

13.38 Air raid alert. The all clear is at 14.08 (147).

14.00 East Group guns assist in repelling an attack via direct observation from Black Hill OP on the left flank of the Devil's Peak line, firing 400 rounds and inflicting heavy casualties (93: 130).

14.00 APV *Frosty* starts Aberdeen patrol (130: 15)

14.30 Official Communiqué:

> We have successfully evacuated our troops, supplies, and essential services from Kowloon. Yesterday the enemy pressed his attack with vigour and in the face of his superior numbers we had to fall back.

It will be appreciated that the bulk of our garrison has, from the beginning, had to be retained on the Island to safeguard our main base. The position we have now reached is as follows: We have retired within our Fortress and from the shelter of our main defences we will hold off the enemy until the strategic situation permits of relief. Emphasis is placed on the word 'Fortress' — every man and woman must contribute a war effort to this end. There is every reason for confidence. Both military and civil authorities have for a long time been working to a situation where the reserves of food, guns and ammunition are ample for a protracted defence on a siege scale. There is every reason for confidence [sic]. The garrison is in good spirits and the staunchness of the civil population is marked. The simple task before every one of us now is to hold firm. Our losses during all the engagements on the mainland have been comparatively light, and the troops gained a valuable time lag for civil defence measures to swing into action. A remarkable rearguard action was fought by about 100 men of an Indian battalion through the streets of Kowloon. They were successfully evacuated this morning in broad daylight on a Star Ferry from the stern of which they continued the action by machine-gun fire in the face of heavy enemy fire. Great praise is due to members of the Government Medical Department and the Auxiliary Medical Corps who voluntarily remained at their posts in Kowloon and are rendering assistance where necessary to the Chinese population. For their own safety the population is warned to keep away from all waterfronts. (147)

16.00   APV *Poseidon* starts Beaufort patrol (130: 14).
16.00   The Japanese make contact with the Ma Lau Tong line (134).
16.00   A shell lands in Connaught Road West near the Tung Shan Hotel, killing thirteen and wounding thirty-nine (131).

17.00   In the afternoon, the matron of Kowloon Hospital, Miss Dorothy Gean, calls the nurses together to tell them that the Mainland is being evacuated, but they are to stay (91: 103). At 17.00, Japanese troops with fixed bayonets enter the hospital (95: 61).
17.00   Official Communiqué:
Nothing further to report since issue of the last communiqué. (147)

17.45   The Japanese attack the Ma Lau Tong line, but fail to penetrate the wire and are driven off with heavy losses. Six-inch howitzers fire on them as they retreat, causing significant casualties. This is the only significant engagement of the day. Presumably the British retreat is so fast that it takes Japanese by surprise (95: 59).

18.00   Orders are given for the Rajputs and 1st Mountain Battery to withdraw from the Devil's Peak peninsula. All mules and ponies and 500 rounds are lost in sinking sampans or to the enemy. One hundred rounds are brought over to the Island (93: 131). In the evening, the Ma Lau Tong line is given up, and two companies of Rajputs (A and C) fall back to the Hai Wan line as the rest of the Punjabis and the Rajputs start crossing to the Island from Lye Mun. Ferries are jammed with desperate civilians.

> Brigadier Peffers instructed Captain Badger and Captain Pardoe to get a car each and proceed to Lyemun, Col. Kilpatrick and myself to get a car each and go to the Tai Koo Dockyard where we would split up transport sent to disperse them on the island, into two parts, keeping half at the Tai Koo Dockyard, and the other half to Lyemun. Captain MacMillan was to proceed to 'D' Bn. HQ at Tai Tam where the troops were to be dispersed on the hillsides. (The idea of two cars at each place was to let one of them act as a messenger between the two points to move transport where required at either place.) Having completed the task at Tai Koo Dockyard and at Lyemun, I went to Tai Tam to see whether assistance was required. Found a seething mob of Indians at the roadside outside the Canadian HQ where they were issued with tea and biscuits. They were a mixture of HKSRA, HK Mule Corps, Rajputs and Punjabis. (Bunny Browne (158))

18.30   A Japanese plane appears over Aberdeen at 1,000 feet and is fired upon by four MTBs (07, 09, 11, and 12) that are waiting for sailing orders. It turns sharply away, emitting a slight glow (143e).

19.00   In the evening, Admiral Chan Chak sinks a Japanese propaganda ship (that had been broadcasting over loudspeakers) in the harbour using limpet mines. Guest: What, in fact, he had done was to draw some limpet bombs from Naval stores and, with three men in a sampan, got as near to the ship as possible. Then two of the men swam to the ship and the bombs did the rest. I began to like my one-legged Admiral more than a little (28: 30).

PHASE I: THE LOSS OF THE MAINLAND   63

23.00 In the darkness, a barge is filled with nine tons of dynamite — including 312 cases of dynamite fuses and detonators (86: 147) — at Green Island. Towed by the P&O tug *Jeanette* under the command of Acting Sub-Inspector Joe Hudson of the Marine Police, it sets off for the central Star Ferry pier two hours earlier than notified. The vessel is also carrying a number of troops who had gone over to load the stores (28: 31). It is accidentally exploded in the harbour by men of the Middlesex regiment firing from a pillbox[98] on the end of the vehicular ferry pier. Phyllis Harrop: 'A terrific explosion shakes the building, throwing me back against the wall . . . before I can open my mouth there is another heavy explosion and it feels as though all hell has been let loose . . . doors and windows fly open, glass crashes everywhere.'

23.45 The Punjabi HQ Company, plus C and D, are ferried to the Island (134).

Roll of Honour for 12 December

ROYAL SCOTS — 2 Killed

Cochrane, David	Private	U
Died of wounds (126).		
Wilson, Frank	Corporal	K
Died 12 Dec. (145: 180). Originally buried Tai Koo Coolie Quarters School (126).		[15 Dec.]

ARTILLERY — 2 Killed

Cheung Wing[99]	Bombardier, RA	U
Muhammad Sharif	Gunner, 1 Mountain Bty. HKSRA	K
1Mountain Bty's 3.7-inch guns were on the Mainland. Possibly killed by a bomb near Peak tram station. See (5: 41).		

PUNJABIS — 2 Killed

(On the retreat through Kowloon or to Devil's Peak)

Adal Sher	Havildar	U
Gul Shah Band	Sepoy	U

VOLUNTEERS — 1 Killed

Stephens, Jack Leslie Corporal, HKVDC (Field Coy. Engineers) U
 (145: 212) mentions Stephens was 'of the Harbour Office': [11 Dec.]
 thus *Jeanette*, 12 Dec.

WINNIPEGS — 1 Killed

Gray, John A. Private U
 Missed last boat to HK. Believed murdered by Japanese (105).[100] [13 Dec.]

POLICE — 4 Killed

Donohue, Patrick Lance Sergeant, HKPF U
 Killed on board *Jeanette*.

Hudson, George Alfred Police Sergeant, HKPF U
 Killed on board *Jeanette*.

Santa Singh Constable, HKPF U
 Killed on *Jeanette* (98: 174). [14 Dec.]

Waryam Singh Constable, HKPF U
 Killed on *Jeanette* (98: 174). [14 Dec.]

CIVILIANS[101] — 7 Killed

Bateson, Harold Australian UX
 Shot by Japanese after surrendering, Kowloon (21: 93)[102]

Buttress, Eric Frank PWD (145: 210) UCWD
 On launch *Jeanette* in the harbour. [13 Dec.]

Clarke, Percy UCWD
 At Hong Kong Harbour. Probably on *Jeanette*.

Dickson, John UCWD
 At Hong Kong Harbour. Probably on *Jeanette*. Harbour Office (145: 210).

Holland, Mrs Jessie Auxiliary Nursing Service UX
 Admitted Queen Mary Hospital 12 Dec. Died same day (145: 79). Probably killed on
 ferry.[103]

Hunter, James UCWD
 Of Leighton Hill, Hong Kong. Harbour Office (145: 211), thus probably *Jeanette*.

Kossick, David UCWD
 Harbour Office (145: 211), thus should presumably be 12 Dec. [15 Dec.]
 on *Jeanette*.

4 Phase II: The Siege of the Island

It had been hoped that the Gin Drinkers Line would hold for at least a week. However, the forcing of the Shing Mun Redoubt within some forty hours of the start of the attack has made the line untenable. In fact, it is fair to question why the Japanese took so long to capture the Mainland.[1]

Of the garrison's approximately 14,000 personnel, it is strange that only some forty-five were allocated to the defence of the Shing Mun Redoubt, and that of the three men who died there, one apparently died later of wounds and the other two were killed as the Japanese captured the final point still occupied.

In the final analysis, delaying the Japanese advance to Tsim Sha Tsui cost the garrison only some sixty-six dead, fifty-seven wounded,[2] and a recorded twenty-seven captured. The Japanese, on capturing Kowloon and the New Territories, claimed that they found 150 bodies, though it is possible that they included some civilian casualties; it is also possible that some of the Indian Other Rank fatalities recorded as occurring later in the conflict in fact occurred on the Mainland.

Some men have become separated from their units. Sergeant Richards[3] and Private Chorley[4] of the Royal Scots recount (133) that their platoon was told to report to Newton of the Rajputs on 11 December. Failing to find him, the two men set off towards the sea, commandeer a sampan on 14 December, and go aground on Waglan Island on the 16th from where they are recovered on the 18th.

With all garrison forces (minus the few stragglers stuck on the Mainland) now back on the Island, the siege consists simply of Japanese bombing and shelling of military and strategic targets.[5] In return, there is considerable counter-battery fire from the coastal guns, but they and the anti-aircraft sites are vulnerable and exposed. Many are put out of action.

During the siege, the Japanese are to make two demands for surrender, and at least one secret reconnaissance of beachfront positions. Stories of an attempted landing prior to 18 December are probably incorrect, as no record of these appears in Japanese documents or post-war interrogations.

What is happening in Kowloon during this time can only be imagined. Almost the only records that exist are from the disciplined hospitals; however, later experience on Hong Kong Island suggests that the Japanese troops are indulging in the same rapes and murders that they would be guilty of later. The number of civilian victims is unrecorded, but Selwyn-Clarke would later estimate the total civilian dead during the fighting at 4,000[6] — though the majority of these would be in the congested urban areas of the Island.

Meanwhile, the Japanese are preparing their assault.

13 DECEMBER SATURDAY

> When Kowloon fell, I was fairly certain that Hong Kong would not last very much longer, but my thought was that it could only be a matter of time before the war was won because I believed then that Japan could never conquer the United States. (Brian Baxter)[7]

By 08.30, the military evacuation of the Mainland is over. Hong Kong Island is under siege. Apart from a request by the Japanese for a British surrender — which is denied as Churchill has ordered Hong Kong to be held as long as possible — artillery fire from the Mainland is the main feature of the day. Belcher's Fort and the 4th Battery HKVDC at Pak Sha Wan come under especially heavy fire.

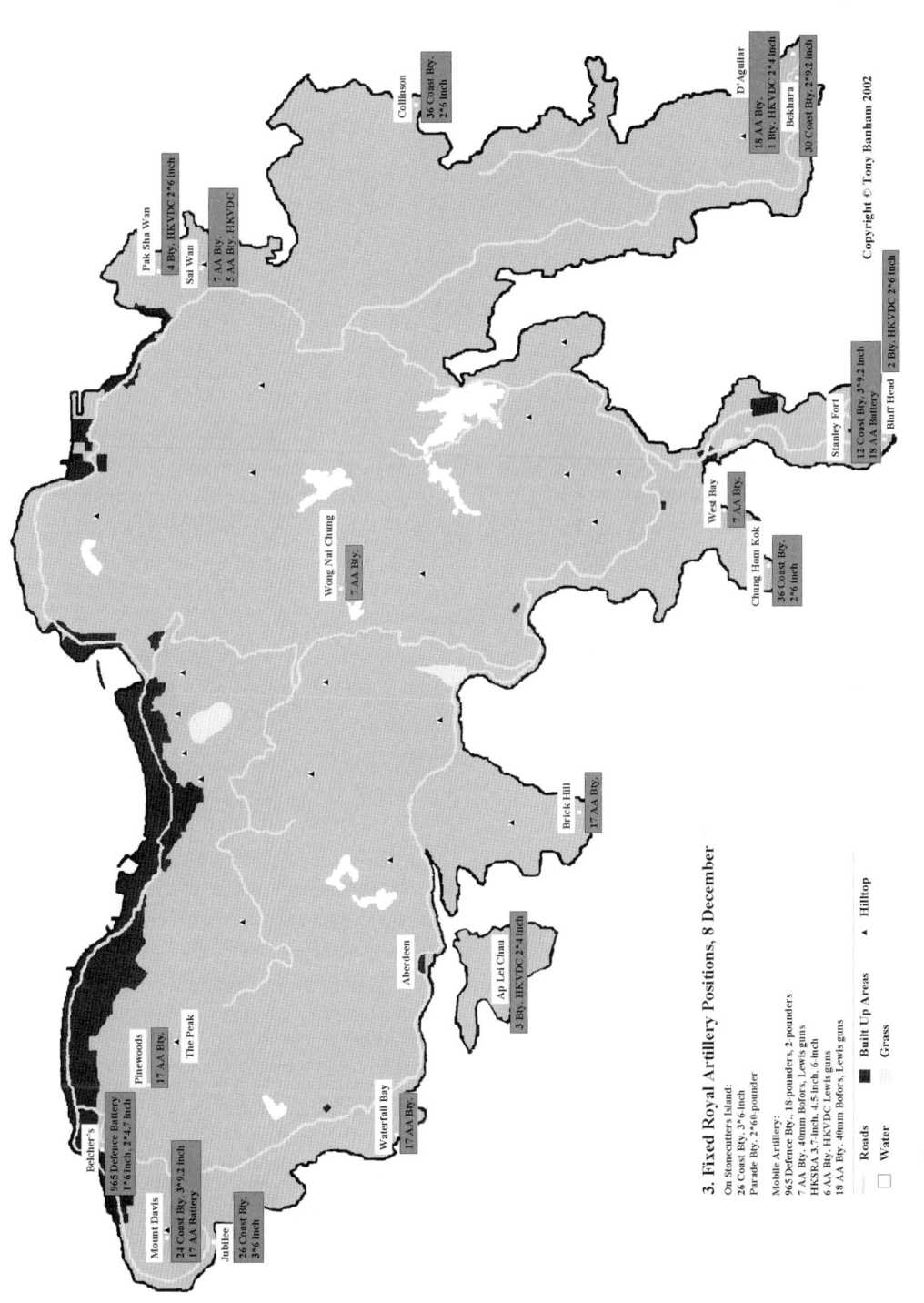

3. Fixed Royal Artillery Positions, 8 December

Sir Mark Young sends a signal to all members of the Civil Defence services:

> I thank you one and all for everything that you have done, and I look forward with certainty to your adding to the high reputation that you have already built up. There is before you a task that can and will be done if you go to it with all your courage and all your might. The defence of Hong Kong against the aggressor is going to be the finest page in the Colony's history. See that your name is written on that page. Good fortune to you all. (147)

In Hong Kong itself there is still an atmosphere of peace: 'The engagement is announced between Beryl June, daughter of Mr and Mrs F. E. E. Booker of the Hong Kong Police and Charles Douglas Neville, only son of Mr and Mrs W. C. Walker of Pyes Hall, Wrentham, Suffolk, England' (147). The newspaper carries the headline 'British Soldier Shoots Down Enemy Carrier Pigeon with Rifle'. However, the war is coming closer.

It has often been noted that sickness, malaria in particular, played a notable part in weakening the defences. On this day alone, the Indian General Hospital (IGH) takes in no less that seventy-one sick (as opposed to wounded) individuals from the Indian armies returning from the Mainland (145: 142). Up to and including today, the Bowen Road British Military Hospital (BMH) has taken 163 wounded and sick (27: 39), and an official communiqué makes the first veiled reference to fifth-column activities on the Island.

Now that the entire garrison is on the island, Maltby splits them into two brigades, eastern and western. East Brigade under Wallis is made up of the Rajputs and the Royal Rifles. West Brigade under Lawson consists of the Punjabis, Winnipeg Grenadiers, and Royal Scots. Both brigades employ units of the HKSRA, Volunteers, and Middlesex. The dividing line between them starts at PB 52 at the north-east corner of Causeway Bay, and goes south to Tai Hang village, Jardine's Lookout, Wong Nai Chung reservoir, Violet Hill, Stanley Mound and Chung Hom Kok.

The Royal Artillery consolidates its positions for the siege. 5 AA Regiment's Wong Nai Chung section moves from there to Tai Hang Wan Fung Terrace. The Lewis guns move back from Devil's Peak to Wong Nai Chung. The 965 Defence Battery Deepwater Bay 2-pounders move to North Shore. The HKSRA 2nd Mountain Battery 3.7-inch gun at Victoria moves to join to others at Stanley Gap, and the two 4.5-inch guns at Coombe Road move to Kellett.

Diary for 13 December

01.30 All the Punjabis are now safely on Hong Kong (20: 10). Major A. J. Dewar and Captain C. G. Turner, RASC, make good use of War Department Vessel (WDV) *Victoria* to aid the evacuation (3: 14).

04.00 The 1st Mountain Battery HKSRA, minus mules, and one company of Rajputs are across (20: 10).

04.30 In the early hours, Maltby decides to evacuate *all* friendly forces instead of leaving the two companies of Rajputs to hold the Hai Wan line as had originally been intended. He phones the Rajput Commanding Officer, Lieutenant Colonel R. Cadogan-Rawlinson, to discuss the matter. They decide to risk it, despite the approach of dawn, as the Japanese would be taken by surprise (95: 60).

05.00 The Extended Defence Officer sends MTBs 07, 09, 11 and 12 to the north-west of Lye Mun to evacuate troops from a rough pier in a bay west of Devil's Peak. Some 260 Rajputs are evacuated to *Thracian* (143e). MTB captain Kennedy: 'The light was creeping into the eastern sky as the first two boats were loaded quietly without fuss. The calmness and bearing of the Indians, all tired men who had been fighting with little rest for nearly a week, made a deep impression on me' (47: 29).

08.30 Military withdrawal from the Mainland is completed with the last Rajput elements setting out on HMS *Thracian* and the MTBs in broad daylight (95: 60).

09.00 The first Japanese demand for surrender is carried across the harbour in a small boat with three Japanese officers (led by Col. Tada), with two British women[8] and two small dogs as hostages. The letter is from Lieutenant General Sakai:

> Since our troops have joined battle I have gained possession of the Kowloon Peninsula despite the good fighting qualities of your men, and my artillery and air force, which are ready to crush all parts of the Island, now await my order. Your Excellency can see

what will happen to the Island and I cannot keep silent about it. You have all done your duty in defending Hong Kong so far, but the result of the coming battle is plain, and further resistance will lead to the annihilation of a million good citizens and to such sadness as I can hardly bear to see. If Your Excellency would accept an offer to start negotiations for the surrender of Hong Kong under certain conditions, it will be honourable. If not, I, repressing my tears, am obliged to take action to overpower your forces. (44: 80)[9]

There is a short wait, during which the participants are photographed and interviewed by reporters Gwen Dew[10] and Vaughn Meisling. The request is summarily rejected. A message from the Governor is conveyed to the waiting Japanese:

> He acknowledges the spirit in which this communication is made but he is unable in any circumstances to hold any meeting or parley on the subject of the surrender of Hong Kong.

Dew and Meisling are escorted away for questioning by policeman Wright-Nooth (71: 55).

09.00 An air attack is made on Aberdeen harbour. HMS *Tern* (143f) reportedly brings down one plane.

09:20 The last Rajput soldier sets foot on Aberdeen after evacuation from the Mainland. They are met by Maltby in person (91: 101). They are assembled in the Tai Tam Gap area and given twenty-four hours' rest before taking over the north-east sector from the Royal Scots (20: 10).

10.00 Belcher's Battery is ordered to destroy lighters lying against Kowloon wharves. The operation is carried out by the upper 6-inch gun, with six being sunk and others damaged. Belcher's Fort and Kennedy Town are also hit by Japanese counter-battery fire, with serious fires being started in West Point (44: 81).

10.30 Official Communiqué:

> The Mainland was successfully evacuated in the night of December 11–12. The position has been stabilised inside the strong defences

Phase II: The Siege of the Island

of the Island of Hongkong and conditions of full siege now exist. The Colony is in good heart. There is plenty of food, arms and ammunition, and the garrison is confident of the outcome. The public continue to behave quietly and to take the situation in their stride. At dusk last night the enemy attacked our troops who still remained on the Mainland at Devil's Peak. The Japanese were decisively repulsed with heavy losses, and were unable to interfere with the withdrawal of our troops to the Island, which had been planned for last night. This withdrawal was consequently carried out without loss and must be accounted a local success for us. Shelling and bombing were both on a light scale and very little damage or casualties resulted. A total of ten bombs dropped on the Island in widely separated areas during the day. We must, however, be prepared for heavier bombardments by the enemy as the situation develops. House-holders are warned that if they leave lights exposed they will be fired on. Under black-out conditions of full siege a certain amount of sporadic light automatic fire (such as, in fact, happened last night) is inevitable, through the necessity to safeguard against possible surprise. Our general position continues satisfactory and we can await events with calm. (147)

10.30   APV *Frosty* is ordered to bring the lighthouse keeper and eight of his staff from Waglan Island to Aberdeen (130: 16).

10.45   There is a five-minute air raid alert (147).

11.00   The Rajputs are concentrated in the Tai Tam–Pottinger Gap area for cover, rest, and reorganisation (139).

13.30   The Waterfall Bay AA gun (presumably an 18 LAA Bofors) brings down an enemy floatplane by range control (93: 132). It sinks in West Lamma Channel. The destruction of the aircraft is also credited to Sapper Bill Bailey[11] of 40 Field Company, RE (91: 107).

14.00   Green Island police and Mr Bailey (custodian of the magazine which *Jeanette* had taken her deadly load) are evacuated by HMS *Thracian* and disembarked at Aberdeen after Bailey's house is hit by two bombs (131).

14.30   Official Communiqué:

> Further news of the successful action at dusk last night has now been received. Just before dark one of our battalions maintaining its position on the Mainland was attacked by the enemy. As explained earlier, this attack broke down under combined artillery and machine-gun fire. During the course of the night our battalion was withdrawn to the island with the loss of only three men missing. Retirements such as this are a most difficult operation and are possible only through close and smooth co-operation between Navy and Army. The enemy's failure to follow up indicates the success of the defence, and the trivial losses suffered by our battalion is an indication of the complete success of the combined operation. The position now is that the full garrison stands on the defence of the Island, confidently awaiting further events. One large seaplane was shot down into the sea to the South of the Island about 1.30 to-day. The public are warned to keep off the streets an under cover as much as possible, particularly after dark. (147)

14.36   There is an eight-minute air raid alert (147).

16.00   Mount Davis and Jubilee area are heavily shelled. The top 9.2-inch gun of Mount Davis Battery is hit by a dud 24-cm shell, damaging the inside of the bore and putting it out of action (93: 132).

16.00   MTBs 08 and 27 are sent from Aberdeen to Green Island to evacuate Royal Engineers there, but no one is found (143e).

17.00   Official Communiqué:

> The populace may rest assured that the Police now have the disorderly elements under complete control. Several of the leaders have been arrested and there is nothing further to fear. A tug with lighter in tow blew up some distance to the West of the Vehicular Ferry Pier at about eleven p.m. on the 12th. The cause is not definitely known. The blast of the explosion shattered windows in the vicinity. There were seven air raids yesterday, but except in one case there were few casualties and little damage either from these raids or from the intermittent shelling. The Military Authorities report no change in the situation since the last communiqué. (147)[12]

17.00   APV *Poseidon* starts Aberdeen patrol (130: 15).

18.00   APV *Perla* starts Beaufort patrol (130: 14).

22.30 Naval authorities and Captain Valentine, HKVDC, report a glider landing on the Peak. Police search, but nothing is found (131).

24.00 The fire brigade, out of its depth with the blazes at West Point, asks for military assistance.

14 DECEMBER SUNDAY

> I rushed up (still during the bombing) and was the first on the spot. I counted four dead and ten wounded, most of them seriously. I did what I could, mostly administering morphia for pain and shock. (Solomon Bard)[13]

King George VI's forty-sixth birthday starts with the shellfire intensifying, and many military targets are hit and damaged. Some non-military targets are also hit, but generally those near British gun sites. Captain Pardoe of the headquarters staff is killed by a shell while visiting units on the Peak. Fired from Kowloon, it makes a direct hit on his car, killing him and his driver instantly (28: 35).[15] Mr Corbally: 'We were approaching Magazine Gap when a shell went into the side of the road some forty yards ahead. The driver backed down the road and clung to the side of the hill, hoping that we should be safer there. They shelled that angle for about ten minutes, and when we went on we saw an officer killed in his car just around the corner' (60: 112).[15] A shell that hits the nursing quarters of St Albert's Convent also kills a 27-year-old nurse, Sister Brenda Morgan.[16] Two guns are put out of action by shellfire at Belcher's Fort. British counter-battery fire targets Lai Chi Kok, Kowloon, Stonecutters Island, and Ma Lau Tong.

In the morning, the Marine Police scuttle their launches in the harbour and Commander F. W. Crowther (of the Royal Naval Dockyards in Admiralty) orders Lieutenant Cole, RN, to look after the Aberdeen dockyards. He is sending him to his death.

The HKVDC HQ moves from Lower Albert Road[17] to Peak Mansions (79: 230). The Hong Kong Naval Dockyard Defence Corps (HKDDC) is added to the list of Auxiliary Units, under the command of the commodore and his officers, by a Government Gazette notification (147).

In occupied Kowloon: 'It is very dark tonight, and repeatedly we hear the shrill, sharp scream of helpless women around us — and we are helpless to aid them!' (117: 31).

The Royal Artillery continues to consolidate its positions. The 5 AA Lewis guns move to the RN Dockyard. The Tai Ho Wan 2-pounder of 965 Defence Battery moves to the Tai Koo area. The HQ of the 1st Hong Kong Regiment is absorbed by RA West,[18] which moves from Wan Chai Gap to Wong Nai Chung Gap. A Counter Battery HQ is also formed at Wong Nai Chung Gap under command of Major G. E. S. Proes, RA, with Tiger Balm and Caroline Hill sections under his direct control. The 1st Mountain Battery moves two 3.7-inch guns to Gauge Basin[19] and two to Tai Tam Fork. They will all be lost when the Japanese invade. Four obsolete First World War vintage Mark 1 18-pounder saluting guns are taken out of store and sent to Stanley for 965 Defence Battery.

By evening of this day, after a week of fighting, Hong Kong is isolated under full siege and all forces on the Island are occupying their defensive positions. Brigadier Peffers realises that Battle HQ is now nearer to the Japanese forces than any other unit, and is vulnerable to attack from across the harbour. He organizes a Battle HQ Defence Force under Captain Charles Turner and Lieutenant Browne, with a platoon of 2/14th Punjabis, a platoon of HKVDC Portuguese, and a platoon of HKVDC Stanley Warders (158).

Diary for 14 December

00.30   East Brigade HQ personnel arrive at their Tai Tam base, the Royal Artillery underground plotting room. It is staffed by the Brigade Commander (Wallis), Brigade Major (Harland), Staff Captain (Belton), two signallers, the Brigade Intelligence Officer, and three clerks. 'The atmosphere was heavy and even with the emergency (draft) plant working and the air vent (emergency exit) open this air was unhealthy and oppressive and made clear the thinking difficult [sic]. One became flushed and had bad headaches' (139).

02.00   Great anxiety is caused by the speed of the fires at Belcher's and Kennedy Town. They are finally brought under control at midday (20: 11).

08.30 Major Ryan of HQRA calls Lieutenant E. H. Field at Belcher's Fort with orders to engage a large junk moving eastwards from the direction of Lan Tau, thought to be carrying Japanese to Stonecutters. This quickly results in counter-battery fire (164).

09.00 A heavy bombardment of Belcher's Fort starts. The lower Battery Observation Post (BOP) is completely demolished, and 965 Defence Battery's two 4.7-inch Quick Firing (QF) guns there are put out of action. The Fort Commander, Lieutenant E. H. Field, Lance Bombardier Palmer, and Master Gunner Cooper are wounded.[20] 'Then all hell was let loose as a shell hissed down the ventilator shaft of the room we were in, and exploded. The Havildar sitting next to the ventilator was killed at once, the BOR next to him was badly wounded, and a Lance Bombardier Palmer had his leg hanging off and, next in line I was peppered with Shrapnel and brick dust': Field (164). Gunner Fateh Muhammad is also killed and hospital records show seven IOR wounded from 965 Defence Battery admitted to IGH on this date (145: 142), one of whom, Mamraz Khan, dies.[21] With the fort effectively out of action, the other Indians are assigned to infantry for local defence (93: 132).

10.30 Official Communiqué:

> It has been a quiet night with nothing of special interest to report. The Police have maintained complete control and the civil population are taking things composedly. The two brief air raids and intermittent shelling yesterday caused a few casualties and comparatively little damage, although in one district there was a serious fire. Communal kitchens in the urban areas fed over one hundred thousand people yesterday, and it is hoped to increase on this number to-day. Further arrangements have been made for the sale of uncooked rice from Government depots. More and more volunteer lorry drivers are required. (147)

11.00 The Pak Sha Wan (4th Bty. HKVDC) and Sai Wan (5th Bty. HKVDC) areas are heavily shelled, with the Pak Sha Wan BOP being permanently knocked out and both guns there being reduced to Case 1 Action.[22] Three ORs are killed, and six injured. The HKVDC 4th Battery Commander, Lieutenant Barnett, is also wounded (93: 133).[23]

12.00   Mount Davis is heavily shelled. One 3-inch AA gun of 17 HAA HKSRA is destroyed by a direct hit, and others are reduced to Case I Action. Nine ORs are killed (93: 132), and four wounded are taken to the IGH (145: 142). Ford: 'a direct hit on the magazine at the AA's position has put one gun out of action, killed nine Indians including our own Havildar and put the magazine hors-de-combat. No. 3 Gun, the pet of the battery, is out of action from a direct hit on the piece from a 240-mm shell . . . Cooper has sustained two crushed legs and seems in a bad way' (15: 64).

14.30   Official Communiqué:

> The Garrison spent a quiet night and weary troops from the Mainland had a much needed rest. These troops were soon deployed with troops already in position. Now that the exact number of casualties incurred in the Mainland fighting has been checked, it has been found that they are even less than originally estimated. This morning there was considerable exchange of shelling between our own and enemy batteries. Two enemy batteries have been silenced. None of our own has been put out of action, although we sustained a few casualties in exposed positions. (147)

15.27   Air raid alarm. All clear at 16.15 (147).

16.00   Aberdeen is bombed, with one bomb hitting the power station (143f).

16.30   Three shells land on telephone cables in Magazine Gap. All main contacts are cut, though they are fixed within twenty hours (95: 77).

16.30   More bombs fall on Aberdeen dock (143e).

18.00   APV *Shun Wo* starts Beaufort patrol (130: 14).

22.30   A 6-inch shell falls near the Aberdeen Industrial School, which the Navy is now using as a base (99: 42), breaking its windows (143e).

Roll of Honour for 14 December

NURSES — 1 Killed

Morgan, Irene Brenda	Sister, QAIMNS	K

Killed by a shell (outside the sisters' quarters, St Albert's Convent).

ARTILLERY — 11 Killed

Fateh Khan	Havildar, 965 Defence Bty. HKSRA	U

Belcher's lower battery.

Ghulam Husain	Havildar, 2 Heavy Bty. HKSRA[24]	U
Hayat Khan	Havildar, 17 HAA Bty. HKSRA[25]	U

Mount Davis.

Muhammad Din	Gunner, 17 HK Bty. HKSRA	U

Mount Davis.

Muhammad Hanif	Gunner, 17 HAA Bty. HKSRA	U

Mount Davis.

Fateh Muhammad	Gunner, 7 AA Bty. HKSRA	U

Wounded Mount Davis. Died in IGH (145: 142).

Muhammad Ali	Gunner, 7 AA Bty. HKSRA	K

Mount Davis.

Muhammad Ashraf	Gunner, 7 AA Bty. HKSRA	U

Mount Davis.

Muhammad Sharif	Naik, 7 AA Bty. HKSRA	U

Mount Davis. (126) states 'Kowloon' but without a date and under 20 Coast Bty. HKSRA.

Niamat Khan	Gunner, 7 AA Bty. HKSRA	U

Mount Davis.

Sarda Alam	Naik, 7 AA Bty. HKSRA	U

Mount Davis.

HEADQUARTERS — 1 Killed

Pardoe, Thomas Martin	Captain, Worcestershire Regt.	K

Killed by shellfire while visiting units.

ROYAL SCOTS — 2 Killed

Burn, Stanford	Major	K	

Shot himself with his revolver (91: 74).[26] (145: 178) says 14 Dec.   [8/16 Dec.]

Taylor, William Trevor	Private	K

Buried No. 2 Crater Borret Road, implying that he died in BRH (126).[27]

ENGINEERS — 1 Killed

Lee Man Fai	Sapper, RE	U

HKDDC — 1 Killed

Fox, Henry Leslie	Private, HKDDC	U[28]

15 DECEMBER MONDAY

> We heard the bomb fall and all dived to the ground — you didn't need much training for that — except for Sequeira. A piece of the bomb hit him under the jaw, and came out above his left temple. (Arthur Gomes)[30]

The day is again a litany of air and artillery attacks. There are eight separate air raid alerts, the longest being from 13.40 to 14.30. In the morning, Aberdeen is bombed and APV *Indira* is sunk (143e). During the day, two more Japanese aircraft are shot down. One falls on Second Street, Sai Ying Poon.

There is systematic shelling of the pillboxes along Hong Kong's northern shore held by C and D Companies of the Rajputs. Three are knocked out and one is badly damaged (15: 70). The Naval Dockyards are also heavily shelled and occasionally bombed (99: 37). Private motoring in the colony is banned and a curfew is ordered from 19.30 to 06.30 (147).

In the evening, beach defence positions are established, including one 2-pounder at PB 56 near the China Fleet Club (now the site of Mass Mutual House), one 18-pounder near Belcher's, and one Bofors at North Point (93: 133). The 5 AA Regiment Wong Nai Chung section moves from Tai Hang back to Wong Nai Chung, and the Albany Road section moves from Albany Road to Caroline Hill.

Later that night, an 'attempted landing' is repulsed. The 6-inch guns at Pak Sha Wan fire at a collection of craft in Kowloon Bay, setting two alight and scattering the remainder. Japanese accounts give no mention of any attack being launched this day, therefore either this was a probe to investigate the defences — the 228th Regiment, for example, imply that they carried out such reconnaissances on the 16th, 17th, and 18th (122) — or (more likely) civilian refugees from Kowloon occupied the boats.

Churchill to Governor Sir Mark Young via telegram:

> We are all watching day by day and hour by hour your stubborn defence of the port and fortress of Hong Kong. You guard a link long famous between the Far East and Europe. We are sure that the defence of Hong Kong against barbarous and unprovoked attack will add a glorious page to British annals. All our hearts are with you in your ordeal. Every day of your resistance brings nearer our certain victory. (147)

Diary for 15 December

00.40 Fort Collinson reports firing at a small boat 1,000 yards northeast (139).

08.00 No. 18 Platoon of 5 Company HKVDC patrols the Mount Davis area. At a house called 'Doman', a Japanese aircraft drops a bomb. It misses the house, but kills Private Sequeira standing outside.

08.06 The Royal Rifles report Japanese parachutes dropped in the vicinity of Tai Tam reservoir. Investigation shows that this was a propaganda pamphlet drop (139).

08.15–12.25 The Pinewood 17 AA HKSRA gun site is bombarded for several hours. One gun is destroyed, and the predictor and height finder are damaged. One IOR is killed and four wounded (145: 142), and the position (on a very exposed on a plateau north of the Peak)[30] is later evacuated (93: 133). The gunners are then attached to the Punjabis as infantry (20: 12).

08.30 APV *Man Wo* starts Aberdeen patrol (130: 15).

09.00 East Brigade is informed that Pilot Officer Thomson is reporting as Intelligence Officer (139).

10.04 Heavy shelling of Sai Wan AA position. This results in one gun being put out of action and the other being damaged (139).

10.30 Official Communiqué:

> During the night there has been nothing of interest to report. The artillery duel continues intermittently. (147)

10.30 East Brigade HQ is visited by His Excellency the Governor, Sir Mark Young. He is assured that the brigade will give a good account of itself (139).

10.48 PB 51 receives a direct hit. There are no casualties, as the crew are already in temporary positions (139).

12.00 Mortar fire starts falling on Central and the Naval Dockyard. The HKVDC 5th Battery at Sai Wan is heavily shelled, and one gun is knocked out (79: 231).

13.00 The Naval Commodore orders that the pom-pom gun from APV *Indira* (sunk earlier) be salvaged (143e).

13.31 PB 51a takes a direct hit. Again there are no casualties (139).

15.30 In the afternoon, a stick of bombs hits the Old Bailey and Caine Road junction, the Pottinger Street and Hollywood Road junction, Wellington Street and the Central Police Station. The ground floor and basement offices of Police Headquarters are destroyed, causing a number of casualties (76: 163). Assistant Superintendent Wilson: 'A number of police officers of various ranks were killed or wounded; my office was set on fire and I was very lucky to get out alive with minor injuries' (132b: Wilson). Phyllis Harrop: 'Thompson created a diversion because he refused to go without his tin hat. Wilson, who shared his office, was very badly shaken but otherwise unhurt. His hair had been singed a bit and his uniform cut in places. Thompson's office was a complete wreck; the bomb had exploded through the grating and just outside his office, blowing everything to bits.' ASP W. R. Thompson's wounds are mainly to his face. The other wounded include Traffic Inspector S. C. Saunders who also receives wounds to the head. The fatalities are Hopkins and two Chinese ATS drivers (49: 76).

17.30 Official Communiqué:

>During the day, our artillery bombarded enemy batteries on the Mainland, and several direct hits were observed. The enemy replied with some sporadic shell-fire. A few enemy planes were observed over the Island, and some were seen to drop leaflets containing the usual Japanese propaganda which invariably shows an astonishing ignorance of British and Chinese psychology. It can now be revealed that the Japanese delegation, which came over from Kowloon under the cover of a White Flag, brought a letter enquiring if H. E. The Governor was willing to negotiate for the surrender of Hongkong. His Excellency rejected this proposal, and replied that he was not prepared in any circumstances to hold any meeting or parley on such a subject. Not only is this Colony strong enough to resist all attempts at invasion but it also has the loyal backing of the resources of the British Empire, of the United States of America, and of the Republic of China. British Subjects, and those who have sought the protection of the British Empire, can rest assured that there will never be any surrender to the Japanese. (147)

18.00 HMS *Thracian* dry-docks in Aberdeen (143e).

18.30 After shells (believed to have been fired by a ship at sea) land at Aberdeen, the MTBs are ordered to sea to engage the enemy. In a confused half-hour engagement from 21.30 to 22.00 they fire torpedoes at unidentified boats (143e).[31]

19.20 PB 52 is reported hit. PB 49 is also suspected hit, and the shelling is reported of PBs 40–47 (139).

19.30 Curfew imposed until 06.30 (147).

21.00 Pak Sha Wan on Hong Kong Island raises the alarm after heavy shelling (44: 81). HKVDC 4th Battery illuminates the water with No. 2 searchlight and gives the alert, claiming that a hundred men with rafts and three rubber boats are attempting to cross the channel. The battery's 6-inch guns fire fifty-eight rounds (93: 133). No. 2 Platoon Royal Rifles also opens fire on the boats from West Fort at Pak Sha Wan (79: 232). The occupants are beaten off with heavy loss, but Japanese batteries return fire knocking out the searchlight.[32]

21.41   Major Bishop, Royal Rifles C Company Commander, no doubt hearing the firing, reports that the enemy has occupied the Pak Sha Wan battery. The report is later learnt to be false.[33] East Brigade War Diary claims that the basis of this report was the assertion by retreating Royal Artillery personnel (presumably 4th Bty. HKVDC) that 'the enemy are as thick as leaves in the battery position' (139).

21.54   Flying Officer Gray[34] in the Sai Wan Redoubt RAF wireless post reports that the landing appears to have been beaten off (139).

22.45   A second crossing from Sam Ka Tsun Bay is reported. Second Lieutenant Sleap claims four boats sunk (3: 17).

24.00   There is a report of Japanese cavalry at Happy Valley, but it turns out to be escaped racehorses. They are mown down by machine guns (95: 76).

Roll of Honour for 15 December

ARTILLERY — 5 Killed

| Cooper, Clarence Bingham | Warrant Officer II, Battery Sergeant Major, 965 Defence Bty. RA | K |

Died of wounds sustained at Belcher's Fort, 14 Dec. Originally buried Colonial Cemetery (126).

| Mamraz Khan | Gunner, 965 Defence Bty. HKSRA | U |

Probably from Belcher's. Admitted IGH wounded on 14 Dec. Died at BMH (145: 142).

| Dara Singh | Gunner, 4 Medium Bty. HKSRA | U |

Died in hospital (145: 141).

| Muhammad Firoz | Gunner, HKSRA | U |

| Silver, William Edward | Gunner, 7 Bty. 5 HAA Regt. RA | U |

Killed by shellfire at Sai Wan. Originally buried Colonial Cemetery (126).

HONG KONG CHINESE REGIMENT — 1 Killed

| To Wei Kei | Private, HK Chinese Regt. | U |

PHASE II: THE SIEGE OF THE ISLAND   83

VOLUNTEERS — 3 Killed

Fernandez, Ignatius Miguel   BQMS, 4 Bty. HKVDC   U
   Presumably by shellfire.

Schnepel, Frederick   Lance Bombardier, 4 Bty. HKVDC   K
   Presumably by shellfire.

Sequeira, Luiz Romano   Private, HKVDC 5 Coy.   K
   Killed by a bomb fragment near Mount Davis.

RAOC — 1 Killed

Chung Koon Yau   Private, RAOC   U

RAMC — 1 Killed

James, Morgan John   Private   U
   Possibly at the Command Observation Post at the Peak (3: 16).

POLICE — 2 Killed

Baker, Albert Victor   Inspector, HKPF   K
   Shot himself, believed connected with having been gassed in First World War (141).[35]

Hopkins, Albert Leslie   Inspector, HKPF   K
   Killed by a bomb in the compound of Central Police Station (141).

ROYAL NAVY — 1 Killed

Lilley, Thomas   Able Seaman, HMS *Tamar*   K
   Admitted Queen Mary Hospital (as 'Lilby') 12 Dec. (145: 82). Died of wounds 15 Dec. (145: 196).

CIVILIANS — 1 Killed

Bookeyah   UX
   Eleven-year-old Indian girl, admitted to St Stephen's Relief Hospital 10 Dec., died 15 Dec. (145: 93).

16 DECEMBER TUESDAY

> What did upset me a little bit was that there was a little, maybe a football field that had been dug up . . . and the PWD vans were picking up dead people on the streets, pulling in and just emptying the dead bodies into this hole. Now I'm convinced that while we

> were watching... some of those dead bodies weren't dead. Whether it was movement of a dead body... there was movement amongst one or two of them. And I believe they covered them with lime. (Bill Bethell)[36]

The bombardment intensifies. A Japanese bomb makes a direct hit on the Bowen Road Hospital kitchen, and another falls on the officers' mess on McDonnell Road (27: 42). Seventeen planes bomb Mount Davis in the afternoon, and a single bomb in one built-up area (Shau Kei Wan) causes 150 serious civilian casualties (20: 12).

The Rajput War Diary reports: 'H.E. The Governor visited TAIKOO Hqrs during the morning and reporters with BOXER visited in the afternoon wanting "copy" regarding the action on DEVILS PEAK' (140).

Japanese artillery focuses mainly on British artillery sites and pillboxes along the northern shore from Pak Sha Wan to North Point. Pillbox 39 of D Company, Middlesex is hit by several shells that overfly Pak Sha Wan (139). By nightfall, more than half of the pillboxes between Lye Mun and Happy Valley are destroyed with some casualties (96: 33). In the afternoon, the shelling turns to Mount Davis, and the Battery Plotting Room is put out of action by a dud 24-cm shell which crashes down a ventilation shaft and does significant damage (93: 133). Solomon Bard:

> It was an incredible shock. It fizzed, and — worried of the possibility of sympathetic detonation from the shells still falling — we evacuated the room. The major [Anderson] was fully and completely in charge and handled the tricky situation well. I remember distinctly that he gave all the orders (he instructed me to stay to the end in case I was required). I also remember that one Warrant Officer (a rather fat one) had broken down under the strain of being next to a hissing shell and was totally useless. I do not remember his name. (132b: Bard)

Central is also targeted, with the Gloucester Building and Hong Kong Bank being damaged by shelling.

During the day two more Japanese aircraft are shot down. One is brought down over Lye Mun, crashing in the sea with its pilot escaping from the wreckage. The other is damaged over South Island, and is last seen losing height over the Mainland.

The batteries are firing back, and this day includes the only other likely engagement with a Japanese naval vessel. Templer at Bokhara:

> A large Japanese destroyer came just within our range. We engaged her and fired about 10 salvoes. Immediately on opening fire she started to zig zag and put out a smoke screen. As soon as a salvo was fired she at once altered course thus making the rounds already fired fall away from her. However, the last round fired at extreme range, 20,000 yards, fell right behind her counter. I saw her stern lift in the air and she proceeded much slower but still out of our range. (150)

In the afternoon, a gang of men demanding 'protection money' from residents of Staunton Street are intercepted by police who take 'drastic action' against eight of them (131).

The 5 AA Albany Road section moves from Caroline Hill to Stanley Prison. One 3-inch AA gun is moved from the dockyard to Hatton Road (but it is not used). The 25th Medium Battery moves the two Tiger Balm guns to Stanley Gap Road.

During the night the Sai Wan AA gun and Mount Davis are both shelled again (93: 134).

Diary for 16 December

00.29 Sai Wan OP reports a big fire in Shau Kei Wan (probably the rubber factory) (139).

01.12 Pak Sha Wan Battery is back in action with one gun and twenty gunners (139).

04.00 HMS *Thracian* attacks Japanese boat concentrations being prepared for the invasion. She runs aground at Uk Kok, but is later refloated. 'At first I was certain we had been torpedoed. It was pitch dark, there was no moon and we were at action cruising stations. Suddenly there was a shuddering crash; the ship's bottom was ripped open and the forward compartment flooded': Petty Officer Peter Paul (91: 116). She enters Aberdeen and docks.

09.00 There is a 35-minute air raid alarm, the first of seven of the day (four in the morning and three in the afternoon). Central Police Station is hit again, causing a number of casualties (76: 163).

Lye Mun Gap and the Sai Wan 6-inch position come under low-level and dive-bombing attacks (139). At Lye Mun, Riflemen Ray Smith, Russel Coates, and Aldon MacNaughton, and Sergeant John Coleman, of C Company Royal Rifles, are wounded (132b: Smith).[37]

Japanese shelling and air attacks on British positions on the Island intensify. In one hour, 230 shells hit the Naval Dockyards (the area around today's Admiralty) (99: 35).

09.30   A Japanese plane force lands in Tathong Channel and the pilot escapes; the kill is claimed by the Wong Nai Chung 3.7-inch section (20: 13).[38]

09.30   Maltby visits East Brigade HQ to discuss artillery plans. He also inspects the Windy Gap and Obelisk Hill defences (139).

10.00   Official Communiqué:

> It has been a quiet night with no change in the position since issue of the last communiqué (147).

10.30   Another plane is brought down over Lamma — claimed by the Brick Hill 3.7-inch section (93: 133) — and crashes in a gully (20: 13).

11.15   East Group Royal Artillery engage a large concentration of enemy motor transport and troops at Customs Pass. This is one of many shoots at that target, and appears to be effective (139).

13.30   A high-level bombing attack starts at Aberdeen dockyard, aimed at HMS *Thracian*. There are many casualties at the dockyards, including Lieutenant Cole, and *Thracian* also takes some casualties after a near miss. 'The *Thracian* had a near miss, killing a few, but she herself was not seriously damaged': Commander F. W. Crowther (99: 37). *Thracian* is then disarmed, as damage from the earlier grounding is considered too bad to fix (15: 70).

Splinters from the bombs also set MTB 08 on fire, and she later blows up. The Naval Armament Tug *Gatling* at the dockhead is also hit, and most of the crew (who are volunteer merchant service officers from Jardine Mathieson's floating staff) are killed (143e). The final casualty list from the *Gatling* is six dead and four wounded (143f), one of the wounded being the Chief Engineer, J. Gunn (145: 196). HMT *Alliance* is also damaged by a near miss (133).

14.00 11 Platoon (B Coy. Punjabis) HQ near Central market is bombed, injuring Jemadar Dhani Ram and Havildars Tota Ram and Bhima Ram (140).

15.50 Sai Wan OP reports two direct hits on the No. 1 AA gun, though the gun is still in action (139).

17.00 Mount Davis is finally evacuated under shellfire in parties of five. Regimental Sergeant Major Ford: 'BSM Barlow[39] and myself established order in the battery plotting room . . . we evacuate the mount and repair to Felix Villas.'

17.30 Official Communiqué:

> There has been a sharp artillery duel with the enemy throughout the day, with our guns maintaining their ascendancy. We succeeded in silencing two of the enemy's gun positions this morning, and another one this afternoon. Our batteries suffered no damage. A Japanese plane was shot down over Lyemun this morning. The enemy pilot succeeded in extricating himself from the wreckage in the water and was last seen paddling towards the mainland shore in a collapsible rubber boat. Our anti-aircraft batteries winged another plane this afternoon on the south side of the Island. This plane was last seen rapidly losing altitude over the Mainland, and it is thought unlikely that it could possibly have returned to its base. There have been a number of air raids throughout the day. Damage and casualties have been on a light scale. (147)

18.25 Pak Sha Wan and Sai Wan come under fire again. Two Other Ranks are wounded at Pak Sha Wan. This battery is later reinforced by one sergeant and seven gunners from 20th Coast Battery RA (93: 133).

19.30 East Brigade reports that King's Road, Braemar, has been heavily shelled. The road is damaged and partly blocked by derelict cars and lorries and many dangling overhead electric tram cables (139).

21.59   The alternative positions of PBs 47 and 48 are reported as receiving direct hits. A paint factory south of the road is reported as being on fire. Much of the fire is later shown to have come from four easterly huts of North Point refugee camp (139).[40]

Roll of Honour for 16 December

HKDDC — 6 Killed

Dawson, Kenneth David	Private, HKDDC	U
Lost in Naval Armament Tug *Gatling*.		[18 Dec.]
Forster, John Garnett	Private, HKDDC	U
Lost in Naval Armament Tug *Gatling*.		[18 Dec.]
Jones, Roland Lewis	Private, HKDDC	U
Lost in Naval Armament Tug *Gatling*. Killed by escaping steam post explosion (133).		[18 Dec.]
Lane, Richard	Private, HKDDC	U
Lost on Naval Armament Tug *Gatling*.		
Ramsey, J. E.	Private, HKDDC	U
Lost on Naval Armament Tug *Gatling*.		
Tillman, Henry[41]	Sergeant, Dockyard Police, HKDDC	U

MIDDLESEX — 1 Killed

Jousiffe, Arthur William	Private	U
Killed in pillbox shelling? (126) says 'Missing south of The Ridge area Dec 16'.		

ENGINEERS — 2 Killed

Wong Sau	Sapper, RE	U
Wong Yer	Sapper, 40 Coy. R.E.	U

ROYAL NAVY — 2 Killed

Cole, George Reginald	Lieutenant, HMS *Tamar*	K
Killed by bombing at Aberdeen (145: 197).		
Trethake, Wilfred	Stoker Petty Officer, HMS *Tamar*	K
Died of wounds (from Aberdeen bombing?) Ex-*Thracian*, at RN Hospital (145: 197).		[17 Dec.]

MERCHANT NAVY — 1 Killed

Jewell, Anthony Michael[42]	Master, SS *Yatshing*	K
(133) states that Jewell died on *Gatling* on 16 Dec. (126) concurs that he was HKDDC.		

CIVILIANS — 2 Killed

Cheong Kin Cho UCWD [6 Dec.][43]

Jorgensen, Jorgen Ship's Captain UX
  Nationality unknown, admitted St. Paul's casualty clearing station 16 Dec. died same day (145: 92).

17 DECEMBER WEDNESDAY

> It was then a case of keeping them off the Island as long as we could. But on the night of the 17th December the Japanese first obliterated all the pillboxes along the North Shore. (Bunny Browne)[44]

There are bombing attacks on Chung Hom Kok and Western Market. A bomb at Tai Koo docks hits a house and kills twenty seamen sheltering inside (131). The shelling also continues, focused largely on Central,[46] but there is a pause for a truce as a second demand for surrender is made and — like the first — summarily rejected.

The Royal Artillery prepares for the coming invasion, sending one 965 Defence Battery 18-pounder to the Belcher's area (though it will be destroyed in Wan Chai Market on the 25th) and one to Stanley (where it will be put out of action at Stanley View on the 23rd). The 2nd Mountain Battery takes over Sanatorium from, and hands Tai Tam Hill to, the 1st Mountain Battery. The 25th Medium Battery moves the two Caroline Hill guns to the Jockey Club stables where they will be put out of action on the 20th.

Wallis: 'Informed the G.O.C. situation on north face not very bright. Many PBs hit and destroyed, Lyon Lights hit and communications cut [though] continuous efforts being made to repair and maintain them' (139).

In the evening, concentrations of enemy land and sea transports are shelled in the region of Kai Tak. Later, unknown to the British, Lieutenant Zempei Masushima[46] and four men cross the harbour to reconnoitre landing sites. Fired upon by Rajput pillboxes, they return safely (95: 72).

Diary for 17 December

01.51 The 6-inch position at Sai Wan is shelled without damage (139).

05.30 The hulk of HMS *Thracian* is deliberately run aground (presumably at Middle Island) (15: 70).

06.30 First light brings a mass air raid.

08.00 Official Communiqué:

> It has again been a quiet night, apart from some shelling in the early hours of the morning. Little damage has so far been reported. (147)

08.10 Fortress HQ informs East Brigade that Mr Harold Sheldon will report for duty to assist in framing charges against the two Royal Scots Mainland deserters (139).

08.25 The Defence Secretary reports that he has found the crew of PB 51a asleep with their Machine guns lying in store. A quick enquiry reveals that the crew were resting after an all-night watch, and the guns were damaged ones that had already been replaced at the post (139).

09.16 The first air raid alert is sounded (147).

09.30 Gloucester Building's clock stops (147).

09.30 The Japanese issue a second request for surrender, which is also rejected. The surrender request is carried in two launches containing Colonel Toda, Lieutenant Miguno, and Mr Othsu. The Japanese promise a truce until 16.00, but receive the reply:

> His Excellency declines most absolutely to enter into any negotiations for the surrender of Hong Kong and he takes this opportunity of notifying Lt.-General Takashi Sakai and Vice-Admiral Masaichi Mimi that he is not prepared to receive any further communication from them on the subject. (15: 91)

09.40 Air raid alarm (147). A force of fourteen Army light bombers make two separate attacks, the first on Shau Kei Wan and Wan

Chai, the second on the Peak, Garden Road, and Central (20: 13).

11.05 No. 1 Company HKVDC at Sanatorium Gap reports that the Japanese have now cleared all obstacles from the runway at Kai Tak (139).

12.30 APV *Frosty* starts Aberdeen patrol (130: 15).

15.00 Official Communiqué:

> The Governor has to-day received a letter from the Japanese Military and Naval Authorities repeating the suggestion that he should enter into negotiations with them for the surrender of Hongkong. In his reply, His Excellency has declined absolutely to enter into any negotiations and has notified the Japanese authorities that he is not prepared to receive any further communications from them on the subject. A heavy bombardment of the Island occurred at about 8.45 a.m. this morning. This bombardment appeared to be directed against buildings in the Central District. At the same time, an air-raid took place and several bombs were dropped. Among the points shelled or bombed were the Gloucester Building, The Hongkong Bank, and other well-known landmarks in the city. Considering, however, the length and severity of the bombardment very little damage was done and very few casualties sustained. This was due to all concerned taking timely cover in ARP tunnels and the ground floors of large buildings. The calm of the civil population was marked. During the bombardment our own batteries actively replied and direct hits were observed. Five enemy guns were silenced. (147)

16.00 After the truce expires, the Japanese continue the bombardment of north shore pillboxes, and fourteen aircraft bomb Central district. The Field Company Engineers at Tai Hang are also heavily shelled.

16.30 Official Communiqué:

> Our Naval patrols are being constantly maintained. They have been attacked from time to time by enemy aircraft, which have been successfully beaten off. We have suffered some casualties. The defences have observed enemy destroyers and torpedo-boats on

patrol, which have made no attempt to attack, and which have remained out of reach of our batteries. Otherwise, there has been no change in the situation since the last communiqué. (147)

17.00 Two Aberdeen boatyards are hit by bombs, killing fifteen people. By the end of hostilities, in Aberdeen alone an estimated 400 Chinese residents have been killed (131).

21.00 Artillery fire starts a severe fire at the Braemar paint works,[47] causing a heavy pall of smoke (20: 13).

Roll of Honour for 17 December

VOLUNTEERS — 1 Killed

Brown, Harold Wilson   Sergeant, 4 Bty. HKVDC   K
 Died of wounds (presumably from Pak Sha Wan shelling), Bowen Road BMH (145: 199).

ENGINEERS — 4 Killed

Brunning, Edward Robert   Sapper, 22 Fortress Coy. RE   U
 Aberdeen (126), which gives 15 Dec. as an alternative date.

Curtis, Reginald Arthur   Sapper, 22 Fortress Coy. RE   U
 Aberdeen (126), which gives 15 Dec. as an alternative date.

Mitchell, Maurice   Staff Sergeant, 22 Fortress Coy. RE   U
 Killed at Aberdeen by a direct hit (126).

Moore, William Charles   Lance Corporal, 22 Fortress Coy. RE   K
 Originally buried Colonial Cemetery (126). Shelling at Tai Hang?

POLICE — 2 Killed

Kirpal Singh   Constable, HKPF   K

Wong Tam   Coxwain, HKPF   U
 'Coxwain' makes Jeanette (on 12 Dec.) a possibility.

CIVILIANS — 2 Killed

Beddow, Herbert Howell   UCWD
 Censor (145: 210)

Lal, D.   UX
 Indian. Admitted St. Paul's casualty clearing station 17 Dec. and died same day (145: 92).

5 Phase III: The Invasion of the Island

The siege has cost the garrison a further fifty-four dead and thirty-eight wounded. More important, it has greatly damaged the defences on the north shore and has tired (and in some cases demoralized) the defenders.

The streets, particularly in the area from Shau Kei Wan to North Point, are covered with debris. Many field telephone lines have been cut (though engineers are later commended for the speed with which they replaced them),[1] and large fires have been started in several parts of town.

Although the defences have been split into West and East Brigades, it is no coincidence that Maltby's two favourite battalions (the Rajputs and Punjabis) are holding the vulnerable north shore. The only talk in China Command is whether the invasion will come from Tsim Sha Tsui (where the embarkation facilities are best) to Central — which is Maltby's belief — or from Devil's Peak (where the water crossing is shortest) to North Point — his officers' best guess. Interestingly, ordinary soldiers are aware of the conversation; Whitehead: 'it was generally assumed by our Top Brass that they would land in the North-West, around the Victoria area, where the channel is narrower. True, the passage opposite Devil's Peak is nearest the Mainland, but it was felt the enemy would not risk a crossing there because of the hazards of sunken shipping' (30: 29).[2] At the last minute, the Royal Scots are moved from Causeway Bay to Wan

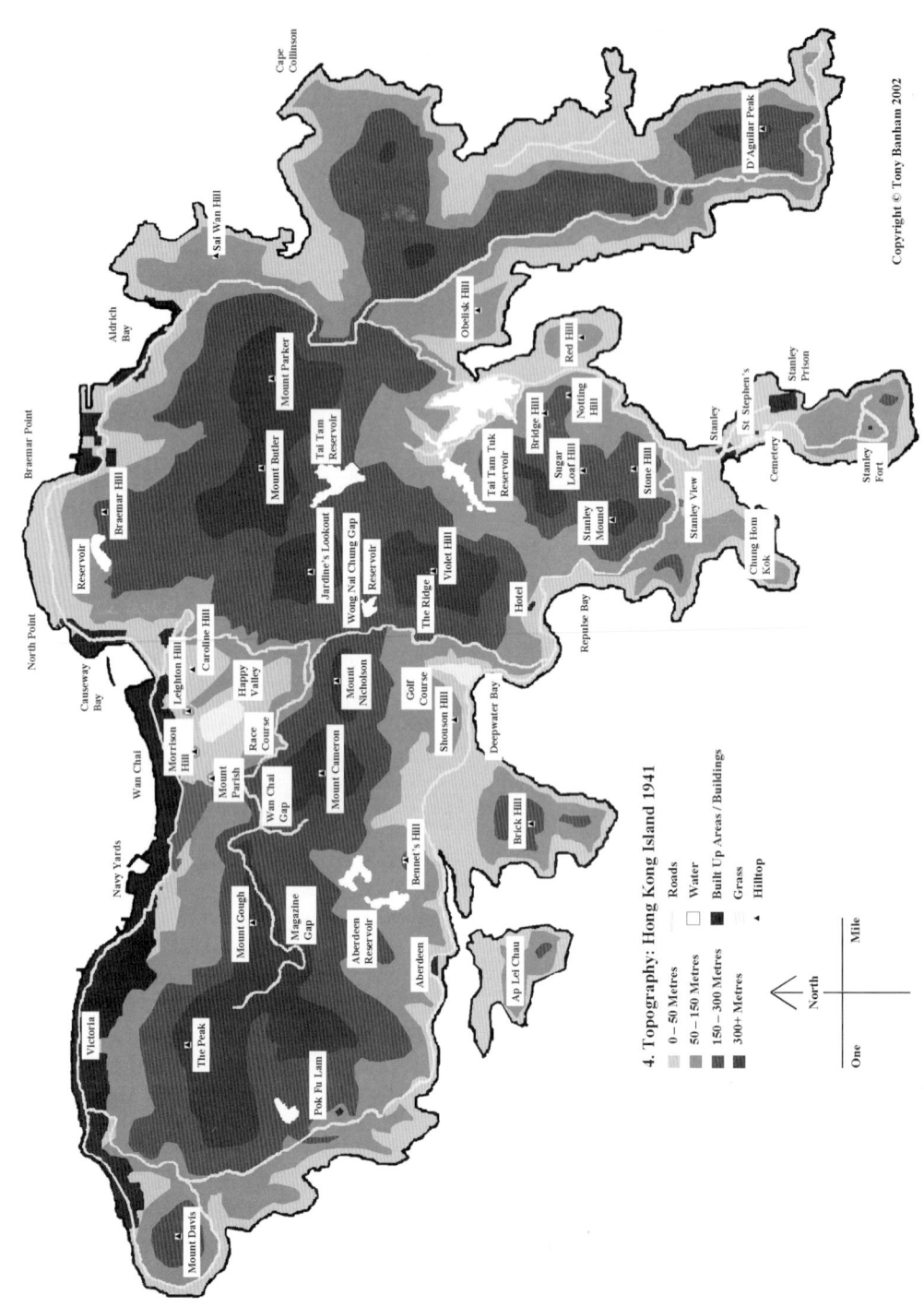

Chai so that they can act as a reserve at a point midway between the two likely points of attack.[3] D Company is at the waterfront, and the other companies are 'put out to grass' near them in no particular formation (132b: Hunter).

Thus on 18 December, as on the 8th, the forces facing the coming onslaught are the Punjabis, Royal Scots, and Rajputs, now rested after their Mainland experience.

In fact, the two halves of the defences are under separate commanders. West Brigade, under Brigadier Lawson, consists of the Punjabis, the Winnipeg Grenadiers, and the Royal Scots. Lawson's HQ, together with the HQ of the Royal Artillery (West),[4] is at Wong Nai Chung Gap opposite D Company of the Winnipeg Grenadiers. Nearby is a medical section, and uphill to the east are an anti-aircraft position and the HQ of 3 Company HKVDC. However, Lawson himself is already questioning the wisdom of holding a headquarters position in an area so likely to become embroiled in fighting. He is planning to withdraw to a more protected position on Black's Link on Friday morning.

East Brigade under Brigadier Wallis is made up of the Rajputs and the Royal Rifles. Brigade HQ is alongside the Royal Rifles' Battalion HQ at Tai Tam Gap. The Rajputs hold the all-important north shore defences between North Point and Shau Kei Wan.

Both brigades employ units of the Royal Artillery, HKSRA, and Volunteers, and the Middlesex hold the coastal pillboxes everywhere except the northern front. While everyone is expecting the attack to come from the north, the two Canadian battalions and the Middlesex are still holding the remainder of the Island's coast for insurance (and to act as a reserve).

18 DECEMBER THURSDAY

> Once the Japs landed in Hong Kong it was sheer chaos. (Steve Smith-Dutton)[5]

It is Hong Kong's last morning of siege. The defences are in place, waiting for the inevitable invasion, as the artillery and aerial bombardment reaches a new intensity.

The shelling continues all day. Mid-Levels, Causeway Bay and North Point are targeted, especially the pillboxes in Causeway Bay and North

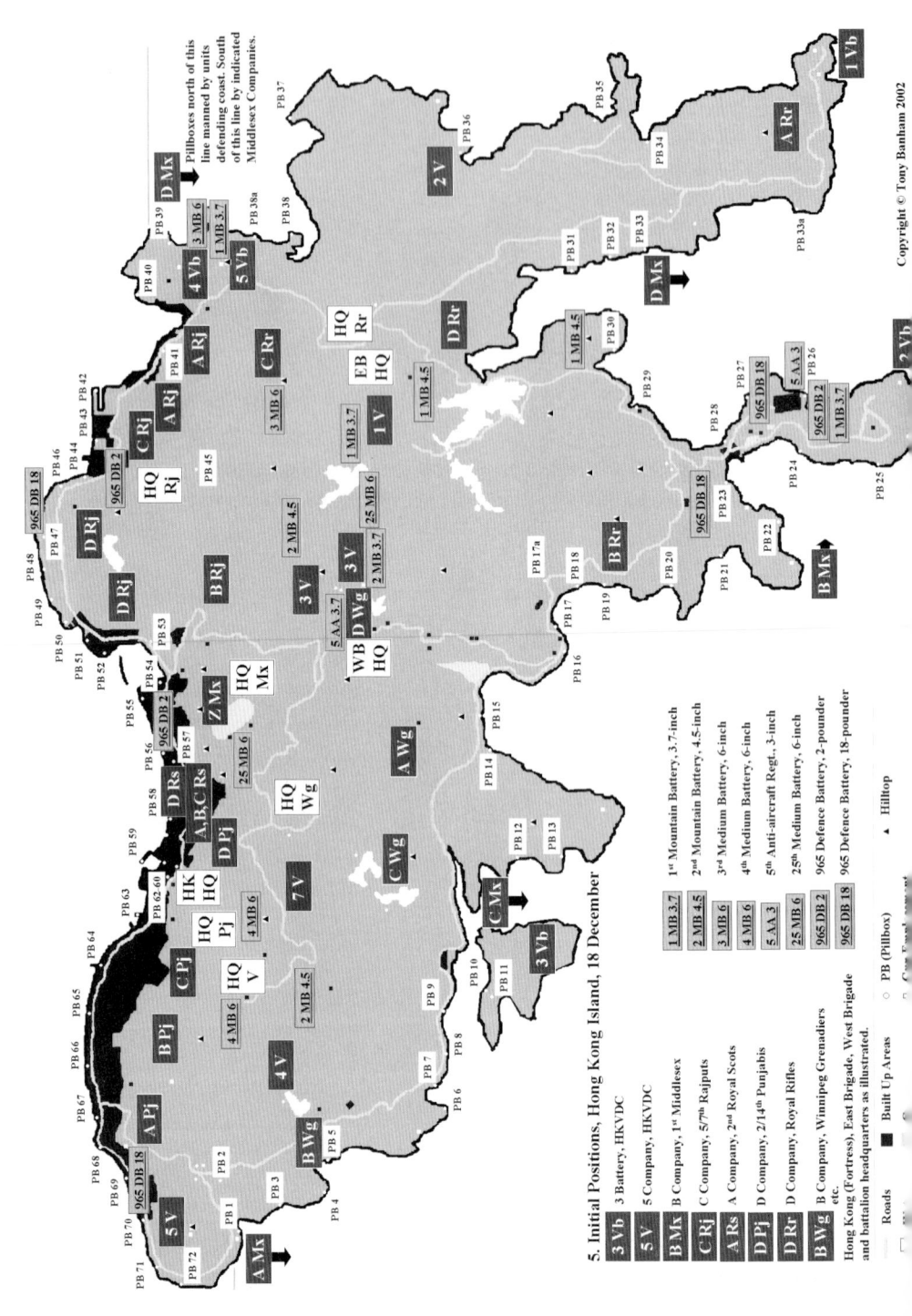

Point. Central is shelled again, damaging the Colonial Secretariat building (44: 82). The Wan Chai police station is hit sixteen times (98: 173).

In return, three Japanese freighters are bombarded by a 60-pounder gun — under command of Lieutenant Vinter (20: 13) — at North Point, which fires some thirty shrapnel rounds from an exposed position on the waterfront. One ship is holed and sunk (93: 134). British guns also put the Japanese battery on Devil's Peak out of action.

The Government knows that the invasion is coming:

> Special Order from His Excellency: From and after 5 p.m. on Thursday, December 18, 1941, no person or vehicle other than one belonging to His Majesty's Forces in the Civil Defence or Essential Services of this Colony shall, except with permission in writing by or on behalf of the Commissioner of Police, enter, be or remain in [the waterfront of Hong Kong Island]. (147)

As darkness comes, visibility falls to zero. It is a wet night, and the north shore is covered by smoke from a burning paint factory and boiling oil tanks, set alight by an earlier bombardment of North Point.

Soon after 19.00, individual telephone calls come in to China Command, claiming strange movements in the harbour. Continuous bombardment interferes with communications, and there are many stories of these early alerts being disbelieved.

By 21.00 however, the Japanese have landed their first wave, estimated at 7,500 men (3: 19). They overwhelm the initial defences they encounter,[6] bypassing any significant points of resistance in their race to get to high ground, and approach Wong Nai Chung Gap.

At this time it is not generally realized that the Japanese have invaded.[7] John Whitehead[8] of the Royal Artillery, for example, driving a Morris lorry to Braemar point comes under such heavy fire that, with three Indian soldiers on board, he gingerly heads back to Causeway Bay. At North Point, he is surprised to see stationary vehicles littering the road, and it is not until the Indian sitting next to him is shot in the chest that he realizes the Japanese are on the Island. Abandoning the vehicle, he sees it hit by a mortar or grenade, killing the other two Indians (30: 28). The battle for Hong Kong has started in earnest.

The fighting is confused on both sides. The 965 Defence Battery Tai Ho Wan 2-pounder is lost in the Tai Koo area sometime during the fighting, as is one of the 1st Mountain Battery's 3.7-inch guns that they had moved during the day to Sai Wan Redoubt (the other gun had been moved to Stanley, where it would see action until the surrender).

The Japanese clearly value speed over all else, and with their attack on the 5 AA Battery HKVDC position on Sai Wan Hill, the massacres of prisoners begin. They continue as the Japanese encounter the first civilians — ARP and St John's Ambulance men captured in the North Point area and murdered by Colonel Doi's men[9] — and the non-combatants of the Advanced Dressing Station at the Salesian Mission in Shau Kei Wan, whom Tanaka's men[10] surround this night and butcher the next day (27: 27).[11]

During the night, West Brigade establishes a defensive line running south from Causeway Bay, leaving the western part of the Island in British hands. A platoon of the 1st Middlesex is ordered to link up with the company of Rajputs at Tai Hang to protect the route to Central. This line is reasonably solid as far south as Wong Nai Chung Gap, but there it lacks depth.[12] East Brigade tries the first probing counter-attacks with C Company Royal Rifles, but these falter in the light of strong resistance.

By midnight, the Japanese have smashed through the 5/7th Rajputs, causing it to all but disintegrate it as a fighting unit. At the easternmost point of their bridgehead, they have encountered HKSRA and Royal Rifles units, which after some initial skirmishes, they largely ignore (their focus being south and west). At the westernmost point, they bump the Middlesex and the Hugheseliers[13] (defending the power station). They make no serious attempt to break through,[14] but instead just drive south until, as the 19th is about to begin, they bump 1 Company HKVDC in Quarry Gap and 3 Company HKVDC just to the north of Jardine's Lookout.

By this time, the Japanese are occupying a salient running from outside the North Point power station to Sai Wan Hill in the north, to the northern tips of Jardine's Lookout, Mount Butler and Mount Parker in the south.

Diary for 18 December

00.23   The beach defence guns move back to the police station as they are under heavy shellfire (139).

01.00   Aberdeen comes under fire from the sea, and the Industrial School is hit (20: 13).

Phase III: The Invasion of the Island

08.30 Official Communiqué:

There has been no change in the general situation after a relatively quiet night. The Governor has received a telegram from the Secretary of State for the Colonies in the course of which, after expressing the fullest approval of the reply returned to the Japanese Commander's request to negotiate terms of surrender, His Majesty's Government sends the following message; 'The stirring conduct of all defenders of the fortress is being watched with admiration and confidence by the whole Empire and by our allies throughout the World. Hold On.' The Governor has replied: 'All concerned in the defence of Hongkong have received with gratitude the message from His Majesty's Government contained in the telegram. We are going to hold on.' (147)

08.30 Governor Sir Mark Young makes a tour of inspection with the Commissioner of Police. He sees that the whole of King's Road has been blown to bits with no pillbox left standing, and that dead and dying are lying all over the streets (131).

09.30 There is a direct hit (probably a shell of 6-inch calibre) on the Tai Tam HQ. Three police casualties result (139).

10.00 A major bombing attack on Victoria commences. The Anglo-Persian Company's oil storage tanks are set on fire at North Point (20: 13). The paint factory at Braemar is already burning, and even in daylight the visibility on the north shore becomes very poor (15: 100).

11.00 Twenty-four Punjabis are killed and thirty-six wounded when a 500-pound bomb hits their HQ in Garden Road (140).

12.00 Two 18-pounder guns of 965 Defence Battery are destroyed by shellfire on Braemar northern shore defences (20: 14). One gun is smashed and on the road. The other is upside down (139).

12.44 Stanley Barracks is bombed (139).

13.15 Central market, being used as a food distribution centre, is hit by a bomb falling through the skylight by a million to one chance, with two more falling immediately outside. Six people

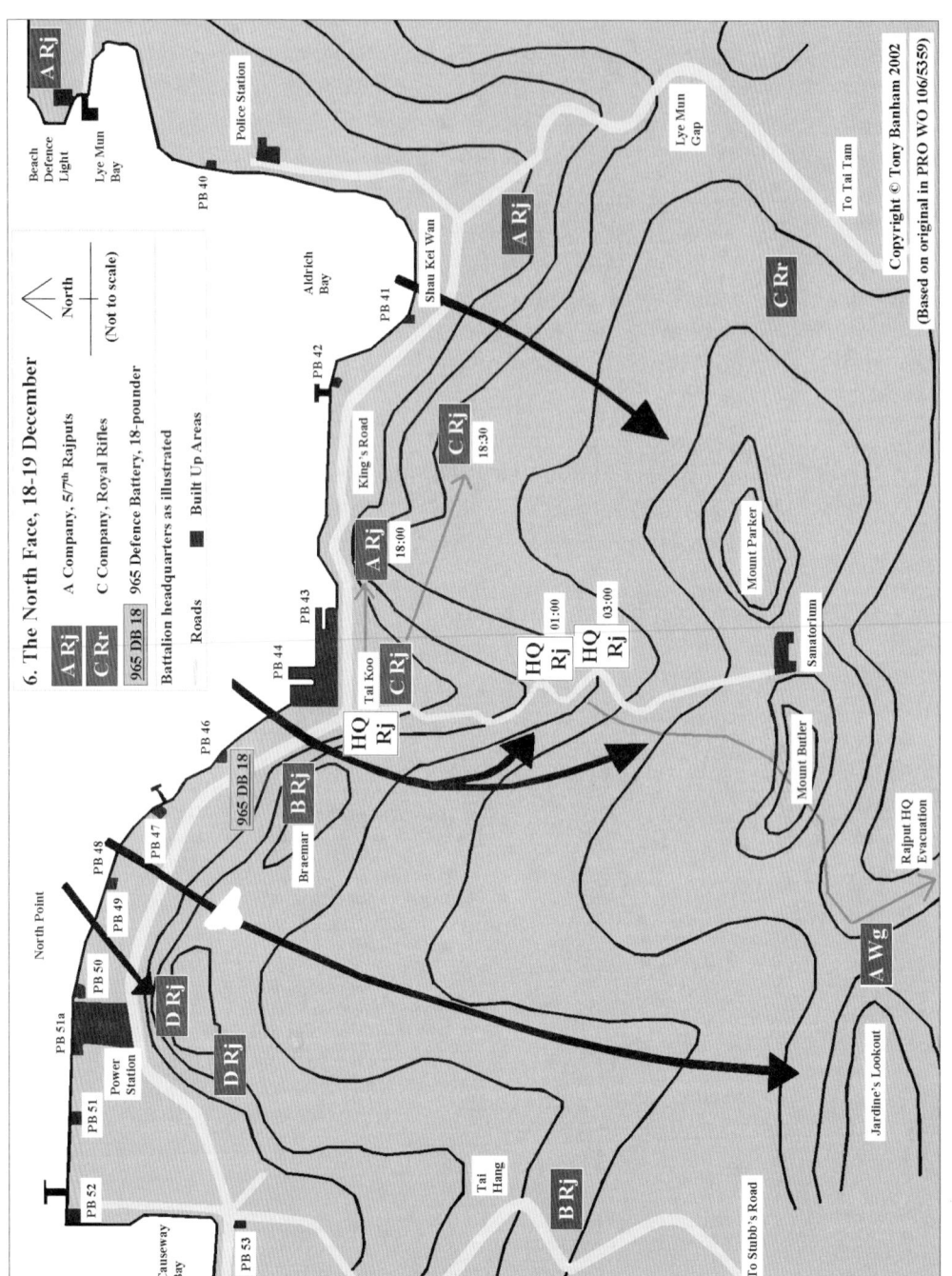

are killed inside, as are many others queuing for food outside, and there are hundreds of casualties (60: 135). 'The earth opened. Bright lights rolled against us like waves of flame. We tried to drop to the earth but the earth rose up to meet us faster than we could fall. Repercussion after repercussion shook the building. Walls spread outward, shuddered back into place' (42: 23).[15]

14.30 Official Communiqué:
> There is no change in the situation. The central district and lower levels of the city were bombed in the course of the morning. There was some enemy shelling towards the east of the Island. Some damage has resulted but although reports are as yet incomplete casualties are again light. (147)

14.55 Middlesex reports that PB 54 and PB 55 (and Causeway Bay in general) are being heavily shelled (139).

15.00 Further air raids begin. Sai Wan Hill (5 AA Battery HKVDC) is one target (20: 14).

16.00 About 40 per cent of the telephone lines to the north shore pillboxes (broken by shelling) have been repaired. All Rajput companies and East Brigade HQ are in communication again (139).

16.30 Fortress HQ states that rice will be unloaded from SS Haldor in Tai Koo docks between 18.00 and 23.59 (139).

17.00 The Hong Kong waterfront is closed by order to civilians and civilian traffic (147).

17.00 Large numbers of Japanese troops (perhaps 200) are observed approaching the Devil's Peak pier. An artillery duel starts (20: 14) and Lye Mun is heavily shelled.

17.00 Wallis visits D Company Rajputs in North Point, and the Hugheseliers (139).

17.00 Official Communiqué:
> A continuous exchange of artillery fire has been maintained with the enemy. Direct hits were observed and one enemy battery was completely demolished, while five more were silenced. Japanese

nuisance air raids have continued throughout the day and some damage has been caused. A small oil dump in the neighbourhood of West Point received a direct hit and was set afire. The enemy attacked the Power Station and though some bombs fell near, no serious damage was caused. One enemy plane was shot down into the sea off the south shore of the Island near Lamma Island, while another was badly damaged and was last seen with dense smoke pouring from it. It is highly improbable that this machine ever regained its base. (147)

17.10   APV Shun Wo starts on the Beaufort patrol (130: 14).

17.55   Two new ex-HKVDC officers, Lammert and Matthews,[16] report to the Rajputs and are assigned to companies (139).

19.00   Three HKVDC armoured cars are sent to Tai Tam Gap as a mobile reserve for East Brigade. The other two cars remain at Leighton Hill (20: 14).

19.00   Traffic on the north shore road is difficult due to debris, shell holes, wrecked vehicles and electric cables (139).

19.00   Three vehicles at Brigade HQ (Wong Nai Chung Gap) suddenly burst into flames. This is considered to be one of the more serious fifth-column attacks (95: 83).

19.00   The first wave of the Japanese 228th (Doi) Regiment embarks east of Kai Tak in several scores of collapsible assault boats. Each boat holds fourteen men and is powered by oars alone (although subsequent waves cross in power boats or collapsible assault boats towed by power boats) (122). The 230th (Shoji) Regiment embarks west of Kai Tak, and the 229th (Tanaka) Regiment embarks at Devil's Peak peninsula.

19.00   Second Lieutenant Newman of the Middlesex, in PB 37 at Lye Mun, telephones that a number of craft are approaching under cover of a smokescreen. This information is relayed to Lieutenant Colonel Home at the headquarters of the Royal Rifles of Canada, but he frankly disbelieves it (139).

19.30   No. 5 AA Battery on Sai Wan Hill reports that it has been heavily shelled for the past hour by a 9-inch howitzer, and that the structure will not stand further damage (20: 14). Bosanquet notes: 'there was another crump. We dashed for the iron stairway

PHASE III: THE INVASION OF THE ISLAND   103

but stopped dead in our tracks. The shell had hit the half-open metal gates of the gun pit. Beneath the twisted metal was the mutilated body of the sergeant who had taken over from me. Beside him lay a bombardier, horribly wounded (29: 33).[17]

19.30   Ex-police sergeant Jessop, a watchman at the Tai Koo Docks, reports Japanese landings there (72: 55).[18]

19.45   A sentry at the junction of the Lye Mun and Island roads reports 'a large party of Chinese had passed through and headed towards Sai Wan Fort' (100: 59).[19]

20.00   PBs 41 and 42 at Shau Kei Wan are shelled (20: 14).
20.00   Three pillboxes in Wan Chai are shelled (79: 236).
20.00   A. Hutton-Potts (at Lye Mun): 'the barrage was indeed terrific, we counted the number of shells that fell . . . they averaged . . . one every four seconds.'
20.00   Major Bishop sends 15 Platoon Royal Rifles forward to Lye Mun (66: 151).
20.00   The Rajputs report that the Japanese, 'approaching in small boats towed by ferry steamers — 10 to 12 to each ferry', are about to land at PB 43 and PB 44 in Tai Koo Docks. Although PBs 40–42 cannot be reached, A Company Rajputs at Quarry Point report that those pillboxes and the 3-inch mortars are all in action and there is heavy firing from Aldrich Bay (139).

20.30   The 230th (Shoji) Regiment land 500 yards east of North Point. They advance along Sir Cecil's Ride during the night and approach the top of Jardine's Lookout.[20] However, not all the fighting is easy. Colonel Doi reports: machine-gun fire was as intense as ever . . . anti-tank Company lost so many men that only one gun could be manned . . . failed to establish contact because of rampaging enemy Bren carriers (15: 99).

The 228th (Doi) Regiment land at Tai Koo (at the foot of Braemar Hill). Their 2nd Battalion leads in groups of fourteen in collapsible boats. They rush inland, storming past the Rajput positions. In doing so they capture the sugar factory and overrun C Company Rajputs. Further west, D Company puts up a strong resistance, though Captain Newton is killed (early next morning), together with the majority of his men. B Company, under

Captain R. G. Course, move in from the west towards Tai Hang, hoping to contact D Company. Kishi Engineering Company, fighting as infantry, captures an AA position held by a platoon of Rajputs, after many casualties. The Rajputs try two company counter-attacks, which fail. Their HQ loses its position, regains it, and then loses it again. Individual pillboxes fight until overwhelmed, while the survivors are forced inland towards Mount Butler. Rawlinson escapes to reach East Brigade HQ at Tai Tam Gap, and others from B Company reach Leighton Hill. There are very few Rajput survivors from C Company. The 228th advances inland to Mount Butler and Quarry Gap.

The 229th (Tanaka) Regiment land at Sai Wan (Shau Kei Wan) (95: 80). They overrun No. 2 Platoon Royal Rifles, and capture Lye Mun Barracks and the 3rd Medium Battery HKSRA 6-inch howitzer (27: 26). The 229th advance inland to Mount Parker and Sai Wan Hill.

> The first landing was at and in the precincts of the [Tai Koo] Dockyard. I had one post there. By that time there were ground troops and the Japanese came across and bumped the Punjabis[21] who were manning machine guns and then they bumped my post. They threw grenades and one of my youngest soldiers was killed in that action. He must have been around sixteen, and he caught a grenade between his chest and the gun. The Japanese then overran Tai Koo Dockyard and the troops had to withdraw. (Captain Botelho (15: 98))

20.30 At the power station, Lance Sergeant A 179 Morrison notices ten or twelve invasion barges crossing from Kowloon Bay to Tai Koo sugar refinery (131).

21.00 The Rajputs report that the Japanese are landing all around PB 43 and that PB 44 has already been overwhelmed (139).

21.30 The commander of the Rajputs reports difficulties contacting the Lye Mun fixed beam (20: 14). Captain Caesar Otway, Corporal Harry Pelham and four sappers are manning this position when it is overrun by a grenade attack that kills two of the sappers and leaves Pelham with a bullet in his hand (91: 131). At around this time,[22] Otway reports sampans lighting smoke flares in the harbour, and motorboats and small craft plying between Devil's Peak and Lye Mun pier (20: 14).

21.30   The 229th attack 4th Battery HKVDC at Pak Sha Wan, overrun No. 1 gun, but fail to consolidate their advantage.[23] In the confusion, Lieutenant H. T. Buxton collects what men he can find and withdraws towards Lye Mun Barracks. However, they are ambushed on the way and Buxton and others are killed. There is only one survivor. Meanwhile, Captain Barnett (just back from hospital, and commanding the 4th Battery) orders the nine remaining gunners to fire at Shau Kei Wan, where he now realizes the Japanese have landed. These positions will hold out until the 21st.

21.30   The barrage stops. Hutton-Potts: 'we heard a burst of machine-gun fire from the pillbox ... I saw a lot of figures running towards us. I turned to "Davy"[24] and said "there are your coolies" and then I suddenly realized it was the Japanese' (94: 71).

21.30   Lieutenant G. M. Williams's and J. E. D. Smith's platoons of C Company Royal Rifles are ordered to occupy Mount Parker to block the Japanese advance (14: 77). Cambon: 'As I remember, we seemed to spend the day climbing hills, not knowing where we were, receiving conflicting orders and always being shot at by someone, sometimes by automatic weapons, more commonly by the odd sniper fire and occasionally light mortars' (38: 14).

21.30   The 229th overrun[25] the 5 AA Battery HKVDC at Sai Wan Fort. Six gunners are killed in the fight. Sergeant Bosanquet[26] reports:

> ... the door burst open. It was the man who had gone out for fresh air. 'The Japs are in the gun pits', he shouted. 'Christ', I said, 'they must have killed the sentries.' No one answered. Lolly[27] and those who were with him were at the door in seconds. 'Everyone out,' he shouted. 'Follow me, quick!' And he was gone. Agonizing moments passed before we had gathered our equipment. Just as we were ready, a hand-grenade came hurtling through the door. There was a blinding flash, a deafening explosion ... some were wounded and blinded. The rest of us did what we could for them, but if anyone was to survive, we had to get out before another grenade was thrown. (29: 34)

Some thirty men escape, but the wounded and stunned are left behind. In the first known massacre of the invasion — though not the last — twenty 5 AA Battery prisoners are bayoneted.[28]

Two, Bombardier Tso Hin-Chi and Gunner Chang Yam-Kwong, survive by feigning death (95: 86).

The 229th then advance to Lye Mun Gap, threatening the East Brigade HQ at Tai Tam Gap.

21.40 The Pak Sha Wan Battery opens fire on some launches heading towards Tai Koo (93: 135).

22.00 Artillery fire is put down on Tai Koo Docks, the sugar factory,[29] and the area of the abandoned PBs 47–48 (139).

22.00 Confused fighting is occurring east and west of the Rajputs' Tai Koo HQ. They fall back on the track to Sanatorium Gap, but later fight their way back to the old position (139).

22.05 The Middlesex are ordered to send a mobile machine gun platoon to North Point to form a defensive flank from PB 49 (outside the power station) to join up with D Company Rajputs at Braemar Hill (20: 14).

22.30 Brigadier Wallis reports that the Commanding Officer of the 5/7 Rajputs is still at the Tai Koo HQ. Wallis plans to recapture the Sai Wan Redoubt at bayonet point (15: 101).

22.34 Captain Penn of No. 1 Company HKVDC is informed of the landing. He goes to Quarry Gap and orders the light machine gun (LMG) section under Sergeant E. L. Curtis (who will be killed before midnight) to occupy a knoll on the eastern slope of Mount Butler. Corporal F. M. Thompson and six men man the weapons pits near PB 45. The remaining fifteen men take positions astride the Gap, with the Vickers gun under Sergeant J. P. Murphy on the right, and the LMGs about twenty-five yards forward on Tai Koo Path.

22.35 Nos. 13 and 15 Platoons of C Company, Royal Rifles, attack Sai Wan Fort, but are forced to retreat (100: 60).[30]

22.40 Major Stewart (No. 3 Coy. HKVDC on Jardine's Lookout) receives word of the invasion and asks for reinforcements. These come from the Winnipeg Grenadiers HQ Company under Captain

Phase III: The Invasion of the Island 107

Bowman. Lawson sends three platoons (one from each of the Winnipeg's A, B and C coys. — his reserve 'flying column') to set up roadblocks at strategic points. Lieutenant G. A. Birkett's platoon is ordered to take the summit of Jardine's Lookout (but delays until next morning because of impossible climbing conditions). Lieutenant Charles D. French's platoon takes the gap between Jardine's Lookout and Mount Butler, using a broken catchwater as a trench. Lieutenant William Vaughan Mitchell's platoon is at Stanley Gap.

22.42 The crew of PB 55 in Causeway Bay reports that the alternative position they are holding is being shelled and sniped at (20: 14).

22.55 The Japanese are reported in the vicinity of the Sai Wan Redoubt. The 1st Mountain Battery HKSRA 3.7-inch howitzer under command of Lieutenant E. A. Bompas (midway between the barracks and the redoubt) is overrun. He rallies some Canadians of C Company Royal Rifles and attempts to recapture the piece, but fails (93: 135). Bosanquet: 'He led the bewildered Canadians and bedraggled me to the defence of the howitzer position. When we got there, we found utter confusion, but I was able to use the field telephone and report to Gunner HQ what had happened to my battery' (29: 35).

23.30 The second Japanese wave attacks (79: 236).
23.30 Wallis reports that the Mount Parker HKSRA 6-inch guns are still in action (20: 14).
23.30 Field:

> Major STEWART telephoned that a Platoon of Canadians was on its way from Coy. H.Q. at STANLEY GAP along the catchwater path. I was to meet them and give any assistance required. Leaving L/Sjt WHITE in charge, I took two men and met the Canadians about 150 yards from the pill-boxes and led them back to the pill-boxes. Lt. BIRKETT (from Capt. BOWMAN's Coy, WINNIPEG GRENADIERS) introduced himself and told me that he was to take up a position around the pill-boxes until dawn and then to move up to the summit of JARDINE'S LOOKOUT. I handed over

the open positions and ordered my men to get as much rest as possible but to be ready for any alarm. I remained with Lt. BIRKETT during the night. At 0200 hrs. on Dec 19th I saw red flares (similar to those I hade seen while on STONECUTTERS ISLAND put up behind LAICHIKOK by the enemy) in the direction of Capt. HOLMES' positions on CLEMENTI'S RIDE on the N.W. slopes of JARDINE'S LOOKOUT. I informed Coy. H.Q. by telephone. Shortly before dawn Lt. BIRKETT sent a patrol to the ridge 100 yards S.E. of P.B.1. There was no sign of the enemy. He then moved off for the summit of JARDINE'S LOOKOUT. I had then no information that the enemy had penetrated to the WONGNEICHONG GAP area. (133)

23.38 On a report from Bompas, East Group RA puts down fire (directed by Fielden at the Sai Wan 6-inch position) on the west slopes of the Sai Wan Redoubt in support of a planned counter-attack by C Company Royal Rifles. '[Home of the Royal Rifles] with whom constant touch was maintained by constant visits from the Brigade Commander and Brigade Major, indicated that his C Company was still in position. As time passed however it was certain that in actual fact, Lyemun Gap — the AA redoubt and the 6-inch howitzer position at Saiwan were all in enemy hands' (139).

23.45 Japanese forward troops make contact with the first HKVDC outpost on Sir Cecil's Ride. Lance Corporal D. Hung's section defends energetically.

23.59 The Rajput HQ finally abandons its position (139).

24.00 All Japanese troops are across.
24.00 B Company Rajput is moving to the area of PB 53, a machine-gun platoon of the Middlesex is around PB 50, and one platoon of B Company Rajputs is still holding out at North Point (20: 14).
24.00 All C Company Royal Rifle positions are under attack (100: 60).

PHASE III: THE INVASION OF THE ISLAND   109

Roll of Honour for 18 December

VOLUNTEERS — 28 Killed

Buxton, Henry Thomas	Lieutenant, 2 Bty. HKVDC	K
Killed withdrawing to Lye Mun barracks.[31]		
Campos, Henry Maria	Gunner, 4 Bty HKVDC	K
Pak Sha Wan. Either killed at No. 1 gun, or by the earlier bombardment.		
Greaves, S. E.	Gunner, 4 Bty. HKVDC	K
Pak Sha Wan. Either killed at No. 1 gun, or by the earlier bombardment.		
Rocha, Antonio Joao	Lance Bombardier, 4 Bty. HKVDC	U
Missing believed killed at Pak Sha Wan Fort (126).		

(Sai Wan Hill fighting (6) and massacre (14). Most bodies were found in a trench in 1949.)

Bakar, A.	Gunner, 5 AA Bty. HKVDC	K
Bannister, Edgar Wallace	Sergeant, 5 AA Bty. HKVDC	U
Cause of death unknown.		
Broadbridge, William Edward	Gunner , 5 AA Bty. HKVDC	K
Chan U Chan	Gunner, 5 AA Bty. HKVDC	K
Cheung Wing Yee	Gunner, 5 AA Bty. HKVDC	K
Fincher, Ernest Francis[32]	Bombardier, 5 AA Bty. HKVDC	K
Said to have been killed by a bomb (48) or shell (29: 33).		
Ho, Algernon	Gunner, 5 AA Bty. HKVDC	K
Awarded posthumous BA in 1942 (23: 300).		
Kwok Wing Ching	Gunner, 5 AA Bty. HKVDC	K
Lao Hsin Nain	Lance Bdr., 5 AA Bty. HKVDC	K
Leung Fook Wing	Gunner, 5 AA Bty. HKVDC	K
Litton, John Letablere	Gunner, 5 AA Bty. HKVDC	K
Ozorio, Manuel Heleodoro[33]	Gunner, 5 AA Bty. HKVDC	K
Paterson, Ernest Manuel	Gunner, 5 AA Bty. HKVDC	K
Poon Kwong Kuen	Gunner, 5 AA Bty. HKVDC	K
Reed, Francis Oswald	Gunner, 5 AA Bty. HKVDC	K
Stokes, George Donald	Gunner, 5 AA Bty. HKVDC	K
Stone, William	Gunner, 5 AA Bty. HKVDC	K
Tsang Ka Pen	Gunner, 5 AA Bty. HKVDC	K
Tse Wai Man	Gunner, 5 AA Bty. HKVDC	U
Missing believed killed at Sai Wan Fort (126) on Dec 18.		[21 Dec.]
Ulrich, Albert	Gunner, 5 AA Bty. HKVDC	K
Ulrich, Peter	Gunner, 5 AA Bty. HKVDC	K
Wilkinson, Joseph Nelson	Gunner, 5 AA Bty. HKVDC	K

Zimmern, Andrew	Lance Bombardier, 5 AA Bty. HKVDC	K
Noronha, Francisco Antonio Killed by grenade Tai Koo Docks? Aged 21.	Private, 6 Coy. HKVDC	U

RAJPUTS — 31 Killed

(The majority of these are from A Coy. at Shau Kei Wan, C Coy. at the sugar factory, and D Coy. holding the waterfront. B Coy. were a little behind the lines at Tai Hang.)

Badan Singh	Sepoy	U
Bhartu Singh	Sepoy	U
Chhanga Singh	Sepoy	U
Durga Singh	Sepoy	U
Ghulam Muhammad	Sepoy	U
Harbal Singh	Sepoy	U
Iqbal Khan	Sepoy	U
Janak Singh	Sepoy	U
Kailash Bakhsh Singh	Sepoy	U
Khan Muhammad Killed Tai Koo HQ (126).	Sepoy 13015	U
Khan Muhammad	Sepoy 19468	U
Krishan Pal Singh	Lance Naik	U
Malkhan Singh	Sepoy	U
Maru Singh	Sepoy	U
Matthews, Eric Arthur	Second Lieutenant	U
Muhammad Yar	Sepoy	U
Mulaim Singh	Sepoy	U
Raghu Nath Singh Killed Tai Koo HQ area (126).	Sepoy	U
Rajpal Singh	Sepoy 18171	U
Rajpal Singh Presumably died in hospital, but records lost.	Sepoy 11726	K
Rameshwar Singh	Subadar	U
Randhir Singh	Lance Naik	U
Risal Singh	Sepoy	U
Saidal Khan	Lance Naik	U
Sant Bakhsh Singh	Sepoy	U
Sohan Singh	Sepoy	U
Sulaiman Khan	Lance Naik	U

Phase III: The Invasion of the Island

Surendar Singh	Sepoy	U
Talukdar Singh	Sepoy	U
Thakur Parshad Singh	Sepoy	U
Vir Singh	Sepoy	U

ARTILLERY — 22 Killed

Bennett, George   Lance Bombardier, 7 Bty. 5 HAA Regt. RA   U
    Captured and murdered, Sai Wan.[34]   [19 Dec.]

Coughlan, Reginald Edmund   Sergeant, 7 Bty. 5 HAA Regt. RA   K
    Captured and murdered, Sai Wan.[35]   [19 Dec.]

Macdonald, Kenneth Henry   Lance Bombardier, 7 Bty. 5 HAA Regt. RA   U
    Captured and murdered, Sai Wan. See note for Coughlan.   [19 Dec.]

Rhoden, William   Gunner, 7 Bty. 5 HAA Regt. RA   U
    Captured and murdered, Sai Wan.[36]   [19 Dec.]

Taylor, Frank Williams   Sergeant, 7 Bty. 5 HAA Regt. RA   K
    Killed by shellfire at Sai Wan. See also (29: 33). Originally buried Colonial Cemetery (126).

Ward, George Robert   Gunner, 7 Bty. 5 HAA Regt. RA   U
    Captured and murdered. Sai Wan.[37]

Butts, Trevor   Gunner, 12 Coast Regt. RA   U
Pak Sha Wan. Unburied (126).

Jones, Thomas Parry   Gunner, 12 Coast Regt. RA   U
Pak Sha Wan. Unburied (126).

Seabrook, Leonard   Gunner, 24 Heavy Bty. 12 Coast Regt. RA   U
    24 Heavy Bty was stationed at Mount Davis. Pak Sha Wan. Unburied.   [8 Dec.]
    18 Dec. (126).

Wong Ping   Gunner, RA   U

(The following six probably at the overrun Sai Wan Redoubt 3.7-inch gun)[38]

Ali Muhammad	Gunner, 1 Mountain Bty. HKSRA	U
Afsar Khan	Gunner, 1 Mountain Bty. HKSRA	U
Dheru Khan	Gunner, 1 Mountain Bty. HKSRA	U
Ghulam Haidar	Gunner, 1 Mountain Bty. HKSRA	U
Khan Muhammad	Gunner, 1 Mountain Bty. HKSRA	U
Nur Khan	Gunner, 1 Mountain Bty. HKSRA	U

Puran Singh   Gunner, 25 Bty. HKSRA   U
    DOW, IGH (145: 143)   [19 Dec.]

(The following three possibly Wong Nai Chung Gap RA HQ, in which case the date should be the 19th)

Muhammad Khan	Gunner, HQ. 1 HK Regt. HKSRA	U
Niaz Muhammad	Gunner, HQ. 1 HK Regt. HKSRA	U
Sardar Muhammad	Gunner, HK Regt. HKSRA	U
Downes, Leslie	Lance Sergeant, 965 Defence Bty. HKSRA	U

Killed at North Point electric power station. Unburied (126).

(Probably Sai Wan 6-inch gun)

Qasim Khan	Gunner, 3 Medium Bty. HKSRA	U

PUNJABIS — 33 Killed [39]

Adal Khan	Barber	U
Agyar Ram	Lance Naik	U
Amir Afzal	Sepoy	U
Anant Ram	Sepoy	U

Killed miniature range HKVDC HQ, body unidentifiable (126).

Bhag Singh	Sepoy	U
Damodar Chand	Sepoy	U

Killed miniature range HKVDC HQ, body unidentifiable (126).

Faqir	Sweeper	U
Ghanam Rang	Havildar	U
Ghulam Ali Khan	Sepoy	U
Ghulam Khan	Sepoy	U
Hardayal Singh	Sepoy	U
Jagat Ram	Sepoy	U

Admitted and died of wounds same day, IGH (145: 147).

Jagat Singh	Naik	U
Kanshi Ram	Havildar	U
Karnail Singh	Sepoy	U
Khushia	Barber	U
Lachhu	Barber	U
Milkhi Ram	Sepoy	U
Muhammad Din	Sepoy	U
Musa Khan	Sepoy	U
Panjab Singh	Sepoy	U
Paras Ram	Sepoy	U

PHASE III: THE INVASION OF THE ISLAND

Prabhu Ram	Sepoy	U
Puran Singh	Sepoy	U
Rais Khan	Sepoy	U
Rangin Khan	Sepoy	U
Saudagar Singh	Sepoy	U
Shankar	Sepoy	U
Taj Muhammad	Sepoy	U
Tara Singh	Naik	U

Killed at section post near golf course Sha Tin (126).

Turra Baz Khan	Havildar	U
Wakil Singh	Sepoy	

Admitted same day and died of wounds, IGH (145: 147)

Zari Shah	Sepoy	U

HKDDC — 2 Killed

(Tai Koo Dockyards.)

Allah Bakhsh	Sergeant, Dockyard Police, HKDDC[40]	U
Pahlwan	Constable, Dockyard Police, HKDDC	U

ENGINEERS — 12 Killed

Body, Raymond Henry John	Sapper, 22 Fortress Coy. RE	U

Missing Braemar searchlight detachment, 18 Dec. (126). [18/19 Dec.]

Bostock, Joseph	Sapper, 22 Fortress Coy. RE	U

Missing Braemar searchlight detachment, 18 Dec. (126). [18/19 Dec.]

Bryan, David Mark	Lance Sergeant, 22 Fortress Coy. RE	U

Missing Braemar searchlight detachment (126). [18/19 Dec.]

Currier, Alfred John	Sapper, 22 Fortress Coy. RE	U

Missing Braemar searchlight detachment, 18 Dec. (126). [18/19 Dec.]

Hudson, John Thomas	Sapper, 22 Fortress Coy. RE	U

Missing Shau Kei Wan. Possibly Sanatorium Gap–Gauge Basin area (126).

King, Harry Joseph Frederick	Sapper, 22 Fortress Coy. RE	U

Missing Shau Kei Wan area (126).

Lam Yung Kam	Sapper, 22 Coy. RE	U
Lee Shek Chuen	Sapper, 22 Coy. RE	U
Murray, Edward	Sapper, 22 Fortress Coy. RE	U
Price, William Alfred	Sapper, 22 Fortress Coy. RE	U

Missing. Possibly from Braemar searchlight detachment (126).

Walsh, Albine   Lance Corporal, 22 Fortress Coy. RE   U
    Missing Braemar searchlight detachment, 18 Dec. (126).   [18/19 Dec.]
Ward, William   Sapper, 22 Fortress Coy. RE   U
    Killed in Shau Kei Wan area (126).

ROYAL RIFLES — 1 Killed

Irvine, Gordon   Rifleman   U
    No. 17 Platoon, D Coy. Killed by same shell that wounded Captain Gavey. See (95: 124).

POLICE — 8 Killed

(Three police casualties when the Tai Tam HQ is hit by a shell.)

Fong Iu Nin   Constable, Chinese Coy. HKPF Reserve   U

Kesar Ali   Constable, Indian Coy. HKPF Reserve   U

Johnson, Albert Joseph   Sub-Inspector, HKPF   U
    Body found on Mount Cameron (141).[41]

Kala Singh   Constable B. 358, HKPF   U
    Admitted Queen Mary Hospital 18 Dec. Died same day (145: 80).   [23 Dec.]

O'Connor, Thomas   Inspector, HKPF   U
    Had been with Johnson in Shau Kei Wan (141).[42] Killed in North Point area (98: 175).[43]

Porritt, Thomas Arthur   Lance Sergeant, HKPF   U
    Last heard of having been wounded by a bomb in Quarry Bay.[44]

Ross, Malcolm Kenneth   Police Sergeant, HKPF   U
    Missing from Quarry Bay (145: 212). Killed in North Point area (98: 175).

Willison, Frank Louis   Lance Sergeant, HKPF   U
    Killed in Quarry Bay.

CIVILIANS — 3 Killed

Baldwin, Alice Adeline[45]   UCWD
    ARP Telephonist; of 35 Humphreys Buildings, Hanoi Road, Kowloon. Widow of James Baldwin.

Seath, William Petrie   UCWD
    At Mount Parker Road, Taikoo.
    Air Raid Warden; of 15 Braemar Terrace, Tai Koo. (Worked for Tai Koo Sugar (145: 212))

Bassant Kour   UX
    Died in Queen Mary Hospital, aged 6 months, having been admitted with mother (145: 71).

6

Phase IV: The Forcing of Wong Nai Chung Gap

One hundred and forty men have been killed on 18 December, in the first few hours following the invasion. A further 451 will be killed this day, the biggest single loss of the fighting. On top of this, some 200 more[1] will be captured.

To understand this phase of the battle, one first needs to understand the defence. The west side of the valley is held by Lawson's headquarters. The bottom is held by the headquarters of D Company Winnipeg Grenadiers, and a medical section. The east side of the valley is held by 3 Company HKVDC, with 7 Platoon at the north end of Jardine's Lookout, twenty members of 9 Platoon holding the two pillboxes covering the middle area, and 8 Platoon — with the remainder of 9 Platoon — holding a variety of positions on Blue Pool Road, Stubbs Road, Wong Nai Chung Gap, the southern end of Sir Cecil's Ride, and Stanley Gap. Near the latter, co-located with 3 Company HQ, is an AA position of 5 AA Regiment.[2]

The battle for Wong Nai Chung Gap itself consists of three phases:

Firstly, soon after the Japanese land, four platoons from the Winnipeg Grenadiers HQ Company are sent forward to reinforce 3 Company HKVDC. McCarthy's platoon is on Sir Cecil's Ride, due west of the 9 Platoon HKVDC pillboxes; Birkett's platoon is told to try and gain the summit of Jardine's Lookout; French's platoon is in the col north-east of Jardine's Lookout at the foot of Mount Butler; Mitchell's platoon is at Stanley Gap. The initial Japanese attack falls on these troops, plus Lawson's HQ and the D Company Winnipeg Grenadier positions.

Secondly, once it becomes clear that the Japanese are attacking the area in force, A Company Winnipeg Grenadiers is also deployed, attacking towards Mount Butler. In a series of largely isolated skirmishes, almost the entire Winnipeg Grenadier force is pushed back, captured or destroyed by the end of the day.

Lastly, the remainder of the fighting here is simply a series of attempted counter-attacks (so disjointed as to amount to little more than reinforcement attempts) by a variety of units. These come from the Royal Engineers with a party of seventy, A Company Royal Scots, sailors from HMS *Thracian*, and later B, C, and D Company Royal Scots and the Winnipeg Grenadiers. 'And the reason for this waste of effort and loss of life was that there had been no concerted plan to counter-attack' (92: 118). How much of this problem is rooted in the loss of Lawson, and the lack of a replacement for 24 hours, is a matter for conjecture.

Interestingly, the Japanese perceive their attacks on the position as equally piecemeal. Shoji: 'I am certain that the areas around the 5-Junction Road[3] were subjected to confused attacking by different units such as the Shoji Butai,[4] the Doi *Butai*, the Iwabuchi *Butai* plus the Divisional artillery directly attacked artillery under the direct commands of GOC Div and OC Infantry Group respectively ... That the Tanaka *Butai* had passed near 5-Junction Road on the same day in the afternoon is quite certain' (148).

Wallis decides, on hearing that the Gap is under attack, to withdraw his Tai Tam Battalion HQ and all his East Brigade forces to Stanley and the hills immediately north. This decision has often been criticized. It has been pointed out that allowing the Japanese to split East Brigade and West Brigade down the middle was an example of divide and conquer, and led to the defenders' eventual defeat. In fact, however, it appears this is a clear case of Wallis understanding that victory is impossible, and that the best he can do is hold out as long as possible. He correctly identifies the Stanley Peninsula as offering the best hope for long-term defence.

Lieutenant Browne at Fortress HQ states:

> So my own opinion is that anybody who thought after our hurried evacuation from the Mainland that we were then fighting the Japanese to win was a fool. We were clearly fighting on, to inflict as much damage to the Japanese forces as we could. So Wallis' decision to move such forces as there were on the east of the island, which in any case were scattered in small pockets, to Stanley, so as to defend it as long as possible, makes sense to me. (132b: Browne)

Wallis himself justified his decision as follows:

> Enemy MAY attempt landing on SOUTH, but having obtained a lodgement more likely to follow it up. Our own troops scattered from STANLEY VIEW to SHEKHO are therefore useless. Piecemeal use of Platoons proved valueless and the same may result by using isolated Companies against enemy on such dominating ground ... soundest course appears to be to concentrate all available Infantry ... in STONE HILL–STANLEY VILLAGE area. Withdraw mobile artillery i.e. GAUGE BASIN–TAI TAM FORK and RED HILL to STANLEY peninsula. Brigade HQ to move to STONE HILL where an exchange exists. (139)

Equally, in withdrawing East Brigade HQ to this area, he has moved as far west as he can without encroaching on West Brigade territory. He does not know that his peer, Lawson, is already dead, and may not know that the West Brigade territory immediately to his flank is not well defended. It would, arguably, be fairer to question Maltby's wisdom in making such a strategic area the border between the two brigades.

19 DECEMBER FRIDAY

> HMS *Tern* was attacked often by planes and then scuttled ... with George Bristow, [I] swam to HMS *Robin*. (Tom Middleton)[5]

While the Japanese 230th Regiment heads south for the gaps, the 228th does most of the street fighting in the Japanese beachhead (79: 237), and thousands of civilians suffer as a result. Zaza Hsieh, a student at Hong Kong University living in Causeway Bay, recalls:

> [we thought that] a safer place would be our grandmother's house on Leighton Hill Road, next to the racecourse in Happy Valley. In

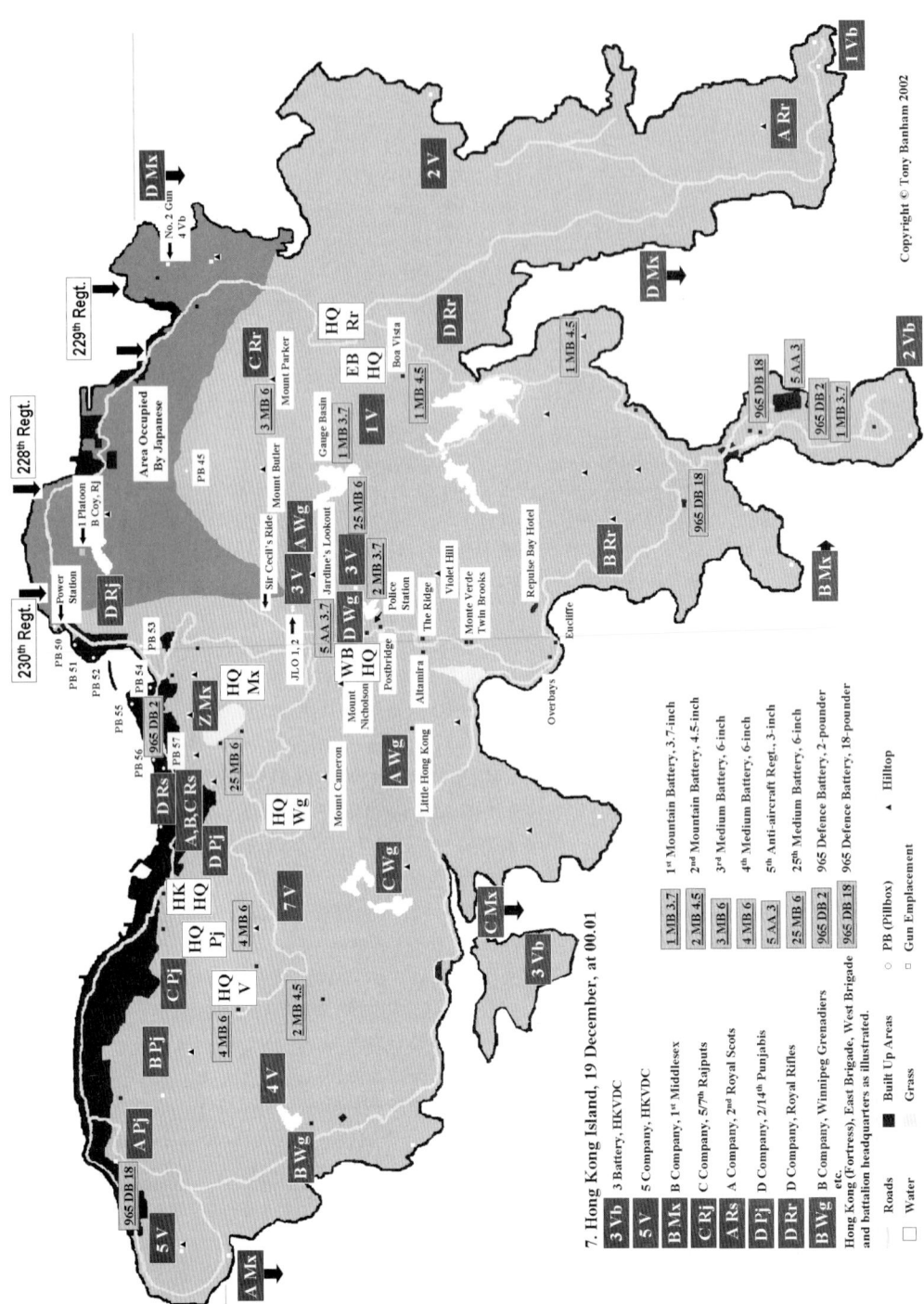

> our hurry to get there, we stepped over many dead bodies. People were shot in the streets, in cars and trucks, and even in ambulances. It was a terrifying sight. Reaching our grandmother's house, we met cousins and friends who had also gathered there thinking it was safer ground. That very night, there suddenly came loud banging on the door. Three Japanese soldiers entered, armed with guns and bayonets. In the darkness — the electricity was out — they shone their flashlights at our faces and hands. When they saw a wrist watch they snatched it. They were also looking for women. When a soldier approached my oldest sister, who was sitting on the floor holding her two-year-old baby, she quickly pinched the baby and he started to cry. That was enough of a distraction that the soldier turned his attention elsewhere. They pulled three of the women upstairs and raped them. (23: 40)

Dr Li Shu Fan later estimates the number of rapes as over 10,000 (52: 111). As the Japanese push inland in the darkness, they capture and behead members of the St. John's Ambulance Brigade and ARP (79: 237).

In the urban areas immediately west of the beachhead, the resistance is strong. The power station holds out as long as humanly possible, blocking any easy advance to the west. The easternmost pillbox of the three in Causeway Bay manned by Z Company Middlesex is demolished by shellfire. Second Lieutenant T. C. Harris and most of his crew are killed (96: 38). The next pillbox is also evacuated, with Lieutenant K. E. Young and his crew taking a new defensive position just to the north of Leighton Hill.

B Company Rajputs are withdrawn from their forward positions north of Leighton Hill, and occupy Chinese Cemetery Ridge to its south-east, together with a small party of sixteen men from the Royal Scots and sixteen from the Middlesex Battalion HQ (96: 36).

A Punjabi company is ordered to the Mound (a high ridge north of Jardine's Lookout, overlooking Caroline Hill) to link the Grenadiers at Wong Nai Chung Gap to the Rajput and Middlesex positions in the Tai Hang and Leighton Hill districts. They suffer casualties while attacking. Now the defenders' line starts to stabilize running south from Causeway Bay, through Mount Nicholson, to Deep Water Bay. Several counter-attacks are launched in an attempt to disrupt the Japanese advance, but these fail.

Shelling continues on the north shore, and PB 39 is hit, killing Middlesex Privates O'Mahoney and Roarty (139). Meanwhile, the bombing and artillery attacks on the city increase: 'Over 70 bombs dropped, mostly in the centre of town . . . fatal casualties were under 25 in number' (147).

On the eastern side of the Island, in the pre-dawn darkness, Brigadier Wallis orders the two platoons of A Company Royal Rifles to re-take Sai Wan Hill. They reach the top but are unable to scale the walls of the old fort and retire under heavy fire.[6] The HKVDC gun positions at Pak Sha Wan, bypassed on the initial landing, are surrounded but resistance continues even as guns are put out of action. The Royal Rifles are sent to Mount Parker but find that units of the Japanese 229th are already in position. As the day progresses, the positions holding out in the Japanese beachhead are snuffed out, and the chance of any successful counter-attack in that area diminishes.

Even before the fighting in the Japanese beachhead is over, and while preparations are being made for an in-depth defence of Victoria, it is clear that the focus of the day will be Wong Nai Chung Gap. By 07.00 Brigadier Lawson reports that his Wong Nai Chung Gap headquarters is surrounded. The Japanese have penetrated as far south as the police station, and start to consolidate their position around Gauge Basin and towards Tai Tam. The Japanese marching south on Sir Cecil's Ride are temporarily thrown into confusion by extremely heavy fire from Canadian positions at the eastern foot of Mount Nicholson, but within three hours, Lawson is dead and the Japanese hold the Tai Tam Gap area.

There is confusion in the Gap itself. Signalman Allister:

> We left our gear, everything, took only our rifles and hastily left the pillbox, feeling naked, abandoned, bewildered. [The Commanding Officer's] fear and mine were one. Fright left me weak, so weak that the rifle itself felt heavy. Fog and drizzle had thickened the darkness . . . it throbbed with violence and bloodletting. Men were dying all around, invisibly, horribly. *Go! Where? No one knew. Run! Forward? Backward? Right? Left?* (118: 27)

Then the first shelter of the Wong Nai Chung Gap Medical Aid Post (MAP), holding ten Chinese stretcher-bearers, is captured. The second — holding an RAMC officer, a sergeant, and three privates — will finally be captured after a twenty-four-hour siege. The Chinese are murdered.[7] 'After a series of explosions we were able to see the St John's bearers with the Indian constable,[8] all in some degree injured, come out of their shelters and surrender. Although the bearers were fully dressed, complete with Red Cross brassards, the Japanese killed everyone' (38: 181). The British escape after being tied up — except for the officer, Captain Beauchamp Depinay Barclay, who is never seen again (57: 8), and Private Evans, who disappears as they make their escape up Sir Cecil's Ride.

Later, the Japanese admit to suffering 800 casualties in taking Wong Nai Chung Gap. The garrison also suffers badly, and 149 casualties from the evacuated Windy Gap collecting post and Tai Tam Gap advanced dressing station are admitted to the BMH alone on this day (57: 8). Babin:

> I was taking five wounded soldiers from Tai Tam Gap advanced dressing station to Bowen Road Hospital in Victoria. With me was a British guide, supplied by the RAMC. On the way, the ambulance was fired upon by the Japanese. Bullets from machine-guns shattered the windshield. I managed to run the ambulance between the wreckage of burned vehicles that lined the side of the road, sheltered somewhat from the Japanese who were on top of the hill. Taking stock, I discovered that I had been wounded on the forehead and right hand, that Bickley (the guide) had received shattered glass from the windshield full in the face and was bleeding profusely, moaning that he could not see.[9]

The whole north-east quadrant of the Island is now firmly in Japanese hands, and they are making inroads south from Tai Tam Gap towards Bridge Hill, and from Wong Nai Chung towards the Repulse Bay Hotel.[10] Tai Tam Gap falls, and East Brigade decides they have no option but to evacuate to Stanley and the hills immediately north. However, it is too late to withdraw the 4.5-inch howitzers at Gauge Basin, and the commander of the 1st Mountain Battery HKSRA at Red Hill misinterprets the command and destroys his guns.

During the afternoon, the seriousness of the situation is finally understood. The HKDDC are sent from Aberdeen to support the Middlesex machine-gun positions on the south-east spur of Bennet's Hill, and all available naval ratings are sent to hold the ridge south of Staunton Creek under Commander Pears[11] (143f). Haines of the HKDDC: 'We hastily dug shallow trenches, received two machine guns and a supply of grenades, in addition to our rifles. Food was brought to us daily via a hill-track' (132b: Haines).

Clearly the Japanese are advancing faster than anticipated, and moves must be made to protect Victoria. Maltby orders a force of 150 RASC men to hold Bennet's Hill and thence move to Brigade HQ (Wong Nai Chung Gap). One section of the Middlesex under Second Lieutenant Wynter-Blyth also takes up a position on Bennet's Hill in support of C Company Winnipeg Grenadiers. Another section under Second Lieutenant Newton[12] covers Pok Fu Lam reservoir supporting A Company Winnipeg Grenadiers (96: 37).[13] Two hundred men from HMS *Thracian* are sent to take over defence of the Little Hong Kong ordnance base area, and RAF personnel are ordered to serve in an infantry capacity to defend the makeshift naval base at Aberdeen where the navy is ordered to scuttle all ships with the exception of HMS *Cicala*, HMS *Robin*, and the motor torpedo boats.

The artillery tries to move back, but several guns are too slow and are lost to the Japanese. The 5 AA regiment Albany Road section moves from Stanley Prison to Stanley Fort. The 965 Defence Battery Tai Tam Bay 18-pounders move back to the Stanley area, as do their promontory, Island, and Deep Water Bay 2-pounders. The two Stanley Bay 18-pounders at Braemar are destroyed by shellfire there before the Japanese landing. The RA East Group moves to Stanley Fort, but RA West Group, together with the Counter Bombardment Group, are wiped out at Wong Nai Chung. The HKSRA 2nd Mountain Battery loses its three 3.7-inch guns at Stanley Gap, and its 4.5-inch guns at Tai Tam Hill. The HKSRA 25th Medium Battery also loses two guns at Stanley Gap Road. The 3rd Medium Battery loses two guns at Sai Wan, and the 1st Mountain Battery loses two 4.5-inch guns at Red Hill and two 3.7-inch guns at Gauge Basin. Further west, the Japanese also attack the 3rd Medium Battery's 6-inch howitzers below Mount Parker.

Fighting continues as some areas bypassed by the Japanese (including positions on Jardine's Lookout, Wong Nai Chung Gap, Mount Butler, and the power station) continue to hold out. However, by early evening all but the Wong Nai Chung Gap shelters have been taken.

In the evening, the situation is still confusing in the Wong Nai Chung Gap area. Postbridge (a house on the Repulse Bay Road just south of Wong Nai Chung Gap) is held by a party of 1st HK Regiment, including Major J. P. Crowe, Captain A. G. Atkinson, Capt. A. S. Avery, Captain W. H. Hoyland, Lieutenant J. S. M. Vinter, four British other ranks, twenty-five Indian other ranks, and a small naval party from HMS *Thracian* under Lieutenant Commander Jack Grenham (93: 136).

At night, Japanese forces move south as far as Gauge Basin, Stanley Gap, Violet Hill, Middle Spur, and even Shouson Hill, and occupy the garage of the Repulse Bay Hotel.

Diary for 19 December

00.10   Carruthers's armoured cars and two trucks leave the Middlesex camp to relieve the power station (21: 149).

00.15   The main body of Japanese attack Lance Corporal Hung's 3 Company HKVDC position on Jardine's Lookout (north slope). He withdraws his section to a prepared position further south. There, a few minutes later, there is a fierce battle, annihilating Japanese units attempting to cut the wire. Eventually, under a shower of hand grenades, the Japanese crawl under the wire and hand-to-hand fighting results. Captain Holmes is killed. Sergeant E. Zimmern is wounded and gives the order to withdraw further. He is killed while covering this withdrawal, as is Lance Corporal E. Hing.

00.30   Corporal F. M. Thompson and six men from HKVDC No. 1 Company HQ reserve man weapon pits near PB 45 below Mount Butler (3: 23). They are attacked and three men (two wounded) return to Quarry Gap while a further man returns via Mount Parker (79: 242).

00.40   A lone survivor from PB 39 is reported. It is assumed that PBs 37–39 have been captured (139).

01.00   The Mount Butler Knoll and Quarry Gap are simultaneously attacked. There are only two survivors from the Knoll (79: 242). Their leader, Sergeant E. L. Curtis of No. 1 Company HKVDC, is killed. After fighting at the Gap, No. 1 Company HKVDC falls back, with a total of nineteen casualties, towards Tai Tam Bungalow (No. 1 Coy. HQ, by the Tai Tam reservoir, about 1,500 metres south of Quarry Gap), and order an HKSRA artillery bombardment of the Gap (3: 23).

01.00   Japanese divisional commander Lieutenant General T. Sano comes across to Hong Kong Island.

01.00   After overrunning Newton's D Company Rajputs, Doi's troops surround the power station and the Hugheseliers.

01.00   The Rajput HQ survivors fall back to the sanatorium valley (139).

01.00   The Royal Rifles attack led by an artillery officer (Bompas) fails to re-take the Sai Wan Hill howitzer position and falls back (20: 15). PB 37 is ordered to switch on its Lyon light to aid the Canadians and blind the Japanese (139). The Royal Rifles are supported by two 6-inch howitzers, which have to be abandoned (106: 131).

01.30   C Company Royal Rifles is ordered to fall back (100: 61).

01.40   Lieutenant Umino's patrol captures the forward position on Jardine's Lookout, but he and five men are killed (148).

01.45   Major Paterson[14] reports that the power station is entirely surrounded. He is ordered to hold out for as long as possible (20: 15). The position is defended by Paterson's 'Methusaliers' (four officers and sixty-six men, together with Volunteers from the Electric Company and the China Light and Power Company, and Free French)[15] all of whom are over 55 years old. Behind an armoured car under the command of Second Lieutenant Carruthers, a Middlesex platoon of twenty-four men, commanded by Lieutenant Ewan C. Graham,[16] drives forward along King's Road in three trucks to try to relieve the power station. A direct hit is scored on Carruthers's armoured car by an anti-tank gun, killing W. Park and H. W. Smits (79: 238). 'The vehicle lurched from a direct hit that stopped it. Three men emerged from the rear door and ran for cover, but a machine-gun opened up — it had a slower rate of fire than our Bren — and they rolled over in a lifeless flop' (30: 28). The lorries are destroyed, but the men reach the power station by running down side streets. Half the Middlesex are shot down on the way. The six Middlesex who reach the defenders are Corporal Dan Cavill, Lance Corporal Wally Coleman, Bandsman Bill Tunmer, Private Tommy Tucker, Private Harry Cooke, and Private Ron Parker (Z Coy.), plus Sergeant Miller and Corporal Meakin (96: 35).[17]

> Our little force was joined from time to time by stragglers from Army units, but a power station is an impossible place to defend,

Phase IV: The Forcing of Wong Nai Chung Gap

especially when it has to be kept running during the fighting. We did what we could, and were commended for our efforts, but in the end, after suffering heavy casualties, we were forced to shut down'. (Corporal R. P. Dunlop (2: 146))

02.00   The Sai Wan gunners are ordered to retire to the Mount Parker 6-inch gun position. They put the Sai Wan 6-inch guns out of action first (93: 135).

02.00   Lawson orders four platoons of Winnipeg Grenadiers (under Lt. G. A. Birkett) to reinforce Jardine's Lookout, currently held by two Volunteer platoons, No. 7 split between three positions on the northern slope under Captain L. B. Holmes, and No. 9 split between two pillboxes on the southeast slope under Lieutenant Field. Difficult conditions mean that Birkett and his men do not reach the summit till dawn, and they find the Japanese already there (95: 89).

02.00   The Rajput HQ comes under attack at their new position, and they fall back to a position higher on Mount Butler (139).

02.30   B Company Rajputs falls back to a position north-east of Leighton Hill, having been unable to penetrate past Braemar Point (3: 21). The Middlesex are still holding PBs 53 and 54 in Causeway Bay (20: 15).

02.30   The last Rajput pillbox in the invasion area (north shore) falls (21: 152).

02.55   The Shau Kei Wan Observation Post reports PB 40 still firing (139).

03.30   Colonel Shoji catches up with the commander of his 3rd Battalion on the north-east slopes of Jardine's Lookout (95: 89). He orders the 2nd Battalion to attack east through the Lookout to Wong Nai Chung Gap, and the 3rd to attack to the right and capture the north slope of Mount Nicholson.

03.30   The Rajputs' new HQ position on Mount Butler comes under attack. Cadogan-Rawlinson decides to move over Mount Butler via Jardine's Lookout to Tai Hang and join up with his B Company. At the col between Butler and Jardine's Lookout, he meets French's Winnipeg Grenadier platoon (139).

04.00	Maltby orders a party of seventy British and Chinese Royal Engineers to reinforce the Wong Nai Chung Gap area as infantry under Lieutenant Colonel Walker (20: 15).
04.00	The Middlesex HQ reports that the Japanese are working round the hills by Tai Hang village, moving east, and that D Company Rajputs are still near the reservoir. Maltby orders the Punjabis to send a Company to fill the gap between the Winnipeg Grenadiers and the Middlesex (20: 15).
04.00	Wallis orders 2 Company HKVDC to counter-attack in Sai Wan. However, fearing that his troops on the east of the Island are being cut off, he cancels this order. Instead, 1st Battery and 2 Company are withdrawn to Stanley, where they arrive in the afternoon (94: 84).
04.00	D Company Middlesex decides to move to Obelisk Hill to prevent any Japanese advance down the Tai Tam–Stanley Road. They are joined there by Lieutenant Scantlebury, much cut about by wire after just escaping with his life from PB 37 (139).
04.30	Major Marsh of the Middlesex phones the HKRNVR to ask for help in clearing Postbridge of suspected fifth columnists (130: 21).
05.00	Lawson briefs Major A. B. Gresham to take A Company Winnipeg Grenadiers from Wong Nai Chung Gap across Jardine's Lookout to secure Mount Butler. There, at dawn, they force scattered Japanese sections to withdraw. D Company platoons are then overrun with only a few men escaping.
05.00	A small Japanese party is encountered near the Filter Beds (20: 15).
05.15	A truck taking part of B Company Punjabis to Stubbs Road runs off the road and into a nullah. Ten men are detained in hospital, though eight join the company later (140).
05.20	Dulley takes a party of HKRNVR (Grenham, Morahan, McDouall, Rutherford, Cockle, Price, Blakeney, Sommerfelt, Mack, Lamble, and Castleton) on a lorry to Postbridge (130: 21).
06.00	The Winnipeg Grenadiers recapture Mount Butler.[18]

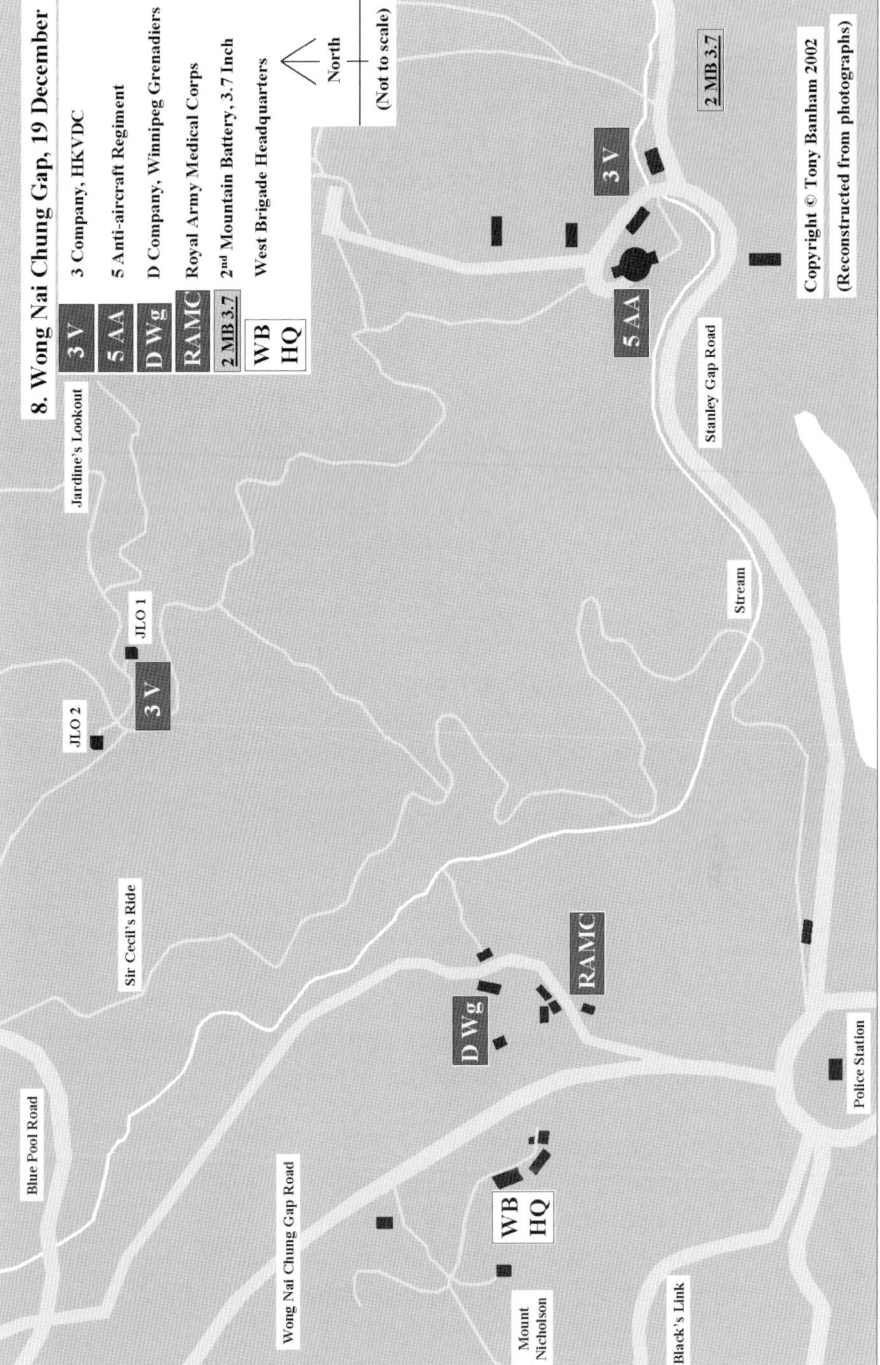

06.00   The RE party arrives at Wong Nai Chung Gap but cannot proceed to West Brigade HQ as it is under intense machine gun and mortar fire (20: 15).

06.25   The 7 AA gun site at Wong Nai Chung Gap reports that it is under attack from the north, and asks for assistance from Stanley Gap (93: 135).[19]

06.30   Japanese advance troops at Jardine's Lookout unexpectedly come into contact with Lance Corporal R. Ma's section. They bunch up on the Ride and are destroyed by fire from Lieutenant Field's position. Eventually the Japanese outflank Ma's position and take it in a bayonet charge. Of the nine men in the section, five are killed and three wounded (3: 26).

06.30   At dawn, Lieutenant G. A. Birkett and Lieutenant Charles French lead Nos. 17 and 18 Platoons of the Winnipeg Grenadiers towards the summit of Jardine's Lookout. A fierce fight starts with the Japanese who are crawling up the other side. They take the hill, but are then hit by another Japanese battalion just north of the Gap and are surrounded. Birkett, covering his unit's withdrawal, is hit twice and finally killed.

French's platoon takes the gap between Jardine's Lookout and Mount Butler, using a broken catchwater as a trench. Lieutenant McCarthy's platoon is astride the Ride, just below the pillboxes, and Lieutenant William Vaughan Mitchell's platoon is at Stanley Gap.

06.30   At dawn, the survivors of 5 AA Battery HKVDC move to the West Bay AA gun site (29: 36).

06.50   The Navy takes over infantry positions in the Aberdeen/Little Hong Kong area, thus freeing A Company of the Winnipeg Grenadiers for other duties (20: 15).

07.00   The Japanese approach Wong Nai Chung Gap from the bed of the stream, and drive back Corporal M. S. Lau's section. Lau, with three men, holds out for thirty minutes. The three men are killed, but Lau escapes to Deep Water Bay Road and joins up with B Company Middlesex there (79: 246).

07.00   The Japanese assault the Winnipeg Grenadiers' HQ shelter at

Phase IV: The Forcing of Wong Nai Chung Gap

Wong Nai Chung Gap, and capture the medical shelter some 75 yards away.

07.00 The Advanced Dressing Station at the Salesian Mission[20] at Shau Kei Wan is surrounded by the 229th. Captain Martin Banfill of the Canadian Medical Corps surrenders. Two injured Rajput officers[21] are murdered in their ambulance as it arrives at the dressing station (21: 145). The Japanese round up the assorted male medical staff (medical orderlies, ambulance drivers, cooks etc.), and separate them from two British nurses, Mrs Tinson[22] and Miss Lois Fearon.[23] They then march the male prisoners up Mount Parker, passing a wounded Volunteer crawling to the dressing station. The Japanese bayonet him. The men are halted on the hillside.

Cadet Medical Officer Thomas: 'suddenly the Japanese soldiers started to bayonet our unsuspecting men from the rear amidst cheers from enemy onlookers ... bodies kicked into a ditch.' Leath: 'I saw that Sergeant E. Watt, RAMC, had been bayoneted. He fell to the ground and was stabbed several times while lying there' (38: 164). Altogether about eight Canadians (including a medical officer), ten RAMC (one officer, three NCOs, and six privates (27: 40)) and three St John's Ambulance men are murdered. Osler Thomas[24] is one of only three men to survive the massacre — the others being Corporal Norman Leath, RAMC, and Captain Martin Banfill.[25]

The female nurses, Tinson and Fearon, are marched towards Lye Mun Fort. Nurse Lois Fearon: 'I said I was 39 and we gathered from the laughter that went up from the Japanese that I was too old to serve the purpose to which the Chinese girls were to be put.' However, after being kept standing in the rain for two hours, they are released (95: 87).

07.00 Lawson telephones Lieutenant-Colonel White (commanding Royal Scots in Wan Chai) and tells him that his HQ is surrounded.[26] Thirteen minutes later, White sends Captain K. J. Campbell's Royal Scots A Company in trucks up Wong Nai Chung Gap road. The trucks come under fire[27] (with Campbell and Lieutenant Hart being wounded, and Lieutenant Fenwick killed) and the troops continue on foot, fewer than a dozen reaching Lawson. These include Sergeant Arnott, Sergeant Corbitt, Corporal Campbell, Lance Corporal Glover, and a few privates.

None are to survive. The rest of the company (fifteen out of seventy-five) fall back, with all company officers being casualties (92: 115).

07.00   Then the Japanese attacking the power station bring up mortars, one of which explodes inside the building, killing Edward Des Voeux. After a two-minute bombardment, they charge. Coleman and Tunmer[28] are overwhelmed. Eventually the men decide to fight their way out. Five run for the cover of a destroyed bus outside in King's Road. They hold the bus for a further two hours but all are hit. A Japanese sword wounds Corporal R. P. Dunlop.[29] Private Vincent Dare Sorby[30] is shot in the legs; Tam Pearce, Private John Roscoe, and Private 'Paddy' Geoghan are also shot. Private Cahagan kills a Japanese officer and four men and survives (79: 240). Joan Crawford:[31]

> Father ordered the station to be shut down and evacuated … climbed over the wall into Electric Road … at the end of Electric Road we were halted by machine gun fire from a pillbox. Everyone scattered, and still with my soldier, some of us got into an empty bus hoping to drive off … in the fighting in and around the bus many men were killed and wounded. Mr. Dunlop escaped being beheaded here, his life being saved by a rucksack he was wearing … Mr. Dunlop sat and dripped blood from a terrible wound across his shoulder … I shall never forget looking down on the ground where Mr. Sorby, the manager, was lying. He had been shot in both knees, he was shivering, and his face was a terrible grey colour. We were not allowed to touch him. (15: 107)[32]

Post-war, a scroll was written to be presented to Des Voeux's next of kin. Unfortunately they could not be traced. The scroll read: 'The scroll commemorates Pt. Sir E. Des Voeux, Hong Kong Volunteer Defence Force, held in honour as one who served his King and Country in the world war 1939–45 and gave his life to save mankind from tyranny. May his sacrifice bring the peace and freedom for which he died.' He was 77.

07.00   Captain Penn, the CO of No. 1 Company HKVDC, reports that the Japanese have overrun the No. 1 Platoon position (139).

07.30   The Japanese take the police station[33] at Wong Nai Chung Gap. They then attack up the hill (Parkview Road)[34] towards Stanley

Gap and Lieutenant E. L. Mitchell's platoon of Winnipeg Grenadiers together with two sections from No. 3 Company under the popular Lieutenant D. J. Anderson. Others attack from the east, above Reservoir Path. Many of the Winnipeg Grenadiers and 3 Company are killed (including Anderson) (79: 247), though the Mitchell brothers survive capture at this time. 'The hills were spotted with clumps of soldiers. Units were fragmented, mixed, leaderless' (118: 28).

07.30 The senior naval officer, Commodore A. C. Collinson, orders a daylight attack on Japanese ferries (carrying two battalions of the divisional reserve, and artillery units) near Devil's Peak by the second MTB flotilla.[35]

08.00 The 7 AA guns (3.7-inch) at Stanley Gap are finally captured.[36] Colonel Doi: 'Two British soldiers were holding out in a small structure with its iron door closed at the [Stanley Gap] anti-aircraft gun position. Despite all our efforts to capture it and persuade them to surrender they refused, so we left them there overnight. The next morning, getting no response to our repeated call, we broke down the door and found that the two had killed themselves with their pistols' (122).[37] The Japanese then work their way towards Gauge Basin and presumably take the Stanley Gap 6-inch and 3.7-inch howitzer positions and the Tai Tam Hill 4.5-inch howitzers as nothing further is heard from these (93: 135) until their shells start hitting British positions (20: 16).[38] Japanese records confirm that they captured 'four medium howitzers, two anti-aircraft guns, and a warehouse[39] in which provisions were stored' in this action (122).

08.00 No. 3 Battalion 230th, resting at a depression near the anti-aircraft position, come under sudden artillery fire from the HKSRA position on the racecourse and suffers heavy losses (148).

08.00 All communications with RA Central at Wong Nai Chung Gap are lost. Major W. T. Temple, Major G. E. S. Proes, and Captain Fox are presumably killed at this time, as is Second Lieutenant B. E. Platts who is manning an OP in the area of Jardine's Lookout (93: 135).[40]

08.00 Postbridge comes under fire.

08.00 The Royal Rifles (under Penn) on Mount Parker come under severe pressure (20: 16), as do the gunners of the 3rd Medium Battery HKSRA 6-inch howitzers (under Bompas) below.

08.15   Lieutenant Field of 3 Company HKVDC holds a position on the south-west of Jardine's Lookout (with nineteen volunteers). Field: 'We had six machine guns, one sub-machine gun and 48 hand grenades . . . we had practised throwing beforehand with suitable stones.' (133). They occupy two pillboxes on either side of a catchwater.[41] The Japanese advance up it twice, but are beaten back; once by Private Jitts who takes the sub-machine gun into the catchwater. Coming round a bend, he comes face to face with five Japanese. Though seriously wounded he kills them all and captures their LMG. Lance Corporal N. Broadbridge and Private Terry Leonard[42] are also in this action. Private E. B. Young is killed by mortar fragments coming through the gun apertures (79: 248).

08.20   The Japanese effectively have control of Stanley Gap (3: 27).

08.30   Gandy receives orders to send MTBs to machine-gun Japanese craft crossing with troops (143e).

08.30   Lieutenant Blaver reports that all firing from 5 Platoon (Royal Rifles) positions on Mount Parker has ceased. It is assumed that Lieutenant Williams, Sergeant Hughes, and their men are killed or taken prisoner at this point (100: 64).

08.40   Gauge Basin reports enemy movements between Mount Parker and Mount Butler. Some men are seen working their way towards Jardine's Lookout (93: 135).

08.45   6 Platoon of 2 Company HKVDC is in action from Pottinger against Japanese moving from Lye Mun to Tai Tam (139).

08.45   Six MTBs in pairs led by Lieutenant R. R. W. Ashby (HKRNVR) attack after forming up behind Green Island. The first pair in is 07 and 09. They sink one ferry and set another ablaze. MTB 07 is hit by a shell and towed back by 09. The second pair is 12 and 11. MTB 12 receives a direct hit on the bridge, killing Lieutenant J. B. Colle and Sub-Lieutenant D. McGill (both HKRNVR) (91: 149), crashes at full speed into the sea wall by Chatham Road near Kowloon Docks. MTB 11 is also hit, six of her crew are killed, and Petty Officer Spirit is wounded (145: 195). The final pair is recalled, as by now it is realized that further attacks are suicidal, but MTB 26 fails to receive the signal, and is last seen stopped off North Point. Lt. D. W. Wagstaff,[43] Sub-Lieutenant J. C. Eager,[44] and Leading Seaman Bowden go down with all hands. However, several Japanese troop-carrying ships are sunk and Ashby is later awarded the DSC for this action.

> At 08.45 on Friday December 19th, 1941, acting on instructions received through you from XDO to Proceed into Harbour & shoot anything inside I slipped ROBIN and proceeded with the other MTB in my subdivision (MTB 09) from Aberdeen into East Lamma Channel through Sulphur Channel into the Harbour at 30 knots. With 09 keeping station one cable astern I proceeded along the outside of the boat boom and passed the Naval Dockyard. On nearing North Point I came under heavy machine-gun fire and this was my first indication that the Japanese had actually landed and established themselves on Hong Kong Island. I continued towards Kowloon Bay and sighted numbers of landing craft in threes crossing from East of Holt's Wharf and making for the area west of Tai Koo Sugar Refinery. These landing craft which appeared very frail (probably portable) were in threes towed by the leading boat of each three which had an outboard motor. Each boat contained from 12 to 15 men.
>
> I immediately signalled to 09 to attack independently and increasing to full speed (37 knots) I went in to attack. Aircraft now started diving on me with machine-gun and cannon fire.
>
> I opened fire on the landing craft with all five Lewis guns at 100 yards range, with excellent effect, and passed down the leading string at a distance of about five yards, firing continuously. I dropped two depth charges, which failed to explode owing to insufficient depth of water. However, this made no difference as the landing craft capsized in my wash and there appeared to be no survivors.
>
> I then came under machine-gun fire from both shores and from wrecks in the harbour, from howitzers, and light artillery fire from both shores, also from cannon and machine-gun fire from aircraft. The boat was hit several times and a cannon shell exploded in the engine-room, putting the starboard engine out of action and killing the leading Stoker.[45] I ordered the telegraphist to the engine-room to investigate. My speed was reduced to 22 knots. However, I turned and attacked a second bunch of landing craft with machine-gun fire at point-blank range with most satisfactory effect. Another cannon-shell now put my port engine out of action

and my telegraphist[46] was killed by machine-gun fire. My speed was reduced to 12 knots and I was making water in the engine-room, so I had no alternative but to try to extricate myself and endeavour to reach my Base. I headed for the Naval Yard under intense machine-gun and howitzer fire and under attack from three aircraft. I directed fire against the diving aircraft and tracers were observed to enter the fuselage of two of them, one of which made off towards Kowloon low down and did not return. After passing the Naval Dockyard firing slackened off, 09 re-joined then and I was able leave Harbour by Sulphur Channel. After rounding Mt. Davis my centre and last engine gave out and I ordered 09 to take me in tow. The crew were able to plug most of the bullet holes below the water line and by pumping it was possible to keep the boat afloat.

    I secured alongside ROBIN at 10.00 and was able to repair all damage except one torpedo rail which had been severed by a shell. In addition to landing craft & aircraft, Japanese on wrecks in the harbour were also machine-gunned. (143a).

09.00   French's Winnipeg Grenadiers are attacked from both sides at Mount Butler Gap. French is killed.

09.00   D Company Royal Rifles at Obelisk Hill is ordered to fall back to Stanley (139).

09.30   Sergeants Barton and Phillips (of the Corps of Military Staff Clerks) attempt to escape from Lawson's HQ. Phillips is killed instantly; Barton is seriously wounded (21: 164).

10.00   Lawson reports to Maltby that because his headquarters position is surrounded, he plans to evacuate to Black's Link. Captain H. A. Bush is ordered to cross to the D Company shelters on the other side of the road to provide covering fire as Lawson and his men, including Woodside (his intelligence officer) break out. The HQ is abandoned, and Winnipeg Grenadier Sergeant R. Manchester sees Lawson cut down by machine-gun fire. All other HQ staff including five Middlesex attached to the headquarters for intelligence duties (Bandmaster Walter Kifford, Bandsman Davies, Bandsman Dillon, Drummer Enderby, Drummer Klintworth) are also killed. Bush later goes back under fire and establishes that the shelters are deserted.[47] The Japanese find

Phase IV: The Forcing of Wong Nai Chung Gap 135

Lawson's body two days later and believe that he had died from loss of blood after being shot in the thigh (27: 28).

10.00 Lieutenant Kerfoot of the Punjabis is sent with three carriers to cover the evacuation of the West Brigade HQ, but arrives a few minutes too late. He is killed, and the driver and gunner of his carrier are wounded (24: 204).

10.00 The Japanese penetrate into the Tai Tam catchment area, forcing the withdrawal of East Infantry Brigade. The Cape Collinson, Bokhara, and Chung Hom Kok batteries are ordered to blow up their guns and evacuate personnel to Stanley. Templer at Bokhara: 'Lomax and Master Gunner Berry[48] destroyed guns with one round (1010 pounds) in muzzle and one fired from breech end. Plotting room and table destroyed with Gun Cotton slabs. Searchlights thrown down cliff. Instruments in BOP broken up with sledgehammers. Battery marched into Stanley' (150).

Orders are also given that the Parker, Gauge Basin, Tai Tam Fork, and Red Hill guns should retire to Stanley. The anti-aircraft guns at Gauge Basin are lost, as are the 4.5-inch howitzers as the order to 'get them out of action' is understood as 'put them out of action'. The commander of these guns is said to have been killed (106: 132).[49]

10.00 D Company of the Winnipeg Grenadiers holds on in Wong Nai Chung Gap, re-enforced by a few of the seventy British and Chinese sappers sent to their aid.[50] The company commander, Captain A. S. Bowman, organizes a counter-attack. It is initially successful, but the Japanese forces re-multiply, take back disputed ground, and kill Bowman as he leads a retreat back to the shelters.

10.00 Three Japanese companies attack the A Company Winnipeg Grenadier positions on Mount Butler. Sergeant W. J. Pugsley relates: 'at about 10.00 I noticed that our troops on Mount Butler were falling back, and almost immediately noticed Japanese troops in large numbers coming over the mountain. CSM Osborn now took charge.' A Company are surrounded.

> Almost immediately, I saw a Japanese soldier, about 150 yds away, creeping through the long grass towards us. I shot him and he began screaming. Seconds later, I was readying myself to shoot at another Jap creeping through the grass, when I myself was shot. The Jap who shot me was further up the hill. I am left-handed and

just before I pulled the trigger, a bullet struck me, entering near my left collar bone, and exiting out the back of my shoulder, just above the arm pit, effectively paralysing my left arm ... at the same time my brother Alf was wounded. (132b: Matthews)

10.00   A master gunner arrives from Fire Control East, Bokhara, with orders for 1 Battery HKVDC to blow up their guns and march to Fort Stanley (23: 34).

10.00   B Company Middlesex is ordered to retire to Stanley. The order is initially disbelieved, and then confirmed. PBs 21, 22, 29, and 30 are ordered to evacuate. A fresh HQ is established near PB 24 at Stanley, and the crews of 21 and 22 under Second Lieutenant King, are put into positions astride No. 1 Bungalow.[51] The crews of 29 and 30 are put in temporary positions near the new HQ, and the crew of 23 moves back to a position on the beach (139).

10.15   Cadogan-Rawlinson reaches Bridge Hill shelters with his second in command, adjutant, quarter master, motor transport officer, and a nucleus HQ. He also reports seeing the 4.5-inch howitzers present but unattended at Tai Tam Hill (139).

10.20   C Company Royal Rifles falls back to Tai Tam Gap (66: 156).

10.30   A naval party from *Thracian* drives up to the Wong Nai Chung Gap from Aberdeen under Commander A. L. Pears in three trucks commanded by the *Thracian*'s First Lieutenant Joe Dines, Lieutenant Tom Quilliam, and Lieutenant Dobson respectively. They are ambushed. 'Grenades were lobbed down on us from the Japs over the road, and bullets were coming in both from the hillside on our right and across the Valley on our left' (Tom Quilliam (78: 127)). Quilliam and Cullum[52] are the only men unhit of the thirty-two men in the second lorry (78: 127). Six men link up with the Royal Scots eight hours later;[53] the others are never seen again. Captain C. E. Otway, commanding a small mixed unit, also tries to dislodge the Japanese but fails.

11.00   Colonel Kidd moves A and D Companies (Punjabis) to a position east of Leighton Hill and towards Tai Hang, to relieve pressure on the Rajputs' D Company (3: 33).[54]

PHASE IV: THE FORCING OF WONG NAI CHUNG GAP   137

11.00   Lieutenant Bompas and Second Lieutenant J. S. B. Eddison engage the enemy over open sights at Gauge Basin and continue until small arms fire causes them to disengage. Bompas is then ordered to disable his guns and retire to Stanley.

11.30   Young visits Maltby and tells him that every day gained is a direct help to the Empire's war effort (20: 17).

11.30   Penn and No. 1 Company HKVDC withdraw (139).[55]

11.45   East Brigade HQ at Tai Tam Gap is closed down on Maltby's instruction, and moves back to Stone Hill (20: 17).

12.00   On Jardine's Lookout, the Japanese succeed in crawling through the catchwater and dropping grenades through the loopholes of pillbox JLO 1 (wounding seven of the eight occupants), but they are wiped out by the defenders in JLO 2. Field moves the survivors into the open. Private E. D. Fisher leads a party from JLO 2 to relieve JLO 1,[56] but is fatally wounded in the attempt. Field: 'P.B. 2 organised a first attempt to relieve us. A party led by Pte. E. D. FISHER tried to come up the main path, but FISHER was wounded fatally and the attempt failed. A second party then approached from the rear and surprised the enemy killing all three remaining. This party was led by Cpl. RIX (Section Commander of the Canadians from Lt. MCCARTHY's Platoon). One of the Canadians was killed' (133).

12.00   The Royal Scots report that one company in a counter-attack has reached a point 200 yards north of the Wong Nai Chung Gap shelters, where they are holding out with only thirteen effectives left (20: 17).

13.00   The last British troops of East Brigade leave the Tai Tam Gap area as they withdraw to Stone Hill (20: 16).

13.00   A seventy-strong force of RASC and others moves to Bennet's Hill (20: 17).

13.30   Maltby orders a general advance to commence at 15.00. As part of this initiative, Kidd of the 2/14 Punjabis is ordered to attack north towards the North Point power station, but the orders never reach him as he is in thick fighting east of Leighton Hill (20: 17).

14.00 The Winnipeg Grenadier HQ Company under Major Hodkinson is told to clear the Gap and carry on to Mount Parker (66: 162).[57]

14.30 Lieutenant Colonel White is told by Fortress HQ that Wong Nai Chung Gap is lightly held. He tells Captain Pinkerton of the Royal Scots, with D Company, to follow the route up the Wong Nai Chung Gap that A Company had failed on seven hours earlier. On Pinkerton's left, Lieutenant F. L. Stanier's C Company moves through the valley. Meanwhile, Captain Douglas Ford's B Company moves by Black's Link around the south of Mount Nicholson to the Gap. The companies are to meet at the Gap and then attack Jardine's Lookout. Captain A. M. S. Slater-Brown leads the Royal Scots' attack with their last three Bren carriers, with D Company on foot behind. They reach the point (200 yards north of the Gap) where Captain Campbell's A Company had been ambushed. The wreckage of their burnt-out lorries blocks the road. As they stop, they are ambushed in turn with heavy machine-gun and mortar fire from positions on Jardine's Lookout previously captured by the Japanese from the Volunteers. A mortar bomb hits the first Bren carrier, killing Slater-Brown and Second Lieutenant Bell (the battalion Intelligence Officer) and causing other casualties (92: 116).

Captain Pinkerton and his men (D Coy. Royal Scots, one platoon under 2nd Lt. Fairbairn and the other under Ford, plus Field Coy. Engineers of the HKVDC acting as infantry under Capt. K. S. Robertson and Lt. I. P. Tamworth attached to D Coy.) finally break into the Gap and reach the police station, which has just been re-occupied by the Japanese. Second Lieutenant J. A. Ford finds Pinkerton badly wounded on the steps up to the police station. A final attack starts after B Company appears from Black's Link, but it fails. Casualties include Second Lieutenant A. K. McKenzie, HKVDC, who is blinded by a gunshot wound (145: 4), and Second Lieutenant V. R. Gordon.[58] The Royal Scots fall back to positions on the lower slopes of Mount Nicholson (15: 118). They are unable to reach the Gap, where elements of 3 Company HKVDC are still holding out (79: 252).

Captain Bush gives a graphic account of the confusion of the situation around the D Company (Winnipeg Grenadiers) position in Wong Nai Chung Gap:

> The position was being fired upon from all sides. It might be compared with the lower part of a bowl, the enemy looking down and occupying the rim. The main road running through the position was cluttered for hundreds of feet each way with abandoned trucks and cars. The Japanese were using mortars and hand grenades quite heavily. Casualties were mounting, but at the same time reinforcements were trickling in, in the form of stragglers, so that at the end of the day, while the killed and wounded were approximately twenty-five, the effective fighting force was about the same . . . A Platoon of Royal Scots passed through, from which later two men returned and reported that all the others had been wiped out (14: 86).

The Royal Scots Platoon had in fact reached Sir Cecil's Ride, but had fallen back immediately as they found no support.

Lieutenant Colonel White orders that these counter-attacks cease until nightfall (92: 116).

14.35 To V2 from Commodore Hongkong.

> The attack carried out by flotilla was most gallant and an inspiration to everybody. Regret losses incurred but like you proud of their devotion to duty 1435/19 (143e).

15.00 The ordered counter-attack on the Japanese beachhead is attempted. While the Royal Scots attack Wong Nai Chung Gap, two Punjabi companies (B and C) advance from east of Leighton Hill towards North Point power station. The Rajputs (B Coy. and survivors from D) advance east from Leighton Hill. B Company of the Winnipeg Grenadiers is ordered to advance across the Gap eastwards in a line running from Sir Cecil's Ride to Middle Spur. The Punjabis B Company (under Maj. Kumta Prasad) makes considerable headway, succeeds in reaching Tai Hang but is then driven back with heavy casualties to a line north-west of Leighton Hill.

15.00 The 1st Battery HKVDC and No. 2 Company HKVDC arrive at Stanley, having evacuated the Shek O peninsula, but minus Bombardier P. Wilson, who went back for supplies but was never seen again (3: 31).

15.00 The Japanese attacking Field on Jardine's Lookout give up infantry attacks and switch to mortars.

15.00   West Group RA — lost earlier at the Wong Nai Chung Gap HQ — is re-formed at Wan Chai Gap under Major Duncan (20: 16).

15.15   On Jardine's Lookout,[59] the Winnipeg Grenadiers A Company's ammunition is running low and the position is hopeless. Major Gresham, the company commander, decides to surrender but is killed by machine-gun fire while waving a white flag.

> 'We retreated back in the direction from which we had come. Some of our Company were further up the hill, near the top, and we were about half way up the hill. The guys at the top of the hill yelled that we were completely surrounded. All of a sudden, Japs appeared, seemingly out of nowhere and an officer started waving a sword at us, implying that we should surrender. Stan Stodgell responded by shooting and killing the Japanese officer . . . a barrage of grenades and mortars followed. (132b: Matthews)

Private J. D. Pollock: 'Grenades started to come over. CSM Osborn kept throwing them back at the Japs'; and later Pugsley: 'a grenade dropped down beside him'; Corporal W. A. Hall: 'Osborn on my right threw himself on it'; Pugsley: 'saved the lives of myself and at least six other men'. Matthews:

> I was with a group that included Sgt. Major Osborn, who was about twenty feet away from me. I saw something land near Osborn, perhaps a grenade, but it looked bigger to me, more like a mortar. I dropped to the ground and covered my head with my arms. The explosion lifted me off the ground. If I had been standing, I am sure that I would have been killed. When I looked up, Osborn was gone, but the guys further up the hill said that he had thrown himself on the mortar, probably saving my life. (132b: Matthews)

Osborn is killed and posthumously awarded the Victoria Cross.[60] Shortly after this action the Japanese overrun the position and take the few survivors (there were approximately 60 casualties) prisoner.

16.00   The Japanese attack The Ridge.[61] They are repulsed, but mortar fire continues.

16.00   Colonel Tanaka's Regimental HQ (having been lost near Tai Tam reservoir) links up with his 2nd Battalion east of Wong Nai Chung Gap. After dark, they cut the road linking the Gap to Repulse Bay.

228th Regiment cross a destroyed bridge in the New Territories — est. 8 Dec. (Source: *Mainichi Shimbun*)

Abandoned British Morris 8 cwt trucks at Salisbury Road, Kowloon — est. 13 Dec. (Source: *Mainichi Shimbun*)

Destroyed Vickers Vildebeest at Kai Tak — est.13 Dec. (Source: *Mainichi Shimbun*)

Crowds after the fall of Kowloon — est. 14 Dec. (Source: *Mainichi Shimbun*)

A Japanese Type 45' 24 cm Howitzer near Kowloon — est. 17 Dec. (Source: *Mainichi Shimbun*)

Commercial Press printing house at North Point — est. 19 Dec. (Source: *Mainichi Shimbun*)

Destroyed pillbox at Braemar Point — est. 19 Dec. (Source: *Mainichi Shimbun*)

Japanese artillery unit overlooking the Power Station — est. 19 Dec. (Source: *Mainichi Shimbun*)

Wanchai viewed from east of Causeway Bay — est. 23 Dec. (Source: *Mainichi Shimbun*)

Japanese engineers inspect a Bren Carrier, Causeway Bay — est. 24 Dec. (Source: *Mainichi Shimbun*)

PHASE IV: THE FORCING OF WONG NAI CHUNG GAP 141

16.00   The Royal Rifles complete their withdrawal from Mount Parker and Tai Tam Gap to Stanley.

16.00   The handful of survivors still inside the North Point power station are overrun and Captain J. K. Jacosta is killed, though a few (including Lt. Graham and Sergeant Fox of the Middlesex (96: 36)) manage to reach Leighton Hill as Major Paterson surrenders.

16.30   Leighton Hill reports that it is being heavily shelled (20: 17).

16.30   A and D Punjabi Companies attack from Caroline Hill[62] up to a col about 1,000 yards north-east, from where they can see North Point. There is fierce hand-to-hand fighting (with thirty men being killed or wounded), but being unable to contact the Rajputs, they withdraw to the racecourse, from which they are transported back to Victoria that evening (24: 205).

17.00   Hodkinson reaches the deserted West Brigade HQ (66: 163).

18.00   Having evacuated twelve walking wounded to Tai Hang Road under Lance Corporal Broadbridge,[63] Field collapses from loss of blood and Lance Corporal K. C. Hung is shot through the shoulder. At dusk, the handful of men remaining surrender.[64] This ends the organised defence of Jardine's Lookout.[65]

18.20   The crew of PB 53 in Causeway Bay withdraw, with their officer dead and 50 per cent of the crew casualties (20: 17).

19.25   A party from Stanley of 100 men of 1st Mountain Battery and 3rd Medium Battery HKSRA, under command of Major E. De V. Hunt and Major Feilden, arrives from Stone Hill Brigade HQ, together with two HKVDC armoured cars. They attempt to capture the police station but fail. Feilden is killed. Lieutenant Colonel J. L. C. Yale of the 1st HK Regiment, who is a member of this party, is reported as wounded and presumably dies here (93: 136). Hunt is lost next day looking for Yale (90: 215). They do not make contact with Postbridge.

20.00   The HQ Company of Sutcliffe's[66] Winnipeg Grenadiers is still pressing their 14.00 attack south via Black's Link to the Wong

Nai Chung police station, then 'onwards to Mt. Parker'. The station is attacked at 20.00, and when they start up the knoll the small force of two officers and twenty-four men meet a hail of grenades from the forty or so Japanese defending the position. Hodkinson is killed and most of the force is wiped out. The few survivors under Sergeant Paterson try to hold off the Japanese, but are overrun.

20.00 The RASC party (and mixed elements) from Bennet's Hill, now 150 strong, joins the RAOC party at The Ridge (20: 17). The Volunteer ASC men are under Major Flippance, Captain Strellet, and Captain Davies (3: 35).

20.31 H.E. The Governor has sent the following message to all H.M. Forces in Hong Kong:

> The time has come to advance against the enemy. The eyes of the Empire are upon us. Be strong. Be resolute and do your duty.
>
> Mark Young Governor 2031/19

21.00 The China Fleet Club comes under heavy mortar fire (20: 17).

22.00 Lieutenant Colonel W. J. Home (commanding the Royal Rifles) is told by Wallis to commence a counter attack at 05.00 on the 20th. One company of the Royal Rifles is ordered to depart from Stanley View, recapture the Gap, join up with West Brigade, and capture Violet Hill. With them will be three Bren carriers of the HKVDC and two Middlesex platoons. A further Royal Rifle company will guard the right flank on Stanley Mound as the others attack on the road to Repulse Bay, and to the east of Violet Hill. No. 2 Company HKVDC is ordered to support the attack from Stanley Mound (139).[67]

22.00 Police Sergeant A 40 Youe is in charge of a police Lewis gun team at the Lee Theatre, Percival Street, Causeway Bay. Apart from Leighton Hill, the nearest supporting Middlesex machine-gun team is also on Percival Street, near Russell Street, under Sergeant Gilham (131).

23.00 Briggs at Aberdeen:

That evening at 11 p.m. I was woken to go to the sick bay as a number of badly wounded had been brought in, among them men from HMS *Thracian* whom I had seen going off into the hills in trucks that morning ... It is strange how one reacts in times of emergency. As I entered the sick bay that night I saw a man with terrible face wounds and my reaction was 'Oh no, not that'. I found myself walking right through the room in a kind of daze, out through another door and in again at the first door, and as I passed the shattered face again, the naval dentist asked me to help him with the patient. As soon as I started helping my feeling of horror left me and I was able to clean his mouth and make him comfortable. He had been shot in the mouth, and teeth and moustache were very mixed.(35: 99)

23.30　Postbridge is evacuated. Captain Avery of the HKSRA dies of wounds here, and Major Crowe and Captain Atkinson of the Royal Artillery are wounded. Mr G. G. Tinson, the owner of the house — who had won the MC in the First World War — is also mortally wounded by a sniper (130: 21). At midnight, Commander Dulley is also killed by a mortar. The surviving party treks across to West Admin Pool.

24.00　The Commissioner of Police reports secret information that there may be landings in Central District and Kennedy Town (20: 17).

Roll of Honour for 19 December

HKDDC — 5 Killed

Abdullah	Private, HKDDC	K
Karan Din	Private, HKDDC	K
Muhammad Sharif	Private, HKDDC	K
Shirin Gul	Constable, Dockyard Police, HKDDC	U
Siraj Din	Private, HKDDC	K

POLICE — 22 Killed

Allah Jawaya	Lance Sergeant, HKPF	U
Bakhshish Singh	Constable, HKPF	U
Balwant Singh	Constable, HKPF	U
Bog Singh	Constable, HKPF	U

Dula Singh	Constable, HKPF	U
Fazl Illahi	Constable, HKPF	U
Jag Mal Singh	Constable, HKPF	U
Jernail Singh	Constable, HKPF	U
Jogindar Singh	Constable, HKPF	U
Karam Singh	Constable, HKPF	U
Kartar Singh	Constable, HKPF (120)	U
Kartar Singh	Constable, HKPF (1328)	U
Kehar Singh	Constable, HKPF	U
Kishan Singh	Lance Sergeant, HKPF	U
Lachhman Singh	Constable, HKPF	U
Muhammad Din	Constable, HKPF	U
Nand Singh	Constable, HKPF	U
Nur Husain Shah	Constable, HKPF	U
Post, Edward George	Inspector, HKPF	U
With A. J. Johnson.[68] Still alive, hurt, on 19th. Implied murdered by Japanese (141).		[18 Dec.]
Pyara Singh	Constable, HKPF	U
Sung Shui Ching	Seaman, HKPF	U
Surjan Singh	Constable, HKPF	U

HEADQUARTERS — 5 Killed

Black, Marvin	Sergeant, Canadian Army	K
Probably Wong Nai Chung Gap		
Jewitt, Charkes L.	Sergeant, Corps of Mil. Staff Clerks, Canadian Army	U
Wong Nai Chung Gap (Brigade HQ) (126).		
Lawrie, John Ferguson	Second Lieutenant, General List	U
Attached to 5 AA. Last known at Wong Nai Chung Gap AA position (126).		
Lawson, John Kelburne	Brigadier, Royal Canadian Regt.	K
Killed Wong Nai Chung Gap.		
Phillips, William E.	Sergeant, Corps of Mil. Staff Clerks, Canadian Army	U
Wong Nai Chung Gap with Lawson (21: 163). See also (100: 262).		

PHASE IV: THE FORCING OF WONG NAI CHUNG GAP   145

WINNIPEGS — 65 Killed

(Jardine's Lookout, Stanley Gap, Mount Butler, where B Company started with sixty-five men and is said to have ended with five)

Abgrall, Harvey	Private	U
Aitken, John A.	Private	U
Killed Jardine's Lookout (126).		
Atkinson, William	Private	U
Killed Mount Blount (126).[69]		
Baptiste, Edgar H.[70]	Private	U
Barron, Oliver A.	Private	U
Beltz, Charles M.	Corporal	U
Last seen Mount Butler (126).		
Birkett, George Allan	Lieutenant	U
Summit of Jardine's Lookout.		
Bowman, Alan S.	Captain	U
Counter-attack at Wong Nai Chung Gap (21: 167). Killed at about 08.00.		
Brady, James	Private	U
Killed by shelling of 'Black Hole'[71] (136) (19 'Bradley').[72]		
Carberry, Samuel Robert	Private	K
Killed Mount Blount (126).		
Chaboyer, Marcel	Private	U
Crawford, William	Private	U
Last seen Mount Blount (126).		
Davis, Albert Henry	Private	U
Shot in the head Wong Nai Chung Gap? (21: 193). Last seen with Gresham (126).		
Donovan, Valentine A.	Private	U
Shot in the head (77: 5), Wong Nai Chung Gap, at Brigade HQ (126).		
Dunsford, Edward C.	Sergeant	U
Killed Mount Blount (126).		
Folster, Herbert T.	Private	U
Folster, Donald H.	Private	U
Brother of the above. Killed Wong Nai Chung (126).		
French, Charles D.	Lieutenant	U
Between Jardine's Lookout and Mount Butler.		
Frobisher, Donald	Private	U
Gagne, Louis	Private	K
Killed on road above Brigade HQ, Wong Nai Chung (126).		
Geekie, Victor	Private	U
Jardine's Lookout (126).		
Grace, Robert W.	Private	U

Granger, Albert A.	Private	U

Probably murdered at 'Black Hole'. See (21: 158). (126) says Jardine's Lookout.

Gresham, Albert B.	Major	U

Shot at 15.15 trying to surrender A Company attempting to get back to Wong Nai Chung Gap from Mount Butler (14: 82).

Hallett, Lloyd M.	Private	U

Jardine's Lookout (126).

Hardisty, William L.	Private	U

Killed at Repulse Bay (126).

Johnson, Cecil H.[73]	Private	U

Wong Nai Chung Gap (126).

Johnson, Harvey	Sergeant	U

(126) states 'Mount Blount'.

Johnson, Lorn W.	Private	U

Chalk trench Mount Cameron (126).

Jonsson, Theodore	Private	U

Last seen Mount Blount (126).

Kelso, Henry	Corporal	U

Wong Nai Chung (126).

Kelso, John R.	Corporal	U

Wong Nai Chung (126).

Kilfoyle, Wesley N.	Private	U

Murdered by Japanese, being too badly wounded in stomach to march (136).[74]

Land, Gordon S.	Private	U

Killed on Jardine's Lookout by a bullet to the head (132b: Matthews).[75]

Land, Roy Clarence	Lance Corporal	U

Bayoneted to death near Wong Nai Chung Gap AA position (136).[76]

Law, George	Private	U

Mount Butler (126).

Lousier, Ernie J.	Private	U

Last seen Wong Nai Chung Gap, buried by RAMC (126).[77]

Lowe, James A.	Private	U

Jardine's Lookout (126).

Maxwell, Ralph C.	Private	U

Wong Nai Chung (126).

McCorrister, Mervin S.	Private	U

Last seen Jardine's Lookout (126).

McGowan, Robert C.	Private	U

Killed Wong Nai Chung Gap (126).

Morgan, Albert W.	Lance Corporal	U

Last seen Mount Blount (126).

O'Neill, Dori J.	Private	U
Murdered at 'Black Hole' (136).[78]		
Osborn, John R.	Warrant Officer II, Company Sergeant Major	U
VC. Killed by grenade retreating from Mount Butler.[79]		
Owen, Richard	Private	U
Killed Wan Chai Gap (126).		
Pare, Gabriel J.	Private	U
Killed on road above Brigade HQ, Wong Nai Chung (126).		
Parenteau, Walter J.	Private	U
Paterson, George H.	Sergeant	U
Killed on Black's Link attacking the Wong Nai Chung police station (66: 164).		
Peppin, Louis	Private	U
Pontius, Ira W.	Private	U
Killed Wong Nai Chung (126).		
Poulsen, Aage L. P.	Private	U
Last seen Wong Nai Chung near AA Bty., Stanley Gap (126).		
Shkolny, Max	Private	U
Last seen Jardine's Lookout (126).		
Silkey, Samuel	Private	U
Killed Jardine's Lookout (126).		
Simpson, Kenneth	Private	U
Killed Jardine's Lookout (126).		
Smith, Cecil E.	Private	U
Killed with Rogers (126).		
Smith, Charles	Lance Corporal	U
Shot in the forehead on Mount Butler (21: 169)[80]		
Smith, Robert C.	Private	U
Specht, William J.	Private	U
Killed Jardine's Lookout (126).		
Starrett, Ewart G.	Corporal	U
Killed Wong Nai Chung (126).		
Stodgell, Stanley F.	Private	U
Killed Mount Blount (126).		
Tarbuth, Lyle T.	Captain	U
Wounded, then killed in the Mount Butler/Jardine's Lookout boundary (14: 82).		
Tompkins, John E.	Private	U
Whalen, Bernard B.	Private	U
Bayoneted to death near Wong Nai Chung Gap AA position (136).		
Williams, Jack	Lance Corporal	U
Killed trying to carry Tarbuth to safety (14: 82). On Mount Blount (126).		

Wright, Roland F.　　　　　　　Private　　　　　　　　　　　　　　U
　Killed attacking high ridge overlooking Caroline Hill.[81]

ROYAL RIFLES — 16 Killed

(2 Platoon A Company, overrun at Lye Mun (west fort) or counter-attacking Sai Wan Hill (nine killed)?)

Arseneau, Jules　　　　　　　　Rifleman　　　　　　　　　　　　U
　(126) gives a date of 15 Dec., stating 'buried at Stanley cemetery'.

Beacroft, Ronald R.　　　　　　Rifleman　　　　　　　　　　　　U
　Killed at Lye Mun (126).

Calder, George　　　　　　　　Rifleman　　　　　　　　　　　　U
　Buried Tai Tam Gap (126).

Crosman, Philip G.　　　　　　Rifleman　　　　　　　　　　　　U

Cuzner, John Gerry　　　　　　Sergeant　　　　　　　　　　　　U
　Murdered by Japanese at C Coy. HQ (100: 304). (126) concurs: 'Killed Lyemun'.

Cyr, Euclide　　　　　　　　　Rifleman　　　　　　　　　　　　K

Halley, George　　　　　　　　Rifleman　　　　　　　　　　　　U
　Last seen Mount Parker (126).

Harrison, Argyle C.　　　　　　Lance Corp.　　　　　　　　　　　U
　Murdered at the Salesian massacre (100: 63).

Harrison, Edwin E.　　　　　　Corporal　　　　　　　　　　　　U
　Last seen Mount Parker (126).

Hickey, Charles　　　　　　　　Rifleman　　　　　　　　　　　　K
　Last seen Lye Mun (126).

Hopgood, Leslie Revelle　　　　Rifleman　　　　　　　　　　　　K
　Last seen Sai Wan (126).

Hughes, Harold B.　　　　　　　Sergeant　　　　　　　　　　　　U
　With Williams, Mount Parker. See (100: 64).

McRae, George W.　　　　　　　Corporal　　　　　　　　　　　　U
　Last seen Mount Parker (126). See (14: 78).

Oakley, Raymond J.　　　　　　Rifleman　　　　　　　　　　　　U
　Murdered at the Salesian massacre (100: 63).

Williams, Gerard Mott　　　　　Lieutenant　　　　　　　　　　　K
　Trying to hold the summit of Mount Parker, together with his sergeant (Hughes) (14: 78).

Woodside, Arnold R.　　　　　　Lieutenant　　　　　　　　　　　U
　Killed with Lawson (75: 31)　　　　　　　　　　　　　　　　[23 Dec.]

SIGNALS — 8 Killed

(Two of the eight RCCS riders were shot by snipers (21: 161). Three attached to Rajputs (21: 110))

Damant, Robert   Signalman, RCCS   K
    Killed in Wan Chai. Buried at 562 The Peak (142).[82]

Greenberg, Hymie   Signalman, RCCS   K
    Killed in Wan Chai. Buried 562 The Peak (142).

Sharp, Charles   Sergeant, RCCS   K
    Killed in Wan Chai. Buried at 562 The Peak (142).

Cooke, Reginald John   Sergeant, Royal Corps of Signals   K
    Died in hospital (145: 130) of wounds on the 19th. Buried No. 1   [8/25 Dec.]
    Crater,[83] BRH (142).

Griffiths, Owen   Lance Corporal, Royal Corps of Signals,   U
                                                          HK Signals Coy.
    Killed Tai Koo sugar factory area (126).

Hodson, Harry Stacey   Signalman, Royal Corps of Signals   K
    Killed in Wan Chai. Buried at 526 Coombe Road, The Peak (142).

McLaren, John Dryburgh   Signalman, Royal Corps of Signals,   U
                                                          HK Signals Coy.
    Killed at North Point (142) on 19/20 Dec. 1943 (sic). Tai Koo sugar   [8/25 Dec.]
    factory (126).

Thomas, Ernest R.   Signalman, Royal Corps of Signals,   U
    Despatch driver killed at Wong Nai Chung Gap (21: 163). Body seen (142). Buried
    (126).

MIDDLESEX — 22 Killed

Bond, Owen[84]   Lance Corporal   K
    Killed North Point Electric, King's Road (126).   [8/25 Dec.]

Burgess, James   Sergeant   U
    Killed at Wong Nai Chung shelters (126).

Coleman, Walter James   Lance Corporal   U
    Killed in power station   [18 Dec.]

Davies, Robert James   Bandsman   U
    Killed with Lawson.   [8 Dec.]

Deamer, Ronald Arthur   Private   K
    Killed in Causeway Bay PB 53, King's Road (126).   [18 Dec.]

Dillon, David   Bandsman   U
    With Lawson   [23 Dec.]

Endersby, George John   Drummer   U
    Attached West Infantry Brigade (145: 153) Z Coy., at Wong Nai Chung   [18/19 Dec.]
    Gap with Lawson.

Grossmith, Arthur Walter	Lance Corporal	U
Attached West Infantry Brigade (145: 153).		[8 Dec.]
Harris, Thomas Crosskey	Second Lieutenant	K
Killed in Causeway Bay PB 53 (Z Coy.), King's Road (96: 38).		[18 Dec.]
Kifford, William E	(Warrant Officer I, Bandmaster)	U
Z Coy., Wong Nai Chung Gap attached to HQ. With Lawson.		[18/25 Dec.]
Klintworth, Ernest	Drummer	U
Attached West Infantry Brigade (145: 153). Killed with Lawson in Wong Nai Chung Gap.		[18 Dec.]
Liborwich, Samuel	Private	K
Originally buried No. 1 Crater, Borret Road (i.e. BRH) (126).		[18 Dec.]
Merton, Sidney Arthur	Drummer	U
Attached West Infantry Brigade (145: 153) with Lawson.		[8 Dec.]
Minchin, Dennis Richard	Drummer	U
Missing Wong Nai Chung area (126).[85]		[8/25 Dec.]
Moggridge, Albert Charles	Corporal	U
Missing vicinity of North Point Electric (126).		[18 Dec.]
O'Mahoney, Desmond	Private	U
Killed in PB 39.		
Parsons, James Arthur	Drummer	U
Attached West Infantry Brigade (145: 153).		[8 Dec.]
Phelan, Sylvester	Corporal	U
Missing area south of The Ridge, 20 Dec. (126).		[18 Dec.]
Radley, Thomas Charles	Corporal	U
Killed by direct hit on his PB in Causeway Bay (91: 185) (Z Coy.).		
Ramsden, Henry	Warrant Officer III, Platoon Sergeant Major	K
Killed on 18th, according to the Middlesex Regt. (96: 423). Cause unknown.[86]		[18/25 Dec.]
Roarty, John	Private	U
Killed in PB 39.		
Zaccardello, Nicolo	Private	U
Killed north face (126).		[18 Dec.]

ARTILLERY — 61 Killed

(Up to four RA officers killed 'in counter battery office at WNCG HQ' (11: 214))

Platts, Baron Edmund	Second Lieutenant, RA	U
Killed in an OP on Jardine's Lookout.		
Dickinson, John William	Gunner, 12 Coast Regt. RA	U
Pak Sha Wan. Unburied (126).[87]		
Page, Patrick George	Gunner, HQ 12 Coast Regt. RA	U
The Ridge (126).		

PHASE IV: THE FORCING OF WONG NAI CHUNG GAP   151

Robinson, John Walter   Gunner, 12 Coast Regt. RA   U
   Mount Davis football ground (126).

Smith, Samuel   Lance Bombardier, 12 Hvy Bty.   U
                             20 Coast Regt. RA
   The Ridge (126).

Yeatman, Benedictus Godfrey   Captain, 12 Coast Regt. RA   K
   Sai Wan Hill (126).

Aldridge, Walter George   Bombardier, 7 Bty. 5 HAA Regt. RA   U
   Wong Nai Chung Gap AA site.[88]

Andrus, Leslie   Bombardier, 7 Bty. 5 HAA Regt. RA   U
   Wong Nai Chung Gap AA site. Unburied.

Barsby, John Alfred   Lance Bombardier, 5 HAA Regt RA   U
   Wong Nai Chung Gap AA site. Unburied.

Chable, Ernest George   Lance Bombardier, 7 Bty. 5 HAA Regt. RA   U
   Wong Nai Chung Gap AA site. Unburied.

Cooper, Geoffrey Samuel   Gunner, 7 Bty. 5 HAA Regt. RA   U
   Wong Nai Chung Gap AA site. Unburied.

Delahunt, Peter   Gunner, 7 Bty. 5 HAA Regt. RA   U
   Wong Nai Chung Gap AA site. Unburied.

Griffiths, Samuel Richard   Gunner, 7 Bty. 5 HAA Regt. RA   U
   Wong Nai Chung Gap AA site.[89]

Hasler, Leonard Frederick   Lance Bombardier, 7 Bty. 5 HAA Regt. RA   U
   Wong Nai Chung Gap AA site. Unburied.

Holland, William Henry   Gunner, 7 Bty. 5 HAA Regt. RA   U
   Wong Nai Chung Gap AA site. Unburied.

Idle, Jack   Gunner, 7 Bty. 5 HAA Regt. RA   U
   Wong Nai Chung Gap AA site. Unburied.

James, Robert   Gunner, 7 Bty. 5 HAA Regt. RA   K[90]
   West Bay. Shot in error. (126) states James was originally buried guard room Stanley Fort on 17 Dec.

Kirby, Edward   Bombardier, 7Bty. 5 HAA Regt. RA   K
   Wong Nai Chung Gap AA site.[91]   [22 Dec.]

Lavelle, Ernest Christopher   Gunner, 7 Bty. 5 HAA Regt. RA   U
   Wong Nai Chung Gap AA site. Unburied.

McCann, Arthur   Gunner, 7 Bty. 5 HAA Regt. RA   U
   Wong Nai Chung Gap AA site. Captured wounded in leg, then murdered.

Macintyre, Samuel   Gunner, 7 Bty. 5 HAA Regt. RA   U
   Wong Nai Chung Gap AA site. Unburied.

Milner, Albert   Gunner, 7 Bty. 5 HAA Regt. RA   U
   Wong Nai Chung Gap AA site. Unburied.

Mullen, Thomas   Gunner, 7 Bty. 5 HAA Regt. RA   U
   Wong Nai Chung Gap AA site. Unburied.

Williams, Leslie Harry	Lance Bombardier, 7 Bty. 5 HAA Regt. RA	U
Wong Nai Chung Gap AA site. Unburied.		
Gardner, Eric	Sergeant, 8 Coast Regt. RA	U
Killed Lye Mun Barracks square (126).		
Feilden, Lucien Jack	Major, RA (HKSRA)	K
Killed attacking Wong Nai Chung Gap police station.[92]		
Proes, Geoffrey Ernest	Major, RA	U
Missing Wong Nai Chung Gap area, 19 Dec. (126).		[19/25 Dec.]

(1st Mountain Battery probably Gauge Basin 4.5 crews)

Abdul Latif	Gunner, 1 Mountain Bty. HKSRA	U
Faqir Muhammad	Gunner, 1 Mountain Bty. HKSRA	U
Fateh Muhammad	Gunner, 1 Mountain Bty. HKSRA	U
Kishan Singh	Havildar, 1 Mountain Bty. HKSRA	U
Muhammad Rafiq	Gunner, 1 Mountain Bty. HKSRA	U
Talib Husain	Gunner, 1 Mountain Bty. HKSRA	U

(Probably the crews of the 3.7-inch guns at Stanley Gap, fighting for the AA position in Wong Nai Chung Gap)

Abdul Hamid	Gunner, 2 Mountain Bty. HKSRA	U
Akbar Khan	Gunner, 2 Mountain Bty. HKSRA	U
Ghulam Muhammad	Gunner, 2 Mountain Bty. HKSRA	U
Luqman Khan	Gunner, 2 Mountain Bty. HKSRA	U
Muhammad Yusuf	Gunner, 2 Mountain Bty. HKSRA	U
Munawar Khan	Gunner, 2 Mountain Bty. HKSRA	U
Swaran Singh	Cook, 2 Mountain Bty. HKSRA	U
Yusuf Ali	Gunner, 2 Mountain Bty. HKSRA	U

(Mount Parker)

Jogindar Singh	Gunner, 3 Medium Bty. HKSRA	U
Rulia Singh	Cook, 3 Medium Bty. HKSRA	U
Ali Dad	Gunner, 4 Medium Bty. HKSRA	U
Charan Singh	Naik, 4 Medium Bty. HKSRA	U
Ghulam Mohi-Ud-Din	Gunner, 4 Medium Bty. HKSRA	U
(126) states 'Kowloon' though without a date and under 20 Coast Bty. HKSRA.		
Mehar Singh	Gunner, 4 Medium Bty. HKSRA	U
Mian Waris	Gunner, 4 Medium Bty. HKSRA	U

PHASE IV: THE FORCING OF WONG NAI CHUNG GAP   153

(Probably Stanley Gap 6-inch guns)

Atma Singh	Gunner, 25 Bty. HKSRA	U
Sama Singh	Gunner, 25 Bty. HKSRA	U
Avery, Alfred Stuart	Captain, 1 HK Regt. HKSRA	U
Killed at Postbridge.		
Fox, John Henry	Captain, 1 HK Regt. HKSRA	U
Killed in the RA HQ at Wong Nai Chung Gap.[94]		
Muhammad Khan	Gunner, HQ, 1 HK Regt. HKSRA	U
Muhammad Shafi	Gunner, HQ, 1 HK Regt. HKSRA	U
Sher Muhammad	Gunner, HQ, 1 HK Regt. HKSRA	U
Sucha Singh	Gunner, HQ, 1 HK Regt. HKSRA	U
Temple, Webb Tatham	Major, RA Commanding, 1st HK Regt. HKSRA	U
Killed in the RA HQ at Wong Nai Chung gap.		
Gurbakhsh Singh	Lance Naik, 25 Light AA Bty. HKSRA	U
Muhammad Sadiq	Gunner, 20 Coast Bty. HKSRA	U
Sarwar Khan	Gunner, 17 HAA Bty. HKSRA	U
Sohan Singh	Gunner, 1 HAA Bty. HKSRA	U

VOLUNTEERS — 55 Killed

Anderson, Donald James   Lieutenant, 3 Coy. HKVDC   K
  Schoolmaster. East of Jardine's Lookout. Killed with the Winnipegs in the battle of Wong Nai Chung Gap (23: 160).[94]

Chung Yew Mun   Private, 3 Coy. HKVDC   U
  Missing believed killed at Wong Nai Chung Gap (126).

Cox, Charles William   Private, 3 Coy. HKVDC   U
  KIA at north Jardine's Lookout (126).

Edwards, Percy   Private, 3 Coy. HKVDC   U

Fisher, E. D.   Lance Corporal, 3 Coy. HKVDC   K
  Killed trying to come to aid of JLO 1.

Fox, Owen Williams   Private, 3 Coy. HKVDC   K
  KIA area of village north of Jardine's Lookout (126).

Gosling, Richard George   Private, 3 Coy., HKVDC   U [20 Dec.]
  Probably murdered at Wong Nai Chung Gap with Lim and MacKechnie, in which case 19 Dec.[95]

Hall, Stephen   Private, 3 Coy. HKVDC   K
  KIA at Stanley Gap AA site area (126).[96]

Hing, Edward Joseph   Corporal, 3 Coy. HKVDC   U
  Killed at JLO 3. 'Area of village north of Jardine's Lookout' (126).

Ho, Albert Lionel Private, 3 Coy. HKVDC U
  Wong Nai Chung Gap (126).
Hoffman, James Joseph[97] Private, 3 Coy. HKVDC K
  KIA Stanley Gap AA site area (126).
Holmes, Leslie Benjamin Captain, 3 Coy. HKVDC K
  Schoolmaster. Killed outside JLO 2.
Hung Kai Chiu Corporal, 3 Coy. HKVDC K
  Shot in back from Mount Nicholson at JLO 2.
Izatt, Samuel Private, 3 Coy. HKVDC K
  Killed JLO 2 (126).
Jitts, Geoffrey Clayton Private, 3 Coy. HKVDC K
  DOW defending JLO 2 in catchwater. Commendation.
Lau, George Private, 3 Coy. HKVDC U
  Missing believed killed area of village north of Jardine's Lookout (126).
Lau Tsun Sze Private, 3 Coy. HKVDC U
  KIA at south end Sir Cecil's Ride, Wong Nai Chung Gap (126).
Leung Tak Chiu Private, 3 Coy. HKVDC U
  Missing believed killed at south end Sir Cecil's Ride, Wong Nai Chung Gap (126).
Lim, A. Private, 3 Coy. HKVDC U
  Missing believed killed at south end Sir Cecil's Ride, Wong Nai Chung Gap (126).
Lim, J. Percy Felix Private, 3 Coy. HKVDC U
  Missing believed killed at south end Sir Cecil's Ride, Wong Nai Chung Gap (126).
Lim Kim Huan Lance Corporal, 3 Coy. HKVDC U
  Kicked in the head until dead, Wong Nai Chung Gap (136).[98]
Lim Seang Teik Private, 3 Coy. HKVDC U
  Missing believed killed at south end Sir Cecil's Ride, Wong Nai Chung Gap (126).
Lo Wing Cheung Private, 3 Coy. HKVDC U
  Missing believed killed at south end Sir Cecil's Ride, Wong Nai Chung Gap (126).
Mackechnie, George Morris Private, 3 Coy. HKVDC U
  Murdered at Wong Nai Chung Gap (136).[99]
Maher, Antonio Pedro Private, 3 Coy. HKVDC U
  KIA area of village north Jardine's Lookout (126).
Markham, William Private, 3 Coy. HKVDC U
  KIA area of village north Jardine's Lookout (126).
Reed, Arthur Augustus Private, 3 Coy. HKVDC U
  KIA area of village north Jardine's Lookout (126).
Reed, Edgar Vincent Private, 3 Coy. HKVDC U
  Chartered accountant. Brother of the above. One died in hospital (145: 127).[100]
Young, E. B. Private, 3 Coy. HKVDC U
  Killed by mortar splinters coming through the gun apertures, JLO 1.
Young, William Lance Corporal, 3 Coy. HKVDC U
  Murdered at Wong Nai Chung Gap (136).[101]

PHASE IV: THE FORCING OF WONG NAI CHUNG GAP   155

Zimmern, E.	Sergeant, 3 Coy. HKVDC	U

Killed at JLO 3. KIA area of village north Jardine's Lookout (126).

Alves, Henrique Alberto	Private, 6 Coy. HKVDC	U

Tai Koo Dockyards?

Marques, Carlos Antonio	Lance Corporal, 6 Coy. HKVDC	U

Tai Koo Dockyards?

(All Hughes Group presumably killed at North Point power station)

Andrews, A.	Private, HKVDC Hughes Group	U

Missing believed killed at Sanatorium Gap (126).

Des Voeux, Sir Edward Alfred	Private, HKVDC Hughes Group	U

North Point power station by mortar.

Hone, A.	Private, HKVDC Hughes Group	U
Jacosta, Frederic Marie	Captain, HKVDC Hughes Group	U

North Point power station (First World War veteran).

Muir, Albert William	Private, HKVDC Hughes Group	U
Pearce, Tam E.	Private, HKVDC Hughes Group	U

North Point power station — battle of the bus.

Rodgers, Robert Augustus	Private, HKVDC Hughes Group	U
Sim, James	Private, HKVDC Hughes Group	U
Wilson, Peter Bruce	Bombardier, 1Bty. HKVDC	U

Went back to Shek O for supplies. Not seen after.

Andrews, Harold Hector	Private, 1 Coy. HKVDC	U
		[18 Dec.]

Missing believed killed Mount Parker (126).

Curtis, Edward Lea	Sergeant, 1 Coy. HKVDC	U
		[18 Dec.]

Killed at knoll on eastern slope of Mount Butler.

Goldman, Reginald	Private, 1 Coy. HKVDC	U
		[18 Dec.]

Buried at Tai Koo Road 600 yards north of Sanatorium Gap (126).

Greenevitch, Voldemar[102]	Private, 1 Coy. HKVDC	U
		[18 Dec.]

Missing believed killed at Sanatorium Gap (126).

Humphrey, Percy Harold Robert	Private, 1 Coy. HKVDC	U
		[18 Dec.]

Missing believed killed at Sanatorium Gap (126).

Jessop, John Edward	Lance Corporal, 1 Coy. HKVDC	U
		[18 Dec.]
Job, Arthur Ernest	Private, 1 Coy. HKVDC	U
		[18 Dec.]

Killed on Mount Parker, according to (4: 155), which gives the unlikely date of 17 Dec.[103]

Kjaer, K. S.	Private, 1 Coy. HKVDC	U
		[18 Dec.]

Buried at Tai Koo Road, 600 yards north of Sai Wan (126).

Van Leeuwen, Henri	Private, 1 Coy. HKVDC	K
		[18 Dec.]

Killed after 00.45 acting as a runner taking a message to PB 45 (140).

Walker, John Michael	Private, 1 Coy. HKVDC	U	
Missing believed killed at Sanatorium Gap (126).			[18 Dec.]
Wylie, L.M.	Lance Corporal, 1 Coy. HKVDC	U	
Missing believed killed at Sanatorium Gap (126).			[18 Dec.]
Park, William	Private, HKVDC A/C[104] Platoon	U	
Killed in direct hit on Carruther's A/C King's Road.			[18 Dec.]
Smits, Henry Walter	Private, HKVDC A/C Platoon	U	
Killed in direct hit on Carruther's A/C King's Road.			[18 Dec.]
Lammert, Lionel Ernest	Second Lieutenant, HKVDC (att: Rajputs)	U	
Believed to have been decapitated after capture in Causeway Bay (72: 94).			

PUNJABIS — 5 Killed

(Tai Hang village)

Gulat Shah	Sepoy	U	
Missing mainland (126).			
Kerfoot, Robert Gaskell	Second Lieutenant	K	
Killed attempting to cover the evacuation of West Brigade HQ (24: 204).			
Lakha Singh	Sepoy	U	
DOW (from 18 Dec. 1941), IGH (145: 147).			
Murad Ali	Sepoy	U	
Missing Mainland (126). If this were true, the date of 19th would be in doubt.			
Nasar Ullah	Sepoy	U	
Admitted Queen Mary Hospital 19 Dec., died same day (145: 85)[105]			[25 Dec.]

ENGINEERS — 12 Killed

(Searchlights and Wong Nai Chung Gap)

Husselbee, Samuel Richard	Sapper, 22 Fortress Coy. RE	U	
Killed Wong Nai Chung searchlight detachment 19 Dec. (126).			[8/25 Dec.]
Killeen, Peter Nicholas	Lance Corporal, 22 Fortress Coy. R.E.	K	
Shau Kei Wan searchlight detachment (126).			
O'Hanlon, Edward	Sapper, 22 Fortress Coy. RE	U	
Missing Wong Nai Chung searchlight detachment 19 Dec. (126).			[8/25 Dec.]
Phillips, Arthur William Harry	Sapper, 22 Fortress Coy. RE	U	
Killed Wong Nai Chung Gap on roadside (126).			
Rogers, William	Sapper, 22 Fortress Coy. RE	U[106]	
Bailey, William Reginald	Sapper, 40 Fortress Coy RE	K	
Killed Wong Nai Chung Gap at junction of roads 19 Dec. (126).			[8/25 Dec.]
Holliday, Donald[107]	Lieutenant, Royal Engineers	K	
Attached 40 Fortress Coy. (145: 115). East side Wong Nai Chung Gap (126).			

Murray, Donald Maitland   Major, Royal Engineers   K
   Attached 40 Fortress Coy. (145: 115). East side Wong Nai Chung Gap (126).

Roberts, George William   Warrant Officer II, Mechanist Quarter   K
                                         Master Sergeant, 40 Fortress Coy. R.E.
   Killed South side Wong Nai Chung Gap (126).

Russell, Frank Watterston   Corporal, 40 Fortress Coy. RE   U
   Missing east side Wong Nai Chung Gap (126).

Shipman, Cecil Ernest   Lance Corporal, 40 Fortress Coy. RE   U
   Missing east side Wong Nai Chung Gap (126).   [19/20 Dec.]

Chang Fat   Sapper, 40 Field Coy. RE   U

ROYAL SCOTS — 23

(A Company ambush north of Wong Nai Chung Gap and B, C, D at the Gap.)

Angus, George   Private   U
   East side Nicholson Camp near St Albert's Hospital (126).

Arnott, John Orr   Sergeant   U
   A Coy. Killed at Wong Nai Chung Gap at Lawson's Brigade HQ.

Bain, Thomas Morris   Lance Corporal   U
   South side Black's Link near Wong Nai Chung Gap (126).

Barr, Peter Buckley   Private   U
   East side Nicholson Camp about 200 yards from St Albert's Hospital (126).

Bell, McCallum   Second Lieutenant   K
   Killed by mortar, with Brown leading D Coy. up Wong Nai Chung Gap road.[108]

Brown, Alexander McArthy Slater Captain   U
   Killed by mortar, leading D Coy. up Wong Nai Chung Gap Road.

Brown, James   Corporal   U

Calder, Arthur Willis   Lance Corporal   U
   (145: 182) claims he was wounded on 19.12   [8/20 Dec.]

Campbell, Norman Nicholson   Corporal   U
   A Coy. Killed at Wong Nai Chung Gap at Lawson's Brigade HQ.

Corbitt, George Henry Douglas Lance Sergeant   U
   A Coy. Killed at Wong Nai Chung Gap at Lawson's Brigade HQ.

Dudgeon, Thomas   Private   U
   Killed Wong Nai Chung area (126).

Ellis, Alfred Richard   Private   U
   Missing Wong Nai Chung area (126).

Fenwick, Michael Forster   Second Lieutenant   U
   A Coy. Killed in Blue Pool Valley (126) trying to relieve Lawson's Brigade HQ at Wong Nai Chung Gap.

Glover, David Cairns   Lance Corporal   U
   A Coy. Killed at Wong Nai Chung Gap at Lawson's brigade HQ.

Gray, George E.	Lance Corporal	U
Missing 19th (145: 179). Wong Nai Chung area (126).		[19/25 Dec.]
Morrow, William	Private	U
Killed Wong Nai Chung area (126).		
Naysmith, John	Private	U
Killed Wong Nai Chung Gap at Lawson's Brigade HQ.		
Reedie, James	Private	U
Missing Wong Nai Chung area (126).		
Ross, Charles	Private	U
Missing Wong Nai Chung area (126).		
Ross, William James	Lance Corporal	K
Died in hospital (145: 134), killed (145: 180). Buried behind SAH (126).		
Stewart, George Retson	Lance Corporal	K
Recorded in hospital records as died of wounds 19 Dec. 1941.[109]		[8 Dec.]
Swettenham, George Faulkner	Second Lieutenant	U
Killed near Jardine's Lookout, where Royal Scots met Punjabis (92: 122); see (145: 178).		[23 Dec.][111]
Whitton, Thomas	Corporal	U
Missing, Wong Nai Chung area (126).		

RAJPUTS — 99 Killed

(North shore defence, and counter-attack from Leighton Hill)

Abdul Aziz	Sepoy	U
Abdul Ghani	Subadar	U
Possibly at Salesian massacre.		
Abdul Ghani	Sepoy	U
Abdul Hamid	Sepoy	U
Abdul Rahim	Sepoy	U
Ahmad Khan	Sepoy, 21433	U
Ahmad Khan	Sepoy, 11518	U
Ali Ahmad	Naik	U
Ali Muhammad	Naik	U
Allah Ditta	Sepoy	K
Allah Yar Khan	Sepoy	U
Ambler, Philip	Captain	U
Anrudh Singh	Sepoy	U
Killed ridge north-west of Tai Koo HQ area (126).		
Ata Jilani	Havildar	U
Atar Singh	Sepoy	U

Babu Singh	Sepoy	U
Bagh Ali	Sepoy	U
Baka Muhammad	Sepoy	U
Bostan Khan	Sepoy	U
Dhan Raj Singh	Sepoy	U
Fateh Khan	Sepoy	U
Fateh Muhammad	Sepoy	U
Fazl Ahmad	Sepoy, 15866	U
Fazl Ahmad	Sepoy, 11625	U
Fazl Dad	Lance Naik	U
Fazl Muhammad	Sepoy	U
Firoz Din	Sepoy, 9962	U
Firoz Din	Sepoy, 21152	U
Ghulam Ali	Sepoy	U
Ghulam Haidar	Sepoy	U
Ghulam Muhammad	Sepoy	U
Ghulam Rasul Killed North Point Coy HQ area (126).	Naik,	U
Gulia Khan	Sepoy	U
Gul Zaman	Naik	U
Habib Khan	Sepoy	U
Hasan Muhammad	Sepoy	U
Hashmat Khan	Sepoy	U
Hukam Singh	Sepoy	U
Indar Pal Singh	Lance Naik	U
Jahan Khan	Sepoy	U
Kalka Singh	Sepoy	U
Karam Illahi	Sepoy	U
Karam Khan	Sepoy	U
Khuda Bakhsh	Sepoy	U
Lakhu Singh	Naik, Indian Order of Merit	U
Lal Bahadur Singh	Sepoy	U
Mahendra Singh	Sepoy	U
Malang Khan	Cook	U
Mangal Singh	Lance Naik	U
Mansabdar Khan	Havildar	U
Maqtul Singh	Havildar	K

Maskin Muhammad	Sepoy	U
Misri Khan	Sepoy	U
Muhammad Afzal	Sepoy	U
Muhammad Ali	Sepoy	U
Killed North Point Coy. HQ area (126).		
Muhammad Bakhsh	Sepoy	U
Muhammad Firoz	Sepoy	U
Muhammad Hayat	Sepoy	U
Muhammad Husain	Sepoy	U
Muhammad Ibrahim	Sepoy,	U
Muhammad Khan	Sepoy, 20333	U
Muhammad Khan	Sepoy, 20347	U
Muhammad Sadiq	Sepoy	U
Muhammad Shafi	Lance Naik	U
Muhammad Shafi	Sepoy	U
Muhammad Sharif	Naik	U
Muhammad Sher	Water Carrier	U
Narayan Singh	Sepoy	U
Nawab Ali	Sepoy	U
Nazar Singh	Sepoy	U
Nazir Khan	Sepoy	U
Nazir Muhammad	Lance Naik	U
Newton, Harold Robert	Captain	K
Killed by machine gun west of sugar factory, early morning.		
Niranjan Singh	Sepoy	U
Niwaz Khan	Havildar	U
(126) states 'Kowloon' but without a date.		
Nur Muhammad Khan	Sepoy	U
Parbat Singh	Sepoy	U
Phul Singh	Subadar	U
Possibly at Salesian massacre.		
Pokhar Singh	Naik	U
Killed ridge north-west of Tai Koo HQ area (126).		
Raghu Nath Singh	Sepoy	U
Raghu Nath Singh	Lance Naik	U
Rahmat Khan	Lance Naik	U
Rahm Dad	Sepoy	U

Ramjas Singh	Sepoy	U
Killed ridge north west of Tai Koo HQ area (126).		
Ram Niwaz Singh	Sepoy	U
Ram Parshad Singh	Sepoy	U
Ratan Singh	Jemadar	K
Possibly at Salesian massacre.		
Sandilands, Donald Ian	Captain	K
Sheo Ram	Sweeper	U
Sher Abbas	Naik	U
Sher Dil	Sepoy	U
Sher Muhammad	Sepoy	U
Sher Singh	Sepoy	U
Sikandar Khan	Havildar	U
Sohbat Khan	Sepoy	U
Surkhru Khan	Naik	U
Umar Din	Sepoy	U
Wali Muhammad	Sepoy	U
Zamin Pal Singh	Sepoy	U

RAF — 2 Killed

Dickenson, Derrick Leslie	Corporal	US
Killed in a fifth-column ambush near Shouson Hill (41: 37).[111]		[20 Dec.]
Stockham, Herbert Richard	Corporal	K
Killed in a fifth-column ambush near Shouson Hill (41: 37). Buried garden 526 Coombe Road (126).		

RASC — 4 Killed

Kelly, Daniel	Driver, RASC	K
Missing (145: 190). Probably killed at Salesian massacre, see (21: 145).		[8/25 Dec.]
Melville, David Shearer	Private, RCASC	K
Died in hospital (145: 138) after being wounded driving Col. Hennessy's car to Wong Nai Chung Gap (100: 259).		
Newsome, Ambrose	Private, RCASC	U
Wong Nai Chung (30e) (126).		
Ng Chung Sze	Private, RASC[112]	K

RAMC — 13 Killed

Barclay, Beauchamp D'Epinay	Captain	U
Disappeared after the Wong Nai Chung Gap MAP massacre.		[19/25 Dec.]

Buchan, Robert   QMS   K
    Salesian Mission massacre (57). A First World War veteran aged 46.   [18 Dec.]
Dunne, John Charles   Private   K
    Salesian Mission massacre (57)   [18 Dec.]
Evans, Frank   Private   U
    Disappeared on Sir Cecil's Ride after escaping the Wong Nai Chung Gap MAP (38: 182).
Langley, Ivan   Private   K
    Salesian Mission massacre (57)   [18 Dec.]
McFarquhar, George Alexander Private   K
    Salesian Mission massacre (57)   [18 Dec.]
Mohan, Hugh Leslie   Private   K
    Salesian Mission massacre (57)   [18 Dec.]
Newton, Arthur   Corporal   K
    Salesian Mission massacre (57)   [18 Dec.]
Reid, Robert Westie   Private   K
    Salesian Mission massacre (57)   [18 Dec. 1940]
Tilbury, Stanley   Private   U
                                                                     [18 Dec.]
Watt, Ernest   Sergeant   K
    Salesian Mission massacre (57)   [18 Dec.]
Webb, Albert Edward   Corporal   U
                                                                     [18 Dec.]
Williams, Arthur Charles   Private   K
    Salesian Mission massacre (57)   [18 Dec.]

ROYAL NAVY — 31 Killed

Chan, Chi Hing   Ordinary Seaman, HKRNVR   UP
Dulley, Hugh W. M.   Lieutenant Commander, HKRNVR   UP
    Killed at Postbridge by Japanese mortar at midnight.
Kempton, Dennis   Sub-Lieutenant, HKRNVR   UP
    Killed with *Thracian* party in third lorry attacking Wong Nai Chung   [23 Dec.]
    (130: 22).
Merry, L. G.   Lieutenant, HKRNVR   UP
    Killed with *Thracian* party in first lorry attacking Wong Nai Chung   [20 Dec.]
    (130: 22).
Gregory, Robert Henley   Sub-Lieutenant, 52A HKRNVR   K
    Killed by an exploding gun at the mine-watching station (114: 37).
Lai, Fook Hing   Able Seaman, HKRNVR   UP
Colls, J. B.   Sub-Lieutenant, HKRNVR   UP
    Killed on MTB 12.

Phase IV: The Forcing of Wong Nai Chung Gap

Elliot, Thomas Killed on MTB 12.	Petty Officer Stoker, MTB 12	UP
McGill, George Spedding Killed on MTB 12.	Sub-Lieutenant, HKRNVR	UP
Bowden, George William Killed on MTB 26 — Coxwain.	Leading Seaman, HMS *Tamar*, RN	UP
Brown, Frederick Alfred Killed on MTB 26.	Leading Stoker, RN 26	UC
Eager, J. C. Killed on MTB 26 (79: 252).	Sub-Lieutenant, HKRNVR	UP [20 Dec.]
Wagstaff, Donald William Killed on MTB 26.	Lieutenant, HKRNVR	UP
Whitter, Jack W. S. Killed on MTB 26.	Able Seaman, RN 26	UC
Donachy, William	Petty Officer, HMS *Hong Kong*, RN[113]	UP
McDade, James McNie Most probably an MTB crewmember, in which case it should be 19 Dec.	Leading Telegraphist, HMS *Hong Kong*, RN	UP [1 Dec.]
Shorrock, James	Petty Officer Stoker, HMS *Hong Kong*, RN	UP
Barker, Reginald MTB 07. Recorded as DOW, RN Hospital (145: 197).	Leading Stoker, HMS *Tamar*, RN	K
Duckworth, Tom G. Killed by machine-gun fire from Japanese aircraft, MTB 07, morning (145: 197).	Telegraphist, MTB 07	UP
Ayles, Bertie Killed single-handedly attacking a Japanese machine gun at Wong Nai Chung Gap (133).	Petty Officer, HMS *Tamar*, RN	UP
Davies, John Henry	Able Seaman, HMS *Tamar*, RN	UP
Muir, James Morton	Stoker 1st Class, HMS *Tamar*, RN	UC
Newburn, Walter J. J. Died in RN Hospital (145: 197).	Petty Officer, HMS *Tamar*, RN	UP
Randall, Robert Payne	Able Seaman, HMS *Tamar*, RN	UP
Thatcher, William Edward Died in RN Hospital (145: 197).	Master at Arms, HMS *Tamar*, RN	UP
Price, Charles Luke	Petty Officer, HMS *Tarantula*, RN[114]	K
Butlin, Frederick	Ordinary Seaman, HMS *Thracian*, RN	UC
Foster, John Daniel This is probably the Foster, G. A. admitted to Queen Mary Hospital 20 Dec. and died 21 Dec. (145: 76).	Ordinary Seaman, HMS *Thracian*, RN	UC
Hyland, James	Stoker 1st Class, HMS *Thracian*, RN	UP
Parsons, Henry James	Petty Officer Stoker, HMS *Thracian*, RN	K

Reynolds, Clifford   Able Seaman, HMS *Thracian*, RN   UP
Slark, Henry Walter   Able Seaman, HMS *Thracian*, RN   UC

CIVILIANS — 3 Killed

Tinson, George G. N., MC   UCWD
  Hong Kong Auxiliary Communications Corps; killed by mortar at Postbridge, Repulse Bay Road.
Orloff, E. N.   UX
  Killed in Salesian massacre (23: 16).
Harrison, Dr   UX
  Killed in Salesian massacre (21: 146).

7 Phase V: Pushing the Line West and Encircling Stanley

The Japanese attacking Hong Kong, like the Russians attacking Berlin four years later, had realized that there should be a focus for their attack. In Berlin it was the Reichstag; in Hong Kong, Victoria. Both attacking forces correctly surmised that the capture of their objective would lead to almost immediate surrender. To the Japanese, while splitting east and west had been strategic, taking Stanley was simply a sideshow to the real attack on Central.

The initial Japanese focus is on consolidating their hold through the centre of the Island. Although East and West Brigades never succeed in joining up after the 19th, skirmishes continue on the Repulse Bay Road until the 23rd. In fact the fighting for positions on the road south from Wong Nai Chung Gap — especially the withdrawal from The Ridge (which was still being reinforced from East Brigade as late as the 21st) — is one of the most complex actions to describe. It consists of quite large groups of men retreating from one position, getting separated, some returning to the position from which they started, others joining more and more disparate groups in the other positions along the road, and yet others being captured by the Japanese. Many of the latter meet their ends at Eucliffe; the wounded left behind at each spot are also generally murdered.

The Ridge itself is a high protuberance from the western face of

Violet Hill. The road south from Wong Nai Chung Gap to Repulse Bay has to deviate round it, thus the one and only large house on this feature in 1941 has a clear field of fire up this road, almost as far as the police station (which is just hidden by a bend in the road). Anyone holding The Ridge and Altamira on the other side of the road can clearly stop advances down it. This is why such a large RASC/RAOC force is sent to hold the position, though the Japanese advance via Violet Hill instead of the road reduce its value enormously.

The details of the fighting that occurred at this spot are unclear as there are so few survivors, but a photograph of the building taken in 1946 clearly shows rows of machine-gun bullet holes across the front, tell-tale pockmarks around every window, and the north-eastern corner of the building blown in by a mortar bomb.

The first attempt to withdraw from The Ridge — by the RASC — is intercepted by the Japanese and the survivors return to where they started. Some make it back to Twin Brooks, others to Overbays, and some even as far as the Repulse Bay Hotel. Those captured on the way are taken to Eucliffe.

In the final analysis, it appears that at least 99 men lose their lives in The Ridge/Overbays/Eucliffe massacres.[1]

As they remove the defenders from the north–south road, the Japanese are simultaneously pushing westwards towards Central, and south towards Stanley.

The westwards advance is held up by West Brigade holding a long north–south line. Initially the line runs from Causeway Bay, through Mount Nicholson, to Deep Water Bay. Soon the line will be pushed back.

In the northern sector, where the garrison largely fights from static positions, Leighton Hill becomes the dominant feature of the defence. The Japanese are held up by serious street fighting in Causeway Bay and Wan Chai as the Middlesex and Punjabis, augmented by elements of the Rajputs separated from East Brigade, Volunteers, artillery men, marines, and any other men fit enough to fight, desperately attempt to prevent a breakthrough. When Leighton Hill finally falls on the 24th, Morrison Hill and Mount Parrish fall soon after and the way through to Central starts to clear.

In the middle sector, the Royal Scots and Winnipeg Grenadiers make several attempts to counter-attack Wong Nai Chung Gap. However, these fail, and then Mount Nicholson falls quickly thanks to a lack of prepared defensive positions. From its peak, the Japanese dominate Middle Gap

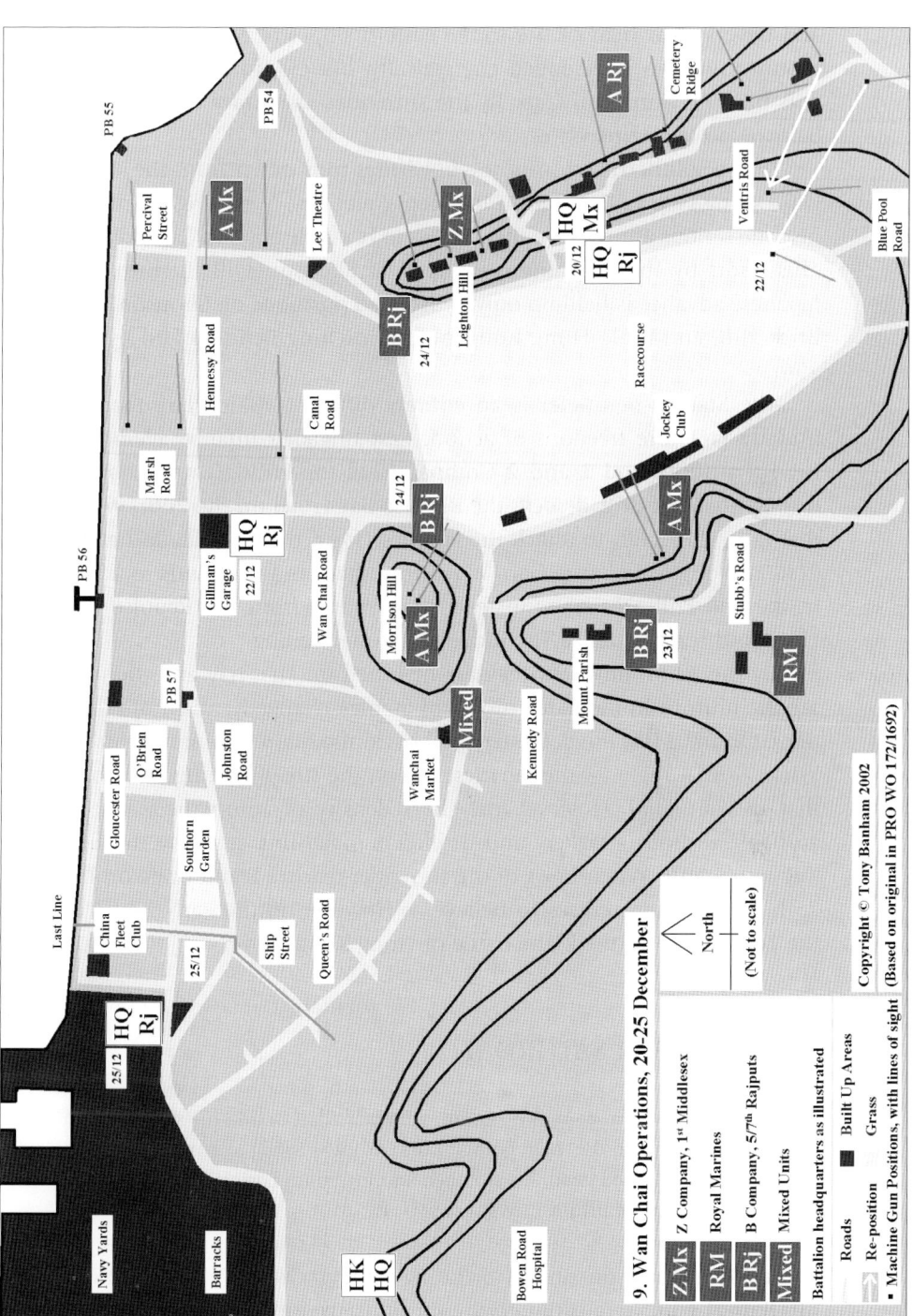

and have a clear field of fire to the eastern slopes of Mount Cameron. Mount Cameron is defended energetically, but eventually the garrison falls back to Wan Chai Gap. By the surrender, they have been pushed half-way to Magazine Gap.

In the southern sector, in the bowl that runs down from the Wong Nai Chung Gap police station to Deep Water Bay, West Brigade makes just one serious effort — on the 20th — to break through to East Brigade. This effort by the Punjabis is stopped at Shouson Hill. In turn, the Japanese advance is held up only by isolated positions on Shouson Hill, Brick Hill, and Little Hong Kong, before reaching Bennet's Hill by the 25th.

The Stanley perimeter is an entirely different affair. Here there is initially far more freedom of action. East Brigade's infantry elements, the Royal Rifles and 1 and 2 Companies of the HKVDC, try to break through to West Brigade near the Repulse Bay Hotel on the 20th. When that fails, they plan to attack the Japanese from the right flank, on the 21st, at Wong Nai Chung Gap. When this attack in turn grinds to a halt in the Red Hill area, they instead attack north from the Repulse Bay Hotel and reach as far as The Ridge that same evening.

By the 22nd, however, they are hemmed in. That day and the next see the hilltops immediately north of Stanley change hands more than once. On the 24th, the defenders pull back into Stanley peninsula itself. When — that night — the Japanese attack, the street fighting resembles that in Wan Chai. However, the sheer density of automatic weapons available to both attackers and defenders make this arguably the first 'modern' battle. When news of the surrender reaches Stanley late on the 25th, the garrison refuses to believe it. However, in the early hours of the 26th it is confirmed. The battle of Hong Kong is over.

20 DECEMBER SATURDAY

> I remember Willie Starrett, who was right beside me saying: 'I am going to die, I am going to die'. As I was trying to comfort him, he collapsed dead; his stomach and intestines basically falling on the floor. (Clifford L. Matthews)[2]

Some 200 garrison prisoners (including some of Osborn's platoon from Mt. Butler) who were captured the previous evening, and left overnight

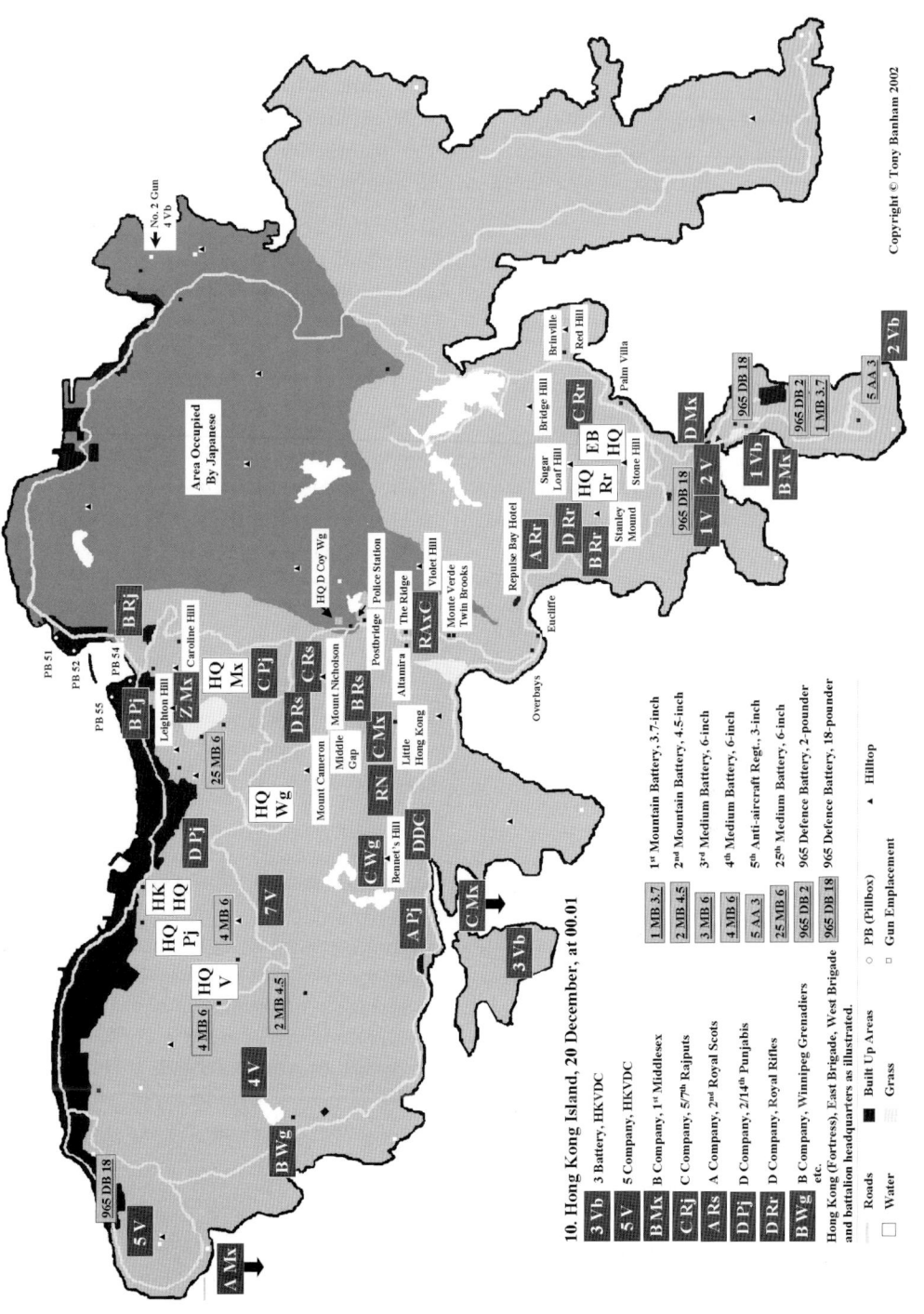

in 'the Black Hole of Hong Kong' (a one-room building measuring 16 feet by 22, and said to have been a garage or an old battery mess hall)[3] are let out to march to North Point. Others imprisoned here include Private Leslie Adams, and Harry Atkinson Winnipeg Grenadiers. During the night, probably at 06.00 (136), a British shell hits the building, killing two Grenadiers (Brady and Starrett), two HKVDC, and several regulars (136).[4] When the Japanese open the door, Lieutenant William Vaughan Mitchell of the Winnipeg Grenadiers asks that his brother, Lieutenant Eric Lawson Mitchell, receive medical attention first. Both are murdered, together with other wounded including Dori O'Neil and Tage Agerbak.[5]

Before dawn, A and D Companies Royal Scots dig in on the eastern slopes of Mount Nicholson, and B and C Companies take positions on their left. B Company Rajputs bridges the gap to B and C Company Punjabis, and Z Company Middlesex holds Leighton Hill (3: 34).

Although Wallis is out of contact with Fortress Headquarters most of the day (139), he receives an order from Maltby to attack westward. This is one arm of a pincer movement, in which A Company Punjabis are charged with striking east along the south coast to relieve the Repulse Bay Hotel, and East Brigade are ordered to attack west to meet them. The Punjabis get as far east as Shouson Hill, and are pinned down by a strong Japanese position there. East Brigade gets as far as the Repulse Bay Hotel, only to find a battle already in progress at the Repulse Bay Hotel garage, the Japanese having occupied Violet Hill and taken the garage before dawn.

> When I told the G.S.O. 'I'[6] early on 20 Dec that I considered the enemy were in the VIOLET HILL–MIDDLE SPUR area in some strength (probably a [battalion] and mortars) he seemed astonished and incredulous. He came back at me with remarks such as — 'Mr (?) Thesseder[7] who has just spoken to me from such and such a bungalow, says there are hardly any Nips in his area. He thinks the situation is all right, etc'. He seemed to suggest that one's reports were alarmist or panicky. It seemed to me that there was a passionate desire to minimise what was obviously a serious situation. One had an unpleasant feeling ones reports were not trusted — that this erroneous outlook was responsible for piecemeal attacks being ordered on strongly held difficult positions such as WONG NEI CHONG GAP[8] with resulting failure. (139)[9]

Exactly what happened at the garage of the Repulse Bay Hotel is unclear, as different versions give the initiative to the troops in the hotel itself, the HKVDC, and the Royal Rifles:

1. 'Grounds started to organise an attack on the garage to free the prisoners . . . He was to recapture the garage, and the five prisoners were released, but he was killed leading the attack' (95: 109).
2. 'Brigadier Wallis orders A Company Royal Rifles under Major Young, and two Platoons of 2 Company HKVDC (6 Platoon, Lt. D. L. Prophet, and 7 Platoon Lt. W. Stoker) to assist . . . The garage was shelled by a howitzer at Stanley View and a successful attack was launched by No. 6 Platoon HKVDC' (3: 36).
3. 'Within an hour [of 08.00] A Company [Royal Rifles] had cleared the garage — 26 Japanese were killed during this encounter' (100: 71).

It seems probable that the battle was in fact started by the troops in the hotel under Lieutenant Grounds of the Middlesex, and that the Royal Rifles and HKVDC either joined in the end of the fight or (possibly) started a second round of it. Perhaps the most consistent description is that of a hotel resident, Siu-Feng Huang:

> When I called up my office, the hotel telephone operator asked me to look down my window and told me that the Japs were already in the garage. You remember where the garage was. Well I had seen those soldiers nearly 20–30 in number but at the same time I saw a gardener was watering in the garden so I thought they were Br soldiers. By the way I forgot to tell you I met Mr Choy and his family at RBH [Repulse Bay Hotel]. He is the father of that Miss Choy who worked in YW [ie. YWCA] HK. I rushed down to see Chow and Tsao and found them and the Choys and many others much frightened in the corridor. Several days ago there came about 30 Br soldiers to be stationed at RBH. Now they were ready to fight. All the guests went to take shelter in the dugout. Nearly 15 ms after we got into the dugout, fighting began [with] rifles, machineguns and trench mortar. The Japs retreated about 2 PM while the Br were reinforced by about 200 Canadian soldiers. (156)

While early on this day an aircraft is reported as having been forced down south of Lamma by the West Bay AA section in action at Stanley (93: 137), civilian areas continue to be bombed and shelled, killing military personnel and civilians alike: 'Mrs Nina Goldin, Mrs Valentine Horowitz, Mrs Barbara Veronkin died suddenly on Saturday, December 20, in Peak Mansions' (147).[10]

Hospitals also come under fire, with the Hong Kong Sanatorium reporting picking up a shell fragment the size of a saucer, weighing over a pound, in the operating theatre itself (52: 98). Later, they take a direct hit: 'I heard a burst of shrapnel overhead. Nurse Bow suddenly screamed and stumbled forward, dripping with blood. I rushed over and caught her in the nick of time. On the operating table, I extracted twenty-two shell fragments from her chest, abdomen, and thighs. She was not yet married, and she was marred for life' (52: 102). The Indian General Hospital in Happy Valley is overrun, and St Stephen's Relief Hospital starts taking convalescent patients (57: 8). Things become worse for the civilians when the water supply to Victoria is cut off.

In Kowloon, civilians are becoming used to the dominating presence of the Japanese military: 'The Japanese across the street came for some cots and mattresses. From now on they will be coming to us for everything they want. We have given them four radios that some friends left in our care' (117: 34).

A rumour surfaces, put about by British Military HQ as a 'morale booster', that 60,000 Chinese troops are on the way to relieve Hong Kong. Meanwhile, a deputation of police present the Commissioner of Police with the following proposition: in view of their manifold duties in the maintenance of internal security, police should not to be used as military units, since the police are neither trained nor, for the most part, armed for modern warfare. Also, the order directing police not to evacuate stations in the face of strong attacks made by Japanese military forces but to hold out to the last man was not justifiable — especially as the military forces often abandon them. The proposition is accepted (131).

RA West Group — destroyed the previous day — re-forms at Wan Chai Gap, where survivors of the HKSRA 25th Medium Battery join them after losing the two guns at the Jockey Club stables. The Lewis guns of 5 AA Regiment are attached to the 2/14th Punjabis. Two 18-pounders of the 965 Defence Battery under Second Lieutenant E. G. Phillips help infantry around Repulse Bay, firing over open sights at enemy on Middle Spur and Violet Hill. Four mortars are destroyed, and many casualties observed.

As the garrison belatedly reorganises to address the current situation, the HKDDC and Commander Pears's party return to Aberdeen. The

HKDDC are then sent to take over the pillboxes in Deep Water Bay to free troops for other duties (143f), and sappers from Fortress Royal Engineers are sent up to Wan Chai Gap to take over defensive positions for the same reasons. Canadian and Volunteer troops hold the Eucliffe mansion near the Repulse Bay Hotel.

In the afternoon, Major Neve goes out in a car with two other officers on reconnaissance. They run into an ambush and are hit with grenades as they debus. Signalman Allister at Shouson Hill: 'We met and saluted an open car full of high brass, who returned the salute — their last. We heard the rattling blast of machine guns and stood transfixed' (118: 34). All the officers are severely wounded; Neve is taken to Queen Mary Hospital where he dies on 23 January (28: 40).

By late evening, the Japanese dislodge the Royal Scots from their positions on the lower slopes of Mount Nicholson and gain the summit. Captain Ford's company moves back to the St Albert's Hospital position of Battalion HQ, and most of the Winnipeg Grenadiers, minus D Company, organize on the slopes of Mount Cameron (95: 122).

Diary for 20 December

00.00 The combined ASC unit under Lieutenant Colonel Fredericks is formed into an infantry unit with Major F. Flippance (HKVDC), Captain D. L. Strellett and Captain R. R. Davies. They move up to The Ridge, which is also used as an RAOC headquarters (3: 25).

Captain Hutton-Potts: 'The Ridge, which was . . . approximately 500 yards from across the valley up to Wong Nei Chong Gap. It was occupied by the Ordnance Corps and was stuffed full of machine-guns, Bren guns, Lewis guns, everything you could think of — rifles, hand grenades, telescopes, field glasses' (15: 118).

01.35 Under Major E. de V. Hunt, a mixed bag of two Volunteer armoured cars and about 100 members of the HKSRA reach Wong Nai Chung Gap police station from Repulse Bay. They find that the Japanese have left it (after an artillery bombardment). The force disperses under fire from remaining Japanese positions in the area.

04.00	The Royal Scots estimate the Japanese to be one battalion strong in the vicinity of Jardine's Lookout (20: 18).
04.00	Blaver's platoon of the Royal Rifles (B Coy, 9 Platoon) is ordered to support Williams's Platoon (No. 5) on Mount Parker. They retire at 09.00 having found the high ground occupied by Japanese (14: 78).
06.00	The retreating Postbridge party arrives on foot at West Admin Pool.
06.30	By dawn, the Japanese have consolidated their positions after having found yesterday's resistance stronger than expected. The 228th have one battalion in the Wong Nai Chung Gap area ready to advance towards Deep Water Bay, and one battalion still on the north shore. The 229th have both their battalions in the Stanley Gap area, preparing to move towards Repulse Bay. The 230th have all three battalions in the Jardine's Lookout area, preparing to attack westwards with a final objective of High West. During the day, Japanese artillery pieces brought across to Hong Kong include mobile howitzers and three light tanks.
06.30	British forces in the Repulse Bay Hotel[11] notice Japanese troops maltreating prisoners[12] on the other side of the road outside the hotel garage. The hotel guests also see them.
06.30	At dawn The Ridge comes under heavy mortar fire. An advanced RASC party under Captain Strellet tries to evacuate to Shouson Hill, but are driven back to The Ridge with casualties (3: 35).
07.15	The Winnipeg Grenadiers withdraw from the Mount Nicholson area to regroup at Middle Gap (20: 18).
07.45	General Maltby hears that the Repulse Bay Hotel garage has been occupied (20: 18). He orders that the hotel be defended.
08.00	Canadian staff officer Colonel Hennessey is about to go for breakfast in a basement in Mount Austin Barracks. He sees smoke rising from behind the building and goes upstairs with Captain Davies to investigate. A shell bursts in the upstairs room of number 8, The Peak. Davies is killed instantly, and Hennessey is carried to the War Memorial Hospital where both legs are

amputated before he dies. Lucien Brunet of the Canadian Postal Corps:

> We couldn't tear the door off but we finally got a wide plank and brought it up stairs. Colonel Hennessy and Captain Davis had come down to the apartment we had been living in on the ground floor. One of the shells had hit the outside of the building and caved the whole wall in. Davis was dead from concussion. Hennessy was laying there and he was conscious, and both his legs were just literally hanging by shreds of skin and flesh, maybe five or six inches above the ankle. (100: 261)

08.00 The Royal Artillery reports that two Royal Scot Companies are digging in on the northeast slopes of Mount Nicholson (20: 18).

08.00 The advanced guard of Home's Royal Rifles attack towards Wong Nai Chung and Violet Hill leaves Stanley View (139).

09.30 The Repulse Bay Hotel comes under siege. At this time the troops at the hotel consist of a platoon of C Company Middlesex commanded by Second Lieutenant P. Grounds, some naval ratings and some HKRNVR, perhaps fifty men altogether. Grounds calls Fortress HQ to report the situation. He is ordered to put civilians in the lowest floors (20: 18) and hold the hotel at all costs (as it guards the coast road). Second Lieutenant Grounds organises an attack on the garage to free the prisoners, but is hampered by civilians rushing about waving white flags. Fighting is almost hand-to-hand, but casualties are low as there is plenty of cover. He re-takes the garage and releases the prisoners (four naval ratings and a Middlesex private), but is killed.[13]

09.30 Gough, Kellet and Austin batteries heavily shelled (93: 136).

09.30 Official Communiqué:

> Yesterday afternoon we launched a successful counter-attack against the enemy in the neighbourhood of Wongneichong Gap. The Japanese were thrown back from this key-point, which previously had been in their hands for a short period, and we have since maintained our lines. There has been no further enemy advance and throughout the night we remained in control of the situation. Heavy shelling of the mid-levels of the city took place towards dusk yesterday and there was some damage. Enemy bombing attacks throughout the day were relatively ineffective. (147)

10.00	The Middlesex machine gunners of C Company on Bennet's Hill are in action against an advancing enemy. Second Lieutenant Mace (commanding) is wounded and Sergeant Bedward takes over (96: 38).
10.00	The Middlesex report that the crews of pillboxes 12, 13, and 15, which had been withdrawn to stiffen up the landward defences, are opposing an advance on to Bennet's Hill (20: 18).
10.00	A Company Punjabis are ordered to move from Aberdeen, via Island Road, and clear the Japanese from the vicinity of the Repulse Bay Hotel (20: 18).
10.00	It is clear that the Japanese are passing round and over Violet Hill, and are already on Middle Spur and in buildings south west of the Repulse Bay Hotel (139).
10.45	The Middle Spur OP is reported surrounded, and Austin barracks is reported on fire (93: 136).
11.00	The Punjabis' A Company, about forty strong, advance from Aberdeen and attack Shouson Hill (together with naval elements) (20: 18). Later, Major Charles Boxer and Alf Bennett arrive in a staff car. Bennett:

> Charles and I were in a bunker and he suddenly said to me 'we're doing nothing here. Let's go and see what's going on'. So we got a vehicle and a driver and drove out — I cannot remember where to — I think it was Repulse Bay but I honestly don't know. I remember we walked away from the car — foolishly perhaps — over some empty landscape and there were Indian bodies lying around. We stood there side by side — foolishly I suppose — there were no soldiers in sight. I fired off some shots into a bush. Then suddenly Charles was shot — he fell down. I remember thinking how odd it was that he in khaki would be shot, and I in blue was not. (132b: Bennett).

Or, Baxter:

> It was reported to General Headquarters on the island that several Japanese soldiers had been captured and were being held in a house on Shouson Hill. Boxer was sent to interrogate them, and was driven from Headquarters to do this. By the time he arrived at the house the Japanese had recaptured it. Boxer got out of the car,

walked towards the house, and was met by a thrown hand grenade. Whilst trying to guard his face his arm was shattered. (132b: Baxter)[14]

11.00 Confused fighting is in progress while Home waits at Frederick's house. A message arrives that a strong Japanese party is in possession of the Repulse Bay Hotel garage, and the Royal Rifles are asking for artillery support. The 18-pounder under Lieutenant Phillips at Stanley View is brought to bear,[15] but firing is soon called off when a further message is received that the Royal Rifles are in possession of the building. The Royal Rifles' party then attack over the hills towards Wong Nai Chung Gap, but make no headway (via the catchments) towards their objective of Violet Hill, or even Middle Spur. A company leave a platoon in Eucliffe, and the remainder fall back to the hotel. They are covered by two Middlesex Platoons, one from B Company under Falconar, and one from D Company under Sergeant Harvey. These suffer losses near Middle Spur (139).

12.00 After a spirited defence by Middlesex machine gunners, the northern part of Brick Hill[16] is in Japanese hands (96: 38).

12.00 Fortress RE is reorganized into three sections — two covering Wan Chai Gap, and the third in reserve (20: 18).

12.30 Lieutenant Colonel Wilcox at Stanley reports that some 300 Japanese with artillery are moving south from Tai Tam Gap. Wallis orders 1 Company HKVDC to occupy the Palm Villa and Stone Hill areas to block the advance to Stanley (139).

13.00 A composite Middlesex rifle platoon reaches Wallis (139).[17]

14.30 Official Communiqué:

> Operations have been proceeding satisfactorily to-day. Parties of the enemy have been mopped up in the Repulse Bay area and our troops have pushed the enemy forces back across Happy Valley. A message has been received from General Yu Hon-mow, from which it appears that his forces are now within a very short distance of Hong Kong, and that the relief of the garrison may be expected in the near future. During the morning, a force of three bombers

escorted by six fighter aircraft was seen to carry out a dive-bombing attack on the Japanese in the north of Kowloon. (147)

16.00   The main Japanese infantry attack of the day (an attack on The Ridge from Violet Hill) is launched and beaten off (3: 35). The Japanese also attack the Mound, and a company of Royal Scots sent to aid the Punjabis there suffers heavy casualties.

16.00   Telephone lines to D Company (Winnipeg Grenadiers) are cut. Captains Billings and Bush, leaving Lieutenant T. Blackwood in command, wait for darkness and then retrieve a relatively undamaged vehicle from the tangle on the road, and coast down into the city and Battalion HQ where they report the situation.

17.00   In thick mist, Captain Douglas Ford's company of Royal Scots evacuate their exposed positions on the east face of Mount Nicholson. The 228th occupy its eastern slopes[18] and fire down on the Royal Scots (north of the hill) and the Winnipeg Grenadiers (south).

17.00   (139) reports that 'All efforts to make progress in the Repulse Bay area failed, the enemy being too strong and holding the high ground from the outset . . . danger of the enemy capturing STANLEY MOUND . . . cutting the road between STANLEY and Repulse Bay and then destroying sub-units in detail'.

17.30   Official Communiqué:

> There is no change in the situation on the Island. Operations are continuing. (147)

18.00   One gun detachment from the HKSRA 25th Medium Battery Caroline Hill section (based at the Jockey Club stables) arrives at Wan Chai Gap reporting that they were in close contact with the enemy and escaped after disabling the guns.

18.00   Major Oyadomari reports to Colonel Shoji: 'landing and advance had encountered unexpectedly strong resistance . . . rumour that Shoji's regiment had been annihilated at the Gap.'

19.00   Major Manners (rtd.) phones[19] from the Repulse Bay Hotel to say that the Canadians have arrived. They have 140 men under Major Young (20: 19).[20]

Phase V: Pushing the Line West and Encircling Stanley 179

19.30 Lieutenant Colonel Sutcliffe launches a counter-attack, sending C Company Winnipeg Grenadiers from Wan Chai Gap via Black's Link. They are pushed back (3: 37).

20.00 The Senior Naval Officer Aberdeen reports to HQCC that A Company Punjabis are still tied to the ground north of Brick Hill, and that Major Boxer has been wounded — making the third General Staff Officer wounded in that locality that day (20: 19).

21.00 D Company Royal Rifles falls back to Stanley View in heavy rain and poor visibility after failing to assault Violet Hill from the East.[21] The Royal Rifles, apart from A Company now in the vicinity of the Repulse Bay Hotel, and 1 and 2 Company HKVDC, are therefore back where they started the day (139).

22.00 Colonel H. B. Rose takes command of Wes Brigade. Lieutenant Colonel E. J. R. Mitchell, OBE, replaces him as commander of the HKVDC.

22.30 MTBs 10 and 11 try to sink the SS *Apoey* (believed to have a Japanese party onboard) at No. 13 buoy.

22.30 Wallis finally gets through to Fortress HQ and explains the situation. He is told to hold on to the area controlled, including the Repulse Bay Hotel, and do what he can to get through via Gauge Basin (139).

Roll of Honour for 20 December

RAJPUTS — 2 Killed

| Course, Richard George | Captain | K |
| Ghulam Muhammad | Sepoy | U |

HEADQUARTERS — 2 Killed

Davies, Roslyn	Captain, RCAPC	K
Mount Austin Barracks by shellfire.		
Hennessy, Patrick	Colonel, RCASC	K
Mount Austin Barracks by shellfire.		

RAOC — 2 Killed

Bonney, Robert John Ball   Captain, RAOC   U
Killed in ambush[22] on Repulse Bay Road.

Hitchcock, Ronald Augustus   Private, RAOC   U
Attached to the Royal Scots.

SIGNALS — 2 Killed

Cornish, Frederick David   Signalman, Royal Corps of Signals   K
Died in hospital (145: 130).[23] Killed Wan Chai, buried No. 1 Crater,   [8/25 Dec.]
Bowen Road (142).

Spinks, George Henry   Signalman, Royal Corps of Signals,   K
                    HK Sig. Coy.
Killed in Wan Chai. Buried at 562 Coombe Road, The Peak (142),   [8/25 Dec.]
20 Dec. (126).

RAF — 5 Killed

Allen, Alfred   Corporal, RAF   US
Missing The Ridge area (126).

Chapman, Cecil   Sergeant, RAF   US
Missing The Ridge area (126).

Fawcett, John Vernon   Aircraftsman 1st Class, RAFVR   US
Missing The Ridge area (126).

Gealy, David Norman   Aircraftsman 1st Class, RAFVR   K
Possibly DOW from the Shouson Hill ambush of the 19th? Missing The Ridge area (126).

Weare, Alan Joseph   Aircraftsman 1st Class, RAFVR   US
Missing The Ridge area (126).

VOLUNTEERS — 2 Killed

Cullen, William Francis   Private, RASC Coy. HKVDC   U
Missing believed killed Repulse Bay Hotel garages (126).

France, Norman Hoole   Gunner, 2nd Bty HKVDC   K
Reader in History at Hong Kong University (23: 299). Killed by a sniper, Stanley (101).

RASC — 2 Killed

Glen, Thomas George   Corporal, 12 Coy. RASC   U
Missing (145: 190).

Logan, James Bartholomew   Private, RASC   K
Missing (145: 190). Killed at junction of Repulse Bay Road and Island Road (126).[24]

PUNJABIS — 6 Killed

(Probably Shouson Hill)

Arjun Singh	Sepoy	K
Bakhshi Ram	Sepoy	U
Died on 20 Dec. of wounds from 18 Dec., IGH (145: 147).		[18 Dec.]
Ghulam Qadir	Sepoy	U
Died on 20 Dec. of wounds from 17 Dec., IGH (145: 146).		[18 Dec.]
Munshi Ram	Sepoy	U
Died on 20 Dec. of wounds from 18 Dec., IGH (145: 147). Buried QMH (126).		
Surayan Singh	Sepoy	K
Surjan Singh	Sepoy	K

HKDDC — 3 Killed

Abdul Karim	Constable, Dockyard Police, HKDDC	U
Muhammad Ramzan	Constable, HKDDC	U
Taj Din	Constable, Dockyard Police, HKDDC	U

ARTILLERY — 24 Killed

(Attack on Wong Nai Chung Gap from Repulse Bay)

Hunt, Edward William De Vere	Major, 1 HK Regt. HKSRA	U
Killed looking for Yale at Wong Nai Chung Gap (90: 215). Last seen alive 'nullah east of road' (126).		
Karam Din	Gunner, 1 HK Regt., HKSRA	U
Murzanir Khan	Havildar, HQ 1HK Regt., HKSRA	K
Umar Din	Gunner, 1 HK Regt., HKSRA	U
Yale, John Corbet	Lieutenant Colonel, 1 HK Regt., HKSRA	K
Killed in attacking Wong Nai Chung Gap (90: 215).		
Pinu Khan	Lance Naik, Depot Bty., HKSRA	U
Abdul Satar	Gunner, 2 Mountain Bty. HKSRA	U
Alam Sher	Gunner, 2 Mountain Bty. HKSRA	U
Bostan Khan	Havildar, 2 Mountain Bty. HKSRA	U
Haji Muhammad	Gunner, 2 Mountain Bty. HKSRA	U
Karam Illahi	Gunner, 2 Mountain Bty. HKSRA	U
Muhammad Din	Gunner, 2 Mountain Bty. HKSRA	U
Muhammad Husain	Gunner, 2 Mountain Bty. HKSRA	U
Muhammad Sarwar	Gunner, 2 Mountain Bty. HKSRA	U

Muhammad Shafi	Gunner, 2 Mountain Bty. HKSRA	U
Muhammad Yusof	Lance Naik, 2 Mountain Bty. HKSRA	U
Muhammad Zaman	Gunner, 2 Mountain Bty. HKSRA	U
Niaz Ali	Gunner, 2 Mountain Bty. HKSRA	U
Nur Alam	Gunner, 2 Mountain Bty. HKSRA	U
Saif-Ur-Rahman	Gunner, 2 Mountain Bty. HKSRA	U
Wali Muhammad	Lance Naik, 2 Mountain Bty. HKSRA	U
Karim Dad	Gunner, 3 Medium Bty., HKSRA	U

(126) states 'Kowloon' though without a date and under 20 Coast Regt. HKSRA.

Pritam Singh	Gunner, 17 HAA Bty., HKSRA	U
Stirrup, Harold	Lance Bombardier, 8 Coast Regt. RA	K

Guard Room, Stanley Fort, 20 Dec. (126). [8/25 Dec.]

HONG KONG CHINESE REGIMENT — 1 Killed

Chan Cheuk	Private, Hong Kong Chinese Regt.	U

WINNIPEGS — 18 Killed

Agerbak, Tage	Corporal	U

Left for wounded and killed with the Mitchells.

Deslaurier, Leon	Private	U

Last seen Stanley Gap (126).

Ferguson, Charles E.	Sergeant	U

Last seen Black's Link (126).

Goodman, Oscar	Private	U

Last seen Stanley Gap (126).

Grantham, William O.	Private	U
Grierson, Hugh L.	Private	U

Last seen Wong Nai Chung Gap (126).

Matte, Thomas	Private	U

Last seen Mount Blount (126).

Mitchell, Eric Lawson	Lieutenant	K

Murdered by Japanese (21: 171).

Mitchell, William Vaughan	Lieutenant	U

Brother of the above. Murdered by Japanese (21: 171).

Morris, John L.	Private	U

Killed Mount Blount (126).

Prieston, William A.	Private	U

Killed Wong Nai Chung (126).

Procinsky, Peter	Private	U
Wounded on Black's Link (126).		
Shatford, Howard E.	Private	U
Killed on Black's Link, Mount Nicholson (126).		
Smelts, Edgar Charles	Private	U
Bayoneted (126).		
Starrett, William J.	Lance Corporal	U
Killed by shell at 'Black Hole' (136).[25]		
Teasdale, Gowan	Private	U
Killed at artillery post near Mount Blount (126).		
Walker, Norman C.	Private	U
Buried Black's Link (126).		
Whiteside, Edwin Ernest	Private	U
Killed Wong Nai Chung (126).		

ROYAL SCOTS — 10 Killed

Brannan, John Hutchison	Private	U
Greig, James	Private	K
Died in hospital (145: 132)[26]		
Greig, Walter Robertson	Private	U
Admitted Queen Mary Hospital 20 Dec., died same day (145: 77).		[8 Dec.]
Lee, John Peters	Private	U
Died Royal Naval Hospital, 20 Dec. (145: 196).		[8 Dec.]
Lowe, William Edmund	Private	K
Died of wounds (126).		
McCormack, Robert	Private	U
Killed Black's Link, Nicholson end (126).		
Middleton, Herbert Kitchener	Lance Corporal	U
Killed Sir Cecil's Ride area (126).		
Milne, Robery	CSM	U
Killed Little Hong Kong near road, north side (126).		
Morrison, James	Private	U
Killed Blue Pool Road area (126).		
Watson, Charles William	Private	U
Killed Blue Pool Road area (126).		

MIDDLESEX — 6 Killed

Alexander, Kenneth William	Private	K
Originally buried Industrial School, Aberdeen, east end of front (126).		
Chamberlain, James	Private	U
Killed Stanley area (126).		

Hogan, John   Private   K
    Originally buried Eucliffe gardens, Repulse Bay (126).
Hooper, Roy Mildon   Private   U
    Originally buried garden of no. 15 Shouson Hill (126).
Grounds, Ronald Leslie   Second Lieutenant   U
    MiD. Killed rescuing prisoners from Repulse Bay Hotel garage. Buried at back of hotel
    (145: 19).   [21 Dec.]
Taylor, Christopher   Private   K
    Originally buried garden of Government Quarters, Leighton Hill (126).[27]

ENGINEERS — 1 Killed

Foo Hong Ting   Sapper, 40 Coy. RE   U

ROYAL RIFLES — 2 Killed

Grieves, Willis J.   Rifleman   U
    KIA at Repulse Bay Hotel (126).[28]
Tapp, Harry J.   Rifleman   U
    KIA at Repulse Bay (126).

ROYAL NAVY — 2 Killed

Price, Thomas John   Lieutenant, HKRNVR   UP
    (130: 27) suggests 20 Dec., attempting to return to Deep Water Bay base. [19 Dec.]
Slay, Edward T. W.   Sub-Lieutenant, HKRNVR   UP
    Shot through head by sniper at Repulse Bay Hotel (114: 51).[29]

CIVILIANS — 3 Killed

Goldin, Mrs Lina[30]   U C W D
    Peak Mansions. Russian. Admitted War Memorial Hospital 20 Dec.   [1–31 Dec.]
    Died same day (145: 94).
Horowitz, Mrs Valentine   UX
Veronkin, Mrs Barbara   UX

21 DECEMBER SUNDAY

> It was a strange feeling, reading the list of names of people that I met — or saw — for a few days, in much tension, and then — we went our separate ways. (Gloria Baretto)[31]

In the morning, East Brigade tries to attack Wong Nai Chung Gap from Tai Tam. The plan is to move up the Island Road to Tai Tam crossroads, then attack due west through the valley to Stanley Gap. It is realized that in order to be successful, Notting Hill, Red Hill, and Bridge Hill should first be captured as they cover the advance (3: 38). This results in confused fighting around the three hills, but by early evening it is clear that the attack has ground to a halt. At this time fresh orders are received from Maltby insisting that the Repulse Bay Hotel area be secured. As the initial attack stalls, East Brigade sends a force of A Company Royal Rifles from the hotel up the Repulse Bay Road towards Wong Nai Chung Gap. They get to the point around 300 yards south of the police station, at the site of The Ridge and Altamira. However, the Japanese are too well established. From this time onwards, the troops at Stanley are cut off from West Brigade. The Japanese have finally driven a wedge through the island.

The Japanese are also attacking, and they appear as far south as Stanley Mound. Corporal Charles Goddard's section of the Middlesex is told to support a depleted company of Royal Rifles to counter-attack. He finds them in low morale at the foot of Stanley Mound, but leads them in an attack that removes the Japanese from the summit before nightfall (91: 191).

Just south of Wong Nai Chung Gap, leaving some twenty Canadians and forty RASC (half of whom are HKVDC ASC Unit) behind, a number of British and Canadian soldiers depart The Ridge and the house opposite, Altamira. In the darkness, all but twelve are captured and taken to the newly abandoned Eucliffe. The final position within the Japanese beachhead is abandoned when, after three days of fighting, Barnett finally surrenders the HKVDC 4th Battery position at Pak Sha Wan.

East Brigade troops are still funnelling into Stanley. Four pack howitzers of 1 Mountain Battery HKSRA are brought in, but without their sights and ammunition which were dumped at Tai Tam Tuk Reservoir. Templer celebrates his fortieth birthday by trying to retrieve them: 'Thick bush around, could not find sights or Ammo so sent back

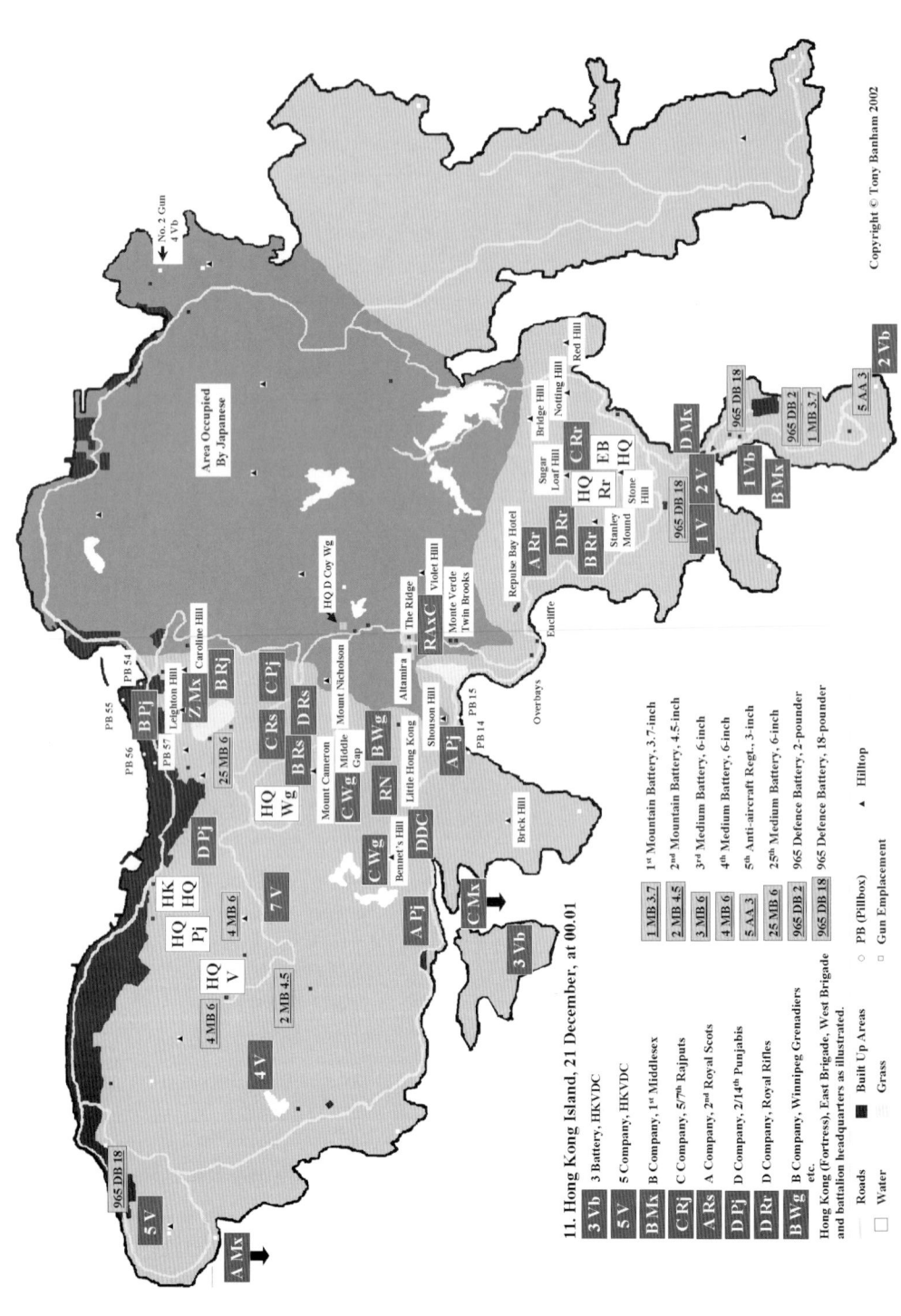

for Sgt Hanger HKSRA to tell me where they had thrown it. Japs all round. As Hanger was pointing out where the ammo had been thrown, a Jap sniper shot him through the heart (he was carrying a revolver and I a rifle and Jap thought he was the officer)' (150). While other troops arrive, Cadogan-Rawlinson and Lieutenant Offer depart Stanley by motor torpedo boat to rejoin and take command of B and D Companies Rajputs in the Tai Hang area. Major Browning, Captain Cole, and Lieutenant Poltock stay at Stanley (139).

In Victoria, electricity and gas are cut off. The civilians now have no light, heat, or water. The artillery and bombing exchanges continue. In the afternoon, the Navy gives what help it can. *Robin* fires fifty rounds of 3.7-inch howitzer at Middle Spur (143f), and *Cicala* shells Japanese attacks on Brick Hill. The Waterfall Bay AA section is shelled, with one IOR being killed and one wounded (93: 138). The ammunition dump at Mount Austin is hit and explodes (131). In retaliation, Company Sergeant Major E. J. Soden and C Company of Middlesex at Aberdeen shoot down a Japanese bomber. It crashes into the sea.

On the western front, the Winnipeg Grenadiers attack the Japanese positions on Mount Nicholson without success. The Royal Scots on the north side of Mount Nicholson move towards the Mound on the right of the Punjabis, but are forced back to the filter beds after heavy fighting.

The British north/south line is now:

West side of Causeway Bay	C Company Punjabis
Leighton Hill	Z Company Middlesex, B Company Rajputs
Wong Nai Chung village	B Company Punjabis, The Royal Scots
Top of Mount Cameron	C Company Grenadiers
Mount Cameron to Bennet's Hill	D and B Companies Grenadiers
To the coast	RN, HKVRNR, RE, and remnants of Middlesex A Company

A message is sent to the 23rd Army from the Imperial Headquarters in Tokyo stating that the 38th Division is to be deployed to the South Pacific, and that hostilities in Hong Kong are to be resolved as soon as possible (76: 40). The Japanese commanders have been served notice: victory is expected, and is expected now.

Diary for 21 December

00.30   Stanley reports 'all quiet' (93: 137).

03.00   C Company Winnipeg Grenadiers is in position at Middle Gap for a 07.00 attack towards Wong Nai Chung Gap (20: 19).

06.00   The Middlesex reports the Japanese are attacking PB 14 and Brick Hill (20: 19).

06.00   Hearing that A Company Punjabis have still made no progress at Shouson Hill, Maltby orders Lieutenant Colonel Kidd to send a senior officer to take command, and Kidd himself decides to take on the task (20: 19). As a result, he is killed[32] leading the Punjabis up the west face in the face of heavy fire from the summit (44: 94). There are heavy losses, only eight Punjabis survive (all wounded), and only four are left standing (95: 123). Two houses near the top of the hill — whose occupants witness this attack — hold out until the surrender (they are occupied by the RASC, and some twenty men of the RNVR, under Cap. A. J. Dewar, RASC).[33]

07.00   Brigadier Rose orders a counter-attack on Mount Nicholson. C Company Winnipeg Grenadiers attacks from Middle Gap, and B Company attacks from three sides. B Company are forced to withdraw as of the ninety-eight men engaged they have lost all officers, seven NCOs, and twenty-nine men. The Japanese are too well dug in on the east slope of Mount Nicholson. Colonel Doi: 'at dawn on the 21st, the enemy counter-attacked, with about four hundred men, but they were repulsed after fierce fighting . . . this fighting cost one company about forty per cent in casualties, including the company commander and platoon leaders' (122).

07.00   Wallis gives the order to advance, at 09.00, through Tai Tam Road to Tai Tam crossroads and Stanley Gap to engage the Japanese at Wong Nai Chung Gap from the flank. The plan is that they will attack at Notting Hill, hoping to break through to Wong Nai Chung Gap via Gauge Basin and Stanley Gap. Major MacAuley commands the advanced force of B Company Royal Rifles, together with 1 Company HKVDC. Major Templer,

Lieutenant Bompas, and Pilot Officer Thomson are detailed to act under MacAuley to add strength to the force. The main body consists of HQ, C and D Companies Royal Rifles, and 2 Company HKVDC (139).

08.00 Lieutenant Tressider at Repulse Bay Hotel provides an overview of the situation there: enemy 450 strong on Stanley Mound and overlooking Repulse Bay with HQ at Wong Nai Chung Gap with three machine guns and a heavy mortar (20: 19).

08.15 Sutcliffe orders the Winnipeg Grenadiers to fall back to Mount Cameron.

08.30 Official Communiqué:

> There has been no substantial change since yesterday afternoon. Both sides are fighting with great stubbornness, and the enemy is attempting to re-inforce his diminished positions on the South side of the Island. We have maintained our lines with difficulty. (147)

09.00 Major H. Marsh reports from Little Hong Kong that the Japanese can be seen moving from Wong Nai Chung Gap to the crest of Mount Nicholson (20: 20).

09.15 Wallis' advance is led by Second Lieutenant B. S. Carter with ten riflemen of No. 1 Company HKVDC, followed by a platoon of Royal Rifles, and strengthened by a section of Vickers guns from No. 2 Company under Lieutenant E. M. Bryden (79: 256).[34] It is a hot and steamy morning after the night's rain, and they come under fire from Red Hill and Bridge Hill, but press forward. Near 'Brinville', the Bren carriers of No. 3 Platoon HKVDC come under fire and one man is killed. A section of Royal Rifles under Lieutenant Fry (together with Lt. Bompas HKSRA) is sent to occupy Red Hill. The Japanese are driven out of Cash's bungalow by Captain Penn's light machine guns.

09.50 A 500-pound bomb falls just below Jardine's Corner, blocking the road to Volunteer HQ (20: 20).

10.00   The Punjabis in the Garden Road/Kennedy Road area are ordered to face south-east to cover a possible breakthrough from the region of Wan Chai Gap (20: 20).

10.00   HMS *Cicala* is ordered to Deep Water Bay to shell Japanese positions. After many air attacks the last of nine bombers scores hits. Three bombs finally strike her, killing the gunner's mate (91: 163) and wounding three others (143f). She sinks slowly in Lamma Channel. The crew escape aboard MTB 10 to serve as infantry around Bennet's Hill. However, MTB 10's First Lieutenant R. B. Goodwin is injured by a shell fired by a Japanese field gun from a hill above Deep Water Bay: 'As I stood against the wheelhouse there came a violent blow on my right thigh, and at the same time the flesh was hauled forward until the skin burst and the strain was suddenly released. A jagged steel splinter had passed through my thigh, and while its entry was marked by only a small puncture, its exit made a hole that could easily accommodate a small fist' (45: 17).[35]

10.30   The Bren Carriers and No. 1 Company HKVDC are held up around the Brinville track junction by fire from Red Hill. The right platoon of the Royal Rifles is held up south of 1 Company, pushing a fighting patrol under Bompas up Red Hill through Brinville. The centre platoon is held up in a catchwater — again by fire from Red Hill — and the left platoon is working slowly up Notting Hill (139).

10.30   After a renewed attack along King's Road, and after mortar fire against the naval dockyards from a position near the power station, the Japanese land in Causeway Bay. A Lewis gun position held by No. 6 Company HKVDC at Watson's Factory, Causeway Bay is overrun. The Portuguese are captured, disarmed and then released. They make their way back to the lines to continue the fight (3: 41). The Middlesex and Rajputs hold on to the line from Leighton Hill to the shore, and the Rajput's colonel is transferred from Stanley to the northern sector by motor torpedo boat. The garrison finally decides to abandon the ineffective pillboxes guarding the shoreline, in order to have more available mobile troops; this frees up D Company Punjabis to move to Wan Chai Gap (3: 41).

PHASE V: PUSHING THE LINE WEST AND ENCIRCLING STANLEY 191

11.00   The Japanese place a heavy mortar on King's Road near the power station, and bombard the Royal Navy Yard (20: 20).

11.30   The Volunteers (2nd Lt. Carter and his ten men) reach the top of Notting Hill, while the Royal Rifles, ably led by MacAuley and Templer, follow and operate two 3-inch mortars against the Japanese at Cash's bungalow. Edwards believes he can capture the crossroads by rushing them with the carriers, and at that moment Captain Penn, Second Lieutenant J. Redman, and Sergeant N. L. White are wounded, leaving Edwards in command of 1 Company HKVDC. There is still no sign of Bompas's patrol (139), and it is later realized that he and Fry have been killed leading the Red Hill attack.[36] The Bren carriers under Edwards push forward to near the crossroads. They engage a Japanese battery on the slopes beyond the reservoir. Edwards goes forward with 1 Company and is killed along with Corporal J. M. Houghton.[37] On Edwards's death, Second Lieutenant Blackaby of the Middlesex is sent up from Stanley to take command of 1 Company, which has now lost all officers except Second Lieutenant Carter (139). The remainder fall back to the carrier's position under Sergeant G. Lemay.

12.00   At noon, A Company of the Middlesex are ordered into the line, with two sections of guns going to Aberdeen to reinforce the naval party under Commander Millet, and the remainder (under Captain Flood) being ordered to Leighton Hill (96: 40).

12.00   The Japanese mount a gun at no. 163, King's Road (20: 20).

13.00   Wallis gets through to Maltby. He says that from where he is speaking he can see the Royal Rifles nearing the top of Bridge Hill,[38] in a hand-to-hand grenade battle, and that 'they were really doing their best that day at any rate and fighting gamely'. Maltby replies that all available men should be sent to Repulse Bay in an effort to break through to West Brigade (139). Templer is ordered to assemble what men he can find. Captain Clarke on Bridge Hill eventually drives the Japanese off by setting fire to the undergrowth (3: 39).

13.00   The Japanese holding the crossroads between Red Hill and Bridge Hill are virtually wiped out as MacAuley's forces capture Notting Hill.

13.00   Mortaring of the north shore defences continues, with PB 59 receiving, oddly, 59 direct hits (20: 20).

14.00   Lieutenant E. M. Bryden of No. 2 Company HKVDC sets up his Vickers guns and fires at the crossroads, Lemay having by now fallen back.

14.15   Official Communiqué:

> The position is at present substantially unchanged. The enemy continues to press on land and from the air, but our troops are defending their positions with the utmost stubbornness and determination. Whenever opportunity offers, or can be made, our troops deliver counter-attacks to gain local successes, and are inflicting heavy casualties. (147)

14.30   Two companies of Japanese occupy the whole length of Mount Nicholson (20: 20).

15.30   Major Templer of the 8th Coastal Regiment, RA, leaves the Red Hill battle area with thirty to forty men and the remaining carriers, to head for the Repulse Bay Hotel (139).

16.00   Three Japanese light tanks are spotted on the road near Tai Tam Tuk dam, and Bryden engages them.

16.00   After pushing forward from The Ridge and across the golf course at Deep Water Bay, Doi's forces are attacking PB 14[39] and Brick Hill.

16.00   General Chiang Kai Shek sends a message to Maltby saying that it is hoped that twenty bombers will operate at once against Japanese aerodromes (20: 21).

17.00   Young sends a telegram to admiralty:

> Military situation is now as follows:– Enemy hold key positions in hills and G.O.C. advises that we are very rapidly approaching a point at which only remaining resistance open to us will be to hold for short time only a small pocket in centre of city leaving bulk of fixed population to be overrun. I feel it will be my duty to ask terms before this position is reached. If H.M. Government feels able to give assent please cable single word ABILITY repetition ABILITY. Governor. Ends. 0521Z/21.

He receives the reply:

> Your message 0521 has been received. It crossed a message from the Prime Minister, who is temporarily out of reach as follows: Begins:–
>
>> To C. in C. and Governor of Hong Kong. The eyes of the world are upon you. We expect you to resist to the end. The honour of the empire is in you hands. Ends. In spite of conditions you and G.O.C. are facing, the difficulties of which are clearly understood, H.M.G.'s desire is that you should fight it out as in Prime Minister's message. 1439A/21. (15: 130)

17.00 The Japanese on Red Hill are strongly reinforced. Major MacAuley orders a withdrawal to Palm Villa. He is wounded at about this time (139).[40]

17.00 Major Templer arrives at the hotel to take command of all forces around Repulse Bay. He leads A Company Royal Rifles,[41] driving (via Eucliffe, with only three lorries reaching this point thanks to fire from Middle Spur (139)) to within 300 yards south of Wong Nai Chung Gap where he finds the remains of vehicles from the naval counter-attack, with the bodies of the ratings lying on the tarmac. He splits his force into two Platoons, one to hold the high ground above Postbridge, and one to attack, from there, the police station. Discovering that their jammed Bren guns[42] (just out of storage) prevent them from making an attack on the Japanese positions, he leaves about fifty survivors of Major Young's A Company pinned down at Altamira house (opposite The Ridge just south of the Gap), with instructions to reinforce the RAOC group at The Ridge, and returns to the Repulse Bay Hotel by bicycle (150). Hours later, a party from A Company Royal Rifles under Major Young does manage to reach The Ridge as reinforcements. The remainder of A Company tries to get through, but they are forced back to the hotel area with the HKVDC Scottish platoons. Eucliffe is evacuated as the local situation deteriorates (3: 37).

17.30 Official Communiqué:

> The enemy has been very active all day, but is being held. (147)

18.00   Wallis realizes that the attack cannot succeed (139). Bryden's party is recalled, thus ending the fight for Red Hill. It is realized that further advance is impossible as the Japanese are too well established there. Thus ends the last attempt to relieve the Gap.

18.00   Sergeant Lemay's party is ordered to proceed to the Repulse Bay Hotel to help in the defence. They set off in the two remaining Bren carriers. By dusk, sixty more Royal Rifles are at Repulse Bay Hotel, and the rest are scattered north-east of Stone Hill.

20.30   Major Templer[43] reports that there are still 100 RASC and RAOC personnel at The Ridge, where Lieutenant Johnston's A Company platoon tries to hold the catchwater between The Ridge and Violet Hill, but fails with many casualties. Fifty A Company Royal Rifles personnel are in Altamira house, while sixty to seventy more from A Company are still at the Repulse Bay Hotel (139).

22.00   Home, at the Stone Hill HQ of East Brigade, formally requests Wallis that he be allowed to speak directly to Governor Sir Mark Young, saying that 'his battalion was dead beat and he felt further resistance would only result in the wasting of valuable Canadian lives'. Wallis dissuades him (139).

22.30   A decision is made to evacuate The Ridge. Eight officers — including Lieutenant Colonel Fredericks, Major Mould, Captain Blaker, and Pigott (94: 102) — and 120 men attempt to leave (leaving six officers and thirty-five wounded men behind), but the evacuation fails as they run into Japanese fire. Some of them make it to Overbays (20: 21).[44]

Roll of Honour for 21 December

MIDDLESEX — 1 Killed

Hills, Albert James	Private	U
Died on 21st (145: 152), though (17) maintains 23rd.[45] (139) says 20th with Falconar.		[23 Dec.]

PUNJABIS — 25 Killed

(Mainly Shouson Hill, with some Causeway Bay)

Amar Nath	Sepoy	U
Anant Singh	Sepoy	K
Bahadur Singh	Havildar	K
Dara Singh	Sepoy	U
Darbara Singh	Sepoy	K
Diwan Singh	Jemadar	K
Gandharb Singh	Naik	U

    Died on 21 Dec. of wounds from 20 Dec., at IGH (145: 148).

Gian Singh	Sepoy	U
Gurbachan Singh	Sepoy	K
Gurdayal Singh	Naik	K
Gurdayal Singh	Sepoy	K
Hamir Singh	Sepoy	K
Hazara Singh	Sepoy	K
Jagat Singh	Sepoy	K
Khera Singh	Sepoy	K
Kidd, Gerald Ralph	Lieutenant Colonel	K

    Attacking Shouson Hill. [22 Dec.]

Niranjan Singh	Havildar	U
Palla Singh	Sepoy 13490	K
Palla Singh	Sepoy 19184	K
Panjab Singh	Sepoy	K
Pyara Singh	Sepoy	K
Sharam Singh	Sepoy	K
Shingara Singh	Lance Naik	K
Swaran Singh	Sepoy	U
Teja Singh	Sepoy	U

VOLUNTEERS — 8 Killed

Burson, Herbert   Lance Corporal, 1 Coy. HKVDC   K
    Reservoir? Ex-Lane Crawford employee (141). Originally buried by Island Road near HKSRA Bty (126).

Edwards, Richard   Second Lieutenant, 1 Coy. HKVDC   K
    Killed leading 1 Coy attacking battery by reservoir.

Egan, Ronald John	Private, 1 Coy. HKVDC	K

Killed by gunshot at the reservoir in a motor-cycle sidecar (21: 175).

Houghton, John Mayo	Corporal, 1 Coy. HKVDC	U

Killed with Edwards attacking battery by reservoir. Buried Red Hill (126).

Stephens, J. R.	Sergeant, 1 Coy. HKVDC	K

Shot while observing battery by reservoir (140).

Cuthill, George Hamilton	CQMS, RASC Coy. HKVDC	U
Hoselitz, Rudolf	Private, HKVDC Hughes Group	U

Doctor. DOW (from power station?) at North Point camp (126).

Skinner, Leslie Douglas	Sergeant, HKVDC Fortress Signals	U

Missing from North Point 19/20 Dec. 41 (142). (126) gives 21 Dec. as date.

ARTILLERY — 12 Killed

Thomas, David	Gunner, 7 Bty. 5 HAA Regt. R.A.	U
Bompas, Eric Ainsley	Lieutenant, RA 1 (HK) Regt. HKSRA	K

Killed Red Hill with Fry of Royal Rifles

Holmes, Clifford	Staff Sergeant, RA att. 1 (HK) Regt. HKSRA	K

Originally buried WMH near tennis courts (126).

Arjun Singh	Gunner, HQ Bty. HKSRA	U
Chand Singh	Gunner, 1 AA Regt. HKSRA[46]	U
Kaka Singh	Gunner, 5 Mountain Bty. HKSRA[47]	U
Abdul Majid	Gunner, 1 Mountain Bty. HKSRA	U
Hanger, Thomas	Sergeant, 1 Mount Bty. 1 (HK) Regt. HKSRA	K

Shot through heart at Tai Tam Tuk reservoir (150). Red Hill battery position (126).

Jagat Singh	Gunner, 1 Mountain Bty. HKSRA	U
Kundan Singh	Gunner, 1 Mountain Bty. HKSRA	U
Nand Singh	Gunner, 1 Mountain Bty. HKSRA	U
Nasib Singh	Havildar-Major, 1 Mountain Bty. HKSRA	U

ROYAL SCOTS — 9 Killed

Buglass, George	Private	U

Killed between Sir Cecil's Ride and Tai Hang Road (126).

Campton, Robert	Lance Corporal	U

Killed between Sir Cecil's Ride and Tai Hang Road (126).

Hunter, Harry Douglas	Lance Corporal	K

Died in hospital (145: 132). Buried behind SAH towards Nicholson (126).

Macalister Hall, William Peter	Private	U

Killed Blue Pool Road area (126).

Macrae, William   Lance Sergeant   U
  Killed Wong Nai Chung area (126).

Shevlin, John   Private   U
  Missing Blue Pool Road (126).

Stanton, Richard John   Lieutenant   K
  DOW (145: 131) from 19 Dec. when attacking Jardine's Lookout under Glasgow (92: 121).[48]

Taylor, James   Corporal   K
  Died in hospital (145: 134). Originally buried behind SAH (126).

Vipond, William   Private   U
  Missing 21st (145: 179). Missing Blue Pool Road, 21 Dec. (126).   [12 Dec.]

ROYAL RIFLES — 7 Killed

Barnett, Clifford G.   Rifleman   U
  Killed at Palm Villa (126).

Delaney, Joseph   Rifleman   U
  Last seen Notting Hill (126).

Fry, William S.   Lieutenant   U
  Killed Red Hill with Bompas of HKSRA.

Major, Kenneth J.   Rifleman   U
  Buried Notting Hill (126).

Murphy, Raynold   Rifleman   U

Thompson, Morton George   Rifleman   K

Trites, Leverette J.   Rifleman   U
  Killed Bridge Hill (126).

WINNIPEGS — 19 Killed

Cooper, Kenneth S.   Private   U
  Buried on Black's Link (126).[49]

David, James A. V.   Lieutenant   U
  Probably shot in the head. See (21: 193).

Eccles, Norman C.   Lance Corp.   U
  Buried on Black's Link (126).

Edgley, Charles   Private   U
  Mount Nicholson (126).

Foster, Russel M.   Sergeant   U
  Mount Nicholson. Buried by Chunchman, RAMC (126).

Fryatt, Walter B.   Warrant Officer II, Company Sergeant Major   U
  Buried on hill Black's Link (126).

Girard, David	Private	K
Hooper, Ronald Jamieson	Lieutenant	K
Shot in the chest by a sniper, Wong Nai Chung Gap (21: 193).		
Kellas, William A.	Private	U
Last seen Jardine's Lookout (126).		
Larsen, Robert E. A.	Private	U
Buried Black's Link (126).		
Lawrie, Keith R.	Private	U
Mount Nicholson (126).		
Little, Francis	Private	U
Mount Nicholson (126).		
McBride, William Ferguson	Private	U
Buried Black's Link (126).		
Meades, Raymond A.	Private	U
Buried Black's Link, Mount Cameron (126).		
Rodgers, Edward Herbert	Sergeant	K
Wiebe, Henry	Private	U
Buried Black's Link (126).		
Willis, Charles	Private	U
Last seen Black's Link (126).		
Woods, Albert T.	Lance Sgt.	U
Killed Middle Gap, Black's Link (126). By LMG fire (155).		
Young, Hugh	Lieutenant	K
Buried on hill Black's Link (126).		

RASC — 3 Killed

(Possibly with HKSRA Battery)

Diwan Khan	Sepoy, Hong Kong Mule Coy. RIASC	U
Faqir Muhammad	Saddler, Hong Kong Mule Coy. RIASC	U
Siraj Din	Sepoy, Hong Kong Mule Coy. RIASC	U

RAJPUTS — 2 Killed

Fateh Singh	Sepoy	U
DOW from 16 Dec., IGH (145: 144).		
Ram Lal Singh	Sepoy	U

RAMC — 1 Killed

Loynes, John Thomas	Private	U

HKDDC — 1 Killed

Ibrahim	Constable, Dockyard Police, HKDDC	U

ENGINEERS — 1 Killed

Wong Kee	Sapper, 22 Coy. RE	U

ROYAL NAVY — 5 Killed

Lai, Milk	Ordinary Seaman, HKRNVR	UP
Ricketts, John Michael	Petty Officer, HMS *Cicala*, RN	UC

Presumably the 'gunner's mate', killed by bombing.

Barr, Robert Lindsay	Able Seaman, HMS *Tamar*, RN	UC
Bowers, Herbert Ivan	Telegraphist, HMS *Tamar*, RN	UP
Mackay, James	Leading Stoker, HMS *Tern*, RN	UP

22 DECEMBER MONDAY

> I heard today that my pal Peter Grounds, 2 Lieut in the Mx, who was with me on the OCTU at Singapore last summer has been killed at Repulse Bay. Rumour says that he led his Platoon to rescue some other prisoners of the Japs at the Repulse Bay Hotel; the Japs were killed, the prisoners were rescued but Peter was killed. I'll miss his cheerful face around. (E. H. Field)[50]

In the early morning, the Royal Artillery carries out orders to destroy remaining oil installations by gunfire. Texaco oil depot, Tai Kok Tsui, and Kowloon Naval oil tanks are destroyed (93: 138). RA West Group moves to the Victoria Gap area.

In the north of the western line, the Royal Scots hold the line from Wan Chai Gap to the Filter Beds, though by early afternoon the Japanese are digging in on the northern lower slopes of Mount Cameron, within one hundred yards of the Royal Scots forward positions.[51]

The Punjabis, Middlesex, and Rajputs hold the line from the Filter Beds to the shore at Causeway Bay. The Middlesex position on Leighton Hill, together with seven survivors of 3 Company HKVDC, is still holding out. The Punjabis pull back to the racecourse after heavy shelling, and the Rajputs adjust their part of the line accordingly (44: 99). In the

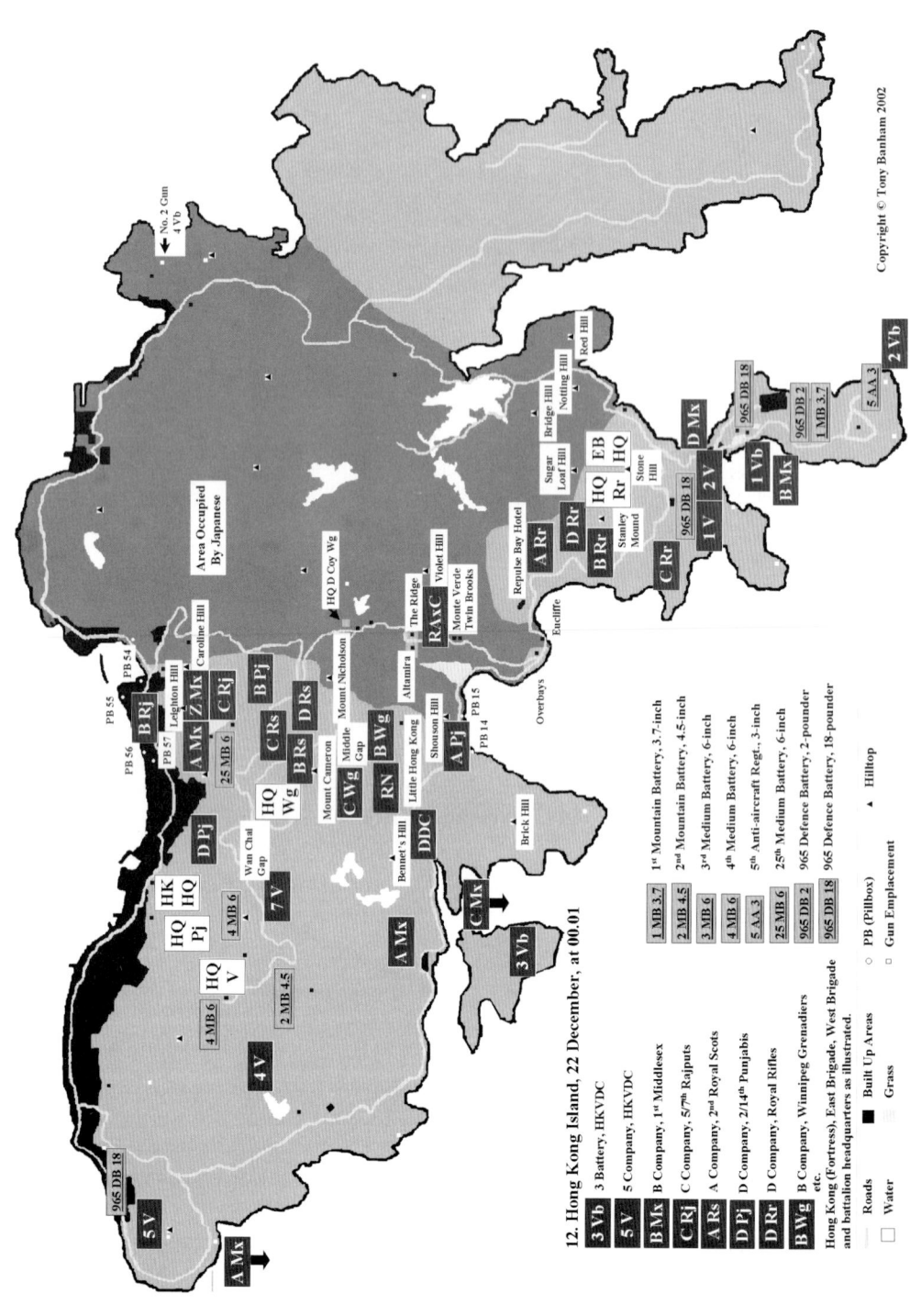

afternoon, the Japanese force a hole between the left flank of the Royal Scots and the right flank of B Company Punjabis, but do not press home this advantage (which is large as the Punjabis are down to eight men). B Company Middlesex plug the hole.

Because of suspected Japanese massing between Mount Cameron and Little Hong Kong, 4 Company and 7 Company HKVDC are brought up to man the line between Wan Chai Gap and Mount Kellet. Lieutenant G. H. Calvert, HKVDC, collects all available men to help hold the line.

The Canadians on Mount Cameron are heavily dive-bombed in the morning. They are also heavily mortared, as are the Royal Scots on Stubbs Road, from the western slopes of Jardine's Lookout.

The western line now runs (north to south):

C Company Punjabis
Z Company Middlesex, at Leighton Hill
B Company Rajputs
B Company Punjabis
Royal Scots
C Company Winnipegs on Mount Cameron
D and B Companies Winnipeg from Mount Cameron to Bennet's Hill
Mixed units to coast (A Coy. Middlesex, RE, HKRNVR, etc.) (79: 258)

The main fighting of the day is in the quadrilateral described by Mount Nicholson, Mount Cameron, The Ridge, and Repulse Bay.

Much of the ground the Japanese have captured still has elements holding out. The HKSRA 17 AA are still hanging on to the seaward end of Brick Hill. Elements of the Royal Navy still hold several houses on the top of Shouson Hill. A mixed bag of British forces (about sixty men comprising Major Marsh and eighteen Middlesex, five Winnipeg Grenadiers, fourteen HKVDC, Major Dewar and twenty naval ratings, and Hamlen of the RASC) hold the Little Hong Kong ordnance depot.

Major Lyndon, the Brigade Major at Wong Nai Chung Gap, tells Lieutenant Blackwood that he is going to try to get through Japanese lines to Battalion HQ. Inexplicably he turns back, and is then shot dead by a sentry (95: 130). Before noon, this small group of Winnipeg Grenadiers (commanded by Cap. R. W. Philip and Lt. Blackwood) are forced to surrender due to exhaustion and lack of food.[52] Of a total of forty men, including Lieutenant Tamworth, holding the position, thirty-six have serious wounds and four minor.[53] Major Evan Stewart of the 3 Company HKVDC also finally abandons his company headquarters, having held out without food since the 19th. His company has suffered about 80 per cent casualties.

In the south, Repulse Bay comes under heavy mortar fire from the Japanese on Middle Spur. Lieutenant Prophet takes 6 Platoon of the Volunteers to the ridge immediately south-west of the hotel, and engages the Japanese positions with machine gun-fire. Meanwhile, Sergeant Lemay attacks them with the Bren carriers. Eventually one carrier is knocked out at the entrance to the hotel, the other at South Bay Road bridge.

The Repulse Bay Hotel is now under very intense siege. It is decided that the troops should be evacuated to Stanley to allow the civilians at the hotel to safely surrender.

At Stanley itself, East Brigade is already establishing defence in depth. Initially a 'Forward Area', under Lieutenant Colonel Home, is set up, running from east to west:

- 1st Middlesex covering the catchwater just north of Palm Villa
- One 2-pounder detachment of 965 Defence Battery at Palm Villa
- B, C, D Companies Royal Rifles, plus 2 Company HKVDC, from Palm Villa to Stone Hill, Stanley Mound, and Stanley View.

A 'Support Area' is established in Stanley Village and jail under Lieutenant Colonel Wilcox, consisting of:

- B and D Companies Middlesex under Martin Weedon
- Survivors of No. 1 Company HKVDC
- Stanley Platoon HKVDC
- Two 18-pounders and two 2-pounders (both 965 DB)

The 'Reserve Area', under Lieutenant Colonel Shaw, is at Stanley Hill and Fort, with:

- 1 Battery HKVDC, 2 Battery HKVDC, 30 Battery, 36 Battery (with small arms)
- Two 18-pounders, two 3.7-inch howitzers (under Maj. Forrester of 965 DB)
- The 9.2-inch and 6-inch fixed guns

Stanley Mound and Stone Hill are abandoned after heavy mortar and infantry attacks, and the Japanese take possession.

British and Canadian prisoners who had escaped from Altamira and Overbays are taken to Eucliffe Mansion (below what is now Garden Mansions) where the Japanese 3rd Battalion has established its HQ. Roped together in threes they are shot. Company Sergeant Major Hamlen, RASC, who is shot through the mouth and survives: 'we knew that we were going to be shot because on top of the bank were pools of blood and at the bottom of the cliff, near the sea, were dozens of dead bodies ... then a firing squad came and we were all shot ... bullet passed through my neck above the left shoulder ... force of the bullet hitting me knocked me clear from the others and I rolled down the cliff' (15: 146). Later, fifty-three bodies are found in the area, shot, bayoneted, or beheaded.

Meanwhile at sea, HMS *Robin* is dive-bombed and damaged. One man is killed and three wounded (143f).

Diary for 22 December

04.30   Nurse Briggs at Aberdeen: 'The captain sent word that Freddie Dalziel and I, with all the patients, were to leave at first light in the R.A.F. ambulance for the Queen Mary Hospital in hope of getting through without being ambushed. Fortunately we got through but there were signs that there had been fighting on that road' (35: 100).

05.00   Lieutenant Colonel Macpherson commanding the RAOC depot on The Ridge is given the order to fall back to Repulse Bay after darkness falls (3: 42).

07.00   There is a further counter-attack on Mount Nicholson[54] by the Winnipeg Grenadiers from Middle Gap. But the Japanese are well dug in on the slopes, and at about 08.15 the Canadians fall back (79: 258).

07.30   The Japanese under Colonel Shoji close in on D Company Winnipeg Grenadiers at Wong Nai Chung Gap after a severe mortar attack. Only about twelve men (under Capt. Philip) are still defending. Philip — who has lost one eye already (21: 167) — tells them to surrender, but some make a break for it. The

Japanese find thirty-seven wounded at these positions, and three more at the D Company HQ on the other side of the road. They also find Lawson's body, and record that he had bled to death after a wound to his right leg.

08.30   Official Communiqué:

> It has been a relatively quiet night and our positions have been maintained. Abortive attempts by small parties of the enemy to land on the north shore of the Island during the early part of last night were successfully beaten off. (147)

09.00   The Japanese start an attack in the Middle Gap area. The Winnipeg Grenadiers then fall back further to Mount Cameron,[55] where they are heavily mortared and dive-bombed. Mount Nicholson Camp (north of Mount Nicholson itself, and held by the Royal Scots) is also bombarded (3: 45).

09.15   The supply of water from Tai Tam pumping station to Stanley stops, and Major Berridge, RE, is ordered to make repairs (139).

10.00   The Japanese attack The Ridge but are driven off with heavy casualties.

10.00   PB 27 reports that the Japanese are on the forward slopes between Stanley Mound and Red Hill (139).

10.30   More Japanese land on Hong Kong as their forces push towards Central (79: 258).

10.30   Maltby places Brigadier Wallis in direct command of Stanley Garrison (20: 21), ordering him to hold onto existing positions and send any help possible to the Repulse Bay Hotel. They agree that Stanley is to be held as long as 'ammunition food and water were obtainable' (139).

10.30   Canadian troops in the Mount Cameron area are heavily dive-bombed and mortared (20: 21).

11.00   There is heavy shelling of the Upper Levels police station (72: 55).

12.00   At midday, a shell hits the operating theatre in the hospital at

Stanley, killing an RAMC private. Another shell lands outside a ward, killing and wounding several patients being transferred to another part of the building (27: 43).

12.20   Major J. P. Crowe returns from hospital and takes over command of RA West Group (93: 139).

14.00   Maltby hears that a British 18-pounder at Repulse Bay has knocked out several Japanese mortar positions on Violet Hill,[56] as the Japanese infiltrate down to threaten the Royal Rifle positions on Sugar Loaf and Stanley Mound (20: 22).

14.00   The road between Repulse Bay Hotel and Stanley (used up till this time to evacuate wounded from the former, and bring up water from the latter) is no longer passable (139).

14.00   The Middlesex position[57] just north of Palm Villa is pushed out in a machine-gun and grenade attack, but West of the Middlesex, together with the Royal Rifles, succeed in recapturing the position (139).

14.30   Official Communiqué:

> The enemy continues to press his attack with great energy, and he has succeeded in bringing up some fresh troops. Our forces are defending their positions resolutely with every means at their command. (147)

15.00   The Ridge comes under heavy artillery and mortar fire. Captain Strellett tries to surrender but has the white flag shot out of his hands. Colonel MacPherson then tries, and falls fatally wounded (15: 147).

16.00   6 Platoon HKVDC withdraws from the Violet Hill area, leaving only a section under Sergeant T. Stainton to watch the area (3: 44).

16.00   Middlesex HQ withdraws from Leighton Hill in the face of very heavy mortar fire (20: 22).

16.20   East Brigade asks Fortress HQ to send Very light pistols and cartridges, and 2-inch mortar ammunition, if an MTB carrying 3.7-inch howitzer ammunition is being sent that night (139).

17.00 Official Communiqué:

    The position remains unchanged since the last communiqué. (147)

18.00 The Japanese massacre thirty civilians at numbers 42B and 44B Blue Pool Road. They include Chao Yut and Mr Sit (both of the Ministry of Communications).

18.00 The Japanese drive the Royal Rifles off Stanley Mound and Stone Hill (139).

18.15 Wallis tells Maltby of his plans for a Royal Rifles counter-attack at first light. The attack will be supported by all fire available against the summits of Stone Hill and Stanley Mound, and will be supported by all Middlesex positions in the Support Area, and No. 2 Company HKVDC from south of Stanley View (139).

19.00 The police party acting as a guard at the military hospital at the Jockey Club is withdrawn to prevent — in the event of a Japanese breakthrough — an armed party being found in the hospital (131).

19.30 6 Platoon HKVDC moves out again detailed to hold the bridge crossing the Lido road at all costs from 20.00 to 03.00. They occupy the bridge after removing Japanese snipers (3: 44).

19.30 Overbays is evacuated, but about thirty-five men are left behind by accident (20: 22).

20.00 The Japanese attack the bridge, overrunning Corporal Sharp's section before being driven off by a bayonet charge (3: 44).

20.00 The Winnipeg Grenadiers on Mount Cameron come under strong mortar and artillery attack after a day of dive-bombing (15: 41).

20.00 The Rajput HQ moves back to Gilman's Garage, Wan Chai (140).

21.00 Splitting up into small parties, about forty men of the RASC and RAOC parties leave The Ridge. They leave two men, including Major C. S. Clarke, to guard MacPherson and the thirty or so wounded (79: 260).[58] Captain Strellett's party reaches 'Twinbrooks',[59] where they hold out until surrendering on the 24th. Company Sergeant Major S. D. Begg's party head for

Repulse Bay, but are fired upon and escape down the cliff at Eucliffe. Taking cover in a cave, they find several Canadians, and are later joined by Company Sergeant Major Hamlen (3: 42). Later, the Japanese attack The Ridge and murder the wounded, whose bodies are found after the surrender by Lieutenant Colonel Lindsay Ride.

21.10 Major Trist (commanding the Canadians and Royal Engineers on Mount Cameron, some 130 strong) runs forward and finds that the Japanese have captured a machine gun and mortar on the right flank. Lieutenant Colonel Sutcliffe orders a withdrawal to Wan Chai Gap. The Japanese themselves (under Doi) receive 9.2-inch fire from Stanley, and 20,000 rounds of .303 from Major H. Marsh's C Company of the Middlesex from Little Hong Kong (95: 128). 'Our effort to hold Mt. Nicholson was harassed by enemy gun fire from Red Pillar Promontory and by machine gun fire from the area south of Mt. Nicholson' (122).

22.00 The evacuation of military personnel from Repulse Bay Hotel[60] starts down a drain discovered by a Dutch engineer, Jan Marsman. The drain leads from the hotel to Lower Beach Road, and then past the Lido up to Island Road. Benny Proulx of the HKRNVR leads the first party down, but they make so much noise that Major Templer decides to lead the others to Stanley on the open road.

24.00 After the soldiers depart, Japanese troops enter the hotel, now just occupied by civilians.[61] One member of the hotel staff, the 'Number 1 Boy', is bayoneted (44: 98). The soldiers then approach the wounded with fixed bayonets, but nurse Elizabeth Mosey blocks their way. They turn away and, at this 'hospital' at least, no murders are committed. However, the civilians find a Rifleman Riley of the Royal Rifles still in the hotel, drunk. To avoid recriminations they dress him in ordinary clothes and pass him off as a civilian (14: 102). [62]

24.00 The Japanese attack the two platoons of Second Lieutenant Cheesewright's[63] and Private Matthews'[64] (C Coy. Middlesex) pillbox on the eastern shore of Repulse Bay (15: 137). During the night, the Middlesex evacuate all five of these pillboxes and march to Stanley (the others in the party included Sgt. Manning) (96: 41).

24.00 Some men left behind at Overbays are found by RAOC Quartermaster Sergeant Singleton. He tells them that the house is being surrendered in order to give the responsibility for the wounded to the Japanese. The men are ordered to pile up their arms (95: 117).

24.00 D Company Middlesex establishes positions on the catchwaters north of Stanley Road (139).

Roll of Honour for 22 December

RAMC — 1 Killed

McIndoe, Harry   Private   K
  Buried at Stanley. Almost certainly the private killed by shellfire at   [23 Dec.]
  Stanley College.

HEADQUARTERS — 2 Killed

Clarke, Charles Sydney   Major, General List   K
  Killed at The Ridge, where he stayed to look after MacPherson   [19/25 Dec.]
  (132b: Browne)

Lyndon, Charles A.   Major, Royal Canadian Armoured Corps   U
  Shot by own men while returning to lines unexpectedly.

PUNJABIS — 1 Killed

Ganda Singh   Sepoy   U
  (145: 76) says admitted to Queen Mary Hospital 20 Dec., died 22 Dec.   [29 Dec.]

RAJPUTS — 1 Killed

Amir Muhammad   Jemadar   U
  Killed at 16.00 by same mortar attack that wounds Lieutenant Offer (140).

ROYAL SCOTS — 9 Killed

Alexander, Robert Hunter   Private   U
  Killed Wan Chai area (126).

Buchanan, Alexander   Private   K
  Died of wounds in hospital (145: 131). Buried No. 2 Crater, Borret Road (126), thus
  BRH.

Callender, John Taylor   Corporal   K
  Died in hospital (145: 131).[65]

PHASE V: PUSHING THE LINE WEST AND ENCIRCLING STANLEY   209

Clark, John Harvey	Private	U
Admitted same day, and died Queen Mary Hospital (145: 73).		
Henderson, William	Private	U
Missing Sir Cecil's Ride area (126).		
Marshall, William	Bandsman	U
Killed Sir Cecil's Ride area (126).		
Galley, Thomas	Private	U
(145: 180) 22 Dec. Killed Sir Cecil's Ride area (126).		[21 Dec.]
Thomson, Thomas Crookston	Private	U
(145: 180) 22 Dec. Killed Sir Cecil's Ride area (126).		[21 Dec.]
Williamson, Charles	Lance Corp.	K
Died in hospital (145: 134). Originally buried behind SAH (126).		

SIGNALS — 1 Killed

Fairley, J. Lloyd   Signalman, Royal Canadian Corps of Signals   K
    Died in hospital (145: 137) of wounds (142). Buried No. 2 Crater, Bowen Road.

ARTILLERY — 5 Killed

Ali Muhammad	Jemadar, Depot Bty. HKSRA	U
(126) states 'Kowloon' though without a date and under 20 Coast Bty. HKSRA.		
Aurangzeb Khan	Gunner, 2 Mountain Bty. HKSRA	U
Fazl Dad	Gunner, 2 Mountain Bty. HKSRA	U
Admitted WMH 22 Dec. and died same day (145: 94).		
Sarfaraz Khan	Gunner, 3 Medium Bty. HKSRA	U
Burn, Jonathon	Gunner, 8 Coast Regt. RA	K
Originally buried Guard Room, Stanley Fort, on 22 Dec. (126).		[8 Dec.]

RAOC — 23 Killed[66]

(All presumably at The Ridge/Overbays/Eucliffe)

Adams, John Samuel Russell	Sergeant, RAOC	U
Burroughs, Sydney Gilbert	Captain, RAOC	U
Cole, Dennis Roy	Private, RAOC	U
Duffield, Sampson John	Staff Sergeant, RAOC	U
Dulson, Harry	Private, RAOC	U
Harland, Harry	Private, RAOC	U
Hearn, James Nelson	Warrant Officer II, Squadron Quartermaster Sergeant, RAOC	U
Johnson, Jack	Lance Corporal, RAOC	K

MacPherson, Robert Archibald	Lieutenant Colonel, RAOC	K
DOW after trying to surrender The Ridge.		
Martin, Albert George	Corporal, RAOC	U
Morries, Horace	Warrant Officer I, Sub-Conductor, RAOC	U
Nicholson, William	Sergeant, RAOC	K
Pennington, Arnold	Lance Corporal, RAOC	U
Simms, John Scott	Corporal, RAOC	U
Standing, Herbert	Lance Corporal, RAOC	U
Stopforth, Clifford	Private, RAOC	U
Taylor, David Alexander	Private, RAOC	U
Originally buried south garden no. 5, The Ridge (126).		
Thrush, Francis Robert	Corporal, RAOC	U
Wallington, Charles Thomas	Lieutenant, RAOC	U
Wynne, Richard Alfred	Lieutenant, RAOC	U
Eucliffe. See (137).		
Desroches, Gerald G.	Corporal, RCOC	U
The Ridge (126).		[19 Dec.]
Jackman, George	Staff Sergeant, RCOC	U
The Ridge (126).		[19 Dec.]
McGuire, Frank C.	Private, RCOC	U
The Ridge (126).		[19 Dec.]

WINNIPEGS — 10 Killed

Boyd, David V.	Lance Corporal	U
Last seen Wong Nai Chung (126).		
Dowswell, Melvin S.	Private	U
Killed Wong Nai Chung (126).		
Foord, Frank M.	Private	U
Mount Cameron (126).		
Hargreaves, John	Private	U
Kasijan, Mike	Private	U
Buried Wan Chai Gap (126).		
Long, John	Sergeant	U
Reported killed by a shell on Mt. Cameron on 12 Dec. (1: 70).		
MacFarlane, George	Private	K
Died in hospital (145: 138).		
Piasta, Henry	Private	K
Killed Mount Cameron (126).		

Swanson, Edwin   Private   U
   Last seen Wong Nai Chung (126).

White, Thomas C.   Private   U
   Died at Repulse Bay (126).

VOLUNTEERS — 19 Killed

White, Norbert Leyburn   Sergeant, 1 Coy. HKVDC   K
   DOW sustained at bottom of Red Hill previous day

Rouban, Michael John   Lance Bombardier, 5AA Bty HKVDC   K

Flegg, Jack Sydney   Staff Sergeant, PWD Corps HKVDC   U
   Bayoneted, 'with his assistant', at Tai Tam reservoir (114: 40).

Rathsam, Henry Walter   Private, 3 Coy. HKVDC   U
   KIA area of Leighton Hill, 22 Dec. (126).

(All presumably at The Ridge/Overbays/Eucliffe)

Brown, Conrad   Private, RASC Coy. HKVDC   U

Elliott, Frank   Private, RASC Coy. HKVDC   U
   Missing believed KIA at Repulse Bay Hotel garages (126).[67]

Fox, George Edmond   Private, RASC Coy. HKVDC   U

Hillier, Wilfred Samuel   Sergeant, RASC Coy. HKVDC   K
   Ex-Watson's employee (141). Initially buried Repulse Bay Hotel about 18 Dec. (145: 19).[68]

Jorge, Francis   Private, RASC Coy. HKVDC   U
   Killed Repulse Bay Hotel garage area (126).

Joseph, H. B.   Private, RASC Coy. HKVDC   U

Kern, E.   Private, RASC Coy. HKVDC   U
   KIA Repulse Bay Hotel garages (126).

Lyen, Edmund Symlov   Private, RASC Coy. HKVDC   U
   KIA Repulse Bay Hotel garages (126).

McCallum, Duncan   Sergeant, RASC Coy. HKVDC   U

Mann, A.   Company Quartermaster Sergeant,   U
                               RASC Coy. HKVDC

Minhinnett, John Denniford   Private, RASC Coy. HKVDC   U
   KIA Repulse Bay Hotel garages (126).

Peters, William Henry   Private, RASC Coy. HKVDC   U
   Missing believed KIA at Repulse Bay Hotel garages (126).

Prew, Albert George   Private, RASC Coy. HKVDC   U
   Missing believed KIA at Repulse Bay Hotel garages (126).

Rapp, Frederick Austin   Private, RASC Coy. HKVDC   U

Zaharoff, Victor Isidor   Private, RASC Coy. HKVDC   U
   Killed at Eucliffe (126).

RASC — 8 Killed[69]

(All presumably at The Ridge/Overbays/Eucliffe)

Cullen, Edward James   Driver, RASC   U
   Missing (145: 190).

Cullen, William Jamieson   Driver, 12 Coy. RASC   U
   Killed The Ridge (126).[70]   [8/25 Dec.]

Jacobs, Edward   Driver, 12 Coy. RASC   U
   Missing (145: 189). Killed The Ridge (126).   [8/25 Dec.]

Kingsford, Edward Cyril   Corporal, 12 Coy. RASC   U
   Missing (145: 188).

Kloss, Rudolph Leopold   Captain, RASC   U
   Reported as killed (145: 187) at The Ridge (94: 106).[71] Head of NAAFI.   [8/25 Dec.]

Wilson, Robert Henry   Driver, 12 Coy. RASC   U
   Missing (145: 188).

Berger, Max   Private, RCASC   U
   Killed at The Ridge (126).   [19 Dec.]

Jackson, Albert   Corporal, RCASC   U
   The Ridge (126).   [19 Dec.]

ROYAL RIFLES — 18 Killed

(Likely Stanley Mound/Sugarloaf, and some at Overbays and Eucliffe)

Bate, Ernest   Rifleman   U
   KIA and buried Stanley Mound (126).

Doyle, Joseph L.   Rifleman   U
   Last seen at Spanish house between Repulse and Deep Water Bays (126). Eucliffe?

Fitzpatrick, John J.   Corporal   U
   Possibly the 'Jack' mentioned in Skelton's diary, in which case killed by a shell.[72]

Gallant, Benjamin J.   Rifleman   U
   KIA and buried Stanley Mound (126).

Gallant, Clement   Rifleman   U
   Last seen at Repulse Bay (126). Eucliffe?

Gammack, Maurice   Rifleman   U
   KIA and buried Stanley View (126).

Keating, Edward R.   Rifleman   U
   KIA and buried Stanley Mound (126).

Latimer, Lorne   Corporal   K
   Killed putting the Vickers gun at Palm Villa back into action (100: 80).

McNab, Lorne R.   Sergeant   U
    Last seen at junction of Repulse Bay and Island Road (126). Eucliffe?

Newell, Lorne R.   Rifleman   U
    Buried Stanley Mound (126).

Noel, William H.   Rifleman   U
    KIA and buried Stanley Mound (126).

Pollock, Duncan M.   Rifleman   U
    KIA and buried Stanley Mound (126).

Rooney, Leonard   Rifleman   U
    KIA and buried Stanley Mound (126).

Ross, James F.   Lieutenant   U
    KIA and buried Stanley Mound (126).

Sannes, Aksel   Lance Corporal   K
    Recapturing the Vickers guns on Sugar Loaf Hill (100: 81).

Smith, William J.   Lance Corporal   U
    KIA and buried Stanley Mound (126).

Sullivan, Fergus   Rifleman   U
    KIA and buried Stanley Mound (126).

Wonnacot, Alfred   Sergeant   K
    Buried Notting Hill by Rifleman Savage and Major MacAuley (126).

ENGINEERS — 6 Killed

Ashley, Charles   Sapper, 40 Fortress Coy. RE   U
    Killed west side Wong Nai Chung Gap (126).

Byres, Stephen   Sapper, 40 Fortress Coy. RE   U
    Killed west side Wong Nai Chung Gap (126).   [22 Dec. 1951]

Murray, Thomas   Sapper, 40 Fortress Coy. RE   U
    Missing south side Wong Nai Chung Gap (126).

Shale, John   Sapper, 40 Fortress Coy. RE   U
    DOW (126).

Todd, Bernard Williams   Sapper, 40 Fortress Coy. RE   K
    Buried north end North Point camp 22 Dec. (126).   [8/25 Dec.]

Cheung Sun Hon   Sapper, 22 Coy. RE   U

MIDDLESEX — 1 Killed

Connolly, Oliver John   Private   U
    Buried at Repulse Bay Hotel grounds (126).

CIVILIANS — 2 Killed

Dobbs, Francis E. L.   UCWD
   Killed fighting with the HKVDC.[73]

Rozario, Mrs M.   Portuguese   UX
   Died in the Matilda Hospital aged 80.

ROYAL NAVY — 1 Killed

Dallow, S.   Warrant Officer, HKRNVR   UP
   Possibly mentioned (54: 52), in which case killed at the Repulse Bay Hotel.[74]

23 DECEMBER TUESDAY

> As we heard it the Officer (Jap) in charge had a brother that had been wounded (another officer) and everything that could be done was done for him and this officer knew that. They got every one out of bed and into the cafeteria (where all tables had been removed) then they brought in 2 tables and set up machine guns on them and started playing with them. By then we were all sitting on the floor while they searched the hospital. After about 2 hrs we went back to our rooms, where we were told to keep away from the windows and he was going to leave guards but had left orders that no one was to be hurt and the hospital was to carry on with the wounded. That was Dec. 23. Then on Xmas day we were brought in 2 beers each. We were very very fortunate it was that officer. (Ray Smith)[75]

In the west, the day starts with the fall of Mount Cameron. West Brigade's whole line then comes under attack, at Leighton Hill, at the Royal Scots' positions, and in the Bennet's Hill/Little Hong Kong area. The Japanese try to take Wan Chai Gap but are beaten off by Royal Scots and Royal Marines from the dockyard. The Rajputs are pushed back at the Happy Valley racecourse under heavy pressure, but the line holds. The Middlesex on Leighton Hill are now under almost continuous attack. During the morning, twenty-five wounded Rajputs from hospital are formed into a new platoon under Jemadar Shah Muhammad at Leighton Hill.

    At St Albert's Convent on Stubbs Road (being used as a 400-bed auxiliary hospital) Japanese refrain from harming the captured inmates after finding one of their own men there.[76] Other histories often comment

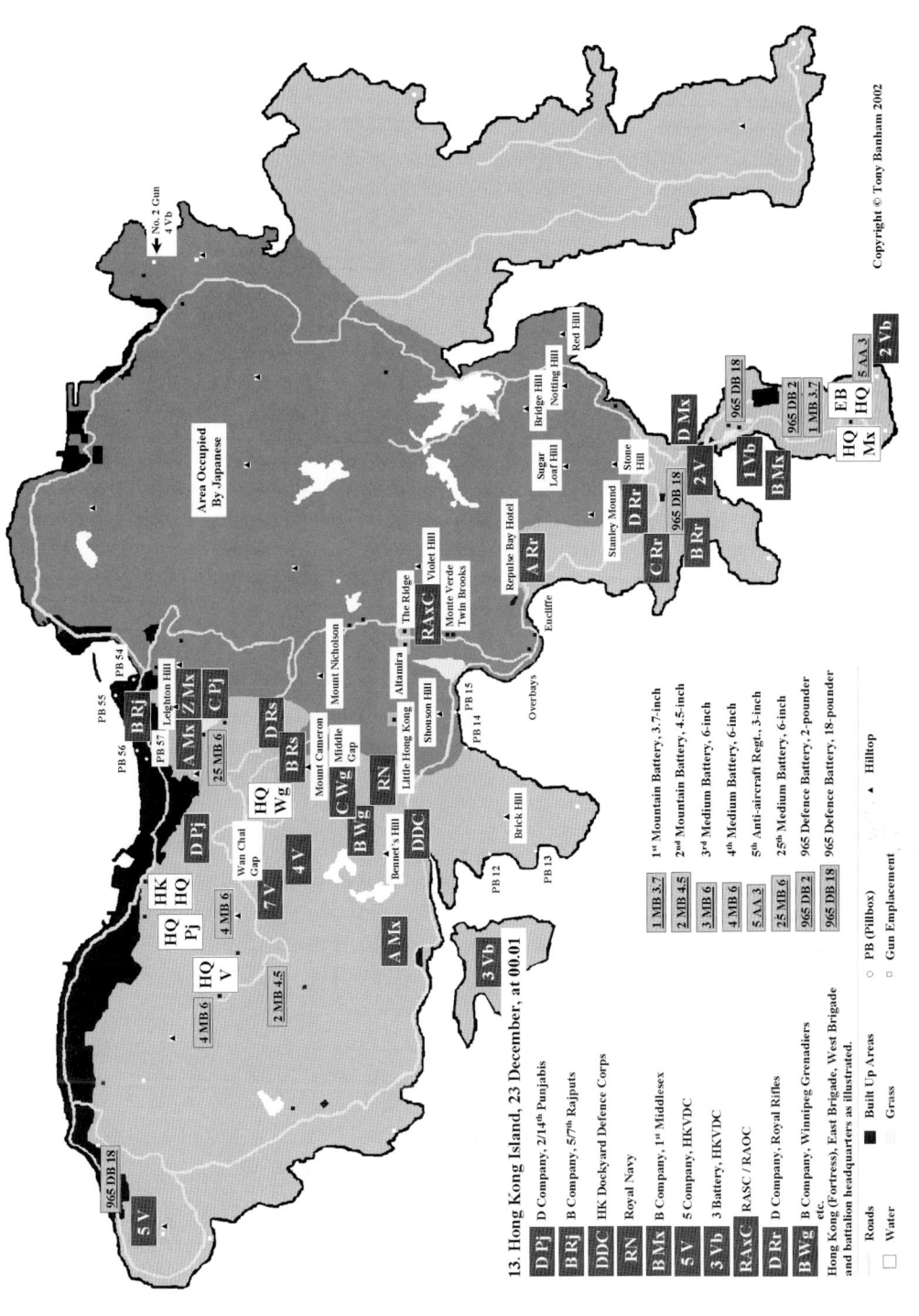

that there was only one recorded example of British wounded receiving aid from Japanese troops. This was the case of Private Jimmy Edulji Mogra, HKVDC, son of Mrs Waki Mogra of Hong Kong. Private Mogra had been born and raised in Japan, and was picked up after calling to them — in Japanese — for water.[77] The St Albert's example, it must be said, is the only one on record on Japanese wounded receiving aid from the British. However, this is a result of the fact that the British were largely in retreat and seldom occupied ground on which fighting had previously occurred.

In the late afternoon, Marsh (of Middlesex C Coy.) gets through to PB 14 — south of Little Hong Kong[78] — on the phone for the last time and talks to Sergeant George Rich. Sergeant Rich, Corporal 'Timber' Wood, Lance Corporal George Bailey, Private Reg Bosley, Private Don Burke, Private Bill Ball, Private Walter Bywaters, Private Eddie Edwards, and Private Harry Newbury are engaging Japanese 20 yards away. There are no survivors from this pillbox. Nearby, eight ammunition lorries escorted by an armoured car (under the charge of the ever-busy 2nd Lt. Carruthers) manage to drive from the ordnance depot at Little Hong Kong to the northern perimeter. Six return safely.

Accidents also take their toll: 'In the change-over of one of the posts in the Flagstaff area, the incoming relief accidentally fired a Bren Gun and shot one of the Punjabis being relieved. I had to get Major Goring to come up from the Battle Box to pacify Havildar Nurkhan in charge of the Punjabi section who was naturally furious': Bunny Browne (132b: Browne).[79]

By this time, the debris of war is all over the Island. John Whitehead reports, while driving near Wong Nai Chung towards Tai Tam, coming under heavy fire and seeing Sikh and Muslim dead (presumably HKSRA) on a ridge there (30: 32). Leiper notes the effects of bombing: 'There was a dreadful shambles all around the Helena May institute, where a stick of bombs had fallen. Collapsed walls and other debris blocked the path between the institute and the Peak Tram track and, as I clambered over this, I saw three dead bodies and various parts of others lying around' (5: 82).

In urban areas, fighting takes place in Hennessy, Perceval, and Blue Pool Roads. The Japanese soldiers continue with their attacks on the civilian population. The tenant of a Happy Valley apartment, Phyllis Harrop, returns home to find the amah raped and forty people killed by Japanese in her block of flats. A police patrol under Luscombe clears looters from Causeway Bay early in the morning, but comes under heavy Japanese fire as they cross Jardine's Bazaar. Two officers are wounded. Looting on the Island was by now a serious problem. Bethell: 'The looting was horrific. You could see from where we were at the back of the police station the fighting on the roof . . . and people were just being flung off the roof onto the streets' (132a: Bethell).

For East Brigade, the day starts when Brigadier Wallis sends the Royal Rifles to re-take Stanley Mound and Stone Hill. They succeed with heavy casualties after three hand-to-hand attacks, but fall back under intense shelling and withdraw to Stanley. The Japanese then press forward to attack Stanley View where they destroy one 965 Defence Battery 18-pounder from the Repulse Bay section. Stanley View is held by the Scottish Volunteers of 2 Company HKVDC. Private Walker's section of No. 6 Platoon fight off the initial attacks, but later, heavier attacks fall on Corporal Sharp's section on the hill overlooking Island Road. Sharp is killed. Prophet then withdraws the Platoon to join No. 7 (Lt. Bryden) on the ridge between Chung Hom Kok and Stanley View.[80] No. 2 Company is then brought back to Stanley (44: 99). During this time, more than 1800 Japanese shells land on Stanley Fort (15: 155), and fifty to sixty patients are transferred from St Stephen's to the hospital at Stanley prison (27: 43).

Wallis plans a Commando-style raid on Tai Tam crossroads. The plan is to take a motor torpedo boat carrying a raiding party of RNVR and Middlesex volunteers under Captain West (armed exclusively with Thompson sub-machine guns and grenades), and land them on the east side of Red Hill to conduct a surprise attack. The plan is called off when it is found that no motor torpedo boat can be spared (139).

B Company Royal Rifles is ordered to take up a position across the Chung Hom Kok peninsula to prevent the Japanese occupying it and firing at Stanley from another angle.

An attempt by the Middlesex to link up from Stanley to the Repulse Bay area is unsuccessful. It is lead by Lieutenant M. H. Falconar, who runs into heavy machine-gun fire. Falconar and four of his men are killed, two wounded (96: 39).

Prime Minister Winston Churchill telegraphs Governor Mark Young:

> There must be no thought of surrender. Every part of the Island must be fought and the enemy resisted with the utmost stubbornness. The enemy should be compelled to expend the

utmost life and equipment. There must be vigorous fighting in the inner defences and, if need be from house to house. Every day that you are able to maintain your resistance you help the Allied cause all over the world, and by a prolonged resistance you and your men can win the lasting honour which we are sure will be your due.

In the evening, a counter-attack at Stanley Mound is supported by mobile artillery and 2nd Battery HKVDC at Bluff Head.

During the night, Home demands to speak to Maltby and tells him that his unit was unfit for further fighting, and that 'continued resistance could only endanger further Canadian lives'. In the presences of Wilcox, Maltby tries to encourage him to continue, saying:

(i) We were a formidable force holding a strong though badly overlooked position. A position it would be costly for the enemy to attack.
(ii) We had ammunition, food and water enough (in spite of water damage which was and could be repaired). That no other troops dreamt of surrender.
(iii) Anyhow we were paid as soldiers to fight and now was our chance. We were containing a strong enemy force, thereby relieving pressure on our sorely pressed comrades elsewhere on the Island.
(iv) We all knew what our gallant Prime Minister expected of us. [Wallis] added that he felt sure the Prime Minister of Canada also expected us to fight on. Furthermore, to surrender in such circumstances would be an action on the part of a Unit Commander which [Wallis] had never before heard of in British history. Such an action [Wallis] said he considered dishonourable.[81]

At the same time, George Verrault of the Canadian Signals notes in his diary: 'Now it's every man for himself for we can no longer count on our officers. Because of their uselessness we have suffered immense losses. The guys are resigned to their lot, but I can't bring myself to give up all hope. It seems impossible that I die. I ask mother in the heavens to help us' (14: 92).

Meanwhile, the Japanese re-group for another attack tomorrow.

Diary for 23 December

00.10 During the night, the Japanese overrun Mount Cameron (defended by 100 Winnipeg Grenadiers of C Coy. and thirty Royal Engineers) in suicidal attacks after intense bombardment. The Grenadiers retreat to Wan Chai Gap, and then on to Magazine Gap. Lieutenant Colonel F. D. Field (RA) goes forward to Wan Chai Gap with a reserve force of forty men of the Royal Marines under Major Farrington. Nos. 4 and 7 Companies of the HKVDC are brought forward to man the line there (44: 99).

01.00 Mount Cameron is reported as definitely held by the Japanese (93: 139).

01.20 The water supply from Tai Tam reservoir is cut (79: 263).

02.00 Parties of Canadians arrive in Aberdeen reporting that they have been driven off Mount Cameron and Bennet's Hill. Commander Pears then takes three naval Platoons to the crest of Bennet's Hill and holds it until shellfire becomes too intense (143f).

Haines of the HKDDC: 'Fighting raged around us in the hills but by an act of Providence the Japs did not attack our position. Had they done so, we would have been easy prey. Apart from one part day at Stonecutters Island having instruction in rifle and revolver shooting, the great majority of us had no military experience whatsoever' (132b: Haines).

02.30 C Company Winnipeg Grenadiers move from their position in the area of Bennet's Hill to Aberdeen. There they find ten Navy personnel, one Royal Marines officer, forty-three HKDDC, and fourteen RAF. Later they are ordered back towards Bennet's Hill (95: 129).

03.00 Having successfully covered the withdrawal from the Repulse Bay Hotel, No. 6 Platoon HKVDC falls back from the bridge they had been defending. They encounter a Japanese force near Frederick's house before retiring to Stanley.

03.45   The Royal Engineers report that their rear party is still in position on Mount Kellet (20: 22).

04.00   A new mobile artillery HQ is formed at Victoria Gap, that at Wan Chai Gap having withdrawn with the infantry (93: 139).

07.00   Eight Middlesex machine guns put down supporting fire on the crests of Stanley Mound and Stone Hill in support of a Canadian attempt to recapture the positions. This reveals the Middlesex positions, and PB 27 plus positions near St Stephen's College and No. 1 Bungalow all come under artillery fire (139).

07.30   The Royal Rifles are back in possession of Stanley Mound (139).

08.00   The Rajputs, after suffering heavy casualties and being short of ammunition, fall back. This exposes the right flank of Z Company on Leighton Hill (79: 264).

08.00   As forces withdraw, the wounded at Overbays are left for the Japanese who promptly murder them (20: 22).[82] Private L. Canivet:

> the Japs stormed the house using hand grenades and a small portable machine gun. The wounded men downstairs were literally murdered in cold blood. Our white flag was torn down, and our interpreter was bayoneted and pinned to a door to die. The Japs came upstairs and kicked open the door of the room we were in, there being about thirty of us. First they sprayed the room with machine gun fire and followed it up with a barrage of grenades . . . we got as many of the wounded out of the windows as possible and then jumped out ourselves. (95: 117)[83]

08.30   Official Communiqué:

> Fighting continues all along the lines held yesterday, with a local success for us in the South. Small parties of our administrative personnel, not normally equipped or trained for active combat but now fighting in advance posts, have shown great determination and courage; in many cases beating off enemy units attempting to over-run their positions, and in other cases fighting to the last. The value to operations as a whole of such fine resistance cannot be overestimated. (147)

09.00	Little Hong Kong magazine reports that the Japanese are advancing in strength both there and on Bennet's Hill (79: 264).
09.00	The Japanese attack all along the Royal Scots' front, but they are beaten off (92: 124).
09.22	Z Company, Middlesex at Leighton Hill reduced to forty men and six Vickers machine-guns as Japanese infiltrate the houses to the east (20: 23).
09.30	The Japanese enter St Albert's Convent Hospital on Stubbs Road. Rifleman Smith: 'I had three good friends (Malcolm Nicholson, George Baker, and Ralph Coleman) who were to be discharged so they were back in uniform when the British Officer in charge made an announcement over the P.A. that those being discharged get back into Hospital Blues as he had to surrender the Hospital' (132b: Smith).
10.00	Leighton Hill is heavily shelled (79: 264). Z Company loses sixteen men during the day (96: 42).
10.10	Wallis reports to Maltby that the Japanese have succeeded in driving the Royal Rifles off Stanley Mound after their previous counter-attack, and that they have eighteen officers killed, wounded, or missing, and only 350 men left. The Royal Rifles are therefore ordered to withdraw after dark to new positions with one company at Maryknoll, one further back at St Stephen's, and one in reserve near the preparatory school (139).
10.27	The 40-mm Bofors gun on the cricket ground is shelled and withdrawn to Government House. Later it is moved to Victoria Recreation Club (93: 139).[84]
11.00	Leighton Hill is heavily shelled and mortared again (79: 264). The guns move into the Lee Theatre (20: 23).
12.00	The line runs from PB 55 to the Lee Theatre, Leighton Hill, Canal Road, north end of the racecourse, Morrison Hill, Mount Parrish,[85] west of St Albert's, Wan Chai Gap, and Bennet's Hill (3: 48).

13.30   Wan Chai Gap and Magazine Gap are heavily dive-bombed (79: 264).

13.30   It is reported that around 250 Japanese troops are in the area of St. Albert's Convent (20: 23).

14.30   Official Communiqué:

> Fighting continues along last night's lines with undiminished intensity. As a result of continuous attack, there was a slight enemy penetration in the central sector in the Mount Cameron direction: this penetration has been contained by our troops since early this morning. Enemy bombardments from aircraft, mortars and artillery of all calibres continue on our positions, Briefly, the situation is substantially unchanged. (147)

15.00   A scratch reserve force of convalescents (Royal Scots, gunners, signallers) is assembled at Fortress HQ. They are sent forward to occupy the Lee Theatre in Causeway Bay (79: 264).[86]

15.00   The Japanese attack across the Happy Valley racecourse. They are repulsed with heavy losses.

15.30   Heavy shellfire falls on all Middlesex machine-gun positions in the Stanley area. Bridge Hill is lost (139).

16.45   Shellfire knocks out the army's last communications with the UK. Communication from now on is via the Navy's radios (20: 23).

17.00   Official Communiqué:

> Two enemy attacks have been beaten off with heavy losses to the Japanese. Our casualties were light. The situation remains unaltered and we have maintained our lines. (147)

17.30   A party of Royal Scots under Sergeant Richardson[87] secures a foothold on the western slope of Mount Cameron (92: 125).

19.00   As ordered, the Royal Rifles have withdrawn to their new positions (139).

19.30   Company Sergeant Major Begg's group start their swim from Repulse Bay to Stanley. The phosphorescence in the water gives

PHASE V: PUSHING THE LINE WEST AND ENCIRCLING STANLEY   223

20.00   No. 2 Company HKVDC takes up positions at Chung Hum Kok (139).

20.30   C Company Winnipeg Grenadiers, reinforced by eighty more men, returns to Aberdeen reservoir (95: 129).

Roll of Honour for 23 December

VOLUNTEERS — 9 Killed

Barton, William Maurice   Private, Armoured Car Platoon HKVDC   K
   Died in hospital (145: 126).

Maxwell, Ronald Douglas   Private, 3 Coy. HKVDC   K
   Killed in Wan Chai (*South China Morning Post* 10 Mar. 1993). By shrapnel (23: 232).
   Buried in St John's Cathedral grounds.[88]

Cunningham, Albert Laing   Corporal, RASC Coy. HKVDC   K
   Driver 74. Admitted to Queen Mary Hospital 19 Dec. 1941, died 23 Dec. 1941 (145: 74).

Delcourt, Armand   Private, RASC Coy. HKVDC   K[89]
   Said to have died of wounds from The Ridge, but actually murdered   [21 Dec.]
   at Eucliffe (137).

Bonner, Horace William   Corporal, RASC Coy. HKVDC   K
   Killed at Overbays (126).   [22 Dec.]

White, Nowell Bernard   Lance Corporal, RASC Coy. HKVDC   U
   Killed at Overbays (126).   [22 Dec.]

Zimmern, W. A.   Corporal, RASC Coy. HKVDC   UX
   Killed at Overbays (126). (94: 101) states that Zimmern was killed in the drive of Overbays.

Sharp, William   Lance Corporal, 2 Coy. HKVDC   U
   Killed on Stanley View (overlooking Island Road).

Calman, Alexander[90]   Private, 2 Coy. HKVDC   U
   Killed at Eucliffe (126).   [23 Nov.]

WINNIPEGS — 5 Killed

(Mount Cameron)

Blanchard, Robert   Private   K
   Killed Bennet's Hill shelter (126).

Osadchuck, Nicholas A.	Private	U

(136) reports that he was bayoneted near Wong Nai Chung Gap AA position (as 'Osadchuk'), in which case 19th.[91]

Rutherford, George Alexander	Private	K

Buried Repulse Bay (pillbox) (126).

Shore, William	Private	K
Vickers, Jack F.	Corporal	U

MIDDLESEX — 21 Killed

(Little Hong Kong, Leighton Hill, breaking out of Stanley towards Repulse Bay)

Bailey, Joseph William	Lance Corporal	U

Presumably 'George' Bailey who died defending PB 14.[92]   [8/25 Dec.]

Ball, Walter John	Private	K

Said to have died defending PB 14 with Private Burke. His brother T. E. died 12 Aug. 1940.   [31 Dec.]

Bosley, Reginald Caleb	Private	K

Killed defending PB 14.   [25 Dec.]

Boyd, Douglas Clifford	Private	U

Killed Morrison Hill area (126).

Burke, Daniel	Private	K

Killed defending PB 14.   [8/25 Dec.]

Bywater, William	Private	U

Presumably 'Walter' Bywater who was killed defending PB 14. Willian's first name and Walter Ball's (above) appear to have been transposed.   [25 Dec.]

Cummings, Henry Harry	Private	U

Killed Morrison Hill area (126).

Edwards, Edward John	Private	K

Killed defending PB 14.   [25 Dec.]

Falconar, Maurice Hall	Lieutenant	K

Killed by machine gun, trying to bridge from Stanley to Repulse Bay. Stanley Mound (126).

Groves, Albert Arthur	Private	U
Hitchins, Henry Ronald	Private	U

Killed Morrison Hill area (126).

Lewis, Charles Frederick	Private	U

Killed with Falconar. Morrison Hill.

Merry, John Albert	Private	K

D Coy. Originally buried Stanley Prison 27 Dec. (126).

Newbury, Henry	Private	U

Presumably 'Harry' Newbury who was killed defending PB 14.   [25 Dec.]

Perry, John Thomas	Private	U
DOW from shelling of No. 1 Bungalow, Stanley (139).[93]		
Pigott, Richard Stephen	Second Lieutenant	U
Attached HK Chinese Regiment (145: 151). Killed Overbays area (126).		[22 Dec.]
Rich, Jack	Sergeant	K
Killed defending PB 14.	[25 Dec.]	
Stutz, Winston George	Private	K
Hit in stomach by three machine-gun bullets. Died on the march back to Stanley. Stanley Mound area (126).		
Warner, Charles Alfred	Private	U
Killed with Falconar.[94]		
Wood, William Henry	Corporal	K
Killed defending PB 14.		[25 Dec.]
Young, Harold Alexander	Lance Corp.	U

SIGNALS — 2 Killed

Somerville, George	Sergeant, Royal Corps of Signals, HK Sig. Coy.	K
Admitted WMH 23 Dec., died same day (145: 97).		[8/25 Dec.]
Southwell, Frederick Jesse	Lieutenant, Royal Corps of Signals	K
Admitted WMH 23 Dec., died same day (145: 97).		

ROYAL RIFLES — 39 Killed

(Stanley Mound/Stone Hill, with some from Overbays and Eucliffe)

Acorn, John M.	Rifleman	U
Acorn, Joseph A.	Rifleman	U
Allen, Louis	Rifleman	U
Last seen at Eucliffe (126).		
Andrews, Albert L.	Rifleman	U
Last seen Repulse Bay Hotel, dead in a pillbox (126).		
Atwood, Percy C.	Rifleman	U
Last seen at Repulse Bay (126).		
Beattie, Leonard	Sergeant	U
Best, William	Rifleman	U
Last seen at Repulse Bay (126).		
Bouley, Narcisse	Rifleman	U
KIA and buried Stanley View (126).		
Briand, Rannie	Rifleman	U
Buried at Repulse Bay (126).		

Bujold, Hubert	Rifleman	U
Buried at Repulse Bay (126).		
Chatterton, Orrin James	Rifleman	K
Collins, Alger R.	Corporal	U
Stone Hill (126).		
Doucet, Edgar	Rifleman	U
Firlotte, John F.	Rifleman	U
Geraghty, Oliver	Lance Corporal	U
Buried Stone Hill (126).		
Jackson, Ray	Rifleman	K
Last seen Stone Hill (126).		
Jacques, Daniel	Rifleman	U
KIA at Repulse Bay (126).		
Lapointe, Joseph P.	Rifleman	U
Lebel, Valmont	Rifleman	U
Last seen at Repulse Bay (126).		
Linn, James W.	Rifleman	U
Missing at West Palm Villa (126).		
McGrath, William J.	Rifleman	U
Buried Stanley Mound (126).		
McIsaac, Joseph	Rifleman	U
Last seen at Repulse Bay Hotel (126).		
McWhirter, John	Rifleman	U
Last seen at Repulse Bay Hotel (126).		
Martel, George H.	Corporal	U
Last seen at Spanish house, Deep Water Bay (126).		
Martin, Paul	Rifleman	U
Meredith, Eddie	Lance Corporal	U
Last seen at Repulse Bay (126).		
Mohan, James W.	Lance Corporal	U
Last seen at Repulse Bay Hotel (126).		
Moore, Walter L.	Rifleman	U
Last seen at Repulse Bay (126).		
Pratt, Porter	Rifleman	U
Last seen Lye Mun (126).		
Reid, Colin	Rifleman	U
Last seen wounded in the blazing Overbays house (126).		
Robertson, Oscar	Rifleman	U
Last seen at Repulse Bay (126).		
Scobie, Garnet	Rifleman	U

Sommerville, Reginald D. Last seen at Repulse Bay (126).	Corporal	U
Thorn, Raymond F. Buried saddle between Stone Hill and Stanley Mound (126).	Lieutenant	U
Travers, Charles W. KIA at Repulse Bay (126).	Lance Sergeant	U
Vigneault, Laureat Last seen near water tank, Stanley View (126).	Rifleman	U
Vincent, Robert L.	Lance Corporal	U
Watts, Eric G. Last seen at Repulse Bay Hotel (126).	Rifleman	U
Wills, John Rifleman J. J. McLean saw him killed, Deep Water Bay (126).	Rifleman	K

RAOC — 4 Killed

Jack, Andrew Missing Overbays (126).	Lance Sergeant, RAOC	U [22/23 Dec.]
Percy, William Herbert Missing Overbays (126).	Private, RAOC	U [22 Dec.]
Singleton, John Henry At Overbays?	Warrant Officer II, Squadron QuarterMaster Sergeant, RAOC	U [22 Dec.]
Stonor, John Anthony Killed Overbays (126).	Lance Corporal, RAOC	U [22 Dec.]

RASC — 5 Killed

Aitken, Charles Edgar Missing (145: 189). Killed Magazine Gap (126).	Warrant Officer II, Squadron QuarterMaster Sergeant, RASC	U
Armitage, George Doran Victor Killed at junction of Repulse Bay Road and Island Road (126).[95]	Driver, RASC	U [8/25 Dec.]
Halder, Laurence Arthur	Lance Corporal, 12 HK Coy. RASC	U
Iggleden, Percy Frederick Missing (145: 188). Killed at junction of Repulse Bay Road and Island Road (126).	Warrant Officer I, Staff Sergeant Major, 12 Coy. RASC	U [8/25 Dec.]
Mann, Henry Charles Missing (145: 190). Killed at junction of Repulse Bay Road and Island Road (126).	Sergeant, 12 Coy. RASC	U [8/25 Dec.]

RAJPUTS — 2 Killed

(Northern line)

Altaf Ali	Sepoy	U
Kamal Khan	Sepoy	U

ARTILLERY — 6 Killed

Arjun Singh Gunner, 1 Mountain Bty. HKSRA U
   Died in hospital (145: 141)

Bachan Singh Gunner, 1 Mountain Bty. HKSRA U

Jit Singh Gunner, 2 Mountain Bty. HKSRA U
   Probably buried at Queen Mary Hospital (126).

Swaran Singh Lance Naik, 2 Mountain Bty. HKSRA U
   Died in hospital (145: 141).

Ratan Singh Gunner, 36 Mountain Bty. HKSRA U
   Presumably 3 Medium Bty.

Flanders, John Gunner, 8 Coast Regt. RA K
   Killed in St Barbara's Church, Stanley (93: 142) on 8 Dec. (150). [8/25 Dec.]
   (126) says 23 Dec.

ROYAL SCOTS — 12 Killed

(Wan Chai Gap, defending Northern Line, attacking Mount Cameron)

Collie, John Gibb Private U
   Buried behind St Albert's Hospital towards Mount Nicholson camp (126).

Drysdale, Andrew Gillies Corporal U
   (145: 180) Killed 23 Dec. Hennessey Road, Causeway Bay/ [24 Dec.]
   Wan Chai (126).

Foster, John Willie Private U
   Reported missing 23rd (145: 179).[96] [23/24 Dec.]

Johnson, Harry Lance Corporal U
   Missing, Mount Nicholson camp (126).

Mouat, Andrew Private U
   DOW (126).

Napier, Robert Dickson Private U
   Buried behind St Albert's Hospital towards Mount Nicholson camp (126).

Newsome Jack Renton Private U
   Missing Mount Nicholson camp area (126).

Redpath, Thomas Lance Corporal U
   D Coy. Attached HQ China Command. (145: 168) Husband of K. Y. Redpath of Hong
   Kong.

Shields, David   Private   U
  Killed Mount Nicholson camp area (126).

Webster, Frank   Private   U
  Missing Mount Nicholson camp area (126).

Wilson, Albert   Lance Corp.   U
  Buried behind St Albert's Hospital (126).

Wiseman, William   Corporal   U
  DOW (126).

PUNJABIS — 1 Killed

Fazl Karim   Lance Havildar,   U
  Possibly killed by accident with a Bren gun outside Brigade HQ.

ENGINEERS — 2 Killed

Fooks, Herbert John   Sergeant, 22 Fortress Coy. RE   K
  Killed north side of Repulse Bay Hotel, 23 Dec. (126).   [8/25 Dec.]

Lee, John   Sapper, 22 Fortress Coy. RE   U
  Missing, possibly Overbays area, 23 Dec. (126).   [8/25 Dec.]

POLICE — 1 Killed

Wong Chung   Constable, HKPF   U[98]

ROYAL NAVY — 5 Killed

Menhinick, Digby Collins   Sergeant, Royal Marines HMS *Tamar*   K
  Originally buried No. 2 Crater, Borret Road (i.e. BRH) (126).

Gibbs, W   Warrant Officer, HKRNVR   UP
  KIA area of Repulse Bay, 22 Dec. (126).

Goldenberg, I L   Warrant Officer, HKRNVR   UP
  KIA area of Repulse Bay, 22 Dec. (126).

Oliver, George Kenneth   Sub-Lieutenant, HKRNVR   UP
  KIA area of Repulse Bay, 22 Dec. (126).

Jenkinson, John Oliver   Ordinary Seaman HMS *Thracian*, RN   UC
  Admitted Queen Mary Hospital 20 Dec. Died 23 Dec. (145: 79).   [19 Dec.]

CIVILIANS — 2 Killed

Si Pani Mohd   UCWD
  According to (145: 140) Sipana Mohd was 'others', number 14625, and died in hospital.[98]

Whealan, Peter   Brother   UX
  Killed during an ambulance mission in Causeway Bay with Private A. B. Carvalho, Field Ambulance (132b: Ride).

24 DECEMBER WEDNESDAY

> I was at the bottom of the slope when I heard a burst of Bren gun fire from the trench and started to go back up the hill to find out what was going on. I got within a short distance when a mortar shell exploded in the trench. All that was left of the occupants was a bloody mess of corpses — all with the exception of Sawyer who was standing in the ruins dazed and bewildered but, otherwise, unharmed. (Roger Rothwell)[99]

At Argyle Street camp in Kowloon, Dr Newton notes: '950 Canadian, British and Indian troops. 150 of them wounded' (95: 157).[101]

On the Island, the Middlesex are finally pushed off Leighton Hill, and to the west, a bombing raid starts on the Naval Dockyards (15: 157). Nearby: 'On Xmas Eve 1941, about ten captives including myself, were all locked in a room in the St. John's Ambulance headquarters at Tai Hang Road. During our stay there, we had in our possession only dog biscuits and water' (132b: Fallon).

The skirmishes in the Causeway Bay/Wan Chai area degenerate into particularly nasty street fighting. The Jockey Club premises (being used as a temporary hospital) are overrun by Japanese. Nurse Redwood:

> Suddenly we heard machine-gun fire fairly near. And it was getting nearer. What now? Nearer and nearer it came. We knew by the noise that it was right outside. Both in the main road and in the valley side. Then in the distance we heard another sound. Again machine-gun fire, but a much different tempo. This could only mean one thing. The Japanese were driving our troops back. This we thought was the end of us. Right in the path of an advancing enemy. (95: 142)

Four Chinese nurses are raped (witnessed by Lance Corporal Harry Harding who, shot in the legs, is hiding in a wicker basket), together with six members of the European nursing staff. Nurse Connie Sully: 'The Japanese came, shone their torches round and picked up four girls

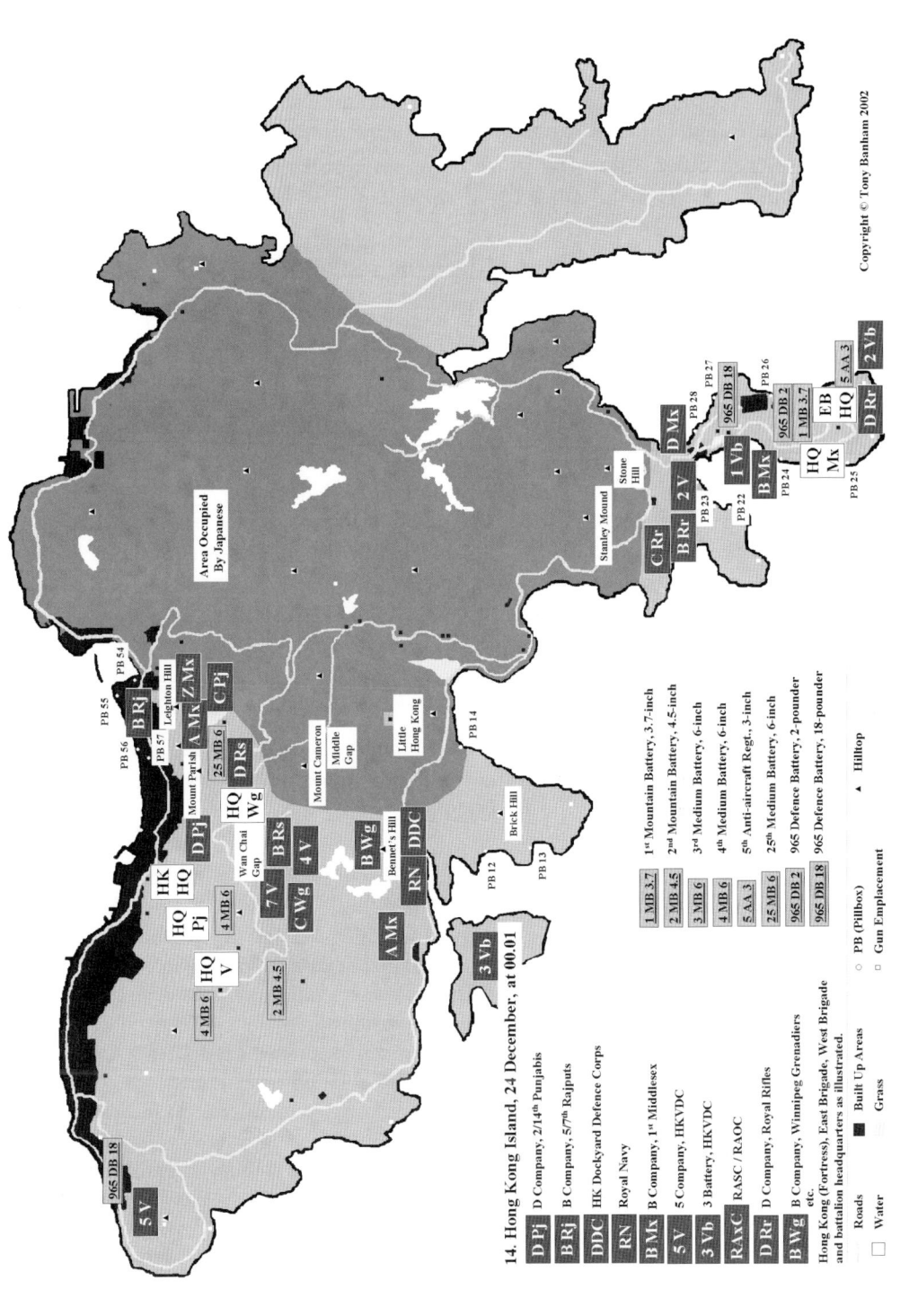

14. Hong Kong Island, 24 December, at 00.01

and made us go up stairs. One girl, she had been sick and, I put my foot in it. I said, "this girl's sick, she's very sick". They didn't take much notice, and eventually (the three of us saying she must go down) they did and unfortunately for us we were all right. It wasn't very nice. But if you'd tried to do anything you would have got a bullet' (167). Two women, Tania Tckencho and Olive Grenham, escape by playing dead (91: 218). Sir Selwyn Selwyn-Clarke… 'I was able to collect them shortly afterwards and take them to the Queen Mary Hospital for treatment, and that none of them became pregnant or developed venereal disease. The mind of one of them however, was permanently affected' (32: 68).[101] Dr J. A. Selby manages to distract the Japanese from massacring the patients (3: 55).[102]

At dawn, A Company Royal Scots also occupy the northern slope of Mount Cameron, but they will be driven off both slopes by the end of the day. In artillery movements, the 2nd Mountain Battery HKSRA moves two guns at Kellet to Peak School, and a Bofors of 18 LAA Battery assists infantry in an attack on the Graigengower Cricket Club pavilion which it shells effectively. In the morning the gun at Mount Austin is temporarily put out of action by a bomb; in the afternoon, the Bluff Head Battery is bombarded and the No. 2 gun put temporarily out of action; and in the evening, an observation post is set up on the top floors of the old Hong Kong Bank building.

The civilians at the Repulse Bay Hotel are herded up and marched to Eucliffe, where they see the bodies of roped and murdered British prisoners, and witness more executions:

> The hundred and fifty of us — mothers with a baby in one arm and the other hand held over head, feeble old Dr. Arlington, children of four and five and ten, crying and frightened — were marched up a side trail to a hillside castle, which the Japanese had taken over as their local headquarters. Along the way we saw some of the bodies of soldiers and naval reserves we had known during the siege. When we came to the hillock on which the castle stood we saw, beside it, many of the British officers and men who had marched out of the Repulse Bay Hotel in the dark hours that same morning. Some of them were in agony from bayonet wounds, inflicted in idle thrusts by their captors. All of them were still being tortured. (Marsman (54: 80))

PHASE V: PUSHING THE LINE WEST AND ENCIRCLING STANLEY   233

Siu-Feng Huang: 'When we passed Eutongsen's garden, we began to see dead soldiers here and there lying along the highway. From RBH to the Gap — you remember the highest spot in the midway from HK to RBH — I think there were at least 100 in uniform and lying in different forms ... It is a tragic sight that I don't like to describe. But I can tell you it just showed the barbarity and narrowmindedness of the Japs' (156).

From there, they march to Wong Nai Chung Gap. At that point, the less fit board lorries to a paint factory in North Point, the others walk and arrive in the evening. Civilians and military personnel come under fire from fifth columnists as far west as Pok Fu Lam, where Mrs Orloff (wife of the medical officer killed at the Salesian Mission massacre) is shot, and dies in the operating theatre (132b: Bard).[103]

In the evening Japanese artillery fire starts a large fire in the area of the China Fleet Club.[104] Firemen ask for military assistance, but none is forthcoming. During the night, anti-personnel mines are laid on the roads leading to Wan Chai and Bowrington (96: 44) in a desperate last attempt to prevent the Japanese entering Victoria through the Naval Dockyards — today's Admiralty.

At Stanley, the situation is getting tense: 'Early on December 24th [Wallis] and [Harland] visited Battalion HQ Royal Rifles of Canada. There they found [Home], [Price] and several senior Canadian officers collected. The atmosphere was tense and sullen. Lt. Col. Home said that it was the considered opinion of all officers and the battalion as a whole that useless casualties were being caused by continuing to fight.'[105]

> [Wallis] once more reiterated the reasons why we should fight on [see previous day], no matter how tired we were. But argument was futile. He then said he would try and arrange for the R.R.C. to move out under white flag to (say) REPULSE BAY, but all other tps would [troops] fight it out. The R.R.C. said they did not wish to surrender alone. [Wallis] said all others were in good heart and would never surrender. [Home] suggested that his unit could perhaps go to a less exposed area such as the Southern end of the Peninsula. [Wallis] explained the FORT had a large enough garrison and he needed no more tps to hold rocky ground where landings were impossible'. (139)[106]

In 1948, Price was asked by the Canadian authorities to comment on Wallis's statements. The body of his reply is quoted here in full:

January 27, 1948

PERSONAL AND CONFIDENTIAL
Lt. Col. G. W. L. Nicholson
Deputy Director
Historical Section (G.S.)
Department of National Defence
Ottawa, Ontario

Dear Col. Nicholson:

I must apologize for not having answered your letter of the 13th of January. I have been away and also I wanted to take some time to consider the copy of extracts from the report of the Historical Section, Cabinet Office, London.

This account is written is such a manner as to create a wrong impression as to intent and motive.

There were plenty of Canadian officers who had battle experience in the first war and who were competent to judge as to the possibility of a successful outcome of the defence of the island. Consider the facts — The Island had been split in two by vastly superior Japanese forces. On the eastern brigade front, which included the Stanley Peninsula, the Royal Rifles and one Company of the Hong Kong Volunteer Defence Force were the only troops who had fought continuously day and night, without rest, since the landing on the 17th and were still carrying all the fighting. By the 21st they had been greatly reduced in fighting strength and by the 23rd to a strength of around 500 all ranks. (It might be interesting to note that when troops in this sector were marched out of Stanley fort as Prisoners of War, they numbered over 2000.)

The enemy controlled the sea and the air. 3" Mortar ammunition had run out. Only one battery of 18 pdr. guns were available for artillery support. Only L.M.G.'s and rifles were left to fight with.

The men had been fighting without much food and practically no sleep and were dead tired. They were obviously in no condition to put up a spirited defence without some rest. A request that they be given 24 hours rest was a reasonable one particularly as it was judged that there were ample troops available who had participated up to date only to a comparatively small degree in the battle and also as the plan then was to contract the front held by a retirement to the Stanley Peninsula itself.

This is part of the story.

The other part casts a reflection on Brig. Home and senior Canadian officers which I greatly resent and about which I protested to General Maltby when I was with him at Argyle St. Officers P.O.W. Camp, Kowloon, in 1942-1943.

In my opinion Brig. Wallis' report is not to be relied upon. He was then in such a state of great nervous excitement and I believe his mental state was such that he was incapable of collected judgement or of efficient leadership. The insinuation in his report is that Brig. Home suggested a complete and final withdrawal of the Canadian force from the fighting. This is untrue and I so told General Maltby.

What happened was this. It was known definitely by December 21st that Brig. Lawson and Col. Hennessy had been killed and that consequently, Brig. Home became the senior Canadian officer in the Colony. As such he inherited responsibilities which he took very seriously and which caused him great anxiety.

It required no great military genius to predict the outcome of the battle once the Japanese had landed on the island with their control of sea and air and great superiority in weapons and men. He felt, I think rightly, that he would be derelict in his duty to his men and to the Canadian Government if he did not communicate his conclusions to the highest authority. Also neither Brig. Home nor his officers had any faith in Brig. Wallis' judgement or in his conduct of operations. And who had better right than he had? He and his men were bearing the brunt of the fighting[107] and knew from first hand knowledge the strength and armament of the forces against them. The Higher Command had consistently shown an inability to grasp the realities of the situation and to pursue tactics which might have prolonged the struggle but could not have altered the final result.

At the meeting on the morning of the 24th, reported by Brig. Wallis, the question of capitulation of the Colony was discussed but never was any suggestion made of a separate final withdrawal of the Canadian forces.

It was after this meeting that the Royal Rifles were withdrawn and came into action again on Christmas day after some six hours rest only.

Generally speaking, there are certain inaccuracies which should be corrected:-

1) Brig. Home on the 21st was called by Lt. Col. Sutcliffe who informed him that he had received and answered a cable from the Minister of National Defence and also that Brig. Lawson and Col. Hennessy had been killed. Lt. Col. Sutcliffe reported that

his battalion had been terribly decimated and also that he had had some argument with Higher Command about useless attacks which his regiment was ordered to make. He asked Brig. Home if he could not do something to stop what he considered was a useless waste of lives.

    2) I cannot believe that Brig. Home asked Brig. Wallis to see the Governor. This does not make sense as we were cut off from the other sector and there was no practical way of carrying this out.

    3) So far as I can remember, Brig. Home and I were the only two Canadian officers present at the meeting with Brig. Wallis on the 24th.

    If there are any further details you think might serve to clarify the situation, I will be glad to let you have them if I can furnish the information.

Sincerely yours,

sgd John H. Price

After days of fighting in the Stanley Mound area, the Royal Rifles at Stanley withdraw into Stanley Fort[108] for a much-needed rest. Brigadier Wallis then establishes three lines of defence for Stanley:

(1) 2 Company HKVDC towards Chung Hom Kok, 1 (Stanley) Platoon of HKVDC under Lieutenant Fitzgerald east of Stanley, some Middlesex machine gunners in support of No. 1 Bungalow, and Royal Rifles from A Company towards Tai Tam Road down to PB 27. Stanley village is held by ten men of 2 Company HQ.
(2) Across the Stanley Peninsula close to the north of St Stephen's College and the old police station, 1 Company HKVDC (under Cpl. E. C. Drown) and a platoon of Middlesex.
(3) Across the peninsula from St Stephen's Preparatory School to the prison, manned by 1 Battery HKVDC (under Capt. Rees), another section of 1 Company HKVDC under Sergeant Murphy, and another platoon of the Middlesex.

Japanese forces launch the first attack on Stanley along the Tai Tam Bay road. Although they lose heavily, they put the two 965 Defence Battery Tai Tam Bay 18-pounders[110] and the two Deep Water Bay section 2-pounders there out of action and breach the first Stanley line. Luckily, in view of what was to happen next morning, Dr Hackett arrives at the St

Stephen's Relief Hospital to take twelve of their most seriously wounded patients back to the prison hospital. He also takes Captain Lynch, Captain Spence, Ashton-Rose, Dr Balean, and several orderlies (38: 169).

In the afternoon, Captain West of the Middlesex places his troops (a mixed bag of RA and RASC) in position in Stanley Cemetery. While doing this, he is killed, together with Corporal Rymer and Corporal Winfield (139).

No one on either front can now doubt the seriousness of the situation. The Japanese will be victorious.

Diary for 24 December

04.00   The Royal Rifles are manning the first line of Stanley's defence (15: 154), from PB 27 on Tai Tam Bay, through St Stephen's, to West Bay. B and D Companies of the Middlesex man the line through Stanley police station together with the Stanley platoon[110] HKVDC (20: 23). Stanley police station[111] itself is defended by Sergeant Simpson and Lance Sergeant Whitley, with a mixture of Chinese and Indian policemen armed with a Lewis gun and grenades in addition to their side arms. To their east is a Middlesex section with four Vickers machine guns (72: 63).

04.45   The Japanese launch a small probing attack at Chung Hom Kok (100: 162).

07.15   Stubbs Road is reported as being held by Japanese; it is shelled by RA guns (93: 139). In Stubbs Road is an entrance to the ARP tunnels which catacomb the more densely populated part of the centre of town. 'Thus they were able to infiltrate through the tunnels and come out behind the lines in Queen's Road Wan Chai. Major Farrington of the Royal Marines went out with a small party of thirty to forty men to try and stop the Japs infiltrating along these tunnels but was killed[112] together with most of his party' (28: 43).

09.15   The Japanese reinforce the northern part of Mount Cameron, where they now have around 300 men (20: 24).

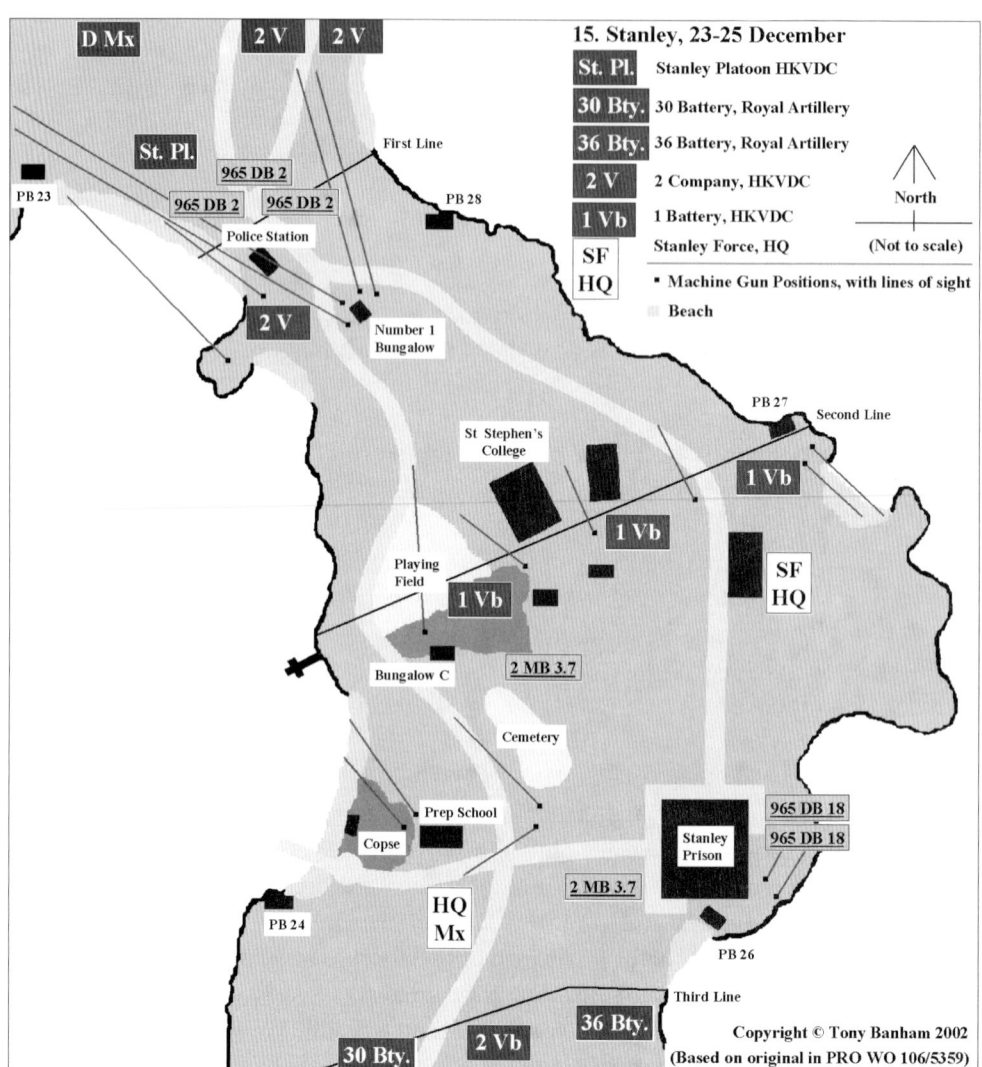

PHASE V: PUSHING THE LINE WEST AND ENCIRCLING STANLEY   239

09.30   Lieutenant A. B. Corrigan, a platoon commander of C Company Winnipeg Grenadiers, is ordered to establish the location and strength of Japanese positions on the southern slope of Mount Cameron. Corrigan described the hand-to-hand fighting that develops: 'too close to permit the firing of my rifle ... wield it club fashion ... knock the rifle and bayonet out of the hands of one of the Japanese ... run through another of the enemy ... flash of a sword being raised ... grasped the blade ... both lost our footing ... two shrill cries ... forgotten that I carried a pistol ... managed to fire ... ended the weary struggle' (95: 138).

09.30   Official Communiqué:

> There has been no further Japanese advance since the last communiqué. The slight enemy penetration in the direction of Mount Cameron is being firmly held. Our lines remain intact. (147)

09.30   Wallis reports to Maltby that the Royal Rifles will be withdrawn to Stanley Fort to recuperate (139).[113]

10.00   The Rajput's line in Wan Chai is reported as 'PARISH HILL–MORRISON HILL (1Mx)–CRAIGENGOWER CRICKET PAVILION–cross rds WONG NEI CHONG–MORRISON HILL RD–CANAL RD (1 Mx.) — SEA' (140).

11.00   A Japanese flag is seen flying on top of a house by the junction of Stanley and Island Roads (139).[114]

11.30   An intelligence report from a Rajput Jemadar, who was captured by the Japanese at Lye Mun but escaped, is submitted to Fortress HQ by East Brigade (139).

12.00   At midday, an infantry attack on Leighton Hill is beaten back with severe losses.

12.00   All communications with Stanley are cut (93: 140).

12.00   St Stephen's Hospital is now holding more than 400 patients. This number is reduced to 280, and the staff to sixty, by further transfers to Stanley Fort and Stanley prison (27: 43).

12.00   One 6-inch howitzer at Mount Austin is put out of action by a bomb (20: 24).

13.00　A party of fifty British ORs of 12 Coast Regiment RA under command of Lieutenant A. E. Clayton are sent to assist the Middlesex in Causeway Bay and take their places in the line (93: 139).

14.30　Official Communiqué:

> Contact has been maintained along the whole front and minor patrolling encounters have ended in our favour. Our position on Mount Cameron is maintained. Naval oil tanks in enemy hands in Yaumati were set ablaze and are still burning. (147)

14.45　The Brick Hill HKSRA AA is section reported as surrounded and under attack (93: 140).

15.00　Leighton Hill reports that it is now being attacked from three sides (79: 271) by about 200 men. This attack develops after a severe bombardment by artillery, mortars, and dive-bombers (20: 24). 'Outnumbered ten to one': George Tann, 1st Middlesex (171).

16.00　A battalion of Shoji's regiment reach the top of Mount Cameron preparatory to attacking the allies on the next day (95: 139).

16.45　The Middlesex Regiment is finally forced off Leighton Hill, which it has been holding since the 18th as part of the north/south line. One machine gun and crew are lost as they cover the withdrawal towards Canal Road (95: 137). The survivors join the Rajputs in a line from Mount Parish to the north-west corner of the racecourse, and then to the sea. Commanding officer Captain Man, together with Company Sergeant Major Jock Ure and Company Sergeant Little[115] find themselves occupying a VD clinic in Wan Chai. Two members of Corporal Broadbridge's section from 3 Company HKVDC (Ptes. L. A. Fox[116] and H. Wong) are cut off, but both eventually escape to China.

17.00　Company Sergeant Major S. D. Begg and two other (Canadian) survivors of The Ridge finally reach Stanley after swimming for twenty-two hours.

17.30   A detachment from 1st Battery HKVDC consisting of three officers and about thirty men (93: 140) is sent to reinforce the St Stephen's College line.

17.30   A Royal Marine patrol reports that the Royal Scots are at Wan Chai Gap, and no Japanese are on the road to its north-east (20: 24).

17.30   Official Communiqué:

> Continued enemy pressure has made no impression on our lines. Strong patrol activities have been maintained by both sides. The situation has not materially altered since this afternoon. (147)

18.00   A Japanese artillery barrage succeeds in knocking out two of the B Company Middlesex machine-gun positions on the eastern slopes of Morrison Hill.[117] The seven guns there are under the command of Captain Flood. But Major R. E. Moody collects thirty spare men and with them reinforces the positions and holds out until the surrender.

18.00   Two civilians captured at the Repulse Bay Hotel (Hon. A. H. L. Shields, an unofficial member of the Executive Council, and Major C. M. Manners,[118] manager of the Kowloon Wharf & Godown Co.) secure permission to pass through Japanese lines to talk to British Military HQ to report that the scale of the Japanese forces they have observed leads them to believe that further resistance would be suicidal. They spend the night under Japanese guard before setting off (95: 145).

18.00   An intense artillery and mortar bombardment starts on the forward and support positions at Stanley (139).

18.30   No. 1 Battery HKVDC takes up its positions at Stanley as infantry under a pale moonlight: 'I have seen films and pictures of war, but never in all my life have I seen anything like the sights, or heard the noise such as came from Stanley Village that night. There were six or seven machine-guns of our own, then the Japanese joined in with their machine-guns, rifle fire, Tommy-guns, and mortars, seeming never to stop. Our machine-guns were firing one tracer in five and it was quite a sight to watch': Sergeant L. Millington, 1 Battery HKVDC (94: 123).

19.00   A party of clerks, signallers, military police, etc. is formed at

	Fortress HQ under Major R. E. Moody and is sent to assist the Middlesex at Morrison Hill (20: 24).
19.00	A large fire starts on the waterfront near the China Fleet Club, hindering forward movements (20: 24).
19.30	Lieutenant A. E. Clayton is killed in action in Canal Road (93: 139).
20.50	In the evening, a second attack on Stanley is supported by three tanks. The leading two tanks are destroyed by a 2-pounder anti-tank gun of 965 Defence Battery stationed on the road, but 2 Company (Scottish) HKVDC are forced back into Stanley village, losing most of their men wounded or killed. The Stanley Platoon also loses some 50 per cent (44: 100). The gun and another at Stanley police station are overrun from the Maryknoll direction.
21.30	Cheesewright, at No. 1 Bungalow, reports that 2 Company HKVDC in front of him are coming under attack (139). The Scots' commanding officer, Major H. R. Forsyth, is recommended for the Victoria Cross by Wallis for refusing to leave his position after being wounded as Japanese overwhelm the line. The defenders fall back to the bungalow.
22.00	Reports indicate a general movement of the Japanese from the Mount Cameron/Nicholson area northwards towards the racecourse (20: 24).
22.00	Central comes under 3-inch mortar fire, targeting Victoria Barracks, Fortress HQ, and the RN Yard (20: 24).
22.30	Major Forsyth is again wounded seriously and Company Sergeant-Major T. Swan is killed, and Forsyth is carried to the schoolhouse adjoining Stanley old police station.[119] 'Impossible to make head or tail of the fracas in the village. The whole narrow isthmus was rocketing fire like a burning munition dump. Nearby, on our left, a house was surrounded, Bren guns blazing from each quarter and automatics returning the fire at point-blank range. All over the place were similar close exchanges. I had never guessed that a real battle could be so like a gangster film': Gunner Bertram, 2 Battery HKVDC (101: 126).[120]

24.00   MacKenzie of 1 Battery HKVDC:

> There was a short lull at midnight, then weird howls (Japanese war cries) as the enemy advanced, held at bay for a while by our battery's machine-guns. The left half of our line was presently subjected to mortar fire every four minutes. Then an incendiary bomb landed near Sergeant Leslie Millington's machine-gun, lighting the whole scene brilliantly over a wide area, and setting off the ammunition in boxes and belts. Those of us still alive lay low, as sharpshooters were picking off any soldiers lit by the glare. Nearly all those on that extreme left wing became casualties'. (23: 35)

24.00   The Japanese attack south of Wan Chai Gap, making a small penetration (3: 49).

Roll of Honour for 24 December

VOLUNTEERS — 23 Killed

Alexander, William	Gunner, 1 Bty. HKVDC	K
Originally buried Bungalow C.[121]		
Smith, John Reginald	Gunner, 1 Bty. HKVDC	K
Bone, Adam	Sergeant, 4 Bty. HKVDC	K
Lacey, John Truman	Company Quarter Master Sergeant, 1 Coy. HKVDC	K
Originally buried Bungalow C.		

(2 Coy at Stanley first line)

Blackman, Donald	Private, 2 Coy. HKVDC	K
Coull, David	Private, 2 Coy. HKVDC	K
Ford, William	Private, 2 Coy. HKVDC	U
KIA Stanley. Buried at west side of black bathing hut (126).		
Forsyth, Henry Russel	Major, 2 Coy. HKVDC	K
Killed defending Tai Tam Road, Stanley. MiD.		
Gill, John Cawthra	Private, 2 Coy. HKVDC	K
Kerbey, Geoffrey Holman	Private, 2 Coy. HKVDC	U
Originally buried Tai Tam Bay (126).		
Mackie, William Craigie	Sergeant Pipe Major, 2 Coy. HKVDC	U
Killed Stanley (91: 206). Buried at west side of black bathing hut (126).		
McCormick, Charles James	Private, 2 Coy. HKVDC	K
Buried at west side of black bathing hut west of preparatory school (126).		

Newhouse, Geoffrey	Private, 2 Coy. HKVDC	U
With 2 Coy, Stanley first line. Buried at Tai Tam Bay (126).[122]		
Pospisil, Alois	Private, 2 Coy. HKVDC	U
Missing believed killed in area of Chung Hom Kok (126).		
Swan, Thomas	Company Sergeant Major, 2 Coy. HKVDC	K
Fort Road, Stanley, helping Forsyth.		
Thomson, James Milne	Private, 2 Coy. HKVDC	K
Watson, Kenneth De Wolfe	Private, 2 Coy. HKVDC	K
Carr, George Wynfield	Private, Stanley Platoon HKVDC	U
KIA at Stanley (126).		
Crossan, James Joseph	Private, Stanley Platoon HKVDC	U
KIA at Stanley (126).		
Gowland, Cuthbert Mercer	Private, Stanley Platoon HKVDC	U
McLeod, Angus	Private, Stanley Platoon HKVDC	U
Murphy, G.	Private, Stanley Platoon HKVDC	U
Pearce, T. H.	Private, Stanley Platoon HKVDC	U

ARTILLERY — 16 Killed

(These four probably all Stanley)

Hakam Singh	Gunner, 965 Defence Bty. HKSRA	U
Kirpa Singh	Gunner, 965 Defence Bty. HKSRA	U
McCarthy, George Egbert	Gunner, 965 Defence Bty. RA	K
Originally buried top of cutting near pumping station, Stanley Fort (126).		
Sadhu Singh	Gunner, 965 Defence Bty. HKSRA	K
Originally buried below St Stephen's College (126).		
Wassan Singh	Gunner, 24 Heavy Bty. HKSRA	K
Clayton, Arthur Edmondston	Lieutenant, 1 HK Regt. HKSRA	U
Craigengower–Canal Road. Unburied (126).		[25 Dec.]
Bashar Ahmad	Gunner, 1 Mountain Bty. HKSRA	U
Ghanzanfar Ali	Gunner, 1 Mountain Bty. HKSRA	U
Ghulam Husain	Gunner, 1 Mountain Bty. HKSRA	U
Imam Din	Gunner, 1 Mountain Bty. HKSRA	U
Lal Khan	Gunner, 2 Mountain Bty. HKSRA	U
Muhammad Amir	Gunner, 17 AA Bty. HKSRA	U
Munsib Khan	Naik, Depot Bty. HKSRA	U
Rahmat Khan	Cook, 4 Medium Bty. HKSRA	U

Ronson, Albert Miller   Lance Sergeant, 8 Coast Regt. RA   U
 St Stephen's Hospital. Unburied (126).   [24 Nov.]

Brown, Henry   Gunner, 12 Coast Regt. RA   U
 Craigengower–Canal Road. Unburied (126).

MIDDLESEX — 22 Killed

Bourdon, Edgar Ernest Benjamin Private   U
 Killed Brick Hill vicinity, 24 Dec. (126).   [8/25 Dec.]

Brown, Joseph Ernest   Private   U

Cheal, Sidney William   Lance Corporal   K
 Kennedy Road behind HQ China Command (126). By mortar   [19 Dec.]
 bomb hitting trench.

Colbron, George Richard   Private   K
 Originally buried garden of Government Treasurer, Leighton Hill (126).

Davy, Frederick Albert   Lance Corporal   U
 Missing, Stanley area (126).

Emery, Douglas Thomas   Private   K
 Killed Government House (126).

Logan, William Mitchell   Private   U
 Killed Morrison Hill area (126).

How, Sidney John   Private   K
 Originally buried Bungalow C.

Mackinlay, William Andrew   2nd Lieutenant   K
 Died in hospital (145: 135). Buried No. 2 Crater, Borret Road (i.e. BRH) (126).

Murphy, James Michael   Private   K
 Killed Bennet's Hill area (126).

Onslow, Lawrence Samuel   Drummer   U
 Z Coy Leighton Hill? Missing. Wong Nai Chung area (126).[123]

Roberts, William Henry   Private   K
 Originally buried Barton's Bungalow, Stanley (126).   [8 Dec.]

Rymer, Arthur Williams   Corporal   K
 Originally buried Bungalow C.

Saw, Albert Edward   Private   K
 Killed North Face (126).

Speleers, Allan   Lance Corporal   U
 Killed Stanley area (126).

Stevens, William Austin   Private   U

Stewart, Gordon Langly   Private   U

Ward, Lord Frederick   Private   U
 Killed Murray Barracks. Possibly buried GOC's garden (126).

West, Douglas[124]   Captain   K
    D Coy at Stanley. Killed in copse. Originally buried Bungalow C.   [25 Dec.]
Williamson, Charles Kenneth   Captain   K
    Barton's Bungalow area, south Stanley (126).
Wilson, James Henry   Corporal   U
    Attached West Infantry Brigade (145: 153). Escaped from Lawson's bunker?[125]
Winfield, Eric   Corporal   K
    Originally buried Bungalow C.

ROYAL RIFLES — 3 Killed

Dupont, Elroy George   Rifleman   K
    Killed Stanley Prison, 25 Dec. (126).
Lyster, Franklin N.   Lieutenant
    KIA — (154) says Stanley Mound — and originally buried at Stanley View (100: 97).
Scott, Arthur Beresford   Lieutenant   U
    Originally buried at Stanley View (100: 97). KIA Stanley Mound (126).

PUNJABIS — 1 Killed

Lal Bad Shah   Sepoy   K

ENGINEERS — 2 Killed

Kelly, Desmond Stanley   Lance Sergeant, 22 Fortress Coy. RE   K
    Admitted WMH 21 Dec. Died 24 Dec. (145: 95).[126]
Bacon, Wilfred Thomas   Sapper, 22 Fortress Coy. RE   U
    Killed Kennedy Road (126). Probably by the mortar attack.   [19 Dec.]

ROYAL SCOTS — 10 Killed

Bailey, Francis Joseph   Lance Corporal   U
Cooper, Eric Baron   Private   U
    Admitted WMH 24 Dec. and died same day (145: 94).[127]   [23 Dec.]
Digney, Joseph Stanley   Private   U
    Reported missing 19th (145: 179). Killed east side Nicholson Camp Road near SAH (126).
Hammond, John   Private   U
    Missing Black's Link/Wong Nai Chung (126).
Hastie, Andrew   Private   U
    South-east of junction of Blue Pool and Tai Hang roads (126).
Higgins, William   Private   U
    Missing 19th (145: 179). East side Nicholson Camp Road near SAH (126).
King, John   Private   U
    Killed north Mount Cameron area (126).

Maxwell, Andrew Gordon   Private   U
    East side Nicholson Camp Road near SAH (126).

McCaffray, John   Private   K
    Killed in a slit trench behind HQ China Command, Kennedy Road (126). [19 Dec.]

Ritchie, Robert Wilson   Sergeant   U
    Killed Hennessey Road, Causeway Bay/Wan Chai (126).

RAOC — 3 Killed

Bliss, Ronald Ernest[128]   Lance Corporal, RAOC   U

Ewens, Frank William   Lance Sergeant, RAOC   U

Rudder, Arthur Wilfred   Lance Sergeant, RAOC   U

RAVC — 1 Killed

Fisher, Handel Ashton   Corporal, RAVC   K
    Possibly killed by a mortar in a slit trench on Kennedy Road.[129]   [19 Dec.]

WINNIPEGS — 3 Killed

Carcary, William T.   Private   U
    Killed Stanley village (126).[130]

Warr, Leslie M.   Lance Corp.   U
    Admitted WMH 23 Dec., died 24 Dec. (145: 97).

Wilson, William J.   Private   U
    Last seen Little Hong Kong (126).

ROYAL NAVY — 1 Killed

Young, Frank   Petty Officer, HMS *Tamar*, RN   UP

CIVILIANS — 2 Killed

Orloff, Mrs.   UCWD
    Shot by fifth columnists on Pok Fu Lam road. Died during fighting,   [24 Dec. 1942]
    i.e. Dec. 1941 (132b: Bard).

Yip Yeung[131]   UCWD

POLICE — 2 Killed

Dar Din   3628, RN Dockyard Police   UX
    Admitted to Queen Mary Hospital 24 Dec., and died same day (145: 74).

Teja Singh   Constable B.162, HKPF   U
    Admitted to Queen Mary Hospital 24 Dec., and died same day (145: 90). [22 Dec.]

25 DECEMBER THURSDAY

> I was firmly of the opinion on the morning of the 25th December with Japanese coming ever closer to our positions, that it would be my last day on earth. I had no idea of surrender. (Lieutenant 'Bunny' Browne)[132]

'Hongkong is observing the strangest and most sober Christmas in its century-old history' (147). So reads the headline in the penultimate wartime *South China Morning Post*, which also carries the more sober message: 'Cases are occurring where there is considerable delay before deaths are reported to the Burial Service staff. Members of the public can help greatly if every time they see a dead body they report at once to the nearest Police or A.R.P. station (147).' Dead civilians are becoming a health hazard in built-up areas. Dr Li Shu-Fan: 'The usual way of disposing of corpses was simply to lay them out on the streets. Every tenement in town was packed with people who were keeping indoors because of the bombardment. There was no room for the dead indoors, and of course no coffins were obtainable' (52: 103). His hospital, the Hong Kong Sanatorium, also ran out of room in the mortuary, and he later describes burying nineteen unidentified Chinese in a trench outside the hospital while under shellfire from the nearby Leighton Hill area (52: 106).

The Governor sends a Christmas message:

> In pride and admiration I send my greeting this Christmas day to all who are fighting and all who are working so nobly and so well to sustain Hong Kong against the assaults of the enemy. Fight on. Hold fast for King and Empire. God bless you all in this your finest hour . . . Let this day be historical in the grand annals of our empire. The Order of the Day is to hold fast.

By this time, the garrison-held territory is restricted to the western third of the Island, plus Little Hong Kong and the Stanley and Chung Hom Kok peninsulas.

At Stanley, 1 Battery HKVDC holds the line from Prison Road to Fort Road. The battery has been reorganized into four infantry sections. On the extreme right, Sergeant Millington's section lines Prison Road, Lieutenant H. S. Jones has a section covering the road entrance to the college, and on his left two sections under Second Lieutenant H. G.

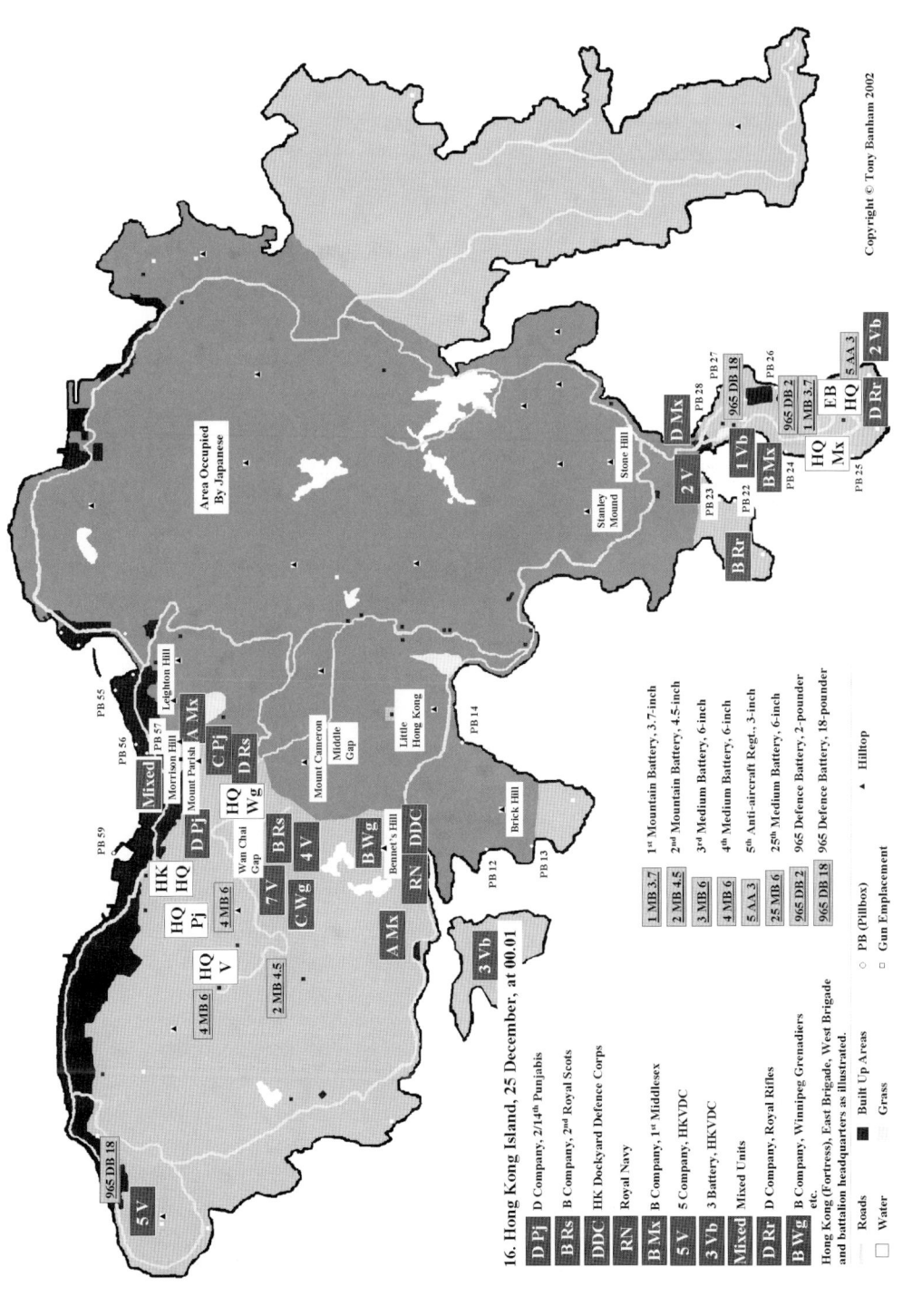

Muir hold the middle ground around Bungalow C and the lower slopes at the south end of the college football ground. They await the next attack.

Soon after midnight, it comes. PB 28, manned by C Company Middlesex, just forward of the first line at Stanley, is knocked out. Sergeant Sheehan, in command, and the entire crew, with the exception of Private Foley, are killed (96: 45).[133]

As the fighting intensifies, the 1st Battery HKVDC on the St Stephen's College line is finally overrun. Lieutenant H. S. Jones (whose section is at the school entrance), Second Lieutenant Muir, and thirty-three other ranks are killed, while Captain F. G. Rees and three other ranks are wounded.

In the pre-dawn hours, the Japanese push the Stanley defenders back beyond St Stephen's College. At the college itself, now an overcrowded temporary hospital, the most sadistic massacre takes place. At the same time, the Japanese try to penetrate west of Bennet's Hill.

At midday, the Royal Rifles make a final suicidal assault on Japanese positions in the grounds of Stanley College, and to the west, Bennet's Hill finally falls, effectively making the defence of Aberdeen impossible.

Two platoons of D Company, Middlesex, bypassed on Maryknoll, attempt to withdraw to Repulse Bay in the early hours. They are surrounded. Lieutenant Scantlebury and Second Lieutenant Newman are both captured and killed, together with the majority of the two platoons (96: 46).

Virtually all the remaining artillery pieces are lost. The Promontory and Island 965 Defence Battery 2-pounders are lost in Stanley, as is one HKSRA 1st Mountain Battery 3.7-inch howitzer. Tai Tam Hill 1st Battery 4.5-inch guns are put out of action, as are the Kellet and Sanatorium guns from 1st and 2nd, and the 4th Medium Battery guns at Mount Gough and Mount Austin.

In the urban areas, Mount Parish and Wan Chai market come under heavy attack. The Japanese (under Shoji) push into Wan Chai house by house, but meet stiff resistance from the China Fleet Club in Fleet House, together with mines in the road and intelligent use of Bofors L60 40-mm guns in the anti-personnel capacity.

At Wan Chai market[134] itself, the 965 Defence Battery Repulse Bay section 18-pounder is destroyed. The Japanese are soon reported as far west as the edge of the Naval Dockyards of HMS *Tamar*. The house-to-house fighting in Wan Chai intensifies to the point where the line is breaking. In the west the Rajputs are pushed back a little to the west of the racecourse, which is virtually abandoned, but some elements of the Middlesex hold on to the top of Morrison Hill until the surrender.

Mount Parish, held by the Middlesex and Rajputs, falls in the afternoon (44: 101) — leaving the way to Victoria open along Kennedy Road — and Maltby surrenders Hong Kong in mid-afternoon.

People react to the surrender in different ways:

> Colonel Bowie, the Chief Surgeon, stripped me, preparatory to putting me in a plaster from my neck to my hips. Before he could do that, Hong Kong surrendered and I sent for the Hospital Chaplain. I had my marriage license in the breast pocket of my tunic, and I asked him to marry me to my fiancée. Thus it came about that I was married naked under a sheet ... My Colonel's wife, Mrs Vi White went through to a nurses' dining room where they (believe it or not) were having Christmas lunch, and snatched their Xmas cake from them, 'Sorry' she explained, 'there's a wedding going on next door' ' (132b: Hunter).[135]

Later, there is a final official communiqué:

> The garrison of Hongkong, having fought until all reserves were expended and until all means of support were exhausted, were ordered to cease active hostilities. The authorities are in contact with the Japanese Military Authorities and further instructions will be issued in due course. (147)

But even as the surrender comes, the battle isn't yet over. In Stanley, fighting continues for some time as elements on both sides choose to disbelieve the news.

Wallis, in particular, refuses to believe the verbal surrender order. In his War Diary he records:

> About 2000 hrs[136] a car arrived draped with a white flag containing:– Lt. Col. R. G. LAMB, R.E. Lieut. J. T. PRYOR, Ft. H.Q. Staff. I knew Lt. Col. LAMB slightly. I had also spoken on the phone with him several times during the last 3 days as he was apparently attached to 'G' Branch. But I thought I had detected in his voice excitability and a certain casualness and an attitude which seemed to convey 'oh well — it will be the same either way, so do as you like'. Lt. PRYOR I thought of unusual appearance, an officer I did not know.[137]

> These officers stated that the G.O.C. had informed H.E. the Governor and C-in-C that further resistance was impossible. That H.E. the Governor, the G.O.C. and several senior officers (Lt. Cols STEWART 1 Mx and WHITE, 2 R.S.) had gone to Japanese H.Q. to negotiate.
> They said my orders were to surrender and hand over all arms and equipment without destruction.
> In view of the G.O.C.'s personal talks with me during the last week and a conversation as late as early on 25 Dec 41, in which he had impressed on me never to give up so long as amn, food and water were available, it seemed a doubtful story. Could I trust these officers? Surely the G.O.C. would have given me some confidential warning to enable me to destroy big guns and importantly equipment in time.
> Nevertheless I realised that it might be a true bill. Conditions elsewhere might have rapidly become untenable and the G.O.C.'s hand been suddenly forced.
> But, yet these officers had no written instructions. (139).

The gunners at Mount Davis claim not to have received the part of the surrender order that tells them not to destroy their weapons, and bury their side arms and destroy their 9.2-inch gun by the simple expedient of ramming a shell nose-first down the muzzle, and firing another at it from the breech (132b: Bard). The gunners of 3 Battery HKVDC, cut off at Ap Lei Chau island, send an officer and a gunner to the 'mainland' (i.e. Hong Kong Island) to see why cars are driving with their headlights on again. They return with news of surrender, and the guns are disabled and all vital parts are thrown into the sea (132b: Wright).

HKVDC 'Z' Force (loosely attached to SOE), who had been operating independently behind Japanese lines since 9 December (blowing up trucks, damaging Japanese communications, and setting up booby traps), note Japanese warships in the harbour on Christmas Day. The three senior members (Teasdale, Holmes, and Thomson) — feeling that a group of seven would be too conspicuous — order the four junior members to surrender while they themselves escape (161). During the night, Corporal Holmes makes his way to a pipe factory in Tsuen Wan and single-handedly blows up Japanese lorries parked there with time-bombs (44: 79).

Meanwhile, at sea, the five Motor torpedo boats leave Hong Kong and move north into Mirs Bay. There they are scuttled (together with a naval supplies launch on its way from Singapore to Hong Kong) off the island of Peng Chau. Seventy-five on board are helped by villagers to escape to Wai Chow and freedom. Eventually, after five months, the remnant of the 2nd MTB flotilla — numbering thirty-one men — reach Glasgow, Scotland.[138]

Diary for 25 December

00.00 The Stanley Platoon (HKVDC) falls back. The Japanese now control the beach at Stanley Bay. Of the twenty-eight men of the Stanley Platoon, fourteen have been hit, whilst every man of the Scottish party has been killed or wounded. Every man of 5 Platoon HKVDC is killed or wounded in Stanley.

00.00 The Japanese attack Bennet's Hill and dig in on the northern slopes (20: 24).

01.00 At Stanley, the Japanese break through on the east side of Stanley towards the prison. Gunners and Middlesex holding the third line inflict heavy casualties, but also lose heavily (3: 51).

02.00 The Japanese now attack along Prison Road, engaging Sergeant Millington's section. They then continue the attack across the school football field (now St Stephen's College sports field), where the machine guns cause them heavy casualties. 'I swung the gun over; the Japanese were coming in waves in the fading light — running, falling, rising and running again. We emptied a couple of [Lewis gun] drums; in a minute the gun was searing hot. Were they so sure of themselves now, that losses no longer mattered?' (101: 132). The struggle then moves to the ridge south of the football field (3: 52).

Gunner Inglis and Lance Bombardier Stafford[139] are aiming their 2-pounder over open sights at the advancing Japanese along Prison Road from a position near the Chinese school. Gunner 'Red' Bullen takes up position on top of the school with a Tommy gun until he is mown down.

03.00 Japanese forces trying to infiltrate west of Bennet's Hill are held up by HKVDC and HKRNVR supported by a 4.5-inch howitzer at the 'Sanatorium' (79: 272).

04.00   The 17th HAA Battery, HKSRA, under Lieutenant F. H. Fairclough on Brick Hill, comes under attack. The Punjabis in front of the guns hold the Japanese off for twenty minutes while the 3.7-inch guns are brought into play in an artillery role. The Punjabis abandon their trenches. The Commanding Officer, Captain Bartram, goes out in front with a Thompson sub-machine gun and a bucket of grenades, but is killed whilst defending the position. The Japanese are held off for a further three hours (95: 184).

04.00   The left gun of the right section protecting Stanley is destroyed by a charge, killing two men (139).

05.00   Scantlebury's Maryknoll position is believed to be out of action (139).

05.30   At the north end of Chung Hom Kok, B Company Royal Rifles under Captain Royal join forces with 2 Company HKVDC under Lieutenant Bryden (139).

06.00   A Bofors gun is taken down to Morrison Hill and used in an anti-personnel role to help the Middlesex to shell the Japanese out of the Craigengower and Civil Service clubs (3: 57) south of Canal Road (20: 24).

06.00   Two lorry loads of Japanese troops drive into the Wan Chai mines laid overnight during the early morning advance to Magazine Gap (96: 44).

06.00   A truce is arranged so that certain Europeans can be moved out of Happy Valley (the scene of heavy shelling and mortar fire). The Japanese ignore the truce and shell and dive-bomb Gloucester Road, Hennessey Road, Mount Kellet, Austin, and the Peak all morning (93: 140), and the Matilda and War Memorial hospitals in the afternoon (8: 26). In Aberdeen, MTB 08 is also blown up by a shell, but there are no casualties.

06.00   Japanese soldiers burst into the St Stephen's Casualty Hospital (a 400-bed reserve hospital in the main building of St Stephens College, Stanley). Lieutenant Colonel Black, Captain Whitney, and Sergeant Anderson go out to meet them. The two officers are taken away, and their bayoneted bodies are later found in the staff lavatory and sitting room respectively (38: 174).[140] The Japanese order everyone out. They shoot Sergeant Parkin in the head when he tries to escape, and bayonet or shoot all patients in bed who are too slow — of simply incapable of — getting out. An uncertain number of men[141] die in this manner. 'As they came in I saw them bayonet wounded soldiers in bed': Padre Barnett (15: 166).[142]

06.30   Japanese forces have penetrated along the northern sea front to a position where they threaten to outflank the defenders holding the Lee Theatre area. Lieutenant Colonel Stewart starts preparing a second line of defence running from O'Brien Street to Wan Chai market and then Mount Parish (3: 57).

06.30   As dawn rises over Stanley, Japanese storm the ridge at the point immediately south of the tennis courts, overrunning two of the Middlesex guns. On the right, Sergeant Millington is killed. Lieutenant Jones rallies his men to retake the position, but is then killed himself together with many of his section. The two sections on the left fall back to the preparatory school.

06.30   Second Lieutenant Muir's section holds on to Bungalow C and repulses all attacks until the Japanese bring up a flame-thrower. The section falls back, but then retakes the bungalow in perhaps the bitterest hand-to-hand fighting of the battle. Eventually the Japanese prevail through sheer weight of numbers. There are no survivors from Muir's section (79: 268).[143]

06.30   As the sun rises, the two Scottish platoons on Chung Hom Kok peninsula (acting as a link between B Company Royal Rifles, with approximately sixty-five all ranks, who are still holding the south of the peninsula, and the main force at Stanley) find themselves virtually surrounded by Japanese forces, which have also captured Chung Hom Kok Fort. Prophet takes a section of twelve men to attack positions on the summit of Chung Hom Kok Height. Only Private I. F. Grant actually reaches the summit, and he is killed there. Meanwhile their positions have come under constant mortar and machine-gun fire. Prophet and Bryden decide to hold the position until nightfall, and then make an orderly withdrawal (3: 53).

06.30   The Japanese attacking Stanley are in Tweed Bay and in the copse near the preparatory school (44: 100). Surviving British forces at Stanley retire to the fort for a last stand.

06.30	A heavy artillery concentration knocks out three more of the Middlesex machine guns on Morrison Hill, killing Second Lieutenant Wynter-Blyth and several men (96: 44).
07.00	Japanese advanced units are reported as far west as the China Fleet Club[144] (79: 273). Maltby discounts this report (20: 25).
07.00	Twenty-seven people attend the early service at St John's Cathedral (15: 163).
07.00	The Japanese reach the Maryknoll Mission in Stanley, bringing six British officer prisoners an hour later (38: 176).
07.00	Captain Weedon launches a counter-attack to drive the Japanese out of the copse, attacking from the east and driving them into a Chinese shrine which they attack with grenades. Blackaby and three men are killed, and Weedon is wounded (139).
07.30	The HKSRA 17th AA Battery on the southernmost point of Brick Hill is overrun. Lieutenant Fairclough continues the defence from the gun position itself. Wounded, he feigns death after the Japanese appear, and later swims to Aberdeen (later still he escaped from the Sham Shui Po POW camp) (93: 140). However, most of the Indian gunners perish.
07.30	Beattie (HKRNVR) re-takes the peak of Bennet's Hill after it has been deserted by the Canadians (130: 28).
07.45	Two Middlesex parties under Company Sergeant Majors Overy and Tibble[145] attempt to clear the Stanley bungalows. They are driven back to a position overlooking the cemetery. Winter[146] is killed in this engagement (139).
08.00	Fifty-six attend the next service at St John's.
08.00	In Wan Chai, the Japanese hold a line from the south end of Canal Road to the east arm of Causeway Bay, with snipers in buildings further forward (20: 25).
08.00	The Japanese launch a fierce attack on the positions east of Bennet's Hill (79: 272).
08.00	By this time only two officers of B and D Companies Middlesex, Second Lieutenant King and Second Lieutenant Whitham[147] remain. Captain West of D Company,[148] Captain Williamson of B Company, Second Lieutenant Blackaby of C Company, have

been killed, and Captain Weedon of B Company wounded (96: 46).

08.30 The formation of a new line is reported to Fortress HQ. Running from the Ruttonjee Sanatorium (then the Royal Naval Hospital — which at that time was almost on the waterfront and 'suffered almost a hundred hits from shells and heavy machine gun bursts' (32: 66)), through Wan Chai market, to the junction of Hennessey and O'Brien Roads in Wan Chai (79: 273).

08.30 There is another clash between Wallis and Home in which — according to Wallis — Home states that his men have had no rest, many of them only pulling back to the fort late at night, and Wallis states that they cannot be inactive when the Middlesex, Royal Artillery, and HKVDC 'fight a battle as infantry for which they were not trained'. Major Parker is ordered to counter-attack Stanley with D Company Royal Rifles:

> Attack Coy to move into position by a track and route out of view of the enemy, down to the N.E. corner of the PRISON — thence EAST of TWEED BAY Hospital and the rocky ground at [Map Reference] 256456. Then advancing to attack from the EAST from the ground just NORTH of the PRISON CLUB. The attack to be supported by fire by all weapons in the Reserve Line which could bear. 1 Mx [Middlesex] at the PREP SCHOOL to co-operate on the left flank as opportunity offers. (139)

09.00 A Company Royal Scots is driven off the foothold on Mount Cameron and falls back to Wan Chai Gap (3: 58).

09.00 Shields and Manners report to Maltby under a white flag. Their advice to surrender is rejected and they return to Japanese captivity. However, the Japanese offer an impromptu three-hour truce. During the truce, the Middlesex commander, Lieutenant Colonel H. W. M. Stewart, visits Fortress HQ to discuss the situation. There he finds Captain Freddie Guest burning secret documents (95: 145). Guest's mentor in this task is General 'One-Arm' Sutton, adventurer and inventor (36: 256).[149]

09.00 At St Stephen's, the surviving patients and staff are taken upstairs and put into different classrooms. Eighty-six patients and staff are put in one room of 100 square feet. Riflemen E. J. Henderson[150] and J. McKay are taken out separately and are later found dead and mutilated, with their eyes, ears, and tongues cut out.

Five British nurses (Smith, Buxton, Begg, Simmons, Gordon) are put in a room with five Chinese ladies (wives of British soldiers). Some twenty-five Chinese stretcher-bearers are then murdered. Anderson: 'The St. John Ambulance Brigade[151] men were all put in one room and systematically butchered, one only remained alive to tell us what happened' (38: 173).

11.00 St. John's Cathedral records read 'some shelling. Attendance nil'.

11.00 The Japanese are in possession of the Stanley cemetery (139).

11.30 Eddison and Challinor of the Royal Artillery try to move — by Scammel lorry — the two 18-pounders at Tweed Bay and the two 3.7-inch howitzers north-west of the prison to a safer position in the Reserve Area. One dismantled 3.7 is put in the lorry and one 18-pounder is towed behind it as it sets off up the hill. It comes under heavy fire and, with casualties, is abandoned (139).

12.00 A Japanese artillery barrage starts. Their infantry then attack the Rajputs on Mount Parish, and the Royal Scots position in Wan Chai Gap. Albert Rodrigues of the HKVDC Field Ambulance: 'In the falling of the gap, Col. White was severely wounded in both legs . . . While I was cleaning them up and stitching the open wounds etc. — Capt. Ford told me that they could not keep the Japanese back much longer. He told me to get the ambulance fully loaded and with engine running to leave as soon as he told me the Japanese were breaking through' (132b: Rodrigues).[152]

By this time, the outer perimeter in Wan Chai is held by the remains of Z Company Middlesex, fourteen men of A Company Royal Scots, seven men of D Company Royal Scots, and a few stragglers. The second line of defence (on the eastern edge of Central under command of Lieutenant Colonel Stewart) is held by seventy Middlesex, fifty Punjabis, and some more stragglers. Both lines are being overwhelmed, and Royal Marine units in the rear are engaging Japanese patrols that have slipped through the lines.

12.00 D Company of the Royal Rifles make a final, almost suicidal, assault on Japanese positions in the bungalows between Stanley College and the cemetery. Parker: 'I was given a guide to conduct me and my Company to the Stanley Prison, the start line of my attack. I was to make a frontal advance to occupy the ridge beyond the cemetery and re-take the Indian Quarters on the right' (75: 40). But the Japanese defence is equally tenacious and heavy losses are taken (44: 101).

> The Canadians were reckless enough, but they were half-trained troops who had been through some rough experiences in the hills. We watched them fan out around the nearest red-and-yellow bungalow, from the porch of which hung a Japanese flag. They wove a kind of Indian circle around it, which suddenly faltered and broke, as dark blue smoke blossomed from the windows. The Nips inside had opened up at close range, and they had plenty of hand-grenades too. The attacking line wavered and broke, as men rushed downhill to cover. Everywhere else it was the same — the attack was spent almost as soon as begun. (101: 129)

Sergeant MacDonell:

> Within seconds we were upon the enemy . . . we took up positions in and around the houses and began to repel the Japanese counter-attack which now developed in some strength. Shells began to explode through the roof and walls of the houses. With ammunition running low, and the houses literally being shot to pieces around us, I received an order to pull back. (14: 95)[153]

Phil Doddridge:

> As I recall, on Christmas Day, when we left the Fort, although the Japs had bombed the building we were in over night, there was no mortar fire at that precise time. They did, however, follow us all the way to the cliff with mortar fire, and down into the Village, especially by the prison, where a huge pile of boxes marked 'TNT' had been stacked beside the prison wall. Shells were landing inside the prison, striking the wall from the inside near the pile of TNT. When we retreated back up the hill and across the 'level' space to return to the Fort, we were shelled again, all the way, even though it was getting dark. When we reached the Fort we were told that the Colony had surrendered. It is stated that 44 men staggered

back up the hill after the battle. I thought [Parker] counted 45. That helps to confirm my memory of what happened. I think I told you this before, but I'll say again, I'll never forget [Parker's] face as he counted the ragged remnants of the battle, with tears streaming down his face. (132b: Doddridge)

13.00   The Belcher's 18-pounder is sent to take up position near Wan Chai market to support the Middlesex. One of its targets is Japanese in a nearby air raid tunnel (93: 140).

13.00   Wan Chai market is successfully held by Middlesex and Rajputs against the Japanese advance, but Mount Parish is reported fallen (79: 273). Shah Mohammad's Rajput platoon there falls back to the meat market (140).

13.00   The O'Brien Street Line is established, held by sixty to seventy men of the Middlesex, with small parties from the Navy, the Engineers (20: 25), and a platoon of Rajputs under Mehar Khan on Ship Street (140).

13.00   The last radio communication from Fortress HQ is received at Stanley (139).

13.00   Assistant Superintendent Luscombe arrives at the Wan Chai police station only to find that — without notice — military units have withdrawn to Stewart Road and the police station is now forward of the front lines (131).

13.40   The Punjabis and Middlesex defending Kennedy Road have only six mobile guns left (79: 273).

14.00   Tanaka sends in all that is left of the 229th Regiment to surround Bennet's Hill. Within an hour, the Winnipeg Grenadiers there are forced to surrender (79: 272). But as the position is overrun, the wounded are not given a chance. Private James Fowler: 'thrusting their bayonets through the many wounded men lying on the ground' (95: 151).

14.00   Captain Crozier observes a large number of Japanese massing on Chung Hom Kok Height, and the 2 Battery HKVDC 6-inch guns at Bluff Battery in Stanley open fire to good effect. The Japanese return fire and knock out a 2 Battery gun (3: 54).

14.30   Communication with Wallis is reported lost. Forces holding the

PHASE V: PUSHING THE LINE WEST AND ENCIRCLING STANLEY 261

west are heavily shelled and dive-bombed. Aberdeen harbour is under heavy artillery fire. Only five MTBs remain. One waits south of Ap Lei Chau, and a launch belonging to HMS *Cornflower* (the pre-war training ship of the Hong Kong Naval Volunteer Force) prepares to reach it, carrying Admiral Chan Chak, Flight Lieutenant Max Oxford, Mr D. M. MacDougal (Head of Department of Information), Major Arthur Goring (Indian Army), Superintendent W. Robinson (Indian Police), Captain Peter MacMillan (RA), Captain Freddie Guest (Middlesex Regiment) and nine others. At about 17.00, the launch leaves boat leaves to take the men to the motor torpedo boats to make their escape to China. Montague: 'Meanwhile the motorboat had left, but unfortunately chose to leave by the South East Channel. Here they came under heavy fire (machine-guns and rifles) from the Japanese who had captured the A/A battery on the South West Point of Brick Hill. The boat was riddled and disabled. Colonel S. K. Yi and messers HARLEY and FOSTER were killed.[154] Captain DAMSGARD? was shot in both legs.' The launch is fired upon from a Japanese position on Brick Hill.[155] Several men are killed; others (including Admiral Chan Chak) are injured. The survivors swim to Ap Lei Chau and (after the MTB fires upon them) Freddie Guest swims out to it and explains the situation. Other motor torpedo boats approach from Stanley under fire (28: 68).

14.30   Wan Chai Gap is overrun (3: 58) after heavy dive-bombing, though a few Royal Scots are still being dive-bombed in positions just to the west. Colonel Rose, commanding Western Brigade from Magazine Gap, tells that he can only hold out for another twenty-four hours. Magazine Gap also comes under incendiary, mortar, and small arms fire (20: 25).

14.30   Canal Road is evacuated, and the defence withdraws to the O'Brien Street line (20: 25).

14.45   The Middlesex Battalion HQ set up at Murray Barracks.

14.50   Captain Man: 'the line is breaking' (20: 26). The Middlesex also withdraws to the line along O'Brien Street, just to the east of the Southorn playground.

15.00   The six British officers held captive at the Maryknoll Mission (including Lt. Lawrence, RE) are murdered (38: 177), together with a number of other ranks.

15.15   The fighting in Wan Chai is now officially described as 'confused' (93: 140). Maltby advises H.E. the Governor that further military effort is useless (20: 26).

15.25   General Maltby advises all Commanding Officers to surrender.

15.30   At the Naval Dockyards on the north coast of the Island, Crowther:

> That afternoon, at about 3.30 p.m. I was standing to with about twelve sailors by a large shell hole in the dockyard wall on the east side, facing the enemy who were then about 200 yards down the road with nothing between us, as they had broken through. We only had rifles (I had a revolver) but no machine guns or hand grenades, and I was wondering what sort of a show we would put up when I was informed to cease-fire. We had surrendered. (99: 38)

15.30   Official surrender.

Goodwin, recovering in the University Hospital: 'One of the VADs, a vivacious little French girl,[156] came over with eyes streaming tears to announce, "they've surrendered"' (45: 19).

15.40   News of the surrender reaches West Brigade HQ (Magazine Gap). They refuse to believe it until Colonel Newnham confirms the order.

16.30   Nurses Begg, Buxton, and Smith are taken from their room at St Stephen's. They are repeatedly raped, then mutilated and murdered.[157]

16.43   The British finally raise the white flag. The Japanese refuse to believe it and continue firing. Lieutenant Colonel White, Captain Douglas Ford, and Private G. King pass through the lines at Wan Chai Gap to meet the Japanese. After conferring at the Japanese HQ in Tai Hang, General Maltby and Governor Sir Mark Young

PHASE V: PUSHING THE LINE WEST AND ENCIRCLING STANLEY   263

cross the harbour from Queen's Pier under a white flag and formally offer a surrender to Sakai. They meet in the Peninsula Hotel, now named the 'Toa' by the invaders (95: 150).

17.00 Nurses Gordon and Simmons in St Stephen's are moved to a room with nurses Fidoe and Andrews-Loving. Fidoe and Gordon are taken out and repeatedly raped, lying on the bodies of five dead St. John's Ambulance personnel.

18.00 The formal laying-down-of-arms by the British garrison at the Japanese army HQ at Tai Hang commences. British, Indian, and Canadian troops of West Brigade are then concentrated in Murray Barracks, where they sleep.

18.00 Three Middlesex machine-gun sections are ordered to take positions along the Stanley wire (139).

21.00 Prophet and the survivors of the Scottish platoons swim to Stanley from their positions on Chung Hom Kok, not knowing that the surrender has already been made.

22.00 Lieutenant Colonel R. G. Lamb RE and Lieutenant J. T. Prior drive down from Fortress HQ to Stanley to order Wallis to stop fighting. Wallis refuses to believe the news,[158] and fighting at Stanley goes on. Major Harland is sent to get written confirmation of the surrender order. Japanese losses are heavy meanwhile. British troops remain in battle positions there, now in a line in the high ground in front of the fort. The Japanese are facing them in the scrub about one hundred yards in front of the fort (95: 152).

Roll of Honour for 25 December

VOLUNTEERS — 53 Killed

Black, George Duncan   Lieutenant Colonel, HKVDC HQ   K
   Murdered by Japanese in the St Stephen's massacre.

Begg, Eileen   Nurse, Nursing Detachment HKVDC   K
   Murdered by Japanese in the St Stephen's massacre.

Buxton, Alberta   Nurse, Nursing Detachment HKVDC   K
   Murdered by Japanese in the St Stephen's massacre. Husband killed on 18th (141).

Smith, Marjorie Mary   Nurse, Nursing Detachment HKVDC   K
  Murdered by Japanese in the St Stephen's massacre.

Cheng Kam Shing   Private, 4 Coy. HKVDC   K
  Died in hospital (145: 126).

Leung Chik Wai   Lance Corporal, 4 Coy. HKVDC   K
  Died in hospital (145: 126).

Ng Po Lau   Corporal, 4 Coy. HKVDC   K
  Died in hospital (145: 126).

Fateh Muhammad   Private, Special Guard Coy. HKVDC   K

Ghulam Husain Shah   Private, Special Guard Coy. HKVDC   K
  KIA Stanley area (126).

(2 Coy Chung Hom Kok)

Grant, Ian Farquharson   Private, 2 Coy. HKVDC   K
  Killed summit of Chung Hom Kok Height. Employed by Butterfield & Swire (145: 210).

Hearne, Henry John   Private, 2 Coy. HKVDC   K

Hobbs, Bertram Carmichael   Private, 2 Coy. HKVDC   U
  KIA Maryknoll (126).

Mackay, Colin Hector   Private, 2 Coy. HKVDC   U
  KIA and buried at Chung Hom Kok (126).

Thom, Charles Stuart   Lance Corporal, 2 Coy. HKVDC   U
  KIA and buried at Chung Hom Kok (126).

Bliss, Arthur Sidney   Gunner, 1 Bty. HKVDC   K
  Killed at Stanley. Body found on wire near internment camp (141).[159]

Buckingham, Harry William   Lance Bombardier, 1 Bty. HKVDC   U
  KIA at science block, St Stephen's College (126).[160]

Butlin, Strathmore Tatham   Gunner, 1 Bty. HKVDC   K

Collins-Taylor, Douglas Harvey   Lance Bombardier, 1 Bty. HKVDC   U
  KIA at science block St Stephen's College (126).

Duffy, Jocelyn Tierney   Gunner, 1 Bty. HKVDC   U
  KIA at science block, St Stephen's College (126).

Floisand, Alfred   Gunner, 1 Bty. HKVDC   K

Gerzo, Samuel Daniel   Gunner, 1 Bty. HKVDC   K
  Killed with Harry Millington. Originally buried St Stephen's College.

Griffiths, Ronald Hannam   Gunner, 1 Bty. HKVDC   K

Ho Lok Kee   Gunner, 1 Bty. HKVDC   U

Jones, H. S.   Lieutenant, 1 Bty. HKVDC   K
  Stanley. Trying to retake Millington's position. Originally buried at St Stephen's College.

Johnson, Lloyd George   Gunner, 1 Bty. HKVDC   U
  KIA at science block, St Stephen's College (126).

Kossakowski, Z.[161] Gunner, 1 Bty. HKVDC K
 Awarded a posthumous engineering degree by Hong Kong University (23: 17). Killed by flame thrower, Bungalow C (78: 167).

Lander, John Gerard Gunner, 1 Bty. HKVDC K

Lawson, W. Graham Gunner, 1 Bty. HKVDC K
 Killed with Harry Millington. Originally buried at St.Stephen's College.

Lipkovsky, Boris Gunner, 1 Bty. HKVDC U
 KIA science block, St Stephen's College (126).

Lodge, Cyril John Gunner, 1 Bty. HKVDC U

Lyon, David Gunner, 1 Bty. HKVDC K

McCabe, Lawrence Hugh Gunner, 1 Bty. HKVDC U
 KIA garden of bungalow, St Stephen's College (126), which gives alternating date of 24 Dec.

Millington, Henry James Sergeant, 1 Bty. HKVDC K
 Killed Stanley. Prison Road

Muir, Hugh Gordan Second Lieutenant, 1 Bty. HKVDC K
 Stanley. Bungalow C (Barton's bungalow). Originally buried there.

Nash, Robert Charles Gunner, 1 Bty. HKVDC K

Orr, Douglas Bombardier, 1 Bty. HKVDC K
 Part-time lecturer in geography at Hong Kong University (23: 299) Originally buried Bungalow C.

Rudrof, Wladyslaw Pawel Gunner, 1 Bty. HKVDC K
 Originally buried Bungalow C.

Samuel, Herbert Gunner, 1 Bty. HKVDC K
 Killed in Stanley (101).

Sayers, M. W. Gunner, 1 Bty. HKVDC K

Smith, Charles Abercrombie Gunner, 1 Bty. HKVDC K
 Bungalow C (Barton's bungalow). Originally buried there. Shot above left eye (78: 167).

Stafford, A. B. Gunner, 1 Bty. HKVDC K
 Buried Stanley cemetery (126).

Stone, Geoffrey Paul Lance Bombardier, 1 Bty. HKVDC K
 Bungalow C (Barton's bungalow). Originally buried there.

Thomerson, Godfrey Lance Corporal, 1 Bty. HKVDC U
 Missing believed killed at science block, St Stephen's College (126).

Yung Yue Wang Gunner, 1 Bty. HKVDC U
 Missing believed killed at science block, St Stephen's College (126).

Wilkens, Kurt Gunner, 1 Bty. HKVDC U

Wyllie, Roy Leslie Gunner, 1 Bty. HKVDC K

Gaubert, Edward Arthur Corporal, 1 Coy. HKVDC U
 KIA Stanley Village area (126).

Lambert, William Robert   Private, 1 Coy. HKVDC   U
    Buried at Mount Parker (126).

Lowry, George Trevor   Private, 1 Coy. HKVDC   U
    Resident Magistrate, Hong Kong. Missing believed killed area of Stanley village (126).

Potter, John Edward   Warrant Officer II, Company Sergeant   U
    Major, 1 Coy. HKVDC
    Missing believed killed area of Stanley village (126).

Williams, Charles Lloyd   Lance Corporal, 1 Coy. HKVDC   U
    KIA at Stanley village (126).

Bagley, Walter J.   Sergeant, Stanley Platoon HKVDC   U

Lim, John Anthony   Gunner, 4 Bty. HKVDC   U
    Missing believed killed at Stanley (126).[162]

RAJPUTS — 3 Killed

Amar Singh   Sepoy   U
Jaimal Singh   Sepoy   U
Shah-Ul-Hamid   Sepoy   U

ROYAL RIFLES — 26 Killed

Adams, Bryce   Rifleman   K
Baker, John Vincent   Rifleman   K
Bertin, Edmund   Rifleman   U
    DOW, buried St Stephen's College (126).

Cormier, Frank   Rifleman   K
    Originally buried Stanley Fort (126).

Fallow, William   Lance Corporal   U
    Buried St Stephen's Hospital (126).

Forsyth, Delmar William   Rifleman   K

Henderson, Elzie J.   Rifleman   U
    Murdered in St Stephen's College.

Hunchuck, Harold   Rifleman   K
    Originally buried Bungalow C.

Irvine, Bertram   Rifleman   U
    Last seen Stanley village (126).

Irvine, Crandel   Rifleman   U
    Killed at Stanley (100: 268).

Kinnie, Ronald   Rifleman   K
Lafferty, Harvey Reginald   Rifleman   K

PHASE V: PUSHING THE LINE WEST AND ENCIRCLING STANLEY 267

Lyons, Jack J.	Lance Corporal	U
Killed by a shell? (21: 204). Buried St Stephens College (126).		
MacLean, Charles L.	Rifleman	U
Last seen Stanley village (126).		
Major, Wilson	Rifleman	U
Killed at Stanley (100: 270).		
Mann, James Burnett	Rifleman	U
Stanley village (126).		
McClellan, Wendell	Corporal	U
Last seen Stanley village (126).		
McGuire Ralph	Rifleman	K
McKay, John	Rifleman	U
Murdered in St Stephen's College.		
Moir, Andrew	Rifleman	K
Nellis, Leo F.	Rifleman	U
Killed Stanley village (126).		
Noseworthy, Percy R.	Rifleman	U
Killed near St Stephen's College (126).		
Poag, Russel	Lance Corp.	K
Bungalow C (Barton's bungalow). Originally buried there.		
Pollock, Frederick W.	Rifleman	U
Last seen Wong Nai Chung Gap. Killed (126).		
Sheldon, Bertram	Rifleman	K
Surette, Henry Andrew	Rifleman	K

ENGINEERS — 5 Killed

Arundell, Richard	Lieutenant, RE	K
Attached 22 Fortress Company (145: 112). Missing Craigengower area (126).		
Chester, Theodor Alexander	Sapper, 22 Fortress Coy. RE	U[163]
Morris, John Albert	Sapper, 22 Fortress Coy. RE	U
Died at Repulse Bay (126) on 25 Dec.		[8/25 Dec.]
Buick, Albert Latham	Warrant Officer I, 40 Fortress Coy. RE	K
Missing, Maryknoll, Stanley (126).		
Lawrence, Thomas Walter	Lieutenant Quartermaster, RE	K
Murdered at Maryknoll, Stanley (38: 177).		

MIDDLESEX — 48 Killed

(Stanley ridge, Bennet's Hill, Little Hong Kong, Morrison Hill, and Wan Chai defence)

Baker, Thomas Frederick	Sergeant	U
Maryknoll massacre.		

Baldock, Charles Richard	Private	K
Ex- PB 28. Killed by missile (dynamite?) west of St Stephen's at 04.00 with Carpenter (139).		
Barkway, George Rex	Lance Corporal	U
Bedward, Benjamin Harry	Sergeant	K
Killed, with his entire section, defending Bennet's Hill (91: 192).		[8/25 Dec.]
Blackaby, Gurth Silverlock	Lieutenant, 1st Bn. Middlesex Regt.	U
Killed attacking Japanese in copse near the preparatory school (139).		[24 Dec.][164]
Blake, Harry Robert	Private	U
Blanche, Thomas Wilfred	Private	K
Killed near Bungalow C (Barton's bungalow). Originally buried there.		
Braun, Jack Francis	Private	U
Killed at PB 28 in Stanley.		
Broadbent, Joseph Rhodes	Lance Corporal	U
Broome, Thomas William	Private	U
Killed Brick Hill vicinity, 25 Dec. (126).		[8/25 Dec.]
Buller, Alfred Victor	Lance Corporal	U
Burgess, Joseph Thomas	Lance Corporal	U
Killed at PB 28 in Stanley.		
Carpenter, Frederick William	Private	K
Killed at 04.00 on 25th (139). Originally buried at Stanley Bungalow C (145: 18).		[4 Dec.]
Cohen, Bernard	Private	U
D Coy (126).		
Cooper, William George	Lance Corporal	U
Missing north face (i.e. north coast) (126).		
Corrigan, Francis Gerald	Private	K
Killed on Brick Hill with Bedward.		[8/25 Dec.]
Harvey, Thomas Sidney	Sergeant	U
Maryknoll massacre.		
Geary, Edward Charles	Private	K
Bungalow C (Barton's bungalow). Originally buried there.		[8 Dec.]
Ginsburg, Leonard	Lance Corporal	K
Served as 'Winter'. Killed at around 07.45 attacking the Stanley bungalows (139).[165]		[8/25 Dec.]
Irwin, Richard	Private	U
Missing Little Hong Kong area (126).		
Johns, Thomas Henry	Sergeant	K
Killed attacking the Japanese in a copse near the preparatory school.		
Jones, Alfred	Private	K
Jones, John David	Private	U

Kelly, Percy Cecil   Private   U
    Killed at PB 28 in Stanley.

Lane, Eric   Lance Corporal   U
    Wounded at the new PB 23 position, and killed while returning for medical aid (139).[166]

Lewis, Sidney George   Private   U
    Middlesex says 25 Dec. (96: 419).   [8/25 Dec.]

Luty, Victor   Private   K
    Killed attacking the Japanese in a copse near the preparatory school.

Malham, Reginald   Private   K
    Middlesex says 25 Dec. (96: 420), and DOW (145: 152).[167]   [8/25 Dec.]

Martin, Robert Alfred James Private   U
    Escaping Maryknoll to Repulse Bay?   [8 Dec.]

McAlpin, George Henry   Private   U

Merry, James   Private   U
    Middlesex says 25 Dec. (96: 421). Killed evacuating PB 27 (139).[168]   [8/24 Dec.]

Mills, William   Lance Corporal   U

Morton, George Robert   Sergeant   U
    Maryknoll massacre.

Mould, Sidney Charles   Private   U

Newman, Sidney Gordon   Second Lieutenant   U
    Killed at Maryknoll. See (135), CO 980/52.   [8/25 Dec.]

North, Henry John   Private   U
    Probably Maryknoll massacre (see 98).[169]   [8/25 Dec.]

Orton, Henry Bertram   Private   U
    Killed at PB 28 in Stanley.

Powell, Ronald Ernest   Private   U
    Escaping Maryknoll to Repulse Bay?   [8 Dec.]

Price, Ernest Frederick   Private   U
    Escaping Maryknoll to Repulse Bay?   [8 Dec.]

Priest, Thomas James   Private   U
    Escaping Maryknoll to Repulse Bay? Killed PB 37 (126).   [8 Dec.]

Read, Leslie George   Private   U
    Escaping Maryknoll to Repulse Bay?   [8 Dec.]

Rimell, Leonard Albert   Private   U
    Missing North Point Electric area (126).

Scantlebury, Victor Archibald Lieutenant   U
    Killed at Maryknoll. See (135), CO 980/52.

Sells, Thomas John   Lance Corporal   U
    Killed at PB 28 in Stanley.

Sheehan, John Joseph   Sergeant   U
    Killed at PB 28 in Stanley.[170]

Steeds, James Thomas   Private   K
    Missing Happy Valley area (126).
Toomey, Francis William   Private   K
    Killed attacking the Japanese in a copse near the preparatory school.
Vince, Charles   Private   U
    Escaping Maryknoll to Repulse Bay?[171]   [8 Dec.]
Wynter-Blyth, Patrick   Second Lieutenant   K
    Killed by shellfire on Morrison Hill (96: 44). Originally buried [23 Dec.]
    'in quarry' there (126).

WINNIPEGS — 8 Killed

Barrett, Wilfred   Private   U
    Buried foot of Mount Cameron (126).
Caswill, Gabriel J.   Private   U
    Killed Magazine Gap (126).
Kelly, Lawrence   Private   K
    Died in hospital (145: 138).
Maltese, James   Private   K
Matthews, Denis   Private   K
    Buried Ordnance House on road from golf course to Wong Nai Chung Gap (126).[172]
Ouelette, Joseph   Private   K
Ross, Victor   Private   U
    Killed Magazine Gap (126).
Woytowich, Frank[173]   Private   K
    Killed Bennet's Hill shelter (126).

RAMC — 2 Killed

Parkin, William   Sergeant   U
    Shot dead trying to escape St Stephen's massacre (38: 170)   [18 Dec.]
Witney, Peter Norman   Captain   K
    Murdered by Japanese in the St Stephen's massacre

ROYAL SCOTS — 1 Killed

Moore, Theodore   Lance Corporal   U
    Killed Wong Nai Chung area (126).

SIGNALS — 6 Killed

Birkett, Gerald Anthony[174]   Signalman, Royal Corps of Signals,   U
                                HK Sig. Coy.
    Body found by Padre Davis and buried near SAH, 25 Dec. (126).   [8 Dec.]

Clover, Peter William	Signalman, Royal Corps of Signals, HK Sig. Coy.	U
Missing, believed killed (142). Buried SAH, 25 Dec. (126).		[15 Dec.]
Fleet, Alfred	Signalman, Royal Corps of Signals, HK Sig. Coy.	U
Body found by Padre Davis and buried near SAH, 25 Dec. (126)		[8 Dec.]
Howell, Joseph Edward	Signalman, Royal Corps of Signals, HK Sig. Coy.	U
Killed at Stanley by shellfire (142). 25 Dec. (126).		[8/25 Dec.]
Palmer, Herbert Slader	Lance Corporal, Royal Corps of Signals, HK Sig. Coy.	K
Died in hospital (145: 130). BRH, of wounds sustained in Wan Chai (142).		
Sproul, William Lamont	Signalman, Royal Corps of Signals, HK Sig. Coy.	U
Missing 25 Dec. (126).		[8/25 Dec.]

RASC — 2 Killed

Abdul Rahman	Sepoy, HK Mule Coy. RIASC	U
(126) states 'Kowloon' but with no date.		
Hickey, Overton Stark	Captain, RCASC	U
Stanley massacre; killed while trying to protect the nurses (107: 378).		

ARTILLERY — 98 Killed

Beadle, John Patrick	Gunner, 8 Coast Regt. RA	U
Believed killed at Maryknoll (150), which also gives alternative dates of death of 23/24 Dec.[175]		
Ingleton, Thomas Dixon	Warrant Officer II, Bty Sergeant Major, 8 Coast Regt. RA	U
Missing Stanley area (126).		
Larthe, Michael Rex	Gunner, 8 Coast Regt. RA	U
Missing Maryknoll area (126).		
Marsden, William	Gunner, 8 Coast Regt. RA	U
Missing Maryknoll area (126).		
Pritchard, William Charles	Lance Bombardier, 8 Coast Regt. RA	U
Missing Maryknoll area (126).		
Stutt, Samuel James	Gunner, 8 Coast Regt. RA	K
KIA, Stanley guardroom, 25 Dec. (150).[171] (126) states 23 Dec.		[8 Dec.]

(In last 24 hours fighting, 1 officer of 12 Coast Regt., 1 Sergeant, and 8 ORs lost helping Middlesex as infantry)

Dobb, Charles Edward	Gunner, 12 Coast Regt. RA	U
Stanley Road area (cremated) (126).		

Drury, Herbert	Sergeant, 12 Coast Regt. RA	U
Craigengower–Canal Road. Unburied (126).		
Ford, Christopher	Gunner, 12 Coast Regt. RA	U
Craigengower–Canal Road. Unburied (126).		

(Stanley 2-pounders, Wan Chai market 18-pounder)

Climo, Reginald Thomas	Sergeant, 965 Defence Bty. RA	U
Killed Stanley police station. Unburied. Possibly cremated (126).		[8 Dec.]
Gurditt Singh	Gunner, 965 Defence Bty. HKSRA	U
Hamad Ullah	Lance Naik, 965 Defence Bty. HKSRA	U
Kaha Singh	Gunner, 965 Defence Bty. HKSRA	U
Muhammad Husain	Gunner, 965 Defence Bty. HKSRA	U
Roscoe, Ronald	Gunner, 965 Defence Regt. RA	U
Originally buried east of Chung Hom Kok military road (126).		
Ward, Eric Phillip	Lance Bombardier, 965 Defence Bty. RA	U
(126) states that he was killed at Stanley police station, was unburied and possibly cremated.		
Sayid Khan	Lance Naik, 1 HK Regt. HKSRA	U
Dost Muhannad	Gunner, HKSRA	U
Shakar Khan	Gunner, HKSRA	U
Tara Singh	Gunner, HKSRA (14240)	U

(Stanley 3.7-inch)

Abdul Haq	Gunner, 1 Mountain Bty. HKSRA	K
Ali Muhammad	Havildar, 1 Mountain Bty. HKSRA	U
(126) states 'Kowloon', though without a date and under 5 AA Regt. HKSRA.		
Allah Bakhsh	Gunner, 1 Mountain Regt. HKSRA	U
Malik Jan	Gunner, 1 Mountain Bty. HKSRA	U
Sher Bahadur	Havildar, 1 Mountain Bty. HKSRA	U
Taj Muhammad	Gunner, 1 Mountain Bty. HKSRA	U
Munshi Khan	Gunner, 1 HAA Bty. HKSRA	U
Ibrahim Khan	Gunner, 2 Mountain Bty. HKSRA	K
Allah Yar Khan	Lance Naik, 2 Mountain Bty. HKSRA	U
(126) states 'Kowloon', though without a date and under 5 AA Regt. HKSRA.		
Niranjan Singh	Gunner, 2 Mountain Bty.	U
Sardar Ali	Gunner, 2 Mountain Bty. HKSRA	U
Sultan Ahmad	Havildar, Mountain Bty. HKSRA	U
Saudagar Singh	Gunner, 3 Medium Bty. HKSRA	U

Thakur Singh	Gunner, 4 Medium Bty. HKSRA	U

(7 AA West Bay)

Barkat Ali	Gunner, 7 HAA Bty. HKSRA (7271)	U
Harnam Singh	Gunner, 7 HAA Bty. HKSRA	U
Malkhan Singh	Lance Naik, 7 AA Bty. HKSRA	U
Muhammad Karim	Gunner, 7 AA Bty. HKSRA	U
Muhammad Khan	Havildar, 7 AA Bty. HKSRA	U
Sher Muhammad	Gunner, 7 AA Bty. HKSRA (7152)	U
Sher Zaman	Lance Naik, 7 AA Bty. HKSRA	U
Wilayat Khan	Gunner, 7 HAA Bty. HKSRA	U
Farman Ali Tweed Bay Hospital (126).	Gunner, 8 AA Bty. 1 HK Regt. HKSRA	K
Tara Singh	Gunner, 8 Heavy Regt. HKSRA (7132)	U
Amir Ali	Havildar, 10 Heavy Bty. HKSRA	U

(126) states 'Kowloon' though without a date and under 5 AA Regt. HKSRA.

Kartar Singh	Gunner, 12 Heavy Bty. HKSRA (12957)	U
Kartar Singh	Gunner, 15 Mountain Bty. HKSRA (15380)	U

(Southern tip of Brick Hill 17 HAA)

Bartram, Harry Bob Killed defending Brick Hill.	Captain, 5 HAA Regt. RA	K
Akbar Ali	Gunner, 17 HAA Bty. HKSRA	U
Ali Ahmad	Gunner, 17 HAA Bty. HKSRA	U
Barkat Ali	Gunner, 17 HAA Bty. HKSRA (6580)	U
Fateh Muhammad	Gunner, 17 HAA Bty. HKSRA	U
Gulab Khan	Gunner, 17 AA Bty. HKSRA	U
Ilam Din	Gunner, 17 HAA Bty. HKSRA	U
Inayat Ali	Gunner, 17 HAA Bty. HKSRA	U
Jamil Muhammad	Gunner, 17 HAA Bty. HKSRA	U
Khushi Muhammad	Gunner, 17 AA Bty. HKSRA	U
Mehar Khan	Gunner, 17 HAA Regt. HKSRA	U
Mian Muhammad	Gunner, 17 AA Bty. HKSRA	U
Muhammad Akbar	Religious Teacher, 17 AA Bty. HKSRA	U
Muhammad Ali	Gunner, 17 HAA Bty. HKSRA	U
Muhammad Amir	Gunner, 17 AA Bty. HKSRA	U
Muhammad Anwar	Gunner, 17 HAA Bty. HKSRA	U

Muhammad Ashraf	Gunner, 17 HAA Bty. HKSRA	U
Muhammad Sadiq	Gunner, 17 HAA Bty. HKSRA	U
Muhammad Zaman	Cook, 17 HAA Bty. HKSRA	U
Riaz Muhammad	Gunner, 17 HAA Bty. HKSRA	U
Sardar Beg	Gunner, 17 HAA Bty. HKSRA	U
Sarfaraz Khan	Gunner, 17 HAA Bty. HKSRA	U
Shadi Khan	Gunner, 17 HAA Bty. HKSRA	U
Sher Muhammad	Gunner, 17 AA Bty. HKSRA (8828)	U
Wali Muhammad	Gunner, 17 AA Bty. HKSRA	U
Yusuf Ali	Gunner, 17 HAA Bty. HKSRA	U

(18 AA Stanley)

Abdul Satar	Gunner, 18 AA Bty. HKSRA	U
Ali Muhammad	Gunner, 18 AA Bty. HKSRA	U
Faqir Husain	Gunner, 18 AA Bty. HKSRA	U
Ghulam Husain	Gunner, 18 AA Bty. HKSRA	U
Inayat Ali	Gunner, 18 Heavy Bty. HKSRA	U
Muhammad Khan	Gunner, 18 HAA Bty. HKSRA	U
Sadhu Khan	Gunner, 18 AA Bty. HKSRA	U
Tufail Muhammad	Gunner, RA 18/5 HAA Bty. HKSRA	U
Ali Bahadur	Gunner, 20 Coast Bty. HKSRA	U
Ali Sher	Gunner, 20 Coast Bty. HKSRA	U
Imam Din	Gunner, 20 Coast Bty. HKSRA	U
Muhammad Khan	Gunner, 20 Coast Bty. HKSRA	U
Nur Muhammad	Gunner, 20 Coast Bty. HKSRA	U
Pahlwan Khan	Gunner, 20 Coast Bty. HKSRA	U
Rahmat Ali	Gunner, 20 Coast Bty. HKSRA	U
Baghicha Singh	Gunner, 20 Heavy Bty. HKSRA	U
Darshan Singh	Gunner, 20 Heavy Bty. HKSRA	U
Hazara Singh	Gunner, 20 Heavy Bty. HKSRA	U
Bullen, John 'Red'	Gunner, 24 Bty. 1 HK Regt. HKSRA	U

    At Stanley. Covering the withdrawal of the 965 Defence Battery 2-pounder. MiD (30: 46).[177]

Allah Dad	Gunner, 26 Coast Bty. HKSRA	U
Khidar Hayat	Gunner, 28 Coast Bty. HKSRA	U
Gulwant Singh	Havildar, 35 Mob. Coast Defence Bty. HKSRA	U

Gurbakhsh Singh	Gunner, 35 Mob. Coast Defence Bty. HKSRA	U
Gurdev Singh	Lance Naik, 35 Mob. Coast Defence Bty. HKSRA	U
Chanan Singh	Havildar, 36 Heavy Bty. HKSRA	U

NURSES — 3 Killed

Badri Datt	Ambulance Sepoy, Combined Military Hospital IHC	U
St Stephen's massacre.[178]		
Dalip Singh	Nursing Sepoy, Combined Military Hospital IHC	U
St Stephen's massacre.		
Ganga Sagar Dikshit	Havildar, Combined Military Hospital IHC	U
St Stephen's massacre.		

POLICE — 3 Killed

Harnam Singh	Lance Sergeant, HKPF	U
Lam Chi Ming	Constable, HKPF	U
Tang Yau	Constable, HKPF	U

MERCHANT NAVY — 1 Killed

Harley, D	Second Engineer, SS *Yatshing*, Merchant Navy	UT

Killed in *Cornflower*'s boat by Japanese firing from captured AA battery on Brick Hill.

ROYAL NAVY — 21 Killed

Forster, J. J.	Sub-Lieutenant, HKRNVR	UP

Killed in *Cornflower*'s boat by Japanese firing from captured AA battery on Brick Hill.[179]

Cremen, John	Leading Stoker, HMS Redstart, RN	UP
Andrews, Cornelius	Able Seaman, HMS *Tamar*, RN	UC
Bowden, Leonard A.	Petty Officer Telegraphist, HMS *Tamar*, RN	UP

MTB 26? In which case, it should be 19 Dec.

Corpse, William	Chief Petty Officer, HMS *Tamar*, RN	UP
Little, Walter John	Engine Rm. Artificer, HMS *Tamar*, RN	UP
Selman, Albert James	Petty Officer, HMS *Tamar*, RN	UC
Shipp, John James	Able Seaman, HMS *Tamar*, RN	UC
Welsh, Francis	Petty Officer, HMS *Tamar*, RN	UP
Whapshare, Stanley G.	Shipwright 3rd Class, HMS *Tamar*, RN	UP

Williams, John Middleton	Able Seaman, HMS *Tamar*, RN	UP
Deakin, Herbert Thomas	Petty Officer, Stoker, HMS *Thracian*, RN	UP
Egan, George	Able Seaman, HMS *Thracian*, RN	K
Greig, Henry Dollar	Ordinary Seaman, HMS *Thracian*, RN	UC
Harrison, George	Ordinary Seaman, HMS *Thracian*, RN	UC
Henderson, Robert	Ordinary Seaman, HMS *Thracian*, RN	UC
Keith, Robert John	Ordinary Seaman, HMS *Thracian*, RN	UC
Kendall, James Lowden	Stoker 1st Class, HMS *Thracian*, RN	UC
Kingham, John	Able Seaman, HMS *Thracian*, RN	UP
Porrett, Harvey Loveday	Able Seaman, HMS *Thracian*, RN	UP
Thomas, Frederick G.	Stoker 1st Class, HMS *Thracian*, RN	UC

CIVILIANS — 5 Killed

Eales, Harold Gordon ARP.		UCWD
Hast, William Francis		UCWD
Moreton, Eric	The Revd., Methodist Missionary Society	K

In the RNH as 'Asst. Army Chaplain' (145: 196).[180]

Tam Cheung Huen   UCWD
   Husband of Lucy Tam, of St Stephen's College, Stanley. Murdered in massacre (4: 155).

Perritt, William   Captain, Merchant Marine RNH   UX
   Beaten to death by Japanese (see *South China Morning Post*, Monday 15 Sept. 1946).

26 DECEMBER FRIDAY

> When D Company [Royal Rifles] was ordered to clear out '15 or 20' Japanese from Stanley Village, a vigorous soccer game was in progress on the field at Stanley Fort. I remember wondering what world the players were living in to be so unconcerned that the enemy was at our door, and wondered why they were not sent out with us. (Phil Doddridge)[181]

It is a time for reflection. As the Japanese march into the naval dockyards and disarm personnel there (99: 38), Lieutenant Stoker HKVDC, reaches St Stephen's College and takes the four surviving British nurses away (3: 55).[182]

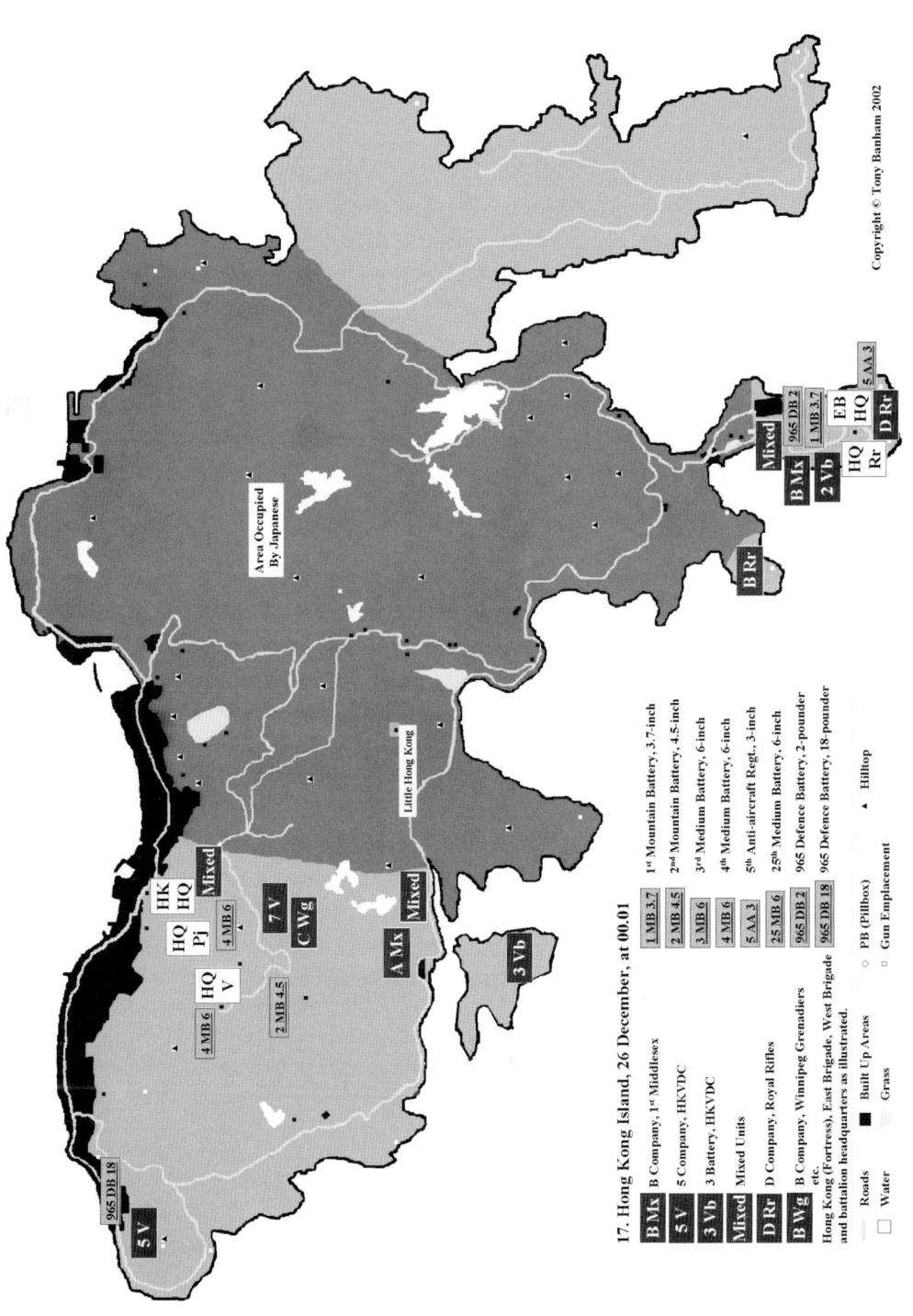

Harland returns from meeting the Japanese in Tai Hang, carrying a written message from Stewart of the Middlesex stating that the Colony has surrendered, and a second directly addressed to Wallis:

> Dear Brigadier,
>
> What I now send to you is the exact words of the G.O.C. General Maltby. Like himself and the Governor who had to go the local Japanese Commander, you will have to do the same. Until you do, no action can or will be taken by the Japanese.
> I am very sorry but there it is,
>
> Yours Sincerely
> (Signed) STEWART. (139)

With the fighting over, both sides are able to take stock. Allied forces bury their dead, in the few places where they have access to them,[183] and the Japanese burn theirs. Civilians emerge from the air raid shelters into bright sunlight. Many of them wish that they'd stayed where they were, as the Japanese now go on a three-day vacation from discipline. 'On the night after Christmas . . . Under pretext of searching for arms or suspects, they broke into house after house at the point of a gun. Once in, they slapped, kicked, murdered, stole, and raped. Throughout the night we heard people wailing and crying in the distance: Save life! Save life! And the desperate beating of hundred of gongs, tins, and pans. The whole of Happy Valley rang from end to end with these pleas for help' (52: 109). The witness, writing in 1964, later concluded: 'Anyone who witnessed the tidal wave of Japanese sex crimes in Hong Kong, or in any other city they captured, could be excused for thinking that the Japanese were by nature a race of sexual criminals' (52: 111).

'The night of the day immediately following the Garrison's surrender, General Maltby and I took the colours of the 1st Middlesex and the 2/14 Punjabis and buried them in the grounds of Flagstaff House': Lieutenant Ian MacGregor, ADC to General Maltby (6: 23).

Diary for 26 December

00.45 Forty-five minutes into Friday, 26 December, Brigadier Wallis finally gives the surrender order at Stanley:

Phase V: Pushing the Line West and Encircling Stanley 279

> By order of His Excellency the Governor and General Officer Commanding His Majesty's forces in Hong Kong have surrendered. Stop. On no account will firing or destruction of equipment take place as otherwise all lives of British hostages will be endangered. Stop. Units will organise themselves centrally forthwith. Stop. (Signed) C. Wallis Brigadier, 0045hrs, 26.12.41. (91: 228)

02.00 Operations cease (139).

02.30 Within two hours all firing has ceased (95: 155).

02.30 Leaving Lt. Col. SHAW, R.A. in local command I then proceeded with my Brigade Major (Maj. HARLAND, 2 R.S.) to the Headquarters of the local 'FRONT COMMANDER' Major M. EGASHIRA. His H.Q. was in a large white Chinese House in STANLEY Village, 400 yards NORTH of STANLEY POLICE Stn at 248471.

Major M. EGASHIRA treated me with courtesy and consideration. We remained prisoners for the rest of the night. Eventually, about 10.00 hours on receipt of confirmation from HONG KONG Japanese H.Q. he released me. He also later released my Brigade Major on the arrival of Capt. JAMES R.A. who remained at the FRONT Comdr's H.Q. where a telephone was connected to the FORT. (139)

11.00 In one of the unluckiest encounters of the war, Police Sergeant Leslie is ordered to lead an anti-looter patrol at 11.00. Going up the stairs of 6 Hospital Road (131) to investigate a robbery, he is shot in the groin and dies of his wounds.

Roll of Honour for 26 December

POLICE — 1 Killed

Leslie, Richardson Barry   Lance Sergeant, HKPF   K
    Shot by looters. Admitted Queen Mary Hospital 26 Dec., died same day (145: 81).[184]

ENGINEERS — 2 Killed

Ho Ling   Sapper, RE   K
    Died in hospital (145: 140) at BRH on 26 Dec. and buried in No. 2   [10 Dec.]
    Crater, Borret Road.

Fox, Thomas		Lance Corporal, 22 Fortress Coy. RE		U
Hospital records state he was admitted to Queen Mary Hospital		[29 Dec.]
19 Dec., and died 26 Dec. (145: 76).

MIDDLESEX — 2 Killed

Anson, Alfred		Private		U
Middlesex says 26 Dec. (96: 408). Killed Overbays area 19 Dec. (126).[185] [8/25 Dec.]

Wragg, Joseph William		Private		K
DOW, Bowen Road BMH.[186]

ROYAL RIFLES — 12 Killed[187]

Boudreau, Vance E.		Rifleman		U
KIA Stanley Mound (126).

Burgess, Walter J.		Rifleman		U
Last seen Stanley Mound (126).

Chalmers, Ralph K.		Rifleman		U
Last seen Wong Nai Chung Gap (126).

Dixon, Alfred A.		Rifleman		U
Buried SSH (126).

Doran, Alexander		Rifleman		U
Last seen Red Hill (126).

Evans, Joseph		Rifleman		K

Long, John R.		Rifleman		U
Last seen Chung Hom Kok (126).

Mahoney, Murray T.		Rifleman		U
Last seen Stanley Village (126).

Main, James S.		Rifleman		U
DOW. Buried St Stephen's College (126).

Moore, Claude		Rifleman		U

Murphy, Claud P.		Rifleman		U

Potts, William G.		Rifleman		U

VOLUNTEERS — 2 Killed

Bell, Robert Sidney		Staff Sergeant, PWD Corps HKVDC		K

Hardwick, Douglas William		Private, 2 Coy. HKVDC		U
DOW, Stanley (126).

ROYAL NAVY — 1 Killed

Rowell, Robert   Able Seaman, HMS *Cicala*, RN   UC
    Admitted Queen Mary Hospital 25 Dec., died 26 Dec. (145: 87)   [25 Dec.]

ROYAL SCOTS — 1 Killed

Urquhart, Hector   Private   K
    DOW (145: 180 says 26 Dec.). Buried No. 2 Crater,   [25 Dec.]
    Borret Road BRH (126).

8 The Week Immediately Following the Fighting

On Saturday, 27 December, the Japanese flag is raised in Central. However, they are still not fully in control of the Island. Lewis Bush HKRNVR, a fluent Japanese speaker with a Japanese wife, is sent at the request of the Japanese to the Little Hong Kong ordnance depot near Aberdeen, where some Royal Engineers are still refusing to surrender. Eventually they emerge and the Japanese take them to Aberdeen, treating them as heroes (95: 163).[1]

Security is lax, and for those willing to take a gamble escape is possible. Corporal Salter of the Royals Scots declined to report to POW camp, instead donning civilian clothes and passing himself off as a Norwegian.[2]

St Stephen's temporary hospital is finally evacuated. British and Canadian casualties go to the British Military Hospital on Bowen Road or to Queen Mary Hospital, Indian forces to Queen Mary Hospital, and light cases to Stanley Fort.

On Sunday, 28 December, the Commanding Officer of the Middlesex sends out a message:

To All Ranks
I am directed by the Commanding Officer to inform you that he wishes all ranks to know how proud he is of your magnificent

behaviour in the short period of hostilities which unfortunately ended in the surrender of the Crown Colony of Hong Kong. The garrison was up against a division and a half of enemy. We had no Air Force and no Navy and, regrettable as it sounds, this was inevitable.

The gallantry, devotion to duty, and the loyalty displayed by all under the most harassing and nerve-wracking conditions has not only earned the praise of HE The Governor and the General Officer Commanding, but the entire civilian population of Hong Kong, who now realise what the Battalion has done. Individual acts of gallantry have been performed but the Commanding Officer finds it difficult to single out any particular soldier as one and all did their utmost and deserve his praise.

The sticking power shown by all is traceable to the high standard of discipline which Colonel Stewart has insisted upon ever since he was honoured with the command of the 1st Battalion. He knows that all ranks, after due consideration, will realise this.

Lastly, while in captivity he looks to all ranks to uphold this fine tradition of unflinching obedience to orders. The time will one day come when we shall reach what we most wish, namely our homes wherever they may be. Time will hang heavily but patience must be exercised.

The Regiment has nothing to be ashamed of. Fortune has not shined on us just lately but remember that all things work together for good.

His thanks are due to all.

Hong Kong 28.12.41 A.G. Hewitt, Capt & Adjt 1MX. (76: 6)

That day, Major Young of the Royal Rifles and the thirty-four men with whom he escaped from Altamira on the 23rd, land at Telegraph Bay (having hidden on the wreck of HMS *Thracian* and on Lamma, in the mean time) and are captured by the Japanese (100: 160).

As the Japanese mount a victory parade of 2,000 men in Victoria led by the Divisional Commander (Lt. Gen. T. Sano) on a white-nosed horse, and their air force gives an air display, the garrison troops and civilians are rounded up. The Royal Naval forces from the dockyard are marched to Murray Barracks and imprisoned with army personnel, and RAMC personnel are ordered to gather at British Military Hospital Bowen Road, but alien internees are released by the Japanese and driven to Repulse Bay Hotel.

Conditions in the hospitals, overflowing with wounded, are

becoming intolerable. Dr Isaac Newton at Argyle Street Hospital: 'I am beginning to find the stench of pus pretty trying. The mortality is going to prove terrific.'

Monday the 29th sees the water supply finally restored in Central (44: 115), and permission is at last given for Commonwealth forces to search for their wounded. Many are found along Repulse Bay Road, tied up and murdered. Others are found bayoneted in pillboxes or shot in ditches. Most who avoided summary execution have already died of wounds (8: 26).

Two thousand two hundred Allied POWs from East Brigade at Stanley are paraded in front of General Sakai and told they will be marching to a new camp the next day (8: 24).

At 01.00 on Tuesday, the HKRNVR party on Shouson Hill is finally taken into captivity. The morning sees the Stanley POWs march north. During the trip, Canadian Rifleman A. Pryce is found alive after having been bayoneted during the fighting.[3] He had locked himself in a concrete shelter on the 19 December and survived on rum. Later, they arrive at the North Point refugee camp (8: 25).[4]

In parallel, 7,000 POWs from West Brigade (and navy) assemble in Victoria in the early morning. They move by ferries to Kowloon and thence to Sham Shui Po, where they arrive some ten hours after assembly (8: 27). 'The whole camp had been stripped of every useful article by looters and had also been bombed. All doors, windows, furniture, and fittings had been taken leaving just hulks of buildings. Even in peace time it was an awful dump, but now it looked as if a typhoon had hit it' (89).

Most men only worry about their personal possessions, but Captain Thompson of the Royal Army Pay Corps has other things on his mind, smuggling HK$90,000 into the camp in a basket covered with clothes.[5]

On the last day of the year, Wednesday, 31 December, in an attempt to restore some urban normality, the Chinese Chamber of Commerce petition Japanese authorities asking for services to be restored and the increasing prostitution stamped out. Hong Kong's first newspaper to be published since 26 December hits the street. It is a Japanese-run English language propaganda sheet called *Hong Kong News*.

What did Hong Kong look like at this time? An American missionary, Bob Hammond, who had been hiding from the Japanese in Kowloon, surrendered and was driven to Stanley Camp some days after. He describes seeing the damaged buildings at the waterfront, and then Happy

Valley and Wong Nai Chung Gap along Wong Nai Chung Gap Road. As they pass the cemetery to the west of the Jockey Club, 'All around us, and especially down in the valley, were hundreds of British and Canadian soldiers lying where they had been killed'. Then through to the Gap: 'We were riding along now on a road that had seen tremendous bloodshed, and all around was evidence of a battle having been fought, burnt lorries, soldiers' equipment, helmets, shoes and clothes scattered everywhere' (12: 53). Others described Leighton Hill and its environs looking like the Somme.

In Sham Shui Po POW camp, the first, inadequate, food is prepared (8: 29). Garrison personnel and civilians alike, start what will be — for those lucky enough to survive the experience — three years and eight months of captivity.[6]

The four junior members of Z Force descend from the hills and surrender to a Japanese pack battery that had seen action in Repulse Bay. Parsons: 'When we got to Kowloon Tong we found ourselves in the midst of a herd of horses and when we reached the corner (white hankies in hand) we met a large contingent on a New Year's morning march. It was like a Walt Disney cartoon. The first file halted and those behind concertinaed into the file in front. One might have laughed under different circumstances.' The Japanese sergeant, who had been a newspaper correspondent in Europe, gives them a note saying:

> If you want *anything to take with you, tell* us tomorrow morning. We will do *anything for you as long as we can.* We all hope your happiness, your new start not as a soldier but as a man of peace. Good NIGHT. We Japanese soldiers think that you are all *Man of Peace* not Man of War. (161)[7]

Roll of Honour, 27 December

ROYAL RIFLES — 1 Killed

Rattie, Alexander   Rifleman   K
   Probably murdered at Eucliffe (137).

ROYAL SCOTS — 1 Killed

Tierney, John   Warrant Officer II, Company Sergeant Major   U
   DOW in hospital (145: 134). Originally buried in front of officer's mess, Murray Barracks (126).

THE WEEK IMMEDIATELY FOLLOWING THE FIGHTING   287

Roll of Honour, 28 December

MIDDLESEX — 1 Killed

Slaughter, John Henry   Lance Corporal   K
   Fatally wounded at 08.30, 25 Dec. manning the rightmost machine-gun in the Stanley
   line (139).

ROYAL RIFLES — 1 Killed

Swanson, Kurt   Rifleman   K

CIVILIANS — 1 Killed

Garton, Mrs F. K.   UCWD
   'Died during hostilities' (9: 172).[8]

Roll of Honour, 29 December

WINNIPEGS — 1 Killed

Orvis, Harry   Private   K
   Admitted Queen Mary Hospital 24 Dec., DOW 29 Dec. (145: 85).   [27 Dec.]

ROYAL RIFLES — 1 Killed

Little, Orval Louis   Lance Corporal   K

MIDDLESEX — 1 Killed

Lusham, James   Corporal   K
   Killed China Fleet Club (126).[9]

ROYAL SCOTS — 2 Killed

Brown, Thomas Archibald   Private   U
   Died of wounds (145: 181). Buried behind SAH (126).
Holmes, Frank   Lance Corporal   U
   Died in hospital (145: 132). Buried behind SAH (126).[10]

ARTILLERY — 3 Killed

Hall, John Joseph   Gunner, 12 Coast Regt. RA   U
   Missing. Last known North Point 29 Dec. 1941 (126).[11]
Stokes, Kenneth Herbert   Gunner, 12 Coast Regt. RA   U
   Missing. Last known North Point 29 Dec. 1941 (126).

Muhammad Azam   Gunner, 1 HK Regt. HKSRA   U

VOLUNTEERS — 1 Killed

Wong Sing Hoi   Private, 4 Coy. HKVDC   U

Roll of Honour, 30 December

WINNIPEGS — 1 Killed

Gunn, John James   Private   K
   Died of septic shrapnel wounds of back, buttock, and scrotum   [29 Dec.]
   (145: 125), (145: 198).[12]

POLICE — 1 Killed

Fazal Shah   Constable, HKPF   U
   Admitted Queen Mary Hospital 27 Dec., died 30 Dec. (145: 75)   [25 Dec.]

Roll of Honour, 31 December

ENGINEERS — 2 Killed

Hyndmam, Edward Filomeno   Sapper, Field Coy. Engineers HKVDC   K
   Admitted WMH on 20 Dec. Died 31 Dec. (145: 95).

Smith, Alfred Edgar   Sapper, 22 Fortress Coy. RE   K
   Admitted WMH on 21 Dec. Died 31 Dec. (145: 97).   [8/25 Dec.]

RAJPUTS — 1 Killed

Abdul Samad   Sepoy   U
   Died of bacillary dysentery (145: 198).

ARTILLERY — 1 Killed

Mian Khan   Gunner, 1 HK Bty. HKSRA   U

POLICE — 1 Killed

Arjun Singh   Constable B.478, HKPF   U
   Admitted to Queen Mary Hospital (as Argan Singh) 18 Dec. (145: 70). [1 Dec.]
   Died December.

9 Conclusion

Post-war, the Battle of Hong Kong was largely forgotten about. In British eyes, the fall of Hong Kong had been overshadowed by many greater tragedies closer to home. Hong Kong people themselves either wanted to put the whole experience behind them, or simply had little time for history in the struggle to survive as China went through its upheavals of civil war and communism. For the Indians, the pain of partition in the wake of British withdrawal dominated the immediate post-war period.

In the mid-1950s, the first general account of the fighting was written by Stewart of 3 Company, HKVDC (3). This had a cathartic effect on many survivors, who needed some sort of recognition of what had happened. Within the next decade, popular works by Luff (91) and Carew (94) appeared, and at last the battle was on the historical radar.

The books that appeared later fell into two main groups: biographies or general histories. Neither ever produced truly comprehensive accounts. The former, by definition, were accounts from a single viewpoint, and the latter were generally based on the same timelines (either that of Maltby's despatch or Stewart's work) fleshed out with interviews. If the book was written in the UK, the interviews were naturally generally with British survivors; if written in Canada, they were generally Canadian. Again, neither was likely to give a comprehensive view.

In the 1980s and 1990s, however, the vast majority of new books to have been written on the subject were Canadian. The majority of these works make almost no mention of any units other than the Winnipeg Grenadiers and the Royal Rifles.

The task of this book, therefore, was primarily to pull together the information in all previous works, reconcile them, and fill in the gaps. With a garrison of only 14,000 defenders, it has been possible to do this — at least in part — at the level of the individual. Completed early in 2002, this is surely one of the last books to be written about the battle with the help of those who were there.

In summary of that battle, General Maltby had been given an impossible task. He was charged with defending a small isolated island, without armour or sea and air cover, against a numerically superior and battle-hardened enemy.

That they held out at all, let alone for eighteen days, is remarkable. Churchill's wish to make invasion as hard as possible for the Japanese — which in the greater scheme of things was an integral part of his eventually successful strategy — was granted. And yet the cost was horrendous.

When I first started this work, in 1990, I came across the documents mentioned in the introduction: 'List of Patients Unlikely to Recover Before 12 Months', and 'List of Patients Unlikely to Become Fit Enough for Further Military Service' (145). At that time the Hong Kong PRO was in Central — in a building now entirely occupied by the Independent Commission against Corruption — and the documents were the crumbling originals. The sense of immediacy I felt as I held them is hard to describe.

In April 2000, I came across those documents again, but this time in the PRO's new purpose-built Kwun Tong offices. They had all been photocopied and bound together in a single 200-page document. Immediacy had given way to convenience, but the content was unchanged. Here are one or two examples from each major unit involved:

Warrant Officer Easterbrook, RN	Peripheral neuritis
Able Seaman Smith, RN	Low wound with faecal fistula
Corporal Green, W. Grenadiers	Shell wound — perineum & rectum
Private Anderson, W. Grenadiers	Great emaciation: fractured tibia
Rifleman Sweetman, Royal Rifles	Depressed fracture of skull

Rifleman Steeves, Royal Rifles	Fractured radius with great loss of tissue and fractured tibia and fibula
Company Sergeant Major Tarrant, RASC	Paralysis — arms and legs
Private Marshall, HKVDC	Haemothorax: general debility
Lance Corporal Long, HKVDC	Amputation of leg
Private Canivet, RCOC	Ununited fracture of humerus; fracture of mandible and general debility
Sapper Moore, RE	Shell wound — left arm: spinal nerve injury
Sapper Stevens, RE	Gun shot wounds — spine
Private Bickley, RAMC	Blinded: both eyes removed
Private Barrett, Middlesex	Loss of patella: stiff knee
Private Wiggins, Middlesex	Amputation of leg
Lance Bombardier Palmer, RA	Multiple wounds — amputation of leg
Gunner Woodfin, RA	Fractured left arm; nerve injury right arm
Signaller Spendelow	Amputation — thigh
Signaller Bates	Shell wounds — shoulder; glenoid cavity
Lieutenant Thompson, RAF	Gun shot wound — neck
Lieutenant Gilmor, Punjabis	Compound fracture of skull
Private Crichton, Royal Scots	Haemothorax; wounds of back; fractured ribs
Private McKay, Royal Scots	Shell wounds — shoulder; paralysis right arm

The last words of this book were written by someone who was there at the time, Inspector Fred Kelly of the Hong Kong Police Force, in a diary he started in January 1942 in Stanley internment camp as a long — and personal — letter to his wife:

> All the time we knew, or at least I did, that we were fighting a losing battle. It was so different to what I'd expected. We didn't stand a chance. (141)

10 Epilogue

Hong Kong really took off from a base of being the most looted city in the world—there wasn't a piece of wood to be seen in Hong Kong when I got back from Shanghai where I'd been a prisoner of war. And the whole city was, well, there was one cable across the harbour, there was some light in one or two buildings on this side (Hong Kong-side) and there was some light at the Peninsula Hotel, which was the Japanese headquarters. But other than that there wasn't any light at all in the place. And it was black. Rats all over the place and the complete and utter destruction you might say, on the Peak. There wasn't a single house that was habitable at all. No doors, no windows. People had left their dogs and big dogs had eaten the little dogs and become so wild that they had to get police with guns to shoot these dogs because it was so dangerous.

And in fact when you look from that ruin it was and how it became one of the most important cities in the world, it's really, it's a miracle. But that was done largely through hard work and I think the fact that Hong Kong didn't wait to say well somebody else must pay for this. We sat down immediately, let's get busy, let's get things going. It is normal here to work hard. It's normal here to take work as something which one is given and should do and wants to do with a view to trying to climb, get higher each time, do something better. This is the point of view of the Hong

Kong citizen generally and that was the main element which caused it to grow the way it has grown."[1]

NOTICE
Will all persons having
Knowledge of the where-
Abouts of the Graves of
Any Allied Service Per-
Sonnel who were killed in
Battle, died of wounds, died in
Hospital or internment camps,
Or under any other circum-
Stances what-so-ever please
Communicate with MAJOR
J. C. RIDDELL, HQ LAND
FORCES, VICTORIA BAR-
RACKS.[2]

HK GARRISON CASUALTIES

True Figures Will Never Be Sorted Out[3]

Appendices

APPENDIX 1. ADDITIONAL CASUALTIES

During the period from the invasion to the surrender, many British and Commonwealth troops were left where they were killed. Many wounded were also left to die as the places where they lay were overrun by the Japanese. After the surrender their bodies were retrieved and buried, but the precise dates of their deaths were not always recorded. For the majority, research has enabled them to be listed on the correct day. The others are listed below:

ENGINEERS — 5 Killed

Yip Wing Mau	Lance Corporal, 22 Coy. RE	(December)	U
Chan Tsan	Sapper, 40 Coy. RE	(18/25th)	U
Fong Fook	Lance Corporal, 40 Coy. RE	(8/25th)	U
Wood, George Heney	Sapper, 40 Fortress Coy. RE	(8/25th)	U

CWGC says 22 Fortress Coy. RE (145: 115) says 40 Fortress Coy.[1]

Yau Kwok Kung	Corporal, 40 Coy. RE	(20/25th)	U

MIDDLESEX — 4 Killed

Grainger, Walter Harold	Private	(8/25th)	U

Attached HK Chinese Regt. (145: 153). Missing area south of The Ridge (126).

Pearce, Ernest Thomas	Sergeant	(8/25th)	U
Wraight, Albert	Corporal	(8/25th)	U
Attached HK Chinese Regt. (145: 153).			
Thompson, William Henry	Corporal	(8/25th)	U
Attached HK Chinese Regt. (145: 153).			

HONG KONG CHINESE REGIMENT — 2 Killed[2]

Leung Shui Ming	Private, Hong Kong Chinese Regt.	(20/25th)	U
Li Fu	Private, Hong Kong Chinese Regt.	(8/25th)	U

SIGNALS — 1 Killed

Dixon, Henry Villiers	Lance Corporal, Royal Corps of Signals, HK Sig. Coy.	(8/25th)	K
Killed at Stanley (142), therefore probably 25 Dec.[3]			

ARTILLERY — 1 Killed

Lee Hon Man	Bombardier, RA	(8/25th)	U

POLICE — 3 Killed

Li Lim Sang	Constable, HKPF	(December '41)[4]	U
Muhammad Amin	Constable, HKPF	(December)	U
Wong Hin	Lance Sergeant, HKPF	(December)	U

RASC — 13 Killed

(All but Focken can be assumed to have lost their lives in The Ridge, Overbays, and Eucliffe massacres)

Benford, Lawrence Albert	Mechanist Staff Sergeant, 12 HK Coy. RASC	(8/25th)	U
Missing (145: 190).			
Chaters, Benjamin	Driver, 12 Coy. RASC	(8/25th)	U
Dean, Percy	Warrant Officer II SQMS, 12 Coy. RASC	(8/25th)	U
Missing (145: 188).			
Dryden, William Elliot	Corporal, 12 Coy. RASC	(8/25th)	U
Missing (145: 188).			
Focken, Frederick John	Captain, RASC	(18/25th)	U
Reported as missing (145: 187). Killed by a landmine at Repulse or Deep Water Bay (126).			

APPENDICES   297

French, Walter George	Mechanist Staff Sergeant, 12 Coy. RASC	(8/25th)	U
Missing (145: 190).			
Knightly, Douglas Haigh	Driver, 12 Coy. RASC	(8/25th)	U
Legg, George C.	Lance Corporal, RASC	(8/25th)	U
Missing (145: 189).			
McMahon, Matthew Oysten	Driver, 12 Coy. RASC	(8/25th)	U
Missing (145: 190).			
Merrifield, George Victor	Staff Sergeant, 12 Coy. RASC	(8/23rd)	U
Missing (145: 188).			
Swan, James	Corporal, 12 Coy. RASC	(8/25th)	U
Missing (145: 189).			
Walker, Denvers Roy	Driver, 12 Coy. RASC	(8/25th)	U
Missing (145: 189).			
Walton, George	Corporal, RASC	(8/25th)	U
Missing (145: 188).			

RAOC — 11 Killed

(All can be assumed to have lost their lives in The Ridge/Overbays/Eucliffe massacres)

Chung On	Private, RAOC	(8/25th)	U
Earley, Alfred	Corporal, RAOC	(22/24th)	U
Holloway, Ernest Douglas	Warrant Officer I, Sergeant Major, RAOC	(22/23rd)	U
Kerley, Harry George	Lance Sergeant, RAOC	(22/23rd)	U
Neale, Reginald A.	Warrant Officer I, Armament Sergeant Major, RAOC	(22/24th)	U
Palmer, Gerald Noel	Staff Sergeant, RAOC	(22/23rd)	U
Paul, John Berry	Corporal, RAOC	(22/23rd)	U
Phillips, William	Corporal, RAOC	(22/23rd)	U
Reynolds, John	Corporal, RAOC	(22/23rd)	U
Saunders, Frank George	Lance Corporal, RAOC	(22/23rd)	U
Wells, Leslie Herbert	Private, RAOC	(21/22nd)	U

CIVILIANS — 9 Killed

December 1–31

Ah Loy			UCWD
Gillen			UCWD
Headington, Alfred John			UCWD

Kwok Kun   UCWD
Li Lin   UCWD
Man Ho   UCWD
Mortan   UCWD
Yau Kwai Shu   UCWD
Lim Ban Sing, Luke   Civilian Medical Service   UX
   Killed by a sniper on his way to a hospital assignment (23: 133), or by shell (23: 16).

APPENDIX 2. THE DEFENDERS ON THE EVE OF INVASION

Army

British and Local Forces
    Headquarters, China Command
    Head Quarters
    G
    Admin
    A
    Q
    Command Royal Artillery
    Command Engineers
    Command Signals
    Command RASC
    Command Ordnance
    Medical Service Branch
    Command Barrack Officer
    Financial Advisor & Army Audit Staff
    Provost Marshall — Corps of Military Police
    2nd Echelon
Royal Artillery
    8 Coast Regiment, RA
        12th Coast Battery
        30th Coast Battery
        36th Coast Battery
    12 Coast Regiment, RA
        24th Coast Battery
        26th Coast Battery

APPENDICES   299

    5 AA Regiment, RA

    965 Defence Battery RA

    Hong Kong & Singapore Royal Artillery (HKSRA), 1st Hong Kong Regiment

        1 Mountain Battery

        1 HAA Battery[5]

        1 AA Regiment

        2 Mountain Battery

        2 Heavy Battery

        3 Coast Battery

        3 Medium Battery

        4 Medium Battery

        5 Mountain Battery

        5 Heavy Battery

        6 Coast Battery

        <u>7 AA Battery</u>

        8 AA Battery

        8 Heavy Regiment

        <u>12 Heavy Battery</u>

        15 Mountain Battery

        17 HAA Battery

        18 AA Battery

        20 Coast Battery

        <u>24 Coast Battery</u>

        25 Medium Battery

        <u>26 Coast Battery</u>

        28 Coast Battery

        <u>30 Coast Battery</u>

        <u>36 Heavy Battery</u>

    Royal Engineers

        HQ Fortress Engineers

        22 Fortress Company, RE

        40 Fortress Company, RE

        RE Services

    2nd Battalion, the Royal Scots Regiment

    1st Battalion, the Middlesex Regiment

    Hong Kong Chinese Regiment

Royal Corps of Signals, Hong Kong Signals Company

Royal Army Ordnance Corps (RAOC)

Royal Army Service Corps (RASC), 12 Hong Kong Company

Royal Army Veterinary Corps (RAVC)

Army Educational Corps

Corps of Military Police

Royal Army Medical Corps (RAMC), 27 Company

Royal Army Dental Corps (RADC)

Royal Army Pay Corps (RAPC)

Queen Alexander's Imperial Nursing Service (QAIMNS)

Royal Army Chaplain's Department

Hong Kong Volunteer Defence Corps (HKVDC)

    Corps HQ

    Supply & Transport

    Corps Artillery HQ

    1st Battery

    2nd Battery

    3rd Battery

    4th Battery

    5th (AA) Battery

    Field Company Engineers

    Corps Signals

    Armoured Car Platoon

    No. 1 Company

    No. 2 (Scottish) Company

    No. 3 (Eurasian) Company

    No. 4 (Chinese) Company

    No. 5 (Portuguese) Company

    No. 6 (Portuguese) LAA Company

    No. 7 Company

    ASC Unit

    Pay Detachment

    Reconnaissance Unit

    Field Ambulance

    Special Guard Company

    Hughes Group

APPENDICES   301

>   Fortress Signal Company
>   Stanley Platoon
>   Nursing Detachment

Canadian
>   Canadian Staff
>   Corps of Military Staff Clerks
>   Canadian Provost Corps
>   Royal Canadian Army Medical Corps (RCAMC)
>   Canadian Army Dental Corps
>   Canadian Service
>   Royal Canadian Corps of Signals (RCCS)
>   Royal Canadian Army Service Corps (RCASC)
>   Royal Canadian Army Pay Corps (RCAPC)
>   Canadian Postal Corps
>   Royal Canadian Ordnance Corps (RCOC)
>   Canadian Chaplains Service
>   Canadian Auxiliary Services
>   Winnipeg Grenadiers
>   Royal Rifles of Canada

Indian[6]
>   Indian Hospital Corps (IHC)
>   Indian Medical Service (IMS)
>   Royal Indian Army Service Corps (RIASC)
>   Hong Kong Mule Corps RIASC
>   5th Battalion, 7th Rajput Regiment
>   2nd Battalion, 14th Punjab Regiment

Royal Navy

HMS *Tamar*
>   Royal Marines (*Tamar*)

HMS *Thracian*

HMS *Thanet*

HMS *Scout*

HMS *Tern*

HMS *Robin*

HMS *Redstart*

HMS *Cicala*

HMS *Moth*

Auxiliary Patrol Vessels

    APV *Minnie*

    APV *Margaret*

    APV *St. Aubin*

    APV *St. Sampson*

    APV *Indira*

    APV *Henriette*

    APV *Shun Wo*

    APV *Han Wo*

    APV *Frosty*

    APV *Poseidon*

    APV *Ho Hsing*

    APV *Teh Hsing*

    APV *Chun Hsing*

    APV *Perla*

Smaller Vessels

    APV *Stanley*

    APV *Britannia*

    HMS *Barlight* (Boom Service Vessel)

    HMS *Aldgate* (Boom Gate Vessel)

    HMS *Watergate*

    HMS *Cornflower* (HQ of HKRNVR)

    Naval Armament Tug *Gatling*

    Jeanette

    RFA *Ebonol*

Minor Vessels[7]

    C410

    Man Yeung (mine layer)

    HMT *Alliance*

    Poet Chaucer

    Waterboat *Wave*

    SS *Matchlock*

    Diesel Launch *Ah Ming*

APPENDICES   303

    Motor Torpedo Boats
        MTB 07
        MTB 08
        MTB 09
        MTB 10
        MTB 11
        MTB 12
        MTB 26
        MTB 27
    Hong Kong Royal Naval Volunteer Reserve
        HKRNVR Headquarters
        HKRNVR Minewatching Stations
    Fleet Air Arm
        Aircraft
            Supermarine Walrus   L2259
            Supermarine Walrus   L2819
    Queen Alexandra's Royal Naval Nursing Service
    Royal Naval Dockyard Police
    Hong Kong Dockyard Defence Corps (HKDDC)

Merchant Navy

SS *An Jou*
SS *Apoey*
SS *Ben Nevis*
SS *Cheng Tu*
SS *Fausang*
SS *Fook On*
SS *Glen Moor*
SS *Henry Keswick*
SS *Hsin Fuli*
SS *Kanchow*
SS *Kau Tung*
SS *Mausang*
SS *Nanning*
SS *Patricia Moller*
SS *Shun Chih*

SS *Soochow*
SS *St. Vincent De Paul*
SS *Tai Ming*
SS *Taishan*
MV *Tantalus*
SS *Tung On*
SS *Whithorn*
SS *Yat Shing*

Royal Air Force

Aircraft:
- Vickers Vildebeeste   K2924
- Vickers Vildebeeste   K2818
- Vickers Vildebeeste   K6370

MI6

Hong Kong Police Force

Indian Company, Police Reserve
Chinese Company, Police Reserve

Fire Brigade

Air Raid Precautions

Auxiliary Services

Auxiliary Services
Auxiliary Communications Service (under postmaster-general)
Auxiliary Conservancy Corps (under urban council)
Auxiliary Civil Pay and Accounts Service (under accountant-general)
Auxiliary Fire Service (under fire brigade)
Auxiliary Labour Corps (under controller of labour)
Auxiliary Medical Corps (under Director of Medical Services)
Auxiliary Nursing Service
Auxiliary Ordnance Corps (under controller of stores)
Auxiliary Quartering Corps (under rating & valuation officer)
Auxiliary Public Works Corps (under director of public works)

Auxiliary Rescue and Demolition Corps (under director of public works)

Auxiliary Supply Corps (under Kowloon-Canton Railway)

Auxiliary Transport Service (under police)

St. John's Ambulance

NAAFI

APPENDIX 3. MASSACRES

As far as can be calculated, approximately 325 of the garrison were killed after capture. This figure is a full 20% of those killed in action, and that percentage may be unmatched in any other battle involving British forces in the Second World War.

Sai Wan Hill

28 Killed: 5 regulars & 23 Volunteers of 5 AA Bty., HKVDC. Some may have died in the fight for the position:

Bakar, A.	Gunner
Bannister, Edgar Wallace	Sergeant
Broadbridge, William E.	Gunner
Chan U Chan	Gunner
Cheung Wing Yee	Gunner
Fincher, Ernest Francis	Bombardier
Ho, Algernon	Gunner
Kwok Wing Ching	Gunner
Lao Hsin Nain	Lance Bombardier
Leung Fook Wing	Gunner
Litton, John Letablere	Gunner
Ozorio, Manuel Heleodoro	Gunner
Paterson, Ernest Manuel	Gunner
Poon Kwong Kuen	Gunner
Reed, Francis Oswald	Gunner
Stokes, George Donald	Gunner
Stone, William	Gunner
Tsang Ka Pen	Gunner
Tse Wai Man	Gunner

Ulrich, Albert — Gunner
Ulrich, Peter — Gunner
Wilkinson, Joseph Nelson — Gunner
Zimmern, Andrew — Lance Bombardier

Of 5 AA RA:
Bennett, George — Lance Bombardier
Coughlan, Reginald E. — Sergeant
Macdonald, Kenneth H. — Lance Bombardier
Rhoden, William — Gunner
Ward, George Robert — Gunner

Salesian Mission

16 killed:

Quartermaster Sergeant, R. Buchan, RAMC
Sergeant E. Watt, RAMC
Corporal A. Newton, RAMC
Private H. L. Mohan, RAMC
Private A. C. Williams, RAMC
Private J. C. Dunne, RAMC
Private G. McFarquar, RAMC
Private R. W. Reid, RAMC
Private I. Langley, RAMC
Rifleman Oakley, Royal Rifles
Lance Corporal Harrison, Royal Rifles
Mr E. N. Orloff, Civilian
Dr. Harrison, Civilian
Subadar Abdul Ghani, 5th Bn. 7th Rajput Regt.[8]
Subadar Phul Singh, 5th Bn. 7th Rajput Regt.
Daniel Kelly, Driver (not confirmed)

Causeway Bay

At least 3 believed killed:

Lionel Lammert, HKVDC
Alice Adeline Baldwin, ARP
William Petrie Seath, ARP

Wong Nai Chung Gap

12 believed killed:
- 10 St. John's Ambulance personnel
- Captain Beauchamp Depinay Barclay, RAMC
- 1 Indian police constable.

Jardine's Lookout

At least 8 believed killed:

3 Coy. HKVDC
- Private Lim
- Private Gosling
- Private MacKechnie
- Lance Corporal Young

Winnipeg Grenadiers
- Private Kilfoyle[9]
- Lance Corporal Land
- Private Osadchuck
- Private Whalen

The 'Black Hole of Hong Kong'

At least 4 believed killed:
- Lieutenant William Vaughan Mitchell, Winnipeg Grenadiers
- Lieutenant Eric Lawson Mitchell, Winnipeg Grenadiers
- Private Dori O'Neil
- Corporal Tage Agerbak

Blue Pool Road

Some 30 civilians killed, including:[10]
- Chao Yut
- Mr Sit

The Ridge

At least 47 killed:[11]

Clarke, Charles Sydney	Major, HQ China Command
Page, Patrick George	Gunner, 12 Coast Regt. RA (Not confirmed)

Smith, Samuel	Lance Bombardier, 20 Coast Regt. RA (Not confirmed)
Cullen, Edward James	Driver, RASC
Cullen, William Jamieson	Driver, RASC
Jacobs, Edward	Driver, RASC
Kingsford, Edward Cyril	Corporal, RASC
Kloss, Rudolph Leopold	Captain, RASC
Wilson, Robert Henry	Driver, RASC
Berger, Max	Private, RCASC
Jackson, Albert	Corporal, RCASC
Adams, John Samuel Russell	Sergeant, RAOC
Burroughs, Sydney Gilbert	Captain, RAOC
Cole, Dennis Roy	Private, RAOC
Duffield, Sampson John	Staff Sergeant, RAOC
Dulson, Harry	Private, RAOC
Harland, Harry	Private, RAOC
Hearn, James Nelson	Warrant Officer II, Squadron Quartermaster Sergeant, RAOC
Johnson, Jack	Lance Corporal, RAOC
MacPherson, Robert Archibald	Lieutenant Colonel, RAOC
Martin, Albert George	Corporal, RAOC
Morries, Horace	Warrant Officer I, Sub-Conductor, RAOC
Nicholson, William	Sergeant, RAOC
Pennington, Arnold	Lance Corporal, RAOC
Simms, John Scott	Corporal, RAOC
Standing, Herbert	Lance Corporal, RAOC
Stopforth, Clifford	Private, RAOC
Taylor, David Alexander	Private, RAOC
Thrush, Francis Robert	Corporal, RAOC
Wallington, Charles Thomas	Lieutenant, RAOC
Desroches, Gerald G.	Corporal, RCOC
Jackman, George	Staff Sergeant, RCOC
McGuire, Frank C.	Private, RCOC
Brown, Conrad	Private, RASC Coy. HKVDC
Elliott, Frank	Private, RASC Coy. HKVDC

Fox, George Edmond	Private, RASC Coy. HKVDC
Hillier, Wilfred Samuel	Sergeant, RASC Coy. HKVDC
Jorge, Francis	Private, RASC Coy. HKVDC
Joseph, H. B.	Private, RASC Coy. HKVDC
Kern, E.	Private, RASC Coy. HKVDC
Lyen, Edmund Symlov	Private, RASC Coy. HKVDC
McCallum, Duncan	Sergeant, RASC Coy. HKVDC
Mann, A.	Company Quartermaster Sergeant, RASC Coy. HKVDC
Minhinnett, John Denniford	Private, RASC Coy. HKVDC
Peters, William Henry	Private, RASC Coy. HKVDC
Prew, Albert George	Private, RASC Coy. HKVDC
Rapp, Frederick Austin	Private, RASC Coy. HKVDC

Overbays

At least 14 killed:[12]

Pigott, Richard Stephen	Second Lieutenant, Middlesex
Doyle, Joseph L.	Rifleman, Royal Rifles
Armitage, George Doran Victor	Driver, RASC
Iggleden, Percy Frederick	Warrant Officer I, Squadron Sergeant Major, RASC
Mann, Henry Charles	Sergeant, RASC
Jack, Andrew	Lance Sergeant, RAOC
Singleton, John Henry	Warrant Officer II, Staff Quartermaster Sergeant, RAOC
Stonor, John Anthony	Lance Corporal, RAOC
Bonner, Horace William	Corporal, RASC Coy. HKVDC
White, Nowell Bernard	Lance Corporal, RASC Coy. HKVDC
Zimmern, W. A.	Corporal, RASC Coy. HKVDC
Percy, William Herbert	Private, RAOC
Reid, Colin	Rifleman, Royal Rifles
Martel, George H.	Corporal, Royal Rifles

Eucliffe

At least 7 dead:

Wynne, Richard Alfred	Lieutenant, RAOC
Gallant, Clement	Rifleman, Royal Rifles

McNab, Lorne R.	Sergeant, Royal Rifles
Delcourt, Armand	Private, RASC Coy. HKVDC
Zaharoff, Victor Isidor	Private, RASC Coy. HKVDC
Calman, Alexander	Private, 2 Coy HKVDC
Allen, Louis	Rifleman, Royal Rifles

The Ridge/Overbays/Eucliffe (not yet precisely placed):

Atwood, Percy C.	Rifleman
Best, William	Rifleman
Briand, Rannie	Rifleman
Bujold, Hubert	Rifleman
Doucet, Edgar	Rifleman
Firlotte, John F.	Rifleman
Jacques, Daniel	Rifleman
Lebel, Valmont	Rifleman
McIsaac, Joseph	Rifleman
McWhirter, John	Rifleman
Meredith, Eddie	Lance Corporal
Mohan, James W.	Lance Corporal
Moore, Walter L.	Rifleman
Benford, Lawrence Albert	Staff Sergeant, Mechanist, RASC
Chaters, Benjamin	Driver, RASC
Dean, Percy	Warrant Officer II, Staff Quartermaster Sergeant, RASC
Dryden, William Elliot	Corporal, RASC
French, Walter George	Staff Sergeant, Mechanist, RASC
Knightly, Douglas Haigh	Driver, RASC
Legg, George C.	Lance Corporal, RASC
McMahon, Matthew Oysten	Driver, RASC
Merrifield, George Victor	Staff Sergeant, RASC
Swan, James	Corporal, RASC
Walker, Denvers Roy	Driver, RASC
Walton, George	Corporal, RASC
Chung On	Private, RAOC
Earley, Alfred	Corporal, RAOC
Holloway, Ernest Douglas	Warrant Officer I, Sergeant Major, RAOC

Kerley, Harry George	Lance Sergeant, RAOC
Neale, Reginald A.	Warrant Officer I, Sergeant Major, RAOC
Palmer, Gerald Noel	Staff Sergeant, RAOC
Paul, John Berry	Corporal, RAOC
Phillips, William	Corporal, RAOC
Reynolds, John	Corporal, RAOC
Saunders, Frank George	Lance Corporal, RAOC
Wells, Leslie Herbert	Private, RAOC

Deepwater Bay Ride (Lyon Light)

At least 6 men believed killed:

Middlesex (137)[13]

St Stephen's College

At least 13 killed. Estimates go up to 99 killed.[14]

56 soldiers said to have been bayoneted in bed:
Names?

2 Riflemen mutilated and murdered:
Rifleman E. J. Henderson
Rifleman J. McKay

3 British nurses raped and murdered:
Mrs Begg
Mrs Buxton
Mrs Smith

4 Chinese nurses raped and murdered:
Names?

1 Canadian killed attempting to aid the nurses:
Captain Overton Stark Hickey, RCASC

2 Medical staff:
Dr Black
Dr Whitney

1 doctor shot in the head while attempting to escape:
Sergeant Parkin, RAMC

25 Indian orderlies and St John's Ambulance:[15]

Badri Datt	Ambulance Sepoy, IHC
Dalip Singh	Nursing Sepoy, IHC

Ganga Sagar Dikshit   Havildar, IHC

1 Civilian:

Mr Tam Cheung Huen

4 Chinese servants (4: 155):

Names?

Maryknoll Mission

At least 8 killed:[16]

Baker, Sergeant, Middlesex

Albert Latham Buick, Warrant Officer I, RE

Harvey, Sergeant, Middlesex

Thomas Lawrence, Lieutenant, RE

Morton, Sergeant, Middlesex

Sidney Gordon Newman, Second Lieutenant, Middlesex

Henry John North, Private, Middlesex

Scantlebury, Lieutenant, Middlesex[17]

Brick Hill

26 believed killed.

17 HAA, HKSRA. Some may have died fighting for the position:

Akbar Ali	Gunner
Ali Ahmad	Gunner
Barkat Ali	Gunner
Bartram, Harry Bob	Captain
Fateh Muhammad	Gunner
Gulab Khan	Gunner
Ilam Din	Gunner
Inayat Ali	Gunner
Jamil Muhammad	Gunner
Khushi Muhammad	Gunner
Mehar Khan	Gunner
Mian Muhammad	Gunner
Muhammad Akbar	Religious Teacher
Muhammad Ali	Gunner
Muhammad Amir	Gunner
Muhammad Anwar	Gunner

Muhammad Ashraf	Gunner
Muhammad Sadiq	Gunner
Muhammad Zaman	Cook
Riaz Muhammad	Gunner
Sardar Beg	Gunner
Sarfaraz Khan	Gunner
Shadi Khan	Gunner
Sher Muhammad	Gunner
Wali Muhammad	Gunner
Yusuf Ali	Gunner

APPENDIX 4. CIVILIAN AIRMEN OPERATING FROM KAI TAK

Robert S. Angle	CNAC
Hugh Chen	CNAC
Sydney H. De Kantzow	CNAC[18]
Frank Higgs	CNAC
Paul Wirt Kessler	CNAC
William McDonald	CNAC
Moon Ching	CNAC
Freddie Ralph	PanAm
William H. Schuler	CNAC
Emil Silvan Scott	CNAC
Charles L. Sharpe	CNAC
Harold A. Sweet	CNAC
Hugh Leslie Wood	CNAC
Jack Young	CNAC

APPENDIX 5. CASUALTY SUMMARY TABLES

Table 1. Fatalities listed in the text as December 1941.

	1	2	3	4	5	6	7	8	9	10	11	12	13	14	15	16	17	18	19	20	21	22	23	24	25	26	27	28	29	30	31	?	Total
HQ																			5	2		2											10
Artillery								1		4		2		1	5			22	61	24	12	5	6	16	98				3		1	1	271
Engineers														11		2	4	12	12	1	1	6	2	2	5	2					2	5	58
Royal Scots									3	1	29	2		2					23	10	9	9	12	10	1	1	1	1	2				115
Middlesex																1			22	6	1	1	21	22	48	2		1	1			4	130
Signals																			8	2		1	2		6							1	20
RAOC															1					2	2	23	4	3								11	44
RASC																			4	2	3	8	5		2							13	37
RAMC															1				13		1	1			2								18
Volunteers												1			3		1	28	55	2	8	19	9	23	53	2			1				205
Royal Rifles																		1	16	2	7	18	39	3	26	12	1	1	1				127
Winnipegs												1							65	18	19	10	5	3	8				1	1			131
Punjabis									1		5	2						33	5	6	25	1	1	1									80
Rajputs										2								31	99	2	2	1	2		3								143
Navy								1							1	2			31	2	5	1	5	1	21	1					1		71
RAF																			2	5													7
Police												1	4		2		2	8	22				1	2	3	1				1	1	3	51
Civilians												7			1	2	2	3	3	3		2	2	2	5			1				9	42
Nurses														1											3								4
HKDDC														1		6		2	5	3													18
Merchant N.																1					1				1								2
RAVC														1						1				1									1
HKCR																																2	4
Total	0	0	0	0	0	0	0	2	4	7	35	19	0	18	14	14	9	140	451	93	94	108	116	89	285	21	2	3	9	2	5	49	1589

Note that this table does not include the 55 St John's Ambulance personnel who died during the conflict at uncertain dates.

APPENDICES   315

Table 2. From Maltby's Despatch (20)

| | Officers |||| Other Ranks ||||
	KIA/DOW	Missing	Wounded	Strength	KIA/DOW	Missing	Wounded	Strength
HQ China Command	2	2	3	33		2	23	285
HQ RA		1		6				233
8 Coast Regt. RA			3	19	19	2	23	285
8 CR Indian						1	4	233
12 Coast Regt. RA	1	1	1	16	15	2	24	200
12 CR Indian					3		3	187
5AA Regt. RA		8	1	23	16	11	10	231
5 AA Indian					24	80	15	332
1st HKSRA	3	7	3	24	2	2	10	30
HKSRA Indian					144	45	103	830
965 Def. Bty. RA			1	3	2	4	8	58
965 Indian					2		4	86
22 Field Coy. RE		1		7	8	20	9	213
40 Field Coy. RE	2			7	2	7	1	220
RE Services		1	1	18	2	5	1	54
2 Royal Scots	12	4	11	35	96	45	188	734
1 Middlesex	10	2	4	36	94	25	110	728
Canadian Staff	2	4	3	14	6	10	5	78
Winnipegs	6	8	12	42	28	222	60	869

Table 2. (Continued)

	Officers				Other Ranks			
	KIA/DOW	Missing	Wounded	Strength	KIA/DOW	Missing	Wounded	Strength
Royal Rifles	6	8	4	41	42	157	160	963
5/7 Rajputs	6	4	7	17	150	109	186	875
2/14 Punjabis	3		5	15	52	69	156	932
RIASC							1	13
Royal Signals	1			7	16	5	14	177
RAOC	3	2	1	15	13	26	4	117
RASC	2		3	24	23	10	11	183
RAVC				2	2			3
RAMC	2	1		28	13	3	3	146
Dental Corps				4				6
RAPC				5			2	25
Military Provost						1		3
Military Police								18
Education Corps								8
Mule Corps			1	3	1	5	5	250
IMS/IHC		1		5		2		55
HKVDC	13	6	13	89	196	139	135	1296
TOTAL	74	61	77	538	971	1,007	1,255	10,438

Note: This table combines three separate tables in the original document, and removes the summation error.

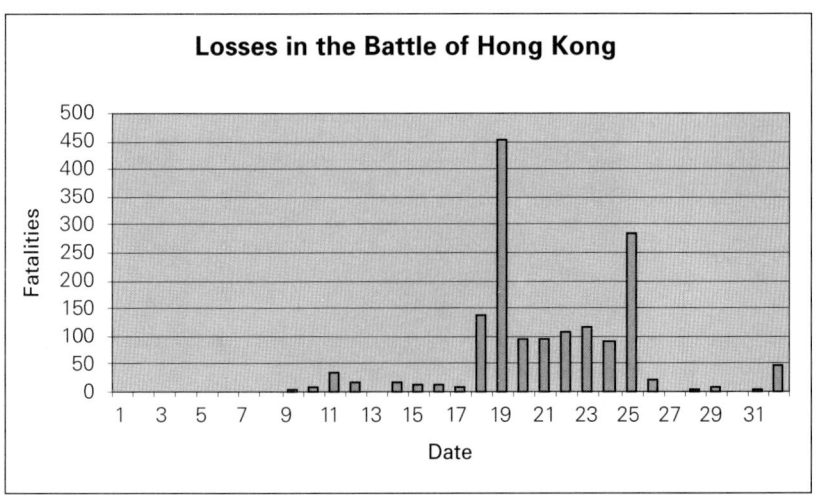

APPENDIX 6. BRITISH MILITARY LOSSES

Maltby's estimate of 2,113 military dead or missing does not correspond well with the approximately 1,560 listed in this book.

While there may well be some slight errors of omission (particularly in Naval and RAF records, and possibly with the Indian army — especially for the Rajputs, who were overrun so effectively and the majority of whose officers were lost), the biggest single anomaly lies in the fact that Maltby's estimate was made very shortly after the battle. Some of the missing simply had not yet turned up, and the majority of the others were in hospitals. It appears that Maltby did not cross-reference the hospital records, but solely made use of the units' individual records that were prepared at the same time.

Take 22 Fortress Company Engineers as a simple example. Of the 219 officers and men they entered battle with on 8 December, they reported 24 missing. Of these, 5 were actually alive (though 3 died before the war was over). Applying the same rough percentages to the total garrison of approximately 12,000, we can estimate that 1,200 would have been listed as missing in total, and of these some 240 and forty would have actually been alive at the surrender.

The War History Division of the Defence Agency of Japan states that the invaders counted 165 bodies on Kowloon side, and 1,555 on the Island. The former is certainly an exaggeration, though the latter is surprisingly accurate.

The CWGC records 190 known graves (i.e. with names on the headstones) from the period 1–25 December at Stanley, and a further 168 at Sai Wan, giving a total of 358. Together, these cemeteries include 621 unidentified individuals (including one from the Royal Navy and one from the Merchant Navy).

Memorials in Hong Kong cover a total of 1,099 losses with no known graves, the RN commemorates a further 64 offshore, and the RAF 5 on the Singapore memorial. In other words:

    358 personnel were identified and buried;
    621 personnel were buried without identification;
    547 bodies were never recovered from the sea and battlefields.[19]

Of that 547, some of the RN losses occurred at sea and the bodies would have been washed away — but the majority of RN deaths occurred on land as infantry. Some bodies — high explosives being what they are — would have been blown to pieces to a degree in which nothing significant remained to be buried. Some were certainly buried where they fell, and others probably disappeared into the cracks and crannies of Hong Kong's hills. They may still be found. Others, victims of massacres and — I suspect — Rajputs at the north shore sea front, would have been thrown into the sea. Eyewitness accounts (e.g. 31: 43) speak of the harbour being full of bodies, and although some claim they were Japanese, as one body looks much like another after a few days in the water.[20]

APPENDIX 7. CIVILIAN LOSSES

The CWGC list of Civilian War Dead in Hong Kong is very short (and many, in fact, appear to have been connected with the garrison), but in (32: 69) Selwyn Selwyn-Clarke estimates civilian dead during the fighting at 4,000 with a further 3,000 having been severely wounded.

    It seems that the deaths of Auxiliary Service members, St John's Ambulance staff, and ARP were seldom officially recorded. The St John's Ambulance state that a total of fifty-five of their members lost their lives during the war (132b: SJA). Other evidence suggests that some of these were killed in North Point during the initial invasion, about ten at Wong Nai Chung Gap (where a memorial to them now stands), and others at Stanley. All, it appears, were murdered.

APPENDIX 8. JAPANESE LOSSES

Japanese losses for the period of fighting are unknown. Estimates range from 675 killed in action and 2,079 wounded in action to 7,000 killed in action and 20,000 woulded in action. The *Hong Kong News* of 29 December 1941 put the figures at 1,996 killed and 6,000 wounded, which — though probably on the high side — is perhaps the most believable estimate as the total attacking force (of the 20,000 or so that actually landed in Hong Kong) is best estimated at 13,000. The bodies of the dead were cremated and their remains sent back to Japan. No list of names is known to have survived the war.

Most of the ordinary soldiers who survived the invasion were later shipped to Palembang, Sumatra, to attack the British and Dutch forces there (the 229th and one battalion of the 230th, via Camranh Bay on 20 January 1942, leaving for Sumatra on 9 February), or to Davao in the Philippines on 18 January, leaving there on 27 January for Guadalcanal to fight the Americans. It is unlikely that many survived.

APPENDIX 9.   HOSPITALS

During the hostilities, the Queen Mary Hospital — manned largely by students of Hong Kong University — dealt with over 1,200 severe casualties, both civil and military (23: 15).

The Canossian Hospital was on Peak Road and was destroyed by Japanese bombs said to have been aimed at a nearby AA position on Albany Road (32: 67). Signs of the bombing are still visible today, though the building itself has been replaced.

St Stephen's College at Stanley (1,420 beds) was a temporary hospital, and scene of the infamous massacre.

Stanley Prison Hospital took wounded from Stanley plus the overflow from St Stephen's.

Hong Kong Hotel (920 beds) was on Pedder Street. The wounded were nursed on mattresses laid out on the ballroom floor (16: 159).

Matilda Hospital was hit 97 times by bombs and shells. Situated on the Peak, it is still in service today.

St Albert's Convent at Rosary Hill (Stubbs Road) was a temporary hospital with 400 beds. It has since been replaced by a housing development.

The Jockey Club was a temporary hospital with 375 beds. It has been redeveloped.

The British Military Hospital on Bowen Road (which had 188 beds and was opened in 1907) is now a school. It was hit an estimated 111 times by Japanese shells during the fighting. It closed on 23 March 1945 and moved to the Central British School, Kowloon, where it reopened on 10 April 1945.

The Royal Naval Hospital is now the site of the Ruttonjee Sanatorium in Wan Chai. In 1941 it was on the waterfront and 'suffered almost a hundred hits from shells and heavy machine gun bursts' (32: 66).

The Indian General Hospital at Whitfield Barracks (with 120 beds) was commanded by Lieutenant Colonel C. Armstrong, RAMC. This moved from Kowloon to Tung Wah East (1,090 beds) on 14 December (110). The building still exists today.

University Hospital took the overflow from the Queen Mary.

The War Memorial Hospital was demolished post-war to make way for housing, though its foundation stone remains.

The Hong Kong Sanatorium in Happy Valley was used as a casualty clearing station and was shelled many times.

St Teresa's Hospital in Kowloon was used for Sham Shui Po prisoners after the surrender. It was closed down on 11 August 1942 and the patients were moved to BRH.

St Paul's Hospital at Causeway Bay (also known as the French Hospital) was hit by more than 200 shells (60: 133). The building still exists.

APPENDIX 10. MILITARY CEMETERIES

Stanley Military Cemetery

This cemetery was opened in the early days of the Colony for the burial of members of the garrison and their families. Closed for seventy years, it was re-opened in 1942 for the burials of those who died in Hong Kong while prisoners of war or in civil internment. After the war, battlefield burials from the 1941 fighting, particularly those of the Hong Kong Volunteer Defence Corps, were moved in.

Those buried in this cemetery include members of the British Army Aid Group, a military organization with a large staff of civilian employees operating in Japanese-held territory in China to facilitate escapes from, and get medical supplies into, the POW camps, to collect military intelligence and to act as an evasion and escape organization for American airmen shot down over Japanese-held territory. The burials from this group are of members who were captured in the course of these activities and subsequently executed.

The cemetery contains 691 burials — 37 Navy, 467 Army, 3 Air Force, 23 Merchant Navy, 98 civilian internees, 41 other civilians (including 39 of the British Army Aid Group) and 22 unknown — of whom 488 are British, 20 Canadian, 5 Indian, 157 Hong Kong, 11 Allied, and 10 entirely unidentified.

Chai Wan War Cemetery And Memorial

This, the principal cemetery for the burial of those who died in the defence of Hong Kong or subsequently in captivity, contains 1,578 graves — 59 Navy, 1,406 Army, 67 Air Force, 18 Merchant Navy, 20 local defence forces, and 8 civilians. 1,013 are British, 283 Canadian, 104 Indian, 33 Australian, 1 New Zealand, 1 Burmese, 53 Hong Kong, 72 Netherlands, and 18 others.

At the entrance to the cemetery stands the Sai Wan memorial bearing the names of 2,071 soldiers who died during the same period but have no known grave. 1,319 of these are from the British Army, 228 from the Canadian Army, 287 from the Indian Army, and 237 from the Hong Kong forces. The sailors and airmen whose graves are unknown are commemorated on the memorials at their home ports or on the Air Force memorial at Singapore.

There are also two special panels on this memorial. The first bears the names of 144 Hindus and Sikhs whose remains were cremated — 9 served in the Hong Kong and Singapore Royal Artillery, 118 in the Indian Army, and 17 in the Hong Kong Police Force. The second commemorates by name the 72 Commonwealth servicemen who died at various stations in China during the two world wars and whose graves are no longer maintainable.

Yokohama

Yokohama war cemetery commemorates 1,556 Commonwealth war dead — including all Hong Kong POWs who died in captivity in Japan — and 182 others.

Others

Many of Hong Kong's civilian cemeteries still contain one or two war graves, and there is one example — a Volunteer — buried outside the cathedral on Garden Road. A few can be found in cemeteries outside Hong Kong and Japan, and the unknown airmen are commemorated on the Singapore memorial. Unknown sailors are commemorated at their 'home ports', which in the case of the Hong Kong war dead are generally Portsmouth, Plymouth, and Chatham.

APPENDIX 11. JAPANESE ARTILLERY RECORDS

Type	Number	Shells Expended
Type 92 Infantry Gun (70 mm)	18	846
Type 94 Quick-Firing Gun (37 mm)	36	6,856
Type 41 Mountain Gun (75 mm)	51	17,449
Type 94 Mountain Gun (75 mm)	11	5,073
Type 'Bo' Mountain Gun (75 mm)	9	3,285
Type 94 Light Mortar (90.5 mm)	36	3,300
150 mm Howitzer	12	4,398
Type '4th year' Howitzer (150 mm)	6	3,468
Type 89 Cannon (150 mm)	16	5,000
Type 45 Howitzer (240 mm)	8	1,970
Bombs dropped		2,473
Incendiaries dropped		98

Source: War History Division, Japan Defence Agency

APPENDIX 12. FATES OF HKVDC AIR UNIT PERSONNEL

Men of the HKVDC Air Unit who died elsewhere on RAF active service abroad.

Private A. M. W. Scott[21]
Sergeant George H. Fowler[22]
Corporal Geoff Polglase[23] (120)
Captain J. F. 'Mickey' Wright[24]
Company Sergeant Major W. E. Peers[25] (120)
J. R. Canning[26] (120)
D. M. Cameron[27] (120)
B. C. Curtis[28] (120)
D. F. Davies[29]
F. Neill[30]

APPENDIX 13. THE HKDDC

The corps was formed shortly after the start of hostilities in Europe, based on a clause in the Admiralty's agreement with dockyard workmen that they would be 'trained in the use of small arms for the defence of the establishment in which they were serving'. All workmen (under the age of 55) who had signed such an agreement were called up, and all the remaining European staff were asked to volunteer. Later, locally recruited Chinese, Indian, and Portuguese staff were admitted.

On the transferral to Singapore of the original commander, Mr R. L. Lawson, in July 1940, Mr C. J. Manning was appointed Commandant.

On 8 December 1941, the European members were mobilized, and the HKDDC was gazetted as an Auxiliary Unit of the HKVDC, though under the direct control of the Commodore Hong Kong. At this time, Collinson approved the appointments of the HKDDC officers (133).

APPENDIX 14. THE BRITISH ARMY AID GROUP (BAAG)

In February 1942, Colonel Ride arrived in Chungking in southern China, having escaped from Sham Shui Po. He proposed to Major General L. E. Dennys, the British Military Attaché in China, that an organization be established to arrange and facilitate the escape of POWs and internees from Hong Kong.

General Chiang Kai Shek gave the proposal his approval and said that China would support it, although the British decided to allocate few resources. The name 'British Army Aid Group' was given, with a cover role of helping refugees in southern China. In March, Ride started to recruit anyone who had escaped, including Captain R. D. Scriven, Indian Medical Service, who had escaped from Sham Shui Po in February, and some SOE agents who had evaded capture. In June, Scriven was replaced in Waichow (in southern China, present Guan Dong province) by Major Clague, and in September, via Chinese agents, contact was established with Sham Shui Po.

BAAG was a unit of the Indian Army under Group E of the Headquarters Intelligence Branch, Delhi.

APPENDIX 15. HKRNVR PERSONNEL TRANSFERRED OUTSIDE HONG KONG

Cornes, Noel Julian Lieutenant	(to RNVR, Fleet Air Arm, HMS *Tern*)	9 July 1942[31]
Dodd, R.A.	(to RNVR)	
Fairbairn, P.C.	(to RNR as Harbour Master, Masawa)	
Gifford-Hull, John G. Lieutenant	(to RNVR, HMS *Gladiolus*)	21 Oct. 1941 UP
Lamont, R. W. C.[32]	(to RNVR, Colombo, Sri Lanka)	
Lammert	(to S.S. RNVR)	
Laycock, E.W.	(to RNVR, HMS *Rodney*)	
Meeke, H. C.	(to RNVR, HMS *Aurora*)	
Milne[33]	(to Royal Australian Navy, HMAS *Lismore*)	
Palmer, A. B.	(to RNR)	
Pollock, A.[34]	(to RNVR, Naval Intelligence Division)	
Walton, A. St. G.	(to RNVR)	

APPENDIX 16. ARRIVAL AND APPOINTMENT DATES OF SIGNIFICANT PERSONNEL

Major-General C. M. Maltby	20 July 1941
Sir Mark Young	11 September 1941
Simon White	24 September 1941 (appointed to command Royal Scots)
Brigadier Wallis	1 October 1941 (appointed to command Kowloon Brigade)
Captain Jones	30 October 1941 (appointed to command C Coy., Royal Scots)
Wing Commander Sullivan	1 December 1941
Admiral Chan Chak	7 December 1941
Colonial Secretary Gimson	7 December 1941

Canadian Forces   16 November 1941

Regimental Sergeant Major   1941
  'Wacky' Jones

Commander Collinson   1941

APPENDIX 17. TABLES OF SHIPS

His Majesty's Ships

Name	Pennant	Built by	In	Fate
Bird Class River Gunboats:				
Tern	T64	Yarrow	1927	Scuttled Hong Kong 19 Dec. 1941
Robin	T65	Yarrow	1934	Scuttled Hong Kong 25 Dec. 1941
Linnet Class Minelayer:				
Redstart		H. Robb	1938	Scuttled Hong Kong 19 Dec. 1941
Aphis Class River Gunboat:				
Cicala	T71	Barclay Curle	1916	Sunk by Japanese at Hong Kong 21 Dec. 1941
Moth	T69	Sunderland	1915	Scuttled at Hong Kong 12 Dec. 1941, salvaged as IJN *Suma* on Yangtse River, mined and sunk 19 Mar. 1945
S Class Destroyers:[35]				
Scout	H51	John Brown	1918	Scrapped 1946
Thanet	H28	Hawthorn-Leslie	1919	Sunk by Japanese navy off Endau 27 Jan. 1942
Thracian	D86	Hawthorn-Leslie	1920	Beached Hong Kong 24 Dec. 1942, slaved as IJN No. 101, retroceded, sold, and scrapped 1945

	Length (feet)	Beam (feet)	Draught (feet)	Displan-ment	Comple-ment	Knots	Main gun
Thracian	276	26.75	8.5–10.75	1220 tons	90	36	4-inch
Thanet	276	26.75	8.5–10.75	1220 tons	90	36	4-inch
Scout	276	26.75	8.5–10.75	1220 tons	90	36	4-inch
Tern	184.75	29	4.25	400 tons	?	?	12-pounder
Robin	150	26.25	3.25	275 tons	?	?	3.7-inch howitzer
Redstart	122.5	26.5	8	346 tons	32	10	20mm
Cicala	238	38	?	615 tons	58	14	6-inch
Moth	?	?	?	?	32–60	?	?

Auxiliary Patrol Vessels

Name	Disp.	Length	Knots	Main gun	AA Gun	Crew
Minnie	740	132	11	12-pounder	2*Bren	41
Margaret	750	137	11	12-pounder	2*Bren	45
St. Aubin	820	135	11	12-pounder	2*Lewis	37
St. Sampson	820	135	11	12-pounder	2*Lewis	37
Indira	1100	178	12	2*12-pounder	1*Pom pom	62
Henriette	750	132	11	12-pounder	2*Bren	38
Shun Wo	350	120	9	6-pounder	2*Bren	41
Han Wo	367	147	9	6-pounder	2*Bren	43
Frosty	780	132	10	12-pounder	2*Lewis	47
Ho Shing	?	?	13	2*12-pounder	2*Lewis	?
Teh Shing	?	?	13	2*12-pounder	2*Lewis	?
Poseidon	?	80	8	6-pounder	2*Bren	17
Perla	?	80	10	6-pounder	Bren	17 (130: 35)

Motor Torpedo Boats

	Length	Beam	Draught	Displacement	Complement	Knots	Main gun
MTB 07	60'4"	13'10"	2'10"	18 tons	9	38	.303 Lewis
MTB 08	60'4"	13'10"	2'10"	18 tons	9	38	.303 Lewis
MTB 09	60'4"	13'10"	2'10"	18 tons	9	38	.303 Lewis
MTB 10	60'4"	13'10"	2'10"	18 tons	9	38	.303 Lewis
MTB 11	60'4"	13'10"	2'10"	18 tons	9	38	.303 Lewis
MTB 12	60'4"	13'10"	2'10"	18 tons	9	38	.303 Lewis
MTB 26							
MTB 27							

MTBs 7–12

British Power Boat Company, Hythe, Hampshire, UK. Built: 1936-1939

MTBs 26 and 27

Thorneycroft Type

War Department Vessels

Harbour launches:

Victoria

Malplaquet

Oudenarde

Fast Motor Launches:

French

Widgeon

Lighters:

Various, for mules and sundry loads

Police Launches

No.	Year	Fate	Length (feet)	Main gun
PL1 (#4)	1936	Scuttled during battle, raised by Japanese	141	3-pounder
PL2 (#5)	1915	Scuttled during battle	100	3-pounder
PL3 (#4)	1929	Scuttled during battle, raised by Japanese, exploded Nov., 45	111	3-pounder
PL4 (#4)	1926	Scuttled during battle, raised by Japanese, hit mine July, 46	111	3-pounder
PL5 (#2)	1922	Survived war. Harbour Patrol Vessel	Hapag class	
PL6 (#3)	1922	Survived war. Harbour Patrol Vessel	Hapag class	
PL7 (#2)	1920	Disappeared during war. Harbour Patrol Vessel	Hapag class	
PL8 (#5)	1928	Disappeared during war. Steam Harbour Patrol Vessel	?	
PL9 (#3)	1925	Found in Canton post-war. Steam Harbour Patrol Vessel	65	
PL10 (#2)	1940	Survived war. Motor boat	43	
PL11 (#3)	1932	Disappeared during war. Shallow water patrol vessel	?	
PL12 (#2)	1940	Survived war. Motor boat	43	
PL14 (#1)	1924	Disappeared during war. Fast motor launch	?	
PL15 (#1)	1934	Disappeared during war. Motor boat	?	
PL16 (#1)	1935	Disappeared during war. Motor boat	?	

The RAF also had at least one Motor Launch.

APPENDIX 18. OCCUPANTS OF REPULSE BAY HOTEL

By the start of the 'siege', the hotel held approximately 200 civilians and some 46 fighting men. The number of the latter grew to around 250 before the military evacuation. This 'Register' is of course only a subset.

Staff

Cordeiro, Annie — Telephonist

Logan, Mrs. Sarah Virtue — Housekeeper

Lu — Cook

Matheson, Miss Marjorie — Manageress

Mosey, Elizabeth — Nurse

Seth, Mr — Director of Hotel

Sing — Number 1 Boy (also known as 'Buffalo')

Civilians

Arlington, Lewis C. — Author

Baker, L. L.

Baker-Carr, D. A.

Baretto, Gloria — NAAFI

Baud, Joseph Marie (Grenoble)

Benson, Father

Boesveld, Henri — ARP (Dutch)

Bond, W. L. — CNAC

Capell, Mrs. and child

Compton, Mimi

Compton, Mr

Da Rocha, Elfreda — NAAFI

Dankwerth, George — Businessman

De Sousa, Emily — NAAFI

Dew, Gwen — Journalist (author of *Prisoner of the Japs*)

Dunnett, Jennie,[36] and infant son Michael

Flanagan, Woulfe — ARP

Gommersall, W. C.

Greenland, Josephine, and son Derek

Guillaume, Baron and Baroness

Hobden, H.

Hogsden

Humphries

King, George

Manners, Major — Retired (died Stanley)

Manners, Mrs

Marsman, Jan (author of *I Escaped from Hong Kong*)

Martin, Jean

Minhinnick, Mrs M. A.[38]

Mladinich, Hugo — Businessman

Needa, Victor — Jockey

O'Gara, Bishop

Ohl, Beatrice Madame

Peterson, Mrs V. I. G.

Proulx, Mrs,[38] and her two sons

Puckle, B. H.

Shields, Andrew — Politician (died Stanley)

Shields, Andrew, Mrs

Simmons (died Stanley)

Spedding, T. A.

Westbrook, Titus

White, C. E.

Wilmer, Mrs[39]

Wilson, Richard — Journalist

Wilson, W. G. M. — Of Asiatic Petroleum Company

Military

Capell, R. S. — HKVDC

Cullum — RN

Dingsdale, Hugh — Police

Grounds, Lieutenant — Middlesex

Guy, Bombardier — RA

Heath, G. E. — RE

Lowry, Lance Corporal (sick bay)

Palfreeman, Denis Creedon — Shanghai Volunteers (in sick bay)

Prophet, Lieutenant — HKVDC

Proulx, Benny — HKRNVR

Riley, James — Royal Rifles

Quilliam, Tom — RN
Templer, Brigadier — RA
Tressider, C. G. — RASC
Slay — HKRNVR
White, John Paul — HKVDC (sick bay)
Zimmerman, Alex — Volunteer

APPENDIX 19.   PERSONNEL AT WEST BRIGADE HQ

These are the personnel recorded as being at West Brigade HQ at 10.00 on 19 December when Lawson decided to 'go outside and fight it out'. Asterisks mark those who are believed to have been present, but proof is not yet available.

Brigadier Lawson, John Kelburne	Royal Canadian Regt.
Sergeant Arnott, John Orr	Royal Scots
Sergeant Black, Marvin	Canadian Army*
Corporal Campbell, Norman Nicholson	Royal Scots
Lance Sergeant Corbitt, George Henry Douglas	Royal Scots
Bandsman Davies, Robert James	Middlesex
Bandsman Dillon, David	Middlesex
Drummer Endersby, George John	Middlesex
Secondnd Lieutenant Fenwick, Michael Forster	Royal Scots*
Captain Fox, John Henry	1st HK Regt. HKSRA[41]
Lance Corporal Glover, David Cairns	Royal Scots
Lance Corporal Grossmith, Arthur Walter	Middlesex
Sergeant Jewitt, Charkes L.	Corps of Mil. Staff Clerks, Canadian Army*
Bandmaster Kifford, William E	Middlesex
Drummer Klintworth, Ernest	Middlesex
Second Lieutenant Lawrie, John Ferguson	General List*
Drummer Merton, Sidney Arthur	Middlesex
Private Naysmith, John	Royal Scots
Drummer Parsons, James Arthur	Middlesex
Sergeant Phillips, William E.	Corps of Mil. Staff Clerks, Canadian Army
Major Temple, Webb Tatham	1st HK Regt. HKSRA
Lieutenant Woodside, Arnold R.	Royal Rifles[40]

(Note: National Archives of Canada, Ottawa, 593 (D1) lists a total of 30 men at this position on 8 Dec.).

APPENDIX 20. JAPANESE ORDER OF BATTLE

Japanese Personnel

Major General Arisue	Chief of Staff HK
General Kitajima	Commander in Chief HK
Lieutenant General Sano	Divisional Commander
Colonel Tokunaga	Commandant of all HK POW camps
Colonel Eguchi	Chief Medical Officer
Oda	Commandant of Stanley Camp
Nagasawa	Oda's deputy
Yamashita	Oda's deputy

HQ 23rd Army

482 Officers and men

Under: Japanese Commander in Chief, South China: Lieutenant General Takaishi Sakai, comprising:

38th Division

Under: Major General T. Sano

228th Regiment

3,038 Officers and men

Under: Colonel Teihichi Doi

Recruited in Nagoya

1 Battalion	Landed at Braemar Point
2 Battalion	Landed at Braemar Point
3 Battalion	

Note. The 228th was transferred from Hong Kong to Davao on 18 Jan. 1942, and thence to Amboina and Timor.

229th Regiment

2,901 Officers and men

Under: Colonel Tanaka Ryosaburo

Recruited in Gifu

1 Battalion	Under Captain Orita Masaru
2 Battalion	Landed at Shau Ki Wan
3 Battalion	Under Major Kehmosu.[42] Landed at Aldrich Bay

Note. The 229th and one battalion of the 230th moved from Hong Kong to Camranh Bay on 20 Jan. 42, and from there to Sumatra.

APPENDICES 331

230th Regiment

2,890 Officers and men

Under: Colonel Toshishige Shoji

Recruited in Shizuoka

1 Battalion

2 Battalion   Landed at North Point

3 Battalion   Landed at North Point

Note. After the Hong Kong operation, the 230th were sent to Camranh Bay, which they left on 18 Feb. 1942 and landed at Java.

Artillery Units

6,259 Officers and men

161 Field Guns, howitzers and mortars

Other Units

8,086 Officers and men

    Inc.   66th Infantry Regiment

             38th Engineer Regiment

First Artillery Group

5,892 Officers and men

42 heavy guns (attached to 23rd Army during operations in Hong Kong)

38th Mountain Artillery Group (3 battalions)

2nd and 5th Independent Anti-Tank Artillery Battalions

One independent mountain Artillery regiment

One heavy field artillery regiment.

The 21st Mortar Battalion.

Of the four divisions across the border, the Japanese selected just one to carry out the invasion. The invading force consisted of nine infantry battalions of the Japanese 38th Division, under Lieutenant General T. Sano, with a heavily augmented artillery component. The 38th Division was battle-hardened and well equipped and comprised the 228th, 229th, and 230th infantry regiments, each having three battalions equipped with landing craft.

The Japanese naval forces included 1 light cruiser, 3 gunboats, 4 minesweepers, 2 other vessels, 3 aircraft (1st Ku JNAF flying G3M), and approximately 300 marines.

The 23rd Army Air Group included some 80 aircraft (others say 34 light bombers,

13 fighters, and 9 other aircraft) and were operating from Canton as:

45th Sentai	Ki 36
10th Independent Chutai	Ki 27
44th Sentai	Ki 51
18th Independent Chutai	Ki 15
14th Sentai	Ki 21

APPENDIX 21. BRITISH ARTILLERY SPECIFICATIONS

Gun	Range	Shell	No.	Unit	Location
3.7-inch howitzer	18,000	20 lb	8	1/2 MB	Mobile
4.5-inch howitzer	21,900	35 lb	8	1/2 MB	Mobile
6-inch howitzer	28,500	100 lb	8	3/4/25 MB	Mobile
40mm AA	16,500	2 lb	2	18 AA	Mobile
3-inch AA	20,000	16 lb	12	5/7/17/18 AA	Sai Wan
3.7-inch AA	32,000	27 lb	2	7 AA	Wong Nai Chung Gap
4.5-inch AA	34,500	55 lb	2	17 AA	Waterfall Bay
2-pounder AT	6,000	2 lb		965 DB	Mobile
18-pounder field	33,300	18 lb	6	965 DB	Mobile
60-pounder	49,200	60 lb	2	26 Bty	Stonecutters
4-inch (naval)	31,350	31 lb[43]	4	1/3 Bty	D'Aguilar/Aberdeen
4.7-inch QF	35,880	50 lb	2	965 DB	Belcher's Lower
6-inch (naval)	40,400	100 lb	15	2/4/26/36/965[44]	
9.2-inch	87,600	380 lb	8	12/24/30 Bty	Stanley/Bokhara/Mt Davis

APPENDIX 22. POPULATION

Chinese	1,420,629
British[45]	7,982
Indian	7,379
Portuguese	2,922
'European'	2,905

American	396
Miscellaneous	2,094
Total:	1,447,307

APPENDIX 23. CANADIAN POPULAR HISTORIES AND BRITISH POPULAR HISTORIES

No serious student of 1941 Hong Kong can fail to notice that Canadian and British 'popular' histories have significantly different 'spins'. Those Canadian works referred to are based on the ideas that:

(a) The Canadian soldiers were one-man armies, who took on the Japanese almost single-handedly

(b) The British officers were incompetent, and preferred to lead from the deepest bunker available

Whereas the British paperbacks claim that:

(c) Canadian soldiers were generally drunk and had no interest in fighting the Japanese

(d) The serious fighting was therefore carried out by British, Indian, and Volunteer troops.

It is worth considering all four points.

For (a) it is true — Canadian soldiers were capable of fighting with great determination (D Coy. Winnipeg Grenadiers at Wong Nai Chung Gap, for example, or D Coy. Royal Rifles at Stanley). However, the same must be said about the Middlesex Regiment (Z Coy. at Leighton Hill, C Coy. at PB 14), the Volunteers (at JLO 1 and 2, and at Stanley), the Rajputs (PB 40), D Coy. Royal Scots at Golden Hill, etc.

(b) is also true. The most extreme example of cowardice on file does indeed concern a British officer (whose name I do not mention for legal reasons, though post-war he was tried and acquitted for treason). However, Maltby himself complained about the number of officers under his command who would *not* stay in their bunkers, and as a result were killed or wounded. Conversely, documents also exist claiming the incompetence of certain Canadian officers.

(c) is true. Both British and Canadian official reports on Canadian drunkenness exist. And yet perhaps the most extreme example on record concerns two British Royal Scots, caught drinking in Wan Chai while their comrades were being slaughtered on Golden Hill.

(d) is true. British, Indian, and Volunteer troops fought hard when they had to, but so did Canadians.

Having discovered that all these generalizations are true, but are also equally true of all nationalities involved, one has to ask why such a polarity should have developed.

It seems that the answer is simple. A British squadron leader's diary records the death of a Royal Scots officer in Kowloon almost as soon as it happened. A British policeman's diary notes the death of a Middlesex officer with whom he had often played rugby. The pre-war British garrison was an extremely tight-knit community; unfortunately the Canadians arrived far to late to be integrated into it.

Troops generally go to battle by unit. It is clear that A Company Winnipeg Grenadiers (for example) would have fought on Jardine's Lookout and been killed or captured without ever seeing another unit of the garrison using their weapons in anger. Equally, the Middlesex on Leighton Hill would probably never have seen a Canadian in action during the entire fighting. Even as POWs, the two nationalities were often in different camps. There were plenty of opportunities for stories to circulate and be embroidered.

In the final analysis, casualty figures[46] imply that all units fought with equal determination. It is true that there were differences in training, but these appear to have had little effect on morale. The British, to a large degree, seem to have continued to demonstrate the First World War mentality of going 'over the top', whether it made sense or not. The Canadians appear to have questioned orders more, offering the opinion that if they were going to be killed, then at least let them sacrifice their lives for some purpose. Had the two groups had more time to become integrated, the Japanese would probably have paid a far higher price for the surrender of Hong Kong.

Notes

INTRODUCTION

1. When numbers of 'killed in action' are mentioned in this work, they include those posted missing who were later declared dead. The uncertainty of the exact number is due to two main factors: firstly, some but not all of the civilians whose deaths are recorded during the fighting appear to have been involved in war-related activities. Secondly, dates of death of members of the Order of St John who lost their lives during the war years in Hong Kong are not recorded; therefore only estimations can be made of the numbers killed in December 1941.

1. THE BACKGROUND

1. In a bizarre coincidence, the wartime cruiser HMS *Galatea* was sunk off Alexandria with horrendous loss of life on 15 December 1941, while Hong Kong itself was being bombed and shelled during the lull between the Japanese capture of Kowloon and invasion of Hong Kong Island.
2. Kai Tak was Hong Kong's main airport until replaced by today's Chek Lap Kok in 1998. Pre-war it housed the RAF, FAA, and HKVDC Air Unit, as well as civilian aircraft.
3. Modern spellings of Chinese names are used throughout.
4. Many women — and their husbands — objected vocally to this evacuation.

Some women joined the essential services to avoid it; others found ways to return to the colony. All these paid the price of internment.
5   Thus a significant number of the Hong Kong Volunteer Defence Corps were in fact conscripts.
6   They were built to prevent enemy vessels entering the harbour. However, the majority of guns were able to fire against land targets as well as sea.
7   To put this in its historical context, the retirement of Hugh Dowding — architect of victory in the Battle of Britain — was gazetted on 1 October 1941. This was two months before the Japanese invasion, but a full year after the famous battle had been won over the skies of London.

2. THE BATTLE

1   The size of the garrison depends entirely on who is counted. The total of regular servicemen and women of the army, navy, and air force, plus HKVDC and HKRNVR, comes to a little over 12,000. However, if the Hong Kong Police, the Royal Naval Dockyard Police, the HKDDC, and civilians in the employ of the services are included, the total is closer to 14,000.
2   A British battalion generally consisted of four companies (comprising a total of sixteen platoons) with a staffing of 30 officers and 992 other ranks. It will be readily appreciated that through disease (malaria and VD to the forefront) and attrition, all Hong Kong's four original garrison battalions were under strength.
3   The 5th Battalion of the 7th Rajput Regiment.
4   Irresponsible TV journalism in 1990s Canada has suggested that the posting of these two battalions to Hong Kong a month before the fighting started was a British idea. It was not. The idea was that of General Grasett, whom Maltby replaced in July 1941. Grasett, himself a Canadian, lectured the Chiefs of Staff in London, and persuaded them in turn to persuade Churchill to overrule his previous directive that Hong Kong should not be reinforced. The Chiefs of Staff's memorandum to Churchill read, in part: 'The Chiefs of Staff heard an interesting account on the present situation in Hong Kong from General Grasett . . . He pointed out the great advantages to be derived from the addition of one or two battalions and suggested that these might be supplied by Canada' (10 September 1941, PRO WO 106/2409). We now know that with the Japanese strategy being what it was, even 'if all their officers had been Napoleons and all their men veterans of the Guard' (24: 215), the defenders could not have affected the issue. As Churchill himself had said on 7 January 1941, 'whether there are two or six battalions in Hong Kong will make no difference to [Japan's decision on whether or not to attack Britain]'. However, the British were perfectly capable of making worse decisions unaided, as witnessed by the debacle — on a far larger scale — at Singapore.

5   This book attempts to leave an audit trail wherever possible for future historians. The first number in parentheses refers to the quoted document, the second — where relevant — to the page. The key is in the bibliography. However, it is not unusual for a description of a particular event to be synthesized from several sources, which may agree on some points but disagree on others. In this case, normally only the most influential source is quoted — despite the fact that the final text may not fully agree with it.

6   The background to this change was not understood by all parties. The Winnipeg Grenadier War Diary reads: 'The possibility of an attack coming from the Japanese occupied territory to the North of Kowloon on the mainland was not apparently given any serious consideration until just prior to the outbreak of war' (155).

7   Wallis was a determined soldier who wore a dark monocle over his left eye (which he had lost in the First World War, in which he had also gained an MC). He had been a trooper in the Royal Horse Guards in 1914, and had transferred to the Indian army in 1917.

8   The senior Canadian officer, Lawson was a career soldier who had won the MC at Passchendaele in the First World War.

9   The site of which is now occupied by the Central Building on Pedder Street.

10 Drummond Hunter states: 'As Battalion Intelligence Officer [Royal Scots], I had observed troopships crowding into Mirs Bay on the China coast on [the] Wednesday or Thursday, and had alerted my superiors' (132b: Hunter).

11 Some works on the subject erroneously use the term HKVDF (Hong Kong Volunteer Defence Force). In fact the HKVDC remained a 'Corps' until a post-war name change on the first of March 1949, to the Hong Kong Defence Force (which effectively amalgamated the HKVDC, HKRNVR, and the HKAAF). A further name change was approved by His Majesty the King on the 1 May 1951, to the 'Royal Hong Kong Defence Force'.

12 Disbanded on the outbreak of war, the Mobile Column under Major H. G. Williams comprised two arms; the Armoured Car Platoon under Carruthers (which was retained as an integral unit) and the Motor Machine Gun Platoon under Captain John Way and Lieutenant Bill Stoker. Personnel from the latter unit generally fought with 2 Coy. HKVDC, although their BSA motorcycle combinations with Vickers guns, and the Bren carriers, were used by other personnel.

13 'The strength of the division which later landed on the Island was given by the infantry commander, Lieutenant General (then Major General) Ito Takeo as rather more than 20,000 men, and we can assume that the total Japanese force was about 60,000 men' (3: 7). Although 20,000 may be the total Japanese force to land, far fewer (perhaps 7,000) were actively involved in the fighting. The figure of 60,000 refers to the entire 23rd Army.

14 Mabel's daughter Barbara Anslow tells me that she and her sisters recently published their mother's memoirs under the title *It Was Like This*.

15 Japanese Army Operations in China, December 1941, reprinted as Appendix 6 of (44).
16 Compton Mackenzie, in (24: 188), puts forward the interesting idea that, as the Canadian battalions were new to Hong Kong and would have been starting from scratch wherever they were posted, they should have been put on the Gin Drinkers Line while the four original battalions stayed on the island in the positions for the defence of which they had been trained. Hunter of the Royal Scots states: '[As to Golden Hill], after 2 years preparing to defend Hong Kong, I had never been on this piece of ground before' (132b: Hunter).
17 One troop of the HK Mule Corps, under Hancock, was attached to the Rajputs.
18 The Hong Kong and Singapore Royal Artillery positions, both Mainland and Island, were as follows: the RA Mainland HQ was at the north end of Waterloo Road. The RA East Group was at Tai Tam Gap, and the RA West Group was at Wan Chai Gap. The 1st Mountain Battery held its 3.7-inch guns at Customs Pass, and split its 4.5-inch guns with two at Red Hill and two at the Sanatorium. The 2nd Mountain Battery had two of its 3.7-inch guns forward at Tai Wai and two at Main Filters. Of its 4.5-inch guns, two were forward at Tai Wai, and two at Main Filters also. The 25th Medium Battery had two guns forward and two at Main Polo. The 3rd Medium Battery maintained two guns at Mount Parker and two more at Sai Wan. Finally, the 4th Medium Battery had two guns at Mount Gough and two at Mount Austin.
19 Some recent works have criticized the level of intelligence reaching Maltby, and the use he made of it. However, it is interesting to note that — unlike the Americans at Pearl Harbour — Maltby was expecting the attack and had made all preparations almost 24 hours before the Japanese were ordered forward.
20 Known as Wong Nei Chong Gap in 1941.

3. PHASE I: THE LOSS OF THE MAINLAND

1 (134) 1 October 1957. This was intended to be a secret interview, but was released to the public relatively recently.
2 Cuthbertson.
3 Burn.
4 Probably Lt. George William Bowes, who died as a POW in Japan, 4 March 1943.
5 Presumably Maj. Leighton William Walker, who became second in command after Burn's suicide. Doddery he may have been, but he is said to have died in heroic circumstances after leaving the sinking *Lisbon Maru* on 2 October 1942.

The *Lisbon Maru* was a Japanese ship that, in the late summer of 1942, was ordered to take POWs from Hong Kong to camps in Japan. On the night of 1 October, it was torpedoed by an American submarine (USS *Grouper* under Lt. Com. Rob Roy McGregor) with great loss of life. It is worth remembering that by the end of the war, 19,000 allied POWs had lost their lives on these transportations.

6. Bill Bethell viewed the arrival of war through a twelve-year-old's eyes. Son of policeman A95, he was to be interned at Stanley Camp. Liberated when he was sixteen, he returned to the UK with his family, to revisit Hong Kong for the first time in 2001. This excerpt is from an interview carried out by the author for TVB Pearl's documentaries of December 2001, *War and Occupation* (169).
7. The Battle Box from which the defence of Hong Kong was managed was near the site of today's British Consulate. The bunker was deep underground. Constructed in 1937, it was reached by thirteen flights of 102 steps in total.
8. The delaying actions of Wallis's mainland brigade give early clues to his character. The Gin Drinkers Line was already manned (or, to be fair, as manned as it was ever going to be), so delaying the Japanese approach (ignoring the casualties imposed) had no strategic value. On this first day of the fighting (as he will on the last), Wallis shows that he is fighting not to win, but to delay the Japanese victory as long as possible as per Churchill's orders. As Compton Mackenzie says (24: 192): 'It was expected that the Mainland Brigade would hold this line for at least a week or ten days; what advantage would have accrued to Hong Kong itself if this dream had been fulfilled is not apparent.'
9. As this incident was recorded by Selwyn-Clarke, it is almost certain to be factual. However, it has not been possible to trace the name of the deceased.
10. This was presumably 2nd Lt. C. B. Burgess of 12 Coastal Regt. RA.
11. Argyle Street and North Point camps, both later POW camps, originally housed refugees from the Sino-Japanese war.
12. The exact position of the boom was presumably across the Tathong Channel (Lam Tong Hoi Hap), the main seaway leading into Hong Kong harbour. It is visible on surviving cine film from the immediate pre-war period.
13. Located at the corner of Gloucester Road and Arsenal Street, it was knocked down in 1982. The site was rebuilt as Fleet House and in 2001 this building is known as Mass Mutual Tower.
14. Two platoons of 3 Coy. were sent to Stonecutters, from which they were withdrawn to Wong Nai Chung Gap on 12 December Holmes's platoon however, was at North Point, and joined the others at Wong Nai Chung on 15 December (133).
15. Before leaving Stonecutters, 3 Coy. were to break into the armoury there and take a quantity of Thompson sub-machine guns. These were to prove effective in Wong Nai Chung Gap (79: 227).

16 Lok Lo Ha was a village near the road and railway some two miles northwest of Sha Tin, and the Pai Tau valley was a village area across from the railway station. Presumably both were consumed by the post-war growth of Sha Tin.
17 All such Royal Artillery entries are from (93: 171) to (93: 174), though the original data can be found in WO 172/1687.
18 Boxer's mistress, and post-war second wife, was the colourful Emily Hahn. Their daughter, Carola, was born eight weeks before the Japanese invasion (48). Boxer himself was an amazing character. His father, like so many, disappeared on the western front in 1915. His mother committed suicide in 1930. Boxer, incredibly, served two years in the Japanese 38th infantry regiment pre-war (67). He passed away in April 2000. The *Guardian* foolishly published a scurrilous article about him in 2001.
19 The Precautionary Period was in fact never declared. See (20: 11).
20 In other records, 'dawn' is often given as a time stamp. For the purposes of this document, dawn is translated to a reasonably accurate 07.00.
21 The Walrus, or 'Shagbat', was Reginald Mitchel's last design before he started on his masterpiece, the Supermarine Spitfire.
22 The two other Vildebeestes were destroyed by the RAF later. It is interesting, however, to note Maltby's comment: 'I had at no time contemplated the serious use of obsolete 100 mph aircraft which would have been shot down immediately by modern fighters' (20: 8). A verse by Varcoe expresses the garrison's lack of confidence in these elderly aircraft:
Brave R.A.F., none understands
How you survived the weather;
The termites in the wings joined hands
To hold the things together! (69: 20)
23 In (54: 13), Marsman claims that the takeoff of this flight was delayed by his late departure from his hotel. Had he been on time, it would have taken off at 08.00, just as the Japanese aircraft arrived over its mooring.
24 Men of the Air Unit fought as ordinary infantry, mainly with No. 1 Coy. However, earlier in the war many had volunteered for RAF duties in the UK. See Appendix 12.
25 These were Sgt. Routledge and Signalman Fairley. Fairley died in Bowen Road Hospital on the 22nd, but Routledge survived and was later decorated for bravery in camp. These two were the first Canadian infantrymen to be wounded in battle in the Second World War. The Jubilee Buildings where they were based was an accommodation block situated beside the sea wall of the camp's waterfront. (131) claims that three British Royal Engineers were also killed in this attack.
26 Lt. Andrews of the Field Company Engineers recalls: 'We had earlier prepared these bore holes. One of them was in a railway cutting and we had had to make a tunnel into the sandstone some 3 feet high, 2–3 feet wide and 12–

14 feet long. Because of the heat we could only work for some 15 minutes at a time and the work took several days. That confined space petrified me' (from a letter supplied by his son-in-law, Dr A. E. Dormer). At time of writing (2002), Andrews — whose father lost his life in the Boer War — is still with us at the ripe old age of 102.

27 This was about a mile north-west of Tai Po, near the present Hong Lok Yuen Estate.
28 The HKRNVR were responsible for a number of regular standing patrols around the Colony.
29 Presumably Lt. J. W. Eastman HKRNVR.
30 Japanese figures do not provide an accurate breakdown of their mainland casualties, or any other. These figures seem a little on the high side. See also the entry for 18.30, for which the same comment holds.
31 Eight MTBs comprised the 2nd MTB flotilla. Six were built by Scott-Paine, and two were the older Thorneycroft type. The flotilla was commanded by Lt. Cdr. G. H. Gandy RN (Rtd.). They were based at the Kowloon Naval Yard MTB Camber, where the torpedo workshops, torpedo store, and engine workshop for running repairs were situated, together with the flotilla office and crews' and maintenance staff's shore accommodation. The officers lived in nearby boarding houses.
32 Appendix 4 lists the pilots involved in this operation.
33 Two-gun Cohen, who rose from a background of petty crime in London's east end to become a Chinese general, was one of Hong Kong's more colourful characters of the time.
34 This is today the site of the Chinese University.
35 On the night of 26 January 1942, *Thanet* was dispatched from Singapore along with the ageing Australian destroyer HMAS *Vampire*. Their mission was to head up the east coast of Malaya to attack a Japanese force consisting of two transports, a cruiser, and four escorting destroyers at Endau. Initially contact was not made. However, in the early hours of 27 January, the two vessels engaged a force of three modern Japanese destroyers. *Thanet* came under heavy fire, and was sunk following hits to her engine room. *Vampire*, after trying to cover *Thanet* with smoke, was forced to withdraw from the area. *Thanet* had fewer than sixty survivors. By coincidence, 100 Squadron (parent of the Vildebeestes at Hong Kong) went into attack in the same action, attacking the Japanese landing forces at Endau on the 26th. They lost the commanding officer and more than half their Vildebeestes in the process, and the remaining aircraft were lost in later actions.
36 MacDonald, who had shared drinks with Boxer and Hahn the previous night (67: 221), wrote an article on his experiences in *The Times*.
37 The Commonwealth War Graves Commission has many records of death dated 8 December. In all cases bar Price there is evidence that these fatalities actually occurred later in the fighting. The fact that Price died in hospital in

Kowloon does indicate that he indeed died before the withdrawal to the Island (12/13 December), but it has not yet been possible to uncover any further details. He may, of course, have died of disease (there is a background noise of natural or accidental death in every garrison). However, the fact that he was an engineer makes it feasible that he was involved in the delaying actions of this day.

38   The documents referred to as (126) are internal files of the CWGC, collated during the period 1945–55. Their vintage must be borne in mind as in many cases there have been updates to our understanding since.

39   The date of 1 December is clearly wrong. Although there are no guarantees, it is possible — though not certain — that Wong was the unnamed *Cornflower* sailor killed on *Indira*. The 'bombing' note tends to support this.

40   Lt. Ralph Stephenson RNVR was second-in-command of APV *Minnie* acting in a minesweeping role. He survived unhurt until receiving a flesh wound late in the fighting while acting as an infantryman (132b: Stephenson).

41   Lo Wai was in the Lung Yeuk Tau district north-east of the Fan Ling crossroads. The correct name is Lung Kwat Tau.

42   (134) largely blames the loss of the Redoubt on Jones's failure to implement the patrols specified by White. Specifically the one that should have taken place: 'At about one hour after dark to South and South-West slopes of Needle Hill and the Shing Mun valley making contact with D Company 5/7 Rajput.'

43   Wo Liu Hang was a small village in the Fo Tan valley.

44   A 'predicted shoot' is one based on calculation only, rather than the alternative of observing and adjusting.

45   (134) describes the weather as 'Dark, slight rain and ground mist'.

46   (134) points out that had this patrol taken the route ordered by White, it would have detected the Japanese massing for the attack.

47   Z Force was a special unit of the HKVDC attached to SOE in Singapore. Its HQ was a bungalow at the Shing Mun reservoir. However, the previous night the entire nine-man force (plus an unidentified Chinese gentleman) had moved to their secret depot — a natural cave some 1,800 feet up Tai Mo Shan.

48   Parsons's brother T. M. was in the HKRNVR and captained MTB 27. Their father, Capt. T. R. Parsons, was also in the HKVDC.

49   The runner (Pvt. Wylie, Royal Scots) locked the 'grille gate' behind him as he left, thus leaving all those inside with no exit apart from the upper grill (134).

50   Basnett died of dysentery and was originally buried in Argyle Street cemetery on 19 April 1942. His brothers Leslie and Robert were also killed during the war. Leslie was in the King's Own Royal Regiment and died on 14 July 1943. He is buried in Poland. Robert was in the Royal Corps of Signals and died on 15 September 1943. He is buried at Kanchanaburi, Thailand.

51   Coyle died in Japan on 7 March 1944. Oddly, he was recorded as belonging to C, rather than A, Company.

52 Wounded in the throat, Jardine crawled out of the redoubt and was rescued by L/Cpl Cook of 17 Platoon D Coy. Royal Scots (92: 101).
53 Interestingly, at about 01.00, Kendall of Z Force made his way through Japanese lines and contacted Bankier to learn the true state of affairs of the redoubt (134).
54 'This Royal Scots party must have left their posts almost immediately on the arrival of the Japanese' (134).
55 The Shing Mun Redoubt still stands today, although much of the surrounding soil has been eroded and the concrete structure in places stands proud of the ground. Marks of the fighting — especially damage caused by the British bombardment — are still clearly visible. The observation post is particularly well preserved, with the location of the steel shutter (see next day) unchanged since 1941, and an amazing amount of shrapnel damage inside from the original blast and a large number of grenades (one of which all but blinded Lt. Thomson) thrown in later.
56 Appendix E of Wallis's report states that, during this fighting, two men of the Royal Scots were found AWOL drinking in Wan Chai. Subsequent fighting prevented their courts martial.
57 Comments without parentheses following a single name indicate the fate of that individual. Comments in parentheses before a name or group of names indicate their possible fates, or clues there to.
58 Haines continues: 'Civilian Dockyard rating was used to determine service rank. As a junior executive officer, I was ranked 2nd Lieutenant. Senior executives were made Captains, and heads of department, Majors' (132b: Haines). Thus the Hong Kong Dockyard Defence Corps (HKDDC) — one of the least researched units defending Hong Kong — was formed. See also Appendix 13.
59 'The whole family of a Y.M.C.A. secretary, except a baby girl, was bombed to death in their home' (117: 22).
60 Wakabayashi himself was later killed in action in Guadalcanal in early 1943 (76: 59).
61 The 'Ls' refer to Lookouts, and were preconstructed trenches at designated sites. The numbering sequence starts at Junk Bay (Tseun Kwan O) on the easternmost point of the Gin Drinkers Line, and they continue in sequence until the last which appears to have been 140. For reference, Lookout 100 is near the redoubt. They appear to have been only a trench, which could be of varying length from short to long enough to encircle a hilltop. In 1941, all commanded excellent views.
62 The captured, including Jones, Willcocks, Thompson, and some twenty-five Royal Scots from inside and outside the redoubt, were taken to Fan Ling. They would rejoin the other POWs in Sham Shui Po on 13 January (89: 225). Although Jones came in for severe criticism over this loss, the Japanese — though somewhat unsure whom they had captured — thought he was a

'splendid officer': 'The commander of the enemy defenders on Hill 251, was, I believe, Captain Johnson, a Canadian. As he was wounded, I ordered the medical officer to treat him. He appeared to be a splendid officer' (122). Interestingly, these were not the first of the garrison to be captured. This dubious honour appears to go to Pte. G. S. P. Heywood of the HKVDC, who was checking a weather station on the border on 8 December See the 1992 reprint of his 1938 book, *Rambles in Hong Kong* (Hong Kong: Oxford Univeristy Press).

63 This fire came from the 9.2-inch guns of Mount Davis, plus the 6-inch and 60-pound guns of Stonecutters Island (134). The Japanese took this as a signal that the redoubt was fully in their hands: 'the bombardment also was conclusive proof that the rest of the enemy had abandoned positions on Hill 251' (122).

64 It is clear that this is Sgt. Robb's party, who then took up a defensive position on the left of D Coy. Rajputs. It was in fact thirteen rather than eighteen men, taking into account the five left behind (134).

65 A Court of Enquiry into the loss of the Redoubt was convened at the Argyle Street POW camp on 8 May 1942 (134).

66 Though Cpl. Mornington Robertson himself perished on the *Lisbon Maru*, 2 October 1942.

67 The reason for the lack of a counter-attack was a focus of the Court of Enquiry held in Camp after the surrender. Rose, in 1957, said: 'Col. White's evidence on this point was also most unsatisfactory but it appears that the real reason [why no counter-attack was carried out] was that most of the Royal Scots had panicked and the troops to the left of the Redoubt were streaming back to Kowloon without ever in fact having been in touch with the enemy. As a result of this the whole defence on the mainland collapsed and the remainder of the Brigade had to withdraw to the Island. Col. White naturally did not want to tell the court this' (134). Rose goes on to point out that D Coy. performed well, and the whole battalion later fought with resolution on the Island.

68 In the Police War Diary it appears that this is a euphemism for summary execution.

69 William Wilkinson died of diphtheria on 2 September 1942.

70 Though Hunter points out that these 'were one or two small, and not every deep trenches. [That was all] — no barbed wire' (132b: Hunter). Hunter was 2IC of D Coy., under Pinkerton.

71 Killed by a stray bullet at Port Said in the Suez Crisis of 1956.

72 35(M) was a previous designation of 965 Defence Battery.

73 The 20 Heavy Battery was founded in 1926 as the 23rd Heavy Battery. This is one of many HKSRA batteries that cannot be reconciled with the batteries that actually existed in Hong Kong at the time.

74 (126) also agrees with the date, and adds: 'Buried "A" Shelter Skeet Ground.' Bard notes: 'I knew Jordan well (I played with him in concerts). He had that

rare condition in which although he could hear music very well, he was somewhat deaf to the spoken voice. So, I believe the sentry story to be true' (132b: Bard). The Royal Scots were certainly alert; Hunter reports: '[On 9 December] I was shot at by my own Royal Scots, as I made my way up the Inner Line to join Don Company. I had to scramble off the track and lie low for a little, after shouting to explain who I was!' (132b: Hunter).

75 Wright was in 3 Bty. HKVDC stationed on Ap Lei Chau.
76 Hewitt, crossing Golden Hill on his escape some nine weeks later, states: 'We passed a group of concrete command shelters from which a nauseating stench of decaying bodies assailed us ... Soldiers had been left to rot where they were killed' (13: 33). Other escapees — e.g. Whitehead (30: 83) — reported identical experiences when crossing former battlefields on both the island and the mainland. The problem persisted; a letter in the *South China Morning Post* in 1946 asked when the Government was going to take care of the skeletons in Wong Nai Chung Gap.
77 On my first ever trip to Wong Nai Chung Gap, I found a Japanese 6.5 mm Arisaka rifle cartridge hanging out of an earth bank just south of the petrol station on the east side. Immediately I understood that all these 'war stories' were real, and there truly was a story worth investigating.
78 Maltby, in the 1957 interview, agrees: 'I am inclined to think that the cause of the panic was the effect of the Japanese 4-inch mortar fire. The Japanese controlling this fire would creep forward, well camouflaged, and dragging a telephone line. Their fire was thus very accurately and quickly directed. The bomb thrown was not effective as a man killer but exploded with a tremendous bang and gave out a terrific blast which was very demoralising' (134). It should be noted in this context that Ford himself was in D Coy., which was not involved in the 'panic' that Maltby describes.
79 Executed by the Japanese, 18 December 1943.
80 Some sources, such as (91: 75), quote 60 killed. This is more likely to be the total number of casualties.
81 'Jimmie Dunlop died on the ridge beside me, calling out "Mother, Mother". I was wounded left arm, and just below right shoulder. Lance Corporal Low dressed my wounds and carried me into the pillbox' (132b: Hunter).
82 Executed by the Japanese, 18 December 1943.
83 See Appendix 12.
84 No doubt the PanAm Clipper. The Supermarine Walruses would have been too small to cause a problem.
85 Much of M. Davis fort survives, around and above the YMCA. Shell damage to the Plotting Room and certain gun mounts is still very visible.
86 Another 35 Royal Scots appear in hospital records as being wounded between the start of the fighting and 17 December.
87 (126) confirms the date, but states 'killed Wong Nai Chung Gap', which is clearly irreconcilable.

88 Note for researchers: The CWGC online register (www.cwgc.org) will only show a single day as date of death; only the paper versions show periods of uncertainty. If the paper records show simply 'December', then the web-based system will default to 1 December. If a range is shown on paper, such as 8/25 December the web-based system will default to 8 December.

89 Believed to have been the first British soldier to have been killed by a sword in the Second World War, though L/Cpl. Murray had been wounded by such a weapon the previous day (92: 98).

90 Maj. Hancock was a British officer in the Hong Kong Mule Corps, an RIASC unit in which only the officers were armed.

91 The wife of Briggs of HMS *Scout*, who had escaped Hong Kong with his destroyer on 8 December.

92 Birch states carefully: 'gun positions alleged to have been already prepared in peace time in the Kowloon-side godowns, and certainly the Japanese were able to bring heavy artillery into action extremely quickly' (44: 81). Stewart, writing of the shelling of the north shore defences, confirms: 'The most accurate fire came from a high-velocity small-calibre gun hidden in one of the Kowloon godowns' (3: 16).

93 Bank of East Asia. HKH is of course the Hong Kong Hotel, and H & SBC is Hong Kong Shanghai Banking Corporation (now HSBC). One original building, The 'Pedder Building', still survives in Pedder Street opposite where the Hong Kong Hotel (The Grips) stood.

94 All on board were killed. Well-known Hong Kong philanthropist Noel Croucher had been invited to join the crew, but luckily declined as he had already been on duty all day (94: 49). The *South China Morning Post* of Thursday, 27 September 1945 claimed that fourteen Europeans had been aboard and that the only piece of wreckage found was the steering wheel — in Connaught Road. (110: 113) and (98: 174) show that two Sikh police constables were also lost on the vessel. (28: 31) claims that a 'large party' of troops were also aboard having been assisting with the loading.

95 One part of HMS *Tamar* lives on, however: the Anglican cathedral, St John's, which was built in 1849, was badly damaged during the war when it served as an officers' club during the Japanese occupation. Many of the old memorial tablets and virtually all the stained glass windows were lost. However, during its post-war rebuilding, the main doors were created from timbers salvaged from the wreck of HMS *Tamar*.

96 Note that the old Kowloon station clock tower, a few yards east of the Star Ferry pier, still shows bullet damage from this encounter (and later damage indicating heavier weapons). One eyewitness (132a: Ozorio) stated that a shell fired from Hong Kong, thus presumably by the garrison after the evacuation was complete, caused the heavier damage.

97 Presumably from Green Island, via *Jeanette*.

98 This pillbox, PB 63 (manned by Z Coy. Middlesex at the time) was

demolished in 1995. This was one of the last to survive in urban areas (although many can still be found today in the hills). Demolition of urban pillboxes started immediately post-war. The *South China Morning Post* for 27 July 1947 carried a short column that stated: 'The clearing away of the pillboxes left by the war is now almost complete.'

99 (154) reports: 'On the shelling of Lyemun Bks. to-day, Capt. Banfill's Chinese driver killed', though there is no proof that this was Cheung Wing.

100 (77: 23), by a member of D Coy., states: 'We had lost one man in Kowloon during the first surprise raid.' Note, however, that many details in this account are inaccurate. (126) states simply his area last seen as 'Kowloon Star Ferry Wharf'. As the Winnipegs were withdrawn from Kowloon on the 12th, this is most probably the date on which Gray actually lost his life. (155) notes: 'Pte Shatford and Pte Grey [sic] were lost on patrol. Pte Grey is presumed to have been killed after reaching Star Ferry Pier. Pte Shatford eventually made his way back to Coy HQ at Wong Nei Chong Gap, having come back to the island with some Indian troops.'

101 Note that the CWGC lists of civilian dead in Hong Kong do not generally include anyone other than British or Commonwealth citizens. The vast numbers of Chinese killed in the conflict in December 1941 (as many as 4,000, according to Selwyn-Clarke) are therefore excluded from the figures presented in this book, except those few individually named in casualty reports.

102 It has not yet been possible to verify this story.

103 Two accounts, (42: 15) and (71: 45), mention a British nurse being killed on the last ferry from Kowloon, though they disagree on some details and provide no name. A more accurate account is probably (86: 146), which describes a nurse called 'Mrs Hollands' as being 'lightly wounded' on this day while serving as a volunteer on a harbour launch under police control, recovering British troops (Lt. Forsyth and his Punjabis) from Kowloon. (98: 174) specifies that she was wounded in the stomach, and was accompanied by another nurse, Mrs Sando. (131) records: 'In spite of the two European ladies being made to lie flat on the deck Mrs Holland received a bullet wound in the abdomen.' Queen Mary Hospital records are unequivocal: she was admitted and was pronounced dead on the same day. 'Buster' Holland, ex-HKVDC, when queried on this matter believed that his family were the only 'Hollands' in Hong Kong at the time, and had no knowledge of this nurse (132b: Holland). However, HK PRO records show a 52-year-old Mr W. E. Holland living on the Peak, and an A. M. Hollomb (which has been corrected by hand to 'Holland?') at Room 509 of the Stag Hotel during the January 1942 'census'.

These are all the facts currently available. Mrs Holland may be an unrecognised heroine. The hospital records state that Mrs Holland lived at 6, Minden Avenue, and give her age as 45.

4. PHASE II: THE SIEGE OF THE ISLAND

1. Historians have often wondered why the Japanese advance on the mainland — in the light of their vastly superior powers — was so slow. Perhaps the most likely reason can be found in *The Business of War* by Sir John Kennedy: 'This extraordinarily cautious attitude was strangely out of keeping with the dash and élan shown by Japanese troops in other sectors . . . These troops, too, had been engaged for the last two years in operations against the Communist Fourth Route Army, and there they had learned that too hasty an advance frequently led to disaster. Several references in personal-experience articles written by officers of this unit to the effect that "the situation greatly resembled a communist guerrilla trap" would indicate that this consideration was at least in the minds of many of the officers and may have carried some weight on influencing the attitude of the expedition commander' (14: 59).
2. This is according to surviving hospital records, which may not be complete. This applies to all estimations of wounded.
3. Died on board the *Lisbon Maru*.
4. Died of dysentery, Sham Shui Po.
5. A surprising amount of the damage inflicted at this time can still be seen in modern Hong Kong. The Lions outside the HSBC headquarters, the low wall north of the Cenotaph, a stone wall beneath the Canossa Hospital, steps at Hong Kong University, the First World War memorial in the botanical gardens, and the Legco building all bear the scars.
6. (32: 69). He adds that a further 3,000 were severely wounded.
7. In 1941, Professor Baxter was a member of the HKDDC.
8. Mrs C. R. Lee, wife of the Governor's secretary, and Mrs MacDonald.
9. Here I quote Birch, but the original is in FO 371/27752 at Kew.
10. Dew later shot several unique cine films of the Japanese invasion of the Island. These were distributed around the Island and never recovered. A few were entrusted to Victor Needa, a well-known Eurasian jockey of the period. In the year 2000, I received a call from a friend enthusing over a one-woman stage show by a Veronica Needa. I made contact as fast as I could, only to learn that (like so many) Victor Needa — her father — had never spoken about the period. Later I heard that Needa had placed them in the safe of the Repulse Bay Hotel, from where they were stolen later in the war.
11. Bailey had little opportunity to take up the offer of a cash prize, as he was killed in Wong Nai Chung Gap on the 19th.
12. In 2002, for the purposes of this book, Warwick Ross was kind enough to ask his 90-year-old father Charles 'Ted' Edwin Ross of the 1941 Hong Kong Ministry of Information, why the announcement of the loss of the *Jeanette* — which, after all, as the biggest explosion ever experienced in Hong Kong, was a very visible event — was not made until 18 hours afterwards.

Unfortunately 'he had no recollection about the announcement or why it was so delayed'.

13 Dr Bard, a member of the HKVDC Field Ambulance, was stationed on Mount Davis and was first on the scene when the No. 3 gun was hit by a large-calibre Japanese shell.

14 Pardoe was initially buried in the Colonial Cemetery, Happy Valley (126).

15 Although I can offer no definitive proof that this report is of Pardoe, it seems more than likely — especially as the context (the next day mentioned being Monday) indicates that it was made on the Sunday.

16 (37: 58) states that Morgan and Kathleen Thompson were walking in the hospital grounds towards the sisters' mess when the shell landed between them, killing Morgan and injuring Thompson. It goes on to say, strangely, that an ambulance came and took Thompson to the Queen Mary Hospital.

17 Where the East Wing of Lower Albert Road Government Offices is now.

18 HQ of the Royal Artillery units forming part of West Brigade.

19 The Gauge Basin gun position is very well preserved, but extremely overgrown. It can be found atop the hillock immediately north-east of the dam across Tai Tam reservoir.

20 Cooper later died of his wounds, and Palmer lost a leg.

21 Note that the IGH records show that Fateh Khan of the 965 Defence Battery died in hospital. However, correlation with CWGC records based on his serial number (7770) shows they believe that Fateh Muhammad was actually the 965 Gunner (rather than Havildar) who lost his life at Belcher's. Fateh Khan (Havildar, 3147), who also died this day, was — according to CWGC — in the HKSRA 17 HAA Battery and was killed at Mount Davis. It is probable that these two have been transposed, thus Fateh Muhammad was actually an IOR at Mount Davis, while Fateh Khan was a Havildar at Belcher's. Belcher's Battery has now completely disappeared under modern development, though one pre-war gun was preserved on site until recent years when it was transferred to the Hong Kong Museum of Coastal Defence.

22 Firing over open sights; in other words, line of sight.

23 Maltby's despatch handles the rout which followed surprisingly graciously: 'At this juncture owing to an imperfectly conveyed message and an error of judgement of the junior officer left in command [Sleap], their personnel were given the option of going to Stanley. All but two Chinese left; seventeen British and Portuguese stayed' (20: 11). A list of missing 4th Bty. personnel compiled on 17 December reads: '4534 — Gnr WL Chung, 4065 — Gnr Tang H, 4630 — Adrult R J, 3070 — L/Bdr Tam Y K, 4532 — Alaraker J M, 3475 — Gnr Tang K M, 5178 — Bau-Kennedy, 4295 — Toang S.W, 2917 — Chan K C, 4047 — Toang K H, 4270 — Chow K C, 4539 — Woo P T M, 4558 — Chan S K, 4563 — Yee M S, 4615 — Ching A, 4641 — Yee S W, 3493 — Freng Y L, 4275 — Young C, 4535 — Freng K, 3451 — Yung F H, 3432 — L/Bdr Ho S, 2854 — Sgt Yeung, 3477 — Gnr Ho S N, 2676 — Bdr Knox T,

4277 — Gnr Kwok K C, 3444 — Kwok M C, 4091 — Lee C C, 3441 — Lam P S, 3446 — Lam P W, 4323 — Lee W C, 3448 — Leung T W, 4561 — Lo P S, 3059 — Lin W C, 4826 — Lewis G M, 4829 — Lo, 3509 — Ma S L, 2621 — Na G K T, 3503 — Pang O L, 3483 — L/Bdr Pau C W, 4105 — Gnr Poun F M, 3796 — L/Bdr Reeoe J W', with the note: 'check and report any not at Stanley'. The fact is that these gun emplacements offered almost no shelter for the troops, and the effect of the shells — bursting on bare concrete — was devastating.

24 No such unit officially exists. This should probably read 2 Mountain Bty.
25 Some Mount Davis fatalities are under 17 AA of the HKSRA, and others under their parent unit, 7 AA Regiment Royal Artillery.
26 A wartime rumour said that Burn had been shot by his own men during the Kowloon fighting. If this were true, 14 December would have been too late. However, Wallis's report speculates: 'I surmise that it was a feeling of disgrace that he was unable to prevent his battalion breaking up near the pencil factory on December 11th which caused the late Major Burn 2IC to take his own life.' (134) confirms that he was sent there to attempt to restore order, thus death at his own hand following failure seems credible. (150) briefly notes his suicide. The fact that he has a known grave makes it likely that he did indeed die after the evacuation to the Island, especially as (126) gives his original burial site as 'White house on west side of Tai Hang Road, Hong Kong'. This is further backed up by (155), which notes the arrival at Blue Pool valley of B and C Coy. Royal Scots under Maj. Burn on 12 December.
27 (126) gives the date as 11 January 1942. Although the RAMC were referred to as 'Rob All My Comrades' in Hong Kong as elsewhere, Bowen Road Hospital was popular. Later in the war, Rothwell of the Middlesex wrote:

> Lord, do not suffer me to go
> Back to the gloom of Sham Shui Po
> Nor yet direct my stumbling feet
> Within the wire of Argyle Street
> Grant, Lord, that I may pack my grip
> And go aboard some friendly ship
> Bound for London or Southampton
> But, Lord, if this prayer is stamped on
> Then, I pray, make light my load
> And let me stay in Bowen Road. (63: 54)

28 (126) gives the date as 24 December.
29 Arthur, then with 5 Coy. HKVDC, is post-war the chairman of the Hong Kong POWs Association (132a: Gomes).
30 Pinewoods is now a barbecue site, but still retains many of its original features. It can be reached from the Peak, by taking a short path down to the north. In May 2000 it was still possible to find fragments of shrapnel from this bombardment.

31 While there are many rumours of the Japanese navy (including destroyers and cruisers) being seen off Hong Kong, and even shelling defensive positions and engaging the Royal Navy, this appears to be one of only two documented incidents (the other being reported from Bokhara). Even in this case, the identity of the engaged vessels is very uncertain. It is generally believed that most of the 'sightings' of Japanese ships were in fact of HMS *Thracian*.

32 There is no evidence in Japanese accounts of an attack being launched this day. Whether this was a probe too small for their records, or simply Chinese refugees from Kowloon, is unknown.

33 This report has sometimes been quoted out of context, as if it was given on December 18th.

34 Executed by the Japanese, 18 December 1943.

35 (98: 173) claims that Baker was killed by a bomb on 16 December. However, the Police War Diary records: 'Acting Chief Inspector Baker was found dead in No. 3 Conduit Road with gun shot wounds in the head in circumstances suggesting suicide' (131).

36 (132a: Bethell). Such emergency cemeteries certainly existed. The Police War Diary, for example, states: '[The officer in charge at Aberdeen] supervised the digging of cemeteries at Apleichau Refuge Dump and the hill side behind Aberdeen Temple for burial of unclaimed bodies' (131). From Bethell's comments it appears he was at the Upper Station — Caine Road — at the time.

37 Coates died of these wounds 5 November 1942, MacNaughton died in Japan 25 January 1944, Coleman died of wounds 18 February 1942.

38 (139) claims that a wing of this aircraft could still be seen sticking out of the sea on 31 December.

39 Killed on the *Lisbon Maru* 2 October 1942.

40 The battle damage was widely remarked upon when North Point refugee camp became a POW camp towards the end of the fighting.

41 The *South China Morning Post* of Tuesday, 18 September 1945 states that he was killed by enemy action whilst in charge of the ammunition ship *Moa Lee*. This may in fact have been the barge pulled by *Jeanette*, in which case the date of death would be incorrect.

42 The *South China Morning Post* of Saturday, 29 September 1945 carried the following notice: 'NOTICE. Will any person having knowledge of the circumstances under which Captain Jewell and six others were killed in Aberdeen in a tug in December, 1941, please communicate with Major J. C. Riddell, China Command, H.Q. Information is particularly required as to the date of death and place of burial. (J. C. Riddell) Major DAAG, H.Q. Land Forces.'

43 This is one of the least certain datings in this book. CWGC records place Cheong's death on 6 December, which makes no sense whatsoever. Having

found no mention of Cheong in any official or unofficial documents, I am forced to guess that this is a simple mistyping of '16'.
44 (132b: Browne).
45 It is amazing to see how much evidence of this shelling is still visible in 21st-century Central. The low north-facing wall of the Cenotaph's enclosure (which was facing open harbour in 1941) has a great deal of poorly patched shrapnel damage, as have the steps on the southern side. The east-facing front of the Legco Building (also damaged by late American bombing) was liberally riveted with shrapnel, which was removed in the late 1970s as it was leaving dark rust stains down the walls. The stone patches that were put in are clearly visible. Most evocatively, the two bronze lions outside the Hong Kong Bank building are full of shrapnel holes. Those who want to know why shrapnel caused such terrible injuries need only see how it has torn through the lions' half-inch thick bronze skin. The eagle-eyed will notice that there are still at least eight pieces of shrapnel — including a fragment of driving band — embedded in the easternmost lion's left rump. Central Police Station is little changed from this time, but the majority of bomb damage was in the compound or in Victoria Prison — off-limits to the more law-abiding of today's population.
46 Pre-war, an Olympic swimmer.
47 Presumably the Paint and Lacquer works at 704 King's Road.

5. PHASE III: THE INVASION OF THE ISLAND

1 However, telephony was still a problem. No. 1 Coy. HKVDC's War Diary reports: 'No. 2 Platoon [Repulse Bay View] had direct communication with me at Coy H.Q. which was entirely satisfactory as far as I was concerned. However, they were under the operations control of [the Royal Rifles] but in order to telephone their [Royal Rifles Company Commander] they had to ring my Coy HQ, ask for D Bn., ask for Fortress, ask for [the Royal Rifles] and ask for their company. This roundabout procedure made telephony practically impossible' (140).
2 The Japanese were indeed concerned about the sunken ships, not as hazards to navigation, but as possible strong points to be held by desperate men to interfere with their invasion fleet.
3 One of the great myths of the battle of Hong Kong in popular writing is that Maltby believed the attack would come from the south (i.e. the open sea). While this had been the foundation for Hong Kong's defence before the Japanese invasion of China, everything had changed by the time Maltby arrived in 1941, and defence for the north shore had finally been built. Maltby, an Indian Army man to a fault, had placed his most trusted units (the Punjabis, Royal Scots, and Rajputs) across the north shore in readiness,

with the Canadian battalions in the rear. My understanding was clarified when shown a map drawn by a Canadian, showing the Royal Rifles and Winnipeg Grenadiers holding the southern beach 'front line' while the Punjabis and Rajputs in the north 'rested in the rear following their exertions on the mainland'. One can only assume that some officer, whether British or Canadian, had thus tried to bolster Canadian *esprit de corps*. Maltby never forgot that a secondary invasion could land on the southern beaches, but there is no evidence that he seriously expected one.

4   Though there is some dispute as to whether these two really were co-located.
5   Smith-Dutton was a Gun Layer with the 7 HAA Bty., 5 AA Regiment. This unit suffered severe casualties on the 18th and 19th, at the Sai Wan AA site and the Wong Nai Chung AA position respectively (132b: Smith-Dutton).
6   Most histories say that the Rajputs, holding the waterfront, were 'wiped out' during this attack. In fact, on the night of 18/19th they lost 130 killed from a strength at 8 December of 892. This is significant number — the 99 lost on the 19th alone being the highest one-day loss of any unit in Hong Kong — but not quite as disastrous as has been portrayed. It is noteworthy, however, that only eleven Rajputs made it to hospital on those two days.
7   At around the turn of the century, papers were found in the attic of a Hong Kong house which was being demolished. These consisted of what appears to be the original hand-written message log of Fortress HQ, and also the message log of the Commander, RAOC. In the former, the first message indicating that a landing had occurred was at 21.45. It said 'Wanchai Gap report M.G. fire from the direction of [North Point]'. In the latter, the first mention is at 24.00 and reads simply: 'Enemy landed Lyemun and Taikoo'.
8   Whitehead later escaped to China and joined Mission 204.
9   228th Regiment.
10 229th Regiment. Plotting the massacres in four dimensions indicates that the majority, though not quite all, were committed by this unit as it moved south.
11 Although the Japanese atrocities in China — Nanjing especially — were well known in Hong Kong, many westerners (in particular, those with experience of Japan) believed that they would behave differently towards them. Ellen Field: 'I thought, for instance, that the Japanese would simply come up to me and say, 'We've won,' or something like that, for at this time none of us really feared them. I believed they would behave decently towards British people; that terms would be agreed' (111: 21).
12 I have been unable to establish why the eastern slopes of Mount Nicholson, overlooking the gap from the west, were — with the exception of West Brigade's bunkers at its foot — not fortified.
13 The Hugheseliers were a group of HKVDC men in their 50s and 60s — mainly with First World War experience — who were formed by Lt. Col. A. W. Hughes into their own unit. Wags named them the 'Methuseliers'.
14 The Japanese tactic was to head south to the high ground. The strategy, on

the other hand, was to take Central. It is interesting to speculate what would have happened had a local commander — like Doi at the Redoubt — decided to act for himself by breaking through the power station defenses and charging west straight towards Central, before most of the garrison even knew the invasion had started.

15 Of all the bombings of civilian targets, this one had the most witnesses and was the most widely reported.

16 Both would be dead within 24 hours. Lammert's father, a Hong Kong auctioneer, was interned in Stanley for the duration. It is said that Lammert hoped till the end that his son was still alive, and that internees who knew he was already dead did not tell him.

17 Most likely Sgt. Wilson, RA, and Bdr. Fincher, HKVDC.

18 The exact timing of the landings is the subject of some debate. Lt. Gen. Ito Takeo (138) states that they occurred at 22.00, though the consensus is closer to a starting time of 20.30. It is possible that the earliest reports refer to some sort of 'Beach Masters' landing, though I have seen no corroboration of this.

19 It must be pointed out that, having only been in Hong Kong four weeks, it is questionable whether the average Canadian soldier could distinguish between Chinese and Japanese people. Nurse Kathleen Christie, herself a Canadian, states: 'they had difficult distinguishing Japanese from Chinese and frequently the sentries' challenges were answered in perfect English, only to discover too late that they were Japanese who had reached them' (95: 123).

20 A first walk along Sir Cecil's Ride in the early 1990s uncovered a number of Japanese rifle cartridges, British bullets (.303 and dubiously hollow-nosed .38s), and shrapnel from British shells and Japanese mortars. Unfortunately, since that time much of the path has been paved. However, after rain, such items still wash down from the hillside. On a mildly hungover walk on 1 January 2001 it was still possible to find a perfectly preserved Japanese rifle cartridge at the edge of the path.

21 In fact Rajputs. The 'youngest soldier' referred to is almost certainly 21-year-old Francisco Noronha.

22 Some sources say 22.00.

23 Nos. 2 and 3 guns (15 and 30 metres north respectively) stayed in the hands of 4 Bty.

24 Sgt. David Gow, HKVDC.

25 Some accounts place this attack at 22.30, but it must in fact have occurred prior to the change of duty at 22.00.

26 Bosanquet later escaped from POW camp.

27 Capt. Goldman, the battery commander.

28 Some sources say twenty (27: 26), others twenty-nine (91: 125). The actual number appears to be two killed in the shelling, six in the initial attack on the position, and a total of twenty (fifteen volunteers and five regulars) in the massacre. Bosanquet describes being sent to Sai Wan with a burial party

approximately one week after the surrender, and finding the bodies of the sentries, others on the road outside, and thirteen more thrown over a wall at the gun site (29: 44).
29 This stood on today's Tong Chong Street.
30 Some sources quoted by (100) claim that Wallis thought the Lye Mun Gap–Redoubt–6-inch howitzer position were still in Canadian hands. Wallis himself (139) states that this was information given to him by Homes.
31 His wife would be murdered at Stanley, 25 December
32 Fincher's wife Irene is mentioned at length in (48).
33 Manuel's niece Anne Ozorio was a major contributor to this book.
34 (126) states: 'Wong Nai Chung AA site. Unburied'. If this were the case, it would indeed be the 19th. However, his colleagues insist he was killed at Sai Wan.
35 (126) states: 'Originally buried near pumping station west of Island Road opposite road to Lyemun.'
36 (126) notes: 'Possibly buried in communal grave on north east slope of Sai Wan Hill (16 bodies).'
37 (126) states: 'Originally buried west slope Sai Wan Hill just above perimeter wire'.
38 The fact that the IGH also took in seven wounded HKSRA gunners this day indicates that there was quite a battle for the piece.
39 The Punjabis are not generally recorded in action until the 19th. However, the fact that the IGH (close to the landing points) took in fifty-one Punjabi wounded on this day is highly significant. Possibly the Punjabis were in action earlier than believed, but it seems that the following undated statement from Guest holds the clue: 'About a hundred and fifty men of the Punjabis and Rajput regiments had taken shelter from the raid in an underground miniature rifle range and a bomb had penetrated the shelter and had killed or wounded practically everybody in it' (28: 40). Further, Mackenzie in (24: 201) states: 'In a particularly heavy [air raid on 18 December] on the Central District a bomb hit an underground miniature range in which 80 Sepoys of the Punjabi headquarters Company were taking shelter. The walls collapsed; 24 were killed and 36 injured.' Despite the claim in (126) that this happened at HKVDC HQ, when I asked Arthur Gomes about the incident he recalled it occurring at the Murray Barracks (132b: Gomes). The Punjabi War Diary (140) states: '11.00 Hrs. Rear Bde. HQ at Volunteer HQ Garden Rd. was struck by a 500 lb bomb. Casualties 24K 36 wounded.' Whichever version is most accurate, it is probable that all except Tara Singh were killed by this incident.
40 The Dockyard Police were raised by separate statute, and there is some uncertainty as to whether they were actually recognized as members of the HKDDC. However, they are attributed to that unit in CWGC records.
41 The *South China Morning Post* of Thursday, 27 September 1945 claims that

he and Willison were killed in Quarry Bay, and that only O'Connor and Post were at Shau Kei Wan. (98: 175) states that Johnson died of wounds sustained in the fighting on Mount Cameron. This would imply 19 December rather than 18 December.
42 Geoffrey Wilson confirms that Shau Kei Wan police station was fought over with police casualties (132b: Wilson).
43 Lance Sergeant A. 175 Jack reports O'Connor and Post leading two groups of police on either side of King's Road when they came under grenade attack. He did not see either again (131).
44 *South China Morning Post*, 27 September 1945. However, (98: 175) states that he died whilst being taken to Queen Mary Hospital for emergency treatment, and (131) reports that he was seriously wounded by a grenade near Quarry Bay station.
45 These two ARP personnel were presumably those beheaded by the 228th.

6. PHASE IV: THE FORCING OF WONG NAI CHUNG GAP

1 It is difficult to estimate the number captured on the evening of the 18th, though 200 may be roughly correct.
2 This AA position is still easily visited. Take the road heading north immediately in front of Park View, and turn left before the bridge instead of continuing on to the service reservoir. At the end of the paved road, force your way through the undergrowth along a little catchwater, and the remains of the position will be on your left.
3 In Japanese records, '5-Junction Road' is Wong Nai Chung Gap, and 'Red Pillar Promontory' is Stanley.
4 *Butai* is Japanese for 'Regiment'.
5 Leading Stoker Tom Middleton joined the complement of *Robin* after *Tern* was scuttled. This was not the first time he had had to swim for it, having been sunk earlier that year — in *Eumaeus* of the Blue Funnel Line — off Sierra Leone by the Italian submarine *Cappellini*. The next ship he would find himself on would be the first transportation (of the 'undesirables', including his friend Bristow again) to POW camps in Japan. This quote comes from an interview kindly conducted for the book by Middleton's son, Tom junior.
6 Most of the attackers were buried in a trench there with the remains of the twenty 5 AA prisoners who were murdered (27: 26). These bodies were finally found in 1949 by 2nd Lt. Mike Cotterill, RA.
7 These were St John's Ambulance. Their post-war memorial was erected about 100 metres south of the MAP.
8 The Indian police constable had been wounded earlier and taken into the MAP. See Sgt. Cunningham's (RAMC) War Crime deposition as reported in

the *South China Morning Post* for Saturday, 15 March 1947. When Cunningham and the others finally surrendered, they were tied to trees, only to be rescued by a sajput sepoy (also a prisoner) who had kept a knife and cut the others down despite being in the midst of an armed Japanese camp.

9   Babin had no option but to turn back. When Bickley was finally treated after the surrender at the Queen Mary Hospital, both eyes had to be removed.

10 As a footnote, Ernest Hemingway and his wife Martha Gellhorn stayed at the Repulse Bay Hotel in the spring of 1941 (67). One wonders what would have resulted had they delayed their visit until the autumn months. Gandt (78) tells the following story of Hemingway's visit to the 7th War Zone after leaving Hong Kong, when a Chinese general asked the British opinion of Chinese infantry:

> 'Johnny's all right and a very good fellow and all that', says Hemingway, affecting a British accent. 'But he's absolutely hopeless on the offensive, you know . . . we can't count on Johnny.'
> 'Johnny?' Asked the general.
> 'John Chinaman', said Hemingway.
> 'Very interesting,' the general said. 'Let me tell you a Chinese story. Do you know why the British staff officer wears a single glass in his eye?'
> 'No,' said Hemingway.
> 'He wears a single glass in his eye so he will not see more than he can understand.'
> 'I will tell the officer when I see him.'
> 'Very good,' the general said. 'Tell him it is a little message from Johnny.'

11 Pears' brother Peter was the celebrated British tenor, 1910-1986.

12 Died on the *Lisbon Maru*, 2 October 1942.

13 Interestingly, the official history of the Middlesex notes that 'The two Canadian battalions were in support of the 1st Middlesex' (96: 31).

14 Known universally as 'J. J.', Paterson's Christian names were actually John Johnstone. A quite incredible character, Wiseman (who shared a hut with him in Sham Shui Po later in the war) notes: 'And he could look after himself. I remember once watching quite fascinated as he caught, plucked, cooked and ate a sparrow!' (51: 64).

15 This unit was formed under Col. A. W. Hughes, chairman of the Union Insurance Co. of Canton (91: 133). He is also recorded as manager of the Union Insurance Co. of Hong Kong (44: 45).

16 Pre-war a director of a London grain exporter (91: 48).

17 Cooke, Parker, Tucker, and Tunmer survived the fighting but died on the *Lisbon Maru*, 2 October 1942. Meakin died as a POW in Japan, 24 December 1942. The North Point power station was, post-war, dismantled and shipped to China.

18 There is some uncertainty about the activities on Mount Butler. Although

largely credited with its recapture, A Coy. Winnipeg Grenadiers may well have actually recaptured the summit of Jardine's Lookout instead. See (81: 481).

19 Some authorities maintain that no assistance arrived. However, it is clear from casualty lists that assistance came from HKSRA, HKVDC, and Winnipeg Grenadiers.

20 The Salesian Mission contained the entire army medical store for China Command, which was moved — via St Albert's Convent — from Kowloon in 1940.

21 Thomas, in the ambulance, confirms that these were Viceroy Commissioned Officers (132a: Thomas).

22 Wife of George Tinson, later killed at Postbridge. Harrop states that eight days after the surrender, 'Alabaster, our Attorney General, has the unpleasant job of breaking the news to Mrs Tinson that her husband had been killed in the battle and that her house had been completely destroyed by mortar fire. When we arrived back at the office we found her in a state bordering on hysterics. No wonder; she had been through quite enough' (49: 100).

23 Fearon had only just arrived from Beijing 'to be safe' (109: 9).

24 Thomas threw himself into the nullah and was shot in the face. He was about to cut his wrists to avoid a lingering death, when Leath crawled over him in an even worse state. This gave Thomas the impetus to survive, and through a series of adventures he evaded capture and ended up joining the BAAG in China (132a: Thomas).

25 Because of his early capture, Banfill did not join the other Canadian POWs in North Point until February 1942. In the meantime, his death had been reported to Canada. On hearing the news, his wife took her own life (63: 35). Seventeen bodies were later found at the massacre site.

26 Lawson had in fact planned to move his Brigade HQ back to the safer Black's Link area this very morning. The speed of the Japanese advance, however, pre-empted that.

27 Shrapnel damage, still clearly visible on both sides of a stone bridge just south of 34 Stubbs Road, is most probably from this ambush.

28 Coleman and Tunmer drowned ten months later on the Lisbon Maru.

29 Died aboard the *Lisbon Maru*, 2 October 1942.

30 Sorby died of these wounds on 15 January 1942 aged 60. Post-war it was revealed that he had left an estate of HK$327,000 — a very large sum at that time. While he was 'only' a private, it should be remembered that he was also the manager of HK Electric, Ltd. He lived at No. 253, The Peak, with neighbours including on one side Gwen Priestwood (at 153) and on the other Sir Atholl MacGregor (at 372).

31 Daughter of Ferdinand Duckworth, the station superintendent, and wife of Ken Crawford.

32 Some 200 POWs captured on the North Face were held in the station garage

overnight with no aid to the wounded. Next day they were marched to the Maryknoll Mission with 200–300 Indians, regulars, and HKVDC.

33 No. 1, Repulse Bay Road, today one of Macau gambling millionaire Stanley Ho's many homes.

34 In 1941 this was known as Stanley Gap Road.

35 Collinson survived the fighting. Rather nicely, the hut that later housed Collinson and other senior naval POWs in Argyle Street camp was known as 'The Aquarium'.

36 However, there was quite a fight for the position, with as many as 16 fatalities from 5 AA alone. Maltby's despatch notes: 'Part of the enemy attack came on to Stanley Gap and involved the 3.7-inch A.A. Section there. The Royal Artillery in the nearest 3.7-inch Howitzer positions [2nd MB, HKSRA] were called on to assist, and leaving their gun positions were drawn into the fighting with their small arms' (20: 16). Whitehead reported many Indian bodies in the vicinity on 23 December: '[Major Rochford-Boyd and I] were driving near Wong nei Chong towards Tai Tam when heavy firing forced us to leave the truck and seek the shelter of a ridge. As we crawled up a slope I saw, just ahead, Sikhs and Muslims lying down. When we drew nearer, I realized they were all dead' (30: 32).

37 It is not clear if this is the case. Stewart confirms that he, CSM White, Sgt. Winch, and four ORs locked themselves in the HQ shelter, but that on the night of the 22nd, 'having been without food for four days and running short of ammunition', they evacuated the position in pairs and returned to lines (3: 29).

38 It was realized that the Japanese were firing British shells because the percentage of 'duds' was so much lower.

39 This warehouse is probably that north of Park View. Take the road running north immediately in front of Park View. Just before the red fire hydrant, some 20 metres south of the service reservoir, climb the bank to your right. Force your way south through the undergrowth and you will find yourself — eventually — standing on its roof. This is also a prime contender for the site of the 'Black Hole'. However, (79: 247) mentions CQMS Fincher holding out in a 'store-shelter' in this vicinity until the front was blown in by a Japanese mortar bomb on the afternoon of the 19th. This description also fits.

40 This is probably the OP that can still be found today just off the track at the top of Jardine's Lookout, underneath the viewing platform immediately west of the trigonometry station. A search of the area in October 2001 revealed one bullet, one broken .303 round, and a large piece of shrapnel — possibly indicative of some sort of action around the position. (148) notes that 'During [20 December], occasionally the peak of Jardine's Lookout received heavy artillery fire from Victoria and Race Course gun positions'.

41 These fortifications and the catchwater still exist not far to the north of Parkview estate.

42 Leonard was secretary of the British Legion in Hong Kong when this book was begun.
43 To trace the Wagstaff story forward and back, the sculptor of the bronze lions (dated 1935) outside today's HSBC headquarters was Wagstaff's father, W. W. Wagstaff. This information was given to me by Wagstaff's son, whom I traced in mid-2001 to a house less than 100 yards from my parents' in a remote north Norfolk village.
44 Eager's father Oscar — a former commandant of the HK Police Reserve — was interned in Stanley, where he was killed by the accidental American navy bombing of Bungalow C on 17 January 1945.
45 Reginald Barker.
46 Tom Duckworth.
47 One brigade shelter from Lawson's position still stands near the garage on the west side of Wong Nai Chung Gap Road. It was refurbished for a visit from Canadian veterans in December 2000. The hillside it is on is arguably the most mosquito-ridden in modern Hong Kong. However, rough and overgrown steps to the south of the garage lead up to the point where Lawson was killed, and where the majority of his HQ shelters are just visible protruding from the soil that has tumbled down the hillside. The lintel shows the impact of heavy machine-gun bullets of around .50 calibre. I found just such a bullet on Mount Nicholson in 1996. David Mather — an expert on the subject — tells me that the most likely weapon would be the Japanese 13 mm model 93 AA/anti-tank MG 1933.
48 Died on the *Lisbon Maru*, 2 October 1942.
49 If he was indeed killed, then Havildar Kishan Singh of 1MB HKSRA would be the most likely candidate. However, it seems unlikely that a havildar would have been in command.
50 The RE commander, Lt. Col. Walker, was in fact rescued by Canadians (Lt. Blackwood and Pte. Morris, Winnipeg Grenadiers) and dragged to the shelters, having been wounded in the legs. National Archives of Canada, Ottawa, DHIST 593 (D1) claims that Walker attempted to drive his car through the Gap, got out when he found it blocked by destroyed vehicles, and was then shot.
51 This bungalow was at the junction of Fort and Prison Roads.
52 Cullum died of malnutrition as a POW, 27 September 1942.
53 One of these was Ron Parry, who wrote: 'After the 2 lead lorries were hit we were unable to get past, and we hid under the lorry for about 8 hours before making our way back to our lines' (132b: Parry).
54 This source actually says B and C Coys., but (20: 17) and (140) state A and D Coys.
55 Wallis in (139) insists that No. 1 Coy. HKVDC's withdrawal was without orders. In fact, he implies that the order had been 'Don't withdraw'. On the same page of his War Diary, he states: '[Wallis] noticed that although he could

get no information from [the Royal Rifles] troops on Mt. Parker early on 19 Dec, these troops appeared to rapidly receive and comply with withdrawal orders.' Rightly or wrongly, Wallis clearly perceived that the Royal Scots, the Royal Rifles, and No. 1 Coy. HKVDC had all let him down. Wallis's comments about the Royal Rifles in particular aroused much resentment post-war. For a discussion of this in the fullest context, see Appendix 23.

56 The clearing immediately north of the upper pillbox is the site of Matheson's old house (78: 120).

57 This order must have made sense — to its originators — at the time. This implies that they seriously believed that the Gap was only lightly held by the Japanese. However, it is difficult to understand why this view was held, following the heavy fighting that had been continuous in the immediate vicinity for the previous seven hours.

58 Who died of wounds received here, 6 January 1942.

59 Although the VC citation puts Osborn on Mount Butler, eyewitnesses claim he was on the southern slope of Jardine's Lookout at the time. The exact position they state is the intersection of a line drawn east from the current reservoir north of the Wong Nai Chung Gap AA position, and north from the westernmost building of Park View. There has been talk of building a memorial at the spot, though at time of writing this is little more than a heap of rough granite cubes.

60 Osborn's VC commendation, the only one of the Hong Kong fighting, reads in the *London Gazette* of 1 April 1946, as follows:

'At Hong Kong, on 19th December, 1941, a Company of the Winnipeg Grenadiers became divided in an attack on Mount Butler. A part of the Company led by C. S. M. Osborn captured the hill at bayonet point, but after three hours owing to the superior numbers of the enemy the position became untenable. C. S. M. Osborn and a small group covered the withdrawal and when their turn came to fall back he single-handed engaged the enemy, exposing himself to heavy enemy fire to cover their retirement. Later the Company was cut off and completely surrounded. Several enemy grenades were thrown which C. S. M. Osborn picked up and threw back. When one landed in a position where it was impossible to pick it up, he threw himself upon it and was instantly killed. His self-sacrifice undoubtedly saved the lives of many of his comrades. C. S. M. Osborn was an inspiring example to all throughout the defence, and in his death he displayed the highest qualities of heroism and self-sacrifice.' Osborn, born on 2 Jan. 1899 at Foulden, Norfolk, England, had enjoyed a varied career including service in the First World War — in which he was gassed — and a spell in the Merchant Navy. Unfortunately, just days before he sailed for Hong Kong, his five-year-old daughter Patricia had an accident in which her clothes caught fire and she was badly burned (21: 40). Osborn died not knowing that she was off the critical list. A statue — ostensibly of Osborn, but actually of an unknown First World War soldier — still stands in central Hong Kong, in Hong Kong Park, near Flagstaff House. Interestingly, his service record (National Archives of Canada File number RG24 Vol. 26734, Regt. No. H6008) doesn't list his citizenship in either the Attestation Paper for enlistment in the Active Forces or on the Official Registration of Death (Province of Manitoba). It seems very possible that he still maintained British citizenship at the time of his death. I am indebted to John Mundie in Canada, who located this file for the purposes of this book.

61 The Ridge is a commanding position a few hundred yards south of Wong Nai Chung Gap, on the east side of the road. At this time it housed just an RAOC unit. It is first referred to as an RAOC position on 11 December in the Commander, RAOC message log (see n. 7 for Ch. 5). Ridge Court is one of the buildings there today.

62 Caroline Hill is today completely flat. However, in 1941 there must have still been some topography as (14) states at 16.30 (approx.): 'Both Coys began the descent of the Eastern Slopes of Caroline Hill.'

63 Broadbridge took with him a message: 'From 9 Pl. 3 Coy. HKVDC To Fortress H.Q. "P.B. 1 & 2 W.N.C. still held. No orders to withdraw. Support required urgently. Three stretcher cases."' He phoned this message from a house in Tai Hang Road and was then ordered to report to the Middlesex on Leighton Hill (133).

64 Other accounts have implied that the Japanese treated their captives as courageous heroes. This is not so. Sgt. George White offered to carry Hung away after the surrender, but Hung elected to stay in the pillbox where 'he could get medical attention'. Hung was not seen alive again. See *South China Morning Post*, 13 March 1947. Winyard saw the killing of MacKechnie and Gosling through jujitsu, Zimmern reported that Lim was 'trampled on his head and bayoneted'. Survivors were thrown into the 'black hole of Hong Kong' (136). This was not, however, the end of 3 Coy. The two sections west of the Gap regrouped under Cpls. Roylance and Mackay and joined the line in Wan Chai (23: 232).

65 In his despatch, Maltby wrote: 'I should like to place on record the superb gallantry of No. 3 (Eurasian) Company at Wong Nai Chung Gap.' The only other two HKVDC units he singled out for praise were 1 Bty. in defence of Stanley, and the Signals section (20: 4). Shoji notes (148) that 3 Battalion, 230th Regiment took 800 casualties in taking the Gap.

66 Sutcliffe was to die of beri-beri and dysentery as a POW, 23 March 1942.

67 It is often claimed that one aim of this attack was to relieve the Repulse Bay Hotel. However, at the time when these orders were given, the Japanese had not yet reached it. Neither is there any evidence that any reports of them having reached the hotel were received by East Brigade before the attack finally advanced from Stanley View at 08.00 on the 20th. The hotel was

simply on the road along which this force planned to attack Wong Nai Chung Gap. When Maltby heard that the hotel was surrounded (some 15 minutes before the Royal Rifles left Stanley View), he ordered A Coy. Punjabis to relieve it from the west, this attack becoming bogged down at Shouson Hill.
68 See 18th.
69 Mt. Blount, from the context, appears to be a part of Jardine's Lookout, possibly near the Wong Nai Chung Gap AA position. The term is not is use today.
70 In 1994, a man claiming to be Baptiste turned up in Canada. His story was that he had suffered terrible head injuries during the fighting, and — through a series of adventures including serving in the Korean war — had only recently realized who he was. There appear to be no mentions of Baptiste — nor any 'unknown' man — in POW records. At time of writing, Canadian authorities have not accepted his claim.
71 See start of 20 December for details of the 'Black Hole'. It is possible that this death, and others ascribed to that location, actually occurred on the 20th rather than the 19th.
72 (126) notes: 'Killed artillery post, Mount Blount'.
73 Johnson came from Yarmouth, Norfolk, England. The Canadian units included a number of British and even Americans.
74 According to (126), this took place at 'Hong Kong Reservoir'.
75 (126) states: 'Mount Blount'.
76 (132b: Matthews) states that Roy Land was killed after attacking the Japanese (with rifle fire and grenades) while others were surrendering, having heard of the death of his brother Gordon. (126) states, as with his brother, 'Mount Blount'. The *South China Morning Post* for 11 March 1947 describes the 'Land incident' in the War Crimes Trials as 'the bayoneting of four Canadians'. The 13 Mar. edition contains the quote: '[after surrendering to the Japanese] Lance Corporal Charles Bradbury, Winnipeg Grenadiers . . . saw one of a group of four Canadians about thirty yards away throw a grenade towards where seven Japanese were visible. The grenade exploded, killing at least four of the Japanese. The three survivors, together with eight or ten other Japanese nearby rushed to the spot where the four Canadians were and bayoneted them to death.'
77 Which gives an alternative date of 20 December.
78 (126): 'Killed Mount Blount'.
79 (126) gives its usual 'Killed Mount Blount'. Although this was the only VC awarded in Hong Kong, there were two other recommendations: Gray of the RAF, and Forsyth of 2 Coy. HKVDC. Mackenzie in (24: 216) states that Ansari had been recommended for the VC for valour during the fighting but, credible though this is, no corroboration has come to light as yet.
80 (126) 'Killed Mount Blount'.
81 (126) 'Killed Mount Blount'.

82 Those buried at 562 The Peak were killed by a shell, having set up their radio in a front room — vulnerable to shellfire — rather than the back (118: 36). However, other records speak of burials at 526 Coombe Road. This is a Wan Chai Gap address, and perhaps more credible.

83 No. 1 and 2 Craters were in fact bomb craters on Borret Road, just below Bowen Road. These were created by the bombing on 17 December (142).

84 CAB 106/88, Captain Scriven 20 December 1941: 'Junction of Deep Water Bay–Repulse Bay road . . . Colour Sgt. Bond was killed and while it is known that a few other ranks escaped, the majority were wiped out.' No other 'Bond' appears relevant, but it is difficult to reconcile these two versions.

85 Although there is no proof, it seems reasonable that Minchin died with Lawson on this day.

86 (126) 'Killed North Point Electric. King's Road. December 19'.

87 Which also gives an alternative date of 18 December.

88 (126) 'Missing. Last known at The Ridge'.

89 (126) 'Possibly buried in communal grave on north east slope of Sai Wan Hill (16 bodies)'.

90 Previously James appeared in both the list of those with known and unknown graves.

91 (126) states Kirby was originally buried in the guard room, Stanley Fort, on 21 December.

92 (126) 'originally buried junction of Black's Link and Deep Water Road'.

93 (126) 'Missing Wong Nai Chung area near Jardine's Lookout'. There is some dispute as to whether RA West was actually co-located with Lawson's HQ.

94 More credibly, (126) states that he was killed at the Stanley Gap AA site area.

95 See Fincher's account in (136). (126) also records 'Pillbox 1 or 2 Jardine's Lookout', which seems to confirm the 19th.

96 (147) for 13 March 1947 claims he was killed at the 'Black Hole' by the mortar attack.

97 The *South China Morning Post* for 19 December 1946 carried four *In Memoriam* notices for 1941. That for Hoffman read: 'In loving memory of my beloved husband and our Dear Father James Joseph Hoffman of HKVDC No 3 Machine Gun Coy who died in action 19th December 1941. Always in our cherished thoughts. Inserted by his loving wife, son and daughters: Freddy, Elizabeth, Mabel and Jeanette.'

98 (126) 'Missing believed killed at south end Sir Cecil's Ride, WNCG'.

99 (126) 'KIA area of village north Jardine's Lookout'.

100 Though (126) claims 'KIA area of village north Jardine's Lookout' for both.

101 (126) claims 'KIA area of village north Jardine's Lookout'.

102 A note from the Manageress of the Repulse Bay Hotel states that an 'Unknown HKVDF [sic] (Grenovitch?)' was buried at the front of the hotel. Greenevitch was also known as Hryniewicz.

103 (126) states: 'Killed in action at Sanatorium Gap. Buried at Mount Parker.'
104 Armoured Car.
105 Hospital records record him under serial 11151 as Nazrulleh Khan, Naik.
106 (126) 'Missing 18 Dec 1941'.
107 Holliday had become engaged to nurse Brenda Morgan — killed by a shell on the 14th — in November.
108 (145: 131) says he died in hospital. Originally buried behind St Albert's Hospital (126).
109 (126) states that Stewart was buried No. 1 Crater, Borret Road 20 December, i.e. he died in BRH.
110 (126): 'Killed near Middle Gap area Dec 23'.
111 This may in fact have been a Japanese ambush, presumed to be fifth column as no one had expected the Japanese to move so far south so quickly. (126) states that Dickenson was 'Missing The Ridge area' on the 20th.
112 In CWGC records as RASC, but presumably Volunteer ASC.
113 The unit 'HMS *Hong Kong*' fails to turn up in any official documentation except CWGC.
114 HMS *Tarantula*, like *Cicala* and *Moth* an Aphis Class River Gunboat, was built by Wood-Skinner in 1916 under pennant T62. Hulked in 1941, it was expended as a target on 1 May 1946 by HMS *Carron* and *Carysfort*. Why one crewmember lost his life in Hong Kong in 1941 is a minor mystery.

7. PHASE V: PUSHING THE LINE WEST AND ENCIRCLING STANLEY

1 These comprised 23 Regular RASC, 19 Volunteer RASC, 38 RAOC, 1 2 Coy. HKVDC, 1 Middlesex, 1 officer of HQCC, and 16 Royal Rifles. A further 15 Royal Rifles who were recorded as KIA in Repulse Bay might also have lost their lives at Eucliffe. Three Artillerymen are also said to have been killed at The Ridge (126), but the dates quoted seem inappropriate. Fifty-three bodies are said to have been found in the Eucliffe area (95: 141), while it is generally accepted that some 30 more died in each of The Ridge and Overbays. The figures match reasonably well.
2 Extract from a short but powerful interview of Pte. Clifford L. Matthews, Winnipeg Grenadiers, kindly conducted for this book by his son John Matthews. Here he refers to the effect of the shelling on the 'Black Hole of Hong Kong'. Interestingly, the garrison included a second Clifford Matthews (of the HKVDC) who went on post-war to propose the popular theory that life on earth evolved from traces brought into the atmosphere by meteorites and dust from space.
3 Described in the War Crimes Trials as being 'a small building situated at the junction of Stanley Gap Road and a road leading up to Jardine's Lookout'

(147). It has still not been possible to confirm the exact site, but most probably this was the building in the flat space immediately west of Parkview. In 1990, the building was still there. A few years later, just the floor existed. Today it is grass.

4. According to Japanese sources, the area was under artillery fire from the racecourse. Doi: 'The moment they spotted anyone near the [Wong Nai Chung Gap AA] gun position they instantly lobbed shells from the artillery position near the race track.' This would imply that the shell was a 6-inch howitzer fired by 25 Medium Battery HKSRA. On the other hand, at least two survivors of the 'Black Hole' are convinced that a mortar bomb was to blame. 'The prisoners, sick and wounded as well as those physically fit, were herded into a kitchen or mess hall, which was being shelled by our own trench mortars' (Sgt. Thomas Marsh, Winnipeg Grenadiers, reported in the *South China Morning Post*, 13 March 1947).

5. (21: 171) transposes the brothers, but relatives insist that the correct version is the one above. Cliff Matthews (Winnipeg Grenadiers, rather than his HKVDC namesake) survives as an eyewitness. Harry Atkinson, another eyewitness, passed away in early 2002.

6. It is not clear whether Wallis is referring to the GSO 1 (Newnham) or the GSO Intelligence (Boxer). The former is probably more likely.

7. Possibly Lt. Tressider.

8. This was the 1941 spelling.

9. Later Wallis adds: 'It was evident that it had not yet been understood how weak in ability the Canadian troops were and how strong was the enemy strength and positions.'

10. Peak Mansions was on the site of today's Peak Galleria.

11. Today's building is a facsimile of the original, which in a monstrous fit of stupidity, was torn down in 1982. The garage on the opposite side of the road is the original.

12. Usually reported as four naval ratings and one Middlesex OR. The naval contingent was probably HKRNVR, including Harrison, Richard Stuart, and C. R. C. Robinson (114: 48).

13. Interestingly, every account of this engagement differs as to who first saw the Japanese at the garage. The longest account, beginning (114: 44), doesn't even mention Grounds, except, probably, in a reference to 'a mortally wounded British officer'.

14. The version of this story that appears in Emily Hahn's *China to Me* (17) is considerably more romantic, and has Charles taking command of the 'leaderless' Punjabis and being shot leading an attack. Baxter's version is arguably the most credible, as there is no evidence that the Punjabis were leaderless, two officers (Thomson and Forsyth) being present. Baxter's version is also similar to Bennett's, and he shared a hut with Boxer, Price, and other officers in Argyle Street. Note that both Boxer and Bennett were fluent

Japanese speakers, though the story of captured Japanese soldiers was probably no more than rumour.

15   Brigadier Wallis having ridden back to Stanley View on the pillion of a motorcycle in order to convey the order. This gun later also destroyed four mortars on Violet Hill (139).

16   Some accounts refer to Brick Hill falling to the Japanese on this day. However, as any visitor to modern-day Ocean Park will note, Brick Hill covers an enormous area. The Middlesex positions that fell this day were very close to the road to Aberdeen. The HKSRA 17 HAA Bty. positions on the southern tip did not fall until Christmas Day. Holidaymakers should note that after capturing both positions, the Japanese bound and bayoneted the survivors.

17   Presumably this was the composite D Coy. Platoon under Witham.

18   The 228th had in fact prepared to attack that night, but the attack was brought forward to 17.00 because they were able to make use of the fog to hide their progress. They succeeded 'without any serious resistance' (122), implying that they simply occupied positions as the Royal Scots left them.

19   Interestingly, the Fortress HQ message log (see Ch. 5, n. 7) only records a single call from Major Manners during the entire battle. This came at 14.10 on 21 December, complaining that firing from Stanley over the Repulse Bay Hotel had hit the servants' quarters. The CRAOC message log reports one outgoing message to the Repulse Bay Hotel (picked up by Major Manners) from The Ridge at 17.45, also on 21 December: 'Messrs Johnson & Blaver have arrived at their destination and are awaiting further instructions.'

20   On this day at the Repulse Bay Hotel, Siu-Feng Huang notes (156) that: 'still we could have our dinner consisting of 3 courses'.

21   Wallis is often accused of a lack of respect for the Canadians in general, but in fact his frustration was mainly with the officers — and most especially with the Royal Rifles' commander, Home (he actually recommended two other officers, MacAuley and Atkinson, for military decorations). Equally, the Royal Rifles often seemed to lack any confidence in officers, whether Canadian or British. In Wallis's account of East Brigade, speaking of the Royal Rifles, he states: 'It was clear from the fighting on 20 and 21 Dec that provided they had good leaders the men were brave enough and would follow.' Weedon — a highly respected Middlesex officer — backs Wallis in this opinion: '[The Royal Rifles] were bewildered and didn't know whether they were coming or going. But if they found an officer who appeared to be in control of the situation — and apparently I fitted the bill in that respect — they glued themselves to him and fought with quite extraordinary tenacity' (91: 200). Of this particular withdrawal, Wallis is contemptuous of D Coy.'s failure to bring back their 3-inch mortars — despite the fact that they were withdrawing over extremely steep and difficult terrain, in wet and slippery conditions, in the dark, under fire, and a 3-inch mortar barrel weighs over 100 pounds. For the sake of completeness, all such controversial elements

of the relationship between Canadians and British in Hong Kong have been included in this work.

22 In the message log of the Commander, RAOC (see Ch. 5, n. 7), a message timed at 10.35 on 20 December reads: 'From DADOS [MacPherson] Ridge. As result of enemy ambush on Repulse Bay Road, following RAOC w/shop personnel believed missing, Capt Bonny (sic), Lieut Wilson, SM Read, S/Sgts O'Toole, Mecking, Cpl Flass, L/Cpl Colebrook. Remainder w/shop personnel at the Ridge.' As this is a hand-written entry, 'Flass' might possibly be 'Bliss' who is listed as lost on 24 December. The remainder survived the war, though 'Mecking' is in fact 'Meekings'.

23 (126) gives a date of 20 December. Clearly he was brought to BRH, but whether he was DOA, or DOW from Wan Chai, is uncertain.

24 Presumably Overbays.

25 (126) again calls this 'artillery post Mount Blount'.

26 (126) notes 'Killed Blue Pool road area', which is presumably where he was wounded.

27 (126) gives an alternative date of 25 December.

28 A note elsewhere in (126) claims that Grieves was last seen at Wong Nai Chung Gap.

29 (145: 19) claims that Slay and others were originally buried at Repulse Bay Hotel on or about 18 December. A note from the manageress states he was buried outside the 'New Wing Pantry'.

30 The notice in the *South China Morning Post* for this day strongly implies that these three were killed by a shell.

31 While researching the occupants of the Repulse Bay Hotel at this time, I sent a provisional list to one of their number, Gloria Baretto. This quote is taken from her reply (132b: Barretto).

32 Kidd's death is officially recorded as 22 December 1941, one of the 218 apparent errors in CWGC Hong Kong records. Some histories insist that this battle took place on the 20th, others on the 21st; however, the engagement in fact spanned both days. Boxer's hospital record is dated 20 December, and other eyewitnesses also give this earlier date. A check of Punjabi hospital records is shows 17 entries for wounds or unknown reasons on the 20th, and 16 on the 21st. Following Kidd's death, Gray took over command of the Punjabis.

33 The AA positions at the summit of Shouson Hill are little altered from the state in which they were left in 1941. As recently as 2001, a Lewis gun magazine and a mortar bomb (blown up on site by the Explosive Ordnance Disposal) were found there. The steep and narrow steel-railed concrete path up which guns were pulled includes a metal loop showing serious shrapnel damage — as do the concrete walls of the site itself. However, access is difficult and may involve crossing through private property. One of the best ways to view the hillside up which the Punjabis attacked is from the cable car at Ocean Park.

34 Wallis had ordered two 2 Coy. machine-gun sections towards Notting Hill to support the advance. He also ordered D Coy. Royal Rifles over Bridge Hill to outflank the Japanese on Red Hill (139).
35 In July 1944, Goodwin — a New Zealander — made arguably the most courageous escape from Sham Shui Po camp.
36 According to Wallis, during this whole action he was acting as a runner, reporting the actions of the forward troops to Home who was in a house that he had made his headquarters (139).
37 (94: 115) maintains that Edwards was killed pulling Houghton to cover.
38 (139) reports that a Japanese officer killed in this fighting carried a photo of an Indian civilian, presumably a fifth-columnist.
39 Held by A Coy. Middlesex. It holds out until the 23rd.
40 (139) goes on to say that the wounding of this officer and F/Lt Thompson, plus the wounding or death of Bompas and all officers of No. 1 Coy. HKVDC in the vicinity, served to undermine morale. Note that later a mortar bomb hit St Stephen's College at Stanley (where Thompson was recuperating), broke his back, and almost killed him. He was lucky to survive the massacre that followed on the 25th (51: 71).
41 (139) states: 'Major TEMPLER R.A. had reported to Bde. Under Ft H.Q. Orders to assume command of [A Company, Royal Rifles], the Comdr of which Coy the G.O.C. had learned had been drunk in the R.B. Hotel during the morning [of Dec 20th]. Unfortunately Major TEMPLER let fall certain indiscreet remarks re Canadian inability to fight in the presence of the Adjutant [Royal Rifles].'
42 Sources vary over whether these were Bren or Lewis guns. Templer, quoted by Wallis in (139), says Bren.
43 Also spelled 'Templar' in some documents.
44 Overbays was owned by Sun Fo, son of Dr Sun Yat-Sen. The location is immediately north of the junction of Repulse Bay Road and Island Road. There is still a house there by that name.
45 (126) states: 'Stanley area Dec 23'.
46 Could be a mistyping for either 1 MB or 7 AA.
47 (90) states that 'A fifth battery was added to the 1st Hong Kong Regiment on 1st December 1941'. These are the only two mentions of it found during the research for this book.
48 Originally buried No. 1 Crater, Borret Road (126).
49 Black's Link fatalities are C Company.
50 Lt. Field of 12 Coastal Reg. RA had been injured on 14 December at Belcher's, with shrapnel wounds to thigh and elbow (164).
51 The Royal Scots were very familiar with this hill. (92: 89) points out that 'for about two years exercises were carried out in the Mount Cameron area'.
52 Penney (75: 31) gives credit for the negotiation of the surrender to Walker of the HKVDC RE. Walker had himself earlier been rescued by two

courageous Winnipeg Grenadiers (Lt. Blackwood and Pte. Morris), who pulled him, badly wounded in the legs, to shelter. The Japanese praised these defenders, saying: 'The enemy fire from these positions was so heavy that not only was the advance checked but our troops were thrown into confusion' (95: 131). However, D Coy.'s positions were shelters rather than pillboxes and not designed for fighting from. The Japanese had therefore been able, early on the 19th, effectively to bypass them.

53 In the War Crimes trial reported in the *South China Morning Post*, Tamworth recounts that as this group of POWs was marched north, the Japanese singled out and bayoneted two or three men including the Canadian-Chinese chauffeur of Brigadier Lawson.

54 The summit of Mount Nicholson can be easily reached by the steps in the concrete catchwater just to the west of the built-up section of Black's Link near Wong Nai Chung Gap.

55 The easiest way to reach the top of Mount Cameron is the concrete steps by a waterfall three-quarters of the way along Middle Gap Road (south from Wan Chai Gap). Today the path is heavily overgrown and almost impassible (the only other human being I've ever met up there was also British!) but the first time I climbed it — in 1994 — I found a live .303 round, a spent Japanese 7.7 mm cartridge, and a large piece of Japanese bomb casing. Records show that 1,000,000 rounds of .303 ammunition was delivered to a single infantry battalion on 11 December, thus there are probably many more remaining on the hillsides. The other path, west from Middle Gap itself, is now quite unpleasant due to scree.

56 The gun was abandoned at about this time, after being disabled, because of heavy machine-gun and mortar fire (139).

57 Presumably Cpl. Goddard's pillbox (C Coy.).

58 Ride of the Field Ambulance was given permission by the Japanese to search for wounded British soldiers five days after the surrender. In the area around The Ridge, Overbays, and Wong Nai Chung Gap, he found over sixty decomposing bodies of men who had been tied up and shot (57: 10). George Lemay reported, 'we went to a place called The Ridge along Repulse Bay Road 21–23. Near the retaining wall of the tennis court we saw a lot of army clothing lying around. When we looked over the wall down to a gully we saw the bodies that were lying scattered close to the wall . . . there is one in particular that I myself dragged by the legs and it parted in the middle. There was another body that I helped carry . . . and its head came off': WO 235/1030.

59 There is still a building by this name at the location.

60 See Appendix 17.

61 Siu-Feng Huang: 'Luckily we have among the guests a Mr Needa whose father might be Portuguese and mother Jap and whose profession was jockey. It was he who met the first Japs who came to the RBH and who acted as the interpreter for the whole community' (156).

62 This led to Riley being interned as a civilian in Stanley, to be repatriated to Canada in 1943 while his more sober comrades suffered in POW camps until August 1945. Interestingly, today he is well remembered by those who were children in camp for his skill in making wooden toys. This was not the first time had been in trouble, as (154) reports that he and Rifleman Wellman were found missing from their posts on 10 December.
63 Died as a POW in Japan, 17 February 1943.
64 Died as a POW in Japan, 18 October 1942.
65 (126) states 'killed Sir Cecil's Ride area' which is presumably where Callender was in fact wounded.
66 See also the list of 11 RAOC who died on unknown dates, but are also believed to have lost their lives at The Ridge, Overbays, or Eucliffe.
67 There is no record of any fighting at the Repulse Bay Hotel garage on this day. While not totally impossible, it seems that this is a (126) euphemism for Eucliffe. All these HKVDC RASC men were probably killed — like their regular counterparts — at The Ridge, Overbays, or Eucliffe.
68 (126) states 'killed Repulse Bay Garage area'.
69 See also the list of 13 RASC who died on unknown dates, but are also believed to have lost their lives at The Ridge, Overbays, or Eucliffe.
70 Edward and this William Cullen were not related. However, Edward Cullen was the brother of another William Cullen, of the ASC Coy. of the HKVDC, who was killed on 20 December.
71 (126) states that he was KIA at Repulse Bay.
72 Last seen Stone Hill (126), though (154) states that he was killed while occupying a position on Stanley Mound. It goes on to mention that Skelton was wounded at the same location.
73 (71: 238) describes how Dodds and his American wife Alice had come from Kunming in south China to Hong Kong for the Christmas holiday, and when the battle started he volunteered and lost his life. Until Alice was repatriated (probably in June 1942 with the other Americans), their two children John and Jennifer were stuck in Kunming with no idea of their parents' whereabouts.
74 (126) concurs: 'KIA at Repulse Bay Hotel'.
75 Ray Smith, C Company Royal Rifles, on the Japanese occupation of St Albert's Convent Relief Hospital, where he had been since being wounded by a bomb on 16 December. Luckily for him, the hospital took in and cared for a badly wounded Japanese officer who later died. (37: 64) describes how, when the Japanese took the hospital, a senior Japanese officer stood weeping by the dead officer's body, thus lending credence to Smith's belief that they were related.
76 Sister Mary Currie is credited with both following the tradition of wrapping the body in a Japanese flag, and ensuring that the Japanese entering the hospital were made aware of this. She was awarded the Royal Red Cross medal (73: 79).

77 Mogra succumbed to his wounds on 4 January 1942 — compound fracture of leg, multiple gunshot wounds, and toxaemia (145: 198).
78 The exact location is believed to have been just under today's Hong Kong Country Club.
79 The main unit charged with defending Fortress HQ was 17 Platoon, D Coy. Punjabis. D Coy's HQ was at 44, Kennedy Road (140).
80 This allowed them to cover Templer's withdrawal to Stanley. Templer's opinion of this platoon: 'A v. good bunch and the only formal unit at the Repulse Bay Hotel' (150).
81 This is from (139) which also states that at about 04.00 on 24 December Wallis finally spoke to Maltby about Home's demand. Maltby declined to speak to Home and asked, 'Will the Royal Rifles fight or not?' From all this it is clear again that Wallis's view of the Royal Rifles as a whole was coloured by the fact that he despised Home.
82 Mackenzie (24: 210) claims that there were a total of 35 British soldiers in the building at the time: a warrant officer of the RAOC and four wounded downstairs, and 30 men upstairs. Canivet and six men got away, leaving 28 dead. This figure of 28 may possibly (Mackenzie's arithmetic is problematic) include four Japanese.
83 There is some uncertainty as to the timing of events at The Ridge, Overbays, and Eucliffe. This book, based (hopefully) on all available information, assumes that The Ridge was overrun on the 22nd, Overbays early on the 23rd, and that the Eucliffe massacre took place on the night of 22/23.
84 As late as Christmas 1999, I bought a 1941 Bofors shell case from a junk shop in Hong Kong's Hollywood Road. Its condition indicates that it had been damaged and then corroded by years outside — very possibly having been buried at one of these sites. It stands on my desk as I write.
85 The Marines were south of Mount Parish (3: 49). The Punjabis and Rajputs held Mount Parish itself. Mount Parish was where the Wan Yan College stands today, east of the Kennedy Road/Queen's Road junction.
86 Demolished in 1991, the site now houses Lee Theatre Plaza.
87 Presumably this is Sgt. Richards, who was lost on the *Lisbon Maru* 2 October 1942.
88 (60: 154) contains a description of what is almost certainly Maxwell's burial.
89 Originally Delcourt was recorded twice in CWGC records, as having a known grave from 23 December and an unknown grave on 21 December.
90 'Alex Calman was my chum since school days living in Kowloon Dock staff quarters — West Terrace. He had an elder sister Barbara "Babs". My record shows no number but in No 2 Coy HKVDC. He was listed as M.B.K. [Missing Believed Killed] 23rd December 1941 in Repulse Bay' (132b: Gomes).
91 However, (126) maintains that he died of wounds *and* was killed at Wan Chai Gap. My interpretation is that he was wounded on the 19th in Wong Nai Chung Gap and died on the 23rd at Wan Chai Gap.

92 (126) states: 'Missing. Last seen at Mount Cameron area.'
93 (126) notes: 'Possibly buried in Old Cemetery Stanley, or St. Stephen's College.'
94 (126) claims: 'Missing. Stanley. South Bungalow area. St. Stephen's College.'
95 This is apparently (126) code for Overbays.
96 (126) bears the following note: 'Missing. St. Albert's Hospital. 23 DEC 1941. Taken away by Japanese.' This implies that Ray Smith's fears of being discovered in uniform may have been well founded.
97 (131) states: 'Upper Levels, 12.30. A Police Reservist was murdered in Caine Road near Peel Street whilst on Street Fountain duty.'
98 To add to the confusion, a Rajput sepoy by the name of Muhammad Khan also had this serial number, but died on 20 August 1943. Mohd, of course, is shorthand for Muhammad. In all cases but this I have converted the name to the longer version. There are other spellings of 'Muhammad' but I have used only this version following the convention used by CWGC. 'Si Pani Mohd' is today buried in Stanley Military Cemetery, with a unique military headstone bearing only the name.
99 Rothwell, of the Middlesex, was at HQ China Command where he was involved in the defence of the headquarters building. According to CWGC records, this mortar attack came on 19 December. However, Rothwell places it on 24 December, which is perhaps more credible. 'Sawyer' is Corporal Ken 'Tom' Sawyer of the RAVC (132b: Rothwell).
100 This gives an idea of the number captured up to that period, although an unknown number of others would have been at North Point, or held in small groups, at this time.
101 Later at Stanley, Leiper noted: 'The names of the nurses who had been raped were known only to the doctors who had taken the necessary action to ensure that there were no living consequences. Their names were never divulged and, by tacit and universal agreement among the internees, there was no speculation on the matter in general conversation' (5: 144). Although it cannot be proven that this is the nurse Selwyn-Clarke refers to, the *South China Morning Post* for 5 August 1947 carried the headline:
SAW JAP HORRORS
Former Hong Kong Nurse Commits Suicide
TRAGEDY IN ENGLAND
over an article which describes the suicide of nurse Ivy Lily Morgan who had 'suffered neurosis through her experience of atrocities'. Her father is quoted as saying that 'she had really been a war casualty'.
102 Interestingly, Allister describes a similar incident immediately after the surrender of Japan when he and other Canadian POWs held in a Japanese camp are successfully distracted by an official as they visit a women's hostel in a half-hearted rape attempt (118: 223).
103 It has proven very hard to get an accurate idea of the extent of the fifth-

columnist problem — despite the fact that they are mentioned so often in the literature. However, Pok Fu Lam seems to have been a hotbed of activity for them, as Wiseman also reports being shot by them there (51: 20).

104 During the installation of air conditioning to the China Fleet Club in 1964, a live Japanese shell was found two feet below the reception room on the ground floor. It weighed some 400 kg and was a metre in length. As this was before the 1972 establishment of the Explosive Ordnance Disposal (EOD) unit, it was removed by the police ballistics division.

105 Home was, of course, absolutely correct. By this time it would have been clear to everyone that Hong Kong would fall sooner or later. Following Churchill's orders might have sent a 'message' to the Japanese, but could never have changed the outcome of the fighting. Having said this, it is clear that many professional soldiers present never considered that it would be anything other than a fight to the death.

106 It is clear from recollections of Canadian ORs that they felt they were bearing an unfair amount of the fighting north of Stanley, while other units (e.g. the Royal Artillery) had troops who were contributing nothing. Wallis was of course using infantry as infantry and artillery as artillery, but bearing in mind that the Royal Rifles were only semi-trained as infantry, it is interesting that he did not consider using the artillery troops as infantry (which he eventually did with 1 and 2 Bty. HKVDC) earlier in the battle.

107 This sentence has been quoted out of context many times. In fact, Price is referring to the Royal Rifles bearing the brunt of the fighting up till this time on the East Brigade front (which — together with 1 and 2 Coys. HKVDC — they did), not the Canadians as a whole bearing the brunt of the fighting in the overall defence of Hong Kong. If one equates the 'seriousness' of the 8–26 December fighting with fatalities, one sees that the two Canadian battalions lost very slightly more men than their two British counterparts (the Middlesex and Royal Scots), but as a percentage of their forces the British losses were very slightly higher.

108 Stanley Fort was occupied by Japanese troops after the surrender. There were many post-war accounts of the ghost of a Japanese officer — complete with samurai sword — being seen in the officers' mess (118: 2).

109 I interpret (139) as stating that these were under Lt. Challinor.

110 The Stanley Platoon's unofficial commander was 'Crumb' Chattey, ex-Adjutant to the Middlesex. Pre-war, Chattey had been found guilty of homosexual activities and imprisoned at Stanley. The Governor agreed to release him as a fighting man, and Chattey displayed extreme gallantry in the battle for Stanley, after which he was re-imprisoned (72: 62).

111 The oldest surviving police station building in Hong Kong, it was a restaurant until the turn of the millennium.

112 Farrington actually survived the war!

113 As an indication of how bad the relationship between Wallis and Home had

become at this point, (139) continues: '[Wallis] stated that he had also considered arresting or shooting Lt. Col. HOME and placing Maj. PRICE (2nd in C) in command.'
114 This house was in fact occupied by West of the Middlesex, who later broke out with his men.
115 Died on the *Lisbon Maru*, 2 October 1942.
116 Fox had been lucky to escape with his life from Jardine's Lookout earlier. The escape from Leighton Hill was — if anything — more difficult. After making it over the border to China, Fox fought with the Chindits in Burma. He escaped with his life once more and, post-war, joined Jardine. His new boss was Field, who had been his commanding officer in 9 Platoon, 3 Coy., HKVDC.
117 A 1931 government map shows Morrison Hill in the process of demolition. It was still in this semi-demolished state in 1941, though today it is completely flattened.
118 Both men died at the age of 62 during their internment at Stanley. Major (Rtd.) Charles Manners, OBE, died on 22 October 1944, and Andrew Lusk Shields died on 24 July 1944.
119 In his usual style, Wallis says: 'All at the Police Stn had held out till the last, except some of the Prison Warders Pl[atoon] whom it is feared were insufficiently disciplined to withstand such an attack' (139).
120 Bertram's book, which gives the most personal and atmospheric account of the Stanley fighting, has the advantage of having been written immediately after the eventual Japanese surrender.
121 Bungalow C (originally known both as Barton's Bungalow and Bungalow 4) still exists.
122 Elsewhere in (126) it states: 'Killed Chung Hom Kok area.' 2 Coy were indeed operating in this area, coordinating with B Coy. Royal Rifles.
123 It is not impossible that Onslow was killed at Lawson's HQ on 19 December.
124 His body was found post-surrender, with six others, by Pte. Wright (8: 23).
125 (126) states: 'Missing Wong Nai Chung area.' May also have been on the 19th.
126 Wakefield states that Kelly was killed outright by a stray bomb at Aberdeen (132a: Wakefield).
127 Of wounds sustained on 23 December (145: 182).
128 Bliss may be the man recorded as 'Flass' in the CRAOC message log, in which case he was presumably lost on 20 December. See n. 22 for 20 December.
129 Browne (132b: Browne) describes seven men, including RAVC, Navy, Royal Marines, Middlesex, and Royal Scots forming part of the HQ Defence Force and being killed by a direct hit on their slit trench on 18 December. He goes on to say that the trench was simply filled in at the time, as no identifiable remains were left. (126) confirms 'Buried behind Kennedy Road behind HQCC with Lance Corporal Cheal HKVDC'. Rothwell, an eyewitness, puts the date as 24 December (132b: Rothwell).

130 It is not impossible that a Winnipeg Grenadier might have become separated from his unit and ended up at Stanley; after all, from Wong Nai Chung police station to Stanley village is only three miles as the crow flies. But Carcary's involvement in the Stanley fighting is not corroborated elsewhere.
131 (133) records a Yip Young of the NSO dying of gunshot wounds at BRH on this day.
132 Browne was at HQ China Command, where he was in charge of local defence.
133 Foley would die on the *Lisbon Maru*, 2 October 1942.
134 The vaguely art-deco building still in use in 2002 is the original.
135 The previous day, Hunter — having recovered from his Golden Hill wounds — was being brought by road to convalesce at the Hong Kong Hotel. During an air raid, the vehicle crashed and his back was broken. He should in fact have left Hong Kong on 6 December, and had prepared the marriage certificate beforehand, but had instead been recalled. By luck his fiancée, Peggy Scotcher, had been seconded from China Command to the Bowen Road Hospital and was there when he was brought in. He remained in his plaster for a full year, but did not see his wife again until August 1945 (132b: Hunter). Peggy was the daughter of Capt. W. J. Scotcher, RASC, also of the garrison.
136 Probably nearer 22.00.
137 Browne: 'Lieut. James T. Prior — King's Own Scottish Borderers. All that I know of him was when I had the next bed to him in Argyle St. A middle-aged man who had been a solicitor in private life. A droll character with a dry sense of humour. His first words on waking up were "One two three up, four five six down" with corresponding movements' (158).
138 One of the escapees, Sub-Lt. Brewer, of HMS *Drake* (a Royal Naval Shore Establishment at Plymouth) was killed in a motor accident on Tuesday, 28 July 1942 on the A1 road in England at the start of his leave. He is buried at Gillingham Cemetery, Kent (8: 22).
139 Died as a POW in Japan, 7 November 1942.
140 Events are here recreated from War Crimes Trials depositions. Existing books describe the massacre as if it all happened at once, with the two good doctors shot at the door. In fact the best way to understand what happened is to remember that the hospital was literally on the front lines. The Japanese soldiers who bayoneted men in their beds were probably being told to 'clear the building, clear the building!' by their NCOs. They did this brutally, but only later did this massacre become deliberately sadistic.
141 Although 56 is the most quoted figure, it is very uncertain. Padre Barnett — ordered by the Japanese to cremate the victims — stated that he disposed of over 120 bodies on a makeshift pyre. However, many of these were the corpses of those killed in conventional fighting.
142 As a footnote, a friend of the author's who was a student at St Stephen's

College in the 1980s told that as children they were informed that the murders took place on the hill outside the main block (which they used as a dormitory). However, although the nurses, three Canadians, and some of the stretcher bearers probably met their ends there, the majority of the murdered were lying in beds exactly where my friend slept forty years later. She also told me that there was a tradition of walking around the main block before retiring for the night, and that this was done every evening of the year except for Christmas Eve when the walk was cancelled and each child was ordered to take a Bible to bed.

143 Wright-Nooth, interned after the surrender in Stanley's Bungalow C, recorded: 'Our Bungalow, which was called Bungalow C, was in an awful condition. Aside from the graves, the vicinity had live small arms ammunition strewn around like so much confetti; may unexploded grenades (mostly Japanese), mortar bombs and rife grenades had been left precisely as they had been abandoned. The building itself had a shell hole through the roof, all windows were smashed and the walls scarred by bullets and shrapnel. The water pipes had burst, the drains were blocked and overflowing, blood was spattered everywhere. Grenades had been thrown inside destroying furniture and setting fire to the wooden floor while smoke had impregnated every room with a black, greyish grubbiness. The bathroom was the worst. It contained so much blood, filth and human excreta that a respirator had to be worn when we cleaned it' (72: 87).

144 This building was on the corner of Arsenal Street and Gloucester Road. It was demolished in 1982 and replaced with Fleet House. Renamed in recent years, it is currently the Mass Mutual building.

145 Died as a POW in Japan, 24 October 1942.

146 Also known as Ginsburg.

147 Died on the *Lisbon Maru*, 2 October 1942.

148 Wright-Nooth continues: 'Everywhere was littered with the debris of war — steel helmets, web equipment, discarded boots and uniforms. A good pair of brown boots attracted my attention and I picked them up to try them for size. I noticed they were of excellent quality, made by Hawkes. Then to my horror I saw the name West marked inside them. They belonged to my friend Captain West of the Middlesex Regiment whom I knew had been killed at Stanley. Months later I learned that he had commanded that part of the last defence line at Stanley of which the bungalow was a part. I could not bring myself to wear them' (72: 87).

149 Guest offered Sutton a place in the 2nd MTB flotilla escape later this day. Sutton, however, refused on the grounds of age (he was nearly 60) and unfitness. Sutton died in Stanley camp, 22 October 1944.

150 Henderson had been the first Royal Rifle to have been wounded, by a bomb splinter while driving a truck to Lye Mun on 9 December (154).

151 The Order of St John lost fifty-four men and women in Hong Kong during

the war, the majority dying at Wong Nai Chung Gap and St Stephen's College. However, as the dates of death were not recorded (with the exception of Potter who died on the *Lisbon Maru*), they are not listed here individually.

152 With the greatest respect to Sir Albert Rodrigues, I must tell the following story: I had spent several hours trying to decode his first handwritten letter to me — which included the above — and mentioned to a mutual friend that Sir Albert could hardly be blamed for his poor handwriting as he was recovering from a stroke. 'Oh no', said the friend, 'Albert's writing was always like that. He's a doctor.'

153 (139): 'Contrary to [Wallis's] orders, [Parker] sent only a small portion of his command (what appeared to be a weak Pl[atoon] of 15–18 O.Rs) by the concealed route round the enemy's right flank through TWEED BAY. Most of the Company advanced N.W. and NORTH across the open fire-swept ground and up through the CEMETERY.' Parker's diary explicitly disagrees, stating: 'I was to make a frontal attack and occupy the ridge behind the cemetery and retake the Indian quarters on the right ... Mr. Breakey had the Indian quarters job on the right, Lieut. Frank Power and Sgt. George MacDonnel led No. 17 & 18 Platoon respectively on the left' (160).

154 We now know that S. K. Yee was not killed, and escaped from Hong Kong at a later date.

155 In (28) Guest states — very credibly — that the firing came from PB 12.

156 Goodwin goes on to describe how she went out to find the body of her husband, who had been killed in the fighting, and was then herself killed by the Japanese. She was almost certainly Mrs Orloff, a nurse whose husband was killed at the Salesian massacre. Bard (see above) describes her as being shot by the Japanese near the university on 24 December, in which case she could not have brought news of the surrender.

157 The preferred Japanese method of restraining nurses resisting rape was — it appears — to batter their heads with steel helmets until movement ceased.

158 (139): '[Wallis] was also considering blowing up the FORT by detonating the magazine should the enemy penetrate into the whole Fort area. Survivors would if time permitted by [sic] harboured with wounded in cover about 255445 near BLUFF POINT. This matter was a last resort and kept secret.'

159 Bliss's wife Phyllis is mentioned at length in (48).

160 (126) states 24 December, but this seems unlikely. 'Killed at science block' may possibly be a euphamism for the St Stephen's massacre.

161 Possibly 'Tsacharoff' in (42).

162 (126) gives a date of 24 December.

163 (126) carries the interesting comment, 'possibly escaped'.

164 CWGC gives 24 December as the date as they believed Blackaby had been killed at Maryknoll.

165 (126) adds: 'Killed rocks West Bay west of sports ground.'

166 (126) adds: 'Killed rocks West Bay west of sports ground.'

167 (126) adds: 'No. 1 Crater Borret Road', i.e. BRH. It gives a date of 20 December. His serial number is in the list of Middlesex personnel treated in military and civilian hospitals. Uniquely, all the entry has is the number; the name and rank are both given as '?', and a note at the end that says 'Died'.
168 (126) adds: 'B Coy. Probable place of burial — Prison burial ground Stanley.'
169 (126) simply states: 'Killed. Stanley area.'
170 His brother Maurice died in a POW camp in Japan, 29 January 1943.
171 (126) notes: 'Missing. Area south of The Ridge.'
172 (126) gives the alternate date of 19 December By the wording, it appears that Matthews was buried at The Ridge, which makes 25 December unlikely.
173 According to a letter to his family, Woytowich was with B Coy. and was killed on 22 December during the Japanese attack on Mount Cameron.
174 Both Birkett and Fleet were attached to Major Gray's force. Fleet's death was predicted by a clairvoyant, and was said to have occurred after the invasion on 18 December (95: 41). The fact that they were buried at St Albert's Hospital (142) makes the date of 8 December highly unlikely. The 18th or 19th are more probable.
175 (126) agrees Maryknoll, but makes no estimate of date.
176 Confusingly, the same document also gives 23 December as date of death. He was initially interred at Stanley Manege.
177 (126) states that he was killed at Stanley police station, was unburied and possibly cremated.
178 It is assumed that these three men are the 'Indian orderlies' mentioned as losing their lives in the St Stephen's massacre on this day.
179 (130: 27) states that Forster was injured by a mortar bomb in Aberdeen on 23 December, and died in Queen Mary Hospital a few days later.
180 The CWGC originally had entries for him on 25 December as a civilian, and 26 December as a padre. His family was from Middlesex, though (150) notes that the Mr Moreton was attached to the Royal Scots. His biographical details are given as:
   Born 5 October 1905, grandson of the Revd. R. H. Moreton, MMS missionary to Portugal.
   1929   Didsbury College.
   1932   Aux Cayes, Haiti.
   1933   Returned to England and returned to life as a Methodist layman, belonging to the Muswell Hill Circuit.
   1936   Re-entered the ministry at Liverpool and then Dormanstown in the Redcar Circuit.
   1938   Accepted call to the English circuit in Hong Kong.
'With his colleague Rev J E Sandbach, he worked, not only amongst civilians, but also amongst the men of the Forces, particularly in the Soldiers' and Sailors' Home. Happily married in 1939, his joy became full when a little son was born. Soon after, when the Japanese attack on Hong Kong began,

Mr Moreton served as an ambulance driver, and in the performance of his duties he suffered a wound on December 18. The wound turned out to be more serious than was at first anticipated, and he died in a Christian hospital [in fact the Royal Naval Hospital in Wan Chai] in Hong Kong on Christmas Day, 1941, having laid down his life for his friends' (65: 164). Today he is buried at Stanley.

181 Doddridge took part in D Coy. Royal Rifles' attack on Bungalow C in Stanley on Christmas Day.
182 (139) contains this entry: 'As far as [Wallis] can now remember it was late on 24 Dec 41 that he learned with astonishment that some European nurses were at ST. STEPHENS SCHOOL. He had thought this hospital had been evacuated to TWEED BAY and STANLEY FORT and had no idea there had ever been any nurses there at all. An ambulance was detailed to rush to this hospital with water and evacuate all nurses. Three [sic] were brought back to STANLEY. Three others as well as Lt. Col. BLACK and another R.A.M.C. doctor were found to have been killed.'
183 The last wounded allied soldier was reportedly found by a burial party, in a hillside gully, approximately a week after the surrender (29: 45).
184 (72) mentions that he died in his sister's arms. She was an Auxilliary Nurse at Queen Mary Hospital.
185 Possibly a victim of the Overbays massacre, though neither date corroborates this.
186 A note in (126) claims that Wragg was originally buried front of the officers' mess, Murray Barracks.
187 The date of death of 26 December seems unlikely for all twelve men. This appears to be an attempt to account for certain individuals who went missing at some point and were not recorded at the time. It is also possible that up to five of these men were victims of the St. Stephen's massacre.

8. THE WEEK IMMEDIATELY FOLLOWING THE FIGHTING

1 This incident is described in full in *The Road to Inamura*.
2 Salter lived in Hong Kong for some time before successfully escaping. See (157). He received much help from the Portuguese wife of Pte. J. Linton of B Coy. Royal Scots, among others.
3 He was found at the C Coy. Royal Rifles bunkers at Lye Mun, not at Wong Nai Chung Gap as often quoted. His companion, Gerry Cuzner, was killed (100: 304).
4 James Bertram, on this march as a member of 2 Bty. HKVDC, describes how there was a spontaneous three cheers for the Middlesex who led the way. In his own words: 'If any battle honours were to be salvaged out of the mess in Hong Kong, we knew where they should go' (101: 138).

NOTES TO PAGES 285-294   381

5   The letter recommending an MBE for Thompson is in the possession of his son, Peter. It goes on to say: 'The possession of this money proved of inestimable value, being used for the purchase of food and amenities for prisoners of war, most of whom were destitute.' The recommendation was approved.
6   (44: 119), quoting Japanese sources, states that 11,241 POWs were captured in Hong Kong. Together with the approximately 1,550 who were killed, that would give a garrison of 12,791. It is unlikely that this includes police (who were interned at Stanley), Chinese volunteer sailors who were dispersed before the surrender, and the Chinese and Portuguese soldiers who disappeared soon after.
7   Wiseman in (51: 53) describes how his friend I. J. 'Kiwi' Blair of the Punjabis (who had helped build up the Z Force stock piles on Tai Mo Shan) had planned to use these to escape, but changed his mind when 'several "Z Force" men arrived in Camp, having walked out of the hills and given themselves up to the first Nips they had met, on the somewhat dubious grounds that once the dump's supplies had been exhausted they had no other choice'. The junior Z Force members were apparently protecting their seniors with this cover story.
8   BAAG received a message from Waterton and other ex-GPO staff interned in Stanley, 27 June 1943, stating simply: 'We and all others of the wireless section are keeping fit. We have received no mail so far. Mrs F. K. Garton died during the hostilities.'
9   This, of course, would imply an earlier date.
10 (126) gives an alternative date of 24 December.
11 Post-war, four bodies were found near Tai Po. Three appeared to be European men, and the fourth a Chinese lady. Some men did simply walk out of North Point (Mulligan, for example). This is speculation, but perhaps Hall, Stokes, and two companions failed on an early escape attempt and met their deaths at Tai Po.
12 (155) states that Gunn was wounded by a mortar bomb at 05.00 on 21 December while visiting the LMG position at Wong Nai Chung Gap with Blackwood (who was also wounded).

10. EPILOGUE

1   Lord Lawrence Kadoorie, quoted in (97: 159).
2   *South China Morning Post*, Saturday, 29 September 1945.
3   *South China Morning Post*, front page headline, Monday 1 October 1945. It should be noted that at least as late as February 1947, the *South China Morning Post* still carried requests for information about wartime graves. The Roll of Honour was produced in that year.

APPENDICES

1. (126) states: 'Dec 25. Killed west side Wong Nai Chung gap' as 40 Coy. The date makes little sense.
2. Activities of this unit during the fighting do not seem to have been recorded. Even its formation, just a few days before the start of hostilities, hardly receives a mention. The next mention of the unit is in BAAG records, thanks to the large number of Hong Kong Chinese Regiment men who escaped to China and rejoined British forces there. Many ended up in Burma with the Chindits.
3. However, (126) gives a date of 30 January 1942, and notes that Dixon was buried at Stanley Military cemetery.
4. These three records in CWGC now show a date of 1 December.
5. As noted in the text, not all HKSRA batteries listed in CWGC casualty returns actually existed. They have been left here for completeness. Key: Plain text — a documented HKSRA unit, underlined text — a regular artillery unit presumed part manned by HKSRA, *italic text* — unknown or errors.
6. Note: Indian officers holding the King's commission were equal to their British counterparts. Viceroy Commissioned Officers, however, were equivalent to the following British ranks:

Subadar Major	= Captain
Risaldar/Subadar	= Lieutenant
Jemadar	= 2nd Lieutenant
Other ranks:	
Dafadar/Havildar	= Sergeant
Naik	= Corporal
Lance Naik	= Lance Corporal
Sepoy	= Private

7. See Appendix 17 for Police Launches.
8. These are the two most likely VCOs mentioned. However, a third possibility would be Jemadar Ratan Singh.
9. Witnesses saw Kilfoyle killed on the march to North Point.
10. A third-hand description of this massacre may be found in (42: 241).
11. After the surrender, Ride states that he saw fifty bodies on the road, six being Middlesex. These may well have been the Middlesex attached to the Hong Kong Chinese Regiment. CWGC internal records also show that five RAF men disappeared near The Ridge on 20 December.
12. It must be accepted that it has not been possible to precisely separate The Ridge, Overbays, and Eucliffe fatalities. This is the best model currently available, though some mistakes are certain to have been made.
13. It is uncertain whether the defenders of PB 14 were killed in combat or after.
14. Some 75–150 bodies were cremated after the surrender (depending on which

account is read), but these included soldiers killed in the fighting around Stanley (965 Defence Bty., for example).

15 The St John's Ambulance staff killed are recorded on a memorial at today's headquarters. Unfortunately no dates of death are quoted; therefore we cannot say which of the fifty-five listed there died in this massacre. The eight Chinese victims quoted are — as usual — apparently unnamed in British records. The real mystery here is: who are the fifty-six or so claimed killed in bed? It is certainly possible that some deaths recorded at other places on the 25th and 26th (especially the list of Royal Rifles on the 26th) in fact lost their lives here. However, it is strange that this most infamous massacre has been the hardest to match with records.

16 Some sources claim as many as eleven or even sixteen; one source says one captain, four or five lieutenants, three sergeants, two corporals, and one private. It is possible that four members of 8 Coastal Regt. RA lost their lives here too.

17 (139) says: 'It is almost certain that both these officers [Scantlebury and Newman], together with Sjts. Baker, Harvey and Morton, were killed at this stage. No reliable report can be obtained and some obviously coloured stories are impossible to believe.'

18 While all the other pilots were American, Kantzow was Australian. Post war he went on to co-found Cathay Pacific Airways.

19 The difference between this total, 1,526, and that in Appendix 5, 1,589, is largely made up by the civilian deaths recorded in the latter number.

20 The Police War Diary states that — at least at Aberdeen — civilian bodies were also dumped in the sea during the night, when collecting them in the day started to prove too dangerous (131).

21 Alec Maxtone Wright Scott, Pilot Officer, 605 Squadron, killed 2 January 1941.

22 Possibly George Henry Fowler, killed with 136 Squadron in India on 16 September 1943.

23 Pilot Officer Polglase was killed on 3 May 1940.

24 A 'John Frederick Wright' was killed with 56 Squadron, 26 January 1942

25 A Pilot Officer 'William Edgar Peers' was killed on 58 Squadron, 15 January 1941.

26 A 'Jack Canning' was killed as a Sergeant with 424 Squadron, 29 June 1943.

27 A 'David McClean Cameron' was killed as a Flying Officer with 422 (RCAF) Squadron on 19 December 1942.

28 A 'Bernard Castle Curtis' was killed as a Pilot Officer with 99 Squadron on 31 July 1941.

29 A 'David Fisher Davies DFM' was killed with 138 Squadron, 8 January 1944.

30 A 'Frederick George Neill' was killed in 221 Squadron on 12 April 1941.

31 Buried at Kirkwall (St Olaf's) Cemetery, Orkney.

32　A 'Robert William Lamont' of HMS *Rosaura* died 18 March 1941.
33　A 'W. Milne R.A.N.' died on 12 September 1944, HMAS *Perth*.
34　An 'Alan Albert Pollock' of HMS *Landrail* died on 5 January 1944.
35　See text for HMS *Tenedos* and HMS *Stronghold*.
36　Married to Pte. F. F. A. Dunnett of the HKVDC ASC.
37　Married to Engineering Capt. F. B. Minhinnick, RN.
38　Married to Bennie Proulx of the HKRNVR.
39　Married to Wilmer of the HKVDC.
40　According to (75: 31).
41　Some sources state that a total of four RA officers were lost here.
42　Kehmosu was later killed in New Guinea, where the entire battalion was annihilated.
43　I am indebted to Tony Williams for filling in many of these details. He points out that the 4-inch (naval) gun's range could be as high as 59,500 feet depending on the mounting, and the shell weight could be up to 35 lb depending on the model. The 4.7-inch QF range could be as high as 50,910, and the 6-inch (naval) range could be up to 77,400 with a 112 lb, shell depending on the model.
44　Collinson, Chung Hom Kok, Bluff Head, Pak Sha Wan, Stonecutters, Jubilee, Belcher's Upper.
45　Including armed forces. These figures were complied by the ARP and are quoted in (79: 212).
46　During the fighting, the Middlesex lost 131 men dead from a strength of 728, or 18 per cent. The Royal Scots lost 115 of 734: 16 per cent. The Royal Rifles lost 127 of 963: 13 per cent. The Winnipeg Grenadiers lost 131 of 869: 15 per cent.

Annotated Bibliography

PUBLISHED SOURCES

(1) *17 Days Until Christmas*. Leo Paul Berard. Privately printed, Canada, 1997.
Berard's useful book covers the period from his joining the Winnipeg Grenadiers in 1933 to leaving the Canadian army in 1965, though the vast majority of the book covers his experiences in Hong Kong and Japan with his original unit. It should be noted that the twelve platoon members listed here are those serving prior to the formation of 'C Force'; by the time of their arrival in Hong Kong, nine of these men were no longer with them. Company Sergeant Major 'T' is of course Tugby.

(2) *A Mountain of Light*. A. Coates. Hong Kong: Heinemann, 1977.
Chapter 16 of this history of Hong Kong Electric covers the 19 December battle for the North Point power station. There are also some interesting photographs.

(3) *A Record of the Actions of the Hong Kong Volunteer Defence Corps*. Major Evan Stewart, DSO. Hong Kong: Ye Olde Printerie, Ltd., 1953.
This is the original book on the subject, written by the wartime commander of 3 Company HKVDC. Most histories written since have largely relied on a timeline based on this book plus Maltby's despatch. A short book, it is unbeatable for anyone wishing to get a basic understanding of the December actions, though it is naturally somewhat biased towards those involving the HKVDC. In a nice twist of fate, the two principals of Ye Olde Printerie pre-war were both Volunteers

(the Labrum brothers). Whilst at Sham Shui Po, they sent a message to their Hungarian partner (technically an enemy) to re-open the Printerie. He did so, together with two Japanese partners who were forced upon him. See (87).

(4)   *A Tear for the Dragon*. John Stericker. London: Arthur Barker, 1958.
Approximately half of Stericker's autobiographical account covers his internment at Stanley. There is little specific information, but good general coverage of diet and camp life. Arthur Barker, who published Robert Graves's 'Claudius' books, and later many of the early books about Hong Kong POWs, was himself captured in Hong Kong as a Captain in the 5th AA Regiment (51: 52).

(5)   *A Yen for My Thoughts*. G. A. Leiper. Hong Kong: South China Morning Post, 1982.
Leiper's book deserves to be better known. A member of 2 Company but also an 'Essential Person', he spent the 18 days working in Chartered Bank during the day, and attached to 4 Company at night. He therefore witnessed the goings-on in Central twenty-four hours per day. His obscene (and probably very accurate) depictions of the effects of shells and bombs hit home with this author, as all were within a short walk of where this book was written; the bloody execution of two Chinese 'looters' post-surrender was almost on the doorstep. The remainder of the book describes life under the occupation.

(6)   *After the Battle*, No. 83. Winston G. Ramsey. London: Battle of Britain Prints International Ltd., 1994.
A 26-page article in a more general magazine, this consists of a quick summary of events brought to life by photographs in the familiar 'then and now' model.

(7)   *An End to Tears*. Russell Clark. Sydney: Peter Huston, 1946.
Arriving with Harcourt's fleet to relieve Hong Kong in August 1945, Clark writes of his impressions — as a journalist — of the Colony's reactions to the removal of the Japanese overseers. The coverage of the last days of Stanley and Sham Shui Po are particularly useful.

(8)   *At the Going Down of the Sun*. Oliver Lindsay. London: Hamish Hamilton, 1981.
A good overall account of the post-1941 experiences of Hong Kong and the POWs in general. Chapter 1 contains a summary of *The Lasting Honour* (95), and chapter 2 is the full story of the MTB escape of 25 December 1941. The remainder covers the camps, the *Lisbon Maru*, and the War Crimes trials.

(9)   *BAAG*. Edwin Ride. Hong Kong: Oxford University Press, 1981.
The son of the British Army Aid Group's founder, Lt.-Col. Ride of the HKVDC Field Ambulance, Edwin Ride describes the BAAG's role from the point when

his father escaped Sham Shui Po till the end of hostilities. Initially formed to facilitate POW escapes from Hong Kong, BAAG's mission was expanded to include assisting USAAF evaders and gathering intelligence from within both occupied territories and the camps. It was remarkably successful until undermined by Anglo/Sino/US politics.

(10) *Battlefields Review*, No. 16, November 2001.
This issue contains five short articles on the conflict, two provided by the current author. The five covered the fighting, a shortened version of *In Oriente Fidelis*, an abridged study of memorials, the story of the writing of *Hong Kong War Diary*, and a brief look at the battlefields as they are today.

(11) *Bloody Shambles*, vol. 1. Christopher Shores, Brian Cull, and Yasuho Izawa. Grub Street, 1992.
This is a superbly researched work on air fighting in the Far Eastern theatre. Volume 1 covers the period from December 1941 to April 1942, and gives arguably the most detailed account of the 8 December attack on Kai Tak.

(12) *Bondservant of the Japanese*. Robert B. Hammond. Privately printed, Pasadena, Calif., 1942.
A slim volume of little practical use to the serious historian.

(13) *Bridge with Three Men*. Anthony Hewitt. London: Jonathan Cape, 1986.
Hewitt's is a very readable account of the adventures of three 'likeable rogues' (himself, Crossley, and Scrivens) escaping from Sham Shui Po and crossing China. Scrivens was a well-known name in post-war Hong Kong, and this gives an interesting sidelight on his personality. However, the eighteen days of fighting are covered by just a few brief sentences.

(14) *'C' Force to Hong Kong: A Canadian Catastrophe*. Brereton Greenhous. Dundurn Press, 1997.
While containing many useful facts on the Canadian contribution, this volume has too many basic mistakes (such as constantly referring to HKVDC as HKVDF), and — for this author — too many attempts to second-guess Maltby. An alternative title to this book might have been 'Maltby's Great Mistakes', but the author's selectiveness in presenting material damages, in part, the work's credibility.

(15) *Captive Christmas*. Alan Birch and Martin Cole. Hong Kong: Heinemann Educational Books, 1979.
This simple work was originally broadcast on radio, and consists very largely of verbatim quotations from published and unpublished works listed in this biography.

(16) *Captive Surgeon in Hong Kong*. Donald Bowie. Hong Kong: Royal Asiatic Society, 1977.
Bowie's book is the central reference on the nutritional and medical histories of POWs in Hong Kong, and the experience of one hospital (the Bowen Road British Military Hospital) in particular.

(17) *China to Me: A Partial Autobiography*. Emily Hahn. Philadelphia: Blakiston, 1944.
By definition a very personal story, but essential reading for anyone interested in the Boxer/Hahn affair. The coverage of the fighting is from the point of view of a privileged civilian, but the post-surrender experiences make fascinating reading — not least because of the author's relationship with the Japanese. By no means can this be taken to depict the experiences of the broader civilian population, or those interned in Stanley.

(18) *Colonial Hong Kong: A Guide*. Stephen Vines. Hong Kong: FormAsia, 2002.
An interesting little book that details many of the buildings mentioned in this account. However, not all 'facts' should be taken at face value. The photograph of Canadians arriving in Hong Kong in 1940 in fact shows RAF personnel arriving in 1945; there is no Anzac cemetery in Sai Wan; those killed at Eucliffe were not captured there.

(19) *Death on the Hellships*. Gregory Michno. Pen & Sword, 2001.
An important book covering a subject — the Japanese transportations and the approximately 21,000 deaths that resulted — that has long been overlooked. Unfortunately the scale of the work means that some errors have crept into the Hong Kong coverage, such as that of the *Lisbon Maru* on pp. 43–7.

(20) *Despatch*. Major-General C. M. Maltby. Supplement to *London Gazette*, 29 January 1948.
The earliest, and generally most accurate (though far from comprehensive), timeline of the December 1941 fighting to be published. It portrays a view of the situation as perceived by Maltby from his Battle Box from invasion to surrender. The release of an unabridged version of this Despatch — in the mid-1990s — created a considerable amount of bad feeling in Canada, as Maltby gave a great deal of credence to Wallis's negative opinion of the Royal Rifles.

(21) *Desperate Siege: The Battle of Hong Kong*. Ted Ferguson. New York: Doubleday, 1980.
A decent general summary of the action, published before the big backlash sparked by *No Reason Why* (66) and the release of the unabridged version of Maltby's report. This is one of the best-balanced books to come from Canadian sources.

Annotated Bibliography 389

(22)   *Diary of a Prisoner of War in Japan*. Georges Verrault. Quebec: Vero, 1996.
George 'Blacky' Verrault was a signaller in the Royal Canadian Corps of Signals. Unfortunately it was not possible to trace a copy of this book, though it has been quoted from at various times through intermediate sources.

(23)   *Dispersal and Renewal*. Edited by Clifford Matthews and Oswald Cheung. Hong Kong: Hong Kong University Press, 1998.
An unusual book, for which Matthews 'bullied' many wartime members of Hong Kong University into each writing a chapter on their wartime experiences. The result does not constitute so much a book as a set of unrelated episodes, some of which, however, make very interesting reading.

(24)   *Eastern Epic*, vol. 1. E. M. Compton Mackenzie. London: Chatto & Windus, 1951.
This is the story, commissioned by the Government of India in 1945, of the Indian effort in the Second World War. Volume 1, *Defence*, was to the best of my knowledge the only volume completed. Pages 183-216 (chs. 16 and 17) cover Hong Kong and appear largely based on Maltby's *Despatch* (20).

(25)   *Eastern Waters, Eastern Winds*. Gillian Chambers. Hong Kong: Royal Hong Kong Yacht Club, 1993.
Chambers was commissioned to write this record of the history of the (Royal) Hong Kong Yacht Club, and did a fine job. The Yacht Club, which adopted Kellet Island as its base in 1940 and is still there today, was the foundation of the HKRNVR — and yet the sailor most quoted for the wartime period is Bunny Browne, a lieutenant of Maltby's HQ China Command. Recommended reading.

(26)   *Eastern Windows, Western Skies*. Jean Gittins. Hong Kong: South China Morning Post, 1969.
In this biographical work, Gittins, the Ho Tung daughter, is clearly writing for the benefit of her descendants. However, there is much of interest here about Hong Kong life in general — though clearly at the top of the social scale. The author, who lost her husband in the 4th Battery HKVDC during the conflict, covers the war years in the second half of Book 2.

(27)   *Eighteen Days*. Colonel D. R. Bennett, RAPC. Hong Kong: The Command Pay Office, 1976.
The body of this book is a general summary of the fighting culled from other sources, and adds little to the body of knowledge. The appendices, however, are interesting — particularly that pertaining to the Pay Corps.

(28)   *Escape from the Bloodied Sun*. Freddie Guest. London: Jarrolds, 1956.
As a Middlesex officer in Maltby's headquarters, Guest saw the battle from the

inside. However, the focus of the book — some 75 per cent — is on the MTB escape of 25 December. Having met Admiral Chan Chak during the fighting, Guest and his colleagues escorted him to the south side of the Island and successfully escaped through China.

(29) *Escape through China*. David Bosanquet. London: Robert Hale, 1983.
Bosanquet, a young man fresh from England starting a career at Jardine, was a sergeant of the ill-fated 5 AA Battery, HKVDC. Lucky enough to get out of the gun site before the massacre, he then escaped with two colleagues from Sham Shui Po, reached England about a year later, and was recruited into MI9. In this book he writes about his experiences during the battle and the voyage back to the UK.

(30) *Escape to Fight On*. John S. Whitehead and George B. Bennett. London: Robert Hale, 1990.
Whitehead's book primarily covers his time with Military Mission 204 in China. However, the first few chapters give interesting coverage of a gunner's life in the pre-war Hong Kong garrison, his experiences during the fighting, and the escape from Sham Shui Po.

(31) *Farewell Hong Kong (1941)*. Christopher Briggs, MBE. Perth, Western Australia: Hesperian Press, 2001.
Of interest as this appears to be the only book covering the departure from Hong Kong on the evening of 8 December 1941 of the destroyers *Thanet* and *Scout*. The author was *Scout*'s First Lieutenant. The majority of the book covers his post-Hong Kong experience, and eventual settling in Australia. See his wife's book, *From Peking to Perth*, below (35).

(32) *Footprints: The Memoirs of Sir Selwyn Selwyn-Clarke*. Selwyn Selwyn-Clarke. Hong Kong: Sino American, 1975.
One of those strong-willed people who returned from the Western Front of 1914–18 determined to put the rest of his life to doing good for others whether they liked it or not, Selwyn-Clarke's biography shows he was not necessarily a likeable person (he was too austere and authoritarian for that) but was certainly sincere. He did his best for the ordinary people of Hong Kong, and clearly the number of deaths among civilian internees would have been much higher without him.

(33) *Four George Crosses Won in Hong Kong 1943–1946*. John Harris. Privately printed, Hong Kong, 1985
This short paper formed the basis of a talk given by Harris in Hong Kong on 5 December 1985 to the officers of the British Forces and retired members of the Canadian Forces visiting. It covers the basic details of the BAAG information-

smuggling ring, and its eventual breaking by the Japanese. While short, it has the advantage of being written by one of the participants in the events described.

(34)   *From Jamaica to Japan.* Thomas S. Forsyth. Manitoba: William R. Warwick, 1995.
Tom Forsyth of the Winnipeg Grenadiers kept a diary of his experiences. Unfortunately it was not possible to trace a copy of this book.

(35)   *From Peking to Perth.* Sis Briggs. Perth, Western Australia: Artlook Books, 1984.
Sis Briggs's book makes a fascinating comparison with that of her husband. Her focus is very much on the pre-war years, and yet her coverage of the events of 1941 is a useful addition to our knowledge.

(36)   *General of Fortune: The Fabulous Story of One-Arm Sutton.* Charles Drage. London: Heinemann, 1963.
Sutton, the 'General' of the title, was the sort of man who just had to wash up in Hong Kong on the eve of war. Having lost the limb in question at Gallipoli, Sutton rose to be one of only three Englishmen to have taken the rank of general in the Chinese Army. Winding up in Hong Kong at the end of his career, he died in Stanley Camp of beri-beri, avitaminosis, and bacillary dysentery.

(37)   *Grey Touched with Scarlet.* Jean Bowden. London: Robert Hale, 1959.
This volume on the Second World War experiences of the army nursing sisters covers Hong Kong on pp. 56–78, and again on pp. 175–84. However, the coverage is far from comprehensive and focuses mainly on St Albert's Hospital, with just a few references to Bowen Road Hospital. St Stephens, Queen Mary, the Royal Naval Hospital, etc. are not covered.

(38)   *Guest of Hirohito.* Ken Cambon. Canada: PW Press, 1990.
The war autobiography of one of the youngest soldiers to serve in Hong Kong. Cambon was 17 when he joined the Royal Rifles. A recommended read, this volume covers both the fighting and the POW years, and has an appendix taken from the War Crimes transcripts in the PRO. 'Bill M.', for those who need to know, was almost certainly Rifleman William S. McAra.

(39)   *Guest of an Emperor.* Martin Weedon. London: Arthur Barker, 1948.
Captain Martin Weedon commanded B Company of the Middlesex and survived the *Lisbon Maru.* Unfortunately the earlier part of his diary, from Christmas Day 1941 to September 1942, was lost in the sinking. This is a shame, as the remaining part of the diary (published here in full and unedited) is one of the most detailed available.

(40) *Hell on Earth.* Dave McIntosh. Toronto: McGraw-Hill, 1997.
McIntosh's six-word summation of Hong Kong, 'a British waste of Canadian manpower', gives a fair idea of the subjectivity of the book as a whole. While correctly allocating responsibility for Canadian involvement to Grasett, he mistakenly labels him 'British'. He also believes that — in 1941 — an attack on Hong Kong was expected to be made from the open sea, and calls Osler Thomas 'Canadian' — which I am sure would give Osler a good chuckle from his Australian home. The remainder of the Hong Kong battle section is the usual quotations from Leath, Banfill, and Barnett, and does nothing to further our understanding. The coverage of the Canadian experience in camp is far more useful.

(41) *History of RAF Kai Tak.* G. L. D Alderson. Hong Kong: RAF Kai Tak, 1972.
This thin volume is all there is, apart from one recently published diary, on which to base the RAF side of the story. As it covers the years 1927–71, there are only two chapters covering the war years.

(42) *Hong Kong Aftermath.* Wenzell Brown. New York: Smith & Durrell, 1943.
Brown was arguably the worst observer of the Second World War, and yet this book does more to capture the atmosphere of wartime Hong Kong than any other. Well worth reading to understand what the experience must have been like, but don't take any 'facts' (especially people and place names, or dates) literally.

(43) *Hong Kong Boy.* Clive and Dorothy Himsworth. Durham, England: Pentland Press, 1999.
The Himsworths' book is the story of Clive's parents at Stanley and before. Told through the medium of reconstructed conversations, it has little value to the historian but would still be useful background reading for any student of the internment. It has an interesting sidelight on one of the fatalities of the 1945 bombing of Bungalow C, though 'Prosser' is of course a pseudonym.

(44) *Hong Kong Eclipse.* G. B. Endacott. Hong Kong: Oxford University Press, 1978.
This is the nearest thing to a 'history book' in this literature. The result of considerable research, it provides the broadest coverage of the Hong Kong wartime experience of servicemen and civilians alike. Essential reading for the serious student.

(45) *Hong Kong Escape.* R. B. Goodwin, OBE. London: Arthur Barker, 1953.
Goodwin of the HKRNVR made the last (1944) escape of a non-Indian POW from Hong Kong, and this volume predominantly covers his experiences of crossing China while suffering from all the deficiency diseases typically associated with being a prisoner of the Japanese.

(46) *Hong Kong Farewell*. Eddie Gosano. USA: Greg England, 1997.
This short biography is useful primarily as an insight into the inequalities of the Macanese/Eurasian community in pre-war and war-time Hong Kong. Gosano, although a trained doctor, was considered by the British as a 'junior' as far as his salary went, but as senior enough to be the BAAG representative in Macau as soon as he had escaped there. As an example: Being a qualified but 'Chinese' surgeon, Gosano earned just 25 per cent of the salary of his Irish anaesthetist, Dr Esmonde. Esmonde also qualified for a five-room flat in the European sector, while Gosano received a four-room flat in the Chinese sector. Like many such disillusioned people, post-war he chose to live abroad — in his case, in the US.

(47) *Hong Kong Full Circle*. Alexander Kennedy. Privately printed, London, 1969.
Only 500 copies of this book were produced, which is a shame as it is the only published first-hand account of the great MTB escape of Christmas Day, 1941.

(48) *Hong Kong Holiday*. Emily Hahn. New York: Doubleday, 1946.
This book is a collection of stories, originally written for the *New Yorker*, of Hahn's experiences in wartime Hong Kong. By itself, although the style is enjoyable, it is not particularly informative. However, read in conjunction with *China to Me* (17), it amplifies many of the characters and incidents in the latter.

(49) *Hong Kong Incident*. Phyllis Harrop. London: Eyre & Spottiswoode, 1943.
Harrop's biography makes interesting reading as it covers many years' experience in China in the thirties. The second half of the book relates her wartime period in Hong Kong, and her eventual safe evasion. Her eyewitness description of the bombing of Central police station is useful, as is the fact that she meets the infamous Mimi Lau on her travels. Purists should note that dates in her wartime diary are not necessarily accurate. Note that many of the books published before the end of the war, such as this one, were reticent to disclose names of those who were still prisoners of war or interned. Sometimes aliases were used. This was also often the case — for obvious reasons — when rape victims were mentioned. And those accused of collaboration, crimes, or anti-social behaviour were also generally referred to by pseudonyms.

(50) *Hong Kong Invaded! A '97 Nightmare*. Gillian Bickley. Hong Kong: Hong Kong University Press, 2001.
The basis of this book is a publication from an anonymous author in 1897, entitled *The Back Door*. It covers an imaginary Franco-Russian attack on Hong Kong and is reprinted here in full, together with materials intended to put it into context. There is an interesting attempt to find parallels with the actual fighting of 1941, but the parallels discovered are naturally limited as the author's reading on this period is rooted in *Captive Christmas* (15), *Ruins of War* (76), and K. D. Bhargava and K. N. V. Shastri, 'Campaigns in South-East Asia 1941–

42', India and Pakistan Combined Inter-services Historical Section, *Official History of the Indian Armed Services in the Second World War 1939–45*.

(51)   *Hong Kong: Recollections of a British POW*. Bill Wiseman. Canada: Veterans' Publications, 2001.
This very readable book covers Wiseman's experiences (as an RASC officer) during the fighting and after. The most useful section for the historian is the set of detailed descriptions of no less than thirty-three of his fellow officers.

(52)   *Hong Kong Surgeon*. Li Shu-Fan. London: Victor Gollancz, 1964.
As the founder of a hospital (the Hong Kong Sanatorium) and a big game hunter, with friends ranging from Ernest Hemingway to Sun Yat Sen, the author was surely one of the more interesting people in the Colony. The book is a full autobiography; chapter 6 covers the fighting, and chapters 7–11 the remainder of the war.

(53)   *Hostages to Fortune*. Tim Carew. London: Hamish Hamilton, 1971.
In this sequel to *The Fall of Hong Kong* (91), Carew examines the fate of those captured, paying particular attention to the *Lisbon Maru* and the early days in camp when diseases were at their most prevalent. There is also a fifty-page recap of the battle for Hong Kong. He occasionally refers to people (see 2nd Lt. Holloway, p. 48) who may possibly be illustrative rather than actual.

(54)   *I Escaped from Hong Kong*. Jan Marsman. New York: Reynall & Hitchcock, 1942.
A propaganda piece from a Dutch/American businessman who would have been on the PanAm Clipper back to Manila on 8 December 1941 had not the Japanese intervened. He describes the siege of the Repulse Bay Hotel, and his escape from the Colony, but as an outsider he can offer little insight into Hong Kong of those times. An alternative view of Marsman himself may be found in (42: 123).

(55)   *I Was a Hell Camp Prisoner*. Robert Wright.
Unfortunately it was not possible to trace a copy of this book.

(56)   *In Enemy Hands: Canadian Prisoners of War 1939–45*. Daniel G. Danocks. Edmonton, Alberta: Hurtig, 1983.
Danocks's work covers Canadian POWs from Hong Kong and elsewhere. Ex-POWs are quoted verbatim, with no attempt to calibrate memories. Although use of the POWs' own words is a powerful vehicle, the lack of even the most basic of checks into the accuracy of statements made more than fifty years after the events reduces the value.

(57) *In Oriente Fidelis*. Peter H. Starling. RAMC Historical Museum: Ash Vale, Hampshire, 1985.
Starling's short history of the medical services' contribution to the Hong Kong fighting derives largely from Bowie's earlier work, with some input from Norman Leath and a short summary of the battle.

(58) *Indian Cavalryman*. Freddie Guest. London: Jarrolds, 1959.
Guest's autobiography includes two chapters on his work at China Command and his escape with the MTB flotilla on 25 December. There is little to be found here not covered in *Escape from the Bloodied Sun* (28).

(59) *Japan and the Indian National Army*. T. R. Sareen. Delhi: Agam Prakashan, 1986.
Indian soldiers captured in Hong Kong were put under great pressure to join the INA (unlike Ghandi, the INA proposed violence as a solution to the British problem). In the vast majority of cases, they refused. Captain Ansari was a case in point; although vocally pro-independence, he was also anti-Japanese. Unfortunately Sareen's work does not investigate the split loyalties that made the Indian lot so hard to bear, but instead focuses on the high-level relationships between the Japanese and the INA. He appears to believe that the Japanese were sincere in offering help to India to rid themselves of the British yoke, and that coercion was not used to persuade captured Indian troops to join them. In both cases he flies in the face of the understanding of British historians. All in all, a thought-provoking work.

(60) *Jesuits under Fire in the Siege of Hong Kong*. Fr. T. Ryan. London: Burns, Oates & Washbourne, 1944.
Although by no means as silly and egotistical as the other missionary accounts, this work has little to offer the general historian of the military aspects of the fighting. Having said that, the scale of the shelling and bombing experienced by the civilian population in December 1941 is better expressed here than anywhere else.

(61) *Kai Tak: A History of Aviation in Hong Kong*. Peter Pigott. Hong Kong: Government Printer, n.d.
Chapter 4 devotes seven pages to the period from the beginning of the Sino-Japanese war to the surrender in 1945.

(62) *Living with Japanese*. Terence Kelly. Folkestone, Kent: Kellan, 1997.
The connection between Terence Kelly — best known for his writings on flying Hawker Hurricane fighters in the defence of Indonesia — and the Battle of Hong Kong may not be well known, but is very strong. After capture and a particularly unpleasant transportation, Kelly ended up at Inoshima camp near Hiroshima,

which was also the home of some one hundred HKVDC prisoners. Kelly gives a clear and interesting portrait of these prisoners and how they were perceived by regular servicemen.

(63)   *Long Night's Journey into Day.* Charles G. Roland. Waterloo, Ontario: Wilfred Laurier University Press, 2001.
Roland's book is a tour de force. Covering all medical aspects of the fighting and the POW experience, he has interviewed hundreds of survivors to build the most comprehensive coverage in existence. Admittedly the focus is on Canadian veterans, but the lessons learned are applicable to all. Recommended reading.

(64)   *Lyemun Barracks: 140 Years of Military History.* Privately printed, Hong Kong, 1987.
Unfortunately it was not possible to trace a copy of this booklet.

(65)   *Minutes of the Annual Conference of the Methodist Church held in Manchester, July*
1942.
Of interest purely for explaining the circumstances of the death of Methodist Minister Eric Moreton.

(66)   *No Reason Why: The Canadian Hong Kong Tragedy — An Examination.* Carl Vincent. Stittsville, Ontario: Canada's Wing, 1981.
A well laid-out book is damaged by a blatant nationalism that is painful to the non-Canadian (and, hopefully, for most Canadians too). The first part of the book examines the reason for Canadians being sent to Hong Kong at all — which could be summarized by saying that Grasett, Maltby's Canadian predecessor, fought tooth and nail for London and Ottawa to agree to this. The second part, covering the fighting, assumes that all Canadians were heroes, and all other nationalities were fools and cowards. Quoting exclusively from post-fighting Canadian sources, this does little to advance our knowledge of the subject. It also amply demonstrates the danger of researching just a small part of a far larger topic. The author puts forward a highly biased view of the efforts of Bompas at Lye Mun, even (apparently) making a joke about his name. There is no evidence that the author realised that, only a few days later, 'Bomp' — a widely respected officer — lost his life in the most gallant manner whilst attempting to prevent Japanese forces reaching Royal Rifles positions.

(67)   *Nobody Said NOT to Go.* Ken Cuthbertson. London: Faber & Faber, 1998.
Cuthbertson's biography of Emily Hahn perhaps relies a little too much on her own writing, but remains a useful work, despite inaccuracies on the Hong Kong aspects, such as claiming that Maltby's six infantry battalions had 13,000 men, or that there were no air raid shelters in Hong Kong.

(68) *Official History of the Indian Armed Forces in the Second World War 1939–45: Medical Services — Campaigns in the Eastern Theatre.* Combined InterServices Historical Section, India and Pakistan. Delhi: Orient Longman, 1964.
A very disappointing book from the point of view of this research. Far from covering the Indian Medical Services — which this work desperately needed — the Hong Kong section (admittedly only 17 pages out of 519) consists of a general summary of the fighting and a few quotes from Bowie. No facts about the IMS in Hong Kong are presented.

(69) *Oriental Odyssey.* Sid Varcoe. Privately printed, Canada, n.d.
This volume of verses by a member of the Winnipeg Grenadiers covers the period from the arrival of the Canadians through to liberation. Although verse was far more of a First World War than Second World War medium, at least three others of the Hong Kong Garrison (McNaughton, Rothwell ,and Potter) are remembered for their works.

(70) *Passport to Eternity.* Ralph Goodwin. London: Arthur Barker, 1956.
Goodwin's second book (with a foreword by Maltby) is a study of the heroic resistance movement within the Hong Kong POW camps, with especial reference to the four George Cross winners and their assistants. The foreword is so interesting — in the light of discussions about Maltby's view on escapes — that it is worth quoting at some length: 'Looking back I feel convinced we made the correct decision in not attempting escapes by small parties or even individuals. In all three camps the general standard of health had reached a very low level [so that further privations would have been fatal]. Therefore our aim, which unfortunately was never to materialise, was that a collection of food, arms and ammunition should be established in the nearby hills, a large diversion should be made by the guerrillas accompanied perhaps by an air raid, and under cover of these there should be simultaneous break-outs from all three camps. One-third of our numbers, owing to their physical state, would have had to be abandoned. Another third we reckoned would probably have fallen in the subsequent fighting, but the remainder, we hoped, would be able to make their way to freedom and so continue to participate in the war. Ambitious, perhaps, but that was our aim.'

(71) *Prisoner of the Japs.* Gwen Dew. New York: Heinemann, 1943.
Dew's reporter's eye captures many details missed by others. An American desperate to cover the war, she managed to be at both the first Japanese call for surrender (at which she was politely arrested by Wright-Nooth — see next entry) and at the Repulse Bay Hotel for the siege. Her coverage of the latter, in particular, is worth reading. Tantalizingly she took many photos and even cine films during the fighting. However, apart from one picture that was used to illustrate the *South China Morning Post* before the surrender, none seem to have survived.

(72) *Prisoner of the Turnip Heads.* George Wright-Nooth. London: Pen & Sword, 1994.

Worth noting as the only coverage of the subject from the point of view of a policeman (with the exception of an unpublished diary in the Hong Kong PRO). The fighting is covered, but the majority of the book is based on the experiences in Stanley internment camp in which the police — despite their militia status — were imprisoned. This book was originally published by Leo Cooper, whose uncle, by coincidence, was on the *Lisbon Maru.*

(73) *Quiet Heroines: Nurses of the Second World War.* Brenda McBryde. London: Chatto & Windus, 1985.

Chapters 10 and 11 of McBryde's useful work cover Hong Kong.

(74) *Road to Inamura.* Lewis Bush. Tokyo: Charles E. Tuttle Company, 1972.

Bush had a Japanese wife and was the Sub-Lieutenant of MTB 08. Fluent in the language, and later transferred to a POW camp in Japan, Bush also wrote *Clutch of Circumstance* and many other works on that country and its people. This is a fascinating book about a fascinating man.

(75) *Royal Rifles of Canada.* Arthur Penney. Privately printed, Canada, 1962.

Written in 1962 as a history of the unit, this book was indirectly responsible for much of the 'Canadianization' of the battle. Penney sticks to his subject with dogged determination (for example, although the book largely focuses on the battle of Hong Kong, he doesn't mention the HKVDC once; Walker of the HKVDC RE unit is mentioned by name, but not by unit). More recent Canadian historians, using Penney as a starting point, have also followed his single-mindedness with far less excuse in works that portray themselves as broad — rather than unit — histories.

(76) *Ruins of War.* Ko Tim Keung and Jason Wordie. Hong Kong: Joint Publishing (HK) Co. Ltd, 1996.

The only one of its kind, this guide takes the reader around all the major wartime sites that still exist in Hong Kong, with photos, maps, and suggestions on how to reach them. It is invaluable for any serious researcher or enthusiast.

(77) *Seared in My Memory.* Bernie Jesse and Norm Park. Privately printed, Canada, n.d.

As the author who recorded this had studied neither the battle nor the location, this largely wasted Bernie Jesse's story, which — as he was survivor of D Company Winnipeg Grenadiers — should have been a useful addition to our understanding of events.

(78)   *Season of Storms*. Robert L. Gandt. Hong Kong: south China Morning Post, 1982.
Gandt's story is a rehash of the basic Stewart/Maltby timeline (3), brought to life by useful interviews of around thirty participants in the fighting.

(79)   *Second to None*. Phillip Bruce. Hong Kong: Oxford University Press, 1991. Bruce's book is a scholarly examination of the history of the Hong Kong Volunteers from inception until a few years before their pre-1997 disbandment. The wartime coverage is largely derived from Stewart's earlier work (3), but is well handled here.

(80)   *Shadow Lights of Sham Shui Po*. Staff Sergeant H. P. McNaughton.
McNaughton fought in Hong Kong with the Winnipeg Grenadiers. Unfortunately it was not possible to trace a copy of this book.

(81)   *Six Years of War*, vol. 1. C. P. Stacey. Ottawa: Dept. of National Defence, 1955.
This official history of the Canadian army covers the Hong Kong operation on pp. 437–91. The account of how the Canadians became involved is one of the best. The summary of the fighting is also very good; the only minor quibble being an exaggeration of Maltby's constant consideration of the possibility — however small — of a Japanese seaborne invasion of the southern beaches of Hong Kong Island.

(82)   *Small Man of Nanataki*. Liam Nolan. New York: E. P. Dutton & Co., 1966. Kiyoshi Watanabe was not the only Japanese to try and help the Hong Kong POWs and internees, but he certainly took more risks than any other. *Small Man of Nanataki* is a biography focusing mainly on his years in Hong Kong and his personal tragedies. This book should be on the 'essential reading' list, if only to prove that — however few — there were exceptions to the brutalities that characterized wartime Japanese in allied eyes.

(83)   *Stanley: Behind Barbed Wire*. Jean Gittins. Hong Kong: Hong Kong University Press, 1982.
Gittins's book focuses primarily, as the title would suggest, on her experiences in Stanley Camp; descriptions of the battle are relegated to just pp. 21–4. However, Gittins's husband Billy was a member of 4th Battery, and the fact that Jean (born Ho Tung) and Billy came from well-established families leads this to being very much a Hong Kong 'insider' account. Jean Gittins's experiences as a member of the Eurasian intellectual elite in pre-war Hong Kong make a fascinating sociological document in their own right.

(84)   *Story of the 2/14th Punjab Regiment (D.C.O.) (Brownlow's) in Hong Kong.* Capt. Macmillan.
Unfortunately this seven-page article adds little to our understanding of this sadly under-represented Indian Regiment.

(85)   *Strange Harmony.* William Sewell. London: Edinburgh House Press, 1946.
'Strange Harmony' is a rather apt title for this atmospheric account. It begins by describing the civilian experience of wartime Mount Cameron (probably Middle Gap Road, in fact), and then moves on to a lengthy description of life in Stanley. However, the author states up front that apart from his family, all other characters are 'synthetic'. This limits the value to a historian, but it is still worth reading and occasionally a historic figure (Sir Vandaleur Grayburn and the Reverend Watanabe being examples) slips through.

(86)   *Sui Geng: The Hong Kong Marine Police 1841–1950.* Iain Ward. Hong Kong: Hong Kong University Press, 1991.
A useful account, though without many details on the war years. However, it includes photographs of several of the wartime establishment of the unit.

(87)   *The Banknote that Never Was.* Francis Braun. Hong Kong: Gulliver Books Ltd, 1980.
The theme of Braun's book is the British Government's first attempt to provide Hong Kong with new currency post-war. However, Braun arrived in Hong Kong before hostilities and being Hungarian was imprisoned with other enemy nationals at Stanley prison after Hungary declared war on the UK on 5 December 1941. His account of this experience, which included being in the prison during the fighting, is the only one I know of.

(88)   *The Bitter End in Hong Kong.* Benjamin A. Proulx. In *The 100 Best True Stories of World War II.* New York: Wm. H. Wise & Co., 1945.
This 16-page story is simply a reprint from *Underground from Hong Kong* (114).

(89)   *The Code of Love.* Andro Linklater. London: Weidenfeld & Nicolson, 2000. Squadron Leader Donald Hill kept a diary of events during the battle for Hong Kong and for a while during his captivity. In order to keep it secret, he wrote it in a numerical code that, according to the cover of the book in which he wrote, was supposedly 'Russell's Mathematical Tables'. Donald survived the camp and brought the diary out with him. However, his experiences were so traumatic that he did not like to talk about them. He died in 1985, and the diary was finally decrypted by Dr P. J. Aston of the Department of Mathematics and Statistics, University of Surrey, in 1996.

(90)   *The Defence of Hong Kong.* Lt. Col. R. J. L. Penfold, RA. *The Gunner,* December 1946.
This five-page article covers each of the artillery regiments present, with a brief summary of their actions during the battle.

(91)   *The Fall of Hong Kong.* Tim Carew. London: Pan Books, 1960.
Such a British book, with all the pros and cons that this entails. Carew clearly focuses on the British troops — especially the Middlesex Regiment — and covers others with a slightly patronizing air. His comments on the Royal Rifles (p. 207), while based on records, provoked some outrage amongst later Canadian historians — especially as D Company was still to make its Christmas Day attack. Other comments (see pp. 171, 189, 191, and 200) are more controversial.

(92)   *The First of Foot: The History of The Royal Scots.* A. Muir. Edinburgh: William Blackwood & Sons, 1961.
Muir covers the inter-war period before beginning his account with the British Expeditionary Force in France in 1940. 'The Hong Kong Tragedy' unfolds in chapter 4, and contains 51 useful pages. The descriptions of the fighting at the Shing Mun Redoubt, and later actions at Mount Nicholson and Mount Cameron, are concise and accurate.

(93)   *The Guns and Gunners of Hong Kong.* Denis Rollo. Hong Kong: Gunners' Roll of Hong Kong, 1992.
An excellent general history, in which chapter 7 covers the 1941 fighting, and appendices 4 and 5 provide useful details of Orders of Battle and wartime movements of artillery. The detailed maps of some gun emplacements are also of interest, as the majority were still in use during the war. Recommended reading.

(94)   *The Hidden Years.* John Luff. Hong Kong: South China Morning Post, 1967.
Luff's book was the first attempt to tell the story, and as such has been re-hashed many times since. A good starting point for anyone interested, it is however far from comprehensive. Having said that, without it we may never have had Oliver Lindsay's later works or many others. We owe him a debt.

(95)   *The Lasting Honour.* Oliver Lindsay. London: Hamish Hamilton, 1978.
Lindsay's first book, although appearing to owe much to Luff, is still the best basic text on the subject. It is as readable as a good novel, and covers all the more important engagements of the fighting. This is the first work that I recommend to people who show interest in the matter. Recommended reading.

(96)   *The Middlesex Regiment (Duke of Cambridge's Own), 1919–52.* P. K. Kemp. Aldershot : Gale & Poden, 1956.
This history of the Middlesex Regiment covers the 1st Battalion in Hong Kong on

pp. 28–56, and the HKVDC (as an allied regiment) in a short summary of the battled in appendix 2. There is also a full roll of honour for the regiment.

(97)   *The Quest of Noel Croucher.* Vaudine England. Hong Kong: Hong Kong University Press, 1998.
Croucher, one of Hong Kong's best-known philanthropists, was born in 1891 in England, and arrived in Hong Kong in 1911. This well-researched biography charts his rise to the position of Chairman of the Stock Exchange, casting many interesting sidelights on the Colony in the middle years of the twentieth century. Chapter 10 covers the war years, and while it is primarily about Stanley camp, the story of why Croucher was not on the *Jeanette* is relevant to this work.

(98)   *The Royal Hong Kong Police (1941–1945).* Colin Crisswell and Mike Watson. Hong Kong: Macmillan, 1982.
Chapter 10 of this comprehensive history gives the best coverage of any book of the HKPF during the war years, and appendix 1 consists of a useful gazetteer of Hong Kong's police stations. There are also some useful photographs of personnel and equipment.

(99)   *The Royal Navy in Hong Kong since 1841.* Kathleen Harland. Liskeard, Cornwall: Maritime Books, n.d.
Harland's book is the best on the subject, but shows how little research has yet been done on the Naval presence in 1941. The coverage of the 1941 period is largely based on the diary of Commander F. W. Crowther, who was later the Senior Naval Officer in Sham Shui Po (POW) camp.

(100)   *The Royal Rifles of Canada in Hong Kong.* Grant Garneau. Sherbrooke, Quebec: Progressive Publications, 1970.
Garneau's good and scholarly work is a must for anyone seriously studying East Brigade or the battle as a whole. Like the vast majority of Canadian works, it needs to be read in the light of a wider understanding of the events to avoid undervaluing the achievements of the other units involved. If I have one complaint it is that the author continually refers to single sources (instead of cross-checking all facts with multiple sources). This is a dangerous tactic, bearing in mind the unique uncertainties and inaccuracies of all source material relating to the battle of Hong Kong.

(101)   *The Shadow of a War.* James Bertram. New York: John Day, 1947.
Bertram's book has the enormous advantage of having been written while memories were still fresh. An Internationalist, Bertram joined 2 Battery HKVDC at the last minute, thus his wartime coverage is quite limited in scope (though descriptions of the Stanley battle are excellent). The later coverage of the POW

experience in Japan would have a broader audience. This book is also available under the title *Beneath the Shadow*.

(102) *The Sinking of the Lisbon Maru*. G. C. Hamilton. Hong Kong: Green Pagoda Press, 1966.
Second Lieutenant Hamilton, brought from the HKVDC into the Royal Scots to replace one of the officer casualties, was himself a survivor of the sinking of the *Lisbon Maru*. Unfortunately it was not possible to trace a copy of this book. Existing copies are in huge demand from relatives of those unlucky enough to have been on board.

(103) *The Story of Government House*. Katherine Mattock. Hong Kong: Government Printer, 1978.
Covering the history of the Governors' residences from 1841 to the time of publication, three chapters detail the period from the Japanese invasion to the British recovery. The story of the rebuilding of Government House by the Japanese, and the mystery of the buried Chinnerys, are well worth reading.

(104) *The Story of the Royal Army Service Corps, 1939–45*. Royal Army Service Corps. London: G. Bell & Sons, 1955.
This huge and professional volume (over 700 well-illustrated pages) examines in detail the many services performed by the RASC in each theatre. Pages 298–304 cover Hong Kong, and all fatalities in all theatres are listed in the Roll of Honour on pp. 657–712.

(105) *The Valour and the Horror*. Merrily Weisbord and Merilyn Simonds Mohr. Toronto: HarperCollins, 1991.
The Hong Kong episode of the TV program on which their book was partly based described the Gin Drinkers Line as a 'white ribbon of concrete'. Enough said. This is for those with a short attention span and little if any interest in the facts.

(106) *The War against Japan: Official History of the Second World War*. London: HMSO, 1957–61.
Volume 1, chapters 7–9, pp. 107–56 cover Hong Kong. Appendix 6 gives the Japanese Order of Battle. A short but accurate account in the impersonal style one would expect from an official history.

(107) *The Women of Stanley*. Bernice Archer. *Women's History Review*, vol. 5, no. 3, 1996.
Archer's paper analyses the roles and contributions to camp life made by the female internees.

(108)   *This Soldier's Story*. George MacDonell. Nepean, Ontario: Baird O'Keefe Publishing Inc., 2000.
MacDonell was a sergeant of the Royal Rifles of Canada. Unfortunately it was not possible to trace a copy of this book.

(109)   *Through Japanese Barbed Wire*. Gwen Priestwood. London: Harrap, 1944.
Priestwood's book is dominated by her experiences in Stanley and in one of the first two (simultaneous) escapes from internment — together with policeman 'Anthony Bathurst' (this was a pseudonym for W. P. Thompson, who at the time when Priestwood's book was published was still operating behind Japanese lines). Posted initially to the Jockey Club as a nurse, she was lucky to escape the atrocities there by volunteering for the seemingly more dangerous job of driving a delivery lorry.

(110)   *Turbans and Traders*. Barbara-Sue White. Hong Kong: Oxford University Press, 1994.
Disappointingly, this interesting book covering the history of the Indian community in Hong Kong devotes only one poorly researched chapter to the war period. The Indian effort in the defence of Hong Kong is by far the least researched, and is worthy of a dedicated study.

(111)   *Twilight in Hong Kong*. Ellen Field. London: Frederick Muller Ltd. 1960.
Field's book is, apart from Hahn's work, the only coverage of life in Hong Kong (from the European point of view) during the occupation. The insights into the work of Selwyn-Clark and 'the small man from Nantaki' are interesting, and so is the description of the activities of an unidentified BAAG agent spiriting British servicemen from the Colony.

(112)   *Twisting the Tail of the Dragon*. Jean Mathers. 1994.
Mathers was the wife of a serving officer of the Punjabis, and spent the entire war in Stanley internment camp. Unfortunately it was not possible to trace a copy of this book.

(113)   *Two-Gun Cohen*. Daniel Levy. New York: St Martin's Press, 1997.
The life story of Cohen, a tough London Jew who moved (via Canada) to become Sun Yat Sen's bodyguard, is utterly unique. By poor luck, he happened to be in Hong Kong as the Japanese attacked, and pp. 200–33 cover the period of the fighting and his internment in Stanley.

(114)   *Underground from Hong Kong*. Benjamin Proulx. New York: Dutton, 1943.
As one of the early escapees, Proulx wrote his book before the end of hostilities. It covers the Repulse Bay Hotel siege in detail, but naturally from a very personal point of view. The majority of the story covers the eighteen days of fighting,

with the escape being simply the last chapter. Like most books written during the war (while key players were still in Japanese captivity), it is short on names.

(115) *Unfading Honour: The Story of The Indian Army.* Major-General J. G. Elliott. New York: A. S. Barnes & Co., 1964.
The neophyte wishing to learn something of the old Indian Army would do well to start with this study. However, with less than four hundred pages to tell the whole story, Elliott could only spare five for Hong Kong before moving on to the larger conflict in Singapore.

(116) *Victoria Barracks 1842–1979.* D. H. Oxley. Hong Kong: British Forces Hong Kong, 1979.
Unfortunately it was not possible to trace a copy of this book.

(117) *We Flee from Hong Kong.* Alice Y. Lan and Betty M. Hu. Grand Rapids, Mich.: Zondervan 1944.
The one redeeming feature of this otherwise dull missionary book is that it describes — briefly — life in Kowloon between the Japanese occupation and the fall of Hong Kong. Living in Grampian Road, Kowloon (near the old Kai Tak airport) the authors were in the middle of the action. The majority of the book, however, covers their escape to America via China.

(118) *Where Life and Death Hold Hands.* William Allister. Toronto: Stoddart, 1989.
Whether this is a 'classic' of Second World War literature is debatable, but it is without doubt the nearest thing to it to have emerged from the Hong Kong campaign (Bertram's book (101) is the only other that would come close). Written by an artist who should never have been near a war, it is at times painfully honest. A Canadian signalman who ended up as a POW in Japan, Allister went on to an interesting career in film and media.

(119) *White Ensign — Red Dragon.* Commodore P. J. Melson. Hong Kong: Edinburgh Financial, 1997.
Melson's book relies heavily on Kathleen Harland's earlier work for the coverage of the war years. This list of His Majesty's Ships in the appendix is useful, though it neglects to mention HMS *Scout*.

(120) *Winged Dragon.* Valerie Penlington. Hong Kong: Odyssey Productions, 1996.
Penlington's history of the Royal Hong Kong Auxiliary Air Force covers the entire period from the first suggestion of forming a flying section of the HKVDC (in June 1930), through to the RHKAAF's disbandment in March 1993. The wartime

period, during which neither unit was operating, is covered in just two pages. However, there is an interesting list of personnel as an appendix.

(121) *Wings Over Hong Kong*. Edited by Cliff Dunnaway. Hong Kong: Odyssey Productions, 1998.
This coffee-table history of aviation in Hong Kong covers the period of the Second War on pp. 129–134, though there are also useful articles on the China Clipper, inter-war aviation, and the Far East Flying Training School. The most useful part of the wartime coverage is a short series of photos, taken from the air, of the Japanese attack on Kai Tak.

UNPUBLISHED SOURCES

(122)   AL 5144. Doi, Box 16. Imperial War Museum, London.

(123)   AL 5084. Monograph 71 Army China Operations, Part 2. Imperial War Museum, London.

(124)   'An Account of War Experiences.' A. Salmon. Endacott MSS, Hong Kong University.

(125)   'Captive Colony' (manuscript). John Stericker. Hong Kong University.

(126)   CWGC Internal Documents.

(127)   Diary of Mabel Redwood. Imperial War Museum, London.

(128)   'Diary of Work at Kowloon Hospital.' Dr Smalley. Endacott MSS, Hong Kong University. (Smalley is himself mentioned in (46).)

(129)   HKRS 170/1/763 HKRNVR (Members of the HKRNVR).

(130)   HKRS 6/1/1706 Historical Records (History of the HKRNVR).

(131)   Hong Kong Police War Diary.

(132)   Interviews:
      (a)   Conversation with the author.
      (b)   Letter or email to the author.

(133)   London PRO ADM 199/1286 (HK Despatches: the HKDDC, the Volunteers, etc.).

(134) London PRO CAB 44/175 (Enquiry into Loss of Shing Mun Redoubt). (It is probable that the name censored from pp. 32 and 33 of this report is Sergeant Robb.)

(135) London PRO CO 980/52 (War Crimes), CO 980/59 (Escapes).

(136) London PRO WO 235/1015 (War Crimes — Wong Nai Chung Gap).

(137) London PRO WO 235/1030.

(138) London PRO WO 235/1107 (War Crimes — Ito Takeo).

(139) London PRO WO 106/5359 (East Brigade War Diary).

(140) London PRO WO 176/1685-1694 / WO 172/1691 (War Diaries).

(141) MB 89 (microfilm) War Time Diary of Inspector Fred Kelly, HK PRO. (The original is held by the Force Historical Records Committee.)

(142) Prisoner of War Diary of Chief Signal Officer China Command, Hong Kong 1941-45, Eustace Levett. HK PRO Library, 940.53 LEV (Royal Signals and all officers POW in Hong Kong).

(143) PRO, London, ADM 199/357:
    (a) Ashby's report of 12 January 1942.
    (b) Kennedy's report of 14 January 1942.
    (c) Collingwood's report of 19 December 1941.
    (d) Parsons's report of 15 January 1942.
    (e) Gandy's report of 8 March 1942.
    (f) Montague's report of 11 February 1942.

(144) PRO, London, FO 916/1082, Kathleen Christie.

(145) Provisional List of British and Foreign (other than Japanese) Casualties, Prisoners of War, and Internees in Hong Kong. HK PRO, HKRS 112-1-1.

(146) RAPC War Diary, Brigadier R. D. Buck, CBE. RAPC Museum, Worthy Down.

(147) *South China Morning Post*, 8-26 December 1941 (minus Saturday, 20 Dec.).

(148) Statement of Major General Toshishige Shoji, OC 230th Regiment.

(149)   'Steering Neutral in Troubled Waters.' Revd. Bourke. Endacott MSS, Hong Kong University.

(150)   Templer's Diary. Imperial War Museum, London.

(151)   'These Defenceless Doors.' R. K. W. Simpson. Hong Kong University Library.

(152)   Transcript of BAAG interview. Author's collection.

(153)   PRO, London, WO 172/1687 Royal Artillery Records.

(154)   War Diaries, Royal Rifles of Canada. National Archives of Canada, Ottawa, DHIST 593 (D3).

(155)   War Diaries, Winnipeg Grenadiers. National Archives of Canada, Ottawa, DHIST 593 (D33).

(156)   WO 208/735. Letter from Siu-Feng Huang to wife.

(157)   WO 208/3035. Interview with Corporal Salter.

FAMILY PAPERS

(158)   Browne Papers (Maltby's HQ Personnel and Functions). Author's collection.

(159)   Coxhead Diaries. Hong Kong Museum of Coastal Defence. (As a note to other researchers, the majority of veterans' families approached for this book had retained documents covering the war years; many even had unpublished diaries.)

(160)   Parker papers (War Diary of Major Parker, D Coy. Royal Rifles of Canada). Held by Ron Parker in Canada.

(161)   Parson papers. Author's collection.

(162)   Ride papers (nominal roll of Field Ambulance; some hospital records).

AUTHOR'S COLLECTION

(163)   Sinclair papers (nominal roll of 5 AA Regiment). Author's collection.

(164)   Diary of E. H. Field, RA. Author's collection.

FILMS, TELEVISION PROGRAMMES, AND RADIO

(165)   *Captive Christmas.* Radio Television Hong Kong. 1978.
This was the radio programme upon which the book (15) was based.

(166)   *Hong Kong '41–'45.* TVB, Hong Kong. 1991
Broadcast to commemorate the fiftieth anniversary of the invasion (a time when many veterans returned for memorial services), this program took a broad brush to the issues, covering the causes of war, the fighting, and the years of occupation in one episode. Considering the breadth, it was not a bad attempt.

(167)   *Horror in the East.* BBC, 2000.
The BBC had originally planned a multi-episode series covering the war in the Far East, to be shown around Christmas 2001 (the sixtieth anniversary of Japanese aggression against the West). One episode was intended to focus purely on Hong Kong. Instead, it metastized into a two-episode series, the first on the theme of the Japanese psyche in attack, the second on their psyche in defence. Disappointing to those 'in the know', but apparently well received in general. The interviews (particularly with Osler Thomas and Nurse Sully) were particularly effective.

(168)   *The Fall of Hong Kong.* Japanese, 1942.
This propaganda film was made in 1942, re-staging the invasion. There is some suggestion that parts may have been shot during the fighting itself, but so far the only cine film known to survive from that period is footage shot by the Japanese from the air. Hahn's description (17) of being taken to see this film in wartime Hong Kong is interesting in its context.

(169)   *The Valour and the Horror.* Galafilm, Inc. Canada, 1991.
The TV program upon which the book was based. The other two episodes (covering Dieppe and the Canadian contribution to RAF Bomber Command) were apparently equally poor, and designed simply to create controversy.

(170)   *They Met in Bombay.* USA, 1941.
Starring Clark Gable and Rosalind Russel as two fictional jewel thieves in Bombay, the film follows their careers as they flee to Hong Kong, where Gable joins the British Army and wins the Victoria Cross.

(171)   *War* and *Occupation.* TVB Pearl, Hong Kong, 2001.
Originally broadcast in December 2001 to mark the sixtieth anniversary of the attack, *War* is arguably the best (though, at twenty minutes, short) chronological coverage of the battle (the author was heavily involved in this episode). *Occupation* is respectable, though tries to cover an impossible three years and eight months in a further twenty-minute slot.

FICTION

(172) *A Handful of Rice.* William Allister. London: Secker & Warburg, 1961.

(173) *Hour of the Dog.* Berkely Mather. London: Collins, 1982.

(174) *If Chance a Stranger.* Charles Fullerton. New York: William Sloane Associates, 1958.

(175) *Invincible.* Jared Mitchell. Toronto: Lester Publishing, 1995.

(176) *No Man Divided.* James L. Bradley. London: John Spencer & Co., n.d.

(177) *Season of Escape.* James Ford, MC. London: Hodder & Stoughton, 1963. Ford's novels are clearly largely autobiographical.

(178) *Sunset.* Douglas Reeman. London: William Heinemann, 1994.

(179) *The Bamboo Wireless.* Martin Booth.

(180) *The Brave White Flag.* James Ford, MC. London: Corgi, 1973.

(181) *The Young Colonials.* Barbara Anslow.

Index

Aberdeen   30, 33, 34, 41, 45, 48, 53, 62, 70–72, 76, 78, 81, 85, 92, 98, 121, 122, 128, 133, 136, 142, 172, 176, 179, 187, 191, 203, 219, 250, 254, 256, 261, 283
Aberdeen Industrial School   48, 58, 76, 98
Aberdeen Island (See Ap Lei Chau)
Aberdeen Reservoir   223
Adams, Private L. (Winnipeg Grenadiers)   170
Agerbak, Corporal T. (Winnipeg Grenadiers)   170
Albany Road   41, 78
Aldgate Gate Vessel   53
Aldrich Bay   103
Alliance, HMT   87
Allister, Signalman W. (RCCS)   120, 173, 405
Altamira   18, 166, 185, 193, 194, 203, 284
Anderson Road   58, 59
Anderson, Lieutenant D. (HKVDC)   131
Anderson, Major L. (RA)   48, 84
Anderson, Sergeant J. (RAMC)   254, 258
Andrews-Loving, Nurse   263
Anglo-Persian Company   99
Ap Lei Chau   52, 252, 261
Apooey, SS   179
Argyle Street Camp   25, 230, 235, 285
Arlington, Doctor   232
Arnott, Sergeant J. (Royal Scots)   129
ARP   98, 119, 237, 248, 260
Ashby, Lieutenant R. (HKRNVR)   132
Ashton-Rose, Captain L. (IMS)   237
Atkinson, Captain A. (HKSRA)   122, 143
Atkinson, Private H. (Winnipeg Grenadiers)   170
Au Tau   38
Auxiliary Medical Corps   61
Auxiliary Quartering Corps   48
Avery, Captain A. (HKSRA)   122, 143

Babin, Rifleman A. (Royal Rifles) 121
Badger, Captain H. (Middlesex) 62
Bailey, Lance Corporal G. (Middlesex) 216, 224
Bailey, Mr 71
Bailey, Sapper W. (RE) 71
Baker, Rifleman G. (Royal Rifles) 221
Balean, Captain G. (HKVDC) 237
Ball, Private W. (Middlesex) 216, 224
Banfill, Captain M. (RCAMC) 129
Bank of East Asia 58
Bankier, Lance Corporal R. (Royal Scots) 39
Barclay, Captain B. (RAMC) 121
Bard, Lieutenant S. (HKVDC) 73, 84, 233, 247, 252
Barlow, BSM W. (RA) 87
Barnett, Captain K. (HKVDC) 75, 105, 185
Barnett, Rev. Captain J. (Canadian Chaplain Service) 29, 255
Barretto, Gloria (NAAFI) 185
Barton, Sergeant T. (Corps of Military Staff Clerks) 134
Barton's Bungalow — See Bungalow C
Bartram, Captain H. (RA) 254
Basnett, Private A. (Royal Scots) 39
Basset, Joyce 28
Battle Box 25, 27, 216
Battle HQ (see Fortress HQ)
Batty-Smith, Captain S. 14
Baxter, 2nd Lieutenant B. (HKDDC) 66, 176, 177
Beacon Hill 52
Beattie, Lieutenant L. (HKRNVR) 256
Bedward, Sergeant B. (Middlesex) 176, 268
Begg, CSM S. (HKVDC) 206, 222, 240

Begg, Nurse Eileen (HKVDC) 258, 262
Belcher's 46, 66, 70, 73–75, 78, 89
Bell, 2nd Lieutenant M. (Royal Scots) 138
Belton, Captain P. 74
Bennet's Hill 19, 121, 122, 137, 142, 168, 176, 187, 190, 204, 219, 221, 250, 253, 256, 260
Bennett, Wing Commander H. (RAF) 176
Berridge, Major R. (RE) 204
Berry, Master Gunner R. (RA) 135
Bertram, Gunner J. (HKVDC) 242, 402
Bethell, B. 23, 84, 217
Bhima Ram, Havildar (Punjabis) 87
Bickley, Private G. (RAMC) 121
Billings, Captain G. (RCCS) 178
Birkett, Lieutenant G. (Winnipeg Grenadiers) 107, 108, 115, 125, 128
Bishop, Major W. (Royal Rifles) 82, 103
Black Hill 60
Black Hole 170
Black, Lt. Colonel G. (HKVDC) 254
Black's Link 95, 134, 138, 141, 179
Blackaby, 2nd Lieutenant G. (Middlesex) 191, 256
Blackwood, Lieutenant T. (Winnipeg Grenadiers) 178, 201
Blakeney, Lieutenant B. (HKRNVR) 126
Blaker, Captain C. (HKVDC) 194
Blaver, Lieutenant C. (Royal Rifles) 132, 174
Blue Pool Road 115, 206, 216
Bluff Head 218, 232, 260
Bokhara Battery 29, 84, 135, 136
Boldero, Lt. Commander J. (RN) 30
Bompas, Lieutenant E. (HKSRA) 107, 108, 124, 131, 137, 189–191, 197

INDEX

Booker, Beryl 68
Booker, Mr & Mrs F. 68
Bosanquet Gunner D. (HKVDC) 102, 105, 107, 390
Bosley, Private R. (Middlesex) 216
Botelho, Captain H. (HKVDC) 104
Bottomley, Major J. (HKVDC) 28
Bow, Nurse 172
Bowden, Leading Seaman G. (RN) 133
Bowen Road 41, 58, 283
Bowen Road Hospital 41, 48, 68, 84, 121, 283, 284
Bowie, Lt. Colonel D. (RAMC) 251, 388
Bowman, Captain A. (Winnipeg Grenadiers) 41, 54, 107, 135
Bowrington 233
Boxer, Major C. (Lincs. Regt.) 27, 45, 84, 176, 179
Brady, Private J. (Winnipeg Grenadiers) 170
Braemar 48, 87, 92, 97, 99, 103, 106, 122, 125
Brick Hill 19, 86, 168, 177, 179, 187, 188, 192, 201, 240, 254, 256, 261
Bridge Hill 19, 121, 136, 185, 189, 191, 222
Briggs, First Lieutenant C. (RN) 27, 31, 390
Briggs, Mrs S. 57, 58, 142, 203, 391
Brinville 189, 190Bristow, Stoker G. (RN) 117
Britannia, APV 53
British Military Hospital (BMH) — See Bowen Road Hospital
Broadbridge, Lance Corporal N. (HKVDC) 132, 141, 240
Brothers Point (see Tai Lam Kok)
Browne, Lieutenant H. 62, 74, 89, 116, 117, 216, 248
Browning, Major J. (Rajputs) 187

Brunet, Corporal L. (CPC) 175
Bryden, Lieutenant E. (HKVDC) 189, 192, 194, 217, 254, 255
Buffalo Hill 25
Bullen, Gunner J. (RA) 253
Bungalow C 250, 255
Burgess, 2nd Lieutenant C. (RA) 25
Burke, Private D. (Middlesex) 216, 224
Burn, Major S. (Royal Scots) 38, 51
Bush, Captain H. (RCASC) 14, 134, 138, 178
Bush, Sub Lieutenant L. (HKRNVR) 283, 398
Buxton, Lieutenant H. (HKVDC) 105
Buxton, Nurse Alberta (HKVDC) 258, 262
Bywaters, Private W. (Middlesex) 216, 224

Cadogan-Rawlinson, Lt. Colonel J. (Rajputs) 12, 69, 104, 125, 136, 187
Cahagan, Private C. (HKVDC) 130
Caine Road 80
Calvert, Lieutenant G. (HKVDC) 201
Cambon, Rifleman K. (Royal Rifles) 105, 391
Campbell, Captain J. (Royal Scots) 129, 138
Campbell, Corporal N. (Royal Scots) 38, 129
Campbell, Major D. (HKDDC) 52
Canal Road 221, 239, 242, 254, 256, 261
Canivet, Private L. (RCOC) 220
Canton (see Guang Zhou)
Canton Road 53
Cape Collinson 79, 135
Cape D'Aguilar 29
Caroline Hill 19, 49, 74, 78, 85, 89, 119, 141

Carruthers, 2nd Lieutenant M. (HKVDC)   13, 123, 124, 156, 216
Carter, 2nd Lieutenant B. (HKVDC)   189, 191
Casey, Private J. (Royal Scots)   39
Cash's Bungalow   189, 191
Castle Peak Bay   29
Castle Peak Road   29, 30, 34, 35, 41, 42, 44–46, 51, 52
Castleton, Seaman Gunner R. (HKRNVR)   126
Causeway Bay   18, 43, 68, 93, 95, 97, 98, 101, 107, 117, 119, 125, 141, 166, 187, 190, 199, 217, 222, 230, 240, 256
Cavill, Corporal D. (Middlesex)   124
Central   13, 18, 19, 80, 84, 89, 91, 93, 97, 98, 101, 143, 165, 166, 204, 242, 258, 283, 285
Central Market   87, 99
Central Police Station   80, 85
Challinor, Lieutenant R. (HKSRA)   258
Chan Chak, Admiral   62, 261
Chang Yam-Kwong, Gunner (HKVDC)   106
Chater Garden   14
Chatham Road   132
Cheesewright, 2nd Lieutenant C. (Middlesex)   207, 242
Cheung Sha Wan   51, 52
Cheung Shiu Tan   31, 32
Chiang Kai Shek   192
China Command (see Fortress Headquarters)
China Fleet Club   26, 58, 78, 142, 233, 242, 250, 256
Chinese Cemetery Ridge   119
Chorley, Private G. (Royal Scots)   65
Christensen, Miss Sessan   25
Chuen Lung   41
Chung Hom Kok   68, 89, 135, 217, 223, 236, 237, 248, 255, 260, 263

Chung Hue Island   45
Chung King   38
Churchill, Sir Winston   66, 79, 193, 217, 218
Cicala, HMS   17, 29, 30, 33, 44, 45, 122, 187, 190
Civil Service Club   254
Clarke, Captain W. (Royal Rifles)   191
Clarke, Major C.   206
Clayton, Lieutenant A. (RA)   240, 242
Clearwater Bay Road   59
Cloudy Hill   25
CNAC   28, 31
Coates, Rifleman R. (Royal Rifles)   86
Cockle, Lieutenant H. (HKRNVR)   126
Cohen, M.   31
Cole, Captain N. (Rajputs)   187
Cole, Lieutenant G. (RN)   73, 86
Coleman, Lance Corporal W. (Middlesex)   124, 130
Coleman, Rifleman R. (Royal Rifles)   221
Coleman, Sergeant J. (Royal Rifles)   86
Colle, Lieutenant J. (HKRNVR)   132
Collinson, Commodore A. (RN)   131
Colonial Secretariat   97
Command Pay Office   48
Conduit Road   29
Connaught Road West   45, 61
Cooke, Private H. (Middlesex)   124
Coombe Road   49, 68
Cooper, Master Gunner C. (RA)   75, 76
Corbally, Mr   73
Corbitt, Sergeant C. (Royal Scots)   129
Cornflower, HMS   30, 34, 261
Corrigan, Lieutenant A. (Winnipeg Grenadiers)   239
Course, Captain R. (Rajputs)   104

INDEX

Coyle, Private H. (Royal Scots)   39
Craigengower Cricket Club   221, 232, 239, 254
Crawford, Joan   130
Crowe, Major J. (RA)   122, 143, 205
Crowther, Commander F. (RN)   73, 86, 262
Crozier, Captain D. (HKVDC)   260
Cullum, Petty Officer H. (RN)   136
Curtis, Sergeant E. (HKVDC)   106, 123
Customs Pass   43, 49, 58, 86

Dalziel, Mr F.   203
Davies, Bandsman R. (Middlesex)   134
Davies, Captain R. (HKVDC)   142, 173
Davies, Captain R. (RCAPC)   174, 175
Deep Water Bay   68, 119, 122, 128, 166, 168, 173, 174, 190, 192
Des Voeux, Private Sir E. (HKVDC)   130
Devil's Peak   23, 49, 54, 57–60, 62, 68, 71, 84, 93, 97, 101, 102, 105, 131
Dew, Gwen   70, 397
Dewar, Major A. (RASC)   69, 188, 201
Dhani Ram, Jemadar (Punjabis)   87
Dillon, Bandsman D. (Middlesex)   134
Dines, First Lieutenant J. (RNR)   136
Dobson, Sub Lieutenant C. (RNVR)   136
Doddridge, Rifleman P. (Royal Rifles)   259, 260, 276
Doi, Colonel   35, 36, 38, 40, 44, 98, 102, 103, 116, 124, 131, 188, 192, 207
Doman   79
Dome Hill   46

Drown, Corporal E. (HKVDC)   236
Dulley, Lt. Commander H. (HKRNVR)   126, 143
Duncan, Major H. (RA)   140
Dunlop, 2nd Lieutenant J. (Royal Scots)   50
Dunlop, Corporal R. (HKVDC)   125, 130

Eager, Sub-Lieutenant J. (HKRNVR)   132
East Brigade   18, 19, 68, 74, 79, 80, 82, 86, 87, 90, 95, 98, 101, 102, 104, 106, 116, 117, 121, 135, 137, 165, 166, 168, 170, 185, 194, 202, 205, 217, 234, 239, 285
East Lamma Channel   52, 53, 133
Eastern Telegraph Company   45
Eastman, Lieutenant J. (HKRNVR)   30
Eddison, 2nd Lieutenant J. (HKSRA)   137, 258
Edwards, Lieutenant R. (HKVDC)   13, 191, 196
Edwards, Private E. (Middlesex)   216
Egashira, Major   279
Electric Road   130
Enderby, Drummer G. (Middlesex)   134
Eucliffe Castle   18, 165, 166, 173, 185, 193, 203, 232, 233
Eurasia Air Corporation   28
Evans, Private F. (RAMC)   121

Fairbairn, 2nd Lieutenant G. (Royal Scots)   138
Fairclough, Lieutenant F. (RA)   254, 256
Falconar, Lieutenant M. (Middlesex)   177, 194, 217, 224, 225
Fallon, Private P. (HKVDC)   230
Fan Ling   13, 27
Farrington, Major C. (RM)   219, 237

Fateh Muhammad, Gunner (HKSRA) 75
Fearon, Miss Lois (ANS) 129
Felix Villas 87
Fenwick, Lieutenant M. (Royal Scots) 129
Fidoe, Nurse 263
Field, Lieutenant B. (HKVDC) 107, 128, 132, 137, 139, 141
Field, Lieutenant E. (RA) 75, 199
Field, Lt. Colonel F. (RA) 219
Fielden, Major L. (RA) 108, 141
Filter Beds (Hong Kong) 126, 199
Filter Beds (Kowloon) 41
Filter Beds House 46, 54
Fisher, Private E. (HKVDC) 137
Fitzgerald, Lieutenant (HKVDC) 236
Flagstaff House 13, 216, 278
Flippance, Major F. (HKVDC) 142, 173
Flood, Captain G. (Middlesex) 191, 241
Fo Tan Valley 33
Foley, Private A. (Middlesex) 250
Ford, Captain D. (Royal Scots) 49, 138, 173, 178, 258, 262
Ford, Lieutenant J. (Royal Scots) 46, 49, 50, 54, 138, 410
Ford, RSME. (RA) 48, 76, 87
Forrester, Major B. (RA) 202
Forster, Sub-Lieutenant J. (HKRNVR) 261
Forsyth, Lieutenant N. (Punjabis) 59, 60
Forsyth, Major H. (HKVDC) 242
Fortress Headquarters 27, 33, 51, 58, 74, 90, 93, 97, 101, 116, 138, 170, 175, 176, 179, 205, 222, 239, 242, 257, 260, 263
Fowler, Private J. (Winnipeg Grenadiers) 260
Fox, Private L. (HKVDC) 240
Fox, Sergeant W. (Middlesex) 141

Frederick's House 177, 219
Fredericks, Lt. Col. E. (RASC) 173, 194
French, Lieutenant C. (Winnipeg Grenadiers) 107, 115, 125, 128, 134
Frosty, APV 53, 60, 71, 91
Fry, Lieutenant W. (Royal Rifles) 189, 191, 196

Gandy, Lt. Commander G. (RN Rtd.) 132
Garden Road 91, 99, 190
Garter Pass 52
Gatling, Naval Armament Tug 86
Gauge Basin 74, 117, 120–123, 131, 132, 135, 137, 179, 188
Gavey, Captain J. (Royal Rifles) 114
Gean, Matron Dorothy 61
Gellman, Private B. (HKVDC) 59
Geoghan, Private 'Paddy' (HKVDC) 130
Gilham, Sergeant S. (Middlesex) 142
Gill's Cutting 29
Gilman's Garage 206
Gimson, F. 15
Gin Drinkers Bay 16
Gin Drinkers Line 12, 13, 16, 17, 21, 33, 36, 39, 40, 43, 65
Glasgow 253
Gloucester Building 58, 84, 90, 91
Gloucester Road 254
Glover, Lance Corporal D. (Royal Scots) 129
Goddard, Corporal C. (Middlesex) 185
Golden Hill 17, 22, 23, 38, 40, 42, 45–47, 49, 50
Goldin, Mrs Nina 172
Goldman, Captain L. (HKVDC) 105
Gomes, Corporal A. (HKVDC) 78
Goodwin, Lieutenant R. (RNVR) 190, 262, 392, 397

Index

417

Gordon, 2nd Lieutenant V. (Royal Scots)   138
Gordon, Nurse A.   258, 263
Goring, Major A. (Punjabis)   216, 261
Government House   14, 221
Gow, Sergeant D. (HKVDC)   105
Graham, Lieutenant E. (Middlesex)   124, 141
Grant, Private I. (HKVDC)   255
Grassy Hill (see Tso Shan)
Gray, Flying Officer H. (RAF)   82
Gray, Major G. (Punjabis)   13, 16, 25, 27, 28, 30, 31, 33, 36, 40
Green Island   63, 71, 72, 132
Grenham, Lieutenant Commander J. (HKRNVR)   122, 126
Grenham, Nurse Olive   232
Gresham, Major A. (Winnipeg Grenadiers)   126, 140, 145
Gripps, The – See Hong Kong Hotel
Grounds, 2nd Lieutenant P. (Middlesex)   171, 175, 199
Guang Zhou   15, 16, 28
Guest, Captain F. (Middlesex)   62, 257, 261, 389, 395
Gunn, Chief Engineer J. (HKDDC)   87

Hackett, Doctor E.   236
Hai Wan Line   53, 62, 69
Haines, 2nd Lieutenant A. (HKDDC)   40, 121, 219
Haldor, S.S.   101
Hall, Corporal W. (Winnipeg Grenadiers)   140
Hamlen, CSM F. (RASC)   201, 203, 207
Hammer Hill   52
Hammett, Captain B. (RA)   48
Hammond, R.   285, 387
Han Wo, APV 31, 53
Hancock, Major F. (HKMC)   56
Hanger, Sergeant T. (HKSRA)   187

Happy Valley   82, 84, 172, 216, 254, 278, 286
Happy Valley Race Course   14, 117, 141, 199, 214, 221, 222, 240, 242, 251
Harding, Lance Corporal H. (Middlesex)   230
Harland, Major H. (Royal Scots)   74, 233, 263, 278, 279
Harley, D. (Merchant Navy)   261
Harmon, Mr T   14
Harris, 2nd Lieutenant T. (Middlesex)   119
Harrop, Phyllis   63, 80, 216, 393
Hart, Lieutenant C. (Royal Scots)   129
Harvey, Sergeant T. (Middlesex)   177
Hatton Road   85
Haywood, 2nd Lieutenant F. (Royal Scots)   50
Helena May Institute   216
Henderson, Rifleman E. (Royal Rifles)   257
Hennessey, Colonel P. (RCASC)   14, 161, 174, 175, 235
Hennessy Road   216, 254, 257
Hewitt, Captain A. (Middlesex)   284, 387
High Junk   53
High West   174
Hill, Squadron Leader D. (RAF)   16, 41, 48
Hindmarsh, Lieutenant D. (HKRNVR)   30
Hing, Lance Corporal E. (HKVDC)   123
Ho Tung, Sir Robert   13
Ho Tung, Lady   13
Hodkinson, Major E. (Winnipeg Grenadiers)   138, 141, 142
Hollywood Road   80
Holmes, Captain L. (HKVDC)   108, 123, 125

Holmes, Corporal D. (HKVDC)   252
Holt's Wharf   133
Home, Lt. Colonel W. (Royal Rifles)   12, 102, 108, 142, 175, 177, 194, 202, 218, 233, 235, 236, 257
Hong Kong Cricket Club   14
Hong Kong Dockyard Defence Corps   52, 73, 121, 172, 173, 219
Hong Kong Hotel   13, 14, 58
Hong Kong Jockey Club   89, 172, 178, 206, 230, 286
Hong Kong Mule Company   12, 62
Hong Kong Police Force   39, 42, 44, 47, 49, 53, 57, 59, 63, 68, 71–73, 75, 85, 97, 99, 120, 143, 172, 206, 217, 248
Hong Kong Royal Naval Volunteer Reserve   48, 126, 175, 187, 201, 207, 261, 285
Hong Kong Sanatorium   172, 248
Hong Kong Shanghai Bank   58, 84, 91, 232
Hong Kong & Singapore Royal Artillery   11, 12, 39, 57, 95, 98, 123, 131, 143, 173, 187, 216, 240, 253
   1 Mountain Battery   16, 49, 58, 62, 69, 74, 89, 97, 107, 121, 122, 141, 185, 232, 250
   2 Mountain Battery   16, 33, 35, 37, 41, 49, 52, 68, 89, 122, 250
   3 Medium Battery   104, 122, 131, 141
   4 Medium Battery   250
   17 HAA   76, 79, 201, 254, 256
   18 LAA   71, 232
   20 Coast Battery   87
   25 Medium Battery   16, 33, 49, 85, 89, 122, 172, 178
   26 Coast Battery   48
Hong Kong Telephone Company   54
Hong Kong University   14, 117, 262

Hong Kong Volunteer Defence Corps   12, 13, 17, 18, 21, 25, 38, 57, 68, 73, 108, 120, 166, 170, 171, 173, 234, 257
   1 Company   16, 48, 51, 59, 91, 98, 106, 123, 130, 137, 168, 177, 179, 188–191, 202, 236
   2 Company   126, 132, 139, 142, 168, 171, 179, 189, 192, 193, 202, 205, 205, 217, 219, 223, 236, 242, 253–255, 263
   3 Company   26, 48, 53, 95, 98, 106, 115, 131, 132, 138, 199, 202, 240
   4 Company   201, 219
   5 Company   79
   6 Company   190
   7 Company   201, 219
   1 Battery   126, 136, 139, 202, 236, 241, 243, 248, 250
   2 Battery   202, 218, 260
   3 Battery   48, 252
   4 Battery   66, 75, 81, 82, 105, 185
   5 Battery   75, 80, 98, 101, 102, 105, 128
   Air Unit   28
   ASC Unit   142, 185
   Field Company Engineers   13, 17, 25, 27, 28, 33, 91, 138
   Hugheseliers   98, 101, 124
   Stanley Platoon   74, 202, 236, 237, 242, 253
   Z Force   38, 252, 286
Hopkins, A. Inspector (HKPF)   80
Horowitz, Mrs Valentine   172
Hospital Road   279
Houghton, Corporal J. (HKVDC)   191
Houstoun-Boswell, 2nd Lieutenant G. (Royal Scots)   50
Hoyland, Captain W. (RA)   122
Hsieh, Zaza   117
Hu Men   15

INDEX 419

Hudson, ASP G. (HKPF)   63
Hughes, Lt. Colonel H. (HKVDC)   38
Hughes, Sergeant H. (Royal Rifles)   132, 148
Hung Hom   26
Hung, Lance Corporal D. (HKVDC)   108, 123
Hung, Lance Corporal K. (HKVDC)   141
Hunt, Major E. de V. (HKSRA)   16, 141, 173
Hunter, Lieutenant D. (Royal Scots)   46, 50, 95, 251
Hurd, Captain E. (Winnipeg Grenadiers)   29
Hutton-Potts, Captain A. (HKVDC)   103, 105, 173

Indian General Hospital   68, 75, 76, 172
Indira, APV   30, 35, 48, 53, 54, 78, 80
Inglis, Gunner J. (RA)   253
Island Brigade   12
Island Road   103, 176, 185, 207, 217, 239
Iwabuchi   116

Jacosta, Captain J. (HKVDC)   141
James, Captain T. (RA)   279
Japanese 10th Chutai   28
Japanese 23rd Army   15, 16, 187
Japanese 38th Division   13, 14, 16, 29, 187
Japanese 45th Sentai   28
Japanese 228th Regiment   25, 29, 36, 38, 78, 102–104, 117, 174, 178, 260
Japanese 229th Regiment   25, 29, 41, 102, 104–106, 120, 129, 174
Japanese 230th Regiment   25, 29, 30, 40, 49, 102, 103, 117, 131, 174
Jardine, Private G. (Royal Scots)   39

Jardine Mathieson   86
Jardine's Bazaar   217
Jardine's Corner   189
Jardine's Lookout   18, 68, 98, 103, 106–108, 115, 116, 119, 122–126, 128, 132, 137–141, 174, 201
Jeanette Lighter   58, 63, 71
Jessop, Mr   103
Jitts, Private G. (HKVDC)   132
Jones, Captain 'Potato' (Royal Scots)   22, 23, 33–36
Jones, Lieutenant H. (HKVDC)   248, 250, 255
Johnson, Sub-Inspector A. (HKPF)   114, 144
Jordan Road   49, 54
Joss House Bay   44
Jubilee Battery   51, 59, 72
Jubilee Buildings   29
Jubilee Reservoir (see Shing Mun Reservoir)

Kai Tak   12, 13, 16, 25, 27, 28, 34, 38, 41, 53, 59, 89, 91,102
Kam Tin (see Sek Kong)
Kendall, M. (HKVDC)   38
Kennedy Road   27, 41, 190, 251, 260
Kennedy Town   70, 74, 143
Kennedy, Lieutenant A. (RNVR)   69, 393
Kerfoot, Lieutenant R. (Punjabis)   135
Kidd, Lt. Colonel G. (Punjabis)   12, 136, 137, 188
Kifford, Bandmaster W. (Middlesex)   134
Kilpatrick, Colonel H.   62
King, 2nd Lieutenant R. (Middlesex)   136, 256
King, Private G. (Royal Scots)   262
King's Park   26, 48
King's Road   87, 99, 124, 130, 190, 191

Kishi Engineering Company   104
Klintworth, Drummer E. (Middlesex)   134
Kowloon   15, 17, 25, 30, 31, 34, 40, 44, 47–49, 51–54, 57, 59–61, 65, 66, 69, 73, 134, 172, 178, 199, 230, 235, 285, 286
Kowloon Bay   31, 78, 104, 133
Kowloon Docks   30, 70, 132
Kowloon Hospital   27, 29, 38, 61
Kowloon Pass   52
Kowloon Railway Station   33
Kumta Prasad, Major (Punjabis)   139

Lady Clementi's Ride   108
Laffan's Plain   29
Lai Chi Kok   44, 51, 73, 108
Lai Chi Kok Road   45
Laird, Lance Corporal J. (Royal Scots)   38
Laloe, Cadet M. (HKRNVR)   30
Lamb, Lt. Colonel R. (RE)   251, 263
Lamble, Cadet R. (HKRNVR)   126
Lamma Channel   190
Lamma Island   26, 47, 48, 51, 86, 102, 171, 284
Lammert 2nd Lieutenant L. (HKVDC/Rajputs)   102
Lan Tau   75
Lau, Corporal M. (HKVDC)   128
Lawrence, Lieutenant T. (RE)   262
Lawson, Brigadier J.   12, 58, 68, 95, 107, 115–117, 120, 125, 126, 129, 134, 135, 144, 148–150, 157, 158, 204, 235, 246
Leath, Corporal N. (RAMC)   129
Lee Theatre   142, 221, 222, 255
Leighton Hill   19, 102, 104, 117, 119, 125, 136, 137, 139, 141, 142, 166, 170, 187, 190, 191, 199, 205, 214, 220, 221, 230, 239, 240, 248, 286
Leiper, Corporal G. (HKVDC)   57, 216, 386

Lemay, Sergeant G. (HKVDC)   191, 192, 202
Leonard, Private T. (HKVDC)   132
Leslie, Lance Sergeant R. (HKPF)   279
Li Shu Fan, Doctor   119, 248, 394
Lido Road   206
Lim K. Chu   40
Little Hong Kong   122, 128, 168, 189, 201, 207, 214, 216, 221, 248, 283
Little, Sergeant J. (Middlesex)   240
Lo Wai   35, 41
Lo Wu   29
Lok Lo Ha   26, 33
Lomax, Captain J. (RA)   135
Lower Albert Road   73
Luen Fat Street   26
Luscombe, ASP E. (HKPF)   216, 260
Lye Mun   54, 62, 69, 84, 86, 87, 101, 102–106, 108, 129, 132, 239
Lynch, Captain J. (RAMC)   237
Lyndon, Major C. (RCAC)   14, 201

Ma Lau Tong   17, 59, 61, 62, 73
Ma On Shan   15
Ma, Lance Corporal R. (HKVDC)   128
McCarthy, Lieutenant J. (Winnipeg Grenadiers)   115, 128, 137
MacAuley, Major M. (Royal Rifles)   188, 189, 191, 193, 213
MacDonald, C.   32
McDonnell Road   84
MacDonnell, Sergeant G. (Royal Rifles)   259, 404
McDouall, Lieutenant J. (HKRNVR)   126
MacDougal, Mr D.   261
McDougall, Lt. Colonel (Royal Scots)   22
Mace, 2nd Lieutenant R. (Middlesex)   176
McEwan, C. (HKVDC)   38

McGill, Sub-Lieutenant D. (HKRNVR) 132
MacGregor, Lieutenant I. 278
Mack, A/Lieutenant A. (HKRNVR) 126
McKay, Rifleman J. (Royal Rifles) 257
McKenzie, 2nd Lieutenant A. (HKVDC) 138
MacKenzie, Gunner N. (HKVDC) 243
MacMillan, Captain P. (RA) 62, 261
MacNaughton, Rifleman A. (Royal Rifles) 86
MacPherson, Lt. Colonel R. (RAOC) 203, 205, 206, 208
Magazine Gap 26, 73, 76, 168, 219, 222, 254, 261, 262
Mainland Brigade 12, 16, 21, 42, 44, 51, 54, 57, 59
Maltby, Major General C. 11–13, 16, 22, 23, 25, 27, 40, 43, 47, 52, 68–70, 86, 89, 93, 117, 122, 126, 134, 137, 170, 174, 185 188, 191, 192, 204–206, 218, 221, 235, 239, 251, 252, 256, 257, 262, 276, 279, 284, 388
Mamraz Khan, Gunner (HKSRA) 75
Man Wo APV 79
Man Yeung Minelayer 34
Man, Captain C. (Middlesex) 240, 261
Manchester, Sergeant R. (Winnipeg Grenadiers) 134
Manners, Major (Rtd.) 178, 241, 257
Manning, Sergeant A. (Middlesex) 208
Marsh, Major H. (Middlesex) 126, 189, 201, 207, 216
Marsman, J. 207, 232, 394
Maryknoll 221, 242, 250, 254, 256, 262
Masaichi Mimi, Vice Admiral 90

Mathers, Captain D. (Punjabis) 45
Matilda Hospital 254
Matthews, 2nd Lieutenant E. (HKVDC/Rajputs) 102
Matthews, Private A. (Winnipeg Grenadiers) 136
Matthews, Private C. (Winnipeg Grenadiers) 136, 140, 146, 168
Matthews, Private C. (HKVDC) 26, 389
Matthews, Private T. (Middlesex) 207
Mau La Tong 53
Mau Tau Kok 12
Meakin, Corporal F. (Middlesex) 124
Mehar Khan (Rajputs) 260
Meisling, Vaughn 70
Mid-Levels 18, 48, 95
Middle Gap 166, 174, 188, 203, 204
Middle Island 90
Middle Spur 123, 139, 170, 172, 176, 177, 187, 193, 202
Middlesex, 1st Battalion 11–14, 18, 63, 68, 95, 98, 101, 102, 106, 108, 121–123, 125, 142, 166, 185, 188, 190, 191,199, 204, 206, 214, 220, 222, 230, 236, 239, 240, 242, 251, 253–255, 257, 260, 261, 263, 278, 284
A Company 187, 201
B Company 128, 136, 177, 201, 202, 237, 241, 256
C Company 175, 176, 187, 207, 216, 250, 256
D Company 84, 126, 177, 202, 208, 237, 250, 256
Z Company 119, 124, 170, 187, 201, 220, 221, 258
Middleton, Leading Stoker T. (RN) 117
Miguno, Lieutenant 90
Miller, Sergeant A. (Middlesex) 124
Millet, Commander H. (RN) 48, 191

Millington, Sergeant L. (HKVDC) 241, 243, 248, 253, 255
Minnie, APV 30, 35, 53
Mirs Bay 252
Mitchell, Lieutenant E. (Winnipeg Grenadiers) 131, 170, 182
Mitchell, Lieutenant W. (Winnipeg Grenadiers) 107, 116, 128, 170, 182
Mitchell, Lt. Colonel E. (HKVDC) 179
Mogra, Private J. (HKVDC) 216
Montague, Commander H. (RN) 261
Moody, Major R. 241, 242
Morahan, Lt. Commander B. (HKRNVR) 126
Morgan, Sister Brenda 73
Morrison, LSA V. (HKPF) 104
Morrison Hill 19, 166, 221, 239, 241, 242, 251, 254, 256
Mosey, Elizabeth 207
Moth, HMS 58
Mould, Major K. (RASC) 194
Mound, The 119, 178, 187
Mount Austin 174–176, 187, 232, 239, 250, 254
Mount Butler 98, 102, 106, 116, 122, 123, 125, 126, 128, 132, 134, 135, 168
Mount Cameron 19, 168, 173, 187, 189, 199, 201, 204, 206, 207, 214, 219, 222, 232, 237, 239, 240, 242, 257
Mount Davis 36, 44, 48, 54, 72, 76, 79, 84, 85, 87, 134, 252
Mount Gough 175, 250
Mount Kellet 68, 175, 201, 220, 232, 250, 254
Mount Nicholson 18, 19, 119, 120, 125, 138, 166, 170, 173–175, 178, 187–189, 192, 201, 203, 204, 207, 242
Mount Parish 19, 166, 221, 239, 240, 250, 251, 255, 258, 260
Mount Parker 98, 104, 105, 107, 120, 122, 123, 125, 129, 131, 132, 135, 138, 141, 142, 174
MTB 07 26, 44, 53, 62, 69, 132
MTB 08 26, 53, 72, 86, 254
MTB 09 26, 53, 62, 69, 132–134
MTB 10 26, 45, 53, 179, 190
MTB 11 53, 62, 69, 132, 179
MTB 12 31, 45, 62, 69, 132
MTB 26 26, 53, 133
MTB 27 26, 53, 72
Muir, 2nd Lieutenant H. (HKVDC) 250, 255
Murphy, Sergeant J. (HKVDC) 106, 236
Murray Barracks 27, 261, 263, 284

Nagy, Von Kobza 14
Namyang 31
Nan Hai 13
Nathan Road 48, 51
Needle Hill 25, 35, 43
Neve, Major G. 173
Neville, Mr C. 68
New Territories 26, 33, 47, 65
Newbury, Private H. (Middlesex) 216, 224
Newman, 2nd Lieutenant S. (Middlesex) 102, 250
Newnham, Colonel L. (Middlesex) 51, 262
Newton, 2nd Lieutenant P. (Middlesex) 122
Newton, Captain H. (Rajputs) 23, 34, 39, 42, 65, 103, 124
Newton, Doctor I. 27, 29, 38, 230, 285
Nicholson, Corporal M. (Royal Rifles) 221
Nicoll, 2nd Lieutenant J. (Royal Scots) 50

INDEX 423

North Point 18, 78, 84, 93, 95, 97–101, 103, 106, 108, 133, 141, 170, 233
North Point Camp 88, 285
North Point power station 18, 19, 98, 102, 104, 106, 119, 122–124, 130, 137, 139, 141, 191
Notting Hill 185, 188, 190, 191
Nurkhan, Havildar (Punjabis) 216

O'Brien Street 255, 257, 260, 261
O'Mahoney, Private D. (Middlesex) 119
O'Neil, Private D. (Winnipeg Grenadiers) 170
Obelisk Hill 86, 126, 134
Offer, Lieutenant J. (Rajputs) 187, 208
Old Bailey Street 80
Orloff, Mrs 233
Osborn VC, CSM J. (Winnipeg Grenadiers) 135, 140, 168
Othsu, Mr 90
Otway, Captain C. (RE) 104, 136
Overbays 18, 166, 194, 203, 206, 208, 220
Overy, CSM R. (Middlesex) 256
Oxford, Flight Lieutenant M. (RAF) 45, 261
Oyadomari, Major 17178

Pai Tau Valley 26
Pak Sha Wan 66, 75, 78, 81, 82, 84, 85, 87, 105, 106, 120, 185
Palm Villa 177, 193, 202, 205
Palmer, Lance Bombardier R. (RA) 75
PanAm Clipper 28
Parade Battery 41, 44
Pardoe, Captain T. 62, 73
Park, Private W. (Middlesex) 124
Parker, Major M. (Royal Rifles) 257, 259, 260

Parker, Private R. (Middlesex) 124
Parkin, Sergeant W. (RAMC) 254
Parsons, Private D. (HKVDC) 38, 286
Paterson, Major J. (HKVDC) 124, 141
Paterson, Sergeant G. (Winnipeg Grenadiers) 142
Paul, Petty Officer P. (RN) 85
Peak Mansions 73, 172
Peak School 232
Peak Tram 58, 216
Peak, The 18, 48, 73, 79, 91, 174, 254
Pearce, Private T. (HKVDC) 130
Pears, Commander A. (RN) 121, 136, 172, 219
Peffers, Brigadier A. 62, 74
Pelham, Corporal H. (RE) 104
Pencil Factory 51
Peng Chau 253
Peninsular Hotel 14, 263
Penn, Captain A. (HKVDC) 16, 106, 130, 131, 137, 189, 191
Percival Street 142, 216
Perla, APV 31, 43, 46, 54, 72
Philip, Captain R. (Winnipeg Grenadiers) 201, 203
Phillips, 2nd Lieutenant E. (RA) 172, 177
Phillips, Sergeant W. (Corps of Military Staff Clerks) 134
Pigott, 2nd Lieutenant R. (Middlesex) 194
Pillbox 12 176
Pillbox 13 176
Pillbox 14 188, 192, 216
Pillbox 15 176
Pillbox 21 136
Pillbox 22 136
Pillbox 23 136
Pillbox 24 136
Pillbox 27 204, 220, 236, 237

Pillbox 28   248
Pillbox 29   136
Pillbox 30   136
Pillbox 37   102, 123, 124, 126
Pillbox 38   123
Pillbox 39   84, 119, 123
Pillbox 40   81, 103, 125
Pillbox 41   81, 103
Pillbox 42   81, 103
Pillbox 43   81, 103, 104
Pillbox 44   81, 103, 104
Pillbox 45   81, 106, 123
Pillbox 46   81
Pillbox 47   81, 88, 106
Pillbox 48   106
Pillbox 49   81, 88, 106
Pillbox 50   108
Pillbox 51   80
Pillbox 51a   80, 90
Pillbox 52   68, 81
Pillbox 53   108, 125, 141
Pillbox 54   101, 125
Pillbox 55   101, 107, 221
Pillbox 56   78
Pillbox 59   192
Pillbox 205   46
Pillbox 206   46
Pillbox 208   46
Pillbox 209   46
Pillbox 210   45
Pillbox 211   46
Pillbox 212   46
Pillbox 213   46
Pillbox 214   46
Pillbox 300   50
Pillbox 308   46
Pillbox 401b   38
Pillbox 402   38, 39, 42
Pillbox 406   42
Pillbox 407   42
Pillbox 408   42
Pillbox JLO 1   107, 108, 115, 132, 137

Pillbox JLO 2   107, 115, 132, 137
Pineapple Hill   36
Pineapple Pass   30
Pinewoods Battery   79
Ping Shan   38
Pinkerton, Captain D. (Royal Scots)   46, 50, 138
Platts, 2nd Lieutenant B. (HKSRA)   131
Po Toi Island   26
Pok Fu Lam   122, 233
Police Training School   52
Pollock, Private J. (Winnipeg Grenadiers)   140
Polo Ground   42
Poltock, Lieutenant W. (Rajputs)   187
Port Shelter   12, 53
Poseidon, APV   34, 43, 53, 54, 61, 72
Postbridge   18, 122, 126, 131, 141, 143, 174, 193
Pottinger Gap   71, 132
Pottinger Street   80
Price, Lieutenant T. (HKRNVR)   126
Price, Major J. (Royal Rifles)   233, 236
Prince Edward Road   52
Proes, Major G. (RA)   74, 131
Prophet, Lieutenant D. (HKVDC)   171, 202, 217, 255, 263
Proulx, Warrant Officer B. (HKRNVR)   207, 400, 404
Prior, Lieutenant J.   251, 263
Pryce Rifleman A. (Royal Rifles)   285
Public Works Department   14, 83
Pugsley, Sergeant W. (Winnipeg Grenadiers)   135, 140
Punjabis, 2nd Battalion, 14th Regt.   11, 12, 16, 17, 21, 25, 27, 31, 34, 39, 43, 57, 60, 62, 68, 69, 74, 79, 93, 95, 99, 119, 137, 166, 168, 172, 178, 187, 199, 216, 254, 258, 260, 278

INDEX

A Company   45, 52, 54, 59, 136, 141, 170, 176, 179, 188
B Company   46, 50, 52, 54, 59, 87, 126, 139, 170, 187, 201
C Company   13, 52, 53, 59, 63, 139, 170, 187, 201
D Company   45, 52, 59, 63, 136, 141, 190
HQ Company   63

Quarry Gap   98, 104, 106, 123
Quarry Point   103
Queen Mary's Hospital   173, 203, 232, 283
Queen's Road   26, 48, 237
Quilliam, Lieutenant T. (RN)   136

Railway Pass   52
Rajputs, 5th Battalion, 7th Regt.   11, 12, 18, 21, 23, 39, 46, 57, 65, 68–71, 84, 89, 93, 95, 98, 102, 129, 141, 166, 190, 199, 206, 214, 220, 239, 240, 251, 258, 260
  A Company   59, 62, 103
  B Company   59, 103, 104, 108, 119, 125, 139, 170, 187, 201
  C Company   62, 78, 103, 104
  D Company   34, 42, 43, 52, 59, 78, 101, 103, 104, 106, 123, 126, 136, 139, 187
Ralph, Lieutenant D. (HKRNVR)   30
Red Hill   19, 117, 121, 122, 135, 168, 185, 189–194, 204
Redman, 2nd Lieutenant J. (HKVDC)   191
Redwood, Nurse Mabel   14, 230
Rees, Captain F. (HKVDC)   236, 250
Repulse Bay   140, 142, 166, 172–174, 176–178, 189, 191, 193, 199, 201–203, 205, 207, 217, 222, 233, 250, 286
Repulse Bay Hotel   18, 19, 121, 123, 166, 168, 170, 171, 173–179, 185, 189, 192–194, 199, 202, 204, 207, 219, 232, 233, 241, 284
Repulse Bay Road   18, 122, 165, 185, 285
Reservoir Path   131
Rich, Sergeant G. (Middlesex)   216
Richards, Sergeant R. (Royal Scots)   65, 222
Richardson, Captain F. (Royal Scots)   49
Ride, Lt. Colonel L. (HKVDC)   207
Ridge, The   18, 140, 142, 165, 166, 168, 173, 174, 178, 185, 192–194, 201, 203–207, 240
Riley, Rifleman P. (Royal Rifles)   207
Rix, Corporal D. (Winnipeg Grenadiers)   137
Roarty, Private J. (Middlesex)   119
Robb, Sergeant R. (Royal Scots)   21, 33, 38, 39, 42
Robertson, Corporal M. (Royal Scots)   43
Robertson, Captain K. (HKVDC)   30, 32, 138
Robin, HMS   26, 53, 117, 122, 133, 134, 187, 203
Robinson, Supt. W. (Indian Police)   261
Rodrigues, Lieutenant A. (HKVDC)   258
Roscoe, Private J. (HKVDC)   130
Rose, Captain W. (Royal Scots)   50
Rose, Colonel H. (HKVDC)   179, 188, 261
Rotary Converter House   52
Rothwell, 2nd Lieutenant R. (Middlesex)   230
Royal Air Force   12, 13, 16, 28, 48, 82, 122, 203, 219
Royal Army Medical Corps.   120, 121, 205, 284
Royal Army Ordnance Corps.   12, 142, 166, 173, 193, 194, 203, 206

Royal Army Service Corps.   11, 122, 137, 142, 166, 173, 174, 185, 188, 194, 206, 237
Royal Artillery   11, 18, 59, 82, 95, 108, 140, 166, 175, 199, 205, 237, 257, 258
   5AA Regt.   26, 48, 57, 68, 74, 78, 85, 86, 115, 122, 128, 131, 172
   8th Coastal Regt.   192
   12th Coastal Regt.   240
   965 Defence Battery   48, 68, 74, 75, 89, 97, 99, 122, 172, 202, 217, 236, 242, 250
Royal Corps of Signals   12
Royal Engineers   12, 21, 71, 72, 116, 126, 128, 173, 177, 187, 201, 207, 219, 220, 260, 283
Royal Marines   166, 214, 219, 237, 241, 258
Royal Naval Dockyards (Aberdeen)   52, 86
Royal Naval Dockyards (Hong Kong)   45, 52, 53, 58, 59, 73, 74, 78, 80, 85, 86, 133, 134, 190, 191, 214, 230, 233, 242, 250, 252, 276, 284
Royal Naval Hospital   257
Royal Navy   59, 128, 187, 188, 201, 217, 222, 260, 284, 285
Royal Rifles of Canada   11, 12, 18, 68, 79, 81, 95, 102–104, 131, 132, 141, 142, 168, 175, 177, 190, 191, 205–207, 220–222, 233–235, 237, 239, 250, 284
   A Company   120, 171, 179, 185, 193, 194, 236
   B Company   174, 188, 202, 217, 254, 255
   C Company   82, 86, 98, 105–108, 124, 136, 189, 202
   D Company   134, 179, 189, 202, 257, 259, 276
Royal Scots, 2nd Battalion   11, 14, 16, 17, 21–23, 25, 30, 34, 39, 40, 41, 44, 45, 47, 52, 54, 57, 68, 70, 90, 93, 119, 136, 137, 139, 166, 173–175, 178, 187, 199, 201, 204, 214, 221, 222, 241, 261, 283
   A Company   12, 33, 36, 42, 46, 50, 116, 129, 138, 170, 232, 257, 258
   B Company   12, 36, 38, 42, 46, 49, 50, 51, 116, 138, 170
   C Company   12, 36, 42, 46, 49, 50, 116, 138, 170
   D Company   12, 38, 42, 46, 49, 50, 95, 116, 138, 170, 258
   HQ Company   42, 46
Royal, Captain W. (Royal Rifles)   254
Russell Street   26, 142
Rutherford, Lieutenant R. (HKRNVR)   126
Ryan, Major C. (RA)   75
Rymer, Corporal A. (Middlesex)   237

Sai Wan   44, 75, 79, 80, 82, 85–87, 90, 98, 101–108, 120, 122, 124–126
Sai Ying Poon   78
St. Albert's Convent   73, 173, 214, 216, 221, 222
St. John's Ambulance   98, 119, 120, 129, 230, 258, 263
St. John's Cathedral   16, 25, 256, 258
St. Stephen's College   172, 217, 220, 221, 236, 237, 239, 241, 248, 250, 253, 254, 257, 259, 262, 263, 276, 283
St. Stephen's Preparatory School   236, 255, 257
Sakai, Lt. General   69, 263, 285
Salesian Mission   98, 129, 233
Salter, Corporal C. (Royal Scots)   283
Sam Ka Tsun   54, 59, 82
San Shui   13

Sanatorium 89, 253
Sanatorium Gap 91, 106, 124
Sano, Lt.-General T. 123, 284
Saunders, Police Inspector S. (HKPF) 51, 80
Sawyer, Corporal K. (RAVC) 230
Scantlebury, Lieutenant V. (Middlesex) 126, 250, 254
Scout, HMS 27, 31
Searle, Assistant Superintendent L. (HKPF) 57
Sek Kong 25, 32, 44
Selby, Doctor J. 232
Selwyn-Clarke, Sir Selwyn 66, 232, 390
Sequeira, Private L. (HKVDC) 78, 79
Sha Tau Kok 29
Sha Tin 16, 34
Sha Tin Pass 42, 52
Shaftain, F. (HKPF) 59
Shah Muhammad, Jemadar (Rajputs) 214, 260
Sham Chun 13
Sham Chun River 27, 29
Sham Shui Po 25, 51, 285
Sham Shui Po Barracks 29, 39, 49, 52, 54, 286
Sharp, Corporal W. (HKVDC) 206, 217
Shau Kei Wan 18, 84, 85, 90, 93, 95, 98, 103–105, 125, 129
Shaw, Lt. Colonel S. (RA) 202, 279
Sheehan, Sergeant J. (Middlesex) 250
Shek O 117, 139
Sheldon, Captain H. 22, 90
Shen Chuan Hsu 15
Sheung Kwai Cheung 36
Shields Mr A. 241, 257
Shih Lung 15
Shing Mun Redoubt 16, 17, 21–23, 33, 36, 38–46, 65
Shing Mun Reservoir 15, 38

Shing Mun Valley 39
Ship Street 260
Shoji, Colonel 102, 116, 125, 178, 203, 240, 250
Shouson Hill 19, 123, 168, 170, 173, 174, 176, 188, 201, 285
Shun Wo, APV 30, 51, 53, 76, 102
Simmons, Nurse 258
Simpson, Sergeant P. (HKPF) 237
Singleton, QMS J. (RAOC) 208
Sir Cecil's Ride 103, 108, 115, 120, 121, 128, 139
Siu-Feng Huang 58, 171, 233
Skeet Ground 38, 42
Skelton, Rifleman S. (Royal Rifles) 212
Slater-Brown, Captain A. (Royal Scots) 138, 157
Sleap, Lieutenant R. (HKVDC) 82
Smith, Lieutenant J. (Royal Rifles) 105
Smith, Nurse Marjorie (HKVDC) 258, 262
Smith, Rifleman R. (Royal Rifles) 86, 214, 221
Smith-Dutton, Gunner S. (RA) 95
Smithfield 60
Smits, Private H. (Middlesex) 124
Smuggler's Path 38
Smuggler's Ridge 34, 44, 46
Soden, CSM E. (Middlesex) 187
Sommerfelt, Lt. Commander A. (HKRNVR) 126
Sorby, Private V. (HKVDC) 130
South Bay Road 202
South China Athletic 14
South Island 84
Southorn Garden 26, 261
Spence, Captain J. (CADC) 237
Spencer, Sister Sybil 29
Spirit, Petty Officer R. (RN) 132
Stafford, Lance Bombardier A. (RA) 253

Stainton, Sergeant T. (HKVDC)   205
Stanier, Lieutenant F. (Royal Scots)   138
Stanley   17, 19, 26, 74, 89, 98, 116, 117, 121, 126, 134–137, 139, 141, 165, 166, 168, 171, 177, 178, 185, 187, 188, 190, 191, 202, 204, 205, 207, 208, 217, 219, 222, 233, 234, 235, 237, 239–242, 248, 250, 251, 253–257, 260, 261, 263, 276, 278, 279, 285
Stanley Barracks   99
Stanley Cemetary   237, 258, 259
Stanley Fort   122, 136, 202, 217, 233, 234, 236, 239, 255, 259, 263, 276, 283
Stanley Gap   49, 68, 107, 115, 116, 122, 123, 128, 130–132, 174, 185, 188
Stanley Gap Road   85, 122
Stanley Mound   19, 68, 142, 178, 185, 189, 202, 205, 206, 217, 218, 220, 221, 236
Stanley Police Station   237, 242, 279
Stanley Prison   85, 122, 202, 217, 239, 257, 259
Stanley View   89, 117, 142, 171, 175, 177, 179, 202, 206, 217
Stanley, APV   31, 53
Stanton, Lieutenant R. (Royal Scots)   52
Star Ferry   59, 61, 63
Stargate   Gate Vessel   53
Starrett, Lance Corporal W. (Winnipeg Grenadiers)   168, 170
Staunton Street   85
Stephenson, Lieutenant R. (HKRNVR)   32
Stewart Road   260
Stewart, Lt. Colonel H. (Middlesex)   12, 252, 255, 257, 258, 278, 284
Stewart, Major E. (HKVDC)   48, 106, 107, 202, 385

Stodgell, Private S. (Winnipeg Grenadiers)   140
Stoker, Lieutenant W. (HKVDC)   171, 276
Stone Hill   19, 117, 137, 141, 177, 194, 202, 206, 217, 220
Stonecutters Island   15, 26, 41, 44–46, 48, 53, 57, 59, 73, 75, 108, 219
Strellet, Captain D. (HKVDC)   142, 174, 205, 206
Stubbs Road   115, 126, 201, 214, 221, 237
Sugarloaf Hill   205
Sullivan, Wing Commander H. (RAF)   12
Sully, Nurse Collie   230
Sulphur Channel   133, 134
Sun Yat Sen, Doctor   31
Supermarine Walrus   16, 28
Sutcliffe, Lt. Colonel J. (Winnipeg Grenadiers)   12, 141, 179, 189, 207, 235
Sutherland, Sergeant S. (Royal Scots)   46
Sutton, General F.   257
Swan, CSM T. (HKVDC)   242

Ta Ku Ling Road   28
Tada, Colonel   69
Tai Hang   68, 78, 91, 98, 104, 119, 125, 126, 136, 139, 141, 187, 230, 262, 263, 278
Tai Hang Wan Fung Terrace   68
Tai Ho Wan   74, 97
Tai Kok Tsui   199
Tai Koo   74, 84, 97, 103, 106, 133
Tai Koo Docks   62, 89, 101, 103, 104, 106
Tai Lam Kok   33, 36
Tai Mo Shan   15, 16, 25, 30, 34
Tai Nam Road   45
Tai Po   25, 28, 29, 31, 34
Tai Po Mai   32

INDEX

Tai Po Road   29–31, 33, 34, 41, 52
Tai Tam   19, 62, 71, 79, 99, 116, 120, 122, 123, 126, 132, 135, 185, 188, 204, 216, 217, 236, 237
Tai Tam Fork   74, 117, 135
Tai Tam Gap   70, 95, 102, 104, 106, 121, 136, 137, 141, 177
Tai Tam Hill   49, 89, 122, 131, 136
Tai Tam Reservoir   123, 140, 219
Tai Tam Tuk Reservoir   185, 192
Tai Wai   51
Tait's Carnival   17
Takashi Sakai, Lieutenant General   90
Tamar, HMS   26, 58, 250
Tamworth, Lieutenant I. (HKVDC)   13, 29, 136, 202
Tanaka, Colonel   98, 102, 104, 116, 140, 260
Tann, Private G. (Middlesex)   240
Tate's Cairn   48, 49, 59
Tathong Boom   26
Tathong Channel   86
Tau Fung Shan Monastery Ridge   33
Tckencho, Nurse Tania   232
Teasdale, 2nd Lieutenant E. (HKVDC)   252
Telegraph Bay   284
Telegraph Hill   34
Temple, Major W. (RA)   131
Templer, Major C. (RA)   84, 135, 185, 188, 191–194, 207
Tern, HMS   45, 53, 70, 117
Texaco Peninsular   38, 42, 199
Thanet, HMS   31
Thomas, C.M.O. O. (HKVDC)   129
Thompson, ASP W. (HKPF)   80
Thompson, Captain A. (RCAPC)   29
Thompson, Captain T. (RAPC)   285
Thompson, Corporal F. (HKVDC)   106, 123
Thomson, 2nd Lieutenant J. (Royal Scots)   33, 36, 39, 42

Thomson, Corporal R. (HKVDC)   252
Thomson, Pilot Officer F. (RAF)   79, 189
Thracian, HMS   31, 53, 69, 71, 81, 85, 86, 90, 116, 122, 136, 143, 284
Tibble, CSM W. (Middlesex)   256
Tide Cove   12, 16, 25, 29, 40, 41, 43, 44
Tiger Balm   49, 74, 85
Tinson, Mrs E. (ANS)   129
Tinson, Mr G.   143
To Kat   13
Toda, Colonel   90
Tota Ram, Havildar (Punjabis)   87
Tressider, 2nd Lieutenant C. (RASC)   170, 189
Trist, Major G. (Winnipeg Grenadiers)   207
Tsim Sha Tsui   23, 57, 65, 93
Tsing Yi   15, 48
Tso Hin-Chi, Bombardier (HKVDC)   106
Tso Shan   25, 35
Tsuen Wan   252
Tsun Wan Wai   42
Tucker, Private T. (Middlesex)   124
Tung Shan Hotel   61
Tunmer, Bandsman B. (Middlesex)   130
Turner, Captain C. (RASC)   69, 74
Tweed Bay   255, 257, 258
Twin Brooks   18, 166, 206

Uk Kok   85
Umino, Lieutenant   124
Upper Levels Police Station   204
Ure, CSM J. (Middlesex)   240

Valentine, Captain R. (HKVDC)   73
Vehicular Ferry Pier   72
Veronkin, Mrs Barbara   172

Verrault, Signalman G. (RCCS) 218, 389
Vickers Vildebeeste 16, 28
Victoria 46, 49, 58, 68, 93, 99, 120–122, 141, 165, 172, 187, 233, 251, 284
Victoria Barracks 242
Victoria Gap 199, 220
Victoria Recreation Club 221
Victoria, WDV 69
Vinter, Lieutenant J. (HKSRA) 96, 122
Violet Hill 68, 123, 142, 166, 170, 175–179, 194, 205

Waglan Island 66, 71
Wagstaff, Lieutenant D. (HKRNVR) 133
Wai Chow 253
Wakabayashi 41
Walker, Lt. Colonel R. (HKVDC) 126
Walker, Major L. (Royal Scots) 22
Walker, Private J. (HKVDC) 217
Wallingford, Sub-Inspector A. (HKPF) 52
Wallis, Brigadier C. 12, 13, 20, 22, 43, 44, 50, 51, 57, 59, 68, 74, 89, 95, 101, 106–108, 116, 117, 120, 126, 142, 170, 171, 177, 179, 188, 189, 191, 193, 194, 204, 206, 217, 218, 221, 233, 235, 236, 239, 242, 251, 256, 257, 260, 263, 278, 279
Wan Chai 18, 19, 22, 26, 90, 93, 103, 129, 166, 168, 206, 230, 233, 237, 239, 240, 250, 254, 257, 258, 262
Wan Chai Gap 19, 74, 140, 168, 172, 173, 177–179, 190, 199, 201, 207, 214, 219–222, 241, 243, 257, 258, 261, 262
Wan Chai Market 89, 250, 255, 257, 260
Wan Chai Police Station 96, 260

War Memorial Hospital 174, 254
Water Police 26
Waterfall Bay 71, 187
Waterloo Road 26, 49, 51
Watson, Lance Sergeant W. (HKPF) 51
Watt, Sergeant E. (RAMC) 129
Weedon, Captain M. (Middlesex) 202, 256, 257, 391
Wellington Street 80
West Battery 44, 53
West Bay 128, 171, 237
West Brigade 68, 93, 95, 98, 116, 117, 128, 135, 141, 142, 165, 166, 168, 179, 185, 191, 214, 261, 262, 263, 285
West Fort 12, 41, 81
West Lamma Channel 71
West Point 70, 73, 102
West, Captain D. (Middlesex) 205, 217, 237, 256
Western Market 89
White, Lance Sergeant G. (HKVDC) 107
White, Lt. Colonel S. (Royal Scots) 12, 22, 35, 39, 42–44, 50, 51, 54, 129, 138, 139, 251, 252, 258, 262
White, Sergeant N. (HKVDC) 191
White, Mrs Vi 251
Whitehead, Gunner J. (RA) 93, 97, 216, 390
Whitley, Lance Sergeant G. (HKPF) 237
Whitney, Captain P. (RAMC) 254
Wilcox, Lt. Colonel 177, 202, 218
Wilkinson, Able Seaman W. (RN) 45
Willcocks, Lieutenant W. (HKSRA) 33, 36, 39, 41
Williams, Lieutenant G. (Royal Rifles) 105, 132, 148, 174
Williamson, Captain C. (Middlesex) 256
Wilson, ASP G. (HKPF) 80

INDEX

Wilson, Bombardier P. (HKVDC) 139
Wilson, Corporal 'Tug' (RAF) 41
Wilson, Mr T. 14
Windy Gap 86, 121
Winfield, Corporal E. (Middlesex) 237
Winnipeg Grenadiers 11, 48, 68, 119, 125, 131, 166, 170, 174, 189, 206, 260
  A Company 107, 116, 122, 126, 128, 135, 140
  B Company 107, 139, 187, 188, 201
  C Company 107, 122, 179, 188, 219, 223, 239
  D Company 23, 41, 42, 51, 54, 95, 115, 116, 126, 135, 173, 178, 187, 201, 203, 204
  HQ Company 106, 115, 134, 138, 141
Winter, Lance Corporal L. (Middlesex) 256
Wo Liu Hang 35
Wood, Corporal W. (Middlesex) 216
Woodside, Lieutenant A. (Royal Rifles) 134
Wong Nai Chung Gap 17–19, 48, 53, 57, 68, 74, 78, 86, 95, 97, 98, 102, 108, 115, 116, 119–122, 125, 126, 128–131, 135–140, 142, 165, 166, 168, 170, 173–175, 177, 178, 185, 187–189, 193, 194, 201, 203, 216, 233, 239, 286

Wong Nai Chung Gap police station 18, 120, 130, 138, 141, 166, 168, 173, 185, 193
Wong Nai Chung Reservoir 68
Wong, Private H. (HKVDC) 240
Wright, 2nd Lieutenant M. (HKVDC) 47, 252
Wright-Nooth, ASP G. (HKPF) 70, 398
Wynter-Blyth, 2nd Lieutenant P. (Middlesex) 122, 256

Yale, Lt. Col. J. (HKSRA) 141, 181
Yatshing, SS 54
Yau Ma Tei 240
Yen Chau Street 28
Yen, Hilda 14
Yi, Colonel S.K. 261
Youe, PSA G. (HKPF) 142
Young, Governor Sir Mark 13, 28, 68, 70, 79–81, 84, 90, 91, 99, 137, 142, 192–194, 217, 236, 248, 252, 262, 278, 279, 284
Young, Lieutenant K. (Middlesex) 119
Young, Major C. (Royal Rifles) 171, 178, 193, 284
Young, Private E. (HKVDC) 132
Yuen Long 30

Zempei Masushima, Lieutenant 89
Zimmern, Sergeant E. (HKVDC) 123